THE AMERICANA ANNUAL

■

2009

AN ENCYCLOPEDIA
OF THE EVENTS OF 2008

YEARBOOK OF THE
ENCYCLOPEDIA AMERICANA

GROLIER

Published 2009 by Grolier Incorporated

Library of Congress Control Number: 23-10041
ISBN-13: 978-0-545-07551-0
ISBN-10: 0-545-07551-3
ISSN: 0196-0180

This annual is also published under the title *The 2009 World Book Year Book*
© 2009 World Book, Inc.

Printed in the United States of America.

STAFF

EXECUTIVE COMMITTEE

President
Paul A. Gazzolo

Vice President and Chief Marketing Officer
Patricia Ginnis

Vice President and Chief Financial Officer
Donald D. Keller

Vice President and Editor in Chief
Paul A. Kobasa

Director, Human Resources
Bev Ecker

Chief Technology Officer
Tim Hardy

Managing Director, International
Benjamin Hinton

EDITORIAL

Associate Director, Supplementary Publications
Scott Thomas

Managing Editor, Supplementary Publications
Barbara A. Mayes

Senior Editor, Supplementary Publications
Kristina A. Vaicikonis

Manager, Research, Supplementary Publications
Cheryl Graham

Administrative Assistant
Ethel Matthews

Editors
Shawn Brennan
Jake Bumgardner
Jeff De La Rosa
Brian Johnson
Daniel Kenis
Nicholas Kilzer
Dawn Krajcik
Pete Kulak
Mike Lewis
S. Thomas Richardson
Kenneth J. Shenkman
Christine Sullivan
Daniel O. Zeff

Contributing Editors
Sara Dreyfuss
Robert Knight
Alfred J. Smuskiewicz

Statistics Editor
William M. Harrod

Manager, Contracts & Compliance (Rights & Permissions)
Loranne K. Shields

EDITORIAL ADMINISTRATION

Director, Systems and Projects
Tony Tills

Senior Manager, Publishing Operations
Timothy Falk

Associate Manager, Publishing Operations
Audrey Casey

Manager, Indexing Services
David Pofelski

Associate Manager, Indexing Services
Aamir Burki

GRAPHICS AND DESIGN

Associate Director
Sandra M. Dyrlund

Manager
Tom Evans

Coordinator, Design Development and Production
Brenda B. Tropinski

Senior Designers
Don Di Sante
Isaiah W. Sheppard, Jr.

Associate Designer
Matthew Carrington

Photographs Editor
Kathryn Creech

Manager, Cartographic Services
Wayne K. Pichler

Senior Cartographer
John M. Rejba

PRODUCTION

Director, Manufacturing and Pre-Press
Carma Fazio

Manufacturing Manager
Barbara Podczerwinski

Production/Technology Manager
Anne Fritzinger

Proofreading
Emilie Schrage

MARKETING

Chief Marketing Officer
Patricia Ginnis

Director, Direct Marketing
Mark R. Willy

Marketing Analyst
Zofia Kulik

CONTRIBUTORS

Contributors not listed on these pages are members of the editorial staff.

ANDREWS, PETER J., B.A., M.S.; free-lance writer. **[Chemistry]**

BAYNHAM, SIMON, B.A., M.A., Ph.D.; senior research associate, Centre for Defence & International Security Studies, University of Lancaster, U.K. **[Africa and African country articles]**

BECK, STEFAN, B.A.; associate editor, *The New Criterion* magazine. **[Literature]**

BERGER, ERIC R., B.A, M.A.; science writer, *Houston Chronicle.* **[Houston]**

BOYD, JOHN D., B.S.; economics writer. **[United States, Government of** the Special Report: Economic Crisis: **The Goverment Jumps In; Economics, U.S.; Economics, World; International trade]**

BRADSHER, HENRY S., A.B., B.J.; foreign affairs analyst. **[Asia and Asian country articles]**

BRETT, CARLTON E., B.A., M.S., Ph.D.; Professor of Geology, University of Cincinnati. **[Paleontology]**

CASEY, MIKE, B.S., M.A.; former assistant editor, *Kansas City Star.* **[Automobile]**

CITRIN, ADRIENNE, B.A.; Manager of Public Relations, Toy Industry Association, Incorporated. **[Toys and games]**

DEEB, MARIUS K., B.A., Ph.D.; Professor, School of Advanced International Studies, Johns Hopkins University. **[Middle East and Middle Eastern country articles; North African country articles]**

DEEB, MARY-JANE, B.A., Ph.D.; Chief of the African and Middle Eastern Division, Library of Congress. **[Middle Eastern country articles; North African country articles]**

DeFRANK, THOMAS M., B.A., M.A.; Washington Bureau Chief, *New York Daily News.* **[Armed forces]**

DILLON, DAVID, B.A., M.A., Ph.D.; architecture and design editor, *The Dallas Morning News.* **[Architecture]**

ELLIS, GAVIN, former Editor in Chief, *The New Zealand Herald & Weekend Herald.* **[New Zealand]**

FISHER, ROBERT W., B.A., M.A.; free-lance writer. **[Labor and employment]**

FITZGERALD, THOMAS, A.B., S.T.M, Ph.D.; Dean and Professor of Church History and Historical Theology, Holy Cross Greek Orthodox School of Theology. **[Eastern Orthodox Churches]**

FRIEDMAN, EMILY, B.A.; health policy and ethics analyst. **[Health care issues]**

GADOMSKI, FRED, B.S., M.S.; meteorologist, Pennsylvania State University. **[Global warming; Weather]**

GOLDBERG, BEVERLY, B.A.; senior editor, American Library Association. **[Library]**

GOLDEN, JONATHAN J., B.A., M.J.Ed.; Chair, History Department at the Gann Academy, New Jewish High School of Greater Boston. **[Judaism]**

GOLDNER, NANCY, B.A.; free-lance dance critic. **[Dance]**

HAVERSTOCK, NATHAN A., A.B.; affiliate scholar, Oberlin College. **[Latin America and Latin American country articles]**

JOHANSON, DONALD C., B.S., M.A., Ph.D.; Director and Professor, Institute of Human Origins, Arizona State University. **[Anthropology]**

JOHNSON, JULIET, A.B., M.A., Ph.D.; Associate Professor of Political Science, McGill University. **[Russia and other former Soviet republic articles]**

KATES, MICHAEL, B.S.J.; associate sports editor, *Chicago Tribune.* **[Sports articles]**

KENNEDY, BRIAN, M.A.; free-lance writer. **[Australia; Australia, Prime Minister of; Australian rules football]**

KILGORE, MARGARET, B.A., M.B.A.; free-lance writer, Kilgore and Associates. **[Los Angeles]**

KING, MIKE, reporter, *The* (Montreal) *Gazette.* **[Montreal]**

KLINTBERG, PATRICIA PEAK, B.A.; Director of Constituent Affairs, Office of Communications, U.S. Department of Agriculture. **[Agriculture]**

KNIGHT, ROBERT N., B.A., M.M.; free-lance writer. **[Bank** Special Report: Economic Crisis: The Banking Meltdown; Bank; **People in the news]**

KOPSTEIN, JEFFREY, B.A., M.A., Ph.D; Professor of Political Science and Director, Centre for European, Russian, and Eurasian Studies, University of Toronto. **[Europe and Western European country articles]**

LAWRENCE, ALBERT, B.A., M.A., M.Ed.; Executive Director, World Chess Hall of Fame. **[Chess]**

MANZO, KATHLEEN KENNEDY, B.A., M.Ed; associate editor, *Education Week.* **[Education]**

MARCH, ROBERT H., A.B., M.S., Ph.D.; Professor Emeritus of Physics and Liberal Studies, University of Wisconsin at Madison. **[Physics]**

MARKSJARVIS, GAIL, B.A.; personal finance columnist, *Chicago Tribune.* **[Stocks and bonds]**

MARSCHALL, LAURENCE A., B.S., Ph.D.; W.K.T. Sahm Professor of Physics, Gettysburg College. **[Astronomy]**

MARTY, MARTIN E., Ph.D.; Fairfax M. Cone Distinguished Service Professor Emeritus, University of Chicago. **[Protestantism]**

MAY, SALLY RUTH, B.A, M.A.; free-lance art writer. **[Art]**

McDONALD, ELAINE STUART, B.A.; free-lance public policy writer and editor. **[State government]**

McWILLIAM, ROHAN, B.A., M.A., D.Phil; Senior Lecturer in History, Anglia Polytechnic University, Cambridge, U.K. **[Ireland; Northern Ireland; United Kingdom; United Kingdom, Prime Minister of]**

MINER, TODD J., B.S., M.S.; Meteorologist, Pennsylvania State University. **[Weather]**

MORITZ, OWEN, B.A.; urban affairs editor, *New York Daily News.* **[New York City]**

MORRING, FRANK, Jr., B.A.; senior space technology editor, *Aviation Week & Space Technology* magazine. **[Space exploration]**

MORRIS, BERNADINE, B.A., M.A.; free-lance fashion writer. **[Fashion]**

MULLINS, HENRY T., B.S., M.S., Ph.D.; Professor of Geology, Syracuse University. **[Geology]**

NGUYEN, J. TUYET, M.A.; United Nations correspondent, Deutsche Presse-Agentur. **[Population; United Nations]**

OGAN, EUGENE, B.A., Ph.D.; Professor Emeritus of Anthropology, University of Minnesota. **[Pacific Islands]**

REINHART, A. KEVIN, B.A., M.A., Ph.D.; Associate Professor of Religious Studies, Dartmouth College. **[Islam]**

RICCIUTI, EDWARD, B.A.; free-lance writer. [Conservation Special Report: Colorado River: Lifeline of the Southwest; Biology; Conservation; Zoos]

ROBERTS, THOMAS W., Editor, *The National Catholic Reporter*. [Roman Catholic Church]

ROSE, MARK J., B.A., M.A., Ph.D.; Executive editor, *Archaeology* magazine. [Archaeology]

RUBENSTEIN, RICHARD E., B.A., M.A., J.D.; Professor of Conflict Resolution and Public Affairs, George Mason University. [Terrorism]

RUBENSTONE, JEFFREY, B.A.; Editor, *Engineering News-Record* magazine. [Building and construction]

RUSSELL, MARY HARRIS, B.A., M.A, Ph.D.; Professor of English, Indiana University. [Literature for children]

SARNA, JONATHAN D., Ph.D.; Joseph H. & Belle R. Braun Professor of American Jewish History, Brandeis University. [Judaism]

SHAPIRO, HOWARD, B.S.; staff writer and travel columnist, *The Philadelphia Inquirer*. [Philadelphia; Washington, D.C.]

SMUSKIEWICZ, ALFRED J., B.S., M.S.; free-lance writer. [AIDS; City; Crime; Drug abuse; Drugs; Medicine; Mental health; Prison; Public health; Safety]

STEIN, DAVID LEWIS, B.A., M.S.; former urban affairs columnist, *The Toronto Star*. [Toronto]

STOS, WILLIAM, B.A., M.A.; free-lance writer. [Canada; Canada, Prime Minister of; Canadian provinces; Canadian territories]

TANNER, JAMES C., B.J.; former news editor—energy, *The Wall Street Journal*. [Energy supply]

TATUM, HENRY K., B.A.; retired associate editor, *The Dallas Morning News*. [Dallas]

TSANG, STEVE, B.A., M.A., D.Phil.; Fellow and Reader in Politics, St. Anthony's College, U.K. [China Special Report: China's Global Awakening]

von RHEIN, JOHN, B.A.; classical music critic, *Chicago Tribune*. [Classical music]

WILLIAMS, BRIAN, B.A.; free-lance writer. [Cricket; Soccer]

WOLCHIK, SHARON L., B.A., M.A., Ph.D.; Professor of Political Science and International Affairs, George Washington University. [Eastern European country articles]

YEZZI, DAVID, B.F.A., M.F.A.; Executive editor, *The New Criterion* magazine. [Poetry; Theater]

WORLD BOOK ADVISERS

Mary Alice Anderson, B.S., M.A. Lead Media Specialist, Winona Area Public Schools, Winona, Minnesota, United States

Ali Banuazizi, B.S., M.A., Ph.D. Professor of Political Science and Codirector of Middle Eastern & Islamic Studies Program, Boston College, Chestnut Hill, Massachusetts, United States

David J. Bercuson, O.C., B.A., M.A., Ph.D. Professor of History and Director, Centre for Military and Strategic Studies, University of Calgary, Calgary, Alberta, Canada

Marianna Anderson Busch, B.A., Ph.D. Professor of Chemistry and Co-Director, Center for Analytical Spectroscopy, Baylor University, Waco, Texas, United States

Anne Innis Dagg, B.A., M.A., Ph.D. Academic Adviser, Independent Studies, University of Waterloo, Waterloo, Ontario, Canada

Jesus Garcia, M.A., Ed.D. Professor of Curriculum and Instruction, University of Nevada, Las Vegas, Las Vegas, Nevada, United States

Marc B. Garnick, M.D. Professor of Medicine, Harvard Medical School, Harvard University; Physician, Beth Israel Deaconess Medical Center, Boston, Massachusetts, United States

Michael F. Graves, B.A., M.A., Ph.D. Professor Emeritus of Literacy Education, University of Minnesota, Twin Cities Campus, Minneapolis, Minnesota, United States

John T. Greene, B.A., M.A., Ph.D. Professor Emeritus of Religious Studies, Michigan State University, East Lansing, Michigan, United States

Alan E. Mann, B.A., M.A., Ph.D. Professor Emeritus of Anthropology, Princeton University, Princeton, New Jersey, United States

Adrian Mitchell, B.A., M.A., Ph.D. Director, Postgraduate Programs, Faculty of Arts, University of Sydney, Sydney, New South Wales, Australia

Jay M. Pasachoff, A.B., A.M., Ph.D. Field Memorial Professor of Astronomy and Director, Hopkins Observatory of Williams College, Williamstown, Massachusetts, United States

Michael Plante, B.A., M.A., Ph.D. Jessie J. Poesch Professor of Art History, Newcomb Art Department, Tulane University, New Orleans, Louisiana, United States

Robert B. Prigo, B.S., M.S., Ph.D. Director of Teacher Education and Professor of Physics, Middlebury College, Middlebury, Vermont, United States

Michael Seidel, B.A., M.A., Ph.D. Jesse and George Siegel Professor of Humanities, Columbia University, New York City, New York, United States

Whitney Smith, A.B., A.M., Ph.D. Director, The Flag Research Center, Winchester, Massachusetts, United States

Ivan Soll, A.B., A.Ph.D. Professor of Philosophy, University of Wisconsin-Madison, Madison, Wisconsin, United States

Scott L. Waugh, B.A., Ph.D. Acting Executive Vice Chancellor and Provost, University of California, Los Angeles, United States

CONTENTS

FOCUS ON

PORTRAITS

From the financial crisis to the election of Barack Obama as president of the United States, 2008 was a year of extraordinary events. On these three pages are stories that the editors picked as some of the most important of the year, along with details on where to find more information about them in this volume.

The Editors

2008

ICE ON MARS

NASA's Phoenix Mars lander, which set down on the planet in May, finds bits of ice under the planet's characteristic reddish dirt. Trenches dug by the lander's robotic arm turn up white material that later disappears, leading scientists to conclude that it was frozen water ice that vaporized after being exposed to the atmosphere. In November, images of Mars made by ground-penetrating radar aboard NASA's Mars Reconnaissance Orbiter reveal vast underground glaciers of water ice up to 1/2 mile 0.8 kilometer) thick. See **Space exploration,** page 357.

TERROR ATTACKS IN MUMBAI

The city of Mumbai, India, is rocked by a wave of terrorist attacks beginning on November 26. Heavily armed men, whom the Indian government later accused of belonging to the Pakistan-based organization Lashkar-e-Taiba, launch attacks at a railway station, a popular restaurant, a Jewish center, and two luxury hotels. At least 170 people are killed and more than 300 others injured before Indian commandos bring the attacks to an end on November 29. See **Asia,** page 61; **India,** page 245; **Pakistan,** page 318; **Terrorism,** page 380.

THE 2008 PRESIDENTIAL ELECTION

On November 4, Illinois Senator Barack Obama, the Democratic candidate, defeats Arizona Senator John McCain, the Republican candidate, to become the 44th president of the United States and the first African American president of the United States. See **Cabinet, U.S.,** page 103; **Congress of the United States,** page 141; **Democratic Party,** page 184; **Elections: A Special Report,** page 196; **Republican Party,** page 345; **United States, Government of the,** page 397; **United States, President of the,** page 408.

THE AFGHAN WAR

The pace of war in Afghanistan escalates in 2008, with U.S. Army estimates of the violence rising by 30 percent over that in 2007. According to some military experts, the Taliban and al-Qa`ida control large parts of the lawless tribal border areas in Pakistan. From these command centers, they stage raids into Afghanistan. By December 2008, the Taliban is active in more than 70 percent of Afghanistan, according to an estimate by the International Council on Security and Development, a British think tank. See **Afghanistan,** page 37; **Armed forces,** page 55; **Asia,** page 61; **Pakistan,** page 318.

ECONOMIC CRISIS

A wave of defaults on subprime residential mortgages, which began in 2007, becomes a flood in 2008, as tens of thousands of people face foreclosure. The housing glut drives down the price of real estate, leaving many people with mortgages greater than the value of their houses and undermining the home building industry. The value of billions of dollars worth of mortgage-backed securities held by investment and commercial banks and other financial institutions plummets, driving some institutions into bankruptcy and others into sales to stronger companies. As the credit contagion spreads from the United States to Europe and then worldwide, the U.S. Treasury and the Federal Reserve, as well as other central banks, step in to contain the crisis. Congress passes legislation authorizing $700 billion to prop up the ailing financial industry. By the end of the year, the U.S. economy and the economies of several other nations are officially in recession, and unemployment rates are climbing to frightening heights. See **Bank,** page 81; **Bank: A Special Report,** page 82; **Congress of the United States,** page 141; **Economics, U.S.,** page 190; **Economics, World,** page 192; **Labor and employment,** page 262; **United States, Government of the: A Special Report,** page 401; and the various country articles.

DISASTERS

A cyclone in Myanmar (also known as Burma) and an earthquake in China together kill more than 155,000 people and leave thousands of others missing or injured in the worst disasters of 2008. Cyclone Nargis deluges Myanmar in May with 20 inches (50 centimeters) of rain and is accompanied by a storm surge 12 feet (3.7 meters) high. A 7.9-magnitude earthquake in China also strikes in May, affecting more than half the country's provinces. See **Asia,** page 61; **China,** page 120; **Disasters,** page 186; **Myanmar,** page 291; and **Weather,** page 410.

OLYMPIC GAMES

China successfully stages the 2008 Summer Olympic Games in Beijing in August, providing spectacular settings and awe-inspiring ceremonies to mark the competitions. Nevertheless, protests over China's control of Tibet accompany the torch relay that precedes the games, and journalists complain over restricted Internet access. Protesters are not allowed to demonstrate during the games. Political analysts note that China's hosting of the games emphasizes the country's reentry as a major player on the world stage. See **China,** page 120; **China: A Special Report,** page 122; **Olympic Games: A Special Report,** page 304; and **People in the news** (Michael Phelps), page 323.

CONFLICT BETWEEN RUSSIA AND GEORGIA

Georgia and Russia on August 7 enter into an armed conflict over South Ossetia, a Georgian breakaway republic that is home to many ethnic Russians. Russia responds with force after Georgia bombs and briefly occupies Tskhinvali, South Ossetia's capital. France's President Nicolas Sarkozy brokers a cease-fire agreement between the two nations a week later. However, the countries break off diplomatic ties after Russia recognizes the independence of South Ossetia as well as Abkhazia, another breakaway republic and home to many Russians. See **Europe,** page 217; **France,** page 228; **Georgia,** page 233; **Russia,** page 347.

MELAMINE SCARE

An international scandal erupts in September after reports surface that some infant formulas made in China are tainted with melamine. Melamine is an industrial chemical that can cause kidney problems. The news reports reveal that at least four infants have died and thousands of others have been sickened. Over the next few months, it becomes clear that not only milk products but also eggs and some foods that contain milk are affected. Manufacturers apparently added melamine to make foods appear to contain more protein. Many countries around the world ban the importation of a variety of foods made in China. See **China,** page 120, and **Food,** page 223.

2008

YEAR IN BRIEF

A month-by-month listing of the most significant world events that occurred during 2008.

JANUARY

2008

A mob mans a burning roadblock in the western Kenyan city of Kisumu on Jan. 29, 2008, in an attempt to prevent the escape of members of the Kikuyu ethnic group. Kikuyu clashed repeatedly with members of the Luo ethnic group for weeks following Kenya's disputed December 2007 presidential election. Hundreds of people died in the violence.

1 A mob torches a church in western Kenya, causing at least 30 people, including many children, to burn to death. It is the worst of several incidents of ethnic violence that have occurred in the wake of Kenya's disputed presidential election on Dec. 27, 2007.

2 The price of crude oil briefly rises to $100 a barrel in a single trade on the New York Mercantile Exchange. It is the first time the price reaches this psychological milestone. Oil costs have been increasing dramatically since mid-2004, when the price per barrel began to consistently exceed $40.

3 In the first contests of the U.S. presidential nomination process— the Iowa caucuses—Senator Barack Obama of Illinois emerges as the Democratic victor, and former

Arkansas Governor Mike Huckabee picks up the Republican win.

6 Five Iranian patrol boats approach three U.S. Navy warships in the Strait of Hormuz between Iran and the Arabian Peninsula. The U.S. ships receive this radio transmission: "I am coming to you. You will explode after a few minutes." United States officials describe the incident as a provocative act and lodge a formal diplomatic protest with Iran on January 10. But they later admit that they are uncertain whether the radio transmission came from the Iranian boats.

8 Senator Hillary Rodham Clinton of New York wins the Democratic presidential primary in New Hampshire. Senator John McCain of Arizona wins New Hampshire's Republican presidential primary.

11 Bank of America, one of the largest U.S. banks, agrees to buy Countrywide Financial, one of the nation's largest mortgage lenders. Countrywide has been hit hard by the U.S. housing slump. The deal is likely to prevent the firm's collapse, which would have a significant ripple effect in the overall economy.

15 The U.S. Department of Defense announces that 3,200 Marines will deploy to Afghanistan in the spring, bringing the total number of U.S. troops there to more than 30,000.

15 Citigroup, one of the largest U.S. banking firms, reports a net loss of about $10 billion for the fourth quarter of 2007. Two days later, Merrill Lynch, another giant U.S. financial services firm, also reports a fourth-quarter net loss of about $10 billion. The losses are mainly due to investments made in high-risk mortgages. Many financial companies are experiencing major declines in profits or outright losses as a result of an on-going mortgage and credit crisis.

15 Former Massachusetts Governor Mitt Romney wins the Republican presidential primary in Michigan. Senator Hillary Rodham Clinton of New York wins Michigan's Democratic primary, but little attention is paid to the contest. The Democratic National Committee voted in 2007 to strip Michigan of its national convention delegates because the state decided to hold its primary earlier than allowed by party rules.

18 Citing instability in the housing and financial markets, sluggish job growth, and high energy costs, U.S. President George W. Bush calls for a $145-billion tax relief package aimed at spurring both business investment and consumer spending. Congressional leaders express optimism that a bipartisan agreement will be reached quickly on the stimulus plan. It is likely to include a one-time tax rebate for individuals and families.

19 In Nevada's presidential caucuses, Senator Hillary Rodham Clinton of New York finishes first among the Democrats, and former Massachusetts Governor Mitt Romney finishes first among the Republicans. In South Carolina, Senator John McCain of Arizona wins the Republican presidential primary.

21 Stock markets around the world plummet on fears that the financial crisis in the United States may have global repercussions. The major stock indexes in China, France, Germany, Hong Kong, India, and the United Kingdom all fall more than 5 percent.

22 In an aggressive move, the U.S. Federal Reserve System slashes the federal funds rate from 4.25 percent to 3.5 percent. This key interest rate is the amount banks charge each other for short-term loans. The unusually large rate cut helps limit a decline in U.S. stock markets.

23 Militants destroy parts of the border wall separating the Gaza Strip from Egypt, and tens of thousands of Palestinians pour into Egypt to buy food, fuel, and other supplies. The breach of the border comes less than a week after Israel tightened a blockade of the Gaza Strip in response to a rise in Palestinian rocket attacks from Gaza into Israeli territory.

26 Senator Barack Obama of Illinois wins the Democratic presidential primary in South Carolina.

29 In Kenya, former United Nations Secretary-General Kofi Annan opens formal negotiations between President Mwai Kibaki and opposition leader Raila Odinga. The talks are an attempt to end weeks of ethnic violence triggered by the presidential election of December 2007, in which Kibaki won a narrow and disputed victory over Odinga. Hundreds of people have died in the violence.

29 Senator John McCain of Arizona finishes first in Florida's Republican presidential primary. Senator Hillary Rodham Clinton of New York wins Florida's Democratic primary, but her victory is seen as largely symbolic. The Democratic National Committee voted in 2007 to strip Florida of its national convention delegates be-cause the state chose to hold its primary earlier than allowed by party rules.

30 Former New York City Mayor Rudy Giuliani drops out of the race for the Republican presidential nomination. Former Senator John Edwards of North Carolina abandons his bid for the Democratic presidential nomination.

30 The U.S. Federal Reserve System reduces the federal funds rate from 3.5 percent to 3 percent, just days after reducing it from 4.25 percent. The action comes amid increased concern that the U.S. economy may be on the verge of recession.

13

1 Suicide bombings at two animal markets in Baghdad, the capital of Iraq, leave nearly 100 people dead.

1 The U.S. oil company ExxonMobil reports a $40.6-billion profit for 2007, the largest annual profit in U.S. history.

3 In a stunning upset, the New York Giants defeat the previously unbeaten New England Patriots 17-14 in the National Football League's Super Bowl XLII.

5 Super Tuesday presidential primaries and caucuses are held in 24 states. Senator John McCain of Arizona emerges as the clear front-runner in the Republican race, with victories in 9 states, including California, Illinois, and New York. Former Massachusetts Governor Mitt Romney wins in 7 states, and former Arkansas Governor Mike Huckabee wins in 5. The Democratic race remains close. Senator Hillary Rodham Clinton of New York notches victories in most of the larger states, including California and New York, but Senator Barack Obama of Illinois wins in 13 states compared with Clinton's total of 9.

5 Dozens of tornadoes tear through Alabama, Arkansas, Kentucky, Mississippi, and Tennessee. More than 55 people are killed.

7 Former Massachusetts Governor Mitt Romney drops out of the race for the Republican presidential nomination.

7 Both houses of the U.S. Congress approve a $168-billion economic stimulus package that includes tax rebates for individuals and families and tax incentives for businesses. President George W. Bush signs the legislation on February 13.

9 Senator Barack Obama of Illinois wins the Democratic presidential primary in Louisiana and caucuses in Nebraska and Washington. On the Republican side, Senator John McCain of Arizona places first in Washington's caucuses, and former Arkansas Governor Mike Huckabee collects victories in Kansas's caucuses and Louisiana's primary.

12 General Motors, the largest U.S. automaker, announces a $38.7-billion loss for 2007, the largest annual loss ever for a U.S. automobile company. The loss is mainly due to a one-time charge to write down deferred tax assets.

12 Film and TV writers belonging to the Writers Guild of America vote to end a strike against studios and networks. An agreement was reached earlier in February over how writers will be paid for the use of their material on the Internet and DVD's. The strike, which lasted 100 days, kept new episodes of U.S. television comedies and dramas from being produced.

12 Presidential primaries are held in Maryland, Virginia, and the District of Columbia. Senator Barack Obama of Illinois wins all three Democratic contests. Senator John McCain of Arizona wins all three Republican contests.

13 Australian Prime Minister Kevin Rudd issues a formal apology to the country's Aborigines for the wrongs done to them by past governments. He apologizes especially for the removal of Aboriginal children from their homes in the 1800's and 1900's.

16 A controversial U.S. surveillance law expires, despite efforts by congressional Republicans to extend it. The temporary law, enacted in August 2007, gave U.S. intelligence agencies the power to eavesdrop on U.S. residents' international phone calls and e-mails for antiterrorism purposes without first getting a warrant.

17 A suicide bombing at a crowded dogfighting event in Kandahar, Afghanistan, kills more than 100 people. The next day, another suicide attack kills more than 35 people in nearby Spin Boldak.

17 The province of Kosovo declares independence from Serbia. The move is condemned as illegal by Serbia and its ally Russia. In the following days, however, the United States and most major European countries recognize Kosovo as an independent country.

A Kosovar Albanian man places an Albanian flag on his roof in Kosovska Mitrovica, Kosovo, to celebrate Kosovo's declaration of independence from Serbia on Feb. 17, 2008. Most Kosovars are ethnic Albanians. Serbia and its ally Russia opposed Kosovo's move, but the United States and most major European countries recognized Kosovo's independence.

17 Westland/Hallmark Meat Company of Chino, California, recalls 143 million pounds (65 million kilograms) of beef because some of the cattle were not properly inspected before slaughter. It is the largest beef recall in U.S. history.

18 Two opposition parties achieve a decisive victory in Pakistan's parliamentary elections. President Pervez Musharraf, who came to power in a 1999 military coup, says that he accepts the defeat of the ruling party, which is allied with him.

19 Fidel Castro announces his resignation as president of Cuba after 49 years in power. On February 24, Cuba's National Assembly names Fidel's brother Raúl president. Raúl Castro has been acting president since July 2006, when Fidel Castro underwent surgery.

19 Senator Barack Obama of Illinois places first in Wisconsin's Democratic presidential primary and Hawaii's caucuses. Senator John McCain of Arizona wins the Republican presidential primaries in Washington and Wisconsin.

21 Thousands of Turkish troops enter northern Iraq to hunt Kurdish rebels who have been staging cross-border attacks in Turkey. The rebels belong to the Kurdistan Workers Party (PKK), which seeks to establish a Kurdish state that would include much of southeastern Turkey. The Turkish offensive lasts until February 29 and achieves its goals, according to Turkey's military.

24 A suicide bombing near Iskandariya, Iraq, kills more than 60 Shi`ite Muslim pilgrims who were on their way to Karbala to observe a religious holiday.

28 After weeks of negotiations, Kenyan President Mwai Kibaki and opposition leader Raila Odinga sign a power-sharing agreement. Under the deal, Kibaki will remain president, and Odinga will assume the newly created position of prime minister. The deal is designed to end the ethnic conflict triggered by the presidential election of December 2007, in which Kibaki won a narrow and disputed victory over Odinga. Hundreds of people have died in the violence.

15

MARCH

2008

A man demonstrates outside the headquarters of the Wall Street firm Bear Stearns on March 26, 2008, protesting its government-backed sale to JPMorgan Chase. The U.S. Federal Reserve financed the deal because it feared that a Bear Stearns collapse would harm the overall economy.

1 A day of intense fighting in the Gaza Strip between Israeli military forces and Palestinian militants leaves dozens of Palestinians and two Israelis dead. The violence began on February 27 and has involved Israeli air strikes, Palestinian rocket attacks on Israeli cities, and an incursion of Israeli troops and tanks into Gaza. The Israeli offensive lasts until March 3.

2 Russian First Deputy Prime Minister Dmitry Medvedev easily wins the country's presidential election. He will succeed President Vladimir Putin in May and plans to appoint Putin as prime minister.

4 Senator John McCain of Arizona clinches the Republican presidential nomination by winning the primaries in Ohio, Rhode Island, Texas, and Vermont. Former Arkansas Governor Mike Huckabee withdraws from the race. On the Democratic side, Senator Hillary Rodham Clinton of New York wins the Ohio, Rhode Island, and Texas primaries. Senator Barack Obama of Illinois wins the Texas caucuses and the Vermont primary.

6 Two back-to-back bombings in a crowded market in Baghdad, Iraq, leave nearly 70 people dead.

6 A Palestinian gunman kills eight Israeli rabbinical students at a seminary in Jerusalem.

8 United States President George W. Bush vetoes a bill that would have prohibited the Central Intelligence

Agency from using waterboarding and other harsh interrogation techniques on terrorism suspects.

11 The U.S. Federal Reserve System announces that it will lend up to $200 billion in U.S. government securities to major Wall Street financial institutions in an attempt to ease the crisis in credit markets. The institutions will be allowed to put up hard-to-sell mortgage-backed assets as collateral. Investors respond favorably to the plan, sending the Dow Jones Industrial Average up nearly 417 points after more than a week of decline.

11 Senator Barack Obama of Illinois wins the Democratic presidential primary in Mississippi.

12 New York Governor Eliot Spitzer announces his resignation, two days after *The New York Times* reported that he had patronized a prostitution service. On March 17, Lieutenant Governor David Paterson succeeds Spitzer and becomes the state's first black and first legally blind governor.

14 Anti-Chinese riots erupt in Lhasa, the capital of China's Tibet region. The riots follow four days of nonviolent marches by Buddhist monks who were marking the anniversary of a failed 1959 Tibetan uprising against Chinese rule. Many regular Tibetans joined the monks' protests, partly because of rumors that security forces were beating and detaining monks, and partly because of simmering resentment over the growing numbers of Han Chinese migrating to Tibet. In the days following the Lhasa riots, protests and clashes spread to other ethnic Tibetan areas of China.

16 JPMorgan Chase, a major Wall Street financial services firm, agrees to buy another major Wall Street firm, Bear Stearns, in a deal backed by the U.S. Federal Reserve System (the Fed). Bear Stearns was on the verge of collapse be-cause of its high exposure to mortgage-backed assets—which had sunk in value as a result of the U.S. housing slump—and its subsequent inability to pay back its lenders. The Fed agrees to provide a $30-billion line of credit to JPMorgan Chase and accept the mortgage-backed assets in Bear Stearns's portfolio as collateral. Federal officials feared that a Bear Stearns bankruptcy would have led to chaos in the overall financial system. The Fed also announces that it will allow

nonbanking financial firms to borrow money directly from the Fed at the rate normally reserved for commercial banks.

17 A bombing near a Shi`ite shrine in Karbala, Iraq, kills more than 50 people.

18 Senator Barack Obama of Illinois, a candidate for the Democratic presiden-tial nomination, delivers a major speech in Philadelphia on race and racial divi-sions in the United States. The speech is in response to the widespread attention being paid to controversial remarks made by Obama's former pastor in Chicago, Jeremiah Wright. Both Obama and Wright are African Americans.

18 In another aggressive move to calm the financial crisis and head off a recession, the U.S. Federal Reserve System lowers the federal funds rate from 3 percent to 2.25 percent. This key interest rate is the amount banks charge each other for short-term loans. Stock markets rally in response, with the Dow Jones Industrial Average jumping 420 points.

23 A roadside bomb kills four U.S. soldiers in southern Baghdad, Iraq, raising the total number of U.S. military fatalities in the five-year Iraq War to 4,000.

24 Pakistan's National Assembly elects Yousaf Raza Gilani as prime minister. Gilani immediately orders the release of top judges who were put under house arrest by President Pervez Musharraf in 2007. Gilani belongs to the Pakistan People's Party (PPP), which opposes Musharraf. The PPP won the most seats in recent parliamentary elections.

25 About 30,000 Iraqi soldiers and police officers launch an offensive in Basra, Iraq, to try to wrest control of the city from Shi`ite militias, particularly the Mahdi Army militia affiliated with the radical cleric Muqtada al-Sadr. Soon after the Basra fighting begins, clashes also erupt between Shi`ite militias and Iraqi and U.S. forces in Baghdad and other cities. For six days, the militias put up heavy resistance. United States and British forces provide some air and artillery support to the Iraqi forces. Hundreds of people die in the fighting. On March 30, Sadr orders his men to withdraw from the streets, and most of the violence in Basra and elsewhere subsides by March 31. Iraqi forces take control of some parts of Basra, but militias remain in control of other areas.

1 The Swiss financial services firm UBS announces an estimated net loss of more than $12 billion for the first quarter of 2008 and a doubling of its write-downs of ailing mortgage-backed assets. The firm's write-downs of such assets since the beginning of 2007 now total about $37 billion.

2 Zimbabwe's electoral commission announces that the ruling party of President Robert Mugabe lost its parliamentary majority in elections on March 29. Results of the presidential election, also held on March 29, have not yet been released. Independent observers predict that a runoff may be necessary between Mugabe and opposition leader Morgan Tsvangirai. The delay in reporting the presidential election results causes tensions to rise in the country.

2 Irish Prime Minister Bernie Ahern announces that he will resign on May 6. He has been under pressure because of government investigations into his personal finances.

4 Texas state police and child welfare officials raid a compound near Eldorado owned by a fundamentalist Mormon sect that practices polygamy. Over the course of four days, more than 400 children are removed from the compound. The officials are investigating allegations that children are being abused, particularly by forcing girls to marry much older men.

6 Fighting erupts in the Sadr City district of Baghdad, Iraq, as Iraqi and U.S. troops try to gain control of areas from which Shi`ite militias are firing rockets and mortars into the nearby Green Zone. The Green Zone is the site of most of Iraq's government buildings as well as the U.S. and British embassies. On-and-off violence in Sadr City continues for several weeks.

8 In testimony before two U.S. Senate committees, Army General David Petraeus, the top U.S. commander in Iraq, recommends that troop withdrawals from Iraq be suspended starting in July, after a current drawdown of 20,000 troops is complete. Withdrawing too many forces too fast could jeopardize the security gains of the past year, he says. On April 10, President George W. Bush says that he will follow Petraeus's recommendation to suspend troop withdrawals. About 140,000 U.S. troops will remain in Iraq after July. Bush also says that starting on August 1, troops will be deployed to Iraq and Afghanistan for 12-month tours instead of 15-month tours.

13 At a meeting in Washington, D.C., officials of the World Bank and the International Monetary Fund call on wealthy countries to respond quickly to a dramatic increase in global food prices. The food crisis is perhaps a greater threat to economic and political stability than the crisis in capital markets, the officials say. Riots have recently broken out in several poor nations in response to high food prices.

14 In Italy, parliamentary elections are held on April 13 and 14. A center-right coalition led by former Prime Minister Silvio Berlusconi wins solid majorities in both houses.

14 Delta Air Lines and Northwest Airlines announce that they will merge, creating the world's largest airline. It will be called Delta and will be based in Atlanta.

15 A car bomb in Baqubah, Iraq, leaves at least 40 people dead. A suicide bomber in Ramadi, Iraq, kills more than 10 people.

16 The U.S. Supreme Court rules 7-2 that Kentucky's method of capital punishment—a lethal injection of three drugs—does not violate the U.S. Constitution.

17 A suicide bombing at a funeral in Iraq's Diyala province leaves at least 50 people dead.

19 Iraqi forces, backed by U.S. and British air and artillery strikes, take control of the last major strongholds of the Mahdi Army militia in Basra, Iraq. The Mahdi Army is affiliated with the radical Shi`ite cleric Muqtada al-Sadr. Militiamen continue to battle Iraqi and U.S. forces in the Sadr City district of Baghdad through the rest of April.

United States Army soldiers lead a man suspected of planting a roadside bomb near their patrol in the Sadr City district of Baghdad, Iraq, on April 23, 2008. Throughout April, Iraqi and U.S. troops battled Shi`ite militias, particularly the Mahdi Army affiliated with the radical cleric Muqtada al-Sadr.

22 Church leaders in Zimbabwe allege that post-election violence in the country has the potential to escalate into genocide. Catholic, Anglican, and Evangelical leaders claim that people who voted for the opposition in the March 29 presidential and parliamentary elections are being abducted and tortured. A partial recount of election results began on April 19 at the request of the ruling party of President Robert Mugabe.

22 Senator Hillary Rodham Clinton of New York wins Pennsylvania's Democratic presidential primary.

23 United States Defense Secretary Robert Gates announces that Army General David Petraeus, the top U.S. commander in Iraq, will be nominated by President George W. Bush to lead the U.S. Central Command. The Central Command oversees all U.S. military activities in the Middle East and Central Asia, including the wars in Iraq and Afghanistan. If confirmed by the Senate, Petraeus will replace Navy Admiral William J. Fallon, who resigned on March 11. Gates also announces that Army Lieutenant General Raymond Odierno will be nominated to replace Petraeus in Iraq.

24 Leaders of Iraq's largest Sunni political bloc, the Iraqi Accordance Front, announce that the bloc is ready to rejoin the country's Shi`ite-led cabinet, though details of the return are still being worked out. The Sunni bloc withdrew from the government in August 2007.

27 Taliban militants try to assassinate Afghan President Hamid Karzai by firing guns and rockets at a military parade he is attending in Kabul. Karzai survives, but three other people are killed.

28 In a 6-3 decision, the U.S. Supreme Court upholds an Indiana law that requires voters to present photo identification at the polls.

30 The U.S. Federal Reserve System lowers the federal funds rate from 2.25 percent to 2 percent. This key rate is the amount banks charge each other for short-term loans.

Children wait in the rain for food at a donation center in Labutta, Myanmar, on May 15, 2008. Cyclone Nargis struck Myanmar on May 2, killing tens of thousands of people and leaving hundreds of thousands of survivors struggling with hunger and homelessness.

1 Suicide bombers attack a wedding convoy in Iraq's Diyala province. More than 40 people are killed.

2 Zimbabwe's electoral commission finally releases the results of the March 29 presidential election. Opposition leader Morgan Tsvangirai won 47.9 percent of the vote, and President Robert Mugabe won 43.2 percent. Zimbabwean law requires a runoff because neither candidate won more than 50 percent.

2 In Myanmar, Cyclone Nargis slams into the Irrawaddy Delta region and the city of Yangon, leaving more than 138,000 people dead or missing and hundreds of thousands of people homeless. In the following days, Myanmar's military government is widely criticized for its slow response to the disaster and its initial refusal to allow international aid workers into the country.

6 Senator Barack Obama of Illinois places first in North Carolina's Democratic presidential primary. Senator Hillary Rodham Clinton of New York wins the Democratic primary in Indiana.

7 Ireland's parliament elects Finance Minister Brian Cowen as the new Irish prime minister. He succeeds Bertie Ahern, who resigned May 6.

7 Dmitry Medvedev is sworn in as president of Russia. He nominates his predecessor, Vladimir Putin, as prime minister. Russia's parliament confirms Putin on May 8. Many observers expect Putin to continue to wield a great deal of power.

7 Violence erupts in Lebanon's capital, Beirut, between Hezbollah militants and supporters of Lebanon's government. The violence stems from government decisions a day earlier to dismantle Hezbollah's private telephone network and fire the head of security at Beirut's airport over alleged Hezbollah ties. Fighting continues in Beirut and elsewhere in the country for about a week. On May 14, the government formally reverses the two decisions that sparked the violence.

20 Thousands of Iraqi troops enter the Sadr City district of Baghdad, meeting almost no resistance from the Mahdi Army militia affiliated with the radical Shi`ite cleric Muqtada al-Sadr. In recent weeks, the Mahdi Army has clashed repeatedly with Iraqi and U.S. forces over control of Sadr City. The Iraqi government and Sadrist aides reached a truce on May 10.

20 Senator Barack Obama of Illinois wins the Democratic presidential primary in Oregon. Senator Hillary Rodham Clinton of New York picks up a victory in Kentucky's Democratic primary.

21 Lebanon's government and the militant group Hezbollah reach a power-sharing deal, ending a political crisis that began in November 2006 when the Hezbollah-led opposition quit the cabinet of Prime Minister Fouad Siniora. The deal gives Hezbollah veto power in the cabinet and provides for General Michel Suleiman, the army chief and a compromise candidate, to be elected president on May 25.

8 Conservative leader Silvio Berlusconi is sworn in as prime minister of Italy. It is his third stint in the country's top job.

10-11 Tornadoes leave at least 20 people dead in Georgia, Oklahoma, and Missouri.

11 In South Africa, a mob in Johannesburg's Alexandra township attacks a group of migrants from nearby African countries. In the following weeks, violence against foreigners spreads to other areas in and around Johannesburg and later to other parts of South Africa, causing more than 60 deaths. The violence is largely motivated by frustration about poverty, with poor South Africans scapegoating immigrants for taking scarce jobs and housing.

12 A powerful earthquake occurs in China's Sichuan province, leaving more than 80,000 people dead or missing and millions of people homeless. A large percentage of the dead are children whose schools have collapsed.

13 A series of coordinated bomb attacks in Jaipur, India, kills more than 60 people.

13 Senator Hillary Rodham Clinton of New York wins West Virginia's Democratic presidential primary.

15 The California Supreme Court rules that same-sex couples have the right to marry under the state Constitution.

25 Phoenix, an unmanned U.S. spacecraft, lands on the northern polar region of Mars. Scientists plan to use Phoenix's robotic equipment to study the history of water on the planet and investigate whether life could survive in the Martian arctic region.

28 Nepal's Constituent Assembly, led by former Maoist rebels, abolishes the country's 239-year-old monarchy and declares Nepal a republic. The Maoists fought against the monarchy from 1996 to 2006.

29 The Texas Supreme Court rules that state officials acted improperly when they removed more than 400 children from a fundamentalist Mormon compound near Eldorado in April. The officials were investigating allegations that children were being abused, particularly young girls being forced to marry much older men. The court rules that the state failed to prove the children were in immediate danger. In the following weeks, nearly all the children are returned to their parents.

31 To resolve an intraparty dispute, Democratic National Committee (DNC) officials agree to seat delegates from Michigan and Florida at the national convention in August, but with only half a vote each. The DNC originally stripped both states of all their delegates because the states decided to hold their presidential primaries earlier than allowed by party rules.

21

JUNE

2008

1 Senator Hillary Rodham Clinton of New York wins the Democratic presidential primary in Puerto Rico.

3 On the last day of the longest and closest presidential primary race in decades, Senator Barack Obama of Illinois clinches the Democratic nomination by gaining the support of several superdelegates and by winning the Montana primary. The superdelegates are mostly current or former party leaders and elected officials. Obama becomes the first African American presidential nominee of a major party. Senator Hillary Rodham Clinton of New York wins the South Dakota primary but falls short in her overall bid for the nomination.

5 Khalid Shaikh Mohammed, the alleged mastermind behind the Sept. 11, 2001, terrorist attacks against the United States, and four other high-level terrorism suspects are arraigned before a U.S. military commission at Guantánamo Bay, Cuba. Each of the men faces 2,973 charges of murder, one for each victim of the September 11 attacks.

6 The U.S. Department of Labor reports that the nation's unemployment rate jumped from 5 percent in April to 5.5 percent in May. Also, the price of a barrel of crude oil on the New York Mercantile Exchange shoots up $10.75 to end the day at $138.54. Stock market investors react pessimistically, sending the Dow Jones Industrial Average down nearly 395 points.

7 Senator Hillary Rodham Clinton of New York ends her run for the Democratic presidential nomination and endorses her opponent, Senator Barack Obama of Illinois.

8 The average retail price of regular unleaded gasoline in the United States reaches $4 a gallon for the first time.

11 Canadian Prime Minister Stephen Harper formally apologizes to the country's *indigenous* (native) peoples for the government's role in forcibly removing indigenous children from their homes and placing them in boarding schools during the 1800's and 1900's.

12 In Cedar Rapids, Iowa, the Cedar River crests at a record 31.2 feet (9.5 meters). Most of the downtown area is underwater, and thousands of people have evacuated their homes. Heavy rains since late May have caused severe flooding along many rivers in Iowa and other Midwestern states. The flooding, which continues through the rest of June, displaces up to 40,000 people and damages millions of acres of farmland.

12 The U.S. Supreme Court rules 5-4 that the foreign terrorism suspects being held at the U.S. naval base at Guantánamo Bay, Cuba, are entitled to the constitutional privilege of habeas corpus—that is, the right to challenge their detention in federal court.

12 Voters in Ireland reject the Lisbon Treaty in a referendum. The intent of the Lisbon Treaty is to reform the institutions of the European Union (EU) to make them more efficient. Because the treaty requires unanimous approval by all 27 EU nations, the Irish vote means that it cannot come into force.

13 Taliban insurgents attack a prison in Kandahar, Afghanistan, blowing up the walls, killing 15 guards, and freeing about 1,200 inmates.

17 Israel and the Palestinian militant group Hamas agree to a six-month cease-fire in and near the Gaza Strip starting June 19. The truce, brokered by Egypt, aims to end Palestinian missile attacks on Israel from Gaza as well as Israeli incursions into Gaza. If the truce holds, Israel plans to ease a blockade of the Gaza Strip that has been in place since Hamas seized control of the territory in June 2007.

17 A car bomb attack in Baghdad, Iraq, kills more than 60 people.

18 North Atlantic Treaty Organization (NATO) and Afghan forces launch an offensive against Taliban militants who are in control of strategically important villages outside Kandahar, Afghanistan. The offensive succeeds in driving the militants out of the villages by the following day.

Buildings and debris pile up in the Cedar River against a partially collapsed railroad bridge in Cedar Rapids, Iowa, on June 14, 2008. The flooding in Cedar Rapids was the worst in the city's history. Heavy rains in May and June caused severe floods along several rivers in the Midwest, displacing up to 40,000 people.

21 Typhoon Fengshen strikes the Philippines, causing the deaths of more than 1,000 people. About 800 of those deaths occur when a ferry, the *Princess of the Stars,* capsizes near Sibuyan Island.

22 Zimbabwe's opposition leader, Morgan Tsvangirai, withdraws from the presidential runoff election against President Robert Mugabe scheduled for June 27. Tsvangirai says that it has become too dangerous for his supporters to vote for him. Since the first round of voting on March 29, the police, the military, and progovernment militias and gangs have killed, beaten, injured, raped, detained, and destroyed the property of many opposition supporters.

25 The U.S. Supreme Court votes 5-4 to strike down as unconstitutional a Louisiana law that authorized the death penalty for the crime of child rape.

26 North Korea submits a declaration of its nuclear activities to China. The next day, North Korea demolishes the cooling tower at its Yongbyon nuclear reactor complex. These actions were called for in an agreement North Korea made in 2007 to end its nuclear weapons programs.

26 In a 5-4 decision, the U.S. Supreme Court strikes down the District of Columbia's handgun ban, ruling that the U.S. Constitution protects an individual's right to own firearms for self-defense.

27 Zimbabwe's presidential runoff election is held, despite the fact that opposition candidate Morgan Tsvangirai withdrew five days earlier. On June 29, President Robert Mugabe is declared the election winner and is sworn in to a new term. On July 1, the African Union calls for a unity government that would include both Mugabe and Tsvangirai.

A customer tries to get the attention of someone inside an IndyMac Bank branch in Pasadena, California, on July 14, 2008, as others wait for the bank to open under federal management. Regulators seized IndyMac on July 11 after depositors withdrew $1.3 billion over 11 business days.

2 Colombian soldiers rescue 15 hostages held by Marxist guerrillas in the Colombian jungle. The freed hostages include former Colombian presidential candidate Íngrid Betancourt and three U.S. citizens.

6 A U.S. air strike near Jalalabad, Afghanistan, reportedly kills 47 civilians traveling to a wedding party.

7 A suicide car bombing at the Indian embassy in Afghanistan's capital, Kabul, kills nearly 60 people.

8 Leaders of the Group of Eight industrialized nations adopt a goal to cut global greenhouse gas emissions in half by 2050.

8 Czech and U.S. diplomats sign an agreement authorizing the United States to install part of a missile defense shield in the Czech Republic. Russia denounces the pact.

9 Iran test-fires nine missiles, including one that Iranian officials claim is capable of striking Israel.

9 The U.S. Senate passes a controversial revision of the Foreign Intelligence Surveillance Act. President George W. Bush signs the bill on July 10. It expands the government's eavesdropping powers in terrorism cases and grants immunity to telecommunications companies that participated in a secret National Security Agency domestic wiretapping program.

10 The U.S. Senate confirms Army General David Petraeus as the new head of the U.S. Central Command, which oversees all U.S. military activities in the Middle East and Central Asia. The Senate also confirms Army Lieutenant General Raymond Odierno to replace Petraeus as the top U.S. commander in Iraq.

11 Federal regulators seize IndyMac Bank, a major U.S. mortgage lender, after a run of $1.3 billion in withdrawals from the bank over 11 business days. It is the first major bank failure since the country's mortgage crisis began in 2006.

11 The price of crude oil on the New York Mercantile Exchange hits $147.27 a barrel in intraday trading—an all-time high.

13 About 200 Taliban-allied insurgents attack a joint U.S.-Afghan military post in eastern Afghanistan. Nine U.S. soldiers and dozens of insurgents are killed.

13 The U.S. Treasury Department and the U.S. Federal Reserve System (the Fed) unveil a plan to stabilize the giant U.S. mortgage finance companies Fannie Mae and Freddie Mac. Their stock prices sank last week due to fears about their financial condition. The plan, which requires congressional approval, would raise the amount that the companies may borrow from the Treasury and would permit the Treasury to buy stock in the companies. Also, the Fed announces that it will allow Fannie Mae and Freddie Mac to borrow money directly from the Fed at the rate normally reserved for commercial banks.

14 The International Criminal Court prosecutor charges Sudan's president, Umar Hassan al-Bashir, with genocide, crimes against humanity, and war crimes in connection with a military campaign against people in Sudan's Darfur region.

14 United States President George W. Bush revokes an 18-year-old executive order that prohibited oil firms from drilling off U.S. coasts. A separate congressional ban on offshore oil drilling remains in place.

15 The euro reaches an all-time high against the U.S. dollar, peaking at $1.6038.

18 United States President George W. Bush agrees to "a general time horizon" for the withdrawal of U.S. troops from Iraq as part of a long-term security accord that the two countries are negotiating. The decision marks a shift from Bush's previous adamant refusals to consider a timetable for troop withdrawal.

19 A U.S. undersecretary of state attends talks involving Iran's chief nuclear negotiator and the European Union's foreign policy chief. It is the highest-level diplomatic contact between Iran and the United States since the 1979 Iranian revolution. The talks, aimed at curbing Iran's nuclear program, are inconclusive.

19 Iraq's largest Sunni political bloc, the Iraqi Accordance Front, ends its yearlong boycott of the country's Shi`ite-led government. The Iraqi parliament approves the appointment of six members of the Sunni bloc to cabinet posts.

21 At their first face-to-face meeting in 10 years, Zimbabwean President Robert Mugabe and opposition leader Morgan Tsvangirai sign an agreement to begin power-sharing talks. It is a step toward resolving a crisis sparked by Zimbabwe's disputed 2008 presidential election. The crisis has involved government-organized violence against opposition supporters.

21 Serbian authorities capture Radovan Karadzic, the Bosnian Serb leader accused of organizing the 1995 massacre of more than 7,000 Bosniaks (Bosnian Muslims) in Srebrenica during the 1992-1995 war in Bosnia-Herzegovina. On July 31, 2008, Karadzic is arraigned on genocide charges before an international criminal tribunal in The Hague, the Netherlands.

23 The U.S. House of Representatives passes a major housing relief bill. The Senate approves the bill on July 26, and President George W. Bush signs it on July 30. The legislation increases the authority of the U.S. Treasury Department to shore up the large U.S. mortgage finance companies Fannie Mae and Freddie Mac. The bill also aims to help homeowners who are at risk of foreclosure to replace their adjustable-rate mortgages with fixed-rate, government-insured loans.

26 A series of bomb blasts in Ahmadabad, India, kills more than 50 people.

28 Three suicide bombers attack targets in Baghdad, Iraq, killing about 35 people. Another suicide bombing in Kirkuk, Iraq, leaves about 30 people dead.

29 Bruce Ivins—a U.S. Army scientist suspected by federal investigators of being responsible for the 2001 anthrax mailings that killed five people—dies of suicide by drug overdose.

29 In Geneva, Switzerland, trade negotiations of the so-called Doha Round collapse when officials from more than 30 countries fail to agree on a pact to reduce global trade barriers.

30 Israeli Prime Minister Ehud Olmert announces that he will not compete in the September 17 leadership election of his party, Kadima, and that he will resign as prime minister after a new Kadima leader is chosen. Olmert faces several corruption allegations, all of which he denies.

AUGUST

2008

6 A U.S. military jury convicts Salim Hamdan—a Yemeni detainee in the U.S. military prison at Guantánamo Bay, Cuba—of providing material support to terrorists. The jury acquits him of conspiring to commit terrorist acts. Hamdan's trial was the first in a controversial military commissions system set up in 2006 to try terrorism suspects.

7 Georgian forces attack Tskhinvali, capital of the separatist region of South Ossetia, after days of border skirmishes with separatist fighters. On August 8, large numbers of Russian troops and tanks arrive in the city and begin driving Georgian forces out. Russia also launches air strikes on targets inside Georgia. In the following days, Russia sends troops to defend Abkhazia, another separatist region; continues its air campaign; finishes expelling Georgian forces from South Ossetia; and initiates a ground invasion deep into undisputed Georgian territory. Hundreds of soldiers and civilians are killed in the war. South Ossetia and Abkhazia are internationally recognized as part of Georgia, but secessionist governments backed by Russia rule both regions.

8 The 2008 Summer Olympic Games open in Beijing with a lavish ceremony featuring some 15,000 performers and 30,000 fireworks.

10 Bolivian President Evo Morales survives a recall vote, winning the support of 68 percent of voters, including most of Bolivia's poor indigenous citizens. However, four department governors who oppose Morales also survive recall votes. These governors, all in Bolivia's wealthier areas, oppose his efforts to implement socialist policies and redistribute land and wealth.

15 Georgian President Mikheil Saakashvili signs a French-brokered cease-fire agreement to end his country's war with Russia and the separatist regions of South Ossetia and Abkhazia. Russian President Dmitry Medvedev signs the accord the next day. However, the two sides disagree over interpretation of the truce terms, particularly the timing and extent of Russian troop withdrawal from undisputed

Georgian territory. In the following weeks, Russian troops pull back from much of the Georgian land they invaded, but they remain in buffer zones around the separatist regions, despite the objections of Georgia and its Western allies.

17 The American swimmer Michael Phelps wins his eighth gold medal at the Beijing Olympics, breaking the record for most gold medals at a single Olympics. The previous record holder was another American swimmer, Mark Spitz, who won seven golds in 1972. Phelps's career Olympic gold medal tally is now 14, also a record. The previous record for career golds was nine.

18 Facing an impeachment movement that began on August 7, Pakistani President Pervez Musharraf resigns. The government has been under his political opponents' control since March. Musharraf's public support began to fall sharply in 2007 because of actions he took to retain power, including ousting Supreme Court judges and declaring a state of emergency in November.

19 Taliban insurgents ambush and kill 10 French paratroopers near Kabul, Afghanistan, on August 18 and 19. Around the same time, other Taliban fighters, including multiple suicide bombers, attack a large U.S. base near the town of Khowst.

19 A suicide car bombing in the Algerian town of Issers, east of Algiers, leaves more than 40 people dead. The next day, two car bomb explosions in the nearby town of Bouira kill more than 10 people.

20 Polish and U.S. officials sign a deal authorizing the United States to locate part of a missile defense shield in Poland. Russian officials denounce the pact and suggest that Russia may respond militarily.

20 A Spanair plane crashes during take-off from Madrid-Barajas Airport in Madrid, killing 154 people.

21 Iraqi and U.S. negotiators agree on draft security terms that call for U.S. combat forces to leave Iraqi cities by mid-2009 and the rest of Iraq by the end of 2011 if condi-

Georgian soldiers run past a building hit by Russian bombardment in Gori, Georgia, on Aug. 9, 2008. Russia defeated Georgia in a war over South Ossetia and Abkhazia, two regions recognized internationally as part of Georgia but controlled by Russian-backed secessionist governments.

tions are relatively stable. The accord requires approval by both governments.

21 Two suicide bombers attack a weapons manufacturing complex in Wah, Pakistan, killing more than 60 people.

22 A U.S.-led air strike near Shindand, Afghanistan, kills as many as 90 civilians, according to Afghan and United Nations reports. The U.S. military puts the number at about 30.

23 Senator Barack Obama of Illinois, the Democratic candidate for U.S. president, names Senator Joe Biden of Delaware as his vice presidential running mate.

24 The closing ceremony of the Beijing Olympics takes place with a cast of thousands. During the games, China won the most gold medals (51). The United States won the most medals overall (110).

26 Russia formally recognizes the independence of South Ossetia and Abkhazia, two separatist regions recognized as part of Georgia by other countries. Georgia and its Western allies denounce the move. Military forces from Russia and the two

regions drove Georgian forces out of the regions earlier in August. Russian forces remain in the two regions as well as in surrounding Georgian territory.

28 Senator Barack Obama of Illinois officially accepts the Democratic nomination for U.S. president at his party's national convention in Denver.

29 Senator John McCain of Arizona, the Republican candidate for U.S. president, names Alaska Governor Sarah Palin as his vice presidential running mate. Palin becomes the second female major-party vice presidential candidate in U.S. history and the first for the Republicans.

30 As Hurricane Gustav crosses the Caribbean—causing especially serious damage in Cuba—New Orleans Mayor Ray Nagin orders a mandatory evacuation of the city. By the time Gustav makes landfall in Louisiana on September 1, about 2 million people have left New Orleans and nearby areas of the U.S. Gulf Coast. The storm causes damage in these areas, but much less than feared. Gustav's overall death toll in the Caribbean and the United States reaches about 140.

SEPTEMBER

2008

President George W. Bush walks to the White House Rose Garden on Sept. 19, 2008, to deliver a statement about the U.S. economy. With him are (left to right) Federal Reserve Chairman Ben Bernanke, Securities and Exchange Commission Chairman Chris Cox, and Treasury Secretary Henry Paulson.

1 Facing low approval ratings, Japanese Prime Minister Yasuo Fukuda announces that he will resign.

1 Rainfall from Tropical Storm Hanna begins to drench Haiti. Over the following days, flooding and mudslides kill hundreds of Haitians.

4 Senator John McCain of Arizona officially accepts the Republican nomination for U.S. president at his party's national convention in St. Paul, Minnesota.

5 The U.S. Department of Labor reports that the country's unemployment rate rose from 5.7 percent in July to 6.1 percent in August.

6 Asif Ali Zardari, leader of the Pakistan People's Party (PPP), is elected president of Pakistan. He is sworn in on September 9.

7 In a drastic step, the U.S. government takes over Fannie Mae and Freddie Mac, U.S. companies that own or guarantee $5 trillion worth of mortgages. They were at risk of failure because of a drop in investor confidence in their ability to absorb losses from the U.S. housing slump. The take-over is necessary, officials say, to prevent the economic chaos that would likely result from the failure of either firm.

7 Canadian Prime Minister Stephen Harper engineers the dissolution of Parliament and the scheduling of a federal election for October 14.

9 United States President George W. Bush announces that by early 2009, U.S. troop levels in Iraq will be cut by 8,000, and U.S. troop levels in Afghanistan will be raised by 4,500.

13 Hurricane Ike slams into the U.S. Gulf Coast, causing massive flooding, property damage, and power losses, especially in the Galveston-Houston area of Texas. The storm continues to cause damage even as it weakens and moves through the U.S. South and Midwest. Before hitting the Gulf Coast, Ike caused much damage in the Caribbean—especially in Cuba, which had already been devastated by Hurricane Gustav in August. Over 100 deaths occur because of Ike, mostly in Haiti and the United States.

14 Wall Street endures a week of extreme and historic turmoil, as three venerable U.S. financial firms—the investment banking icons Lehman Brothers and Merrill Lynch and the insurance giant American International Group (AIG)—either fail or are taken over. The firms have had enormous losses because of their high exposure to mortgage-backed securities, which have sunk in value as a result of the U.S. housing slump. On September 14, Bank of America, a giant U.S. bank, announces that it will buy Merrill Lynch. On September 15, Lehman files for bankruptcy after the U.S. government refuses to finance a buyout of the firm. Lehman's $639 billion in assets makes its bankruptcy the largest in U.S. history. To stave off further collapses, the U.S. Federal Reserve System (the Fed) and other world central banks take steps on September 14 and 15 to broaden financial firms' access to central bank funds. On September 16, in a drastic step, the Fed agrees to lend AIG $85 billion in exchange for an 80-percent stake in the firm. The Fed resorts to this move after failing to persuade private banks to lend to AIG. Federal officials want to keep AIG from defaulting on the huge number of financial insurance policies it provides to investors. In response to the Wall Street crisis, stock markets plummet worldwide. The Dow Jones Industrial Average drops 812 points from September 15 through 17. In Russia, where investors are also worried about falling oil prices, stocks fall especially hard, prompting the government to temporarily halt trading on two Russian exchanges. Late in the week, U.S. officials draft an extraordinary rescue plan that, if passed by Congress, would allow the government to buy up to $700 billion in toxic assets from financial firms. Stock markets zoom up in response, with the Dow gaining 779 points on September 18 and 19.

15 After weeks of talks, Zimbabwean President Robert Mugabe and opposition leaders Morgan Tsvangirai and Arthur Mutambara sign a power-sharing deal. It is an attempt to resolve a violent political crisis sparked by Zimbabwe's disputed 2008 presidential election. Under the deal, Mugabe will remain president, and Tsvangirai will assume the newly created post of prime minister. The composition of the cabinet remains to be determined.

17 Members of Kadima, the lead party in Israel's governing coalition, elect Foreign Minister Tzipi Livni as party leader. She succeeds Prime Minister Ehud Olmert, who faces corruption probes and opted not to run for reelection. On September 21, he submits his resignation as prime minister, allowing Livni to begin negotiating a new governing coalition. Olmert will remain as caretaker prime minister until a new government is formed.

20 A suicide truck bombing at the Marriott Hotel in Islamabad, Pakistan, kills over 60 people, including many foreigners.

21 South African President Thabo Mbeki announces that he will resign. Leaders of his party, the African National Congress (ANC), called for his resignation because of his alleged interference in a corruption case against his political rival, ANC President Jacob Zuma. Mbeki's resignation takes effect September 25. That day, the National Assembly elects ANC Deputy President Kgalema Motlanthe to serve the remainder of Mbeki's term.

22 Japan's ruling Liberal Democratic Party elects Taro Aso, a former foreign minister, as party leader. Two days later, Japan's legislature formally installs Aso as prime minister.

25 Federal regulators seize Washington Mutual (WaMu), a huge U.S. savings and loan corporation, and then sell its operations and its troubled investment portfolio to the U.S. financial firm JPMorgan Chase. WaMu had major losses in its home loan and credit card businesses. Also, its depositors withdrew $16.7 billion after last week's Wall Street upheaval began. WaMu becomes the largest bank to fail in U.S. history.

28 In response to the spreading effects of the U.S. financial crisis, European governments nationalize or arrange bailouts for several European banks on September 28, 29, and 30.

29 The U.S. House of Representatives votes 228-205 to reject a $700-billion rescue plan for the ailing U.S. financial system. Many opponents of the legislation argued that taxpayer money should not be used to bail out companies that made bad investments. Stock market investors, stunned by the plan's surprise defeat, send the Dow Jones Industrial Average down 778 points—the index's largest one-day point drop. However, the next day, investors grow more confident that Congress will eventually enact the plan, and the Dow regains 485 points.

29

1 After much midyear debate, the U.S. Congress allows a 27-year-old offshore oil drilling ban to expire.

1 After attaching several provisions, the U.S. Senate votes 74-25 to approve a bill authorizing the U.S. Treasury Department to buy up to $700 billion in distressed assets from U.S. financial firms. The added provisions include an increase in federal insurance for bank deposits, an array of tax breaks, and a parity requirement for mental health insurance. The U.S. House of Representatives—which rejected an earlier version of the financial package on September 29—votes 263-171 to pass the Senate version on October 3. President George W. Bush signs the bill later that day.

3 The U.S. bank Wachovia announces that it will be bought out by a rival U.S. bank, Wells Fargo. Wachovia, beset by investor worries that it could not cover the huge losses in its mortgage business, saw its stock price plunge in September, and its depositors began withdrawing funds. The Wells Fargo deal trumps an earlier deal announced on September 29 between Wachovia and the U.S. banking firm Citigroup. Wells Fargo plans to acquire all of Wachovia, whereas Citigroup agreed to acquire only parts of it.

6 The world's financial markets endure a terrible week, despite government efforts to shore up financial institutions and stimulate lending. European governments continue to nationalize or bail out troubled banks and announce guarantees of bank deposits. An especially serious crisis is underway in Iceland, where the banking sector is massively leveraged and the currency is depreciating rapidly. On October 6, most global benchmark stock indexes fall 4 percent or more. Russia's index falls 19.1 percent. The Dow Jones Industrial Average falls 370 points to close below 10,000, then falls another 508 points on October 7. On October 6 and 7, the U.S. Federal Reserve System (the Fed) greatly expands its lending to financial firms and also announces that it will make direct loans to nonfinancial firms through the commercial

paper market. This market, where many companies go for short-term loans to fund routine operations, has become nearly paralyzed. On October 8, the Fed, the European Central Bank, and the central banks of Canada, Sweden, Switzerland, and the United Kingdom all cut their benchmark interest rate targets. The Fed lowers the federal funds rate—the target rate for short-term loans between banks—from 2 percent to 1.5 percent. Also on October 8, the British government announces a massive plan to buy shares in British banks. On October 9, Iceland nationalizes its largest bank, just days after nationalizing its other two major banks. Stock markets continue to plummet worldwide. From October 6 through 10, Japan's main stock index falls 24.3 percent, and the United Kingdom's index falls 21.1 percent. The Dow falls 679 points on October 9 to close below 9,000.

8 As called for in a September agreement between Russia and Georgia, Russian troops finish withdrawing from the buffer zones they established in August around the separatist regions of South Ossetia and Abkhazia. The buffer zones were in undisputed Georgian territory. Russia and Georgia fought a war in August over the two separatist regions, which lie within Georgia's internationally recognized borders. Secessionist governments backed by Russia control both regions.

10 A suicide bomber kills more than 100 tribesmen in the Orakzai tribal area of northwestern Pakistan.

10 The Connecticut Supreme Court rules that same-sex couples have a constitutional right to marry.

11 The U.S. State Department removes North Korea from its list of state sponsors of terrorism, after the countries reach an agreement on verifying the dismantling of North Korea's nuclear weapons program.

13 A week of extreme volatility occurs in financial markets, with investors alternately encouraged and discouraged by government actions and by economic news. On October 13, the United Kingdom and the 15

Stock markets worldwide spiked up and crashed down throughout October 2008, as a crisis in financial and credit markets that began in the United States spread to Europe, Asia, and elsewhere.

European nations that use the euro announce several rescue measures for banks, including massive government purchases of bank shares and guarantees of interbank loans. Also, U.S. officials persuade major U.S. banks to accept partial nationalization under a Treasury Department plan to buy $250 billion worth of shares in the banks. In response to the government actions, most benchmark stock indexes in Asia and Europe soar 8 percent or more on October 13, and the Dow Jones Industrial Average shoots up 936 points, its largest one-day point gain. But on October 15, after the U.S. government releases data showing declining retail sales and other weakening economic activity, the Dow sinks by 733 points. World stock markets follow suit on October 16, with Japan's main index falling by 11.4 percent. Also on October 16, Switzerland announces a rescue plan for the Swiss financial services firm UBS.

14 In elections in Canada, Prime Minister Stephen Harper's Conservative Party wins 143 of the 308 seats in the House of Commons—a gain of 19 seats, but still not enough for a majority government.

20 Financial market volatility continues. On October 20, the Dow Jones Industrial Average gains 413 points. On October 21, the U.S. Federal Reserve System announces a plan to make $540 billion in loans available to struggling money-market funds through the commercial

paper market. On October 22, the U.S. bank Wachovia reports a $24-billion loss for the third quarter of 2008—one of the biggest quarterly losses in banking history. Also on October 22, stock markets worldwide tumble sharply, with most benchmark indexes dropping 4 percent or more. The Dow falls 514 points. However, some areas of the credit market show improvement. Stock markets again plummet sharply on October 24.

27 Financial market volatility continues. On October 28, the Dow Jones Industrial Average jumps 889 points on news of improving conditions in credit markets. On October 29, the International Monetary Fund and the U.S. Federal Reserve System (the Fed) announce a total of $220 billion in loans for emerging-economy countries that have seen the value of their currencies fall in recent months. The Fed also cuts the federal funds rate—the target rate for short-term loans between banks—from 1.5 percent to 1 percent. Most world stock indexes rise from October 28 through 30.

28 The euro falls as low as $1.2329 against the U.S. dollar.

29 In Major League Baseball's World Series, the Philadelphia Phillies defeat the Tampa Bay Rays, four games to one.

30 In India, numerous bombings in the state of Assam kill more than 80 people.

2008

United States President-elect Barack Obama, a Democrat, waves to his supporters in Chicago on Nov. 4, 2008, after defeating his Republican opponent, Senator John McCain, in the 2008 presidential election.

3 A U.S. air strike near Kandahar, Afghanistan, reportedly kills about 40 civilians at a wedding party.

4 Senator Barack Obama (D., Illinois) is elected the 44th U.S. president, defeating Senator John McCain (R., Arizona) by 365 to 173 in the Electoral College and by 53 percent to 46 percent in the popular vote. Obama will become the first African American president when he succeeds President George W. Bush on Jan. 20, 2009. In U.S. congressional elections, the Democrats increase their majorities in both the Senate and the House of Representatives. In California, voters approve a ballot initiative to ban same-sex marriages, thus nullifying a May 15 California Supreme Court ruling that legalized gay marriage.

5 After rising 305 points on Election Day, the Dow Jones Industrial Average sinks 929 points on November 5 and 6. Stocks in Europe and Asia also experience steep mid-week declines after enjoying large gains early in the week.

7 The U.S. Department of Labor reports that the nation's unemployment rate rose from 6.1 percent in September to 6.5 percent in October. The department estimates that 651,000 nonfarm jobs were cut from August through October, bringing the total jobs lost so far in 2008 to an estimated 1.2 million.

9 China's government unveils an aggressive plan to spend 4 trillion yuan ($586 billion) on domestic infrastructure and social welfare programs over two years. It is the largest economic stimulus package in the country's history. Asian stock markets rise sharply on November 10 in response to the plan.

10 The U.S. government announces a restructured $150-billion rescue plan for the giant U.S. insurance firm American International Group (AIG) to replace the original bailout extended to AIG on September 16. The new deal includes both loans and capital injections.

12 United States Treasury Secretary Henry Paulson announces that the $700-billion Troubled Assets Relief Program (TARP)—the financial rescue package enacted by Congress in October—will not be used to purchase hard-to-sell mortgage-related assets from financial institutions as originally planned. Instead, he says, TARP funds will be used to inject capital into financial firms and to try to ensure that consumers can get credit card, auto, and student loans. Partly in response to Paulson's statement, the Dow Jones Industrial Average falls 411 points. However, the Dow remains volatile, rising 553 points on November 13. Then, it drops 338 points on November 14 in response to data showing falling U.S. retail sales.

15 Leaders of the Group of 20—which consists of 19 industrialized and developing countries plus the European Union—meet in Washington, D.C., and agree to work together to combat the global financial crisis and economic slump.

15 Somali pirates hijack the *Sirius Star,* a huge Saudi-owned oil tanker, in the Indian Ocean off the coast of Kenya. The ship is taken to waters near Xarardheere, Somalia, and anchored there on November 18. It is the largest vessel captured so far in a wave of Somali piracy in 2008.

16 Iraq's cabinet approves a U.S.-Iraqi agreement authorizing a continued U.S. troop presence in Iraq through 2011. The pact, which has been under negotiation for months, would require U.S. troops to pull out of Iraqi cities by mid-2009 and leave Iraq entirely by the end of 2011, and it would give Iraq's government greater control over U.S. operations. The pact still requires approval by Iraq's parliament and presidential council.

19 The U.S. Labor Department reports that its Consumer Price Index (CPI) fell by 1 percent in October, led by an 8.6-percent drop in energy prices. It was the largest monthly decline in the CPI's 61-year history. In addition, the U.S. Department of Commerce and U.S. Department of Housing and Urban Development report that housing starts fell to a seasonally adjusted 791,000 in October, the lowest level in that survey's 49-year history. The re-

ports help send the Dow Jones Industrial Average down 427 points to close below 8,000. On November 20, the Dow falls 445 points to finish at 7,552, its lowest close since 2003. Then, on November 21, the Dow shoots up 494 points.

23 The U.S. government approves a rescue plan for the huge U.S. banking firm Citigroup, which has had massive losses on its mortgage-backed assets since the U.S. housing slump began in 2006. Under the plan, the government will directly invest $20 billion in the firm and partially guarantee more than $300 billion worth of Citigroup's troubled assets. Stock investors react positively to the plan. On November 24, major European stock indexes climb 9 percent or more, and the Dow Jones Industrial Average jumps 397 points. Asian stocks rise the next day.

24 United States President-elect Barack Obama announces his picks for the top economic posts in his administration. His nominee for secretary of the treasury is Timothy Geithner, president of the Federal Reserve Bank of New York.

25 The U.S. government unveils a program to encourage lending in the consumer finance and housing markets. The U.S. Federal Reserve System (the Fed) will lend up to $200 billion to investors willing to buy assets backed by consumer loans. The Fed will also buy $600 billion in ailing mortgage-related assets from the mortgage finance companies Fannie Mae and Freddie Mac, which the U.S. government took over in September.

26 In Mumbai, India, 10 terrorists armed with machine guns and grenades attack a large train station, two luxury hotels, a Jewish community center, and several other sites. Over the course of three days, the attackers kill at least 170 people and take numerous hostages. On November 28 and 29, Indian police and military forces retake all seized buildings, kill most of the terrorists, and rescue the hostages. The Indian government alleges that the terrorists were linked to an Islamist extremist group based in Pakistan.

27 The Iraqi parliament votes 149-35 to approve a U.S.-Iraqi agreement authorizing a continued U.S. troop presence in Iraq through 2011.

29 More than 300 people are killed during sectarian riots in Jos, Nigeria, on November 28 and 29.

DECEMBER

2008

1 United States President-elect Barack Obama announces his national security team. He will retain Defense Secretary Robert Gates as a holdover from President George W. Bush's Cabinet. Obama also will nominate Senator Hillary Rodham Clinton of New York—his chief rival for the Democratic presidential nomination—as secretary of state; former Deputy Attorney General Eric Holder as attorney general; and Arizona Governor Janet Napolitano as secretary of homeland security. Obama names retired Marine General James Jones as national security adviser.

1 The National Bureau of Economic Research, which dates U.S. business cycles, reports that the nation's economy entered a recession in December 2007. The announcement, combined with other poor economic reports, prompts a 680-point fall in the Dow Jones Industrial Average and similar drops in European and Asian stock indexes.

2 Thailand's Constitutional Court finds that the ruling People Power Party (PPP) and two allied parties committed electoral fraud during the 2007 Thai election. The court orders the parties to disband and bars their leaders from holding office for five years. The ruling forces Prime Minister Somchai Wongsawat to step down. The next day, antigovernment protesters end their weeklong occupation of two Bangkok-area airports. The protesters, affiliated with the People's Alliance for Democracy, have campaigned for months to bring down the PPP-led government.

4 Iraq's presidential council (the president and the two vice presidents) approves a U.S.-Iraqi agreement authorizing a U.S. troop presence in Iraq through 2011. The pact, approved earlier by Iraq's cabinet and parliament, is now fully ratified.

4 Canadian Governor General Michaëlle Jean agrees to suspend Parliament until Jan. 26, 2009, at the request of Prime Minister Stephen Harper. The suspension allows Harper to stave off an effort by three opposition parties to form a coalition that would oust his minority Conservative Party government without new elections. The opposition parties objected to an economic plan proposed by Harper's government late last month.

5 The U.S. Department of Labor reports that U.S. employers cut an estimated 533,000 nonfarm jobs in November, the worst one-month job decline since 1974. An estimated 1.9 million jobs have been lost so far in 2008. The department also reports that the unemployment rate rose from 6.5 percent in October to 6.7 percent in November.

9 Federal agents arrest Illinois Governor Rod Blagojevich on criminal corruption charges. United States Attorney Patrick Fitzgerald alleges that Blagojevich engaged in several "pay to play" schemes for personal gain, including an attempt to sell the U.S. Senate seat vacated by President-elect Barack Obama.

10 The U.S. House of Representatives approves $14 billion in emergency loans to the U.S. automakers General Motors and Chrysler, which are in danger of collapse. However, the next day, U.S. Senate Republicans kill the loan package by preventing it from getting the 60 votes needed to advance to a formal vote.

11 A suicide bomber kills over 50 people at a Kirkuk, Iraq, restaurant.

11 Federal agents in New York City arrest money manager Bernard Madoff on a criminal charge of securities fraud, and the U.S. Securities and Exchange Commission files a civil complaint against him and his investment firm. Madoff is accused of running a giant Ponzi scheme that has caused investors to lose tens of billions of dollars. Under the alleged scheme, returns were paid to investors from the principal contributed by later investors rather than from profits. The investors affected by the scheme include several major hedge funds, foreign banks, and charities.

16 The U.S. Labor Department reports that its Consumer Price Index (CPI) fell by 1.7 percent in November, led by a 17-percent drop in energy prices. It was the largest monthly

Unemployed Coloradans register at a job fair and employment outreach workshops. The U.S. Labor Department reported on Dec. 5, 2008, that employers had cut nearly 2 million jobs since the U.S. economy entered a recession in December 2007.

decline in the 61-year history of the CPI. Also, the U.S. Department of Commerce and U.S. Department of Housing and Urban Development report that housing starts fell to a seasonally adjusted 625,000 in November, the lowest level in that survey's 49-year history.

16 The U.S. Federal Reserve System lowers the federal funds rate—the target interest rate for short-term interbank loans—from 1 percent to a range between zero and 0.25 percent. It is the first time that the rate has been set below 1 percent.

19 United States President George W. Bush announces that $17.4 billion will be lent to the struggling U.S. automakers General Motors and Chrysler, on the condition that the companies prove their financial viability by March 31, 2009. The loans will come from the $700-billion financial rescue package that Congress authorized

in October 2008. On December 20, Canadian officials announce a similar loan package for Canada's automotive sector.

19 The price of crude oil on the New York Mercantile Exchange falls as low as $32.40 a barrel in intraday trading. Oil prices have plummeted dramatically since reaching a record high above $147 a barrel in July 2008. The average retail price per gallon of regular unleaded gasoline in the United States—which hit a record $4.11 in July—is now below $1.70.

27 Israel launches air strikes against the Gaza Strip in response to Palestinian rocket and mortar attacks from Gaza on Israeli communities. The multiple-day air assault is mainly aimed at sites controlled by Hamas militants. Hundreds of militants and civilians are killed in the air campaign. The militants continue to fire rockets, killing a handful of Israelis.

UPDATE

The major events of 2008 are covered in more than 250 alphabetically arranged articles, from "Afghanistan" to "Zoos." Included are Special Reports that offer in-depth looks at the 2008 economic crises in banking and finance, agriculture, and energy. Special Reports are found on the following pages.

SPECIAL REPORTS

FOCUS ON

PORTRAITS

Afghanistan fell into a "downward spiral" of violence in 2008 as Islamic militants fought the government and its foreign supporters, according to an American intelligence evaluation. President Hamid Karzai said on October 29, "We are still a nation deeply in pain and misery" despite the 2001 ouster of the militants' Taliban regime.

In 2008, the Taliban's many loosely organized guerrilla bands continued to attack the Afghan army and police as well as Western troops supporting Karzai's government. They staged suicide attacks in the capital, Kabul; kidnapped and killed foreign aid workers; made roads unsafe with ambushes; and terrorized villagers who did not support them. United States officials noted that, in 2008, the level of violence in Afghanistan had grown by 30 percent from the previous year.

United States General David D. McKiernan, the commander of the 65,000-strong international force helping Karzai's government, rejected the idea that they were losing the war. Some of his North Atlantic Treaty Organization (NATO) nations were reluctant to continue sending troops, but France remained committed after 10 French soldiers were killed on August 18.

Pakistan. American commanders in 2008 accused the Taliban of recruiting fighters across the unmarked border with Pakistan, training troops and staging attacks from there. On June 15, Karzai threatened to send Afghan soldiers across the border after Taliban militants. On August 7, General McKiernan said that Pakistan's Directorate for Inter-Services Intelligence (ISI) had "some complicity" with Afghan militants. In an effort to curtail cross-border raids, U.S. forces fired rockets at reported Taliban camps in Pakistan in late 2008.

The Afghan government accused the ISI of a failed April 27 assassination attempt on Karzai. American intelligence officials said evidence linked the ISI to a July 7 bombing of India's embassy in Kabul that killed 54 people. India, long a rival of Pakistan, developed close ties with the Afghan government after the Taliban was driven out.

The Afghan defense minister said on October 14 that well-trained fighters from Iraq were also joining the Taliban in Afghanistan. American casualties in Afghanistan in 2008 exceeded those in Iraq. Inside Afghanistan, Taliban recruitment benefited from poverty, hunger, and anger over civilian deaths from aerial attacks by Western forces.

Bombing and rocket attacks by NATO forces were used to break up Taliban attacks or to target reported Taliban forces, often when NATO lacked sufficient ground troops. Afghans repeatedly charged that civilian bystanders were killed in air attacks. New York City-based humanitarian organization Human Rights Watch reported in September that civilian deaths caused by airstrikes had nearly tripled from 2006 to 2007.

An Aug. 22, 2008, attack on a western village killed some 90 people according to a United Nations (UN) investigation. The U.S. military initially confirmed 30 militant deaths and no more than 7 civilian deaths, but it later said 33 civilians were among the dead. On November 3, a U.S. aerial attack on a wedding party killed 37 civilians and 26 militants, according to Afghan officials; U.S. officials reported only 20 civilian deaths and accused insurgents of holding the wedding party captive before drawing U.S. forces into a fight.

Suicide bombings attributed to the Taliban hit a number of Afghan cities. On January 14, a suicide squad penetrated Kabul's leading and best-protected hotel, killing six people. Another bomber shot his way into the Ministry of Information and Culture in Kabul on October 30, killing at least two people. Foreigners working in Kabul were increasingly targeted. Nationwide, more foreign aid workers had been killed by August 2008 than in all of 2007.

Officials responded to the need for increased security and development in Afghanistan at a June 12, 2008, meeting of more than 80 countries and aid agencies in Paris. Representatives pledged to provide more than $21 billion in aid to Afghanistan for developing the country's infrastructure while combating poverty, violence, and drugs.

Talking to the Taliban. As the situation worsened in late 2008, the Afghan government began efforts to engage some moderate Taliban leaders in peace negotiations. The top British commander in Afghanistan said in October that a "decisive military victory" over the Taliban was impossible. Saudi Arabia hosted an informal meeting between Afghans and Taliban members in September. A tribal council of Afghan and Pakistani leaders on October 28 agreed to contact militant groups for peace talks. President Karzai appealed for Taliban leader Mullah Omar to return to Afghanistan from his presumed hiding place in Pakistan and work for peace. On November 16, Karzai reiterated his offer, promising to provide security for Omar. Taliban representatives rejected the offer, refusing to meet until foreign troops left the country.

Opium. On August 26, the UN reported that Afghanistan was beginning to make progress in its efforts to reduce cultivation of opium poppies used in the production of illegal narcotics. However, an American counternarcotics official accused corrupt Afghan officials of shielding poppy farmers from prosecution.

Drought. Low levels of rain and snow in late 2007 and early 2008 led to a drought throughout Afghanistan. The authors of a British study estimated in October 2008 that 8.4 million Afghans did not have enough to eat because of drought and rising food prices.   ■ Henry S. Bradsher

See also **Armed forces; Asia; Pakistan.**

AFRICA

On Jan. 31, 2008, at the opening session of the African Union (AU) summit in Addis Ababa, Ethiopia, United Nations (UN) Secretary-General Ban Ki-moon highlighted the successful collaboration between the two organizations in peacekeeping, development, and human rights operations. Tanzania's president, Jakaya Kikwete, took over as AU Chairman from Ghana's President John Kufuor at the summit.

During 2008, the partnership between the two organizations was evident in the war-torn Darfur region of western Sudan, where the UN-AU hybrid mission (UNAMID) cooperated in a bid to bring peace to the region. Since fighting erupted in Sudan in 2003 between black African rebels and militias bankrolled by the Arab-dominated Sudanese regime, more than 300,000 people have died from violence, starvation, or disease, with over 2 million forced from their homes. However, there were repeated delays in sending UNAMID peacekeeping forces to Darfur; in late 2008, barely a third of its planned 26,000 military personnel were in place, and there were no signs of an end to the conflict.

AU armed intervention. On March 25, more than 1,000 AU troops helped the government of President Ahmed Abdallah Mohamed Sambi of the Comoros islands restore central control to the island of Anjouan. In 2007, the island had illegally reelected a local president, Mohammed Bacar, who threatened to break away from the three-island Union.

Food riots. Following demonstrations and riots protesting high food prices in the West African states of Burkina Faso, Cameroon, Niger, and Senegal in early 2008, the UN cautioned that such disturbances "may become common in other places in Africa." The warning was followed on May 5 by violent demonstrations in Somalia when tens of thousands of people rioted in the capital, Mogadishu, over excessive food prices. Many African countries rely heavily on imported basic foods, especially rice; in 2008, strong demand for these same foods from China, India, and other emerging giants caused prices to rise sharply.

According to figures released by the UN on September 10, the international community was falling behind in its efforts to relieve poverty in sub-Saharan Africa. On September 22, a high-level meeting of the UN General Assembly in New York City on Africa's development needs

noted that the continent remained "off track" in its quest to achieve the Millennium Development Goals (MDG's). The MDG's were adopted by world leaders in 2000 to focus attention on improving the well-being of the globe's poorest people.

Bush visit. On a five-nation tour in February 2008, United States President George W. Bush visited Benin, Ghana, Liberia, Rwanda, and Tanzania—all countries that have benefited from U.S. foreign aid. President Bush met with African leaders to discuss possible solutions to such problems as poverty and the diseases of AIDS and malaria.

Sport took on wider African political connotations in the run-up to the 2008 Summer Olympic Games in Beijing when many international politicians and activists called for a boycott. They said that China provided economic and military support to the Sudanese government, which was accused of committing genocide and war crimes in its Darfur region. Africa's tally of medals at the Games totaled 40—12 gold, 14 silver, and 14 bronze. Kenya won the most—5 gold and 9 other medals—and Ethiopia came in second with 7 medals, 4 of them gold.

Pirates. Figures provided in 2008 by the International Maritime Bureau (IMB) showed a sharp increase in piracy around Africa since the mid-1990's. The rapid rise in hijackings and attempted hijackings was blamed largely on the collapse of law and order in Somalia and on political unrest in Nigeria. In Somalia, an al-Qa`ida-allied Islamist insur-gency has kept the country ungovernable for several years.

Zimbabweans line up outside a bank in Harare, the capital, on September 30 to withdraw money. In 2008, inflation in Zimbabwe skyrocketed to record levels, making the nation's currency virtually worthless. By November, inflation was running at 69.7 sextillion percent (1 followed by 21 zeros) a month.

Targets have ranged from private yachts and fishing boats to cruise liners and oil tankers. Ships and their hostage crews were often released after a ransom was paid, a practice which critics claimed encouraged more attacks. Pirates seized more than 40 vessels off Somalia in 2008, despite Western-led navy patrols in the area. In May, the IMB identified the waters off Nigeria's 530-mile (853-kilometer) coastline as another of the world's most dangerous piracy hot spots.

In one of the boldest attacks in 2008, pirates seized the Ukrainian-operated *MV Faina* off the Somali coast on September 25, as it headed toward Kenya carrying 33 Russian-built tanks. The pirates demanded a $20-million ransom from the vessel's owners. Later, on November 15, Somali pirates hijacked the *Sirius Star*, a Saudi supertanker laden with 2 million barrels of crude oil, off the East African coast. The U.S. Navy tracked both

vessels back to Somalia's coast, as negotiations between the ships' owners and hijackers continued late into 2008.

The UN World Food Program announced that its efforts to help famine-struck Somali refugees were being severely jeopardized by the attacks on its aid ships. Meanwhile, security analysts said that the risk from piracy was threatening the entire shipping industry through the Gulf of Aden and the Suez Canal—one of the world's busiest maritime traffic routes.

West Africa. According to the UN Office on Drugs and Crime, countries along the West African coast—including Benin, Guinea, Guinea-Bissau, and Senegal—were in 2008 becoming major transit routes for cocaine from South America to Europe. These countries, which were incapable of policing their coastlines or airspace, were also targeted by drug barons for trafficking heroin.

FACTS IN BRIEF ON AFRICAN COUNTRIES

Country	Population	Government	Monetary unit*	Foreign trade (million U.S.$) Exports[†]	Imports[†]
Algeria	34,355,000	President Abdelaziz Bouteflika; Prime Minister Abdelaziz Belkhadem	dinar (65.85 = $1)	60,510	26,250
Angola	17,313,000	President José Eduardo dos Santos	kwanza (75.00 = $1)	45,030	12,290
Benin	8,067,000	President Thomas Yayi Boni	CFA franc (446.02 = $1)	586	1,085
Botswana	1,758,000	President Ian Khama	pula (6.62 = $1)	5,025	3,403
Burkina Faso	14,425,000	President Blaise Compaoré; Prime Minister Tertius Zongo	CFA franc (446.02 = $1)	617	1,296
Burundi	8,349,000	President Pierre Nkurunziza	franc (1,170.00 = $1)	44	272
Cameroon	18,002,000	President Paul Biya; Prime Minister Ephraim Inoni	CFA franc (446.02 = $1)	3,827	3,714
Cape Verde	523,000	President Pedro Pires; Prime Minister José Maria Pereira Neves	escudo (73.66 = $1)	77	744
Central African Republic	4,157,000	President François Bozizé; Prime Minister Faustin-Archange Touadera	CFA franc (446.02 = $1)	147	237
Chad	10,591,000	President Idriss Déby; Prime Minister Youssouf Saleh Abbas	CFA franc (446.02 = $1)	4,201	1,158
Comoros	712,000	President Ahmed Abdallah Mohamed Sambi	franc (361.35 = $1)	32	143
Congo (Brazzaville)	3,921,000	President Denis Sassou-Nguesso	CFA franc (446.02 = $1)	5,800	2,634
Congo (Kinshasa)	64,827,000	President Joseph Kabila; Prime Minister Adolphe Muzito	franc (541.00 = $1)	1,587	2,263
Côte d'Ivoire (Ivory Coast)	20,092,000	President Laurent Gbagbo; Prime Minister Guillaume Soro	CFA franc (446.02 = $1)	8,476	5,932
Djibouti	838,000	President Ismail Omar Guelleh; Prime Minister Dileita Mohamed Dileita	franc (177.00 = $1)	340	1,555
Egypt	77,243,000	President Mohammed Hosni Mubarak; Prime Minister Ahmed Nazif	pound (5.37 = $1)	24,450	44,950
Equatorial Guinea	538,000	President Teodoro Obiang Nguema; Prime Minister Ricardo Mangue Obama Nfubea	CFA franc (446.02 = $1)	9,904	3,083
Eritrea	4,886,000	President Issaias Afewerki	nafka (15.00 = $1)	12	573
Ethiopia	78,326,000	President Girma Woldegiorgis; Prime Minister Meles Zenawi	birr (9.67 = $1)	1,288	5,165
Gabon	1,457,000	President El Hadj Omar Bongo; Prime Minister Jean Eyeghe Ndong	CFA franc (446.02 = $1)	6,956	2,107
Gambia	1,582,000	President Yahya A. J. J. Jammeh	dalasi (21.00 = $1)	88	271
Ghana	23,542,000	President John Agyekum Kufuor	new cedi (1.15 = $1)	4,162	8,053
Guinea	10,044,000	President Moussa Dadis Camara; Prime Minister Kabine Komara	franc (4,615.00 = $1)	1,128	1,202
Guinea-Bissau	1,454,000	President João Bernardo Vieira; Prime Minister Carlos Correia	CFA franc (446.02 = $1)	113	200
Kenya	37,190,000	President Mwai Kibaki	shilling (68.50 = $1)	4,127	8,540
Lesotho	2,248,000	King Letsie III; Prime Minister Pakalitha Mosisili	loti (11.71 = $1)	853	1,536

*Exchange rates as of Sept. 30, 2008.   [†]Latest available data.

Country	Population	Government	Monetary unit*	Foreign trade (million U.S.$)	
				Exports[†]	Imports[†]
Liberia	3,556,000	President Ellen Johnson-Sirleaf	dollar (49.00 = $1)	1,197	7,143
Libya	6,266,000	Leader Mu'ammar Muhammad al-Qadhafi; General People's Committee Secretary (Prime Minister) al-Baghdadi Ali al-Mahmudi	dinar (1.23 = $1)	42,970	14,430
Madagascar	18,774,000	President Marc Ravalomanana; Prime Minister Charles Rabemananjara	ariary (1,623.84 = $1)	986	1,918
Malawi	13,630,000	President Bingu wa Mutharika	kwacha (142.01 = $1)	604	866
Mali	14,724,000	President Amadou Toumani Touré; Prime Minister Mobido Sidibé	CFA franc (446.02 = $1)	294	2,358
Mauritania	3,342,000	General Mohamed Ould Abdel Aziz; Prime Minister Moulaye Ould Mohamed Laghdaf	ouguiya (226.00 = $1)	1,395	1,475
Mauritius	1,276,000	President Sir Anerood Jugnauth; Prime Minister Navinchandra Ramgoolam	rupee (28.20 = $1)	2,231	3,656
Morocco	31,851,000	King Mohammed VI; Prime Minister Abbas El Fassi	dirham (7.77 = $1)	12,750	28,500
Mozambique	20,854,000	President Armando Guebuza	new metical (23.86 = $1)	2,412	2,811
Namibia	2,091,000	President Hifikepunye Pohamba	dollar (7.77 = $1)	2,919	3,091
Niger	15,367,000	President Mamadou Tandja	CFA franc (446.02 = $1)	428	800
Nigeria	140,923,000	President Umaru Yar'Adua	naira (117.65 = $1)	61,970	38,500
Rwanda	9,548,000	President Paul Kagame	franc (543.85 = $1)	184	637
São Tomé and Príncipe	169,000	President Fradique de Menezes; Prime Minister Rafael Branco	dobra (14,486.72 = $1)	9	66
Senegal	12,507,000	President Abdoulaye Wade; Prime Minister Cheikh Hadjibou Soumaré	CFA franc (446.02 = $1)	1,650	3,731
Seychelles	86,000	President James Michel	rupee (8.04 = $1)	395	823
Sierra Leone	5,915,000	President Ernest Bai Koroma	leone (2,940.00 = $1)	216	560
Somalia	9,007,000	Acting President Aden Mohamed Nur; Prime Minister Nur Hassan Hussein	shilling (1,428.91 = $1)	300	798
South Africa	47,114,000	President Kgalema Motlanthe	rand (7.77 = $1)	76,190	81,890
Sudan	39,076,000	President Umar Hassan Ahmad al-Bashir	pound (2.09 = $1)	8,879	7,722
Swaziland	1,102,000	King Mswati III; Prime Minister Barnabas Sibusiso Dlamini	lilangeni (7.77 = $1)	1,926	1,914
Tanzania	40,675,000	President Jakaya Kikwete; Prime Minister Gilbert Houngbo	shilling (1,160.00 = $1)	2,227	4,861
Togo	6,637,000	President Faure Gnassingbé; Prime Minister Gilbert Houngbo	CFA franc (446.02 = $1)	702	1,201
Tunisia	10,352,000	President Zine El-Abidine Ben Ali; Prime Minister Mohamed Ghannouchi	dinar (1.23 = $1)	15,150	18,020
Uganda	30,730,000	President Yoweri Museveni	shilling (1,640.00 = $1)	1,686	2,983
Zambia	12,255,000	President Rupiah Banda	kwacha (3,505.00 = $1)	4,594	3,611
Zimbabwe	13,242,000	President Robert Gabriel Mugabe; Prime Minister Designate Morgan Tsvangirai	dollar (40,000.00 = $1)	1,520	2,183

Most of Guinea's leading politicians surrendered to military officials in Conakry, the capital, on December 25, finishing a *coup* (overthrow) that began with the death on December 23 of President Lansana Conté, a dictator who ruled for 24 hears. Conté appeared to have died of natural causes. The coup leaders, junior military officers backed by the army's rank and file, named Captain Moussa Dadis Camara the country's new president.

On July 7, British former special forces officer Simon Mann was sentenced to 34 years in jail in Malabo, the capital of Equatorial Guinea, for attempting to kill dictator President Teodoro Obiang Nguema in 2004 and install exiled opposition leader Severo Moto in his place. Mann admitted leading a team of mercenaries from South Africa and attempting to buy weapons in Zimbabwe to use in the plot. He was sentenced to seven years in prison by a Zimbabwean court in 2004 but was extradited to Equatorial Guinea in February 2008. At his trial, Mann said that Sir Mark Thatcher, son of former British Prime Minister Lady Margaret Thatcher, was a party to the conspiracy—a claim denied by Sir Mark.

On August 6, Mauritania's President Sidi Ould Cheikh Abdallahi was overthrown in a bloodless coup. Abdallahi, who was Mauritania's first democratically elected president, had fired several military officers the day before the coup.

Hadijatou Mani, a woman born into slavery, won a landmark victory against Niger's government on Oct. 27, 2008, when a court ruled that it had failed to enforce its own antislavery laws and ordered the government to pay her damages. Anti-Slavery International estimated that there were some 43,000 slaves in the country.

In Ghana, presidential and parliamentary polls were held on December 7. The two main contestants were the governing New Patriotic Party (NPP), led by Nana Addo Akufo-Addo, and the National Democratic Congress (NDC), headed by John Atta Mills. Addo won 49.13 percent of the presidential vote, and the NPP won 109 of the 230 seats in parliament; Mills obtained 47.92 percent of the presidential vote, and his NDC won 113 seats. Because neither presidential candidate won over 50 percent of the vote, a runoff election was held on December 28. However, final results were not expected until after an audit of disputed ballots and a vote in a missed precinct in early 2009.

Central Africa. In February 2008, three African nations of the Great Lakes region—Congo (Kinshasa), Rwanda, and Uganda—agreed to cooperate to protect endangered mountain gorillas and other rare species in the Central Albertine Rift, where the three countries' borders meet. In early 2008, only 720 of the apes remained in the wild, all of them in the Albertine Rift region. However, Congolese rebels seized a base in Congo's

Virunga National Park in October, leaving some 200 gorillas vulnerable to poachers. Stability in the region was severely undermined in late 2008 by an escalation of civil conflict in eastern Congo, which borders Uganda, Rwanda, and Burundi. In Congo (Brazzaville), some 30,000 combatants from the country's civil war (1997–1999) began a long-delayed process of demobilization and reintegration into civilian life in June 2008.

In February, insurgents stormed N'Djamena, the capital of Chad, and attempted to seize the presidential palace. They were repulsed by government troops loyal to President Idriss Déby and by French forces. The International Committee of the Red Cross said that hundreds of civilians were killed in several days of fighting. Thousands of others fled the capital for neighboring Cameroon. In 2008, France had 1,450 soldiers and a squadron of fighter jets stationed in Chad at Déby's request.

Earlier in January, the European Union approved 3,500 peacekeeping troops for Chad and the Central African Republic to protect hundreds of thousands of refugees escaping from the conflict in Sudan's Darfur region. Following a landslide victory by President Paul Kagame's ruling Rwanda Patriotic Front on September 17, Rwanda became the first nation in the world whose women members of parliament (MP's) outnumbered men when 56 percent of the seats went to female candidates. The multiparty election was the country's second since the 1994 genocide committed by Hutu extremists left up to 1 million Tutsis and moderate Hutus dead. On December 18, a UN tribunal convicted Theoneste Bagosora, defense minister at the time, of genocide and sentenced him to life in prison.

Eastern Africa and the Horn. In early 2008, political turmoil in Kenya, East Africa's richest and most developed country, threatened the entire region and beyond. Because of Kenya's role as the region's economic powerhouse, its postelection violence in January and February had repercussions well beyond its borders. Before Kenya's crisis, the five nations of the East African Community (EAC), an organization promoting regional economic growth, expected their combined gross domestic product (GDP) to grow by 6 percent in 2008. (The GDP is the total value of goods and services produced by a country in a year.) However, economic analysts predicted that the unrest would cut the growth rate of the EAC's nations— Burundi, Kenya, Rwanda, Tanzania, and Uganda— nearer to 4 percent.

Against this background, the UN World Food Program (WFP) in July announced that more than 14.5 million people living in Djibouti, Ethiopia, Kenya, Somalia, and Uganda faced famine. The WFP appealed for international food aid to tackle the emergency, as it had done in years past.

Somalia President Abdullahi Yusuf resigned on December 29 in the wake of a power struggle with Prime Minister Nur Hassan Hussein. The resignations came after the parliament backed Nur when Yusuf tried to dismiss him from office.

At least 2.6 million Somalis faced hunger in 2008 due to acute food shortages spurred by a prolonged drought and chronic political instability. Somalia's government and its Ethiopian military backers continued to struggle in 2008 against Islamist insurgents who had controlled much of the country until they were driven from power by Ethiopian and Somali troops in 2006.

Southern Africa. The political and economic crisis in Zimbabwe dominated events in southern Africa during 2008, risking the stability of the whole region. Several African nations, including Botswana and Zambia, refused to accept the result of Zimbabwe's June 27 runoff presidential election, won by President Robert Mugabe against a background of electoral fraud and intimidation.

More than 1,100 people died in a cholera outbreak in Zimbabwe that began in late 2008. The disease, which affected more than 20,000 people, was blamed on the near-collapse of Zimbabwe's health care and water systems.

On September 21, South Africa's President Thabo Mbeki was forced out of office by the ruling African National Congress (ANC). He was replaced by Kgalema Motlanthe pending 2009 elections, which ANC party leader Jacob Zuma was favored to win.

In Zambia, the Aug. 19, 2008, death of President Levy Mwanawasa led to an election on October 30. Acting President Rupiah Banda narrowly defeated Michael Sata, leader of the opposition Patriotic Front. Observer groups from the AU and other international bodies called the vote fair.

On September 5, Angolans voted overwhelmingly for President José Eduardo dos Santos's ruling Popular Movement for the Liberation of Angola in the country's first multiparty legislative elections since 1992. The election was a milestone in Angola's political transition following decades of civil war that ended in April 2002.

A new five-year term was approved by Mauritius's Cabinet for President Sir Anerood Jugnauth, whose first presidential term ended on Sept. 30, 2008. In Mauritius, the president is head of state but holds no executive power.

In contrast to many of its neighbors, Botswana experienced a peaceful transition of power, as President Festus Mogae stepped down in favor of his vice president, Ian Khama, on April 1, after a decade in office. On October 20, Mogae was awarded a $5-million UN prize for African leadership. ■ Simon Baynham

See also **Agriculture: A Special Report; AIDS;** various African country articles.

Agriculture. In the first half of 2008, robust demand for United States farm products from foreign buyers and for renewable fuels production caused prices for wheat, feed grains, oilseeds, and rice to set new record highs. In the second half of the year, projections of good harvests and the global slowdown in trade and commerce triggered by the financial crisis caused prices to decline but nevertheless to remain above historical averages.

World crop production. World wheat production of 684.3 million metric tons in 2008 represented a 12-percent increase over the 2007 statistic, according to a report from the United States Department of Agriculture (USDA) released in December 2008. Favorable weather in wheat-producing regions increased the U.S. wheat crop by 21 percent to 68 million metric tons (2.5 billion bushels). For the first time in two years, drought retreated in Australia, and the country produced a 20-million-metric-ton wheat crop, 54 percent above the 2007 crop. The European Union (EU) harvested 151 million metric tons, a 26-percent increase, and Russia harvested its largest wheat crop ever at 63 million metric tons, a 28-percent increase from 2007. Despite ample supply from the bumper harvest, the 2008 season average wheat price was a record-high $6.71 a bushel.

Coarse grains production including corn, barley, sorghum, and oats totaled 1.0972 billion metric tons. Of this total, 786.2 million metric tons was corn. The U.S. corn crop of 305.3 million metric tons (12 billion bushels) was the second-largest ever. China produced 160.6 million metric tons; the EU, 60.1 million metric tons; Brazil, 55.4 million metric tons; and Mexico, 24 million metric tons. Argentina's corn crop came in at 18 million metric tons and Canada's, at 10.6 million metric tons. The 2008 season average price for corn was $4.00 a bushel, the second highest price ever.

World oilseed production—soybeans, sunflower seeds, cottonseed, and rapeseed—totaled 418 million metric tons, of which 236.5 metric tons were soybeans; U.S. soybean production of 80 million metric tons (2.9 billion bushels) was up 9 percent. Soybean production in Brazil was 59.6 million metric tons; in Argentina, 51 million metric tons; and in China, 17 million metric tons. The U.S. season average price for soybeans was $9.01 per bushel, the second highest on record.

The global rice harvest in 2008 was 434 million metric tons. China harvested 131 million metric tons, followed by India, with 98 million metric tons—its largest crop ever. Indonesia produced 36 million metric tons; Vietnam, 24 million metric tons; Thailand, 20 million metric tons; Japan, 8 million metric tons; and the United States, 6.5 million metric tons. The season average price was a record high $15.50 per hundredweight (100 pounds [45.36 kilograms]).

World cotton production at 112.3 million bales was down 6 percent in 2008 due to a 30-percent drop in U.S. production. The U.S. crop at 13.5 million bales was the smallest since 1989. Production in China in 2008 (37 million bales), in India (24.5 million bales), and in Pakistan (9 million bales) partially offset the U.S. reduction.

Food prices rose dramatically in 2008; U.S. food prices increased 5.5 percent following a 4-percent increase in 2007. Global food prices increased about 40 percent in 2008. Rising prices created hardship, especially in developing countries, where consumers rely more heavily upon basic commodities and spend 25 percent to as much as 70 percent of their income on food. By contrast, Americans spend, on average, about 14 percent of their income on food.

Tightening supplies was the greatest factor in food price spikes. As prices for basic commodities of wheat, feed grains, and soybeans reached record highs in late June, panicked buying began. Ethanol and livestock producers sought corn stocks, whereas importing countries sought other basic commodities to feed their people. Cambodia, Indonesia, Kazakhstan, Russia, Argentina, Vietnam, Ukraine, Thailand, Egypt, and many other countries restricted food exports to the rest of the world. However, such hoarding caused prices to rise even further.

Renewable fuels. Record-high corn prices took a toll on U.S. ethanol producers in 2008. As corn prices in the first half of the year spiraled upward, some ethanol companies locked in supplies at high price levels. The price trajectory reversed course in midyear, however, and by August, corn prices had fallen by 50 percent. VeraSun Energy Corporation of Sioux Falls, South Dakota, one of the nation's largest ethanol producers, filed for bankruptcy on October 31.

In 2007, the last year for which complete statistics are available, global production of ethanol surpassed 13 billion gallons (49.2 billion liters). The United States produced about 6.5 billion gallons (24.6 billion liters), largely corn-based, and second-ranked Brazil, about 5 billion gallons, mainly sugar cane-based. The EU, the world's largest producer of biodiesel, which is made from oilseeds such as soybeans, produced 5.7 million metric tons of the biofuel in 2007. After mid-2008, petroleum prices slid from a high of $147 a barrel to under $50 a barrel. Analysts speculated that the sharply lower petroleum prices would slow the global growth of biofuels production.

Biotech crops. In 2007, global acreage of farmland planted to biotech (BT) crops (also known as "genetically modified," or GM crops) expanded 12 percent over the 2006 acreage. The world's farmers in 2007 planted BT crops on 282 million acres (114.3 million hectares), according to the International Service for the Acquisition of Agri-biotech Applications (ISAAA), an organization that promotes the use of biotechnology in developing nations. Farmers in the United States, Argentina, Brazil, Canada, India, and China led the world in BT plantings in 2007, as in 2006.

The ISAAA report also highlighted a trend in 2008 toward BT varieties with more than one biotech trait. For example, a particular BT plant might be furnished with one gene that endows it with insecticidal properties and another gene that gives it resistance to herbicides; crops so modified are said to contain "stacked genes."

In the United States, especially, farmers turned in increasing numbers in 2008 to BT corn and cotton seed with stacked genes that resist both pests and herbicides. U.S. farmers in 2008 planted 80 percent of corn acreage to BT seed; fully half of this acreage was planted to the stacked gene variety. Similarly, cotton producers planted 86 percent of acreage to BT seed, of which slightly more than half was of the stacked gene variety. Soybean BT varieties are exclusively herbicide resistant; in 2008, 92 percent of U.S. soybean acres were planted to one-gene BT seed.

Organic food. Sales of organic foods and beverages in 2007, the last year for which complete statistics are available, totaled $21 billion, according to the Organic Trade Association (OTA). In its 2007 Manufacturer Survey, the OTA predicted that annual growth in sales of organic foods would average 18 percent per year through 2010. Some analysts suggested, however, that the global economic downturn, which began in late 2008, could dissuade consumers from choosing higher-priced organic products.

New farm law. On June 18, Congress passed the $290-billion Food, Conservation and Energy Act of 2008, overriding President George W. Bush's veto. The law, which covers crop years 2008–2012, allocates nearly $40 billion for farm subsidies. Of that amount, $3.8 billion is for a new permanent disaster program to work in tandem with the federal government's existing crop insurance program.

About two thirds of the farm law's funding is directed to such domestic nutrition programs as food stamps and school lunch programs. Some $60 billion is set aside for international food aid. Various conservation programs, including an initiative to restore and protect the Chesapeake Bay watershed, account for $30 billion of the funding. The law also provides about $1 billion to support development of the nation's renewable energy industry. ■ Patricia Peak Klintberg

See also **Agriculture: A Special Report; Economics, World; Energy supply.**

As prices of basic commodities soar, the poor
of the world are less and less able to afford food.

ECONOMIC CRISIS:
FOOD

By Kristina A. Vaicikonis

I n 2008, troops were sent to guard grain
elevators throughout Pakistan. Fights
broke out among Egyptians standing in
line at bakeries for state-subsidized bread.
Farmers in Thailand armed themselves to
protect their rice crops at night from thieves
who tried to steal the grain as it ripened. And
people in Haiti—some of whom were reduced
to eating "mud" pies made of cooking oil,
vegetable scraps, and clay—tried to oust their
president in the course of food riots. People in
Cameroon, Ethiopia, Indonesia, Mexico,
Morocco, the Philippines, Senegal, and Yemen
also rioted over food, sometimes with deadly
results. By October, the international relief
and development organization Oxfam, based
in Oxford, England, reported that 900 million
people were facing starvation. In the United
States, the Department of Agriculture

Increase in global prices of rice, wheat, and corn

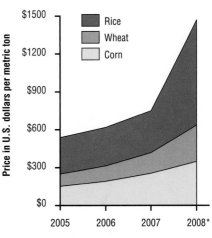

*2008 figure reflects prices in June. Source: International Monetary Fund.

projected that food prices in 2008 would increase by 5 to 6 percent over the previous year and by an additional 3.5 to 4.5 percent in 2009. Although it was clear that major food commodity prices—for wheat, corn, rice, soy, coffee, cotton, dairy products, meat, fruits, and vegetables—had risen to historic levels around the globe, few experts agreed on what should be done to stop the increases.

Why the rise in global food prices?

The cause of the record rise in food prices is complex. On the one hand, there has been an increase in demand for food. According to United Nations (UN) demographers, the growth rate of the world's population has slowed. Nevertheless, the global population reached 6.684 billion in July 2008 and that number was expected to grow by 80 million people annually, according to the U.S. Census Bureau. In addition, more and more people in China and India—which together have a population of about 2.5 billion people—have become members of the middle class. They can afford, and are choosing to buy, better food, which is more labor-intensive and more resource-intensive and thus more costly. People who once subsisted on grains now demand grain-fed meat and dairy products, which require more land and energy to produce.

The supply of food worldwide has not kept pace with the rising demand. The amount of land available for farming is decreasing, because of industrial and residential development. Weather-related problems, such as the extreme drought in Australia from 2002 to 2007 and in Ukraine in 2007—two major wheat-producing nations—have resulted in lower yields.

The author:
Kristina A. Vaicikonis is a Senior Editor of *The World Book Year Book*.

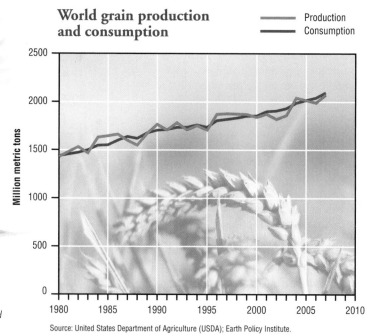

World grain production and consumption

━━━ Production
━━━ Consumption

Source: United States Department of Agriculture (USDA); Earth Policy Institute.

Regional contribution to world crop production

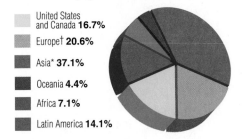

United States and Canada **16.7%**

Europe† **20.6%**

Asia* **37.1%**

Oceania **4.4%**

Africa **7.1%**

Latin America **14.1%**

†Including Asian part of Russia. *Excluding Asian part of Russia.
Source: Food and Agriculture Organization of the United Nations, 2005.

Where the hungry people of the world live (in millions)

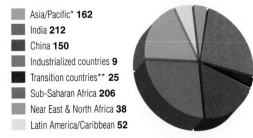

Asia/Pacific* **162**

India **212**

China **150**

Industrialized countries **9**

Transition countries** **25**

Sub-Saharan Africa **206**

Near East & North Africa **38**

Latin America/Caribbean **52**

*Excludes China and India. **Transition countries are those that are experiencing rapid economic growth; this group consists mainly of Eastern European countries and those that formerly belonged to the Soviet Union. Source: Food and Agriculture Organization of the United Nations, data for 2001-2003 (latest available).

In addition, some countries have begun to restrict the export of certain foods to control the rise of their own food costs. Russia and Argentina, for example, have placed restrictions on the export of wheat; Cambodia, China, Egypt, India, and Vietnam restrict rice exports. Such policies increase prices for nations that cannot grow enough grains to feed their people and must import them from other countries.

Other nations and organizations, including the United States and the European Union, subsidize their farmers. They guarantee that farmers will receive set minimum prices for raising key crops. Subsidies were originally intended to ensure that small farmers earn a sufficient profit to enable them to continue farming, even in years when weather destroys a crop or low prices on world markets result in a financial loss. Critics argue that many farms in the United States are run by large corporations that do not need subsidies to survive and that the practice drives up prices for the poor of importing nations—either when they purchase their own food or when donors of food aid purchase it for them.

Africa produces only 7.1 percent of the world's crops, but sub-Saharan Africa is home to 20 percent of the world's hungry people.

The controversy over biofuels

One especially controversial use of subsidies is government support for crops that are used to make *biofuels* (fuels made from plant materials). Biofuels are made from such crops as corn, sugar cane, and rape seed. Because they are a renewable resource, biofuels are considered to be more environmentally friendly than such fossil fuels as petroleum, coal, and natural gas. In 2003, the European Union (EU) mandated that biofuels make up 10 percent of fuel for cars and trucks by 2020. Some EU nations introduced such incentives as tax rebates to encourage production of biofuels.

In the United States, legislation was enacted in 2005 to promote cleaner-burning fuels and decrease U.S. dependence on foreign oil. The U.S. government also offered subsidies to encourage production of the fuel. As a result, from one-fifth to one-third (depending on the source of the estimate) of the 2007 U.S. corn harvest was diverted to the production of ethanol. Ethanol is a type of biofuel composed of

85 percent ethyl alcohol. In the United States, ethanol is made by fermenting sugar from corn. Brazil's ethanol industry—the second-largest in the world after that of the United States—is based on sugar cane. When it was launched in the mid-1970's, and for many years thereafter, the government of Brazil also subsidized the industry.

The UN Food and Agriculture Organization (FAO) and other groups that work to fight global hunger criticize government subsidies for biofuels. According to the FAO, biofuels drive up food costs and divert grains that could be used to feed the hungry while providing only modest environmental and economic benefits. Those in favor of biofuels argue that without ethanol, gasoline prices would rise even higher; that biofuels help reduce greenhouse gas emission; and that only a small portion of grain grown for food is used to make biofuel.

In addition to reducing the country's dependence on foreign sources of oil, the U.S. government also hoped that an increase in the use of biofuel would result in a drop in the price of oil, which skyrocketed during the first nine months of 2008. The rise in oil prices increased the costs

Amount of the United States corn crop used to produce ethanol

Grain Production
Grain for Fuel Ethanol

Million tons

500
400
300
200
100
0

1980   1985   1990   1995   2000   2005 2008

Note: 2008 figure is projected. Sources: U.S. Department of Agriculture; Earth Policy Institute.

of fuel, fertilizers, and chemicals for farmers, as well as the costs of production, packaging, and transportation of goods.

Hope for the future

Is there any hope that food prices will fall again? Most experts agree that a drop in prices will not happen soon. They also believe that it will take a concerted effort by the governments of developed nations to bring food costs down. One development that many scientists believe is necessary is an increase in government spending on agricultural science. The farmers of wealthy nations became more efficient at growing greater quantities of food in the 1960's, 1970's, and 1980's. However, in the 1990's, after staples had become so plentiful that food was stockpiled and exported—and governments paid farmers not to grow more food—funding for research and development decreased.

Farmers in less developed nations now need help in learning how to make the most of their limited agricultural resources, and their governments often cannot afford the cost of such research. Food production in Africa, where many of the world's undernourished people live, has declined over the past 30 years, according to the FAO. In fact, African farmers produce only one-quarter of the average yield that farmers in other areas of the world produce. They need help increasing soil fertility, managing limited water resources and insect pests, developing markets for their products, and improving infrastructure such as roads and bridges to access those markets.

In developed nations, some experts suggest, research into the production of biofuels from cellulose may help to bring costs down. *Cellulosic biofuels* (made from such plants as switchgrass and wood chips) can be grown on land not suitable for other crops, reducing the competition between crops grown for food and those grown for fuel.

Many agricultural experts agree that the world now has the resources and the technical expertise to adequately feed all of the people on the planet. What remains is to formulate policies that will ensure that all countries of the world have access to such resources. However, as global leaders in late 2008 dealt with a continuing, world-wide financial crisis, it appeared doubtful that solving the problem of world hunger would become a top priority any time soon.

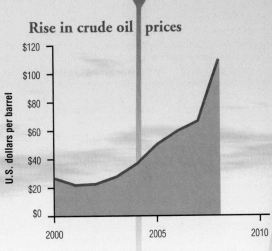

Rise in crude oil prices

*2008 figure represents an average of monthly prices from January through August.
Source: Energy Information Administration.

AIDS. Attempts to develop an effective vaccine against HIV (the virus that causes AIDS) continued to produce discouraging outcomes in 2008. In July, officials at the National Institute of Allergy and Infectious Diseases (NIAID), a part of the National Institutes of Health (NIH), canceled a planned clinical trial of a highly anticipated government vaccine known as Partnership for AIDS Vaccine Evaluation (PAVE) 100. NIAID officials said researchers needed more information about fundamental processes in the immune system before they could develop an effective vaccine.

The decision to cancel the PAVE trial followed the suspension of trials of a similar vaccine developed by Merck & Co., of Whitehouse Station, New Jersey, with government assistance. Studies of that vaccine were halted in September 2007 to prevent harm to the participants. Preliminary findings, confirmed by more detailed analyses published in November 2008, found that the Merck vaccine reduced neither the risk nor severity of HIV infections.

New way to fight AIDS. Researchers at the University of Michigan in Ann Arbor reported in May that they had developed the first new mechanism in nearly 20 years for blocking a substance needed by the AIDS virus for reproduction. The scientists said the finding could lead to a new class of anti-AIDS drugs that would cause fewer side effects than current drugs. The researchers, led by medical chemist Heather A. Carlson, developed a chemical compound that inhibited the action of HIV-1 protease in laboratory tests. HIV-1 protease is an enzyme that helps produce proteins needed to assemble HIV. The new compound prevents protease from producing the proteins.

WHO goal met. The World Health Organization (WHO), an agency of the United Nations, announced in June that it had met its goal of having 3 million people in developing countries on drugs to prevent their HIV infections from developing into AIDS. Despite this milestone, WHO noted that only 31 percent of the people in developing countries who were in immediate need of anti-AIDS medications received them in 2007. Obstacles to using anti-AIDS drugs in poor countries included a shortage of healthcare providers and lack of government funding.

HIV undercounted. The number of new HIV infections in the United States every year is 25 percent higher than previously thought, according to a June 2008 statement by immunologist Anthony Fauci, of the NIH. Fauci said that more accurate counting of certain population groups in various geographical regions of the United States revealed that 50,000 people per year become infected with HIV. ■ Alfred J. Smuskiewicz

See also **Africa; Drugs; Medicine; Public health.**

Air pollution. See **Environmental pollution.**

Albania. Albanian leaders achieved one of their main foreign policy goals in April 2008, when member states of the North Atlantic Treaty Organization (NATO) invited Albania to join the alliance as a full member in 2009. The ruling Democratic Party of Albania, led by Prime Minister Sali Berisha, continued to promote internal reforms in 2008, including reform of the judiciary and of electoral processes. NATO and the European Union (EU) both required such reforms to enable Albania's full integration into these institutions.

In April 2008, Albania's Parliament passed legislation to reform the nation's electoral system. The legislation included measures to promote proportional representation in Albania's 12 administrative districts; to streamline the election of the president in Parliament; and to clarify and streamline parliamentary rules for confidence votes and the calling of new elections.

Albania's *gross domestic product* (the value of all goods and services produced in a country in a year) grew by an estimated 6 percent in 2008. However, as the global economy slowed late in the year, economists predicted that Albania would experience more modest economic growth in 2009. ■ Sharon L. Wolchik

See also **Europe; Economics, World.**

Alberta. See **Canadian provinces.**

Algeria. The Algerian insurgent group called al-Qa`ida in Arab Maghreb Union continued its terrorist attacks in 2008. The group began a string of bombings in Algeria in December 2006. One of the worst terrorist attacks in Algeria in years happened on Aug. 19, 2008, when a car bombing aimed at a police training school killed at least 43 people and wounded 45 others in the northern town of Issers. A number of other deadly bombings occurred that same month.

In February, the Algerian interior ministry announced that authorities had killed a leader of al-Qa`ida in the Arab Maghreb Union and arrested six of his associates who were suspected of involvement in the December 2007 bombings of a United Nations (UN) facility in the capital, Algiers, and a group of foreign oil workers. Those attacks killed 41 people, including 17 UN staff members.

The December 2007 attacks led to a UN investigation of security conditions at UN offices worldwide. The investigative panel, led by Algerian diplomat Lakhdar Brahimi, reported in June 2008 that UN personnel around the world were increasingly likely to be attacked because many groups viewed the UN as a biased tool of the most powerful nations. ■ Alfred J. Smuskiewicz

See also **Africa; Terrorism; United Nations.**

Andorra. See **Europe.**

Angola. See **Africa.**

Anthropology. Research reported in 2008 suggested that the first prehistoric human ancestors arrived in Europe from Africa much earlier than anyone had previously thought. In a paper published in the March 27, 2008, issue of *Nature*, Eudald Carbonell of the University of Rovira I Virgili in Tarragona, Spain, and colleagues reported the discovery of a fossilized fragment of human *mandible* (lower jaw) at a site called *Sima del Elefante* (Cave of the Elephant), in the Atapuerca Mountains of northern Spain. A series of geological dating techniques and the presence of ancient animal fossils in the same layers indicated that the human fossil is about 1.2 million years old. This date is about 400,000 years older than the age of any other human fossil known from Europe.

The Sima del Elefante fossil is a jaw fragment that includes the chin area and a few fragmentary teeth. It resembles early human fossils discovered in 1996 at Gran Dolina, another cave site in northern Spain. The Spanish scientists classified the fossil as *Homo antecessor,* the same species as the Gran Dolina specimens. However, other anthropologists do not accept this classification.

Rudimentary stone flakes, resembling ancient stone tools previously found in Africa, were recovered in association with the jaw. The fossilized bones of antelope and other large mammals were also found in the cave. Many of the animal bones were fractured in ways that suggest the cave occupants broke them open with stone tools to gain access to the calorie-rich marrow inside. Cut marks on the bones indicate these prehistoric people used sharp stone flakes to butcher the animals.

Neandertal brain growth. In September 2008, a team of scientists led by Marcia S. Ponce de León of the University of Zurich, Switzerland, reported that Neandertal brains grew more rapidly in infancy than those of modern human beings. Adult Neandertals possessed much larger heads and brains compared with those of modern people. Scientists had thought that the Neandertals developed larger brains because they had a longer, slower period of childhood growth and development compared with modern people.

The researchers determined the size of Neandertal brains by using computers to produce three-dimensional virtual reconstructions of three Neandertal infant skeletons—those of an 18-month-old and a 2-year-old recovered from Dederiyeh Cave, near Damascus, Syria, and a newborn from Mezmaiskaya Cave, in the Northern Caucasus Mountains of Russia. The reconstructed fossil skulls showed that they were born with a brain about the same size as modern human beings—roughly 400 cubic centimeters in volume.

To determine how fast the brain grew after birth, the researchers examined fossil specimens of older Neandertal children from several sites in Europe. From this comparison, the investigators concluded that Neandertal children had a faster rate of brain growth, especially during infancy, compared with modern people. This early growth spurt alone was responsible for the larger brain and head size seen in adult Neandertals. Scientists are not sure exactly why the Neandertals had such large heads. However, the larger brain of the Neandertals did not give them greater intelligence compared with modern people.

Excavations at Gibraltar show that Neandertals dined on shellfish, seals, dolphins, and fish between 30,000 and 60,000 years ago, according to a report published in the Sept. 23, 2008, issue of *Proceedings of the National Academy of Sciences.* The remains were excavated at two cave sites on Gibraltar. Lead author Chris Stringer of The Natural History Museum in London commented that researchers do not understand precisely how the Neandertals obtained the marine resources. Anthropologists had considered the consumption of marine foods to be a more recent and uniquely modern-human practice. But many bones bear cut marks made by stone implements typically manufactured by Neandertals, proving they consumed seafoods at the sites. ■ Donald C. Johanson

Antigua and Barbuda. See **Latin America; West Indies.**

Archaeology. Several new and important archaeological discoveries were announced in 2008 from Bamiyan, Afghanistan. Bamiyan is the site where two giant sculptures of Buddha were destroyed by Taliban forces in 2001 in spite of international protests. While the ancient statues were destroyed, the site, which was once a large Buddhist monastery, preserves other archaeological treasures in a maze of caves, ruins, and catacombs throughout the mountainous location. In April, a study of Buddhist paintings on cave walls at Bamiyan, conducted by a team of scientists from the European Synchrotron Radiation Facility, showed that the paint was made with a base of walnut or poppy seed oil. The paintings depict scenes with Buddhas in bright red robes sitting among palms with a variety of animals, both real and imaginary. The paintings date from between A.D. 400 and 800, which is notable since the first oil paintings in Europe or any other part of the world were not produced before about 1200.

The remains of another giant Buddha statue were also found hidden nearby, according to reports in September 2008 by Afghan archaeologist Zemaryalai Tarzai. The remains of a 62-foot- (19-meter-) long horizontal statue of the sleeping Buddha were found buried in the foundation of an ancient temple about 1 mile (1.6 kilometers) from where the two giant statues were destroyed seven years before. The statue, which dates to around A.D. 200, is broken into several parts. The discovery of this third giant statue gives hope that an even larger one, described by a Chinese monk around 632, may yet be found in the region.

Ancient American feces. Dried human feces discovered in an Oregon cave site represent the oldest evidence of human occupation in the Americas according to a report published in April 2008 in the journal *Science*. In 2002, University of Oregon (Eugene) archaeologist Dennis Jenkins discovered dried feces in the Paisley caves of southern Oregon. Samples of the preserved excrement were later analyzed by University of Copenhagen geneticist Eske Willerslev, who found that some contained human DNA.

The researchers had the feces dated in 2008 using radiocarbon techniques. To their surprise, the radiocarbon dates showed that the feces were 14,300 years old—making them the oldest human remains ever discovered in the Americas. These remains prove that human beings arrived in the Americas long before the mammoth-hunting Clovis culture of about 13,000 years ago. For decades, archaeologists considered the Clovis people the first Americans. There are a handful of sites in North and South America that have radiocarbon dates older than 13,000 years. Some archaeologists, however, think the sites may be dated incorrectly. None of these sites have preserved human remains. Many scientists agree that

the Paisley cave remains put to rest all debates about whether the Clovis people were the first human beings to arrive in the Americas.

Wari mummies. In August, a Peruvian team of archaeologists discovered a 1,300-year-old tomb of the Wari culture in the Miraflores district of Lima, Peru. The tomb was discovered at a site called Huaca Pucllana, a temple complex used by the little-known Wari people, whose empire flourished from about 600 to 1000, long before the rise of the Inca empire in Peru.

The archaeologists, led by Huaca Pucllana site director Isabel Flores, discovered the mummies of three adults in the tomb, including one of a woman wearing a painted ceramic mask decorated with striking blue eyes. The "Lady of the Mask," as the archaeologists called her, was placed in the tomb in a seated position with her knees drawn up to her chest. Around her body they found pottery and other artifacts usually associated with weavers. Remains of a child, likely a victim of human sacrifice, were also found in the tomb. About 300 Wari tombs have been found in the area. However, this is the first intact tomb discovered. The others had all been looted.

Earliest human tuberculosis. In October 2008, scientists from University College London and Tel-Aviv University in Israel announced that

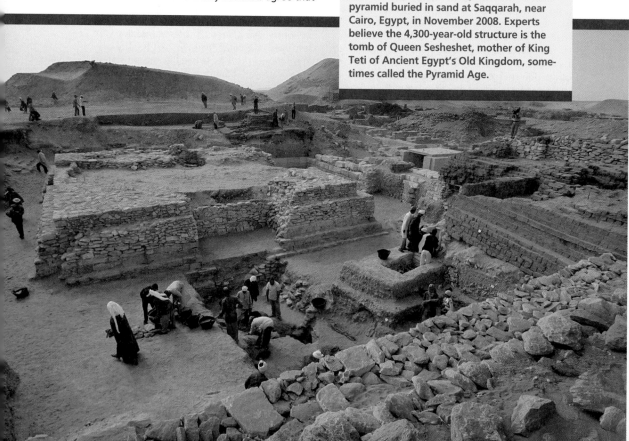

Workers excavate a newly discovered small pyramid buried in sand at Saqqarah, near Cairo, Egypt, in November 2008. Experts believe the 4,300-year-old structure is the tomb of Queen Sesheshet, mother of King Teti of Ancient Egypt's Old Kingdom, sometimes called the Pyramid Age.

they found evidence of tuberculosis (TB) in the bones of a mother and baby excavated from Atlit-Yam, a submerged 9,000-year-old village off the coast of Haifa, Israel. One researcher identified characteristic marks of TB infection on the bones of the mother. More detailed analysis of the bones revealed preserved DNA from *Mycobacterium tuberculosis,* the bacterium that causes TB in human beings. The *Neolithic* (New Stone Age) village dates from about the time that the first cattle were domesticated in the region. The village was submerged by a rise in sea level in the Mediterranean.

Scientists have long thought that the variety of tuberculosis that infects human beings developed from a strain that regularly infected wild cattle. Scientists theorized that when people domesticated cattle, the *bovine* (cattle) TB bacterium evolved to infect human beings through close contact over time. The tuberculosis DNA obtained from the Atlit-Yam bones lacked a particular piece of DNA that is characteristic of common TB strains present in the world today. This is evidence that TB has existed in human populations for a very long time—longer than if it originated from bovine TB. This skeletal evidence supports a more recent theory that suggests that bovine TB developed from human TB rather than the other way around. ■ Mark Rose

Architecture. Art and cultural projects dominated the American architectural landscape in 2008, not surprising considering how the global recession decimated commercial and residential construction. Yet not all of these new projects are museums. This year's roundup included a nature center, a stunning federal courthouse, and the restoration of an iconic 1960's building. Green is becoming the color of choice and "sustainable," a synonym for progressive.

The most anticipated building of 2008 was Renzo Piano's California Academy of Sciences in San Francisco. Tucked beneath a 3-acre (1.2-hectare) sod roof—which is a dramatic expression of sustainability—are an aquarium, planetarium, science museum, and rain forest as well as offices and research laboratories. Piano retained portions of the original 1916 building, yet the building materials and mechanical systems are all environmentally responsive and state-of-the-art. The major complaint, primarily from staff, was that exhibits and research spaces are poorly integrated.

Trinity River Audubon Center in Dallas, designed by Antoine Predock, is less ambitious yet formally inventive. From above, it resembles a bird in flight; on the ground, a series of pinwheeling arms reach out to ponds, swamps, and old-growth forests along the Trinity River. The Center is aggressively green inside and out, from the cypress siding on the classroom wing to the bamboo flooring and recycled blue-jean ceilings in the auditorium and exhibit hall.

Notable new museums in New York City. Devoted to contemporary art, the New Museum, by the Tokyo firm SANAA, is a skewed seven-story tower that resembles a stack of tipsy hat boxes. Located in the historic Bowery on Manhattan's Lower East Side, the $50-million building is sheathed in glass and rugged aluminum mesh; the materials capture both the industrial grittiness of the surrounding neighborhood and the lofty aspirations of the art inside, most of which is edgy and experimental.

The Museum of Art and Design, formerly the American Craft Museum, took over Edward Durrell Stone's idiosyncratic Huntington Hartford Gallery on Columbus Circle. Derided when it opened in 1964—one critic called it "a Venetian palazzo on lollipops"—the building became the focus of a bitter preservation battle that involved most of the city's design establishment. The preservationists lost, and Brad Cloepfil of Allied Works in Portland, Oregon, was commissioned to redesign the Hartford building inside and out. He replaced Stone's Vermont marble with glazed terra cotta and added bands of glass that some observers insist spell HI! Comments about the interior, especially the layout of the galleries and the views of the city, have been more positive.

A Brutalist icon reborn. Far more successful was the restoration of Paul Rudolph's Art and Architecture Building at Yale University in New Haven, Connecticut. The Brutalist icon from the 1960's was nearly burned to the ground by students in 1969 and subsequently chopped up into a warren of bleak, jerry-rigged spaces. (The Brutalists created plain, massive buildings with rough reinforced concrete exteriors.) The $125-million restoration, by Gwathmey Siegel Architects, recaptures the raw power of Rudolph's original design while eliminating the thoughtless and purely expedient additions. As a symbol of shifting architectural fashion, Rudolph's still controversial Art and Architecture Building is perfect.

Federal Center. Springfield, Massachusetts, a battered industrial city in the center of the state, got an extraordinary gift from the federal government in the form of a new courthouse by Moshe Safdie. Located in the heart of downtown, it consists of two concrete and glass semicircles that are bright, inviting, and transparent—qualities often not found in civic architecture. The sculptural shape was determined partly by a desire to preserve two ancient trees on the site. The courthouse was funded through the Design Excellence Program of the General Services Administration, which has over the last two decades dramatically improved the architecture of federal buildings.

Aqua. The recession notwithstanding, downtown Chicago is getting a first-ever office, hotel, retail, and residential tower named Aqua. Designed by local architect Jeanne Gang of Studio Gang, its 88 stories are covered with wave-like balconies—thus the name—that give it a shifting, phantasmagorical appearance. In a city famous for rugged, structurally expressive architecture, Aqua is skyline sculpture.

Awards. French architect Jean Nouvel, known in the United States for his industrial-strength Guthrie Theater in Minneapolis, won the 2008 Pritzker Prize, the profession's most prestigious honor. An innovative modernist of impressive range and unpredictable style, Nouvel has designed the Arab World Institute in Paris; the bullet-shaped Torre Agbar in Barcelona, Spain; and an acclaimed concert hall and culture center in Lucerne, Switzerland.

In addition to kudos for his California Academy of Science in San Francisco, Renzo Piano received the American Institute of Architects Gold Medal for lifetime achievement. The jury described his work as "sculptural, beautiful, technically accomplished and sustainable." They might have added "diverse," because over 40 years he has designed everything from boats to skyscrapers and memorable art museums. ■ David Dillon

The wavelike balconies of the Aqua tower, nearly completed in 2008 in downtown Chicago, give the building a shifting, phantasmagorical appearance that has been compared to sculpture. Designed by Chicago architect Jeanne Gang of Studio Gang, the 88-story structure will house offices, retail space, a hotel, and residences.

Argentina. In March 2008, President Cristina Fernández de Kirchner ran afoul of Argentina's farmers by imposing higher taxes on their agricultural exports, the mainstay of the nation's economy. With world food prices soaring, she had hoped to raise $4 billion as part of her social agenda to redistribute wealth and maintain price controls. Taxes on soybeans, for example, rose to 44 percent of their value. Previously, the tax was pegged at a fixed rate of 35 percent.

The sudden change of the rules seemed unfair to many Argentines and led to four months of protests spearheaded by farmers. Their strikes caused food shortages and interrupted commerce in several areas of the country, costing the government billions in lost revenue. In July, a demonstration in Buenos Aires, the capital, attracted 235,000 supporters on the eve of a Senate vote on the legality of her actions.

Voting drama. On July 17, after an 18-hour debate, Argentina's Senate rejected Fernández de Kirchner's tax increases by a single vote cast by that body's presiding officer, Vice President Julio Cobos. "May history judge me," Cobos said. "If I am making a mistake, I ask for forgiveness."

The deciding vote made Vice President Cobos the only popular facet of a rather unpopular Argentine government. The Fernández de Kirchner administration had lost credibility for its populist politics, lack of financial discipline, and questionable economic choices. In November, Fernández de Kirchner announced plans to nationalize nearly $26 billion in private pension funds as well as Argentina's largest airline in response to the global economic crisis. The plans scared off foreign investors, who saw a government desperate for cash.

Minimum wage hike. Hours after the senate vote, Fernández de Kirchner revoked her March decree. By then, her approval rating, owing largely to this single issue, had plummeted to 20 percent. In an effort to recover support, she raised the minimum wage by 27 percent, an action that benefited an estimated 750,000 workers.

The former president. In August, Fernández de Kirchner faced hostile questions at her first press conference since taking office in December 2007. Among them were stinging allegations that her husband, former President Néstor Kirchner, was "pulling the strings" of her administration. Argentine media have charged that Kirchner was still making big decisions, with Fernández de Kirchner serving largely as a figurehead.

Natural gas terminal. On Aug. 4, 2008, Fernández de Kirchner signed an agreement with Venezuela's President Hugo Chávez for the joint construction of Argentina's first liquefied natural gas terminal, a $600-million project. The two countries also agreed to study the possible construction of an oil pipeline and refinery in Argentina to help resolve the country's worsening energy shortage.

Ex-generals in prison. On August 28, two former military commanders were sentenced to life in prison for "crimes against humanity" during the country's so-called "Dirty War" against political dissidents from 1976 to 1983. General Luciano Benjamin Menendez, 81, and retired General Antonio Bussi, 82, who was already in jail, were convicted of the kidnapping, torture, and murder of Senator Guillermo Vargas Aignasse on March 24, 1976. Six other former military officers and one civilian were also convicted of crimes of that era.

Ex-president charged. On Nov. 28, 2008, Argentines watched on television as former President Carlos Menem, 78, was formally charged with arms-trafficking. Menem was accused of illegally selling weapons to Croatia and Ecuador when they were involved in conflicts in the 1990's. If convicted, he could spend up to 10 years in jail. However, as a sitting senator representing his home province of La Rioja, Menem was immune from imprisonment. The ex-president was too ill to attend the trial, but he participated through video conference. Menem was president of Argentina from 1989 to 1999.

◼ Nathan A. Haverstock

See also **Latin America.**

Armed forces. United States military affairs were again dominated in 2008 by the wars in Iraq and Afghanistan. United States-led forces began operations in Afghanistan in October 2001 and in Iraq in March 2003. In Iraq, President George W. Bush's "surge" of 30,000 combat troops, begun in 2007, helped stabilize conditions, prompting some troop withdrawals. Conditions in Afghanistan, however, deteriorated in 2008 as fighters fielded by a resurgent Taliban penetrated deeply into the country and launched bolder and more numerous attacks.

Iraq security agreement. In November, U.S. negotiators and the Iraqi Cabinet signed a security agreement that set conditions for a continued U.S. military presence in Iraq and gave a timetable for the eventual withdrawal of U.S. and allied troops. The agreement stipulated that coalition forces should be withdrawn from all urban areas by June 30, 2009, and fully withdrawn from Iraq by the end of 2011. The pact acknowledged a degree of Iraqi jurisdiction over crimes committed by foreign service persons off-base and off-duty, a significant Iraqi victory.

Improved security in Iraq during 2008 provided the background for the U.S.-Iraqi accord. Declines in insurgent-perpetrated and sectarian violence resulted in fewer coalition troop casualties and civilian deaths. In the second half of

2008, the death toll among coalition troops—nearly all of them U.S. soldiers—dropped to an average of fewer than one per day. By contrast, in mid-2007, over 100 per month, or an average of about 4 per day, had been dying. Analysts attributed the improved situation partly to the troop surge but also to decisions by many former Sunni insurgents to stop resisting the U.S. presence and a cease-fire by the largest Shi`ite militia. As of Dec. 22, 2008, 4,210 American soldiers had been killed in Iraq.

General David H. Petraeus, the U.S. commander in Iraq, told the U.S. Congress on April 8, 2008, that the security situation in Iraq was "significantly better" than before the surge but remained "fragile and reversible." The last of the five combat brigades from the troop surge returned to the United States in July. On September 10, President Bush announced that an additional 8,000 troops would be withdrawn from Iraq in February 2009 but 5,000 other soldiers and Marines would be sent to Afghanistan.

Command shift. On April 23, 2008, Secretary of Defense Robert M. Gates announced that General Petraeus would leave his Baghdad post and become commander of the U.S. Central Command (CENTCOM), with overall authority for the wars in both Iraq and Afghanistan. General Raymond T. Odierno, the Army's vice chief of staff, replaced Petraeus as commander of U.S. forces in Iraq. Petraeus replaced Admiral William Fallon as CENTCOM commander. Fallon decided to retire early after policy disagreements with Petraeus and the Bush administration over policy in Iraq and Afghanistan and relations with Iran.

On December 1, 146,000 U.S. troops were stationed in Iraq, and approximately 4,200 had died since the 2003 invasion.

Afghanistan. As the situation improved in Iraq, conditions deteriorated in Afghanistan, with a significant increase in attacks by insurgents led by the Taliban. According to intelligence experts, the Taliban, since being ousted by the U.S.-led invasion in 2001, had regrouped in remote mountainous regions of neighboring Pakistan.

On July 13, 2008, Taliban insurgents assaulted a North Atlantic Treaty Organization (NATO) military base near the Afghan-Pakistani border with rocket-propelled grenades and mortars, killing nine U.S. soldiers. (NATO took over command and coordination of the International Security Assistance Force in Afghanistan in 2003.) The attack, the deadliest on a coalition position since 2005, was part of a pattern of accelerated attacks by Taliban-sponsored insurgents in 2008 and increasing casualties among U.S. and NATO coalition troops.

On September 10, the chairman of the Joint Chiefs of Staff, Admiral Michael Mullen, told a congressional hearing, "I'm not convinced we're winning it in Afghanistan; I am convinced we can." Later in September, General David D. McKiernan, the commander of U.S. and NATO forces in Afghanistan, requested 15,000 U.S. combat troops beyond the 5,000 additional troops already pledged for deployment in Afghanistan by the beginning of 2009.

On Dec. 1, 2008, 32,000 U.S. troops were stationed in Afghanistan, serving under NATO command. As of December 22, 625 U.S. troops had died since the war began in 2001.

European deployments. The Bush administration's plans to create an antiballistic missile shield in Europe moved closer to reality during 2008. On July 8, representatives of the United States and the Czech Republic signed an agreement to deploy a sophisticated U.S. radar system on Czech soil. United States and Polish leaders reached a similar agreement on August 14, when the Poles agreed to allow the United States to base 10 interceptor missiles in Poland by 2012. Russian leaders protested, claiming that the antimissile system threatens Russia's sovereignty. United States officials countered that the system was purely defensive and designed to protect NATO allies and Israel from nuclear attack by a rogue nation such as Iran.

Weapons programs. In 2008, the U.S. Department of Defense (DOD) continued developing a variety of new weapons systems, including a joint strike fighter, new classes of nuclear aircraft carriers and destroyers, a new generation of armored fighting vehicles, an Air Force strategic bomber, and the littoral combat ship (LCS), a small, mobile, shallow-draft vessel capable of close-in warfare at high speed along enemy coastlines. The Navy christened and launched two LCS's in 2008 and commissioned its fourth and fifth Virginia-class nuclear attack submarines, *North Carolina* and *New Hampshire*.

In February, the DOD chose Los Angeles-based Northrop Grumman Corporation and a European consortium to build the next generation of aerial refueling tanker jets. Chicago-based Boeing Company, the losing bidder for the $100-billion program, challenged the decision in March. After the Government Accountability Office found "significant errors" in the Air Force's decision-making process, Secretary Gates ordered a fast-track review of the decision. On September 10, however, Gates said that the tanker decision would be left to the new president taking office on Jan. 20, 2009.

The Navy confirmed in July 2008 that it would cancel the DDG-1000 Zumwalt-class destroyer project after completion of the first two ships. Rising costs were cited as the principal factor in the decision. Each Zumwalt ship would cost more than $2.5 billion, twice the cost of the Burke-class destroyer it was intended to replace.

Air Force shakeup. In June, Secretary Gates requested and received the resignations of Secretary of the Air Force Michael W. Wynne and General T. Michael Moseley, chief of staff—the top civilian and military leaders, respectively, of the U.S. Air Force. Gates explained that several incidents, including the inadvertent dispatch by jet in August 2007 of six nuclear-tipped missiles from a base in North Dakota to a base in Louisiana, had broken his confidence in the leadership of the two men. Gates nominated Michael B. Donley as secretary of the Air Force and Norton A. Schwartz to be Air Force chief of staff; both appointments were confirmed by the U.S. Senate.

Personnel strains. The intensity of combat operations in Iraq and Afghanistan produced serious strains on soldiers and their families trying to cope with extended and multiple combat deployments. The number of soldiers diagnosed with post-traumatic stress disorder (PTSD) rose nearly 50 percent in 2007, the DOD disclosed in May 2008, an increase largely attributed to the dual wars that have required tens of thousands of soldiers to serve as many as four combat tours. In a report released in April by the Rand Corporation, a nonprofit research organization that studies U.S. defense policy, experts estimated that treating PTSD in servicepersons would cost $6 billion over the next two years. The report also found that nearly 20 percent of the 1.6 million U.S. veterans of the Iraq-Afghanistan conflicts reported probable traumatic brain injuries during their combat deployments.

In May, the Army announced that 115 soldiers committed suicide in 2007, the largest yearly total in nearly 30 years. The Veterans Administration revealed in February 2008 that more than half the veterans who killed themselves after returning from Iraq or Afghanistan were members of the National Guard or military reserves.

On October 29, Secretary of the Army Peter Geren announced that the army would collaborate with the National Institute of Mental Health on a five-year, $50-million medical study to identify the causes and risk factors of suicide. The army agreed to supply subjects for the study and to make its databases available to researchers.

More than 1,200 U.S. service members stand at attention before taking the Army enlistment oath at the Al-Faw Palace in Baghdad on July 4, 2008. General David Petraeus, the top commander in Iraq, led the mass reenlistment ceremony.

Responding to concerns about mental and physical strains on combat personnel, President Bush announced on July 31 that future Iraq combat tours would be reduced from 15 months to 12 months.

Defense budget. On February 4, the DOD submitted its budget for fiscal year 2009, which began on Oct. 1, 2008. The request totaled $515.4 billion, a 7.5-percent increase over appropriations for fiscal 2008. The proposed level of defense spending, adjusted for inflation, was the largest since World War II (1939–1945), surpassing the military build-up begun by President Ronald Reagan in the early 1980's. The budget included funding for a 3.4-percent pay raise for military personnel and for expansion of the Army and Marine Corps by 12,000 soldiers. It also included a 20-percent increase in spending on weapons systems.

In addition to the DOD budget package, President Bush in January 2008 requested a $70-billion supplemental appropriation for operations in Iraq and Afghanistan.

Command changes. In 2008, the Senate confirmed Army Lieutenant General Ann E. Dunwoody as the nation's first woman four-star general. The Senate also confirmed General Craig R. McKinley as the first four-star general to command the National Guard Bureau.

Appointments. President-elect Barack Obama in late November appointed sitting Secretary of Defense Robert M. Gates to also serve as secretary of defense in his administration, beginning on Jan. 20, 2009. In December 2008, Obama appointed retired Marine General James Jones, a former Supreme Allied Commander of NATO, to serve as national security adviser in his administration.
■ Thomas M. DeFrank

See also **Afghanistan; Czech Republic; Iraq; People in the news** (Ann Dunwoody); **United States, Government of the.**

Armenia. Prime Minister Serzh Sargsyan won Armenia's presidential election on Feb. 19, 2008, with 52.9 percent of the vote. Sargsyan was a close political ally of outgoing President Robert Kocharian, who was constitutionally prohibited from pursuing a third five-year term in office. International observers from the Organization for Security and Co-operation in Europe declared that the elections were conducted "mostly in line with the country's international commitments," though they noted some vote-counting problems.

Thousands of supporters of second-place candidate Levon Ter-Petrosian took to the streets of Yerevan, the capital, to protest the election results. The government responded by detaining a number of opposition leaders and placed Ter-Petrosian under house arrest, but the demonstrations continued. After the crowd and police clashed violently on March 1, Kocharian declared a 20-day state of emergency and arrested additional opposition activists.

On March 8, the Armenian Constitutional Court rejected Ter-Petrosian's claim that the election had been rigged and reaffirmed the official results. Sargsyan was sworn in as president on April 9. Former Central Bank head Tigran Sargsyan, who was no relation to the new president, became prime minister. ■ Juliet Johnson

See also **Asia.**

Art. Two major museums in New York City announced the retirement of their long-time directors and the selection of new directors in 2008. In January, Philippe de Montebello said that he would leave his post as the director of the Metropolitan Museum of Art after more than 30 years. Montebello, a French-born art historian and curator, will retire on December 31, having served longer than any other director of the museum, usually called simply the Met. In September, the Met announced that Thomas P. Campbell, its curator of European sculpture and decorative arts, will succeed Montebello on Jan. 1, 2009.

During Montebello's tenure, the Met nearly doubled in size. Montebello oversaw such notable building projects as the Lila Acheson Wallace Wing for art of the 1900's, which opened in 1987, and new Greek and Roman galleries, which opened in 2007. The Met acquired many masterpieces and major collections under Montebello's leadership, ranging from *Madonna and Child* (about 1300) by the early Renaissance artist Duccio di Buoninsegna to the Annenberg Collection of Impressionist and Post-Impressionist paintings.

In 2006, Montebello reached a groundbreaking agreement with the Italian Culture Ministry that was hailed as a model to settle disputes between museums and national governments over the ownership of artworks and other objects. The Met agreed to return a number of items from its collection that Italy claimed were removed illegally from Italian soil. In return, Italy agreed to lend objects of comparable importance to the Met.

In February 2008, the Solomon R. Guggenheim Foundation in New York City announced that Thomas Krens would step down as its director. On November 4, Richard Armstrong, former director of the Carnegie Museum of Art in Pittsburgh, succeeded him. Krens remained with the foundation as its senior adviser for international affairs, overseeing the development of a satellite museum in Abu Dhabi in the United Arab Emirates. During his 20-year leadership, Krens oversaw the Solomon R. Guggenheim Museum in New York City and an international network of museums that he helped create, including the Guggenheim Museum Bilbao in Spain, which opened in 1997.

Major exhibitions. A comprehensive survey of the American Realist artist Edward Hopper ran through January 2008 at the National Gallery of Art in Washington, D.C. Hopper's spare images of urban and rural life have become some of the most popular artworks of the 1900's. The exhibition of paintings, water colors, and prints included such well-known works as *Drug Store* (1927), *New York Movie* (1939), and *Nighthawks* (1942), Hopper's famous depiction of a late-night diner.

The first full exhibition in 30 years of the life's work of French artist Gustave Courbet opened at the Met in February 2008. The show presented some 130 works by the pioneering artist who helped pave the way for Modernism. The works included early self-portraits; paintings of life in Ornans, the village in France where Courbet was born; and a series of female nudes from the 1860's.

An exhibition devoted to Queen Marie Antoinette of France opened in March 2008 at the Grand Palais in Paris. The show featured more than 300 paintings, sculptures, pieces of furniture, and decorative items. The exhibition presented the story of Marie Antoinette's life—from her childhood in Austria, through her lavish reign as the queen of France, to her tragic end during the French Revolution (1789-1799), when she was guillotined at age 37 in 1793.

Museums in both Chicago and New York City featured works by the American sculptor Jeff Koons in 2008. Koons's best-known sculptures transform common objects, such as balloons and toys, into large-scale art. In May, the Museum of Contemporary Art in Chicago opened a survey of sculpture and paintings by Koons, ranging from the 1980's to the early 2000's. The early works included *Rabbit* (1986), a stainless steel statue of an inflatable bunny; and *Michael Jackson and Bubbles* (1988), a porcelain figure of the pop singer holding his pet chimpanzee. Later works included two monumental sculptures made of highly polished stainless steel, *Balloon Dog (Orange)* (1994-2000), a 10-foot (3-meter) sculpture of a balloon twisted into the shape of a poodle; and *Hanging Heart (Blue and Silver)* (1994-2006). Another sculpture, *Balloon Dog (Yellow)*, drew record crowds when the Met exhibited it and two other works by Koons in its rooftop garden through October.

The exhibition "Afghanistan: Hidden Treasures from the National Museum, Kabul" appeared throughout the summer at the National Art Gallery in Washington, D.C. It displayed more than 200 objects, most on view for the first time in the United States. The exhibition included ivories, gold objects, painted glassware, and bronze and stone sculptures. They dated from 2200 B.C. to A.D. 200

The Clinic of Dr. Gross, an 1875 masterpiece by Philadelphia artist Thomas Eakins, went on display at the Philadelphia Museum of Art in August. The Philadelphia Museum of Art and the Pennsylvania Academy of the Fine Arts joined forces to buy the painting from a local medical school and will share the right to exhibit it.

and had been unearthed from archaeological sites. The Kabul museum lost much of its collection during years of civil war and other conflict in Afghanistan. But museum officials preserved many of the objects in the exhibition by hiding them in a vault under the presidential palace until 2003.

A comprehensive survey of portrait busts by the renowned Italian Baroque sculptor Gian Lorenzo Bernini went on view for the first time in the United States in August 2008 at the J. Paul Getty Museum in Los Angeles. The major international loan exhibition, titled "Bernini and the

Birth of Baroque Portrait Sculpture," featured nearly 60 sculptures, paintings, and drawings.

New museums. The new 63,000-square-foot (5,850-square-meter) Contemporary Jewish Museum opened in downtown San Francisco in June. The Polish-born American architect Daniel Libeskind designed the $47.5-million building to incorporate a landmark 1907 power plant. The new building preserves the facade of the historic plant and adds a tilted extension clad in blue steel panels. The Contemporary Jewish Museum, which was founded in 1984, has no permanent collection. Instead, it hosts a variety of traveling exhibitions and programs.

The Los Angeles County Museum of Art opened its new Broad Contemporary Art Museum in February 2008. The three-story, $56-million building provides 60,000 square feet (5,570 square meters) of column-free exhibition space. It was designed by the Italian architect Renzo Piano, who planned the open space specially for the display of large contemporary art. The new museum takes its name from Los Angeles philanthropist Eli Broad and his wife, Edythe, who donated $60 million to the museum. The museum also unveiled other new facilities, including two refurbished main galleries; underground parking; and a covered concourse linking the museum's east and west sections. A central grand entrance features *Urban Light* (2007), a permanent installation of vintage street lights by American artist Chris Burden.

Museum rescue. In December, Broad pledged $30 million for a bailout of the financially strapped Museum of Contemporary Art in Los Angeles. Broad offered to match the first $15 million raised by the museum's trustees and to donate $3 million per year for exhibits over the next five years.

Weegee discovery. In June 2008, the Indianapolis Museum of Art acquired 210 black-and-white photographs by Weegee, as well as other related documents. Weegee, whose real name was Arthur Fellig, was a legendary New York City photographer known for his images of street scenes. The photographs and papers, dating from the 1930's to the 1960's, were discovered in a trunk at a farmhouse yard sale in southern Kentucky in 2003. They probably once belonged to Weegee's long-time companion, Wilma Wilcox. The photographs spanned Weegee's career, from candid pictures of crime scenes; through shots of audiences in darkened movie theaters and jazz clubs; to photos of strippers and celebrities.

Record auction prices. Despite fears of an economic recession, New York City auction houses sold more than $800 million in Impressionist, Modern, and contemporary art in May 2008. *Triptych, 1976,* by the British artist Francis Bacon, sold for $86.3 million at Sotheby's auction house. It set a world record for a contemporary work of art. The monumental painting of distorted faces, body parts, and other forms consists of three panels, each about 6 ½ by 5 feet (2 by 1.5 meters).

A 1995 painting by British artist Lucien Freud set a world record for a living artist when it sold for $33.6 million at Christie's auction house. The painting, *Benefits Supervisor Sleeping*, depicts one of the artist's regular sitters, Sue Tilley, napping naked on a couch.

Art world losses. Anne d'Harnoncourt, the first woman to run a major American museum, died in June 2008. She was the director and chief executive officer of the Philadelphia Museum of Art in Pennsylvania and an internationally respected art historian. D'Harnoncourt organized major exhibitions that showcased the work of the Romanian abstract sculptor Constantin Brancusi, the French Post-Impressionist Paul Cézanne, and the American Abstract Expressionist Barnett Newman, among others. During her 26-year leadership, d'Harnoncourt also oversaw the renovation of the museum's European, modern, and contemporary collections, as well as the expansion into a neighboring landmark Art Deco building.

One of d'Harnoncourt's greatest acquisitions, *The Clinic of Dr. Gross,* also known as *The Gross Clinic,* went on display at the Philadelphia Museum of Art in August 2008. In 2007, d'Harnoncourt joined forces with the Pennsylvania Academy of the Fine Arts, also in Philadelphia, to buy the painting from Thomas Jefferson University, a local medical school. The Pennsylvania Academy and the Philadelphia Museum of Art now jointly own and exhibit *The Clinic of Dr. Gross,* an 1875 masterpiece by Philadelphia artist Thomas Eakins.

Robert Rauschenberg, an American artist who helped transform art in the 1900's, died on May 12, 2008. Rauschenberg worked as a painter, photographer, and printmaker, as well as a choreographer, composer, set designer, and performer. He invented an art form called the *combine,* which brought together everyday objects, often joined with painted canvases. One combine called *Bed* (1955) consists of a real quilt, sheet, and pillow, all splattered with paint. Another, *Canyon* (1959), features a stuffed eagle mounted on canvas.

Cornell Capa, a Hungarian-born American photojournalist, died on May 23, 2008. During his nearly 30-year career as a photographer, Capa worked for *Life* magazine and Magnum Photos, a member-owned photography agency. He focused largely on politics and social justice issues, covering John F. Kennedy's 1960 presidential campaign and the 1967 Six-Day War in Israel. In 1974, Capa founded the International Center of Photography in New York City, one of the world's leading photography museums. His brother, Robert Capa, was also a famous photographer. ■ Sally-Ruth May

See also **Architecture.**

ASIA

Natural disasters caused widespread suffering across Asia in 2008. The worldwide economic downturn slowed progress toward relieving extensive, persistent poverty.

Disasters. A *cyclone,* a weather system known as a hurricane in the Atlantic Ocean, devastated the Irrawaddy River delta of Myanmar on May 2 and 3, 2008. It left nearly 138,000 people dead and missing. Myanmar's ruling *junta* (military government) was slow to provide relief and obstructed foreign aid as tens of thousands of people suffered hunger and thirst.

Flooding caused deaths in India, throughout Southeast Asia, and into China. The break of a river embankment in Nepal during monsoon season in August flooded India's Bihar state, killing at least 191 people and leaving more than 3 million others homeless. The same heavy rain system caused flooding in Myanmar, northern Thailand, Laos, and Vietnam.

In Afghanistan, a long-term drought and severe winter weather cut wheat crops by 60 percent. Livestock died from lack of water and food. With prices rising for imported food, an

A Laotian man pulls his boat through the flooded Xiengkuane Buddha Park in August 2008. Monsoon rains throughout Southeast Asia caused extensive flooding, raising the level of the Mekong River, which flows through Laos, Cambodia, and Vietnam, to nearly 45 feet (14 meters) above its usual level in the dry season.

FACTS IN BRIEF ON ASIAN COUNTRIES

Country	Population	Government	Monetary unit*	Foreign trade (million U.S.$) Exports†	Imports†
Afghanistan	32,253,000	President Hamid Karzai	afghani (46.78 = $1)	274	3,823
Armenia	2,994,000	President Serzh Sargsyan; Prime Minister Tigran Sargsyan	dram (302.00 = $1)	1,200	2,807
Azerbaijan	8,607,000	President Ilham Aliyev; Prime Minister Artur Rasizade	manat new spot (0.82 = $1)	21,270	6,045
Bangladesh	150,060,000	President Iajuddin Ahmed; Chief Adviser Fakhruddin Ahmed	taka (68.00 = $1)	12,450	16,670
Bhutan	718,000	King Jigme Khesar Namgyel Wangchuck; Prime Minister Jigme Thinley	ngultrum (49.32 = $1)	350	320
Brunei	379,000	Sultan and Prime Minister Haji Hassanal Bolkiah	dollar (1.42 = $1)	6,767	2,000
Cambodia (Kampuchea)	14,656,000	King Norodom Sihamoni; Prime Minister Hun Sen	riel (4,111.00 = $1)	4,089	5,424
China	1,346,606,000	President Hu Jintao; Premier Wen Jiabao	yuan (6.84 = $1)	1,565,900 (includes Hong Kong)	1,270,200
East Timor	995,000	President José Ramos-Horta; Prime Minister Xanana Gusmão	U.S. dollar (1.00 = $1)	10	202
Georgia	4,421,000	President Mikheil Saakasvili; Prime Minister Grigol Mgaloblishvili	lari (1.40 = $1)	2,104	4,977
India	1,144,734,000	President Pratibha Patil; Prime Minister Manmohan Singh	rupee (43.60 = $1)	151,300	230,500
Indonesia	232,269,000	President Susilo Bambang Yudhoyono	rupiah (9,125.00 = $1)	118,000	84,930
Iran	72,048,000	Supreme Leader Ayatollah Ali Khamenei; President Mahmoud Ahmadinejad	rial (8,229.00 = $1)	88,260	53,880
Japan	127,994,000	Emperor Akihito; Prime Minister Taro Aso	yen (109.72 = $1)	678,100	573,300
Kazakhstan	15,367,000	President Nursultan A. Nazarbayev; Prime Minister Karim Masimov	tenge (119.80 = $1)	48,350	33,210
Korea, North	23,059,000	Chairman of National Defense Commission Kim Jong-il Premier Kim Yong-il	won (2.20 = $1)	1,466	2,879
Korea, South	48,877,000	President Lee Myung-bak; Prime Minister Han Seung-soo	won (1,083.50 = $1)	379,000	349,600
Kyrgyzstan	5,336,000	President Kurmanbek Bakiev Prime Minister Igor Chudinov	som (34.80 = $1)	1,337	2,636

*Exchange rates as of Sept. 30, 2008.   †Latest available data.

estimated 8.4 million people did not have enough to eat.

Earthquakes in 2008 shook China, Pakistan, and Japan. The most severe of these rocked China's Sichuan Province on May 12. The 7.9-magnitude quake killed nearly 70,000 people and left another 18,000 missing. China's government responded quickly with relief work and rebuilding. The government later admitted that a number of schools that collapsed in the quake, killing some 10,000 children, had been shoddily built.

At least 215 people were killed by a 6.4-magnitude earthquake that hit southwest Pakistan on October 29. Japan was rocked by two significant earthquakes in 2008. The stronger of the two was a 7.2-magnitude quake that struck northeastern Japan on June 14, killing at least 12 people.

Economic problems throughout the world slowed the growth of many once-booming Asian countries. Much of the boom had been based on exporting to the West, especially from China, Japan, South Korea, Vietnam, Thailand, and

Country	Population	Government	Monetary unit*	Foreign trade (million U.S.$)	
				Exports[†]	Imports[†]
Laos	6,361,000	President Choummaly Sayasone; Prime Minister Bouasone Bouphavanh	kip (8,657.00 = $1)	970	1,378
Malaysia	27,526,000	Paramount Ruler Mizan Zainal Abidin, the Sultan of Terengganu; Prime Minister Abdullah bin Ahmad Badawi	ringgit (3.38 = $1)	176,400	139,100
Maldives	313,000	President Mohamed Nasheed	rufiyaa (12.80 = $1)	167	930
Mongolia	2,670,000	President Nambaryn Enkhbayar; Prime Minister Sanjaa Bayar	tugrik (1,187.25 = $1)	1,889	2,117
Myanmar (Burma)	51,988,000	Chairman of the State Peace and Development Council Than Shwe; Prime Minister Thein Sein	kyat (450.00 = $1)	6,122	2,942
Nepal	27,416,000	President Ram Baran Yadav; Prime Minister Prachanda	rupee (70.25 = $1)	830	2,398
Pakistan	167,947,000	President Asif Ali Zardari; Prime Minister Yousaf Raza Gilani	rupee (75.38 = $1)	18,120	28,760
Philippines	89,681,000	President Gloria Macapagal-Arroyo	peso (45.71 = $1)	49,320	57,560
Russia	141,358,000	President Dmitry Medvedev; Prime Minister Vladimir Putin	ruble (24.65 = $1)	355,500	223,400
Singapore	4,467,000	President Sellapan Rama Nathan; Prime Minister Lee Hsien Loong	dollar (1.42 = $1)	302,700	252,000
Sri Lanka	20,140,000	President Mahinda Rajapakse	rupee (107.72 = $1)	8,135	10,360
Taiwan	23,111,000	President Ma Ying-jeou; Premier (President of the Executive Yuan) Liu Chao-shiuan	dollar (31.53 = $1)	246,500	215,100
Tajikistan	7,292,000	President Emomali Rahmon; Prime Minister Oqil Oqilov	somoni (3.42 = $1)	1,606	2,762
Thailand	65,591,000	King Bhumibol Adulyadej (Rama IX); Prime Minister Abhisit Vejjajiva	baht (34.04 = $1)	151,100	125,200
Turkmenistan	5,232,000	President Gurbanguly Berdimuhammedov	manat (3,733.23 = $1)	7,567	4,516
Uzbekistan	27,890,000	President Islam A. Karimov; Prime Minister Shavkat Mirziyayev	som (1,332.00 = $1)	8,050	4,480
Vietnam	87,009,000	Communist Party Secretary-General Nong Duc Manh; President Nguyen Minh Triet; Prime Minister Nguyen Tan Dung	dong (16,570.00 = $1)	48,560	58,920

Malaysia. With credit drying up and the demand for Asian-manufactured goods from Western countries dropping, governments scrambled to try to continue programs intended to reduce poverty.

Rising prices for food, fuel, and other necessities contributed to widespread hunger and distress. India, Malaysia, and Indonesia were among nations that struggled with fuel prices. The governments of those countries provoked public outcry by cutting subsidies for fuel that were straining government budgets.

As Asian stock markets plunged, few countries were in such a favorable position as China. With $1.9 trillion in foreign exchange reserves, China's government on November 9 announced plans to stimulate its weakening economy by spending some $586 billion by 2010 on infrastructure and social welfare projects. In contrast, Pakistan received temporary international aid for its economy. Other nations increased deficit spending.

Terrorism. Pakistan was torn by suicide bombings and other terrorist attacks in 2008. Some attacks were intended to ward off government efforts to curtail the use of Pakistani territory to support Islamic militants fighting in adjacent Afghanistan. Others were retaliation for earlier official efforts to control domestic extremists.

Bombings in India's northeastern Assam state were apparently related to indigenous inhabitants' hostility to recent settlers. Other parts of India suffered terrorism that officials tied to tensions between the Hindu majority and Muslim minority. On November 26, suspected Pakistani militants launched a three-day series of attacks in Mumbai, India, that left more than 170 people dead.

In Southeast Asia, however, terrorist networks that had killed hundreds of people in the past were believed by experts to be greatly weakened by 2008. Improved police work backed by better intelligence efforts had reduced the number of terrorists tied to the worldwide al-Qa'ida organization. On November 9, Indonesia executed three Islamic terrorists convicted of killing 202 people in the bombings of nightclubs on Bali in 2002.

Territorial disputes were settled in 2008 in two cases, but others remained unsettled. China and Japan announced on June 18 that they would work together to exploit natural gas under a part of the East China Sea where their claims overlapped. The maritime boundary remained unresolved, however.

China and Russia on July 21 signed an agreement over a disputed border where two rivers joined. The agreement, signed in the Chinese capital, Beijing, divided an island where the rivers join.

The Maldives. Asia's longest-serving ruler, President Maumoon Abdul Gayoom, failed on October 8 to secure the 50 percent of votes required for victory in the Maldives' first multiparty elections, taking only 41 percent. Mohamed Nasheed, founder and head of the Maldivian Democratic Party, rallied most of the opposition to defeat Gayoom in the October 28 runoff, winning 54 percent of the vote. Nasheed was sworn in as president on November 11.

Gayoom had suppressed political opposition for most of his 30 years in power, including jailing or banishing Nasheed to remote islands for a total of about six years. Gayoom began political reforms, including lifting a ban on political parties only after riots against his rule in 2003 and 2004, and international pressure for democracy in the islands were brought to bear.

During his presidency, Gayoom shifted the emphasis of the Maldives' economy from fishing to tourism, giving the nation's 313,000 people the highest per capita income in South Asia. On Nov. 10, 2008, Nasheed warned that global warming could cause rising sea levels to submerge many of the low-lying coral atolls that make up the country. He also suggested that tourism earnings would be used to buy land elsewhere to resettle the Maldives' people.

Bhutan became a constitutional monarchy in 2008. Continuing the two previous kings' policy of moving from absolute royal power to a democratic system, King Jigme Khesar Namgyel Wangchuck signed a new constitution on July 18. A national assembly elected on March 24 assumed most governmental powers.

In the election, the royalist Peace and Prosperity Party won 45 of the 47 parliamentary seats. The party's leader, Jigme Thinley, became prime minister, a post he had held twice before by royal appointment.

The formal coronation of the king took place on November 6 in Thimphu, the capital. Wangchuck had assumed royal duties in December 2006 when his father *abdicated* (stepped down). The coronation was delayed until a time considered auspicious by astrologers of the Himalayan nation's Tibetan Buddhist religion.

East Timor. President José Ramos-Horta was critically wounded in an attack on his residence on Feb. 11, 2008, by a renegade military group. An attempt was also made to kill Prime Minister Xanana Gusmão. Presidential guards killed the renegade leader, Alfredo Reinado. Gusmão said the attempts were intended to "paralyze the government and create instability." He accused Reinado, who had left the army in 2006 fighting, of a *coup* (overthrow) attempt.

Neighboring Australia sent more peacekeeping troops to East Timor, which is also known as Timor-Leste. Australia had helped the country gain independence from Indonesia in 1999. Ramos-Horta returned from medical treatment in Australia on April 17, 2008.

A group of international aid organizations reported on October 16 that East Timor faced a food crisis. They noted that more than 70 percent of households surveyed were unable to find enough food during the five months between harvests. More than half of the youngest children were going hungry.

Mongolia. Elections on June 29, 2008, for the State Great Hural, Mongolia's one-house parliament, led to riots. The Mongolian People's Revolutionary Party (MPRP), a reformed version of the Communist party that ruled the nation under the former Soviet Union's direction, won 47 of the parliament's 76 seats. The opposition Democratic Party (DP) won 26 seats. After the DP charged the MPRP with fraud, mobs burned the MPRP headquarters in the capital, Ulaanbaatar. Five people died in the riots.

◼ Henry S. Bradsher

See also **Australia; Disasters; Terrorism;** various Asian country articles.

Astronomy. Astronomers in 2008 confirmed the presence of water ice and snow on Mars, discovered rings around one of Saturn's moons, observed a *supernova* (exploding star) in the act of blowing up, and studied the most distant object visible to the unaided eye.

Polar exploration on Mars. The Phoenix Mars spacecraft made the first-ever landing near the North Pole of Mars on May 25. The robotic craft had been launched by the United States National Aeronautics and Space Administration (NASA) in August 2007. Photographs of soil excavated by Phoenix's robotic arm revealed shiny shards of material that vaporized after exposure to the Martian atmosphere, suggestive of water ice changing into water vapor. (The low atmospheric pressure on Mars causes ice to vaporize rather than melt.) Chemical analysis of the soil in July 2008 provided proof that the material was indeed water. Chemist William V. Boynton of the University of Arizona in Tucson, lead scientist of the team that announced the discovery, noted "… this is the first time Martian water has been touched and tasted."

Instruments on Phoenix also recorded weather events on Mars. Photographs taken in September showed a dust devil, a small soil-containing whirlwind, moving across the Martian terrain. In addition, a laser device probing the atmosphere in September detected snow falling from clouds that were approximately 2.5 miles (4 kilometers) above the surface of Mars. The snow vaporized before reaching the surface.

Rings around a moon of Saturn. Results of observations made with NASA's Cassini spacecraft, announced in March, indicated that Rhea, the second-largest of roughly 60 moons that orbit the ringed-planet Saturn, may be encircled by its own system of rings. That deduction was based on data gathered by Cassini as it flew past Rhea in November 2005. Three instruments on the spacecraft recorded direct impacts of particles of dust making up the rings. Other instruments found electromagnetic disturbances around the moon suggesting that material encircling Rhea was blocking the flow of electrons (negatively charged particles) to detectors on Cassini.

NASA scientists reported that Rhea's rings appear to form a broad disk several thousand miles in diameter and that the rings contain many small pebbles and a few large boulders. The material in the rings is most likely composed of frozen methane and water ice, similar to the rings of Saturn itself. Although Saturn and the other giant planets (Jupiter, Uranus, Neptune) were all known to be surrounded by rings, Rhea was the first moon found to have a ring system.

Exploding star caught in the act. On Jan. 9, 2008, astronomers for the first time detected a massive star just moments after it began exploding. Such explosions, called supernovae, have frequently been observed in distant galaxies. However, astronomers had previously not discovered these unpredictable events until long after the explosions had begun.

The supernova, dubbed SN 2008D, was discovered by chance by astronomer Alicia Soderberg of Princeton University in New Jersey. Soderberg and her team were conducting research on galaxy NGC 2270 using NASA's Swift satellite. While observing the galaxy, the astronomers noticed a sudden burst of X rays, which they recognized as the signal of a new supernova. They immediately mobilized a worldwide collaboration of astronomers to monitor the explosion at various wavelengths of electromagnetic energy. The observations included both space-based and ground-based telescopes.

The observations confirmed predictions made by theoretical astrophysicists that the heaviest stars, consisting of more than eight times the mass of the sun, would generate intense blasts of X rays as they become supernovae. After such a massive star depletes its nuclear fuel, its center collapses into an ultradense ball called a neutron star. The outer layers of the star first fall inward and then rebound off the neutron star, producing an outrushing wave of material that gives off X rays and visible light. As the expanding shock wave plows into gas clouds surrounding the stellar remnant, it also generates radio waves. Soderberg and her collaborators observed these theoretical events as they actually happened in the days after the discovery of SN 2008D.

Most distant visible object. On March 19, NASA's Swift satellite recorded gamma rays generated by a powerful stellar explosion that was 7.5 billion light-years away. A light-year, the distance that light travels in one year, equals 5.88 trillion miles (9.46 trillion kilometers). The outburst, named GRB 080319B, was a type of explosion called a gamma ray burst, in which a dying star ejects powerful jets of material into space.

Alerted by Swift scientists at Pennsylvania State University in University Park, researchers using ground-based optical telescopes also detected the burst, which brightened to a magnitude barely visible to the unaided eye before quickly fading again. Had an observer been looking at the right time in the direction of the burst, toward the constellation Bootes, he or she would have seen the most distant object ever known to be visible to the unaided eye. The most distant object that can normally be seen by the unaided eye is the Triangulum Galaxy (M33), which is 2.9 million light-years from Earth.

■ Laurence A. Marschall

See also **Space exploration.**

Hot greenish or bluish newborn stars are seen beneath a blanket of dust within the Rho Ophiuchi nebula more than 400 light-years away. This false-color image, released in February, and other images of this stellar nursery made by the Spitzer Space Telescope revealed more than 300 young stars, with an average age of only 300,000 years—compared with about 12 billion years for the universe's oldest known stars.

A number of infrared images made by NASA's Spitzer Space Telescope shed light on cosmic mysteries in 2008.

Stars of various ages shine in a Spitzer image, released in August, of a nebula known as W5, about 6,500 light-years from Earth. Bluish dots in the centers of the two dark cavities represent older stars. Pinkish dots along the edges of the cavities represent younger stars. This image supports the idea that new stars form as radiation and winds from massive older stars blow out cavities in nebulae, pushing gas molecules together and causing them to ignite.

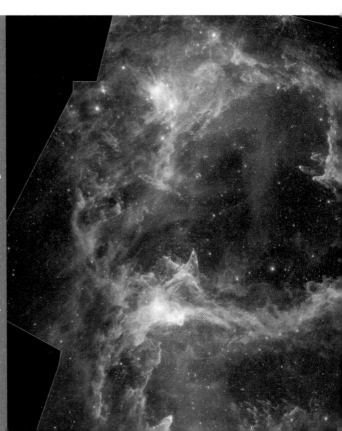

The Milky Way—the galaxy in which Earth and the solar system are located—has two main, dense arms of stars wrapped around a central bar, Spitzer data revealed in June. Astronomers had long thought the Milky Way had four main arms. An image based on 800,000 "snapshots" from Spitzer shows the main Scutum-Centaurus Arm and the Perseus Arm, as well as several minor arms, as they might appear from directly above.

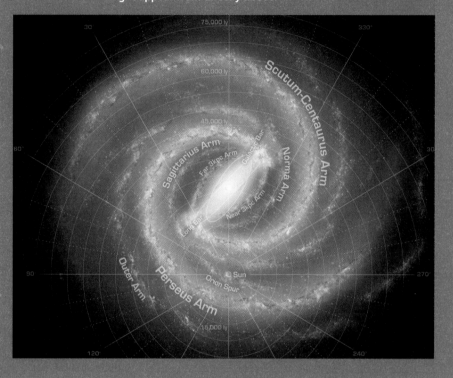

The head of Comet Holmes is seen in a false-color close-up as it appeared in March—five months after the comet mysteriously exploded. Dust particles in the comet's *coma* (atmosphere) appear orange, with particles blown out of the *nucleus* (core) appearing in yellow. The nucleus itself appears as a small bright spot. The Spitzer images of the comet, which brightened by a factor of 1 million on Oct. 24, 2007, gave scientists a rare look at material that was once in the nucleus of a comet.

AUSTRALIA

Australia had a year of mixed economic fortunes in 2008. The year began well with a continuing boom in mineral exports, but the global financial crisis later in 2008 cast a shadow over the country's economic outlook. In the political sphere, 2008 was notable for Labor Prime Minister Kevin Rudd's apology to the Aboriginal people of Australia for past wrongs and work on measures designed to halt climate change.

Economy. Treasurer Wayne Swan delivered his first budget to federal Parliament in Canberra, the national capital, on May 13. Swan forecast that inflation would be contained at 3.25 percent and that employment would grow by 1.25 percent. He also predicted a budget surplus of $21.7 billion and that *gross domestic product* (GDP) would grow by 2.75 percent. (All amounts in Australian dollars unless otherwise noted.) GDP is the total value of goods and services produced in a country during a given year. The global financial crisis later in the year raised doubts as to whether or not these figures would be achieved.

Unemployment rates hit a 33-year low of 4 percent of the work force in February. However, Australia's wholly foreign-owned automobile industry suffered from a fall in the local demand for cars during 2008. In February, the Japanese corporation Mitsubishi announced that it would close its automobile plant in Adelaide, South Australia, with the loss of an estimated 1,000 jobs. In August, Ford Australia announced that 350 jobs would be lost in its plants in Victoria. There was better news from the Japanese automobile manufacturer Toyota, which announced in June that, beginning in 2010, it would produce 10,000 of its hybrid gas-electric cars a year in Australia.

Mining companies continued to benefit from China's demand for Australian minerals in 2008. On May 15, Fortescue Metals Group in Western Australia sent its first-ever commercial shipment of iron ore to China from Port Hedland. In August, Australia-based mining giant BHP Billiton posted a record profit of more than $17 billion.

The Australian dollar on May 22 reached 96.54 U.S. cents, its highest level against U.S. currency since December 1983. By October 2008, the Australian dollar had dropped to a five-year low of around U.S. 60 cents.

The Australian stock market, which had reached an all-time high in November 2007, began 2008 with a sharp fall in January. By October, it had lost more than 40 percent of its value. The media used the term "Black Friday" to describe October 10, when around $100 billion was wiped off the price of Australian shares in the market's biggest one-day fall since "Black Tuesday" in 1987.

Australia's tightly regulated banks suffered less in the 2008 global credit crisis than those in the United States and the United Kingdom. Nevertheless, Prime Minister Rudd announced on October 12 that the federal government would guarantee all deposits in Australian banks and other related financial institutions for three years.

State and federal politics. On September 5, Quentin Bryce became the first female Governor General of Australia. Bryce had enjoyed a distinguished legal and academic career before becoming governor of Queensland in 2003.

The Australian Labor Party, which began 2008 in power in the federal government as well as in every state and territory, experienced a series of setbacks during the year. On May 26, Paul Lennon stepped down as premier of Tasmania. His deputy, Dave Bartlett, took over the premiership. Voters went to the polls in the Northern Territory on August 8 and returned Labor to government with a reduced majority of just one seat. On September 5, Labor leader Morris Iemma quit as premier of New South Wales and was replaced by Nathan Rees. On September 6, the Labor government in Western Australia was defeated in the state elections, and Liberal leader Colin Barnett became premier. The Labor party in the Australian Capital Territory also lost its majority in elections on October 18 but continued in government with the help of the Greens party.

Internal struggles over the leadership of the Liberal Party of Australia came to a head on September 16 when federal leader Brendan Nelson forced a showdown and lost a close vote in a poll of his fellow Liberal members of Parliament. He was replaced by his only challenger, former lawyer and merchant banker Malcolm Turnbull.

Defense and security. In February, Australia reacted swiftly when the president of neighboring East Timor, José Ramos-Horta, was severely wounded in a failed assassination attempt. Ramos-Horta was flown to Darwin in the Northern Territory, where he eventually recovered. Prime Minister Rudd ordered 350 extra military personnel to East Timor and visited the country for talks with Prime Minister Xanana Gusmão.

In June, Prime Minister Rudd's Labor government carried out its election promise to withdraw Australia's 550 remaining combat troops from Iraq. Almost 14,000 Australian soldiers had served in Iraq during the nation's five-year involvement in the war. No troops were killed in combat during this time. The commitment cost more than $2.3 billion. Some military personnel remained behind in Baghdad to support the Australian embassy, and Australia continued its commitment to the war in Afghanistan.

In Melbourne, on September 15, jurors found Muslim cleric Abdul Nacer Benbrika and five of his followers guilty of belonging to a terrorist organization. The prosecution alleged that Benbrika wanted to launch attacks on Australian soil in 2005 and 2006 to convince the Australian government to withdraw its troops from Iraq. Benbrika and his followers had attempted to obtain automatic weapons and materials to produce explosives.

Climate. In 2008, leading Australian economist Ross Garnaut issued a series of reports for the federal government on the possible economic effects of measures designed to combat climate change. In his first report in February, he warned that Australia might need to cut carbon dioxide emissions from 70 to 90 percent by 2050 to prevent dangerous climate changes that could severely impact Australia. Many scientists believe that the build-up of carbon dioxide and other greenhouse gases in the atmosphere, caused by the burning of fossil fuels, causes global warming. Garnaut presented a

further report in July 2008. In his final report, on September 30, Garnaut recommended reducing Australia's carbon emissions by 10 percent of 2000 levels by 2020, though he also discussed the possibility of a 25 percent cut. On Dec. 15, 2008, Prime Minister Rudd announced a plan to cut greenhouse gas emissions from 5 to 15 percent by 2020, but some critics argued that his plan did not do enough to combat climate change.

Minister for Climate Change and Water Penny Wong released the federal government's Green Paper (government report) on the Carbon Pollution Reduction Scheme on July 16, 2008. At the heart of the scheme was a provision for industry to buy and trade permits for emissions up to certain levels. Special provisions were to be made for operators of heavy vehicles and middle- and low-income families who would be financially disadvantaged by the proposed legislation. On October 30, the federal government resolved to push ahead with the plan and predicted that consumer energy bills would rise by an average of $7 a week

Australians watch Prime Minister Kevin Rudd deliver an apology to Australian Aborigines for injustices committed by the government. From about 1910 to about 1970, some 50,000 Aboriginal children, called the "Stolen Generation," were removed from their families and placed in government-run schools.

Population	20,979,000
Government	Governor General Quentin Bryce; Prime Minister Kevin Rudd
Monetary unit*	dollar (1.17 = $1 U.S.)

Foreign trade (million U.S.$)

Exports[†]	142,100
Imports[†]	160,000

*Exchange rate as of Sept. 30, 2008.
[†]Latest available data.

when the scheme was implemented in 2010.

In 2008, Australia had its hottest January on record. According to David Jones, the head of climate analysis at the Australian Bureau of Meteorology, the average temperature across the continent had risen by about 1.8 °F (1.0 °C) since 1950, which was consistent with global warming patterns across the planet. The citizens of Adelaide, South Australia's largest city, sweltered in a heat wave in March as temperatures stayed above 95 °F (35 °C) for 15 days—a record for any Australian state capital city.

Sydney experienced the driest May the city had suffered since record keeping began, with only 0.1 inches (0.3 centimeters) of rain. Nevertheless, water levels in the dams supplying eastern Australia's major cities improved during 2008 and, in June, Sydney eased water-use restrictions that had been in place since October 2003. Despite widespread rain in July 2008, many areas of Australia continued to suffer from drought, especially western New South Wales.

In March, a meeting of state premiers and the prime minister agreed to a federally funded $10-billion scheme to share the waters of the Murray-Darling, Australia's largest river system. Under the plan, a new body would be established by 2011 to decide how much water each state would be allowed to draw from the rivers and how much should be left to improve the environment. Lack of water led scientists to predict great ecological damage to the Coorong, a national park and lagoon system in South Australia at the mouth of the Murray River.

Aborigines. On Feb. 13, 2008, both Prime Minister Rudd and Liberal opposition leader Brendan Nelson issued formal apologies to the Aborigines who had been taken as children from their parents by government agents without parental permission. Prime Minister Rudd estimated that from 1910 to 1970, about 50,000 children had been taken from their families as a result of government policies. Many children were abused in the government-run institutions in which they were placed and raised. A large number of Aborigines belonging to the "Stolen Generation" traveled to Canberra to meet the prime minister and listen to speeches at Parliament House. Others gathered to watch live television broadcasts on large screens set up in cities across the continent.

In the federal budget in May 2008, the government announced that $1.2 billion would be spent on programs in the next five years in an attempt to close the gap between indigenous and nonindigenous Australians. In August, Aboriginal leader Warren Mundine and Fortescue Metals chief Andrew Forrest, one of Australia's richest citizens, announced plans to create jobs for 50,000 Aborigines in the next two years.

Traditional landowners won control of about 80 percent of the Northern Territory's coastline as a result of an Australian High Court decision on July 30. Under the court's 5-2 ruling, anyone wanting to enter Aboriginal land, including beaches and the sea from the high- to low-water mark, will have to obtain permission. Experts noted that the ruling gives Aborigines unprecedented control over commercial and recreational fishing along the coastal areas.

Olympic Games. At the 2008 Summer Olympic Games in Beijing, China, in August, Australian athletes won a total of 46 medals, including 14 gold medals. Australia's female swimmers competed particularly well, with Stephanie Rice winning three gold medals. Australia took sixth place in the gold medal tally and fifth place in the overall medal tally.

Arts. In January, renowned Australian magazine *The Bulletin* ceased publication after more than 120 years. The magazine, which had been losing money and readers for many years, had published many famous Australian authors, including the poet and short story writer Henry Lawson, during its heyday in the late 1800's and early 1900's.

In February 2008, Melbourne-born motion picture producer Eva Orner won an Academy Award for her documentary *Taxi to the Dark Side,* which examined alleged U.S. torture practices in the war on terror. The documentary was shot in Afghanistan, Iraq, and Guantanamo Bay, Cuba. Earlier in February, Australian actor Cate Blanchett won a Golden Globe award for her part in *I'm Not There,* a movie about American singer Bob Dylan. Blanchett was one of 10 prominent Australians invited to Canberra by the Rudd government on April 19 and 20 to lead 1,000 other delegates in discussions on the future of the country.

On March 7, Sydney artist Del Kathryn Barton won the Archibald Prize, Australia's most prestigious award for painting. Her winning work was

MEMBERS OF THE AUSTRALIAN HOUSE OF REPRESENTATIVES

The House of Representatives of the 42nd Parliament first met on Feb. 12, 2008. As of Dec. 5, 2008, the House of Representatives consisted of the following members: 83 Australian Labor Party, 55 Liberal Party of Australia, 9 National Party of Australia, and 3 Independents. This table shows each legislator and party affiliation. An asterisk (*) denotes those who served in the 41st Parliament.

Australian Capital Territory
Annette Ellis, A.L.P.*
Bob McMullan, A.L.P.*

New South Wales
Tony Abbott, L.P.*
Anthony Albanese, A.L.P.*
Bob Baldwin, L.P.*
Sharon Bird, A.L.P.*
Bronwyn Bishop, L.P.*
Chris Bowen, A.L.P.*
David Bradbury, A.L.P.
Tony Burke, A.L.P.*
Jason Clare, A.L.P.
John Cobb, N.P.*
Greg Combet, A.L.P.
Mark Coulton, N.P.*
Bob Debus, A.L.P.
Justine Elliot, A.L.P.*
Pat Farmer, L.P.*
Laurie Ferguson, A.L.P.*
Joel Fitzgibbon, A.L.P.*
Peter Garrett, A.L.P.*
Joanna Gash, L.P.*
Jennie George, A.L.P.*
Sharon Grierson, A.L.P.*
Jill Hall, A.L.P.*
Luke Hartsuyker, N.P.*
Alex Hawke, L.P.
Chris Hayes, A.L.P.
Joe Hockey, L.P.*
Kay Hull, N.P.*
Julia Irwin, A.L.P.*
Mike Kelly, A.L.P.
Sussan Ley, L.P.*
Louise Markus, L.P.*
Robert McClelland, A.L.P.*
Maxine McKew, A.L.P.
Daryl Melham, A.L.P.*
Scott Morrison, L.P.
John Murphy, A.L.P.*
Belinda Neal, A.L.P.
Brendan Nelson, L.P.*
Robert Oakeshott, Ind.
Julie Owens, A.L.P.*
Tanya Plibersek, A.L.P.*
Roger Price, A.L.P.*
Philip Ruddock, L.P.*
Janelle Saffin, A.L.P.
Alby Schultz, L.P.*
Craig Thomson, A.L.P.
Malcolm Turnbull, L.P.*
Danna Vale, L.P.*
Tony Windsor, Ind.*

Northern Territory
Damian Hale, A.L.P.
Warren Snowdon, A.L.P.*

Queensland
Arch Bevis, A.L.P.*
James Bidgood, A.L.P.
Steven Ciobo, L.P.*
Yvette D'Ath, A.L.P.
Peter Dutton, L.P.*
Craig Emerson, A.L.P.*
Michael Johnson, L.P.*
Robert Katter, Ind.*
Andrew Laming, L.P.*
Peter Lindsay, L.P.*
Kirsten Livermore, A.L.P.*
Ian Macfarlane, L.P.*
Margaret May, L.P.*
Shayne Neumann, A.L.P.
Paul Neville, N.P.*
Graham Perrett, A.L.P.
Brett Raguse, A.L.P.
Kerry Rea, A.L.P.
Bernie Ripoll, A.L.P.*
Stuart Robert, L.P.
Kevin Rudd, A.L.P.*
Bruce Scott, N.P.*
Peter Slipper, L.P.*
Alexander Somlyay, L.P.*
Jon Sullivan, A.L.P.
Wayne Swan, A.L.P.*
Chris Trevor, A.L.P.
Warren Truss, N.P.*
Jim Turnour, A.L.P.

South Australia
Jamie Briggs, L.P.
Mark Butler, A.L.P.
Nick Champion, A.L.P.
Kate Ellis, A.L.P.*
Steve Georganas, A.L.P.*
Christopher Pyne, L.P.*
Rowan Ramsey, L.P.
Amanda Rishworth, A.L.P.
Patrick Secker, L.P.*
Andrew Southcott, L.P.*
Tony Zappia, A.L.P.

Tasmania
Dick Adams, A.L.P.*
Jodie Campbell, A.L.P.
Julie Collins, A.L.P.
Duncan Kerr, A.L.P.*
Sid Sidebottom, A.L.P.

Victoria
Kevin Andrews, L.P.*
Fran Bailey, L.P.*
Bruce Billson, L.P.*
Russell Broadbent, L.P.*
Anna Burke, A.L.P.*
Anthony Byrne, A.L.P.*
Darren Cheeseman, A.L.P.
Darren Chester, N.P.
Peter Costello, L.P.*
Simon Crean, A.L.P.*
Michael Danby, A.L.P.*
Marc Dreyfus, A.L.P.
Martin Ferguson, A.L.P.*
John Forrest, N.P.*
Petro Georgiou, L.P.*
Steve Gibbons, A.L.P.*
Julia Gillard, A.L.P.*
Alan Griffin, A.L.P.*
David Hawker, L.P.*
Greg Hunt, L.P.*
Harry Jenkins, A.L.P.*
Catherine King, A.L.P.*
Jenny Macklin, A.L.P.*
Richard Marles, A.L.P.
Sophie Mirabella, L.P.*
Brendan O'Connor, A.L.P.*
Chris Pearce, L.P.*
Andrew Robb, L.P.*
Nicola Roxon, A.L.P.*
Bill Shorten, A.L.P.
Tony Smith, L.P.*
Sharman Stone, L.P.*
Mike Symon, A.L.P.
Lindsay Tanner, A.L.P.*
Kelvin Thomson, A.L.P.*
Maria Vamvakinou, A.L.P.*
Jason Wood, L.P.*

Western Australia
Julie Bishop, L.P.*
Gary Gray, A.L.P.
Barry Haase, L.P.*
Steve Irons, L.P.
Sharryn Jackson, A.L.P.
Dennis Jensen, L.P.*
Michael Keenan, L.P.*
Nola Marino, L.P.
Judi Moylan, L.P.*
Melissa Parke, A.L.P.
Don Randall, L.P.*
Luke Simpkins, L.P.
Stephen Smith, A.L.P.*
Wilson Tuckey, L.P.*
Mal Washer, L.P.*

THE CABINET OF AUSTRALIA*

Kevin Rudd—prime minister
Julia Gillard—minister for education, employment and workplace relations, and social inclusion; deputy prime minister
Anthony Albanese—minister for infrastructure, transport, regional development, and local government
Wayne Swan—treasurer
Simon Crean—minister for trade
Joel Fitzgibbon—minister for defence
Stephen Conroy—minister for broadband, communications, and the digital economy
Stephen Smith—minister for foreign affairs
Chris Evans—minister for immigration and citizenship
Peter Garrett—minister for the environment, heritage, and the arts
Robert McClelland—attorney general
Lindsay Tanner—minister for finance and deregulation
Tony Burke—minister for agriculture, fisheries, and forestry
Jenny Macklin—minister for families, housing, community services, and indigenous affairs
Joseph Ludwig—minister for human services
John Faulkner—special minister of state; cabinet secretary
Penny Wong—minister for climate change and water
Kim Carr—minister for innovation, industry, science, and research
Nicola Roxon—minister for health and ageing
Martin Ferguson—minister for resources, energy, and tourism

*As of December 5, 2008.

PREMIERS OF AUSTRALIAN STATES

State	Premier
New South Wales	Nathan Rees
Queensland	Anna Bligh
South Australia	Mike Rann
Tasmania	David Bartlett
Victoria	John Brumby
Western Australia	Colin Barnett

CHIEF MINISTERS OF AUSTRALIAN MAINLAND TERRITORIES

Australian Capital Territory	Jon Stanhope
Northern Territory	Paul Henderson

a self-portrait that included her children. The annual award is given for achievement in portraiture of a distinguished Australian.

On March 13, the Swedish Arts Council announced that Melbourne novelist Sonya Hartnett was the 2008 recipient of the Astrid Lindgren Memorial Award, the world's largest prize for children's and youth literature. Hartnett is the author of 18 novels for children, young adults, and adults. On June 19, Melbourne author Steven Carroll won the Miles Franklin Award for his novel *The Time We Have Taken.* The award, Australia's most prestigious literary prize, is bestowed annually for a work portraying Australian life.

The heavily publicized motion picture *Australia,* directed by Baz Luhrmann and starring Australian actors Hugh Jackman and Nicole Kidman, was released on November 26. The film was set in the Australian outback and in Darwin in the Northern Territory when the city was bombed by the Japanese during World War II (1939-1945).

Religion. On May 22, Anglican Kay Goldsworthy was consecrated as Australia's first female bishop at St. George's Cathedral in Perth, Western Australia. The ceremony was attended by her husband and twin sons.

Science. In May, a team of scientists at the University of Melbourne announced that they had successfully inserted genes from the extinct Tasmanian tiger into a live mouse embryo. The last known Tasmanian tiger died in captivity in 1936. Despite the success of the project, the scientists stressed that they were still a long way from re-creating a live Tasmanian tiger. ■ Brian Kennedy

See also **Bank: A Special Report; Olympic Games: A Special Report.**

Australia, Prime Minister of.

Australian Labor Party leader Kevin Rudd began his first full year as prime minister of Australia in 2008. On February 13, Rudd issued a formal apology on behalf of the government to the "Stolen Generation" of Aboriginal people who were removed from their parents by government officers from about 1870 to about 1970.

In February 2008, Rudd began a busy year of overseas travel with a visit to East Timor. In March, he visited Papua New Guinea and the Solomon Islands before meeting with President George W. Bush in the United States. In April, he met with Queen Elizabeth II and Prime Minister Gordon Brown in the United Kingdom before going to China for talks with President Hu Jintao. During a visit to Japan in June, he pushed for the establishment of an international commission on nuclear disarmament to be cochaired by Australia and Japan. During that same month, he proposed establishing an Asia-Pacific Union similar to the European Union by 2020.

In September 2008, Rudd spoke to the United Nations General Assembly in New York City on financial stability. He flew to the United States again in November to attend a meeting of world leaders called to discuss the global financial crisis.

■ Brian Kennedy

See also **Australia; Economics, World.**

Australian rules football. The Hawthorn Hawks defeated the Geelong Cats 18 goals 7 behinds (115 points) to 11 goals 23 behinds (89 points) to win the Australian Rules Football League (AFL) premiership in Melbourne on Sept. 27, 2008. The unexpected win was a personal triumph for coach Alastair Clarkson and gave the team its 10th premiership and its first since 1991. Hawks defender Luke Hodge, who had suffered a suspected rib injury in the preliminary final against St. Kilda the previous weekend, was awarded the Norm Smith Medal for the best player on the ground in the grand final. Adam Cooney, a 22-year-old midfielder for the Western Bulldogs, won the Brownlow Medal for the best and fairest player during the season.

In the AFL Queensland grand final on Sept. 21, 2008, the Southport Sharks defeated the Morningside Panthers 18.7 (115) to 15.17 (107). On the same day, the Subiaco Lions beat Swan Districts 22.16 (148) to 14.7 (91) to win the West Australian Football League premiership. On September 26, the North Ballarat Roosters won the Victorian Football League grand final over Port Melbourne 18.12 (120) to 11.9 (75). The Central District Bulldogs defeated the Glenelg Tigers 17.11 (113) to 10.11 (71) to win the South Australian National Football League grand final on October 5.

■ Brian Kennedy

Austria. In July 2008, the ruling "grand coalition" of Austria's two largest parties, the center-left Social Democratic Party and the center-right People's Party, collapsed. The coalition had ruled since January 2007, but Social Democratic Chancellor Alfred Gusenbauer was perceived as a weak leader unable to manage disagreements within his own Cabinet. After his party performed poorly in regional elections, he resigned as party leader.

Transport Minister Werner Faymann became acting party leader. Faymann quickly declared, without consulting his coalition partners, that future changes to European Union (EU) treaties should be put to a popular vote. He also abandoned a coalition agreement to reduce spending on pensions. People's Party leader Wilhelm Molterer withdrew his party from the coalition, forcing the government to call early elections. In August 2008, Faymann was elected Social Democratic Party leader and became the party's candidate for the position of chancellor in a new government.

Elections to the National Council (the lower house of Austria's Parliament) took place September 28. Although both grand coalition members retained their places as the top two parties, both suffered losses. The People's Party received only 26 percent of the vote, and the Social Democrats garnered 30 percent. The far-right Freedom Party and the Alliance for Austria's Future together took 29 percent of the vote. Both rightist parties ran on anti-immigrant and anti-EU platforms.

Analysts disagreed on the reasons for the surge to the right among Austrians. Some claimed that the exclusion of the rightist parties from government had increased their appeal. Others maintained that the vote was more a protest against the long-time dominance of the ruling parties than a clear statement in favor of extreme nationalism. Faymann ruled out working with the rightist parties in government. He formed a new government that was again made up of the Social Democrats and the People's Party and was sworn in as prime minister in December.

Haider. Right-wing nationalist leader Jörg Haider died in an automobile accident on October 11. Haider had been a leading figure in the Freedom Party until a falling out with other party leaders led him to found the competing Alliance for Austria's Future. Known for his flamboyant lifestyle and inflammatory statements on Austria's Nazi past, Jewish Austrians, and immigrants, Haider was long seen as a leading force in the resurgence of right-wing politics in Europe.

Economy. In the face of the global economic crisis, EU economists forecast that Austria's economy would grow by 1.9 percent in 2008, down from 3.1 percent in 2007. ■ Jeffrey Kopstein

See also **Europe.**

Automobile and light-truck sales tumbled in 2008 as the United States auto industry struggled through its worst year in over a decade. By year's end, the failing traditional Big Three automakers—General Motors (GM) Corporation of Detroit; Ford Motor Company of Dearborn, Michigan; and Chrysler LLC of Auburn Hills, Michigan—became embroiled in a controversial government bailout battle in the U.S. Congress.

Through the first nine months of 2008, U.S. auto sales totaled 10.8 million units, down 13 percent from the same period in 2007. Early in 2008, sales fell as gasoline prices rose to historic highs. Sales dropped even further as the credit crunch worsened and consumer confidence declined. Analysts expected 2008 sales to be 13.2 million, compared with 16.1 million in 2007. Although the sales of all major automakers declined, the Big Three suffered the most. Their reliance on pickup trucks and sport utility vehicles (SUV's) made them especially vulnerable to rising gasoline prices that shot past $4 a gallon. GM and Ford saw their stocks sink to the low single digits.

In the fall, the federal government approved $25 billion in low-interest loans administered through the Energy Department to help the companies build more fuel-efficient vehicles. But as auto sales worsened, top executives from the Big Three met with congressional leaders in Washington, D.C., in November to ask for additional help. Congress met later that month in a special session to debate a proposed bailout of the Big Three. In early December, Democratic congressional leaders demanded that the car executives provide a business survival plan in exchange for $14 billion in loans. The proposal passed in the House the following week, but failed in the Senate when negotiations between Democrats and Republicans collapsed over wage and benefit cuts. On December 19, President George W. Bush announced that he had authorized a $17.4-billion short-term loan package, stating that allowing the auto industry to fail is not "a responsible course of action." The money was from the Troubled Asset Relief Program (TARP), the $700-billion measure that passed in October to help bail out financial institutions. General Motors and Chrysler were given a deadline of March 31, 2009, to undertake extensive restructuring of debt and labor costs and prove that they can become profitable. Ford asked only for a loan guarantee in case of a later emergency.

Besides losing sales, the Big Three saw their combined market share drop to 47.4 percent through September 2008, compared with 51.2 percent for the same period a year earlier. The Big Three lost market share despite offering more generous incentives than many competitors. The market share of Japan-based auto companies rose nearly three percentage points to 39.7 percent, while those of European manufacturers edged up slightly to 7.6 percent, and Korean companies' market share improved a bit to 5.3 percent.

The Ford F-series pickup was again the year's most popular light truck, with sales of 392,698 through the first nine months. The Toyota Camry was again the top-selling automobile, with sales of 355,562 through September. Although they were the year's best sellers, sales for the F-series dropped 27 percent and Camry's sales declined 3 percent over the same period a year earlier. Hybrid sales were essentially flat at 255,000 vehicles.

Big Three. GM's sales fell 18 percent to 2.4 million in the first nine months, while its market share dropped to 22.4 percent from 23.8 percent, compared with the same period a year earlier. GM's net loss for the first nine months totaled $21.2 billion, compared with a net loss of $38 billion during the same period in 2007. Although GM's losses were down, in late 2008 the company announced it was running out of cash and faced the prospect of going broke by year's end. Such dismal prospects led GM to suspend its dividend, further reduce its work force, announce the closing of four truck plants, and put several businesses up for sale. The company wanted to sell its Hummer division, its ACDelco replacement parts business, and its technical and manufacturing center in Strasbourg, France.

Ford's sales dropped 18 percent to 1.6 million for the first nine months of 2008, and its market share fell to 14.9 percent, compared with 16 percent for the same period in 2007. Losses during the first three quarters of 2008 totaled $8.7 billion, compared with a net income of $88 million for the same period a year earlier. Ford announced in November that it would cut 2,260 white-collar workers in North America. To raise cash, Ford sold its Jaguar and Land Rover businesses to Tata Motors of India for about $1.7 billion in June. In November, Ford sold 20 percent of its ownership stake in Mazda Motor Corporation of Japan.

Chrysler's sales fell 25 percent to 1.2 million in the first nine months of 2008, and its market share dropped to 11 percent, compared with 12.8 percent for the same period in 2007. The company was taken private in 2007 and was not required to report its finances. In June 2008, Chrysler announced it was closing one of its two minivan plants in St. Louis. During the year, Chrysler and GM discussed a merger, but in November, GM suspended acquisition talks because of its financial problems. GM faced possible bankruptcy by year's end; Chrysler, by early 2009.

Other manufacturers. The economic slowdown even affected Toyota, Japan's largest car maker. Sales in the United States fell 10.4 percent to 1.8 million units through the first nine months of 2008. On December 22, Toyota forecast its first annual loss—$1.7 billion—in 71 years. A surge in the value of the yen, compared with the American dollar, also drove down Japanese exports. However, the Japan-based automaker improved its market share by a half a percentage point to 16.7 percent through the first nine months of the year.

Honda's sales declined slightly, to 1.2 million units through the first nine months of 2008. The Japan-based automaker's market share improved to 11 percent compared with 9.7 percent for the same period a year earlier. Honda benefited from the sales of its small car, the Civic. Sales for the Civic rose to 285,715 units, an increase of 12 percent, compared with the same period a year earlier. In October, Honda began producing Civics at its new assembly plant in Greensburg, Indiana, that was expected to make 200,000 cars a year.

In July, Volkswagen announced it would build an auto plant in Chattanooga, Tennessee. The plant was scheduled to open in 2011 and manufacture 150,000 midsize sedans a year. Through the first nine months of 2008, Volkswagen sold 243,371 vehicles in the United States, a decrease of 1.3 percent, compared with the same period a year earlier. Its market share for the period was 2.3 percent, compared with 2 percent for the same period in 2007. ■ Mike Casey

See also **Economics, United States; Labor and employment; Transportation.**

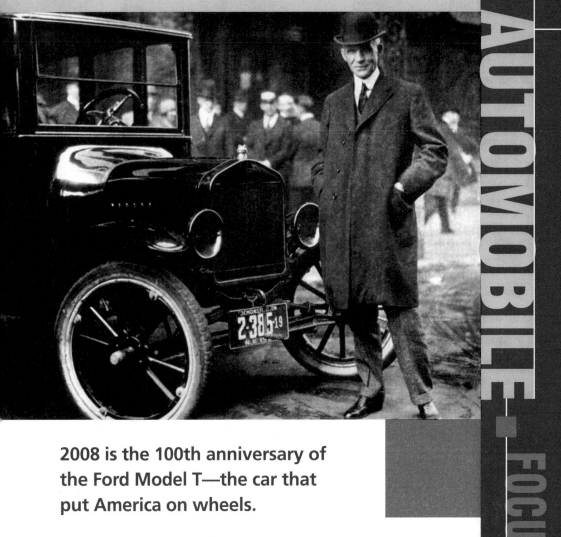

2008 is the 100th anniversary of the Ford Model T—the car that put America on wheels.

In 1908, Henry Ford's Ford Motor Company introduced the famous Model T. Affectionately known as the "Tin Lizzie," this simple, inexpensive car outsold all other cars for almost 20 years. The model changed little from year to year, and from 1914 to 1925, it came in only one color: black. The model's original price of $850 was too high for many customers. To lower the price, Ford and his executives tried new ways to reduce production costs. In 1913, the company established the first moving assembly line at its factory in Highland Park, Michigan. Each worker performed a particular task, such as adding or tightening a part. Using this method, all but the body of the Model T could be assembled in 93 minutes. As the company's production costs fell, Ford passed much of the savings on to his customers. The price of a Model T touring car dropped to $550 in 1913, $440 in 1915, and $290 in 1924. The automobile was now within reach of the average family.

The U.S. economy boomed after a 1920-1921 slump, and people had extra money to spend on cars. Consumers wanted more than just basic transportation. Other companies, especially General Motors, built cars that offered comfort, styling, and speed at reasonable prices. Sales of the Model T declined in the mid-1920's. In 1927, Ford stopped making the Model T. The company introduced the Model A later that year, after more than 15 million Model T's had been sold. In 1928, the Model A became the top-selling car. After that, Ford offered a new model every year, as automakers continue to do today.

FOCUS ON AUTOMOBILE

As gas prices soared in 2008, consumers in the United States demanded fuel-efficient alternatives from automakers.

Reflections of unsold Hummers mark the front grill of another of the low-mileage vehicles at a dealership in Dublin, Ohio, in June. Sales of Hummers, manufactured by General Motors (GM), dropped by about 66 percent in 2008, compared with the previous year.

The Chevy Volt (above), previewed by GM in September, is one of several battery-powered electric cars scheduled to debut in 2010. Able to run for 40 miles (65 kilometers) on a charge from a household outlet, the car will use a gas motor for power and recharging for longer distances.

The hybrid Toyota Prius (left), the most fuel-efficient car sold in the United States, combines a battery-driven electric motor with a gasoline engine that charges the battery and also powers the motor. Toyota sold more than 1 million Priuses worldwide in 2008.

The Honda FCX Clarity, leased in limited numbers in July 2008, has a fuel cell that mixes oxygen from the air with compressed hydrogen gas to create electricity to power the motor. The vehicle gets an estimated 72 miles per gallon (3 liters per 100 kilometers).

Scott Dixon of New Zealand leads the field in the final laps of the Indianapolis 500 race at the Indianapolis Motor Speedway on May 25, 2008. Dixon defeated Vitor Meira of Brazil by 1.75 second, earning a record $2.99 million for his victory.

Automobile racing.

American Danica Patrick became the first woman to win a major series auto race with her victory on April 20, 2008, in the Indy Racing League's (IRL) Japan 300 in Motegi, Japan. Ashley Force celebrated her own breakthrough victory in 2008, becoming the first woman to win a national race in a Funny Car event in the National Hot Rod Association (NHRA) series. She beat her father, John, on April 27 in Commerce, Georgia. Less than a month later, Melanie Troxel also won a Funny Car event to become the first woman to win in both the Funny Car and Top Fuel series.

In National Association for Stock Car Racing (NASCAR) competition, Kyle Busch launched his own assault on history, capturing 7 of the series' first 19 races to grab a big point lead. Busch won eight races to lead in points during the regular season but finished in 10th place in the "Chase for the Championship."

The bitter 12-year rivalry between the two American open-wheel series, IndyCar and Champ Car, ended in February with a reunification of the two series. IndyCar absorbed the drivers and teams of the struggling Champ Car series.

Scott Kalitta became the second Funny Car driver in two years to die on the track after his engine exploded during the final round of racing on June 21 at Old Bridge Township Raceway Park in New Jersey. In response to the accident, the NHRA announced a safety initiative. As a first step, the group reduced the length on the Top Fuel and Funny Car races from 1,320 to 1,000 feet (402 to 305 meters).

Indianapolis 500. Scott Dixon captured the Indianapolis 500 on May 25, taking the lead in his final pit stop by being quicker than driver Vitor Meira of Brazil. Dixon then held off Meira and Marco Andretti over the final 29 laps. The race was plagued by crashes, with 69 of the 200 laps raced under a caution, in part because the field featured 11 rookies—the most in more than a decade—and 9 drivers from the defunct Champ Car series. Dixon, of New Zealand, led for 115 laps, averaged 143.567 miles (231.049 kilometers) per hour, and beat Meira by 1.75 second. Dixon won $2.99 million, a record.

Formula One. Lewis Hamilton of the United Kingdom became the first black driver to win the drivers championship, capturing the 2008 Formula One title by one point over Brazilian driver Felipe Massa. At the age of 23, Hamilton became the youngest driver to win the title.

NASCAR. Jimmie Johnson won the Sprint Cup championship. He finished with 6,684 points, 69 points ahead of Carl Edwards. It was Johnson's third consecutive Cup title, tying him with Cale Yarborough for most consecutive titles. Clint Bowyer won the Nationwide Series title. Johnny Benson won the Craftsman Truck Series title.

In other major developments during the 2008 season, two-time champ Tony Stewart parted with Joe Gibbs Racing to become a part owner and driver of the new Stewart-Haas Racing team in 2009. The race team led by 2007 IRL and Indy 500 champ Dario Franchitti of Scotland was shut down in the middle of his first season with NASCAR by team owner Chip Ganassi due to a lack of sponsorship.

IRL. Scott Dixon won the 2008 IRL driver's title, beating out Helio Castroneves of Brazil by 17 points. Danica Patrick finished sixth, the best finish for a woman driver ever in a major series.

Endurance. Ganassi's team won its third straight Rolex 24-hour race in Daytona Beach, Florida, on January 27. Juan Pablo Montoya of Colombia; Franchitti; Scott Pruett; and Memo Rojas of Mexico led for 252 of the 695 laps, won by two laps, and covered 2,460 miles (3,959 kilometers). Despite a late crash, Audi won its fifth straight Le Mans 24 Hour on June 15, the manufacturer's eighth title in the race. Denmark's Tom Kristensen, Italy's Rinaldo Capello, and Scotland's Allan McNish completed 381 laps and finished with a lead of 4 minutes, 31.094 seconds.

Dragsters. Tony Schumacher won the 2008 NHRA Top Fuel championship. Cruz Pedregon won the Funny Car division, and Jeg Caughlin, Jr., won the Pro Stock Division. ■ Michael Kates

Aviation. Global economic turmoil in 2008 added to the difficulties of the airline industry. The serious downturn in the economy hit all carriers hard, including some that had struggled even during the economic boom times of the early 2000's.

During the first half of 2008, as the price of oil, and, therefore, jet fuel soared to record highs, many airlines scrambled to raise revenue by charging customers for basic services that had once been covered by the price of a ticket. In the early 2000's, airlines began charging for food and drinks that had once been complimentary. Seeing that consumers had, perhaps, become resigned to such charges, carriers in 2008 added fees for such services as checking a bag or booking a ticket.

The fees caused many passengers to try to beat the system. Some passengers avoided checking bags. The large number of passengers carrying bags aboard, however, often led to slow boarding times, as passengers ignored size restrictions and tried to squeeze a too-large suitcase into a small overhead compartment. Passengers also brought their own pillow and blankets to avoid being charged for that service. Web sites sprang up that allowed buyers to compare airline fees for various services. The new charges and fees and staff reductions that left fewer workers to serve passengers pushed customer satisfaction with the airlines to a

three-year low, according to a survey released by the Westlake, California-based marketing firm J. D. Power and Associates in June.

From the airline's side, increases in fuel costs had been substantial. In May 2008, *The Wall Street Journal* reported that with oil at $130 a barrel, the industry faced fuel costs for 2008 that were $24.6 billion higher than a year earlier. By the end of 2008, oil prices had fallen substantially. Reduced demand and a decrease in overly optimistic investment by commodities traders caused a drop from nearly $150 a barrel in July to below $60 a barrel by November. But this drop did not significantly help airlines. Carriers often locked in the price of the fuel purchases in long-term contracts. These contracts meant that many airlines would be paying higher prices for fuel for months to come.

Boeing and Airbus. Like the problems that had beset its European competitor, Airbus, in the past, the Chicago-based plane manufacturer Boeing Company had delay problems in 2008. Although orders for Boeing planes had been very good during the year, the company was forced to push back the date of its first test flights for the new 787 Dreamliner into 2009. That, in turn, pushed back the possible date on which the plane could be delivered to buyers. Adding to delays caused by supply problems, an eight-week strike by Boeing members of the International Association of Machinists (IAM) shut down U.S. manufacturing on the 787. The machinists voted to end the strike in early November and resumed work. Some aviation experts noted that Boeing may actually have benefited from the economic downturn in one sense. Carriers were no longer as desperate for the new planes they had ordered and were more likely to wait for a delayed 787 instead of canceling the order.

Rival manufacturer Airbus, a division of the European Aeronautic Defence and Space Company (EADS), cut jobs and restructured in 2008 to trim costs. The economic downturn had caused airlines to cancel more than 100 orders with the firm. Because Airbus had a production backlog of several years, the cancellations did not affect the company's profits.

Airbus also was involved in a stock scandal. Several high-level managers (or former managers) at Airbus and EADS were indicted in 2008 on charges of insider trading. They were accused of selling large amounts of their stock when they learned of production delays on the Airbus A380. Airbus announced the delays to investors and the general public several months later, and stock prices fell.

Future flight. A new $8.6-billion terminal at London's Heathrow Airport, Terminal 5, was officially opened by Queen Elizabeth II on March 14,

2008. The terminal was opened to the public on March 27. The glass and steel structure, designed by the well-known British architect Richard Rogers, was meant to ease the congestion at Heathrow, which was operating near its maximum capacity and had become noted for delays.

Terminal 5 was built exclusively for London-based British Airways (BA) and was designed to handle around 30 million passengers per year, or around 80,000 per day. The terminal's numerous check-in desks and security lines were designed to allow British Airways to process passengers through these stages in under 15 minutes.

Although the building was promoted as the new face of travel, its early days were inauspicious. Problems with computer software led to chaos at the terminal's opening. Complex computer programs and miles of underground tunnels and belts were supposed to allow baggage to be moved efficiently. By noon of the first operating day, however, more than 20 flights had been canceled because of baggage problems. In the first week, thousands of bags became separated from their owners, and 400 flights had to be canceled because of the luggage system. This led BA to delay moving all of its Heathrow operations to Terminal 5 for several months.

■ Christine Sullivan

See also **Disasters; Transportation.**

Azerbaijan. The Azerbaijani parliament voted on March 4, 2008, to withdraw its 33 peacekeepers from Kosovo, which declared independence from Serbia on February 17. The Azerbaijani government feared that Kosovar independence would encourage separatists in the Azerbaijani enclave of Nagorno-Karabakh, which is populated mainly by ethnic Armenians. On March 5, Azerbaijani and Armenian forces in the disputed region exchanged gunfire in defiance of a 1994 cease-fire, killing an estimated 16 soldiers.

Azerbaijan reopened diplomatic ties with Turkmenistan when the two countries settled a dispute over a gas debt on March 5, 2008. The leaders of the two countries met for the first time in 12 years on May 19.

President Ilham Aliyev won a second term in an October 15 presidential election, reportedly taking 89 percent of the vote. Opposition figures boycotted the election, citing government persecution and media restrictions. Election monitors from the Organization for Security and Co-operation in Europe expressed concern over media bias and vote-counting procedures.   ■ Juliet Johnson

See also **Asia.**

Bahrain. See Middle East.

Ballet. See Dancing.

Baltic States. See Estonia; Europe; Latvia; Lithuania.

Bangladesh. After almost two years under an army-backed caretaker government, Bangladesh held parliamentary elections on Dec. 29, 2008. The main contestants were two women who alternated as prime minister from 1991 to 2006 amid hostility, violence, and rampant corruption.

Sheikh Hasina of the Awami League and Khaleda Zia of the Bangladesh Nationalist Party led their parties after the government dropped corruption charges against them. Their personal antagonism had made normal politics unworkable, and the government sought unsuccessfully to remove them from politics.

Zia had been prime minister from 2001 until her legally mandated resignation in October 2006 in preparation for elections in January 2007. Sheikh Hasina threatened to boycott those elections, accusing Zia of rigging them. The army-backed government postponed the elections.

Cleanup. In 2007, the caretaker government jailed Sheikh Hasina, Zia, and some 150 other prominent people on corruption charges. By mid-2008, some 11,700 other politicians and businesspeople had been jailed for corruption and other crimes. Seeking honest elections, the government removed 12 million names from voter rolls as being duplicates, deceased, false, or otherwise ineligible to vote.

Both the Awami League and the Nationalist Party refused to discuss new elections with the government until their leaders were released. A violent protest in the capital, Dhaka, on August 25, demanded the release of Zia and her son and presumed political heir, Tarique Rahman, so he could travel abroad for medical treatment. In September, officials freed Zia on bail and allowed Sheikh Hasina to return from medical treatment abroad. Their key deputies were also freed on bail.

Elections. In the first test of the cleansed electoral system, the Awami League won 12 of 13 mayoral races on August 4. The League also won a landslide in the December 29 parliamentary elections, taking about 250 of the 300 parliamentary seats and positioning Sheikh Hasina to again become prime minister. The country's election commission praised the vote as "very free and fair."

Economy. Soaring prices for food and fuel sparked street protests during 2008 as study groups found poverty increasing sharply. On some 200 occasions, workers demanding higher wages attacked garment factories, a mainstay of Bangladesh's economy. The government in June announced plans to double subsidies on food, oil, and fertilizer and to increase welfare spending. Bangladeshi officials said the World Bank, a United Nations affiliate, had pledged $1.34 billion in aid in 2008 and 2009.   ■ Henry S. Bradsher

See also **Agriculture: A Special Report; Asia; Disasters.**

Bank. The world's banking industry in 2008 underwent the most severe financial crisis since the Great Depression of the 1930's. Numerous banks staggered under debt and tottered on the edge of *insolvency* (the condition of not having enough cash to pay bills). These conditions prompted governments of the United States, the United Kingdom, Iceland, Switzerland, Germany, and other nations to nationalize many of their banks, sharply reversing market-oriented policies of recent years. (When a government *nationalizes* private companies, such as banks, it buys shares of ownership in the companies.)

Roots of the banking crisis were to be found, economists noted, in the U.S. mortgage market, which underwent an unprecedented boom in the mid-2000's. As the mortgage market heated up, some financial institutions and mortgage brokers abandoned traditional lending practices, such as requiring down payments. This trend away from traditional lending prudence was made possible by Congress's deregulation of the financial industry, starting in the late 1990's.

Ultimately, what transformed a U.S. crisis in-the-making into a global one was the conversion of the financial assets represented by future mortgage payments into securities, which could be traded on financial markets. Heavy international demand for U.S.-based investments magnified this effect. The crisis emerged in late 2007 as rates of *mortgage default* (failure of a mortgage holder to meet payments) soared. Collapse of confidence in U.S. mortgage-backed securities— which soon became known as "toxic securities"— spread and infected the global banking system.

Dominoes fall. In March 2008, rumors that the Wall Street investment bank Bear Stearns was insolvent caused its stock to plummet. (*Investment banks* specialize in selling stocks and bonds, whereas *commercial banks* primarily offer services such as checking and savings accounts.) The Federal Reserve (the Fed), the U.S. central bank, worked out an arrangement for New York City-based J.P. Morgan Chase to acquire Bear Stearns —paying $10 per share for stock that had, as recently as 2006, been valued at $171 per share.

In July 2008, depositors started a run on Indy-Mac, a Pasadena, California-based savings and loan heavily invested in the mortgage market. The Federal Deposit Insurance Corporation (FDIC)—the government entity that insures bank deposits—took over IndyMac on July 11.

A number of major U.S. financial institutions reported huge losses in 2008. Among these were the Wall Street investment banks Lehman Brothers and Merrill Lynch; Seattle, Washington-based savings and loan Washington Mutual; and Charlotte, North Carolina-based commercial bank Wachovia. Lehman Brothers filed for bankruptcy in September. Merrill Lynch was purchased by Charlotte, North Carolina-based Bank of America; Washington Mutual, by JPMorgan Chase; and Wachovia, by San Francisco-based Wells Fargo.

Government action. In October, the administration of U.S. President George W. Bush and Congress responded to the financial chaos by making available $700 billion to buy up "toxic" securities. As the U.S. Treasury began to implement the so-called "bailout" plan, however, officials funneled the money into purchasing stakes in the banks—in effect, nationalizing them— rather than buying up their tainted assets.

On December 16, the Fed lowered its overnight federal funds rate to 0.25 percent, virtually zero, a historic low.

In Europe, the same "toxic" assets weighed down many major banks. Especially hard-hit was Switzerland-based UBS AG, which reported cumulative write-downs of $44 billion. (A write-down is a quantity of debt that banks write off as uncollectible.) In October, the Swiss government approved a $60-billion bailout package for UBS.

Banks in the United Kingdom (U.K.) were also in trouble. Large U.K. banks, including the Royal Bank of Scotland, HBOS, Lloyd's TSB, and Barclays, reported huge losses in 2008. In October, the British government bought shares in these banks, effectively nationalizing them.

Banking systems in Germany, France, and other Western European countries were also shaken. In September, the governments of Belgium, the Netherlands, and Luxembourg jointly bailed out the Belgium-based bank Fortis, contributing a total of 11.2 billion euros ($14.4 billion). Days later, Belgium, Luxembourg, and France mutually bailed out another Belgian bank, Dexia.

In October, the German government bailed out Hypo Real Estate AG, one of Germany's largest banks, with $50 billion euros ($69 billion). It also guaranteed all depositors' bank accounts, as did the governments of Ireland and Greece.

Iceland became the first nation to go bankrupt in the credit crisis of 2008. Iceland's three main banks all tottered on the edge of insolvency by September. Their inability to meet obligations quickly spread panic to other countries. In the U.K., 300,000 depositors had savings in Icelandic banks, attracted by the banks' aggressive marketing and online services.

Iceland's government attempted to shore up its troubled banks with cash, but this measure prompted an international collapse of Iceland's currency, the krona, essentially driving the country into bankruptcy. Iceland's government then hurriedly negotiated loans to attempt to pull itself out of the red.   ■ Robert N. Knight

See also **Economics, U.S.; Economics, World; Iceland; U.S. Government: A Special Report.**

Economic Crisis:
The Banking Meltdown

By Robert Knight

In 2008, financial institutions around the world suffered losses so enormous and far-reaching that governments, including the government of the United States, were forced to intervene in an effort to avoid what many feared could become a worldwide economic depression. The losses were triggered by a mortgage crisis that began in the United States in 2007. That crisis had its roots in an era of deregulation. Fostered by the banking industry and by the U.S. Federal Reserve (the Fed)—the nation's central bank—Congress partially deregulated banking in the late 1990's and early 2000's.

The mortgage crisis was only one of a succession of shocks experienced by financial markets through much of 2008. In March, the New York City-based investment bank Bear Stearns, unable to meet financial obligations, lost the confidence of investors, prompting a steep slide in its stock price. To prevent the firm's complete collapse, the Fed and JPMorgan Chase, a commercial and investment bank based in New York City, struck a deal in which Chase bought a controlling interest in Bear Stearns for $2 per share (later raised to $10 a share). In 2006, Bear Stearns stock had sold for as much as $171 a share. (Commercial banks, which are regulated by the government, offer such services as checking and savings accounts to a wide variety of customers. Investment banks, which are largely unregulated, offer such investment services as stocks and bonds to companies and wealthy individuals.)

Many of the largest and most prestigious U.S. commercial and investment banks continued to rack up huge losses through 2008 due to *write-downs* (losses written off) related to mortgages. By mid-2008, CitiGroup Inc. of New York City, the largest U.S. commercial bank, had reported nearly $41 billion in write-downs. Two major Wall Street investment banks also reported large write-downs by midyear: $32 billion by Merrill Lynch and $12 billion by Morgan Stanley.

From the 1930's until the late 1990's, federal regulations kept commercial and investment banking separate. This separation had been a response to the failure of many banks during the Great Depression of the 1930's. Congress passed the Glass-Steagall Act in 1933 to protect the savings of small investors from the riskier environment of investment banking. However, in 1999 Congress, under intense lobbying pressure from the banking industry, repealed Glass-Steagall. The repeal, sponsored in the Senate by Phil Gramm (R., Texas) and in the House by James Leach (R., Iowa), essentially tore down the walls separating commercial and investment banks. This allowed commercial banks, such as CitiGroup, to maintain their own in-house trading departments and invest in mortgage-backed securities. (A security is a corporate- or government-issued investment instrument that provides evidence of debt or equity.) Like investment banks, the new "mixed-type" banks began to speculate with their own money in higher-risk securities in an attempt to enlarge profits.

An era of "irrational exuberance"

The U.S. mortgage industry in the mid-2000's was, in a phrase coined by former Fed Chairman Alan Greenspan, undergoing a period of "irrational exuberance." After the collapse of Communism in Eastern Europe in the early 1990's, capital went "global." It flowed from country to country in search of opportunity for profits. Because the United States was considered a safe place to invest, capital from around the world flowed into Wall Street, the U.S. center of finance. At the same time, housing prices in the United States, particularly in the booming Sunbelt states, rose

A mortgage meltdown that began in 2007 produced a banking meltdown in 2008, triggering the worst financial crisis since the Great Depression of the 1930's.

The author:
Robert Knight is a free-lance writer.

at an unprecedented rate. As more and more homeowners realized they could sell their properties for huge profits—or pull cash out in home equity loans—the demand for real estate skyrocketed. The feverish cycle of buying and selling inevitably pushed property values ever higher.

The subprime mortgage

Banks quickly recognized the potential for profits in the once heavily regulated home mortgage industry. Lenders, who in the past had thoroughly reviewed the assets of mortgage candidates, relaxed rules—to the point of no longer checking employment and income records. Down payments, the money a buyer puts down toward the purchase price, dropped from 15 or 10 percent to 5 percent; then to nothing; and finally to what became known as the "subprime mortgage."

Subprime mortgages are loans made to home buyers whose credit histories do not qualify them for conventional mortgages. Financial institutions that offered subprime mortgages before the mortgage meltdown that began in 2007 typically assessed higher fees and interest rates to compensate for the higher risk. Expectations of spiking housing values and big sale profits motivated some consumers to take on that kind of risky mortgage debt.

To make such loans more attractive to consumers, some lenders packaged them as adjustable-rate mortgages. Such mortgages typically start out with a low interest rate, which, after a specified introductory period, floats—usually upward.

Depending on the mortgage product and interest rates, consumer payments on adjustable mortgages could double over time. During the housing boom, many consumers and lenders downplayed the dangers of adjustable-rate mortgages, reasoning that homeowners pinched by rising payments could always resell their properties and even make a profit.

The banks, savings-and-loans, and other financial institutions that gave out these mortgages quickly

Falling Home Sales*

Thousands of houses each quarter

Source: United States Census Bureau.
*Number of new houses sold in the United States from January 2000 through September 2008, in thousands per quarter.

Falling Home Prices*

Thousands of dollars

$257,400
$225,700
$165,300

Source: United States Census Bureau.
*Average sale price of new houses sold in the United States from January 2000 through September 2008, in thousands per quarter.

resold them. This turnaround allowed the bank that originated a subprime mortgage to take a fast profit and hand off the risk. The mortgage was bought by an *aggregator*—that is, an institution that bundles mortgages and commercial loans and turns them into bonds or various other securities. These, in turn, are sold to other banks, money markets, and pension funds, at home and around the world, which is how the financial contagion spread to Europe and Asia. (A money market is a market for short-term debt instruments, such as certificates of deposit, commercial paper, and treasury bills.)

The housing boom, which began to deflate in 2007, all but collapsed in 2008. Property values, which once spiraled upward, now slid. Between May 2007 and May 2008, property values in the United States as a whole fell by 15 percent—a drop not seen since the Great Depression of the 1930's. The decline was much higher in some Sunbelt cities, particularly Miami and Las Vegas. As a result, some home owners were making monthly payments on mortgages that were higher than the value of their property. If they had an adjustable-rate mortgage and the interest on the loan rose, their monthly payments increased, even as the value of property decreased. As a result, *defaults* (failure to make payments on time) ballooned.

Defaults led to foreclosure, the lender's legal take-over of a property under a defaulted mortgage. In July, U.S. Secretary of the Treasury Henry Paulson estimated that the number of residential foreclosures in 2008 would be 67 percent greater than in 2007; he predicted that 2.5 million residences would go into foreclosure in 2008.

Mortgage-backed securities

Revenue streams from payments on mortgages fund new mortgages, but in a roundabout way that is facilitated by the global financial structure. As previously noted, mortgages are grouped together and repackaged as mortgage-backed securities (MBS's)—financial instruments somewhat like bonds that investors purchase with the expectation of earning a profit. These securities are only as good as the mortgages they represent, but the risk has traditionally been dispersed and manageable.

However, as the housing boom collapsed and foreclosures rose, faith in MBS's faltered. Because these securities are traded on financial markets, their value can rise or fall, and many went into steep declines. As a result, financial institutions that held large quantities of MBS's, which included many of Wall Street's most venerable investment banks and the nation's largest commercial banks, found themselves confronting enormous losses.

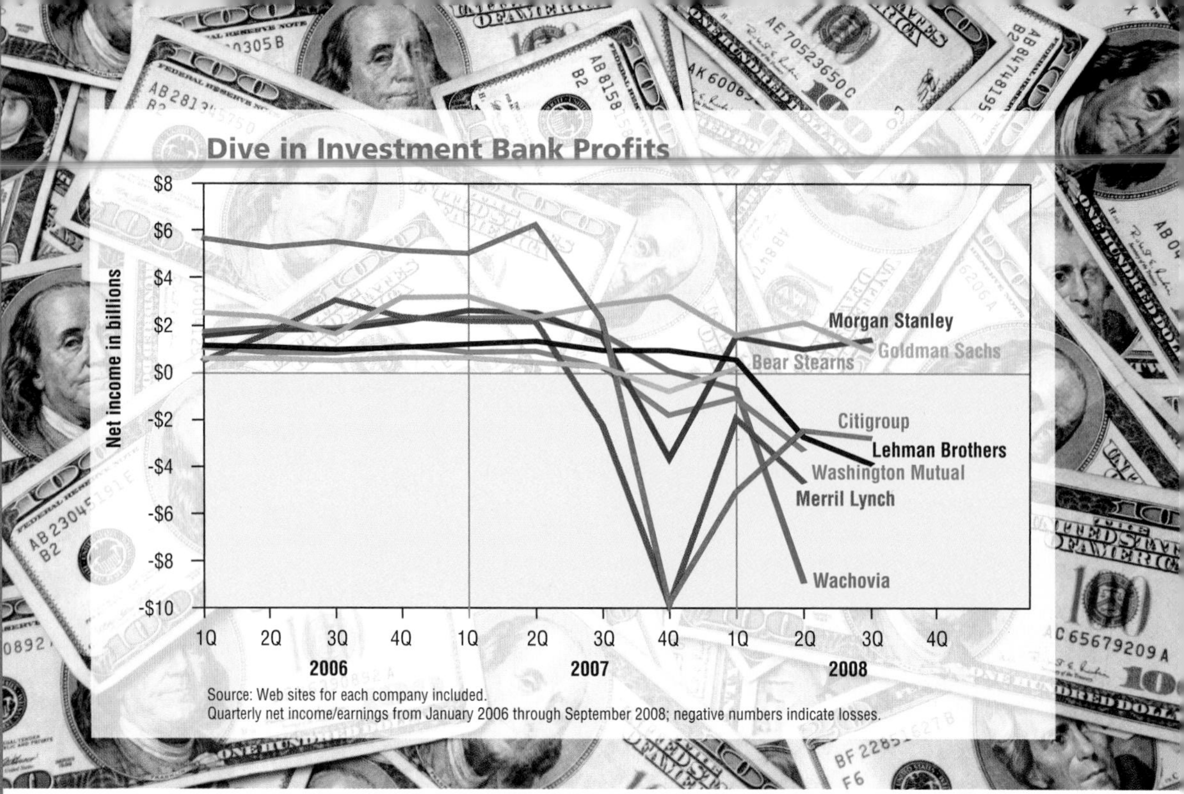

Dive in Investment Bank Profits

Net income in billions

$8
$6
$4
$2
$0
-$2
-$4
-$6
-$8
-$10

1Q 2Q 3Q 4Q | 1Q 2Q 3Q 4Q | 1Q 2Q 3Q 4Q
2006 | **2007** | **2008**

Morgan Stanley
Goldman Sachs
Bear Stearns
Citigroup
Lehman Brothers
Washington Mutual
Merril Lynch
Wachovia

Source: Web sites for each company included.
Quarterly net income/earnings from January 2006 through September 2008; negative numbers indicate losses.

Fannie Mae and Freddie Mac

By mid-2008, it was becoming apparent that the biggest players in the U.S. mortgage market—two government-sponsored enterprises known as Fannie Mae and Freddie Mac—were also deeply mired in the crisis. Fannie Mae (the Federal National Mortgage Association, or FNMA) was created in 1938 to help middle-class consumers get home mortgages. Freddie Mac (the Federal Home Loan Mortgage Corporation, or FHLMC), was created in 1970 to perform a similar function. Both are private-sector corporations with publicly traded stock. However, because they were federally chartered, Fannie Mae and Freddie Mac traditionally enjoyed such special privileges as borrowing at low interest rates and maintaining lower capital reserves than a regular commercial bank.

Fannie Mae and Freddie Mac are, like investment banks, "aggre-gators." They promote *liquidity* (availability of funds) in the mortgage market by buying mortgages from banks, bundling them into MBS's, and selling these securities to such institutional investors as bank trust funds, insurance companies, and pension funds. Fannie and Freddie also held MBS's in their own portfolios of assets.

By mid-2008, Fannie Mae and Freddie Mac were reporting huge losses, causing the value of their stocks to plummet. This alarmed markets and government regulators alike. In 2008, the two entities controlled nearly half of all mortgages in the United States. In late July, Congress passed and President George W. Bush signed major legislation to extend the U.S. Treasury's line of credit to Fannie and Freddie. It did not help. On September 7, the Department of the Treasury placed both Fannie Mae and Freddie Mac under federal management, pledging as much as $200 billion to back their assets.

The move failed to calm the panic sweeping the nation's financial sector. On September 14, the venerable investment firm Merrill Lynch & Co., strapped for cash in the face of huge mortgage-related losses, announced that it had agreed to be taken over by Charlotte, North Carolina-based Bank of America for $50 billion in stock. On September 15, Lehman Brothers, the fourth largest Wall Street investment bank, faced with $6.6 billion in losses so far in 2008, filed for bankruptcy. The announcement sent stock prices tumbling on markets around the world. On September 16, the Fed announced that it was lending American International Group (AIG), the largest U.S. commercial and industrial insurer, $85 billion in return for an 80-percent stake in the firm. The unprecedented bailout was designed to rescue AIG from bankruptcy and to avert the threat of a global financial meltdown. AIG, which insures bank loans and investments around the world, had been crippled by a financial instrument known as a credit default swap.

Credit default swaps

A credit default swap (CDS) is a contract between two parties that is related to a security of some kind, for example, a mortgage-backed security. The seller of the contract promises to guarantee the value of the security should it default. In return, the buyer of the contract pays the seller periodic premiums based upon the value of the security. CDS's have been compared to insurance; in exchange for the premiums, the value of the security is insured, reducing the owner's risk. According to some financial experts, CDS's did start out as a kind of insurance. However, CDS's are unregulated. In fact, in December 2000, the Senate Committee on Banking Chairman Phil Gramm cosponsored the Commodity Futures Modernization Act, which prohibited any governmental regulation of CDS's and other *derivatives* (financial instruments whose values derive from the value of an underlying asset, such as a bond). As a result, investors could buy CDS's without owning the underlying asset; essentially, they were betting that the underlying asset, which they did not own, would default. This allowed them to collect the value of a security they never owned. Economists estimate that at the height of the real-estate boom, the total worldwide value of CDS's exceeded $60 trillion; AIG sold CDS's on more than $440 billion in bonds. Other companies that sold CDS's bundled them

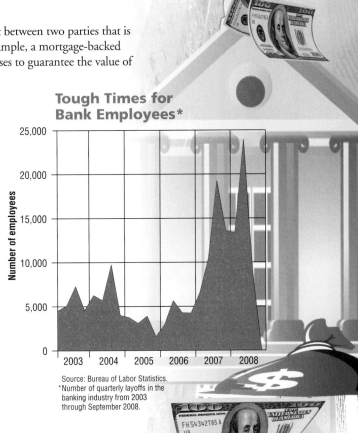

Tough Times for Bank Employees*

Source: Bureau of Labor Statistics.
*Number of quarterly layoffs in the banking industry from 2003 through September 2008.

together and sold them as securities. When the boom crashed and the value of the mortgage-backed securities crashed with it, the buyers of CDS's tried to collect and found that in most cases the CDS's were worthless. Because they were unregulated, no government agency had required the sellers—primarily banks, hedge funds, and AIG—to hold the necessary reserves to back them. So the seller of the CDS was, in effect, betting that the underlying asset would not default, allowing the financial institution to annually collect a percentage of the value of an asset it did not own. Economists suggest that one reason for the current freeze in credit is that banks—unsure of how many CDS's remain outstanding, how much is owed, and the financial conditions of other banks—are unwilling to lend money for fear they will not be repaid. In an industry based on trust, distrust is disastrous.

The drain continues

On September 19, the U.S. Treasury announced that it would guarantee money market funds against losses of up to $50 billion, and the Fed announced that it would provide loans to commercial banks for the acquisition of asset-backed securities from money market funds. These measures were taken because the total value of money market funds—some $3.4 trillion—had declined by nearly $170 billion in one week. "This action should enhance market confidence and alleviate investors' concerns about the ability for money market mutual funds to absorb a loss," declared Treasury officials.

It didn't. On September 21, the last two big independent private investment banks on Wall Street—Goldman Sachs and Morgan Stanley—were granted government permission to transform themselves into commercial banks. In exchange for subjecting themselves to more regulation, the companies gained access to all Fed loan packages. On September 26, JPMorgan Chase took control of most of the assets of the largest U.S. savings and loan institution, Washington Mutual (WaMu); on September 29, the fourth largest U.S. bank, Charlotte, North Carolina-based Wachovia, drowning in liabilities totaling $42 billion, went on the block. It was finally acquired by San Francisco-based Wells Fargo.

Given the urgency of the situation, Federal Reserve Chairman Ben S. Bernanke and Treasury Secretary Henry M. Paulson, Jr., asked Congress for a $700-billion bailout for the collapsing financial sector.* The House of Representatives passed the legislation on October 3. On October 6, stock prices plunged on markets around the world—an indication, according to economists, that the bailout had failed to calm nervous investors. In late November, Paulson was forced to pump $20 billion into CitiGroup on top of $25 billion of the $700-billion bailout that the bank had received just weeks earlier.

Former Fed Chairman Greenspan testified before the House Government Oversight Committee in the fall of 2008 that the current economic crisis had exposed "a flaw" in his view of how markets function. Describing the worldwide financial crisis as "broader than anything I could have imagined," he reversed his long-held economic philosophy and called for the passage of new banking regulations.

*For more information on government intervention in the crisis, see **U.S. Government: A Special Report.**

Baseball. The Philadelphia Phillies captured their first World Series title in 28 years on Oct. 29, 2008, in Philadelphia. They finished off the upstart Tampa Bay Rays 4 games to 1, in a Game 5 that was suspended for rain and finished nearly 48 hours later.

The Rays were considered a 200-to-1 shot to win the World Series before the season began, having never won more than 70 games in any of their first 10 seasons. They became just the second team to go from having the worst record in the league to making the play-offs the following year, joining the 1990 Atlanta Braves.

Also in 2008, Major League Baseball became the latest sports league to introduce instant replay for certain calls. Beginning August 28, umpires could review video footage of potential home runs to determine whether they were fair or foul, whether they cleared the fence, and whether fans had interfered with them. Baseball officials had resisted adopting instant replay for years, fearing that it would slow the pace of the game.

Absent from major-league play in 2008 were slugger Barry Bonds and pitcher Roger Clemens, both at the center of controversies over performance-enhancing drugs. Bonds awaited a March 2009 perjury trial, the charges stemming from his 2003 testimony in a federal investigation into steroid distribution by the Bay Area Laboratory Co-Operative (BALCO). Clemens spent an uncomfortable 3 ½ hours before a United States congressional panel on Feb. 14, 2008, facing Brian McNamee, a former personal trainer who had accused him of using perform-ance-enhancing drugs.

World Series. Philadelphia pitcher Cole Hamels earned the Most Valuable Player award for his performance in the World Series. Hamels pitched six innings of two-run ball in Game 5, which began on October 27. The game was halted with the score 2-2 in the bottom of the 6th inning because of heavy rains, becoming the first World Series game ever suspended. When play resumed two nights later, the Phillies won 4-3, with closer Brad Lidge earning his 48th save of the season in 48 tries.

The Phillies had opened the series with a 3-2 victory behind Hamels on October 22 in St. Petersburg, Florida. The Rays tied the series the

Philadelphia Phillies closer Brad Lidge strikes out Eric Hinske of the Tampa Bay Rays on October 29 for the final out of the 2008 World Series. The Phillies won the series 4 games to 1, earning their first championship title in 28 years.

FINAL STANDINGS IN MAJOR LEAGUE BASEBALL

AMERICAN LEAGUE

American League champions—
Tampa Bay Rays
(defeated Boston Red Sox, 4 games to 3)

Eastern Division	W.	L.	Pct.	G.B.
Tampa Bay Rays	97	65	.599	—
Boston Red Sox*	95	67	.586	2
New York Yankees	89	73	.549	8
Toronto Blue Jays	86	76	.531	11
Baltimore Orioles	68	93	.422	28.5
Central Division				
Chicago White Sox	89	74	.546	—
Minnesota Twins	88	75	.540	1
Cleveland Indians	81	81	.500	7.5
Kansas City Royals	75	87	.463	13.5
Detroit Tigers	74	88	.457	14.5
Western Division				
Los Angeles Angels	100	62	.617	—
Texas Rangers	79	83	.488	21
Oakland Athletics	75	86	.469	24.5
Seattle Mariners	61	101	.377	39

Offensive leaders

Batting average	Joe Mauer, Minnesota	.328
Runs scored	Dustin Pedroia, Boston	118
Home runs	Miguel Cabrera, Detroit	37
Runs batted in	Josh Hamilton, Texas	130
Hits	Dustin Pedroia, Boston	213
	Ichiro Suzuki, Seattle	213
Stolen bases	Jacoby Ellsbury, Boston	50
Slugging percentage	Alex Rodriguez, New York	.573

Leading pitchers

Games won	Cliff Lee, Cleveland	22
Earned run average (162 or more innings)	Cliff Lee, Cleveland	2.54
Strikeouts	A. J. Burnett, Toronto	231
Saves	Francisco Rodriguez, Los Angeles	62
Shut-outs	Matt Garza, Tampa Bay	2
	Roy Halladay, Toronto	2
	Cliff Lee, Cleveland	2
	Jon Lester, Boston	2
	Jesse Litsch, Toronto	2
	C. C. Sabathia, Cleveland	2
	James Shields, Tampa Bay	2
	Kevin Slowey, Minnesota	2
Complete games	Roy Halladay, Toronto	9

Awards[†]

Most Valuable Player............................Dustin Pedroia, Boston
Cy Young...Cliff Lee, Cleveland
Rookie of the Year..........................Evan Longoria, Tampa Bay
Manager of the Year ....Joe Madden, Tampa Bay

NATIONAL LEAGUE

National League champions—
Philadelphia Phillies
(defeated Los Angeles Dodgers, 4 games to 1)

World Series champions—
Philadelphia Phillies (defeated Tampa Bay Rays, 4 games to 1)

Eastern Division	W.	L.	Pct.	G.B.
Philadelphia Phillies	92	70	.568	—
New York Mets	89	73	.549	3
Florida Marlins	84	77	.522	7.5
Atlanta Braves	72	90	.444	20
Washington Nationals	59	102	.366	32.5
Central Division				
Chicago Cubs	97	64	.602	—
Milwaukee Brewers*	90	72	.556	7.5
Houston Astros	86	75	.534	11
St. Louis Cardinals	86	76	.531	11.5
Cincinnati Reds	74	88	.457	23.5
Pittsburgh Pirates	67	95	.414	30.5
Western Division				
Los Angeles Dodgers	84	78	.519	—
Arizona Diamondbacks	82	80	.506	2
Colorado Rockies	74	88	.457	10
San Francisco Giants	72	90	.444	12
San Diego Padres	63	99	.389	21

Offensive leaders

Batting average	Chipper Jones, Atlanta	.364
Runs scored	Hanley Ramirez, Florida	125
Home runs	Ryan Braun, Milwaukee	37
	Ryan Ludwick, Seattle	37
	Albert Pujols, St. Louis	37
Runs batted in	David Wright, New York	124
Hits	José Reyes, New York	204
Stolen bases	José Reyes, New York	56
Slugging percentage	Albert Pujols, St. Louis	.653

Leading pitchers

Games won	Brandon Webb, Arizona	22
Earned run average (162 or more innings)	Johan Santana, New York	2.53
Strikeouts	Tim Lincecum, San Francisco	265
Saves	José Valverde, Arizona	44
Shut-outs	C. C. Sabathia, Milwaukee	3
	Ben Sheets, Milwaukee	3
Complete games	C. C. Sabathia, Milwaukee	7

Awards[†]

Most Valuable Player.............................Albert Pujols, Seattle
Cy Young..................................Tim Lincecum, San Francisco
Rookie of the Year...............................Geovany Soto, Chicago
Manager of the Year...............................Lou Piniella, Chicago

*Qualified for wild-card play-off spot.
[†]Selected by the Baseball Writers Association of America.

---

next night with a 4-2 victory. The series then shifted to a rainy Philadelphia, with Game 3 on October 25 delayed until 10:06 p.m. Eastern time, the latest start in World Series history. The Phillies won 5-4 in the bottom of the 9th inning. They moved to the verge of the franchise's second World Series title with a 10-2 rout on October 26. In that game, the Phillies' Joe Blanton became the first pitcher in 34 years to hit a World Series home run.

Play-offs. The Rays earned their first World Series berth with a 3-1 victory on October 19 in St. Petersburg, eliminating the defending champion Boston Red Sox 4 games to 3 in the American League Championship Series (ALCS). The Red Sox faced elimination in Game 5 on October 16, trailing 7-0 in the bottom of the 7th inning in Boston. But the Red Sox pulled out an 8-7 victory, the biggest postseason comeback since Game 4 of the 1929 World Series, when the Philadelphia Athletics rallied from 8-0 to beat the Chicago Cubs 10-8. Boston won 4-2 in Game 6 on Oct. 18, 2008, to force Game 7.

Boston reached the ALCS by defeating the Los Angeles Angels 3 games to 1 in the American League Division Series (ALDS). The Rays beat the Chicago White Sox 3 games to 1 for their ALDS victory.

The Phillies defeated the Milwaukee Brewers 3 games to 1 in the National League Division Series (NLDS). They beat the Los Angeles Dodgers 4 games to 1 in the National League Championship Series (NLCS). The Dodgers had swept the Cubs in the NLDS, ensuring that it would be a full century since the Cubs last won a World Series championship.

Regular season. The Rays won the American League (AL) East with a 97-65 record, and the Red Sox won the AL wild-card race with a 95-67 mark. The New York Yankees finished 89-73, failing to make the play-offs for the first time since 1993. (Due to a players strike, no play-offs were held in 1994.) The White Sox won the 2008 AL Central in a one-game play-off with the Minnesota Twins. The Angels won the AL West by 21 games, finishing with the best mark in the majors at 100-62.

The Phillies won the National League (NL) East at 92-70, and the Dodgers took a lackluster NL West with an 84-78 mark. The Cubs posted the best record in the league to win the NL Central at 97-64. Milwaukee earned the wild card with a 90-72 record.

No-hitters. Less than two years after being diagnosed with cancer, Red Sox left-hander Jon Lester pitched a no-hitter against the Kansas City Royals on May 19 in Boston. On September 14, the Cubs' Carlos Zambrano pitched a no-hitter against the Houston Astros in Milwaukee. The game had been moved from Houston due to Hurricane Ike.

Jered Weaver and Jose Arredondo of the Angels combined to no-hit the Dodgers on June 28 in Los Angeles. But the game fell short of an official no-hitter, with the Angels pitching just eight innings in a 1-0 loss. It was just the fifth time since 1900 that a team had lost without giving up a hit.

Milestones. Angels' pitcher Francisco Rodriguez set a new major-league record with 62 saves, 5 more than Bobby Thigpen recorded in 1990 with the White Sox. Cincinnati Red Ken Griffey, Jr., became the sixth player to reach 600 homers with his blast in Miami on June 9, 2008, before being traded to the White Sox. Boston's

Manny Ramirez, later traded to the Dodgers, became the 24th player to hit 500 homers, with a May 31 blast in Baltimore.

Numbers slump. Home run totals slipped to their lowest since 1993. Some players attributed the decline in home runs to more vigorous steroid testing, while others pointed to a trend toward larger ballparks or other factors. Other offensive marks declined as well. Boston's Dustin Pedroia led the American League with 118 runs, the lowest total for a league leader since 1992. New York Yankee Alex Rodriguez's .573 slugging percentage was the lowest for a league leader since 1989. Texas Ranger Josh Hamilton's 331 total bases were the lowest atop the American League since 1992.

College. Fresno State University captured its first National Collegiate Athletic Association (NCAA) title with a 6-1 victory over the University of Georgia on June 25, 2008, in Omaha, Nebraska. Fresno State had lost 12 of its first 20 games and had to win its conference tournament just to win a spot in the NCAA finals.

Youth. The United States won its fourth straight Little League World Series Championship title on August 24. A team from Waipahu, Hawaii, beat a team from Matamoros, Mexico, 12-3 in South Williamsport, Pennsylvania. Michael Kates

See also **Sports.**

Basketball. The Boston Celtics completed the greatest single-season turnaround in National Basketball Association (NBA) history in 2008 by capturing the franchise's 17th championship. To win their first title since 1986, the Celtics defeated the Los Angeles Lakers by a record 39 points on June 18, 2008, 131-92, in Boston, to take the Finals 4 games to 2.

Boston had earned the top seed in the NBA play-offs by virtue of its 66-16 record, winning 42 more games in 2007-2008 than it did in 2006-2007. Off-season deals for veteran guard Ray Allen and Kevin Garnett set the stage for the Celtics' run.

In college basketball in 2008, the University of Kansas (Lawrence) captured its first men's National Collegiate Athletic Association (NCAA) title in 20 years with a thrilling 75-68 overtime victory over the University of Memphis on April 7 in San Antonio. It was the first overtime championship game since 1997.

In the women's NCAA tournament, the University of Tennessee (Knoxville) repeated as national champions with a 64-48 rout of Stanford University on April 8, 2008, in St. Petersburg, Florida. Candace Parker, the national player of the year, became the fourth player to win consecutive awards for Most Outstanding Player of the Final Four as the Lady Vols captured their eighth NCAA championship since 1986-1987.

COLLEGE TOURNAMENT CHAMPIONS

NCAA (Men) Division I: Kansas
                Division II: Winona State
                Division III: Washington-St. Louis

        (Women) Division I: Tennessee
                 Division II: Northern Kentucky
                 Division III: Howard Payne

NAIA (Men) Division I: Oklahoma City
                Division II: Oregon Tech

        (Women) Division I: Vanguard
                 Division II: Northwestern

NIT (Men) Ohio State
       (Women) Marquette

MEN'S COLLEGE CHAMPIONS

CONFERENCE	SCHOOL
America East	UMBC*
Atlantic 10	Xavier
	Temple (tournament)
Atlantic Coast	North Carolina*
Atlantic Sun	Belmont*
Big 12	Texas
	Kansas (tournament)
Big East	Georgetown
	Pittsburgh (tournament)
Big Sky	Portland State*
Big South	Winthrop*–North Carolina-Asheville (tie)
Big Ten	Wisconsin*
Big West	Cal State-Fullerton*–Cal State-Northridge–UC-Santa Barbara (3-way tie)
Colonial	Virginia Commonwealth
	George Mason (tournament)
Conference USA	Memphis*
Horizon League	Butler*
Ivy League	Cornell*
Metro Atlantic	Siena*–Rider (tie)
Mid-American	
East Division	Kent State*
West Division	Western Michigan
Mid-Eastern	Morgan State
	Coppin State (tournament)
Missouri Valley	Drake
	Tulsa (tournament)
Mountain West	Brigham Young
	Nevada-Las Vegas (tournament)
Northeast	Robert Morris
	Mount St. Mary's (tournament)
Ohio Valley	Austin Peay*
Pacific 10	UCLA*
Patriot League	American*
Southeastern	Georgia (tournament)
East Division	Tennessee
West Division	Mississippi State
Southern	
North Division	Appalachian State–Chattanooga (tie)
South Division	Davidson*
Southland	Texas-Arlington (tournament)
East Division	Lamar
West Division	Stephen F. Austin
Southwestern	Alabama State
	Mississippi Valley State (tournament)
Summit League	Oral Roberts*
Sun Belt	
East Division	Western Kentucky*–South Alabama (tie)
West Division	Arkansas-Little Rock–Louisiana-Lafayette (tie)
West Coast	Gonzaga
	San Diego (tournament)
Western Athletic	Boise State*–Nevada State–New Mexico State–Utah State (4-way tie)

Professional men. Paul Pierce, who was named the Finals Most Valuable Player, averaged 21.8 points a game in the series. Pierce suffered a strained knee injury during the second quarter of Game 1 but returned before the end of the half to lead the Celtics to victory. In Game 2, Garnett scored 26 points and grabbed 14 rebounds, and Allen pumped in 26, tying the Finals record with 7 three-points. Allen's 22 three-pointers in the series set a new record.

After the Lakers won Game 3 in Los Angeles to close the series 2 games to 1, the Celtics engineered the greatest comeback in a Finals game. Trailing by a Finals-record 21 after the first quarter and by 20 with six minutes left in the third quarter, Boston finally won 97-91. The Lakers won Game 5 in Los Angeles but were blown away when the series returned to Boston.

The Celtics advanced to their first Finals since 1987 by eliminating the Detroit Pistons 4 games to 2. Boston's first two series went seven games, with Boston winning 4 games to 3 over the Atlanta Hawks and then 4 games to 3 over LeBron James and the Cleveland Cavaliers. Boston did not win a road game until Game 3 of the Pistons series in the Eastern Conference finals to take a 2-1 series lead. Boston closed out the series with another win at Detroit, rallying from 10 down in the fourth quarter of Game 6 to win 89-81.

The Lakers swept Denver in the first round, beat Utah 4 games to 2 in the second round, and beat the defending champion San Antonio Spurs 4 games to 1 to reach their first Finals.

WOMEN'S COLLEGE CHAMPIONS

CONFERENCE	SCHOOL
America East	Hartford*
Atlantic 10	George Washington–Temple (tie) Xavier (tournament)
Atlantic Coast	North Carolina*
Atlantic Sun	East Tennessee State*
Big 12	Kansas State Texas A&M (tournament)
Big East	Connecticut*
Big Sky	Montana*
Big South	Liberty*
Big Ten	Ohio State–Iowa (tie) Purdue (tournament)
Big West	UC-Santa Barbara*
Colonial	Old Dominion*
Conference USA	Texas-El Paso Southern Methodist (tournament)
Horizon League	UW-Green Bay Cleveland State (tournament)
Ivy League	Cornell*–Dartmouth–Harvard (3-way tie)
Metro Atlantic	Marist*
Mid-American	Ohio (tournament)
East Division	Bowling Green
West Division	Ball State–Eastern Michigan (tie)
Mid-Eastern	North Carolina A&T Coppin State (tournament)
Missouri Valley	Illinois State*–Drake–Evansville (3-way tie)
Mountain West	Utah New Mexico (tournament)
Northeast	Robert Morris*–Quinnipiac (tie)
Ohio Valley	Southeast Missouri State Murray State (tournament)
Pacific 10	Stanford*
Patriot League	American Bucknell (tournament)
Southeastern	Louisiana State Tennessee (tournament)
Southern	Chattanooga*
Southland	Texas-San Antonio (tournament)
East Division	Lamar
West Division	Texas State
Southwestern	Prairie View A&M*–Jackson State (tie)
Summit League	South Dakota State Oral Roberts (tournament)
Sun Belt	
East Division	Western Kentucky*
West Division	Arkansas-Little Rock
West Coast	Gonzaga San Diego (tournament)
Western Athletic	Fresno State*–Boise State (tie)

*Regular season and conference tournament champion.

Sources: National Collegiate Athletic Association (NCAA); National Association of Intercollegiate Athletics (NAIA); National Invitation Tournament (NIT); Conference Web sites.

In the regular season in the Eastern Conference, the Celtics won the Atlantic Division, Detroit won the Central Division with a 59-23 mark, and upstart Orlando took the Southeast with a 52-30 record. The Western Conference was far more tightly bunched, with no team securing a play-off spot until about two weeks remained in the season. The Lakers' 57-25 mark won the Pacific Division, and New Orleans had the second seed by winning the Southwest Division with a 56-26 record. Utah won the Northwest Division with a 54-28 record.

During the season, the Houston Rockets won 22 consecutive games starting on Jan. 29, 2008, the second longest winning streak in NBA history and 11 short of the mark set by the 1971-1972 Lakers. Kobe Bryant won the Most Valuable Player award, his first.

Professional women. The Detroit Shock won its third Women's National Basketball Association (WNBA) championship in six years, completing a three-game sweep of the San Antonio Silver Stars on Oct. 5, 2008. San Antonio had finished with the league's best regular season record. Katie Smith of the Shock was named the Most Valuable Player of the Finals.

College men. Memphis, whose 38 wins topped the record for a men's team in a single season, appeared poised to win its first national championship. The team led Kansas 60-51 with 2 minutes, 12 seconds to play in the title game. But Memphis (38-2), one of the worst free-throw shooting teams in the nation, missed four of five free throws in the final 1 minute, 12 seconds. Mario Chalmers of Kansas forced the game into overtime with a three-pointer with 2.1 seconds left.

Kansas (37-3), the top seed in the Midwest Regional, advanced to the title game with an 84-65 victory on April 5 over North Carolina, the top seed from the East Regional. North Carolina (36-3) trailed 40-12 late in the opening half but rallied to within 5 before Kansas pulled away. Memphis, the top seed in the South Regional, pummeled UCLA (35-4), the number-one seed from the West Regional, 78-63.

Although 2008 marked the first time all four top seeds made it to the Final Four, the tournament was not lacking a Cinderella story. Davidson College, a small North Carolina school with 1,700 students, was seeded 10th in the Midwest Regional and pulled off three upsets before falling 59-57 to Kansas in the regional final. Riding the outside shooting of Stephen Curry, Davidson beat seventh-seeded Gonzaga in the first round, second-seeded Georgetown in the second round, and third-seeded Wisconsin in the Sweet 16. A last-second three-pointer for the win against Kansas missed.

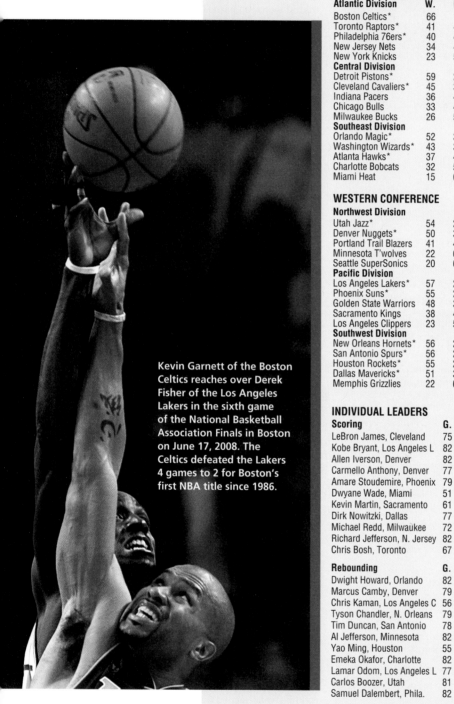

Kevin Garnett of the Boston Celtics reaches over Derek Fisher of the Los Angeles Lakers in the sixth game of the National Basketball Association Finals in Boston on June 17, 2008. The Celtics defeated the Lakers 4 games to 2 for Boston's first NBA title since 1986.

EASTERN CONFERENCE

Atlantic Division	W.	L.	Pct.	G.B.
Boston Celtics*	66	16	.805	—
Toronto Raptors*	41	41	.500	25
Philadelphia 76ers*	40	42	.488	26
New Jersey Nets	34	48	.415	32
New York Knicks	23	59	.280	43
Central Division				
Detroit Pistons*	59	23	.720	—
Cleveland Cavaliers*	45	37	.549	14
Indiana Pacers	36	46	.439	23
Chicago Bulls	33	49	.402	26
Milwaukee Bucks	26	56	.317	33
Southeast Division				
Orlando Magic*	52	30	.634	—
Washington Wizards*	43	39	.524	9
Atlanta Hawks*	37	45	.451	15
Charlotte Bobcats	32	50	.390	20
Miami Heat	15	67	.183	37

WESTERN CONFERENCE

Northwest Division	W.	L.	Pct.	G.B.
Utah Jazz*	54	28	.659	—
Denver Nuggets*	50	32	.610	4
Portland Trail Blazers	41	41	.500	13
Minnesota T'wolves	22	60	.268	32
Seattle SuperSonics	20	62	.244	34
Pacific Division				
Los Angeles Lakers*	57	25	.695	—
Phoenix Suns*	55	27	.671	2
Golden State Warriors	48	34	.585	9
Sacramento Kings	38	44	.463	19
Los Angeles Clippers	23	59	.280	34
Southwest Division				
New Orleans Hornets*	56	26	.683	—
San Antonio Spurs*	56	26	.683	—
Houston Rockets*	55	27	.671	1
Dallas Mavericks*	51	31	.622	5
Memphis Grizzlies	22	60	.268	34

INDIVIDUAL LEADERS

Scoring	G.	F.G.M.	F.T.M.	Pts.	Avg.
LeBron James, Cleveland	75	794	549	2,250	30.0
Kobe Bryant, Los Angeles L	82	775	623	2,323	28.3
Allen Iverson, Denver	82	712	645	2,164	26.4
Carmello Anthony, Denver	77	728	464	1,978	25.7
Amare Stoudemire, Phoenix	79	714	556	1,989	25.2
Dwyane Wade, Miami	51	439	354	1,254	24.6
Kevin Martin, Sacramento	61	417	502	1,443	23.7
Dirk Nowitzki, Dallas	77	630	478	1,817	23.6
Michael Redd, Milwaukee	72	550	402	1,632	22.7
Richard Jefferson, N. Jersey	82	619	542	1,857	22.6
Chris Bosh, Toronto	67	507	472	1,496	22.3

Rebounding	G.	Off.	Def.	Tot.	Avg.
Dwight Howard, Orlando	82	279	882	1,161	14.2
Marcus Camby, Denver	79	230	807	1,037	13.1
Chris Kaman, Los Angeles C	56	173	538	711	12.7
Tyson Chandler, N. Orleans	79	322	606	928	11.7
Tim Duncan, San Antonio	78	237	644	881	11.3
Al Jefferson, Minnesota	82	308	603	911	11.1
Yao Ming, Houston	55	172	422	594	10.8
Emeka Okafor, Charlotte	82	255	621	876	10.7
Lamar Odom, Los Angeles L	77	197	622	819	10.6
Carlos Boozer, Utah	81	197	647	844	10.4
Samuel Dalembert, Phila.	82	304	545	849	10.4

NBA champions—Boston Celtics
(defeated Los Angeles Lakers, 4 games to 2)

*Made play-offs.

Legendary coach retires. Bob Knight, the all-time winningest coach in Division 1 men's basketball, resigned as coach of Texas Tech University on February 4 in favor of his son, Pat, his handpicked successor. The often-controversial Knight, who won three NCAA titles at Indiana University (Bloomington), had coached for 42 years and accumulated 902 wins.

Coaching pioneer dies. Will Robinson, who became the first black basketball coach in Division 1 when he took over the Illinois State University program in 1970, died on April 28, 2008, at age 96.

College women. Playing with an injured left shoulder, Candace Parker scored 17 points and grabbed nine rebounds as Tennessee (36-2), the top seed in the Oklahoma City Regional, routed the Cardinals (35-4), the number-two seed out of the Spokane Regional.

The Lady Vols squeaked their way into the title game when Alexis Hornbuckle put back a missed shot with seven-tenths of a second left to beat Louisiana State University (Baton Rouge) 47-46 on April 6. LSU (31-6) was the number-two seed in the New Orleans Regional. Stanford made the final with an 82-73 victory over Connecticut (26-2), the top seed in the Greensboro Regional.

■ Michael Kates

See also **Olympic Games: A Special Report.**

Belarus. Relations between Belarus and the United States deteriorated sharply in early 2008. On March 7, Belarus recalled its envoy to the United States and expelled U.S. Ambassador Karen Stewart in retaliation for U.S. sanctions on Belarusian oil monopoly Belneftekhim. The United States had imposed the sanctions in 2007 to protest human rights abuses in Belarus. On April 30, 2008, Belarus expelled 10 more U.S. diplomats, escalating the conflict.

In an attempt to mend relations, on August 17, Belarus's President Aleksandr Lukashenko conceded to international demands to release opposition leader Aleksandr Kazulin from prison. Kazulin had been sentenced to 5 ½ years in prison after he ran against Lukashenko in the 2006 presidential election. In response to his release, the U.S. government relaxed its economic sanctions.

Lukashenko permitted 70 opposition politicians to take part in Sept. 28, 2008, parliamentary elections and gave international observers greater access to the proceedings. Opposition candidates won no seats in the 110-member parliament. The vote fell short of international standards, but the European Union acknowledged marginal improvement in the election process by lifting its 1999 travel ban on Lukashenko and 34 other Belarusian government officials. ■ Juliet Johnson

See also **Europe.**

Belgium. Prime Minister Yves Leterme's government—a coalition of Flemish (Dutch-speaking) and francophone (French-speaking) Christian Democratic and Liberal parties and the French-speaking Socialists—struggled to rule during 2008 but suffered considerable setbacks. Leterme resigned on December 19. On December 28, King Albert II asked Herman Van Rompuy, a Flemish Christian Democrat and the speaker of parliament, to form a new government. Van Rompuy agreed. He formed a Cabinet made up of the same five parties that made up Leterme's government.

Leterme had also offered to resign on July 14, when his government was unable to meet a self-imposed deadline for agreeing on reforms to devolve significant powers to Belgium's regions. Belgium's northern region of Flanders, where the country's 60-percent majority Flemish live, favors greater autonomy. The southern region of Wallonia, where the 40-percent minority French speakers live, favors a strong federation. The coalition had only been in power since March, after a government could not be formed following the June 2007 election. The essence of the dispute is a disagreement on resources and power between the two linguistic communities. Flemish-speaking Belgians live in one of Europe's richest regions and resent subsidizing the poor, French-speaking areas. Francophone Belgians worry that any constitutional arrangement granting greater autonomy to the regions will reduce funding for the south.

The "wise men" intervene. In July 2008, the king asked that Leterme remain in office to implement the coalition's economic program. He also assigned a panel of "wise men" made up of three ministers the task of proposing a way to start talks on constitutional reform. In September, the panel submitted guidelines on how the talks should proceed. The nationalist New Flemish Alliance Party withdrew from the government in protest over the plan. The party's defection paved the way for the other Flemish parties to agree to negotiations.

The talks began October 8, as Flemish and Walloon ministers attempted a "rebalancing" of power. In late fall, however, the global economic crisis forced the government to concentrate on maintaining Belgium's economy. Leterme offered his resignation two months later amid allegations of government irregularities in the break-up of Fortis, one of the country's largest banks.

Economy. EU economists projected that, because of the global economic downturn, Belgium's economic growth would slow from 2.8 percent in 2007 to 1.4 percent in 2008.

■ Jeffrey Kopstein

See also **Europe.**

Belize. See **Latin America.**

Benin. See **Africa.**

Bhutan. See **Asia.**

Biology. Scientists found species in 2008 that had never previously been described. New species included a giant elephant shrew from Tanzania and a giant palm from Madagascar.

Giant shrew. The elephant shrew scientists described in January is a giant of its kind. Weighing about 1.5 pounds (0.7 kilogram), it is 25 percent larger than any other elephant shrew. The insect-eating mammal resembles a mouse with a long, flexible snout. However, elephant shrews are not closely related to mice or even shrews. In fact, they form a group of their own that first appeared around 50 million years ago. The newly discovered elephant shrew comes from the Udzungwa Mountains of Tanzania. A scientific team led by Francesco Rovero of Italy's Trento Museum of Natural Sciences announced the discovery in the *Journal of Zoology*.

Strange palm. Scientists also described a giant palm from Madagascar, a large island off the coast of Africa. The palm is another giant among its kind, standing 66 feet (20 meters) high with leaves 16 feet (4.9 meters) wide. The palm was found by the owner of a cashew plantation. There may be fewer than 100 such giant palms.

After growing for a century, the palm blooms from a stem atop its trunk. Hundreds of flowers are pollinated and develop into fruit. The palm uses so much energy in this explosion of growth that it then dies and collapses. Palm authority John Dransfield of the Royal Botanical Gardens at Kew, in London, reported the palm in the January *Botanical Journal of the Linnean Society*.

Back from the dead. In April, researchers announced that they had rediscovered a giant turtle thought to be extinct in the wild. Scientists with the Cleveland Metroparks Zoo photographed a wild Swinhoe's softshell turtle near Hanoi, Vietnam. Weighing up to 300 pounds (136 kilograms), it is the world's largest freshwater turtle.

Scientists also spotted a greater dwarf cloud rat on the island of Luzon, in the Philippines, for the first time in more than a century. A British scientist collected a greater dwarf cloud rat from local people in 1896, but the species was not seen again for 112 years. Then, in April 2008, a team of American and Filipino scientists captured the rat in its natural habitat, high in the rain-soaked mountain forest. The rat, weighing just 6.5 ounces (185 grams), was on a tree branch.

In July, researchers found a tiny Australian frog that was presumed extinct. The armored mistfrog was thought to have been wiped out by the chytrid fungus, which has devastated frogs worldwide. The frog had not been seen since 1991, until several were spotted in a creek. Researchers from Australia's James Cook University took DNA samples that proved the rare frog has survived.

Fungus cure? Bacteria natural to frogs may combat the deadly chytrid fungus. Researchers discovered that frogs that survived the fungus had higher levels of certain bacteria on their skin. Scientists then found that treating sick frogs with high doses of the bacteria boosted the animals' survival rates. A team led by Reid Harris of James Madison University in Virginia described the research at the June 2008 meeting of the American Society for Microbiology, in Boston. A method for treating frogs in the wild is needed, however.

Bat fungus. Another fungus is involved in thousands of bat deaths in the United States. A new disease has killed up to 90 percent of the bats in caves in several northeastern states. The disease is called *white-nose syndrome* because of the moldy white fungus that appears to cause it.

The fungus was a main topic at an August meeting of the National Speleological Society, which is an organization of cavers. Cavers at the Boston meeting were warned to decontaminate their clothing after exploring caves in New York, Vermont, Connecticut, New Jersey, Massachusetts, New Hampshire, Pennsylvania, and Rhode Island.

The disease was first spotted during January 2007 in bats from a cave near Albany, New York. By June 2008, it had spread to Vermont, Massachusetts, and Connecticut. Infected bats seem to starve to death while hibernating, often collapsing just outside of caves to die in the winter cold. The little brown bat, a common cave dweller, has died by the tens of thousands. The endangered Indiana bat has also suffered greatly.

Beneficial bats. The number of harmful insects eaten by bats was demonstrated in two separate studies reported in an April 2008 issue of the journal *Science*. A team led by tropical ecologist Kimberly Williams-Guillen from the University of Michigan in Ann Arbor compared the number of insects eaten by bats with those eaten by birds at a Mexican coffee plantation. In the wet season, bats ate 84 percent more insects and other bugs than did birds. In a study carried out in a Panamanian rain forest, a team led by Margaret Kalka of the Smithsonian Institution found that if bats were kept away from plants by nets, the damage by pests tripled. Plants shielded from birds had only twice the normal damage.

Eat big, digest fast. In the spring of 2008, researchers discovered how crocodiles, alligators, and their relatives—a group of animals called crocodilians—eat such huge meals. Crocodilians can eat animals that weigh as much as 23 percent of their body weight. They often consume victims whole—hooves, claws, bones, and all. It would take most animals so long to digest such food that it would actually decay in their stomachs, making the meal deadly.

The crocodilians' secret lies in their ability to

divert blood flow. Most animals send blood carrying carbon dioxide waste to their lungs, where the carbon dioxide is expelled. Crocodilians usually do the same. After a heavy meal, however, they send such blood to the stomach. There, the carbon dioxide helps the crocodilians make gastric acid, which promotes digestion. Crocodilians can flood the stomach with gastric acid 10 times as fast as mammals. The acid also kills bacteria. The research was described by biologist Colleen G. Farmer of the University of Utah and her colleagues in the journal *Physiological and Biochemical Zoology.*

Real animal magnetism. Research reported in August suggests that cattle, sheep, and similar grazing animals can sense Earth's magnetic field. These animals tend to face the same direction when feeding, and scientists had assumed that they turned to face the wind or the sun. Now, research led by Sabine Begall of the University of Duisburg-Essen in Germany suggests a different explanation. Begall and her team studied more than 8,000 satellite images of cattle and deer herds in several parts of the world. They found that the animals tended to face either the north or south magnetic pole, regardless of the wind or sun. Animals faced the north pole, for example, even when it differed in direction from geographic north. Other animals, including certain fish and birds, use magnetic fields to navigate, but such behavior has not been observed in large mammals. The research was reported in the *Proceedings of the National Academy of Sciences.*

Ant berries. Scientists reported in January on a previously unknown parasite with the remarkable ability to make ants look like berries. The microscopic parasite is a kind of worm that spends part of its life inside ants and part inside birds. The ant is a tree-dwelling species native to tropical American forests that feeds on bird droppings. When ants eat the droppings, they can become infected by eggs from the parasitic worm.

The problem for the worm is that it must move from the ant to the bird. The only way it can make this move is if the ant is eaten, but the birds in question do not ordinarily eat ants. This is where the berry trick comes into play. After infecting an ant, the worm causes the ant's abdomen to swell and turn bright red. The normally active ant becomes sluggish and holds its abdomen upright. This makes the ant look like a berry to the bird, which eats the infected ant and starts the cycle over again. Robert Dudley, a biologist at the University of California, Berkley, reported the discovery with his colleagues in *The American Naturalist.* ■ Edward Ricciuti

See also **Conservation; Global warming; Ocean; Zoos.**

Boating. Francis Joyon of France in 2008 shattered the world record for solo around-the-world sailing by more than 14 days. Joyon made the voyage in 57 days, 13 hours, 34 minutes, and 6 seconds aboard a trimaran. Joyon left Brest, France, on Nov. 23, 2007. When he returned to Brest on Jan. 20, 2008, he had shaved two weeks off the record set in 2005 by Dame Ellen MacArthur of the United Kingdom. A lighter-than-normal boat helped Joyon cut his time. Instead of carrying an electric generator, he used wind turbines and solar panels to power piloting and communication equipment.

America's Cup. The International Sailing Federation lifted a doping ban imposed on Simon Daubney in 2007 because of a positive drug test. The federation said it had based its decision on a Swiss Olympic Association ruling, which stated Daubney had not infringed any antidoping rule. Daubney had helped Swiss syndicate Alinghi win the America's Cup trophy in 2007. However, the World Anti-Doping Agency appealed the ruling and the ban was reinstated on Oct. 2, 2008.

The location of the next America's Cup race remained unclear. The problem centered on an ongoing court challenge against Alinghi by American challenger BMW Oracle Racing over rules for the competition.

World championships. Australians Nathan Outteridge and Ben Austin won the 49er world title on Jan. 9, 2008, in Melbourne, Australia. The United Kingdom's Ben Ainslie won the Finn World Championship on January 29, and Americans Erin Maxwell and Isabelle Kinsolving won the women's 470 world title on January 30. On the same day, Nic Asher and Elliot Willis of the United Kingdom won the men's 470 title.

At Takapuna Beach, Auckland, New Zealand, Tom Ashley from New Zealand won the RS:X men's title and Italy's Alessandra Sensini won the women's title on January 18. Australia's Darren Bundock (helm) and Glenn Ashby (crew) won the Tornado World Championship on February 29. France's Sarah Steyaert won the women's division of the Laser Radial World Championships on March 20, and Canada's Michael Leigh won the men's division on March 28.

Sarah Ayton (helm) with Sarah Webb and Pippa Wilson (crew) of the United Kingdom won the Yngling World title on February 15 in Miami. Poland's Mateusz Kusznierewicz (helm) and Dominik Zycki (crew) won the Star Worlds Championship on April 17. Americans Bill Hardesty, Erik Shampain, Steve Hunt, and Jennifer Wilson won the Etchells World title in Chicago on June 28.

Powerboats. The 100th running of the APBA Gold Cup in Detroit was canceled because of high winds. ■ Michael Kates

See also **Olympic Games: A Special Report.**

Bolivia. On Aug.10, 2008, Bolivians reaffirmed their support for President Juan Evo Morales by rejecting a recall referendum. Two out of three voters approved of "the continuation of change" led by Morales. He had gained wide support by investing windfall profits from Bolivia's natural resources into social programs.

Regional tensions. Morales orchestrated the referendum to break a political stalemate between his own supporters and the eastern lowland residents of four energy- and agriculturally rich provinces: Beni, Pando, Santa Cruz, and Tarija. Earlier in 2008, voters in all four of these provinces approved initiatives aimed at gaining more political autonomy, as well as a larger share of the revenues from gas, oil, and agricultural production in their area.

Constitution. Following the show of support for Morales in August, Bolivia's congress deferred to his wishes and scheduled a national referendum on a new constitution for 2009. The document would grant a "priority" share of revenues from natural resources to indigenous Bolivians.

Violence in Pando. On Sept. 11, 2008, 15 people were killed when opponents of the president tried to stop indigenous Morales supporters from attending a meeting in Porvenir, Pando. The Bolivian army restored order and arrested several people, including the governor of Pando. The Bolivian Congress established a commission to investigate the incident.

Cattle and horses cluster on high ground in northeastern Bolivia during flooding in February 2008. Heavy rains swelled rivers, leaving 60 people dead and 43,000 others homeless and causing millions in damage.

Replacing coca with rice. Morales urged Bolivia's farmers to substitute rice and corn for some of their coca crops during 2008. The move was intended to help the country feed itself at a time of rising grain prices and food shortages. In the Chapare region of the central Bolivian foothills, Morales was still president of the local coca growers federation. Some 35,000 farmers there were each required to plant 2.5 acres (1 hectare) of rice.

As incentives, each farm family was given a $500 loan to plant crops and a $2,000 grant to build a house. The government also invested $450,000 in a plant to process hearts of palm and $455,000 in another plant that will be able to process 60 tons (54.4 metric tons) of rice annually.

Indigenous universities. On August 2, Morales signed a decree establishing three new indigenous universities. One is in the municipality of Warisata in western La Paz department; the others are in Cochabamba and Santa Cruz. The new educational institutions were to offer instruction in the native Bolivian Aymara, Quechua, and Guaraní languages as part of curricula designed to preserve and enhance Bolivia's Indian traditions.   ■ Nathan A. Haverstock

See also **Latin America.**

Books. See Literature; Literature for children.

Bosnia-Herzegovina. In April 2008, Bosnian leaders and officials of the European Union (EU) signed a Stabilization and Association treaty (SAA), regarded as a first step toward eventual EU membership. The signing occurred after the Bosnian national parliament adopted EU-advocated police reforms. The reforms aimed to integrate the country's police forces, previously maintained separately and independently by the two ministates that comprise Bosnia—the Muslim-Croat Federation (MCF) and the Republika Srpska (RS).

The MCF and the RS are creations of the 1995 Dayton Accords, which ended the Bosnian War (1992–1995). The treaty endeavored to preserve Bosnia as a sovereign country while giving its three main ethnic groups—Bosnian Muslims, called *Bosniaks;* Croats; and Serbs—a loose federal structure in which to coexist. The RS is populated mainly by Serbs; the MCF is home to Bosnia's Croat and Bosniak communities. Linking the two ministates is a weak national government headed by a rotating presidency of one Croat, one Bosniak, and one Serb. The Dayton Accords also provided for an International High Representative (IHR), a United Nations-appointed official empowered to enforce Dayton provisions.

Hard-line nationalists in the RS and in the MCF made significant gains in local elections in October 2008. Analysts noted that two politi-

cians, in particular, had contributed to the political polarization: Milorad Dodik, prime minister of the RS; and Haris Silajdzic, the Bosniak member of Bosnia's tripartite presidency. In September, IHR Miroslav Lajcak warned that Serb-Bosniak tensions threatened to split Bosnia apart, and political observers noted that such tensions were impeding the government's reform agenda.

Responding to these developments, EU officials warned in November that negotiations for EU membership could not proceed until Bosnia's central government carried out promised reforms. Also in November, EU officials decided to keep 2,100 European peacekeepers in Bosnia in 2009, despite earlier plans to withdraw troops.

Arrests. The arrests in 2008 of alleged war criminals Radovan Karadzic and Stojan Zupljanin drew praise from the EU and the international community. Karadzic was accused of masterminding the 1995 Srebrenica massacre in Bosnia in which Bosnian Serb fighters killed more than 7,000 Bosniaks. Zupljanin was accused of carrying out ethnic cleansing in northwest Bosnia during the Bosnian War. Both men were arrested in Serbia and delivered to the International War Crimes Tribunal in The Hague, the Netherlands, for trial.
         ■ Sharon L. Wolchik

See also **Europe; Human rights; Serbia.**

Botswana. See Africa.

Bowling. Chris Barnes of Double Oak, Texas, captured his first Player of the Year award in 2008 for his performances during the 2007-2008 season. This was the first season the award was based on a point system rather than a vote of the Professional Bowling Association (PBA) membership and the media.

Barnes edged out six-time Player of the Year Walter Ray Williams, Jr., 64 points to 62. Barnes took the lead for good by winning the 2008 Don Johnson Buckeye State Classic on March 2 in Columbus, Ohio. Barnes led the tour with 18 match-play appearances (in 21 events) and finished second in average (225.18) and fifth in earnings with $142,410.

Norm Duke of Clermont, Florida, became the first bowler to win three straight majors, the final two of the 2007-2008 season and the first of 2008-2009. On Feb. 24, 2008, he beat Ryan Shafer, 202-165, to win the PBA World Championship in Indianapolis. On March 30, he captured the final major of the season, the U.S. Open in North Brunswick, New Jersey, converting a 2-4-5-8 spare to beat Finland-born Mika Koivuniemi, 224-216. He then beat Barnes in the PBA World Championship on October 28 in Wichita, Kansas, 259-189, for his 6th career major and 30th tour title. Duke led the PBA tour in earnings with $176,855. Williams led the tour in average with 228.34 pins per match.

Michael Haugen, Jr., of Cave Creek, Arizona, overcame a 52-pin deficit after six frames to win his first career major, beating Barnes 215-214 at the PBA Tournament of Champions on January 27 in Las Vegas. Sean Rash, from Wichita, Kansas, won the first major of the 2007-2008 season in the United States Bowling Congress (USBC) Masters on Oct. 28, 2007, in Milwaukee. He beat Steve Jaros of Yorkville, Illinois, 269-245, in the final match.

Women's bowling. In the first professional championship match between two African American bowlers (either male or female), Kim Terrell-Kearney of Dover, Delaware, defeated Trisha Reid of Columbus, Ohio, 216-189, in the USBC's U.S. Women's Open on Aug. 6, 2008, in Romeoville, Illinois.

Seniors. Tom Baker of King, North Carolina, won an unprecedented fourth straight Player of the Year award despite not winning a single tournament. Baker led the point standings with 137,165. Kenny Parks of Hammond, Indiana, captured the Senior Masters on June 13 in Tucson, defeating Baker 681-589. In the other major, Wayne Webb, of Sacramento, California, won the Senior U.S. Open on June 20 in Las Vegas, defeating Johnny Petraglia of Manalapan, New Jersey, 204-172 in the finals.　　■ Michael Kates

Boxing. Oscar De La Hoya lost his nontitle welterweight fight against Manny Pacquiao on Dec. 6, 2008, in Las Vegas. The bout was expected to be the final fight in De La Hoya's long and successful career. The 35-year-old fighter left open the possibility that he might return down the road. Pacquiao won the highly publicized fight on an eighth round RTD (referee technical decision) after De La Hoya did not come out for the ninth round.

Pacquiao, who won the World Boxing Council (WBC) lightweight title on June 28 with a ninth-round TKO (technical knockout) of David Diaz, has captured championship fights at five different weight categories. In perhaps Pacquiao's best fight of the year, he won a narrow split decision over Juan Manuel Marquez on March 15 to claim the WBC super featherweight title. Marquez landed more punches but was knocked down in the third round of a bloody, intense fight.

In another notable nontitle fight, Joe Calzaghe of Wales defeated American Roy Jones, Jr., in a unanimous decision in a light-heavyweight fight in New York City on November 8. Calzaghe extended his undefeated record to 46 consecutive victories. After the fight, Calzaghe stated that he was undecided whether he would continue his professional boxing career.

Heavyweights. Russian Nikolay Valuev won the World Boxing Association (WBA) title on August 30 in Berlin over American John Ruiz. Originally, judges scored it a split decision, but the result was later corrected to a unanimous decision when a judge realized he had put the fighters in the wrong order on his card. Ukrainian Vitaly Klitschko defeated Samuel Peter on October 11 in Berlin for the WBC title. Vitaly's brother, Wladimir, holds the heavyweight titles for the International Boxing Federation and the World Boxing Organization.

Mayweather retires. American Floyd Mayweather, Jr., considered by many to be the best pound-for-pound fighter in the world, announced his retirement on June 6. Mayweather compiled a 39-0 record with 25 knockouts and won championships in five different weight divisions. Mayweather had beaten De La Hoya and Ricky Hatton and made more than $50 million in the 18 months before his announcement.

Boxer recovers. Welterweight Oscar Diaz collapsed in his corner after the 10th round of his fight on July 16 in San Antonio and underwent emergency surgery to relieve swelling to his brain. Diaz went into a coma after surgery but awoke from it on September 18 and was upgraded from critical to stable condition.　　■ Michael Kates

See also **Olympic Games: A Special Report.**

WORLD CHAMPION BOXERS

WORLD BOXING ASSOCIATION

Division	Champion	Country	Date won
Heavyweight	Nikolay Valuev	Russia	8/08
Light heavyweight	Hugo Garay	Argentina	7/08
Middleweight	Felix Sturm	Germany	4/07
Welterweight	Yury Nuzhnenko	Ukraine	12/08
Lightweight	Yosuke Kobori	Japan	5/08
Featherweight	Chris John	Indonesia	9/03
Bantamweight	Anselmo Moreno	Panama	5/08
Flyweight	Takefumi Sakata	Japan	3/07
Minimum	Roman Gonzalez	Nicaragua	9/08

WORLD BOXING COUNCIL

Division	Champion	Country	Date won
Heavyweight	Vitaly Klitschko	Ukraine	10/08
Light heavyweight	Adrian Diaconu	Romania	4/08
Middleweight	Kelly Pavlik	United States	9/07
Welterweight	Andre Berto	United States	6/08
Lightweight	Manny Pacquiao	Philippines	6/08
Featherweight	Oscar Larios	Mexico	5/08
Bantamweight	Hozumi Hasegawa	Japan	4/05
Flyweight	Daisuke Naito	Japan	7/07
Strawweight	Oleydong Sithsanerchai	Thailand	11/07

Brazil. On Sept. 2, 2008, President Luiz Inácio Lula da Silva jubilantly raised a small container with the first oil pumped from a huge new off-shore reserve. The ceremony came less than a year after Petrobras, the state-owned oil company, announced the discovery of the "Tupi field," a defining moment in Brazil's economic history. The field lies in the Santos Basin roughly 155 miles (250 kilometers) off Brazil's southern coast.

The Tupi field, the world's largest oil find in nearly a decade, will allow Brazil to satisfy its own oil needs and become a major petroleum-exporting nation. Petrobras plans to invest more than $40 billion over the next four years to retrieve the estimated 5 billion to 8 billion barrels of crude oil and natural gas in the Tupi field.

Expanding and diversifying economy. New investment related to the Tupi field helped stoke the growth of the Brazilian economy, which was expected to grow by 5 percent in 2008. Also contributing to Brazil's economic surge was the government-owned Companhia Vale do Rio Doce S.A.—known as VALE— the world's second largest mining company. Drawing on windfall profits from mineral exports, VALE mounted a $59-billion, four-year investment program to fund its global operations and finance future expansion. In August, the company placed a $1.6-billion order for the construction of 12 new large iron ore carriers with China's Rongshen Ship-Builders and Heavy Industries in Shanghai. Upon their completion, the vessels will carry iron ore (VALE is the world's largest producer) to markets in Asia for steel production.

Shrinking gap between rich and poor. During 2008, a series of heartening statistical studies documented a shrinking gap between Brazil's rich and poor. An April survey found that more than half of Brazil's 190 million people belonged to families considered middle class. The finding marked the first time that Brazil had more middle-class people than poor people. Also in 2008, the World Bank, a United Nations affiliate, announced that the income of Brazil's top 10 percent had increased by just 7 percent, while that of the bottom 10 percent shot up by 58 percent from 2001 to 2006.

Social programs. During that same period, the Brazilian government invested an estimated $15.6 billion in social programs. More than half of this spending was targeted at Brazil's north-east, a long-impoverished area (and birthplace of the nation's current president).

To spur employment, the Bank of the North-east, a government-financed agency, provided more than 330,000 people with small amounts of credit to start or expand small businesses. These loans played a vital role in improving the quality of life, especially in poor neighborhoods of the region's overcrowded coastal cities.

Deadly flooding. In November 2008, heavy rainfall led to landslides and flooding in the state of Santa Catarina, killing at least 109 people. Nearly 80,000 Brazilians were forced from their homes. Itajaí, Brazil's second largest seaport, was closed as a result of the flooding.

Amazon deforestation. The rate of defor-estation in the Amazon basin rose by 69 percent in the 12-month period ending August 2008, the first such increase in three years. In all, 3,088 square miles (8,000 square kilometers) of forest was felled to accommodate farmers and ranchers. The data came from satellite images taken by Brazil's National Institute for Space Research.

In June, Brazilian government agents seized 3,100 head of cattle grazing on an ecological reserve in the northern state of Para. "No more being soft," said Carlos Minc, environment minis-ter, by way of warning to other ranchers. An esti-mated 60,000 cattle were grazing illegally on similarly deforested land. The seized cattle were sold at auction two weeks later. The proceeds went to government food and health programs.

◾ Nathan A. Haverstock

See also **Latin America.**

British Columbia. See Canadian provinces.

Brunei. See Asia.

Building and construction. On

Sept. 18, 2008, the St. Anthony Falls Bridge opened in Minneapolis. The new 1,223-foot (373-meter) span was completed in just 339 days—three months ahead of schedule—using the design-build method in which construction begins before all design details are finalized. The short design and construction period was a significant feat, as similar bridge projects often take well over two years to complete. The white concrete bridge cost $234 million and was designed to last 100 years.

The new St. Anthony Falls Bridge opened with 10 traffic lanes and space for a light railway to accommodate future transportation needs. It underwent intense scrutiny and inspection by the Minnesota Department of Transportation. Com-ponents of the bridge's construction that would normally have taken hours for inspection were checked and rechecked over several days. The bridge included a number of monitoring systems embedded into its design, including vibrating wire strain gauges, chloride sensors, and accelerome-ters to measure stress and shock. The bridge replaced the Interstate-35W bridge that collapsed suddenly on Aug. 1, 2007, killing 13 people.

Retractable stadium roof. During 2008, the Dallas Cowboys organization of the National Football League (NFL) worked to complete their

The Utah State Capitol reopened in January 2008 after a four-year restoration and earthquake-resistant retrofitting. The neoclassical building was constructed between 1912 and 1916.

new stadium for the 2009 season. The Arlington, Texas, sports facility will have one of the largest retractable roofs in the world—410 feet by 256 feet (125 meters by 78 meters). The roof is supported by a pair of arched steel trusses whose sweeping curves form the shape of the stadium. The bases of the trusses extend beyond the stadium's walls in a shape often said to resemble an insect's legs. Rather than have a flat, almost-completely horizontal retracting roof as in similar projects, Cowboys Stadium's roof is curved in an elliptical shape, which is as steep as 23.8 degrees in some places. The parallel arches form the longest single-span roof structure in the world.

The massive retractable roof required a first-of-its-kind rack-and-pinion gear-drive system to move the roof panels at an acceptable rate. This system pulls the panels along tracks, clicking along instead of using a more traditional cable-and-drum design used in smaller retractable roof systems. Construction began in September 2005, and the total cost for the stadium is projected to be $1.3 billion. Cowboys Stadium will seat 80,000 people and has already been named the site of the NFL's 2011 championship, Superbowl XLV.

Record bridge spans the Yangtze. On May 25, 2008, the Sutong Bridge opened, connecting the cities of Suzhou and Nantong in China's Jiangsu Province. At 3,570 feet (1,088 meters), it is the world's longest cable-stayed bridge span. Including the approaches, the entire length of the bridge is 3.7 miles

(6 kilometers). Spanning the Yangtze River, the bridge also boasts the largest concrete piled foundations, the second tallest towers, and the world's longest single cable. Construction began in June 2003 and cost $1.7 billion to complete.

The Sutong Bridge had to contend with the strong currents and heavy traffic of the Yangtze River and the region's harsh climate. The concrete piles were sunk 394 feet (120 meters) into the sandy soils of the river for stability. Massive, wide piles were necessary as it was considered unfeasible to drill 984 feet (300 meters) into solid bedrock, which is the more traditional way of building bridge foundations. The bridge's two 984-foot (300-meter) tall, inverted-Y-shaped towers anchor the cables that support the bridge. The record-length 1,893-foot (577-meter) cable weighs 64 tons (58 metric tons) and is made up of 313 galvanized wires. The bridge has a high and wide navigational clearance, as almost 3,000 ships pass beneath it each day.

Beijing's looping towers. Construction continued in 2008 on the China Central Television (CCTV) Headquarters in Beijing's new business district. The building was described as a tilted union of two skyscrapers, leaning together to meet in a crumpled arch made of right angles. The CCTV Headquarters facade was completed in time to impress during the 2008 Summer Olympics, but interior construction will continue into 2009.

At its tallest, the building is 768 feet (234 meters) high and contains more than 5 million square feet (550,000 square meters) of space. The need to stack 32 large studios of varying size drove the need for an unusual solution and allowed the CCTV towers to have nearly as much floor area as the unfinished Burj Dubai in the United Arab Emirates, which when completed will be the tallest building in the world.

The wrenched architecture of the CCTV Headquarters connects two leaning towers of 46 and 51 stories above the 37th floor and below the 10th. The irregular grid on the building's facades is an expression of the forces traveling throughout its structure, which must be strong enough to withstand earthquakes. Yet the towers present the illusion of instability and appear to be under enormous strain. Begun in 2004, the headquarters' estimated cost is $750 million and will eventually house 10,000 people. The building has no conventional windows, and the distorted form obscures the number of floors from the exterior. Precise engineering was required to achieve this result, and designers used cutting-edge computer software to plan the structure. More than 600 monitoring stations were employed during construction to oversee the final placement of steel.

■ Jeffrey Rubenstone

See also **Architecture; China: A Special Report.**

Bulgaria. In July 2008, officials of the European Union (EU) froze nearly $600 million in aid slated for Bulgaria, which had joined the European association in January 2007. In November 2008, EU officials rescinded $300 million of the total promised aid.

The EU actions followed a series of scandals involving government officials in Bulgaria. In January, a Bulgarian official responsible for distributing EU funds for road building was indicted for demanding bribes; a court in Sofia, the capital, convicted him later in the year. In April, the country's interior minister resigned amid allegations of ties to organized crime.

In October, Prime Minister Sergei Stanishev's coalition government pushed through parliament a conflict of interest law. The EU-recommended legislation required political office holders to declare potential conflicts of interest. Officials of the EU, however, continued to demand broad reforms in Bulgaria's law enforcement agencies and its judiciary. ■ Sharon L. Wolchik

See also **Europe.**

Burkina Faso. See **Africa.**
Burma. See **Myanmar.**
Burundi. See **Africa.**
Business. See **Bank: A Special Report; Economics, United States; Economics, World; International trade; Labor.**

Cabinet, U.S. There were two changes in United States President George W. Bush's Cabinet in 2008. Late in the year, President-elect Barack Obama nominated members of his Cabinet.

New members. Alphonso Jackson, secretary of housing and urban development, resigned on April 18 amid allegations of ethical misconduct. Jackson was accused of retaliating against the Philadelphia Housing Authority by withholding federal funds after the city agency refused to turn over a $2-million vacant lot to a friend. In addition, the U.S. Justice Department had been investigating allegations that Jackson steered housing contracts in New Orleans and the Virgin Islands to friends. President Bush nominated Steve Preston, the administrator of the U.S. Small Business Administration, to replace Jackson. The Senate unanimously confirmed Preston on June 4.

The Senate on January 28 unanimously confirmed former North Dakota Governor Ed Schafer as secretary of agriculture. Schafer replaced Mike Johanns, who resigned on Sept. 20, 2007.

Obama's nominees. In late 2008, President-elect Obama announced that he would retain Defense Secretary Robert Gates as the sole holdover from the Bush Cabinet. Other Cabinet nominees included former Iowa Governor Tom Vilsack as secretary of agriculture; Arne Duncan, chief executive officer of Chicago Public Schools, as secre-

tary of education; Steven Chu, director of the Lawrence Berkeley National Laboratory and a Nobel Prize-winning physicist, as secretary of energy; former Senator Tom Daschle of South Dakota as secretary of health and human services; and Arizona Governor Janet Napolitano as secretary of homeland security. New Mexico Governor Bill Richardson was picked for secretary of commerce, but his nomination was withdrawn in early 2009.

Obama also nominated Shaun Donovan, head of the New York City Department of Housing Preservation and Development, as secretary of housing and urban development; Senator Ken Salazar of Colorado as secretary of the interior; former Deputy Attorney General Eric Holder as attorney general (the head of the Justice Department); Representative Hilda Solis of California as secretary of labor; Senator Hillary Rodham Clinton of New York, a former U.S. first lady and Obama's chief rival for the 2008 Democratic presidential nomination, as secretary of state; Representative Ray LaHood of Illinois, a Republican, as secretary of transportation; Timothy Geithner, president of the Federal Reserve Bank of New York, as secretary of the treasury; and retired Army General Eric Shinseki, a former Army chief of staff, as secretary of veterans affairs.　　　　■ Mike Lewis

See also **United States, Government of the; United States, President of the.**

Cambodia on July 27, 2008, held the most peaceful election in its recent history. The Cambodian People's Party (CPP) headed by Prime Minister Hun Sen won 90 out of 123 seats in the National Assembly. Although the election fell short of international democratic standards, observers noted that irregularities did not change the overall result. They said the long-ruling CPP benefited from recent stability and increasing prosperity.

A political party led by Sam Rainsy, Hun Sen's most vocal critic, won 26 assembly seats. Rainsy accused the government of omitting thousands of his potential supporters from voting lists. Two factions representing Cambodia's former royal rulers won only four seats.

The 2008 naming of Hindu temple Preah Vihear as a world heritage site by the United Nations Educational, Scientific and Cultural Organization (UNESCO) reignited a border dispute between Cambodia and neighboring Thailand. The temple, built in the 1000's when the Khmer empire in Cambodia ruled a wide area, belongs to Cambodia, but the land around the temple has been disputed for decades. Fighting erupted on the land in October 2008, but representatives of the two governments agreed to settle the matter peacefully.　　　　■ Henry S. Bradsher

See also **Asia; Thailand.**

Cameroon. See Africa.

At the request of Prime Minister Stephen Harper, Governor General Michaëlle Jean suspended Canada's Parliament on Dec. 4, 2008. The suspension blocked an attempt by opposition parties to bring down Harper's minority Conservative government. If Parliament had remained in session, Harper would have faced two important votes that he was expected to lose. One was a vote on his economic proposals, and the other was a motion of no confidence from the Liberals. A motion of no confidence would have forced him to resign or ask the governor general to call a new election. Instead, Parliament will return in January 2009 to vote on the economic plan. The challenge to Harper came during an economic slump and a sharp drop in world stock markets, and less than two months after his party had strengthened its position in federal elections.

In October 2008, Canadian voters had gone to the polls for the third time in four years. For the second time, Harper's party, the center-right Conservative Party of Canada, won the most seats in the House of Commons but fell short of a majority. The Conservatives had to form another minority government, Canada's third since 2004. Canadian voters had not chosen three straight minority governments since the 1960's.

Federal election. On Sept. 7, 2008, Prime Minister Harper asked Governor General Jean to dissolve Parliament and call a general election on October 14. Harper, who had governed as the leader of a minority government since January 2006, hoped to gain enough seats for a majority.

Stéphane Dion, the head of the center-left Liberal Party of Canada, faced his first election as the leader of the Official Opposition. The central planks of the Liberal platform were income-tax-

CANADA

cuts and a *carbon tax*, a tax on emissions of carbon dioxide and other gases that are contributing to global warming.

Three smaller opposition parties hoped to gain influence in the election. The left-wing New Democratic Party (NDP), led by Jack Layton, ran its best-funded national campaign ever. The NDP's goal was to replace the Liberals as the main opposition to the Conservatives. The separatist Bloc Québécois, headed by veteran campaigner Gilles Duceppe, put up candidates only in the province of Quebec. The Bloc aimed to keep control of the largest number of seats in Quebec, where the Conservative Party had gained in popularity. Finally, the Green Party of Canada, under Elizabeth May, hoped to elect the first ever Green member of Parliament (M.P.). The party had gained its first M.P. in August when Blair Wilson of British Columbia, a former Liberal and Independent, switched his allegiance to the Greens.

Prime Minister Harper called for the election even though he had supported an act of Parliament in 2006 setting elections every four years. Under the act, the next election would have been on Oct. 19, 2009. The prime minister explained that the minority status of his government hampered it from accomplishing essential work.

In the months before the 2008 election, the Liberals under Dion had repeatedly avoided forc-ing a new election. The Liberals abstained 43 times from parliamentary votes the prime minister had deemed to be *matters of confidence*—that is, legislation so essential that a defeat would require the government's resignation. Dion said that Canadians did not want another election so soon. Political analysts, however, suggested that he wanted to avoid going to the polls until the party's finances improved.

The campaign was marked by a series of verbal blunders by the governing Conservatives and by a deepening economic crisis. Conservative Agriculture Minister Gerry Ritz came under fire for remarks he made in early September to members of the Canadian Food Inspection Agency. Bacteria in sliced meat from a Toronto-area plant had caused an outbreak of listeriosis, a kind of food poisoning. Ritz joked that the crisis was hurting the government "like a death by a thousand cuts, or should I say cold cuts." When he learned that there had been a listeriosis death in Prince Edward Island he stated, "Please tell me it's Wayne Easter." Easter was a Liberal M.P. who served as the Opposition's official agriculture critic. Ritz apologized for his comments, and Harper rejected calls for Ritz's resignation.

In September, Liberal candidate Bob Rae revealed that sections from a 2003 speech given at the start of the Iraq War by Harper, then leader of the Canadian Alliance, were plagiarized from a speech given by Australian Prime Minister

Prime Minister Stephen Harper (center) and other members of Parliament applaud Phil Fontaine, national chief of the Assembly of First Nations, in June 2008. Fontaine accepted Harper's apology on behalf of the Canadian government to Canada's native peoples for wrongs done to them by the country's residential school system.

John Howard. A speechwriter for Harper resigned following the revelations.

The Conservatives viewed Quebec as an electoral battleground where they hoped to gain up to two dozen seats. But many voters in the province opposed Conservative plans to cut funding for art projects and artists whose work was deemed contrary to government policy. The Bloc Québécois also criticized a new Conservative policy that would toughen sentences for young offenders in the criminal justice system. Bloc leader Duceppe called for rehabilitation instead of jail time as a way to reduce crime.

A steep slide in world and Canadian stock markets also hurt the Conservatives' standing with the voters. Prime Minister Harper reassured voters that the fundamentals of the Canadian economy were strong. He accused Dion of panicking after the Liberal leader announced a 30-day action plan to bring business leaders and government officials together following the election to address the problems. Harper also suggested during an inter-

view that the decline in stock prices presented buying opportunities for Canadians. Opponents charged that the prime minister seemed uncaring about the many Canadians whose life savings and retirement accounts had shrunk in value.

As the economic crisis deepened, the Liberals gained in the polls and narrowed the gap with the Conservatives. A recorded television interview, however, hurt the Liberals. In the interview, a few days before the election, Dion fumbled a question about how he would have handled the economic situation if he had been prime minister. The television station had to restart the interview four times as the Liberal leader said he could not understand what was being asked. Prime Minister Harper seized on Dion's difficulty answering and accused him of having no plan. Dion has a partial hearing loss, and he did the interview in English, his second language. His staff blamed his difficulty on his hearing disability, his lack of fluency in the English language, and a question they called poorly worded. They noted he had

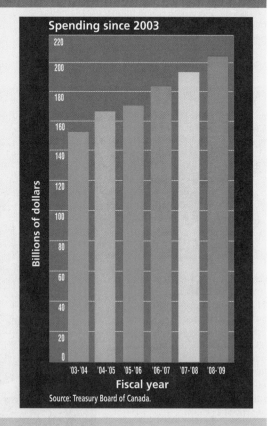

FEDERAL SPENDING IN CANADA
Estimated budget for fiscal 2008-2009*

Department or agency	Millions of dollars†
Agriculture and agri-food	3,154
Atlantic Canada opportunities agency	337
Canada revenue agency	3,737
Canadian heritage	3,422
Citizenship and immigration	1,433
Economic development agency of Canada for the regions of Quebec	287
Environment	1,608
Finance	80,099
Fisheries and oceans	1,682
Foreign affairs and international trade	5,350
Governor general	19
Health	4,732
Human resources and skills development	42,054
Indian affairs and northern development	6,511
Industry	4,200
Justice	1,381
National defence	18,304
Natural resources	2,698
Parliament	563
Privy Council	293
Public safety and emergency preparedness	7,270
Public works and government services	2,343
Transport	4,544
Treasury board	4,685
Veterans affairs	3,398
Western economic diversification	269
Total	**204,372**

*April 1, 2008, to March 31, 2009.
†Rounded in Canadian dollars; $1 = U.S. $0.83 as of Oct. 21, 2008.

Spending since 2003

Source: Treasury Board of Canada.

answered similar questions easily in previous interviews. The Liberals also criticized the TV station for releasing the footage after initially promising not to air it.

The election results gave the Conservatives 143 seats, a gain of 19 seats but 12 short of a majority. The Liberals won 77 seats, including a seat from Montreal won by Justin Trudeau, the oldest son of former Prime Minister Pierre Elliott Trudeau. The Bloc Québécois ran candidates only in Quebec, where it won 49 of the 75 seats. The NDP emerged with 37 seats. Independent candidates won 2 seats. The Green Party increased its share of the national vote from the previous election but won no seats. The Conservatives made gains in the Maritime Provinces (New Brunswick, Nova Scotia, and Prince Edward Island), Ontario, the Prairie Provinces (Alberta, Manitoba, and Saskatchewan), British Columbia, and Nunavut. The Liberals suffered heavy losses in Ontario, New Brunswick, Manitoba, and British Columbia but increased their holdings in Quebec and in Newfoundland and Labrador. The Liberal Party got its lowest share of the popular vote since the 1860's, slightly over 26 percent. The New Democrats won their first seat ever in Quebec during a general election and did exceptionally well in northern Ontario. Voter turnout hit a record low. Just 59.1 percent of eligible voters went to the polls.

On Dec. 10, 2008, Dion stepped down as Liberal leader after just over two years at the helm. The party chose Michael Ignatieff, a former university professor, as interim leader. The Liberals were expected to confirm Ignatieff as their new leader in May 2009.

New Cabinet. On Oct. 30, 2008, Prime Minister Harper formed a new Cabinet, enlarged to 38 members from the previous 32. Because of the economic crisis, he kept Cabinet veterans in positions dealing with the economy, including Minister of Finance James (Jim) Flaherty. The Cabinet included 13 ministers from Ontario, 10 from the Prairie Provinces, 5 each from Quebec and British Columbia, and 4 from Atlantic Canada. Eleven women held posts in the new government, including Leona Aglukkaq, a newly elected M.P. from Nunavut, who became minister of health.

Foreign affairs and political events. The federal election was a successful moment for Harper's Conservatives during a year in which they faced numerous challenges. Foreign Affairs Minister Maxime Bernier resigned on May 26 after less than a year in the post. Bernier's resignation followed a string of blunders. On April 13, he had spoken out against Asadullah Khalid, the governor of Kandahar, Afghanistan. Khalid had been accused of torture and corruption, and Bernier told reporters that Khalid would be gone within weeks. That public pronouncement put Afghan

2008 CANADIAN POPULATION ESTIMATES

PROVINCE AND TERRITORY POPULATIONS

Alberta	3,581,700
British Columbia	4,441,600
Manitoba	1,195,000
New Brunswick	750,500
Newfoundland and Labrador	502,800
Northwest Territories	42,900
Nova Scotia	933,200
Nunavut	31,800
Ontario	12,906,300
Prince Edward Island	139,200
Quebec	7,754,700
Saskatchewan	1,005,900
Yukon	30,800
Canada	33,316,400

CITY AND METROPOLITAN AREA POPULATIONS

	Metropolitan area	City
Toronto, Ont.	5,598,100	2,512,100
Montreal, Que.	3,721,700	1,635,900
Vancouver, B.C.	2,315,600	591,800
Calgary, Alta.	1,179,000	1,037,900
Ottawa-Gatineau	1,174,600	
Ottawa, Ont.		828,200
Gatineau, Que.		248,700
Edmonton, Alta.	1,111,600	758,900
Quebec, Que.	736,900	497,300
Hamilton, Ont.	722,600	510,500
Winnipeg, Man.	717,700	639,200
Kitchener, Ont.	472,700	210,800
London, Ont.	472,000	359,100
St. Catharines-Niagara	395,000	
St. Catharines, Ont.		133,200
Niagara Falls, Ont.		83,600
Halifax, N.S.	387,800	378,300
Oshawa, Ont.	352,500	142,600
Victoria, B.C.	340,800	79,700
Windsor, Ont.	330,800	219,500
Saskatoon, Sask.	246,200	204,600
Regina, Sask.	204,300	179,700
Barrie, Ont.	191,000	141,000
St. John's, Nfld. Lab.	184,600	101,200
Kelowna, B.C.	168,700	111,400
Sherbrooke, Que.	167,800	150,800
Abbotsford, B.C.	166,900	127,500
Greater Sudbury/Grand Sudbury, Ont.	163,000	158,900
Kingston, Ont.	154,400	118,400
Saguenay, Que.	152,000	142,300
Trois-Rivieres, Que.	145,200	127,900
Guelph, Ont.	131,200	118,700
Moncton, N.B.	129,800	65,500
Brantford, Ont.	127,400	91,800
Saint John, N.B.	126,700	67,400
Thunder Bay, Ont.	122,900	109,200
Petersborough, Ont.	119,000	76,300

Source: World Book estimates based on data from Statistics Canada.

MEMBERS OF THE CANADIAN HOUSE OF COMMONS

The House of Commons of the first session of the 40th Parliament convened on Nov. 18, 2008.
As of Dec. 10, 2008, the House of Commons consisted of the following members: 143 Conservative Party of Canada, 77 Liberal Party, 49 Bloc Québécois, 37 New Democratic Party, and 2 Independent. This table shows each legislator and party affiliation. An asterisk (*) denotes those who served in the 39th Parliament.

Alberta
Diane Ablonczy, C.P.C.*
Rona Ambrose, C.P.C.*
Rob Anders, C.P.C.*
Leon E. Benoit, C.P.C.*
Blaine Calkins, C.P.C.*
Rick Casson, C.P.C.*
Earl Dreeshen, C.P.C.
Linda Duncan, N.D.P.
Peter Goldring, C.P.C.*
Stephen Harper, C.P.C.*
Laurie Hawn, C.P.C.*
Brian Jean, C.P.C.*
Jason Kenney, C.P.C.*
Mike Lake, C.P.C.*
Ted Menzies, C.P.C.*
Rob Merrifield, C.P.C.*
Deepak Obhrai, C.P.C.*
LaVar Payne, C.P.C.
Jim Prentice, C.P.C.*
James Rajotte, C.P.C.*
Brent Rathgeber, C.P.C.
Blake Richards, C.P.C.
Lee Richardson, C.P.C.*
Devinder Shory, C.P.C.
Kevin Sorenson, C.P.C.*
Brian Storseth, C.P.C.*
Tim Uppal, C.P.C.
Chris Warkentin, C.P.C.*

British Columbia
Jim Abbott, C.P.C.*
Alex Atamanenko, N.D.P.*
Dawn Black, N.D.P.*
Dona Cadman, C.P.C.
Ron Cannan, C.P.C.*
Jean Crowder, N.D.P.*
Nathan Cullen, N.D.P.*
John Cummins, C.P.C.*
Don Davies, N.D.P.
Libby Davies, N.D.P.*
Stockwell Day, C.P.C.*
Sukh Dhaliwal, Lib.*
Ujjal Dosanjh, Lib.*
John Duncan, C.P.C.
Ed Fast, C.P.C.*
Hedy Fry, Lib.*
Nina Grewal, C.P.C.*
Richard Harris, C.P.C.*
Russ Hiebert, C.P.C.*
Jay Hill, C.P.C.*
Peter Julian, N.D.P.*
Randy Kamp, C.P.C.*
Gary Lunn, C.P.C.*
James Lunney, C.P.C.*
Keith Martin, Lib.*
Colin Mayes, C.P.C.*
Cathy McLeod, C.P.C.
James Moore, C.P.C.*
Joyce Murray, Lib.
Denise Savoie, N.D.P.*
Andrew Saxton, C.P.C.
Bill Siksay, N.D.P.*
Chuck Strahl, C.P.C.*
Mark Warawa, C.P.C.*
Alice Wong, C.P.C.

Manitoba
Niki Ashton, N.D.P.
James Bezan, C.P.C.*
Rod Bruinooge, C.P.C.*
Steven Fletcher, C.P.C.*
Shelly Glover, C.P.C.
Candice Hoeppner, C.P.C.
Jim Maloway, N.D.P.
Inky Mark, C.P.C.*
Pat Martin, N.D.P.*
Anita Neville, Lib.*
Joy Smith, C.P.C.*
Vic Toews, C.P.C.*
Mervin Tweed, C.P.C.*
Judy Wasylycia-Leis, N.D.P.*

New Brunswick
Mike Allen, C.P.C.*
Jean-Claude D'Amours, Lib.*
Keith Ashfield, C.P.C.
Yvon Godin, N.D.P.*
Dominic LeBlanc, Lib.*
Rob Moore, C.P.C.*
Brian Murphy, Lib.*
Tilly O'Neill-Gordon, C.P.C.
Greg Thompson, C.P.C.*
Rodney Weston, C.P.C.

Newfoundland and Labrador
Scott Andrews, Lib.
Gerry Byrne, Lib.*
Siobhan Coady, Lib.
Judy Foote, Lib.
Jack Harris, N.D.P.
Todd Russell, Lib.*
Scott Simms, Lib.*

Northwest Territories
Dennis Bevington, N.D.P.*

Nova Scotia
Scott Brison, Lib.*
Bill Casey, Ind.*
Rodger Cuzner, Lib.*
Mark Eyking, Lib.*
Gerald Keddy, C.P.C.*
Greg Kerr, C.P.C.
Megan Leslie, N.D.P.
Peter MacKay, C.P.C.*
Geoff Regan, Lib.*
Michael Savage, Lib.*
Peter Stoffer, N.D.P.*

Nunavut
Leona Aglukkaq, C.P.C.

Ontario
Harold Albrecht, C.P.C.*
Malcolm Allen, N.D.P.
Dean Allison, C.P.C.*
Charlie Angus, N.D.P.*
Navdeep Bains, Lib.*
John Baird, C.P.C.*
Mauril Bélanger, Lib.*
Carolyn Bennett, Lib.*
Maurizio Bevilacqua, Lib.*
Peter Braid, C.P.C.
Gord Brown, C.P.C.*
Lois Brown, C.P.C.
Patrick Brown, C.P.C.*
Paul Calandra, C.P.C.
John Cannis, Lib.*
Colin Carrie, C.P.C.*
Chris Charlton, N.D.P.*
Michael Chong, C.P.C.*
Olivia Chow, N.D.P.*
David Christopherson, N.D.P.*
Tony Clement, C.P.C.*
Joe Comartin, N.D.P.*
Bonnie Crombie, Lib.
Patricia Davidson, C.P.C.*
Bob Dechert, C.P.C.
Dean Del Mastro, C.P.C.*
Barry Devolin, C.P.C.*
Paul Dewar, N.D.P.*
Ruby Dhalla, Lib.*
Ken Dryden, Lib.*
Kirsty Duncan, Lib.
Rick Dykstra, C.P.C.*
Diane Finley, C.P.C.*
Jim Flaherty, C.P.C.*
Royal Galipeau, C.P.C.*
Cheryl Gallant, C.P.C.*
Gary Goodyear, C.P.C.*
Claude Gravelle, N.D.P.
Albina Guarnieri, Lib.*
Helena Guergis, C.P.C.*
Martha Hall Findlay, Lib.
Ed Holder, C.P.C.
Mark Holland, Lib.*
Carol Hughes, N.D.P.
Bruce Hyer, N.D.P.
Michael Ignatieff, Lib.*
Andrew Kania, Lib.
Jim Karygiannis, Lib.*
Gerard Kennedy, Lib.
Peter Kent, C.P.C.
Daryl Kramp, C.P.C.*
Guy Lauzon, C.P.C.*
Jack Layton, N.D.P.*
Derek Lee, Lib.*
Pierre Lemieux, C.P.C.*
Ben Lobb, C.P.C.
Dave Mackenzie, C.P.C.*
Gurbax Malhi, Lib.*
Wayne Marston, N.D.P.*
Tony Martin, N.D.P.*
Brian Masse, N.D.P.*
Irene Matthyssen, N.D.P.*
John McCallum, Lib.*
Phil McColeman, C.P.C.
David McGuinty, Lib.*
John McKay, Lib.*
Dan McTeague, Lib.*
Larry Miller, C.P.C.*
Peter Milliken, Lib.*
Maria Minna, Lib.*
Rob Nicholson, C.P.C.*
Rick Norlock, C.P.C.*
Gordon O'Connor, C.P.C.*
Bev Oda, C.P.C.*
Robert Oliphant, Lib.
Glen Pearson, Lib.*
Pierre Poilievre, C.P.C.*
Joe Preston, C.P.C.*
Rob Rae, Lib.
John Rafferty, N.D.P.
Lisa Raitt, C.P.C.
Yasmin Ratansi, Lib.*
Scott Reid, C.P.C.*
Greg Rickford, C.P.C.
Anthony Rota, Lib.*
Gary Schellenberger, C.P.C.*
Judy Sgro, Lib.*
Bev Shipley, C.P.C.*
Mario Silva, Lib.*
Bruce Stanton, C.P.C.
David Sweet, C.P.C.*
Paul Szabo, Lib.*
David Tilson, C.P.C.*
Alan Tonks, Lib.*
Dave Van Kesteren, C.P.C.*
Peter Van Loan, C.P.C.*
Joseph Volpe, Lib.*
Mike Wallace, C.P.C.*
Jeff Watson, C.P.C.*
Bryon Wilfert, Lib.*
Stephen Woodworth, C.P.C.
Borys Wrzesnewskyi, Lib.*
Terence Young, C.P.C.

Prince Edward Island
Wayne Easter, Lib.*
Lawrence MacAulay, Lib.*
Shawn Murphy, Lib.*
Gail Shea, C.P.C.

Quebec
Arthur André, Ind.*
Guy André, B.Q.*
Gérard Asselin, B.Q.*
Claude Bachand, B.Q.*
Josée Beaudin, B.Q.
André Bellavance, B.Q.*
Maxime Bernier, C.P.C.*
Bernard Bigras, B.Q.*
Jean-Pierre Blackburn, C.P.C.*
Raynald Blais, B.Q.*
Steven Blaney, C.P.C.*
France Bonsant, B.Q.*
Robert Bouchard, B.Q.*
Sylvie Boucher, C.P.C.*
Diane Bourgeois, B.Q.*
Paule Brunelle, B.Q.*
Lawrence Cannon, C.P.C.*
Serge Cardin, B.Q.*
Robert Carrier, B.Q.*
Denis Coderre, Lib.*
Irwin Cotler, Lib.*
Paul Crête, B.Q.*
Claude DeBellefeuille, B.Q.*
Nicole Demers, B.Q.*
Johanne Deschamps, B.Q.*
Luc Desnoyers, B.Q.
Stéphane Dion, Lib.*

THE MINISTRY OF CANADA*

Jean Dorion, B.Q.
Gilles Duceppe, B.Q.*
Nicolas Dufour, B.Q.
Meili Faille, B.Q.*
Raymonde Folco, Lib.*
Carole Freeman, B.Q.*
Christiane Gagnon, B.Q.*
Marc Garneau, Lib.
Roger Gaudet, B.Q.*
Jacques Gourde, C.P.C.*
Monique Guay, B.Q.*
Claude Guimond, B.Q.
Michel Guimond, B.Q.*
Marlene Jennings, Lib.*
Jean-Yves Laforest, B.Q.*
Mario Laframboise, B.Q.*
Francine Lalonde, B.Q.*
Carole Lavallée, B.Q.*
Denis Lebel, C.P.C.*
Marc Lemay, B.Q.*
Yves Lessard, B.Q.*
Yvon Lévesque, B.Q.*
Luc Malo, B.Q.*
Réal Ménard, B.Q.*
Serge Ménard, B.Q.*
Maria Mourani, B.Q.*
Thomas Mulcair, N.D.P.*
Richard Nadeau, B.Q.*
Christian Ouellet, B.Q.*
Massimo Pacetti, Lib.*
Pascal-Pierre Paillé, B.Q.
Pierre Paquette, B.Q.*
Christian Paradis, C.P.C.*
Bernard Patry, Lib.*
Daniel Petit, C.P.C.*
Louis Plamondon, B.Q.*
Roger Pomerleau, B.Q.
Marcel Proulx, Lib.*
Pablo Rodriguez, Lib.*
Jean-Yves Roy, B.Q.*
Francis Scarpaleggia, Lib.*
Thierry St.-Cyr, B.Q.*
Ève-Mary Thai Thi Lac, B.Q.*
Justin Trudeau, Lib.
Josée Verner, C.P.C.*
Robert Vincent, B.Q.*
Lise Zarac, Lib.

Saskatchewan
David Anderson, C.P.C.*
Kelly Block, C.P.C.
Ray Broughen, C.P.C.
Garry Breitkreuz, C.P.C.*
Rob Clarke, C.P.C.
Ralph E. Goodale, Lib.*
Randy Hoback, C.P.C.
Ed Komarnicki, C.P.C.*
Tom Lukiwski, C.P.C.*
Gerry Ritz, C.P.C.*
Andrew Scheer, C.P.C.*
Bradley Trost, C.P.C.*
Maurice Vellacott, C.P.C.*
Lynne Yelich, C.P.C.*

Yukon
Larry Bagnell, Lib.*

Stephen Harper—prime minister
Marjory LeBreton—leader of the government in the Senate
Jay Hill—leader of the government in the House of Commons
James Flaherty—minister of finance
Josée Verner—president of the Queen's Privy Council for Canada, minister of intergovernmental affairs, and minister for La Francophonie
Lawrence Cannon—minister of foreign affairs
Stockwell Day—minister of international trade and minister for the Asia-Pacific Gateway
Chuck Strahl—minister of Indian affairs and Northern development and federal interlocutor for Métis and non-status Indians
Gerry Ritz—minister of agriculture and agri-food and minister for the Canadian Wheat Board
Gregory Thompson—minister of veterans affairs
Christian Paradis—minister of public works and government services
Peter MacKay—minister of national defence and minister for the Atlantic Gateway
Jason Kenney—minister of citizenship, immigration, and multiculturalism
Diane Finley—minister of human resources and skills development
Jean-Pierre Blackburn—minister of national revenue
Leona Aglukkaq—minister of health
Vic Toews—president of the Treasury Board
Gail Shea—minister of fisheries and oceans
John Baird—minister of transport, infrastructure, and communities
Douglas Nicholson—minister of justice and attorney general of Canada
James Moore—minister of Canadian heritage and official languages
Lisa Raitt—minister of natural resources
Jim Prentice—minister of the environment
Tony Clement—minister of industry
Peter Van Loan—minister of public safety
Beverley Oda—minister of international cooperation
Rona Ambrose—minister of labour

*As of Dec. 10, 2008

PREMIERS OF CANADIAN PROVINCES
Alberta ....Ed Stelmach
British Columbia ....Gordon Campbell
Manitoba ....Gary Doer
New Brunswick ....Shawn Graham
Newfoundland and Labrador ......Danny Williams
Nova Scotia ....Rodney MacDonald
Ontario ....Dalton McGuinty
Prince Edward Island ....Robert W. J. Ghiz
Quebec ....Jean Charest
Saskatchewan ....Brad Wall

GOVERNMENT LEADERS OF TERRITORIES
Northwest Territories ....Floyd Roland
Nunavut ....Eva Aariak
Yukon...Dennis Fentie

President Hamid Karzai in an awkward position. Karzai had come under criticism from Afghans for bowing to the pressure of foreign governments.

Bernier had previously come under fire for getting the name of the president of Haiti wrong, though Canadian troops had served as peacekeepers in Haiti for years. In May, Bernier promised that Canadian military planes would fly aid to cyclone victims in Myanmar. However, no planes were available, and the government was forced to rent an aircraft to fulfill the promise.

Hours after Bernier resigned, his former girlfriend Julie Couillard revealed that the minister had left secret North Atlantic Treaty Organization (NATO) documents at her home and asked her to put them in the garbage for him. In later interviews and in a book released during the election campaign, Couillard said that Bernier had offered to help her obtain a government position and that she suspected someone had installed listening devices in her home. Opponents called Bernier's relationship to Couillard a threat to national security. He admitted leaving the documents at her house but denied any other wrongdoing.

Canadian officials also found themselves at the center of a controversy in the U.S. presidential election. In February, Democratic presidential hopefuls Barack Obama and Hillary Clinton both promised to renegotiate the North American Free Trade Agreement (NAFTA), a treaty that eliminated most trade barriers among Mexico, the United States, and Canada. The candidates criticized NAFTA and charged that it cost thousands of Americans their jobs. But the prime minister's chief of staff, Ian Brodie, inadvertently revealed to reporters that Canadian officials had received reassurance from Clinton's campaign that she had no intention of renegotiating NAFTA. Clinton's campaign denied the story. A reporter cited an unnamed source, later identified as Canada's ambassador to the United States Michael Wilson, who reported similar assurances from Obama's campaign. Foreign affairs specialists suggested the leak could hurt Canadian-American relations. Prime Minister Harper vowed to investigate the leak and to take whatever action was warranted.

The Cadman affair. Harper was criticized for allegedly offering Independent M.P. Chuck Cadman a bribe to help defeat the Liberal minority government in 2005, when Harper was leader of the Opposition. Cadman cast a deciding vote in support of Prime Minister Paul Martin's Liberal government in a confidence motion in May 2005. Cadman said he supported the government because a majority of voters in his district opposed an early election. Cadman was receiving treatment for cancer and died less than two months later. Conservative strategists believed Cadman did not want Parliament to be dissolved because his

health benefits and salary would end during a difficult time for his family. Representatives of the Conservative Party reportedly offered Cadman a million-dollar life insurance policy in exchange for Cadman's vote against Martin's government.

Harper denied the charges, but Cadman's widow reported that her husband had told her about the offer of life insurance. The author of a book on Cadman recorded an interview with Harper in 2005 in which Harper seemed to confirm the offer to Cadman. Harper denied that his statements on the tape confirmed the life insurance offer, suggested that the tape had been altered, and sued the Liberal Party for libel. The libel trial began in September 2008. At the trial, an audio expert hired by the Conservative Party stated that key parts of the tape showed no signs of alteration.

The economy and budget. On February 26, Finance Minister Jim Flaherty unveiled the country's smallest budget in 11 years. It offered Canadians new tax shelters and some relief for the struggling manufacturing and automobile sectors. The manufacturing industry received $1 billion (all amounts in Canadian dollars) in temporary tax relief over three years, with $250 million in funding for the auto industry spread over five years. Other highlights included $500 million for public transit and a permanent $2-billion fund for infrastructure investment—that is, investment in such essential facilities as water supply systems and local roads. On December 20, Prime Minister Harper announced the federal government would provide the Canadian subsidiaries of Detroit's Big Three automakers with $3.29 billion in emergency loans.

Flaherty announced that the previous fiscal year's $10.2-billion surplus would go to pay down the national debt. Federal spending was projected to rise by only 3.4 percent in the 2008-2009 fiscal year, a steep decline from the 14.8-percent increase in spending in the two previous budgets.

In fall 2008, several major banks and other financial institutions in the United States suffered large losses. The U.S. stock market plunged, and individuals and businesses had difficulty obtaining loans. The financial crisis spread to international markets and did not spare Canada. By October 16, the country's main stock market, the Toronto Stock Exchange, had fallen in value by almost 40 percent from its record highs in 2007. Consumer confidence hit a 26-year low. Canada's exports declined sharply as international markets weakened. The Canadian dollar, which had risen in value above the U.S. dollar for the first time in almost 30 years in 2007, slumped to slightly over U.S. $0.80.

Prime Minister Harper had promised during the federal election campaign not to run budgetary deficits during his next term in office. As the economic crisis worsened, however, he suggested that a deficit might be necessary as a last resort.

Prime Minister Stephen Harper celebrates the victory of his Conservative Party of Canada in federal elections on October 14. The Conservatives won an increased number of seats in Parliament but fell short of a majority.

A national apology. On June 11, 2008, Prime Minister Harper issued a formal apology to Canada's native peoples for wrongs done to them by the country's residential school system. From the late 1800's to the late 1900's, residential schools removed about 150,000 First Nations (American Indian), Inuit, and Métis (mixed white and Indian) children from their families and communities. The schools forced the children to learn English or French and adopt European customs and religions as part of an "aggressive assimilation" policy. Emotional, physical, psychological, and sexual abuse of students often occurred at these schools. The government created a $2-billion compensation package for the approximately 86,000 surviving students of the residential schools.

Many First Nations leaders accepted the apology and called for a new era in race relations. Assembly of First Nations National Chief Phil Fontaine told members of Parliament and observers: "The attempts to erase our identities hurt us deeply. But it also hurt all Canadians and impoverished the character of this nation. We must not falter in our duty now. Emboldened by this spectacle of history, it is possible to end our racial nightmare together." ■ William Stos

See also **Canada, Prime Minister of; Canadian provinces; Canadian territories; Montreal; People in the news** (Leona Aglukkaq); **Toronto.**

Canada, Prime Minister of. Prime Minister Stephen Harper's governing Conservative Party of Canada won reelection with an increased number of seats in Canada's Parliament on Oct. 14, 2008. The campaign focused heavily on Harper's image as a strong leader. Public opinion polls consistently suggested that voters considered him the best choice for prime minister among the leaders of the major political parties. The election results indicated progress toward Harper's goal of supplanting the Liberal Party of Canada as the nation's dominant political party. The Liberals are sometimes called Canada's "natural governing party" because they have dominated federal politics since the late 1800's.

Harper's reputation as a strong leader was compromised, however, by a political crisis late in the year. Harper blocked an attempt by opposition parties to bring down his government by asking Governor General Michaëlle Jean to suspend Parliament on Dec. 4, 2008. He then faced weeks of serious attacks from political commentators, opposition leaders, and even members of his own party. Critics blasted him for allowing party politics to undermine national unity. *The Globe and Mail* and other newspapers that had endorsed Harper during the election called for his resignation in editorials. ■ William Stos

See also **Canada.**

Canadian provinces. Every province in Canada presented a balanced budget for the 2008-2009 fiscal year. Nevertheless, some governments warned about coming economic declines in the face of a global financial crisis.

Alberta, Canada's only debt-free province, prospered with revenues from oil and gas as the price of those fuels continued to rise around the world. On April 22, 2008, Alberta Minister of Finance and Enterprise Iris Evans presented the province's 15th consecutive balanced budget. The budget projected an estimated $1.6-billion surplus (all amounts in Canadian dollars). Budget highlights included the elimination of health care premiums on Jan. 1, 2009, saving $1 billion for the people and businesses of Alberta. The budget will also provide Albertans with $300 million in additional tax savings. The spending plan called for expenditures of $22.2 billion over three years for health facilities, schools, roads and other *infrastructure* (essential facilities and services). The budget also included $574 million for efforts to slow global warming over three years and $468 million over three years to fight crime.

The province's savings account, officially named the Heritage Savings Trust Fund but often called the "rainy day" fund, declined in value by about $1 billion in 2008 because of the economic downturn. Premier Ed Stelmach said, however, that Alberta was in a good position to weather the decline.

Stelmach's party, the right-wing Progressive Conservative Association of Alberta, won a crushing reelection victory on March 3. The Conservatives took 72 of the 83 seats in the Legislative Assembly. Stelmach formed the 11th consecutive Conservative government in the province, stretching back to 1971. All the opposition parties lost seats. The centrist Alberta Liberal Party dropped from 16 to 9 seats, and the center-left Alberta New Democratic Party went from 4 to 2 seats. Only 41 percent of eligible voters cast ballots, the lowest turnout in the province's history.

British Columbia. British Columbia's centrist Liberal Party government introduced North America's first comprehensive *carbon tax,* a tax on emissions of carbon dioxide and other gases that cause global warming. The tax on greenhouse-gas emissions, which took effect on July 1, 2008, started at $10 per metric ton (1.1 tons) and was to climb to $30 per metric ton over five years. The provincial government described the carbon tax as "revenue neutral." The government will return revenue from the carbon tax to British Columbians by reducing other taxes for individuals, families, and businesses, which will pay more for gasoline and home heating fuel but will pay less at tax time.

Finance Minister Carole Taylor announced the carbon tax as part of the provincial budget unveiled on February 19. The $37.7-billion budget boosted spending but also increased the provincial debt and forecast slow economic growth.

On October 22, Premier Gordon Campbell announced a 10-point economic plan to deal with the global financial crisis. Under the plan, the provincial government will accelerate income tax cuts and boost spending to respond to the economic slump. Campbell recalled the province's Legislative Assembly for a short session in November, and the Assembly approved his plan.

Two bomb blasts rocked oil and gas pipelines near Dawson Creek in the northeastern part of the province in October. Police suspected a link between the explosions and a letter sent to the *Dawson Creek Daily News* calling oil and gas companies "terrorists" that are "endangering our families." Terrorism experts said the blasts were probably planned by one or two individuals.

British Columbia Attorney General Wally Oppal announced in February that there might be no second trial for convicted serial killer Robert Pickton. Pickton, a hog farmer in the Vancouver suburb of Port Coquitlam, was charged with killing 26 women but was initially tried for only 6 of the murders. After an 11-month trial, a jury convicted him in December 2007 of six counts of second-degree murder, and a judge sentenced him to life in prison. Oppal said the second trial would not proceed if the six convictions were upheld at Pickton's appeal, expected to begin in March 2009.

Manitoba celebrated the first annual Louis Riel Day holiday on Feb. 18, 2008. Riel, a controversial figure in Canadian history, is a hero to many French Canadians and people of Indian ancestry. Riel led two uprisings against the Canadian government in the 1800's by people of mixed white and Indian ancestry called Métis. Some people consider Riel the founder of Manitoba, but others describe him as a traitor. He was found guilty of treason and hanged in 1885.

On April 9, 2008, Manitoba's center-left New Democratic Party government presented a $12.2-billion budget with a projected $96-million surplus. Finance Minister Greg Selinger withdrew $70 million from the province's Fiscal Stabilization Fund, a savings account also known as the "rainy day" fund. Most of the money went to enhance health care, especially to invest in the recruitment, training, and retention of more doctors and nurses. The government paid down the $11.1-billion provincial debt by $110 million. Increases in licensing fees, such as vehicle and fishing licenses, created additional revenues.

New Brunswick. Finance Minister Victor Boudreau of the governing center-left New

Brunswick Liberal Association delivered a balanced budget with a modest surplus of $19 million on March 18. The budget provided $113.3 million in increased health care spending, $63.5 million in new education spending, and funding to hire additional social workers. The province also announced a one-year tuition freeze for publicly funded universities.

On June 4, the New Brunswick government released a *discussion paper* that suggested establishing a carbon tax. A discussion paper is a government document that submits a proposal for discussion without any commitment to action. Public opinion polls showed that many New Brunswickers opposed a carbon tax, fearing that it would raise prices and eliminate jobs. In the federal election on October 14, Liberals lost three of the province's parliamentary seats to the Conservatives. Many political experts blamed the carbon-tax proposal for the Liberals' poor showing in the election.

Newfoundland and Labrador became so prosperous in 2008 that, for the first time in its history, the province failed to qualify for federal equalization payments. Canada's equalization program redistributes federal money to economically disadvantaged provinces so they can provide their residents with services comparable to those in wealthy provinces. On November 3, the federal government confirmed that Newfoundland and Labrador would stop receiving equalization payments in 2008, a year earlier than expected. Oil and gas revenues had revived the provincial economy after a decline in its fishing industry in the 1990's. On April 29, 2008, provincial Finance Minister Tom Marshall had unveiled a balanced budget with a $544-million surplus.

In the October 14 federal election, Newfoundland and Labrador became the only province in Canada without a Conservative member of Parliament. The federal Conservatives lost all three of the province's parliamentary seats. Premier Danny Williams of the Progressive Conservative Party led a successful campaign to defeat the candidates of the Conservative Party—the federal version of his own party—in the election. Williams accused the federal Conservatives of breaking a promise to exclude income from non-renewable energy sources when determining the province's eligibility for equalization payments.

Nova Scotia. Finance Minister Michael Baker presented a cautious budget on April 29, as Nova Scotia braced for an economic slowdown. The seventh consecutive balanced budget, with an estimated $158.5-million surplus, cut taxes by $105 million. Major expenditures included a program to give home-heating rebates to families earning less than $25,000 a year, the creation of 470 additional spaces at the Nova Scotia Commu-

nity College, and 1,000 new long-term-care beds for hospitals. The budget also earmarked $18.6 million for better high-speed Internet connections in rural communities. The center-right Progressive Conservative Party of Nova Scotia headed a minority government, which must enlist the support of one or more other parties to gain a majority in the Legislative Assembly. The Conservatives passed the budget with the help of the centrist Nova Scotia Liberal Party.

On October 16, the province created five new nature reserves to protect old growth forests and wetlands. The reserves, totaling 1,468 acres (594 hectares), will be protected under the Special Places Protection Act of 1989.

Ontario. The economic downturn that began in late 2007 hit Ontario particularly hard. Ontario's economy, based on manufacturing and export-based industries, had lost thousands of jobs over the previous few years. In response, the provincial government proposed massive tax cuts and exemptions for the hardest hit sectors, including $750 million over four years in business tax relief. Finance Minister Dwight Duncan presented a budget on March 25 that stressed job creation and skills development. Key programs included a $1.5-billion, three-year job-training plan, including programs to retrain workers who have lost jobs. Duncan's budget also included $1 billion in new infrastructure expenditures, including new highways, bridges, and transit systems.

Although the finance minister projected a budget surplus in March, the global economic crisis later led the provincial government to change its predictions. On October 22, the government released its fall economic statement and said it would run a $500-million deficit in 2008. Premier Dalton McGuinty of the Ontario Liberal Party said the government would delay expenditures for new projects and slow spending on existing programs.

In 2005, McGuinty had launched a "campaign for fairness," urging the federal government to give Ontario some of the money distributed to needy provinces through the federal equalization program. On Nov. 3, 2008, the federal government announced that Ontario would qualify for equalization payments in 2009 for the first time in its history. The province will receive an estimated $347 million in payments.

On June 16, 2008, the Ontario Legislative Assembly passed a law banning smoking in vehicles when children under the age of 16 are present. The act, which would levy fines of about $200, will take effect on Jan. 21, 2009. The new law continued the government's campaign to curb tobacco use, which also includes a smoking ban in all businesses and government offices throughout the province.

Prince Edward Island. The island's center-left Liberal government, elected in June 2007, presented its first budget on April 23, 2008. The government focused on new spending for public health care. The budget called for modernizing provincial hospitals and replacing five government-owned residential institutions for the care of the elderly. Health organizations praised the budget's promise of $275,000 for programs to assist people dying of an incurable illness who wish to die at home. The budget also provided an additional $2 million in funding to improve cancer prevention and treatment.

On October 17, Premier Robert Ghiz of the Prince Edward Island Liberal Association announced a $1-billion plan to develop wind power to reduce the province's need to import power. The project would produce 500 megawatts of wind power by 2013.

Quebec. On Nov. 5, 2008, Premier Jean Charest asked Quebec's Lieutenant Governor Pierre Duchesne to dissolve the provincial legislature, the National Assembly of Quebec, and call for a provincial election. Charest, who headed a Liberal Party minority government, said he hoped voters would give him a "clear mandate" and a majority. In the election on December 8, Charest's Liberals won a slim majority, taking 66 of the 125 seats in the Assembly. The Parti Québécois, which is committed to the independence of Quebec, won 51 seats. The nationalistic Action Démocratique du Québec (ADQ) dropped from 32 seats to 7, and a left-wing party called Québec Solidaire took 1 seat. After the ADQ loss, Mario Dumont resigned as head of the party.

On March 13, Quebec's government had presented a $62.9-billion "balanced" budget designed to stimulate the economy. Although the budget was technically balanced, Finance Minister Monique Jérôme-Forget withdrew money from the province's "rainy day" fund to offset a projected deficit. Quebec law requires the provincial government to post only balanced budgets. The province predicted 1.5-percent economic growth for 2008. Key budget measures included investment tax credits for the purchase of manufacturing and processing equipment and the elimination of certain taxes for manufacturing companies. The budget also called for the creation of 20,000 new subsidized day-care spaces over five years.

Quebec celebrated the 400th anniversary of its founding in 2008. The celebration included an "architectural megaprojection" show created by theatrical director Robert Lepage from June 20 to September 8. The multimedia show included a sound track and a video projected on the huge grain elevators in the Port of Québec. On August 22, Quebec singer Céline Dion gave a concert on the Plains of Abraham, the site of the British victory in 1759 that helped persuade the French to surrender their holdings in Canada.

The international community of French-speaking nations, known as the Francophonie, held its annual meeting in Quebec in October 2008. French President Nicolas Sarkozy came under fire from Quebec separatists for remarks during the meeting that seemed to suggest France favors a united Canada over an independent Quebec.

Saskatchewan. Finance Minister Rod Gantefoer, of the newly elected right-wing Saskatchewan Party, presented a balanced budget on March 19 that provided money for tax cuts and reduction of the province's debt. The budget called for a $1-billion capital investment for hospitals and other health facilities, schools, and roads and highways. The government increased school operating budgets by $34.6 million. The budget pledged $91.5 million to fund new agricultural risk-management programs to protect farmers against losses due to such causes as bad weather or a sharp drop in a crop's market price. The budget also earmarked funding for skills training and programs to attract skilled workers from other parts of Canada, particularly newly arrived immigrants.   ■ William Stos

See also **Canada; Canadian territories; Montreal; Toronto.**

Canadian territories. Canada moved in 2008 to reinforce its authority over its three northern territories and their coastal waters. On Aug. 26, 2008, Prime Minister Stephen Harper announced a large-scale Arctic mapping program to chart the energy and mineral resources of Canada's Far North. The program will employ ground researchers and aircraft equipped with state-of-the-art sensors to map geological features on and below Earth's surface. Geologists will use the resulting maps to determine where oil and other resources might be found.

Harper announced the mapping program at the start of a three-day visit to Canada's northern territories. In Tuktoyaktuk, Northwest Territories, on August 27, the prime minister announced two measures that would increase Canada's ability to control shipping in its Arctic waters. Under one measure, the government proposed legislation that would greatly expand the area of the Arctic Ocean that Canada considers its national territory for the purpose of preventing pollution. The Arctic Waters Pollution Prevention Act of 1970 forbids ships from dumping waste into Arctic waters within 100 nautical miles of the Canadian coastline. The new legislation would extend that limit to 200 nautical miles. (A nautical mile equals about 1.2 regular miles or 1.9 kilometers.)

The second measure announced by Harper

would require more foreign ships entering Arctic waters to register with the Canadian Coast Guard. Present regulations encourage, but do not require, incoming ships to register. The proposed changes would require all ships entering the 200-nautical-mile zone to do so.

The Canadian Forces conducted a series of military exercises in the Arctic to further reinforce Canada's claims over the area. The largest exercise was Operation Nanook 2008 in August, centered on Baffin Island in Nunavut. In that operation, Canadian Forces rehearsed for emergencies that may arise in the region. The simulated emergencies included an outbreak of disease on a cruise ship, a hostage-taking on a cruise ship, and a fuel spill and fire on a cargo ship. The exercises involved hundreds of military personnel, two warships, and surveillance planes.

Northwest Territories. Federal officials announced the creation of a new national park reserve on April 7. The government creates a national park reserve where land has been set aside for conservation purposes but not all aboriginal land claims have been resolved. The new reserve would be created under a land-claim agreement with the Dene Indians and the Métis, people of mixed Indian and European ancestry. It would create a protected area covering 2,930 square miles (7,600 square kilometers) called the Naats'ihch'oh (pronounced *NAT chee oh)* National Park Reserve. The reserve will lie next to the existing Nahanni National Park Reserve.

On May 22, Northwest Territories Minister of Finance J. Michael Miltenberger presented a balanced budget with a $13-million surplus for the 2008-2009 fiscal year (all amounts in Canadian dollars). Operating expenditures increased $64 million or 5.5 percent. The budget provided funds for five key aims: (1) promoting family well-being through such efforts as early childhood programs and health care; (2) reducing the cost of living in the Far North by subsidizing home construction and investigating ways to cut energy costs; (3) seeking to balance environmental conservation with resource development; (4) improving education and skills training; and (5) finding efficiencies in government operations. The budget invested $180 million in infrastructure projects—that is, services and facilities, such as bridges, roads, and water treatment plants.

Nunavut. During a visit to Iqaluit on Feb. 8, 2008, federal Environment Minister John Baird announced $242 million in funding over seven years for repairs to the territory's transportation facilities. Baird and Nunavut Premier Paul Okalik said the money would be used to repair airstrips and to build small harbors. Most communities in Nunavut are accessible only by air or sea.

Nunavut Finance Minister Louis Tapardjuk unveiled a balanced budget on February 20 with a $4.5-million surplus. Tapardjuk made history by presenting the budget entirely in the Inuktitut language. The government projected total expenditures for 2008-2009 at $1.162 billion. The budget focused on developing tourism programs; funding local building projects; increasing housing allowances for government staff; and cutting taxes for pensioners, students, full-time and part-time firefighters, and businesses.

On November 14, Eva Aariak became the territory's first woman premier. Aariak, a first-term member of the Legislative Assembly, replaced Premier Paul Okalik. Nunavut's Assembly elects the premier from among its own members.

Yukon. Yukon's territorial government unveiled a balanced budget on March 20, 2008, with a theme of improving the well-being of families and communities. Major budget items included $6.67 million to improve community health services; $5.59 million to replace the Whitehorse Correctional Centre; $1.25 million to upgrade municipal infrastructure, including water supply and waste disposal; $10 million for construction of a new hydroelectric power line; and $31 million for reconstruction of the Campbell Highway over three years. ■ William Stos

See also **Canada.**

Cape Verde. See Africa.

Census. The United States Census Bureau estimated that the country's Jan. 1, 2008, population was 303,146,284—a 0.9-percent increase from Jan. 1, 2007. The agency in 2008 projected that the U.S. population would reach 400 million in 2039.

Minorities. The country's minority population—including Hispanics, blacks, Asians, American Indians, Alaska Natives, Native Hawaiians, and other Pacific Islanders—reached 102.5 million on July 1, 2007, the bureau reported on May 1, 2008. This figure was 34 percent of the total population of 301.6 million. The country's 199.1 million non-Hispanic, single-race whites made up 66 percent.

Hispanics were the largest and fastest-growing minority group. From 2006 to 2007, the Hispanic population grew by 1.4 million, or 3.3 percent, to reach 45.5 million—more than 15 percent of the total population. Hispanics may be of any race.

Blacks were the largest racial minority. From 2006 to 2007, the black population increased by 540,000, or 1.3 percent, to reach 40.7 million. Asians were the fastest-growing racial minority. From 2006 to 2007, the Asian population rose by 434,000, or 2.9 percent, to reach 15.2 million.

Four states had minority populations of more than 50 percent in 2007: Hawaii (75 percent), New Mexico (58 percent), California (57 percent), and Texas (52 percent). The District of Columbia's minority population was 68 percent. The states with the smallest minority populations were Maine (5 percent), Vermont (5 percent), West Virginia (6 percent), and New Hampshire (7 percent).

On Aug. 14, 2008, the bureau projected that minority groups would together make up a majority of the U.S. population in 2042—eight years earlier than the bureau had previously predicted. Census officials indicated that the main reason for this change was a high birth rate among Hispanics.

Age. On May 1, 2008, the bureau reported that 37.9 million U.S. residents, or 13 percent of the population, were 65 or older on July 1, 2007. The number of working-age adults (18-64) was 189.8 million, or 63 percent, and the number of children was 73.9 million, or 24 percent. The states with the highest percentages of people 65 or older were Florida (17 percent), West Virginia (16 percent), and Pennsylvania (15 percent). The states with the lowest percentages were Alaska (7 percent), Utah (9 percent), and Georgia (10 percent).

On Aug. 14, 2008, the bureau projected that in 2030, nearly 20 percent of U.S. residents would be 65 or older. The number of people in this age group was projected to be 88.5 million in 2050, more than double the 2007 figure.

Income and poverty. A census report released on Aug. 26, 2008, revealed that real median household income in the United States grew by 1.3 percent from 2006 to 2007, reaching $50,233. The number of U.S. residents in poverty rose from 36.5 million (12.3 percent of the population) in 2006 to 37.3 million (12.5 percent) in 2007. The number of U.S. residents lacking health insurance declined from 47 million (15.8 percent of the population) in 2006 to 45.7 million (15.3 percent) in 2007.

Fastest-growing areas. In late 2007 and in 2008, the bureau announced which U.S. areas had the fastest population growth rates from July 1, 2006, to July 1, 2007. Nevada was the fastest-growing state, with a 2.9-percent increase, and Arizona was a close second (2.8 percent). The Palm Coast, Florida, metropolitan area grew by 7.2 percent, the fastest rate among metropolitan areas. Among counties with populations of 10,000 or more, the fastest-growing were St. Bernard and Orleans parishes in Louisiana (42.9 percent and 13.8 percent, respectively). These increases were mainly the result of people returning after being forced to leave by Hurricane Katrina in August 2005. Similarly, among cities with populations of 100,000 or more, New Orleans grew the fastest (13.8 percent). From July 1, 2005, to July 1, 2006, New Orleans had undergone a monumental 50.6-percent drop in population because of Katrina.   ■ Mike Lewis

See also City; Immigration; Population; State government.

Central African Republic. See Africa.
Chad. See Africa.

Chemistry. The development of a new kind of carbon fiber that is lighter in weight—but 30 times stronger—than Kevlar was announced in August 2008 by scientists at Los Alamos National Laboratory in New Mexico. Kevlar is a *synthetic* (artificial) fiber used as a substitute for steel in cables, tires, and other products. The new fiber had potential applications in both the textile and electronics industries.

Materials scientist Huisheng Peng, as part of a research team led by fellow scientist Quanxi Jia, accidentally created the carbon fiber while he was trying to produce nanotubes. Nanotubes are rolls of carbon atoms that are arrayed in a chicken-wire pattern. They are among the strongest and stiffest materials known. However, practical uses of nanotubes have been limited, partly because the longest tubes made have been only a few millimeters in length.

The fiber created by Peng consisted of long tubes of carbon atoms, which were referred to by the researchers as "colossal carbon tubes" (CCT's). The scientists reported that the CCT's appeared to be double rolls of nanotubes, bonded together with channels resembling those in corrugated cardboard. The researchers added that although CCT's are nearly as strong as nanotubes, CCT's are also flexible and much longer than nanotubes—on the order of centimeters.

The length of CCT's is roughly equivalent to the length of cotton fibers, suggesting that available textile technology and equipment could be used to make the fibers into various kinds of ultrastrong fabrics, such as light body armor. Furthermore, the researchers reported that CCT's are good conductors of electricity, indicating that the fibers could have uses in new kinds of high-strength microelectronics components.

Alligator blood. Alligators are known to be amazingly resistant to infection, despite often living in polluted waters, feeding on diseased prey, and engaging in battles that result in gaping wounds. The explanation for this hardy *immunity* (disease resistance), according to an April report by chemists in Louisiana, is the presence of highly active *peptides* (protein fragments) in the blood of alligators.

Chemist Lancia N. F. Darville of Louisiana State University in Baton Rouge and her colleagues discovered that at least four alligator blood peptides had deadly effects on a number of harmful bacteria and other disease-causing microbes. Working with blood from the American alligator, the scientists first extracted white blood cells and then separated out the proteins from the cells to create peptide test samples. In laboratory experiments, exposure to even tiny amounts of the peptides in these samples killed the herpes simplex virus, *Escherichia coli,* yeast microbes, and even human immunodeficiency virus and the "superbug" referred to as methicillin-resistant *Staphylococcus aureus* (MRSA).

Darville's team concluded that the peptides in alligator blood serve as the crucial first line of defense for these large reptiles. This peptide defense system is important to the alligators, because they otherwise have a slowly acting and primitive immune system.

Although the medical use of unprocessed alligator peptides would sicken or even kill a human being, the scientists said that they hoped continued research with the peptides would lead to the development of new drugs targeting dangerous microbes. Foremost among these microbes would be those, such as MRSA, that are resistant to the effects of traditional antibiotics.

CSI barbershop. Your hair is like a travel diary, recording each of the places you have visited in a way that is almost indestructible. James R. Ehleringer, an environmental chemist at the University of Utah in Salt Lake City, reported in February that natural regional variations in water atoms are incorporated into hair as it grows, providing evidence that could be used to help narrow down the geographic origins of victims of crime or natural disasters. The same kind of data might also be used to challenge the alibis of murder suspects.

Atoms of a chemical element can exist in different versions called *isotopes,* which vary in their number of *neutrons* (electrically neutral particles) and, thus, in their weight. The particular isotopes of oxygen atoms and hydrogen atoms that make up water vary from region to region. For example, tap water in Texas typically has higher percentages of heavier isotopes than does tap water in Montana. After a person consumes water, the isotopes become locked into the hair's *keratin,* the tough and chemically stable protein that is the main component of hair.

Ehleringer and his colleagues examined random hair samples from people in 65 cities across the United States and correlated these data with records of the particular isotopes found in the water in these regions. They determined that tap water accounted for 35 percent of oxygen and 27 percent of hydrogen in the hair's keratin. From these results, the researchers were able to construct maps showing the types of isotopes found in the hair of people in different regions.

The scientists explained that by analyzing the water-derived chemical constituents at different points along the length of a hair—and then by combining this information with the length of time it took for the hair to grow—dates could be matched with places visited by an individual. Such forensic evidence would be a new tool for crime scene investigators.   ■ Peter Andrews

Chess. In October 2008, world chess champion Viswanathan Anand of India successfully defended his title against former world champion Vladimir Kramnik of Russia. The competition took place in Bonn, Germany. In September, 24-year-old Alexandra Kosteniuk of Russia became the women's world chess champion by defeating 14-year-old Chinese chess prodigy Hou Yifan in Nalchik, Russia.

In November, teams from 152 nations competed in the 38th biennial Chess Olympiad in Dresden, Germany. In the open division, Armenia captured the gold medal; Israel, the silver; and the United States, the bronze. In the women's division, Georgia won the gold medal; Ukraine, the silver; and the United States, the bronze.

United States tournaments. Yury Shulman won the U.S. Chess Championship and Anna Zatonskih won the U.S. Women's Chess Championship in 2008. Both events took place in Tulsa, Oklahoma, in May. In August, Enrico Sevillano won first place in the U.S. Open Chess Championship in Dallas.

Young American champions. Samuel Shankland and Darwin Yang won bronze medals in the under-18 and under-12 age divisions, respectively, at the World Youth Chess Championships in Vung Tau, Vietnam, in October. In June, 17-year-old Tyler Hughes won the U.S. Junior Closed Championship and 14-year-old Conrad Holt won the U.S. Cadet Championship. Both tournaments were held in Lindsborg, Kansas.

More than 4,000 students competed in national scholastic chess tournaments sponsored by the U.S. Chess Federation in 2008. At the National High School Championship held in Atlanta in April, Catalina Foothills High School of Tucson, Arizona, won in the team category. Odle Middle School of Bellevue, Washington, won the team title in the National Junior High Championship, held in April near Dallas. Intermediate School 318 in Brooklyn, New York, was the top team at the National Bert Lerner Elementary Championship, held in Pittsburgh in May.

Chess in space. Greg Chamitoff, an American flight engineer aboard the International Space Station, played a number of chess games with mission control centers around the world in 2008. He played one game against the American public, led by students at Stevenson Elementary School in Bellevue, Washington. The public voted on possible moves proposed by the students.

Chess champion Bobby Fischer died on January 17 in Reykjavik, Iceland. He was 64 years old. Fischer had riveted world attention on the island nation in 1972, when, as an American during the Cold War era, he beat defending world chess champion Boris Spassky of the Soviet Union in a match in Reykjavik.   ■ Al Lawrence

Chicago resident Barack Obama, who represented Illinois in the U.S. Senate, was elected president of the United States on Nov. 4, 2008. The event was celebrated with an enormous election night rally in the city's lakefront Grant Park. The president-elect chose two Chicagoans for his staff. Representative Rahm Emanuel was appointed chief of staff, and Arne Duncan, chief executive officer of the Chicago Public Schools, was nominated for secretary of education, a Cabinet post.

Trumped. Construction crews completed pouring concrete for the 92nd floor of the Trump International Hotel and Tower Chicago in August, officially "topping out" the structure at 1,170 feet (357 meters). The planned addition of a nearly 200-foot (61-meter) spire will make the building the city's second tallest. The Skidmore, Owings, and Merrill-designed tower, which contains a hotel and luxury condos, rises on the north side of the Chicago River.

Schools. On September 2 and 3, hundreds of Chicago Public School (CPS) students did not attend classes in support of a boycott led by the Reverend James Meeks. The boycott, which took place on the first two days of the 2008-2009 school year, was intended to attract attention to funding disparities between schools in Chicago and those in wealthier suburbs. Despite the boycott, CPS officials reported that nearly 94 percent of students attended classes on the first day, a record.

Sports. For the first time since 1906, both of Chicago's professional baseball teams reached the postseason. The White Sox won a one-game play-off with the Minnesota Twins to take the American League Central Division crown on Sept. 30, 2008. They lost to the Tampa Bay Rays in the first round of the play-offs. The Chicago Cubs, winners of the National League Central Division, were swept in three games by the Los Angeles Dodgers.

In June 2008, the International Olympic Committee (IOC) named Chicago one of four "Candidate Cities" to host the 2016 Olympic Games. Others included Madrid, Spain; Rio de Janeiro, Brazil; and Tokyo, Japan. Chicago had won a competition to become the U.S. applicant city in April 2007. The IOC planned to choose

the 2016 host city by October 2009.

Transportation. On Sept. 5, 2008, an appellate court ordered the city to cease the demolition of about 600 structures blocking part of a $15-billion expansion of O'Hare International Airport. The ruling stopped bulldozers in the adjacent village of Bensenville while the village appealed an earlier ruling allowing the demolition to continue.

On October 1, the Chicago City Council voted unanimously to lease Midway International Airport to a private group. The city will receive about $1 billion from the $2.5-billion deal. The remainder will go to pay off the airport's debt. The Federal Aviation Administration needs to approve the deal before it can be completed.

On January 17, the Illinois General Assembly approved a plan to give free Regional Transportation Authority rides to seniors as part of a $530-million tax increase package. The package, which headed off service cuts and fare increases for Chicago-area transit, included increases in the real estate transfer tax and in the sales tax in the Chicago area. The 0.25-percent sales tax increase

gave Chicago, at 10.25 percent, the highest sales tax rate in the United States.

Music. On May 5, Chicago Symphony Orchestra officials announced the signing of Italian conductor Riccardo Muti, 66, to a five-year contract as music director beginning in September 2010.

Political landscape. On June 4, 2008, Chicago political fund-raiser Antoin "Tony" Rezko was found guilty on 16 charges at Chicago's Federal Courthouse. Rezko was convicted of soliciting pay-offs from businesses seeking state contracts in exchange for providing access to political connections.

Milestone. Beloved Chicago author, radio host, and activist Louis "Studs" Terkel died on Oct. 31, 2008. He was 96. ■ Ken Shenkman

See also **City; Elections: A Special Report; People in the news** (Riccardo Muti; Michelle Obama).

Children's books. See **Literature for children.**

Chile. In 2008, President Michelle Bachelet Jeria, Chile's first woman leader, found herself embroiled in social issues and a growing debate over moral values. In April, Chile's Constitutional Court halted a program she had instituted to provide free morning-after contraceptive pills to women and to girls as young as 14. The program was meant to curb teen pregnancy in a country where abortion is outlawed and few schools teach sex education. Chile is one of Latin America's most sexually conservative countries.

The court's decision was popular with conservative Chileans who believed the free pills encouraged sexual activity. Conservatives also blamed teen promiscuity on Fotolog, a popular photo-sharing Web site, where parties were advertised that drew as many as 4,500 teenagers. In 2008, 60 percent of Fotolog's nearly 5 million accounts in Chile were in the name of children aged 12 to 17.

Economic stimulus. Using a portion of Chile's $28 billion reserves, President Bachelet announced a $1.15-billion economic stimulus package in early November to help offset the downturn in the economy tied to the downturn in the world economy. The stimulus was meant to expand credit for small and midsize businesses and help bolster home sales. This came after an $850 million package passed in October had proved insufficient.

Increased spending for education. President Bachelet increased Chile's budget for education in 2008, drawing on profits from the nation's copper exports. In May, she unveiled a $6-billion Bicentennial Fund for Human Capital to provide scholarships for 30,000 young Chileans to attend universities abroad over the next decade. The program includes incentives for those who return to work in government, the academic community, and "priority sectors of the knowledge economy."

Salmon sickness. In August, the Chilean government introduced measures to clean up its large salmon industry. During 2008, millions of farm fish died from infectious salmon anemia, a virus encouraged by overcrowded and unsanitary salmon pens. Chile exports more salmon to the United States than any other country but Japan.

Volcanic eruption. In May, more than 4,000 people fled the fishing village of Chaiten after a volcano 800 miles (1290 kilometers) south of Santiago, the capital of Chile, erupted. A thick column of hot gases, smoke, and ash rose 12 miles (19 kilometers) into the atmosphere. Authorities moved quickly to assist the residents of the village, which was largely destroyed two weeks later by the overflow of a river swollen by volcanic matter. Villagers willing to permanently relocate were given about $25,000 per family to buy new homes. ■ Nathan A. Haverstock

See also **Latin America.**

China suffered a major earthquake, winter weather problems, economic setbacks, and regional turmoil in 2008 while winning world applause for staging the Summer Olympic Games.

Earthquake. On the afternoon of May 12, a magnitude-7.9 earthquake hit mountainous parts of western Sichuan Province, killing nearly 70,000 people and leaving another 18,000 people missing. An estimated 5 million others became homeless.

In an unprecedented move, Premier Wen Jiabao and other officials rushed to the scene and appealed for international aid for a country that has a history of covering up natural disasters. The rugged terrain made relief difficult, but officials were widely praised for their efforts. Reconstruction costs were estimated at nearly $150 billion, including the rebuilding of some 3,400 primary schools and the strengthening of 2,600 others.

An estimated 10,000 children died in schools destroyed in the quake. Many buildings near the fallen schools had withstood the earthquake shock, and parents angrily accused the government of having built shoddy schools. In September, a government committee acknowledged that many schools had been quickly and poorly built.

Winter chaos. The worst snow and ice storms in 50 years disrupted central and southern China in January and February. An estimated 800,000 people were stuck for days in the main train station in the southern city of Guangzhou while trying to get home for the Lunar New Year holidays. Electric power and water service failed over wide areas.

Economy. In April, the World Bank, a United Nations affiliate, announced that China's economy had become the world's second-largest in terms of purchasing power. It ranked behind only the United States.

Three decades of rapid industrial expansion and overall economic growth had propelled China into this position. In the first quarter of 2008, China's economy grew at 10.4 percent. By the third quarter, growth had slowed to 9 percent, partially due to world economic troubles and a resulting drop in demand for Chinese exports. The Shanghai stock exchange composite index fell 67 percent by October. Economists feared growth might stay below the 8-percent level needed to absorb young adults entering the labor market.

On November 9, officials announced plans to spend $586 billion by 2010 on infrastructure and social welfare projects to stimulate the economy. The plans were made amid signs that fourth-quarter growth could drop below 6 percent.

Land reform. On Oct. 12, 2008, Chinese Communist Party (CCP) officials approved plans to allow China's estimated 800 million peasant farmers to trade land use rights more freely. The plan would also provide greater legal protection for landholders. Since the Communists came to power in 1949, land had been owned by the state or rural collectives, but in recent decades most farmers were given 30-year land use contracts. Their rights were weak, however, and officials sometimes confiscated land for personal profit. Half or more of the officially reported 90,000 public protests in 2006 were over land grabs.

While stopping short of privatization of land, the 2008 plan was intended to foster rural growth. Economic reforms adopted in 1978 had led to rapid growth in cities, draining the countryside of population and leaving those remaining little better off. The plan set a goal of doubling by 2020 the annual disposable income of rural residents from the 2008 level of about $720.

Tibet. Resentment over CCP control of Tibet and suppression of its Buddhist culture, combined with hostility toward ethnic Chinese settlers dominating Tibetan towns, exploded in 2008.

Trouble began with a March 10 protest in Lhasa, the provincial capital, for the release of Buddhist monks detained on the anniversary of a Tibetan uprising against China. Demonstrations grew over several days. On March 14, protesters began throwing rocks at police officers, who fled. The crowds turned on Chinese migrants and began burning cars and looting stores. Police officers returned to quell the violence. The Chinese media later reported that 18 civilians and a police officer had been killed in fighting in Lhasa; 55 Tibetans were subsequently sent to prison for terms of from three years to life.

Buddhist monks and others in adjacent Tibetan ethnic areas also demonstrated against Chinese control. China's government claimed that 19 people had died in the violence; Tibetan exiles said that at least 200 Tibetans were killed by government troops in Lhasa and elsewhere.

Premier Wen blamed the violence on the Dalai Lama, the Tibetan Buddhist leader who had fled into exile in India in 1959. Periodic talks between representatives of the Dalai Lama and Chinese officials continued after the protests. The Dalai Lama said in October 2008 that he was losing hope of convincing China to allow more autonomy for Tibet. In November, the Dalai Lama met with other exiled Tibetan leaders in Dharamsala, India, to evaluate their policy toward China. Some younger exiled Tibetans argued for a less peaceful approach toward China.

Xinjiang Province in western China was also troubled in 2008. Its historic inhabitants, Uygurs of Central Asian Islamic background, had long been restive under Chinese rule. China typically blamed resistance to its control in the region on international terrorist organizations.

Chinese police cracked down on a March 23 protest that they blamed on separatists. In July, police shot five Uygurs who allegedly sought to wage holy war against China. In August, two Uygurs attacked Chinese troops in Kashgar, killing 16 officers. Following other attacks, Chinese authorities clamped tight controls on the region's Muslim people. Government officials, teachers, and students were forbidden to observe Ramadan, the Islamic holy month of daytime fasting.

Olympics. China provided spectacular settings and ceremonies for the Summer Olympic Games in the capital, Beijing, in August 2008 and was widely praised for its host role. China spent an estimated $43 billion to construct sporting venues, prepare the city's infrastructure, and clean up the environment. Normally polluted Beijing was fairly clean as many factories were closed, construction was halted, and traffic was restricted.

China failed, however, to honor some promises to the International Olympic Committee, including allowing the games to be held in a more open way than its normally tight police-state allowed. Strict efforts were made to avoid antigovernment protests. Authorities worried about foreign demonstrators attempting to disrupt the Games because of China's support for nations accused of human rights violations, such as Sudan. Three remote Beijing parks were designated for protests during the games, but permission was required to hold a protest. All 77 known requests were denied, and some applicants were detained. Chinese citizens who tried to enter Beijing to air long-standing complaints about local corruption and abuse were blocked. Journalists at the games were denied access to some Internet Web sites carrying material disliked by authorities. Internet access in China is typically subject to tight access restrictions.

Human rights. A report released by the United States Department of State on March 11, 2008, noted that China's "overall human rights record remained poor" but dropped China from a list of the world's worst offenders. Chinese officials remained nervous about signs of dissent at the Olympics and elsewhere. They strongly condemned a decision by the European Parliament on October 23 to award its most prestigious human rights prize to Chinese activist Hu Jia. Hu was serving a sentence of 3 ½ years in prison for his essays criticizing Communist Party policies on human rights and other issues.

Contaminated food killed at least four babies in China, sickened thousands of others, and caused widespread scares during 2008. After first suppressing reports, authorities confirmed in September that the industrial chemical melamine had been illegally added to baby formula and other dairy products to hide their low protein content. Melamine can cause kidney problems in infants.

The chemical had been detected in Chinese-made pet food that killed pets in the United States in 2007. Chinese officials promised to reform food safety regulations, but in October 2008, melamine was found in animal feed and eggs as well as milk products. As evidence emerged of a widespread cover-up, some senior government officials and company officers were dismissed. Premier Wen acknowledged that "the government ... has a responsibility" in the matter and announced plans for China's first major food safety law.

Corruption. China's top auditor reported in August that $660 million had been "misused or embezzled" and another $6 billion mismanaged in 2007. In 2008, the head of a Chinese university's anticorruption research institute estimated that some 10,000 corrupt officials had fled the country with up to $100 billion in public funds in the past decade. High profile officials from several Chinese cities were found guilty of accepting bribes in 2008. In October, a Shanghai official and an official from the province of Zhejiang disappeared in Paris. Experts suspected the two men of defecting in the face of possible corruption charges.

Space. China sent its third manned spacecraft since 2003 into orbit in 2008. On September 27, one of the crew took the nation's first spacewalk.

■ Henry S. Bradsher

See also **Asia; China: A Special Report; Disasters; Food; Olympic Games: A Special Report; Space exploration; Weather.**

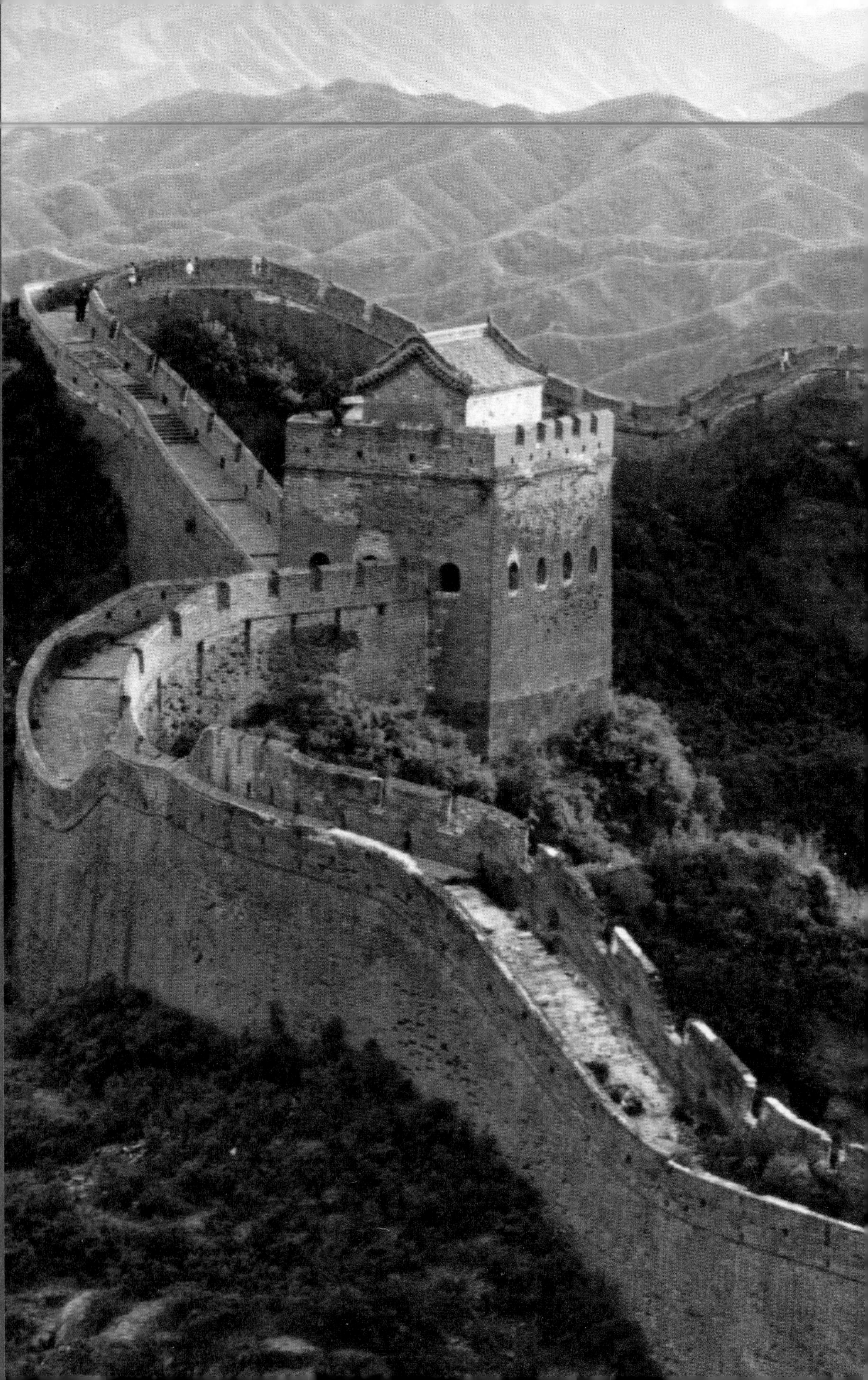

CHINA'S
GLOBAL AWAKENING

After years of struggle and dramatic economic growth, China in 2008 climbed to a new international prominence.

By Steve Tsang

The 2008 Olympic Games in Beijing dazzled the world in more ways than just China's haul of gold medals. The breathtaking new infrastructure, the numbers of highly disciplined people deployed to support the occasion, and the awe-inspiring opening ceremony—all left a strong impression on international observers. China's People's Liberation Army even managed to prevent rain over the stadium during the ceremony: Soldiers fired more than 1,000 rockets carrying silver iodide crystals into the clouds, forcing them to drop the rain before it reached Beijing. Chinese leaders intended the Games to be the "coming-out party" of a China recovered from the

turbulent times of revolutionary leader Mao Zedong (1893-1976). For many people throughout the world, the Beijing Olympics marked the reemergence of China as a major world power.

China's power and influence are generally recognized by political and business leaders worldwide. The nation is not only known as the "workshop of the world" and the fourth-largest economy in terms of *gross domestic product,* but also as one of the five veto-holding permanent members of the United Nations (UN) Security Council. (The gross domestic product, or GDP, is the total value of all goods and services produced in a country in a given year.) By these measures, China, at the start of the 2000's, was not just a rising power but one that has already risen.

Yet, the Chinese government itself often appears not to recognize the nation's status. China generally avoids asserting itself and plays a reactive—rather than proactive—role in the Security Council. Chinese leaders refrain from taking the lead in such trouble spots as Darfur in Sudan, where China has large stakes in the oil sector, or in Myanmar (also known as Burma). As one of Myanmar's largest trading partners and most important supporters, China has more influence with that nation's leaders than any other member of the Security Council. Because of a perception of China as the next superpower, the leaders of other nations tend to magnify China's achievements and look to China for the future. This, in turn, is beneficial to the country's development, as it encourages foreign investment in China and enables Chinese businesses to build their international networks and import advanced technologies and management skills.

The author:
Steve Tsang is a Fellow and Reader in Politics at St. Antony's College, Oxford University, in the United Kingdom.

Yet, despite all of China's achievements, the country's government operates on the belief that China is still in the process of rising. In fact, in 2003, Chinese leaders publicly committed the nation to a policy of "peaceful rise," in which they seek to raise their people from poverty while joining the global economy and improving China's relations with the rest of the world. The reasons behind the discrepancy in perceptions of China are rooted in the complex history and culture of this ancient land.

Risen or still rising?

So has China risen or is it still rising? The conflict lies in the fact that there is no universal agreement on how to judge whether a country has risen. To say that China has risen on the basis of its Security Council membership and international status is essentially an assessment based on a Western-dominated view of the world since the establishment of the UN in 1945. Although China was a founding member of the UN—under the Nationalist Party government of Chiang Kai-shek (1887-1975)—its Communist Party leadership does not accept this—or, for that matter, any—Anglo-American-centric view of the post-World War II (1939-1945) world order.

According to the current leaders of China, China's "rightful place" in the world should be based on a long-term, historical perspective. Over the last 2,000 years, China has enjoyed a long-standing—though period-ically interrupted—position of dominance in the world, both culturally and politically. China was a leader in establishing principles of govern-ment, scientific development, and inventions until the modern era. Many of its contributions—including the magnetic compass, paper, moveable type, gunpowder, and an efficient bureaucracy recruited on the basis of merit—influenced the course of human civilization.

In terms of political power, China's first empire (the Qin Dynasty, 221-206 B.C.) and second empire (the Han Dynasty, 206 B.C.-A.D. 220)

New high-rises replace the old as the fast pace of modernization in 2008 changes the face of Shanghai.

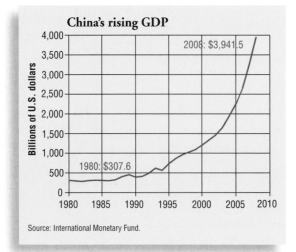

China's rising GDP

2008: $3,941.5

1980: $307.6

Source: International Monetary Fund.

China's *gross domestic product* (GDP—the total value of all goods and services produced in a country in a year) grew dramatically over the past two decades. In 1987, China ranked ninth among the nations of the world in total GDP. By 2007, it was fourth.

were roughly contemporary with the Roman Empire (established in 27 B.C.). Both Chinese empires were "superpowers" of the world within their reach. In Europe, when the power of Rome collapsed, it was never resurrected on a sustainable basis. In China, the glory and might of the first empire was periodically resurrected and expanded further until at least 1912, when the Republic of China was established. This history has resulted in a general belief among the Chinese that a united empire in which China benevolently dominates "all under heaven" is the norm.

In economic terms, China has historically accounted for a much greater percentage of global GDP than it does today. Home to about 25 percent of the world's population throughout most of recorded history (20 percent of the world's population in 2007), China contributed to only an estimated 6 percent of global GDP in 2007. By contrast, it produced 26.2 percent of global GDP 2,000 years ago; 22.7 percent in the year 1000; 25 percent in 1500; and 32.9 percent in 1820. This high point was followed by a period of decline lasting roughly from the mid-1800's to the end of World War II, a period that is perceived by Chinese leaders and taught in Chinese schools as "a century of humiliation." Nevertheless, China ranked fourth among the countries of the world in GDP in 2007. In terms of *per capita* (per person) GDP, however, it ranked much lower— 107th. More than half of the countries of the world have a higher per capita GDP than China.

There is a consensus among Chinese leaders that the country must redress this "humiliation," though there is no agreement about how this can be achieved. An unspoken assumption among many Chinese is that their nation will not have truly reemerged or reclaimed its "rightful place" until it returns to the historical norm in terms of its economic contribution to and importance in the world.

The "peaceful rise" strategy

The Chinese government first presented its concept of "peaceful rise" in November 2003, at an annual economic conference called the Boao Forum for Asia. The slogan became a cornerstone of the policy of Hu Jintao, who became the general secretary of the Communist Party and president of China in the early 2000's. The new policy marked the resurgence of a powerful China confident of its own approach to the modern world and to development. Although the policy was subsequently modified, first to "peaceful development" and then, in 2006, to the promotion of a "harmonious world," its essence has not changed. The new rhetoric was devised primarily to reassure the rest of the world that China's rise would not pose a threat to other nations.

The adoption of the peaceful rise policy does not mean that when its leaders finally decide that China has risen, the country will continue to promote peace rather than competition, instability, or conflict. However, neither does it mean that the concept is part of a sinister plot to mask dangerous intentions. Whether China has in fact already risen or not, the reality is that it is still rising, and rising at a faster rate than any foreign observer or, for that matter, any Chinese leader, predicted when the reform period began in the late 1970's. However, it will be at least several decades before China's power can hope to equal that of the United States, the lone superpower at the end of the *Cold War* (a period of intense rivalry between the Soviet Union and the United States that began in about 1945 and ended with the breakup of the Soviet Union in 1991). Although the Chinese government has never defined the conditions under which it will consider China as having risen, it will almost certainly not be until China has either replaced the United States as the sole superpower or become equal in power to the United States.

Workers at the Bautou Steel factory in Inner Mongolia leave work at the end of their shift. Although China, with a population of 1.35 billion people, has the world's fourth highest gross domestic product (GDP), *per capita* (per person) GDP ranks below more than 100 other countries.

In the early 2000's, the strategic thinking of China's leaders is based on the "24 character" strategy of Deng Xiaoping, the country's most influential leader from the late 1970's to the early 1990's. That strategy instructs the nation to "Observe carefully, secure our position, cope with affairs calmly, hide our capabilities and bide our time, be good at maintaining a low profile, and never claim leadership." Deng's dictum is meant to ensure that China rises to prominence on its own terms while avoiding preemptive reactions from other nations of the world. The policy of peaceful rise is meant to create a favorable international environment in which China can develop into a modern superpower under the leadership of the Communist Party.

As part of the "peaceful rise," the goal of the Chinese government is to increase "comprehensive national strength." Such strength does not involve only the build-up of military capability, though military might is an important element. The goal also involves developing China's economic, political, and *soft power.* (*Soft power* refers to a country's use of its culture, values, or foreign policy to influence others; *hard power* refers to military superiority or economic clout.) Chinese leaders have chosen such a strategy to avoid getting into an arms race with the United States. The Soviet Union engaged in such a policy during the Cold War, and Chinese leaders believe that the move was partly responsible for the collapse of the Soviet Union. China's leaders are determined not to make essentially the same mistake. They also understand that soft power is worth cultivating and that it is more effective when backed by hard power.

Although intended primarily to appease foreign government leaders, the "peaceful rise" strategy also provides a logical basis for China's current foreign policy. Chinese leaders believe that it will take decades for the country to reach a stage of development in which China can assert itself freely and fully. Therefore, a commitment to avoid conflict in the foreseeable future can only help them achieve their goal.

A new ideology of nationalism

Communism in effect ceased to be the state ideology of China some time between the Tiananmen Massacre of 1989, in which protesters called for more democracy and an end to government corruption, and the fall of the Soviet Union in 1991. To fill the void, the Communist Party sought to put in place a new ideological framework that would bind the nation together under the leadership of the party. Without a new ideology, the party feared the country would disintegrate as the Soviet Union had. Chinese leaders also sought to keep Western values and beliefs from captivating Chinese citizens and filling the ideological void.

The Tiananmen Massacre, in which authorities attacked students and other protesters and killed hundreds of them, had caused a tremendous rift between the party and ordinary citizens. Party leaders determined that nationalism was the only important value shared by itself and its critics, and thus the most reliable claim to the loyalty of Chinese citizens. The party quickly asserted itself as the defender of China's national pride.

A protester attempts to block a line of tanks at Tiananmen Square in Beijing on June 5, 1989. The previous day, hundreds of people were killed in the square as government forces put down a demonstration staged in the name of greater democracy and an end to government corruption.

The focus of the new nationalistic indoctrination was to instill in the Chinese people a sense of pride in their country and its development that is inseparable from the leadership of the Communist Party. The party tightly controls the teaching of modern history. Thus, Chinese children are brought up believing China suffered a century of humiliation under Western and Japanese imperialism that began around 1839. In 1839, Chinese officials tried to stop British merchants from illegally importing opium into China, a move that triggered the Opium War. The United Kingdom won the war and received the island of Hong Kong as part of the settlement.

In subsequent wars of the 1800's, China lost Korea and the island of Taiwan to the Japanese, as well as other territories to European powers. It was also forced to adopt the Open Door Policy, which guaranteed the rights of the great powers to trade with China on an equal basis. This provoked strong anti-Western feelings that erupted in a mass movement to attack foreigners known as the Boxer Rebellion. The Manchu dynasty supported the uprising but was forced to capitulate after eight powers jointly invaded China in 1900. The dynasty subsequently tried to reform but was overthrown by a revolution. China's republican experiment suffered from civil wars and a full scale Japanese invasion (1937-1945). National unity, stability, and order were restored after the Communists seized power in 1949. Since then, according to party teachings, it was the Communist Party that saved the Chinese people from the "century of humiliation." To foster such beliefs, the party has revived *xenophobia* (fear of strangers or foreigners) and propagated the story of its "heroic" fight against Japanese imperialism, even though the party in fact played only a marginal role in resisting Japanese aggression in the 1930's and 1940's.

This indoctrination campaign was meant to enhance the party's ability to stay in power in two mutually reinforcing ways. The campaign provided an ideological basis for legitimacy and served as a rallying force for the development of a national aspiration around the leadership of the party. In other words, since 1989 nationalism has been used by the leadership as a way to pursue greater power and prosperity for the nation. More specifically, the party launched an extensive propaganda and educational campaign to instill a new sense of citizenship, one that requires its citizens to affirm the rightness and acceptability of the state, its values, policies, and agencies. At the core of this campaign was the message that China's unique national conditions make it unsuitable to

A mob of Chinese men and boys stand outside the British compound in Beijing during the Boxer Rebellion of 1900. During a surge of anti-Western sentiment in China around the turn of the 20th century, "boxers"—young Chinese men trained in unarmed combat aided by some imperial army troops—attacked foreign businessmen and their families and Christian missionaries. For safety, foreigners retreated into the compounds of diplomatic legations in the capital. They were eventually rescued by an international force.

Construction workers in March 2007 take a break before a billboard depicting the new headquarters of China Central Television in Beijing in March 2007. The $700-million building is thought to be the world's largest and most expensive media headquarters. Designed by Dutch architect Rem Koolhaas, it consists of two interlocking Z-shaped towers that rise 767 feet (233 meters).

adopt Western-style liberal democracy. China's existing political system, in contrast, is essential for political stability, a prerequisite for rapid economic development. By emphasizing China's national confidence and pride and turning past humiliation into a driving force for China's modernization, the Communist Party has turned nationalism into an effective instrument for enhancing its legitimacy. The intention was to instill in the minds of Chinese people a strong feeling of "my government, right or wrong."

The role of the Olympic Games

The success of the nationalist indoctrination campaign manifested itself dramatically in 2008, the year the Communist Party had intended to launch the re-branded modern China on the occasion of the Beijing Olympics in August. The force of nationalism, however, could not be contained until the Games as was originally planned. Somewhat ironically, the indoctrination had generated so much pride that the nationalists asserted themselves in April when the Olympic torch relay outside China was met with unfavorable foreign reactions. The negative responses were directed mainly at the way Chinese authorities organized the relay, guarding it heavily with elite members of the People's Armed Police dressed as torch attendants. Chinese nation-alists reacted strongly when protesters in foreign cities through which the torch passed demonstrated against such government policies as continued Chinese rule in Tibet. (China has occupied Tibet since 1950.) What they ignored was that by sending elite police officers, who often dictated to local police how the torch should be guarded, the Chinese government was interfering in the domestic affairs of the countries through which the torch passed. If such a move had been attempted in reverse, with the country hosting the Olympics sending police officers to tell the Chinese how to guard a torch relay in Beijing, the matter would have created a huge uproar.

The large number of Chinese citizens who responded with strong nationalism during the torch relay sought to show support for their government in the face of foreign criticism. To the Chinese, verbal abuse of China's government by foreigners—no matter how corrupt its citizens privately may consider it to be—was seen as an insult to the country.

Nationalism also asserted itself dramatically in the aftermath of the Sichuan earthquake of May 2008, in which nearly 70,000 people died. By making the rescue operation a Chinese national effort, and holding up for days the access of foreign rescue teams to the scene, the Chinese government ensured that nearly all survivors were saved by Chinese rescue workers. The heroism of the rescue operations conducted by the Chinese themselves was used to galvanize a countrywide movement to rally around the party's leadership in the subsequent relief efforts, even though the government had, in fact, accepted generous foreign aid and donations. Thus, no matter how well or poorly the party actually handled the crisis, and whether bureaucratic corruption and other policy failures were responsible for the collapse of a disproportionately large number of school buildings (as many parents of children who had died charged), the party still emerged from its first major test since 1989 stronger than before.

Just as the astute management of propaganda after the earthquake ensured a positive image of the party, the long-standing indoctrination of nationalism persuaded most Chinese to dissociate their leaders in Beijing from the local officials they blamed. The Chinese government may not be able to silence all grieving parents, but it can divert their anger from the central government to specific individuals or departments at the local level and reduce the negative impact on the credibility of the central government as a whole.

In 2008 the Communist Party demonstrated a remarkable capacity to harness nationalism to support its most important policies. The greatest examples of its success took place during the Olympic Games, as vast numbers of people in the vicinity of Beijing made sacrifices to ensure the success of the event. Factories were closed for weeks to help alleviate the dense air pollution in Beijing. Many farmers, particularly those in Hebei province, faced destitution as water for irrigation was diverted from large tracts of agricultural land to beautify Beijing. Migrant laborers were sent home without compensation, because organizers believed their presence might detract from the appearance of the capital for Olympic visitors.

Workers put finishing touches on the world's largest building, the new terminal at the Beijing International Airport. The Chinese government employed tens of thousands of workers around the clock to complete the terminal for the opening of the 2008 Olympic Games.

Despite the hardships that were imposed and the resentment of those whose livelihoods were affected, for the most part, the public responded as the party leadership required them to.

Nevertheless, the party's heavy reliance on an inherently xenophobic nationalism also leaves it vulnerable to the will of the people. The party leadership may be devoted to its policy of a peaceful rise. However, the new nationalists who basked in the glory of the success of China's Olympic team may expect—and even demand—that the Chinese government be more assertive as China continues to rise. The peaceful rise strategy may require the government to bide its time, hide its capabilities, and desist from claiming leadership, but the nationalists expect it to stand up for the greatness, dignity, and pride of China. Nationalism may need to be contained to sustain China's peaceful rise strategy.

The issue of Taiwan

Whether China's rise will continue to be peaceful is not a question for which there is a definitive answer. Domestic politics as well as the changing fortune of China in the international community will affect how the nation's leaders judge whether China has risen or not. In general terms, the clearest sign that the Communist leadership considers China to have risen will be the resolution of the Taiwan issue to its satisfaction. In 1949, after nearly 20 years of civil war, Communist forces led by Mao Zedong took control of mainland China and formed the People's Republic of China. The Nationalist forces under Chiang Kai-shek fled to Taiwan, where they formed the Republic of China. The United States provided the Republic of China with military, technical, and economic aid and recognized the government in Taiwan as the legitimate government of China. Taiwan held China's seat in the UN.

In 1971, the UN expelled Nationalist China and admitted Communist China. In addition, many nations, including the United States, ended diplomatic relations with Taiwan and established such relations with Beijing. However, the United States continued to provide Taiwan with military aid and maintained unofficial ties with the Nationalist government.

Since 1950, the Chinese government has considered Taiwan a sacred territory that was prevented from reuniting with "mother China" by U.S. support for Taiwan's Nationalist regime. The government in Beijing has maintained this claim despite the fact that the People's Republic of China has never had jurisdiction over Taiwan and that it cannot succeed the government of the Republic of China because the latter still exists. A democratically elected government based on universal suffrage has existed in Taiwan since 1996 (before then, the Nationalist Party was the only legal political party and Taiwan was ruled by martial law). For China to resolve the "Taiwan issue" to its satisfaction, it would have to force the United States to back down over its support for an independent Taiwan. What China's intentions would then be is hard to say. However, for such a scenario to take place, China would have to become the premier power in the world or at least to build up sufficient power to deter the United States from protecting Taiwan.

China in the international arena

Before China reaches this important stage in its reemergence as a superpower, one or more generations of its leaders will probably have come and gone. How successive generations of Chinese leaders view the world and their country's place in it will depend, to a great degree, on how the rest of the world treats China's rise. If Chinese leaders believe the international community perceives China as an enemy and seeks to prevent it from rising peacefully, China will almost certainly react as an enemy. The more constructive way for the international community to deal with China's rise would be to take the peaceful rise rhetoric at face value. At the same time, world leaders should hold China accountable as a responsible stakeholder in international affairs even as it is rising. A good starting point would be to encourage China to live up to its stated policy of promoting a "harmonious world." In problem areas of the world where China has greater influence than other permanent members of the Security Council, China should be encouraged to take a leading role and receive support for doing so.

The Three Gorges Dam near Yichang, in central China, is the largest hydroelectric facility in the world. Completed in 2008, it was built to control flooding and improve navigation on the Yangtze, China's longest river. The project has generated much controversy, as more than 1 million people were relocated and cultural relics and historic sites were lost to the floodwaters. Critics also charge that the project has wrought significant environmental damage.

In Darfur, Sudan, for example, China could be invited to contribute a large force and take over command of the UN peace-keeping operation there. Other permanent members of the Security Council could provide logistical support and expert advice to enable the Chinese to deploy the force over such a great distance. Such a mission would enhance China's military capability as well as give its armed forces valuable and otherwise unobtainable experience in a major overseas operation. If well executed, the mission would also help China spread its influence to Africa and beyond. It would not put China's energy interests in Sudan at risk, as a large presence of the People's Liberation Army—even if the soldiers wore blue United Nations helmets—would deter the government in Khartoum from harming Chinese interests there. But it would achieve another goal: getting China to take a major step in being a responsible stakeholder in world affairs and upholding one of the founding principles of the UN—to stop the spread of a humanitarian disaster.

If China can then be encouraged to continue to take on such missions, over the long term such a role may have a valuable effect on how a later generation of Chinese leaders looks at the world and China's place in it. Success on such a mission could lead to constructive changes in how China plays the role of a superpower.

City. Mayors from around the United States gathered in Miami, Florida, from June 20 to June 24, 2008, for the 76th annual meeting of the United States Conference of Mayors (USCM). The Washington, D.C.-based USCM is a *nonpartisan* (politically unaffiliated) organization made up of mayors of cities with populations of at least 30,000. Among the many topics addressed by the municipal leaders were soaring gasoline prices, problems related to mortgage foreclosures, and sluggish economic conditions.

Gas prices. A survey of 132 U.S. mayors released at the USCM meeting shed light on the relationship between high gasoline prices and local efforts to improve energy efficiency. At the time of the meeting, average weekly U.S. retail gasoline prices were more than $4 per gallon.

In the survey, 90 percent of responding mayors reported that high gasoline prices and other energy costs had significant impacts on their city budgets. Eighty-four percent of the mayors noted that energy costs prompted them to make plans for increasing city revenues, adding fuel-efficient vehicles to city fleets, and modifying buildings for energy efficiency. According to the report, however, the greatest obstacle to improving cities' energy efficiency was insufficient funding from state governments and the federal government.

Mortgage foreclosures. Another study released at the USCM meeting examined how the problem of vacant and abandoned properties was worsened by the increase in mortgage foreclosures. According to the study, which included survey information on 42 U.S. cities, this property problem was a huge drain on city budgets, quality of life, and neighborhood redevelopment.

More than 70 percent of the responding mayors in the survey reported that the number of vacant and abandoned properties in their cities had increased because of the nationwide foreclosure crisis. Almost 30 percent of the mayors responded that efforts to address their property problems had lost ground. Most mayors in the survey noted that federal funds would be useful for acquiring and either rehabilitating or demolishing vacant and abandoned properties.

Sluggish economy. A report released at the USCM meeting revealed that economic growth in U.S. cities over the past 12 months weakened, while consumer prices rose sharply. The report, by Global Insight, Inc., an economic forecasting firm based in Boston, examined economic conditions in 363 U.S. metropolitan areas.

According to the report, officials in one-third of the cities expected employment to decline in 2008. In 80 of the cities, hundreds of thousands of jobs that were lost since the economic recession of 2001 had never been regained.

USCM resolutions. Committees at the USCM meeting passed resolutions on a wide variety of subjects, such as health and human services, criminal justice, environmental protection, economic policy, and international affairs. Passed resolutions included support for national health insurance for all Americans and a request for federal funding to combat gang violence. Other resolutions urged the development of local-state-federal partnerships to study the effects of climate change on water resources; supported reforms in the credit card industry to protect consumers; and condemned the suppression of civil rights by the government of Venezuela.

City livability awards. Mayors Jerry E. Abramson of Louisville, Kentucky, and Roy D. Buol of Dubuque, Iowa, were awarded first-place honors in the 2008 City Livability Awards Program in June. The awards, sponsored by the USCM and Waste Management, Inc., of Houston, recognize outstanding mayoral leadership in implementing programs that improve quality of life in cities.

Mayor Abramson was honored for the "Healthy Hometown Program," a community-wide effort to encourage physical activity and healthy diets. The effort included 150 partners from businesses, schools, and other community organizations. Mayor Buol was honored for the "America's River Project," a $188-million project to clean up and redevelop polluted riverfront property for commercial, recreational, and educational activities.

Climate protection awards. Also in June, mayors Greg Nickels of Seattle and James Brainard of Carmel, Indiana, were awarded first-place honors in the 2008 Mayor's Climate Protection Awards Program. This program, sponsored by the USCM and Wal-Mart Stores, Inc., of Bentonville, Arkansas, recognizes mayors for innovative practices that increase energy efficiency and curb global warming.

Mayor Nickels was honored for the "Seattle Climate Action Now" program, a grassroots campaign aimed at providing residents with information and tools for increasing energy efficiency at home and work and on the road. Mayor Brainard was honored for the "Roundabouts" program, which promoted the development of *roundabouts*, a type of circular road junction designed for more efficient traffic flow.

Chicago crime wave. Calling crime in Chicago "out of control," Illinois Governor Rod Blagojevich said in July that the Illinois state police and National Guard could be used to help the city's police fight a spring and summer spike in violent crime. Jody Weis, superintendent of Chicago police, replied that although assistance from the National Guard would be unnecessary, he was open to the idea of using state troopers in the city's anticrime efforts.

50 LARGEST CITIES IN THE UNITED STATES

Rank	City	Population*
1.	New York, NY	8,304,869
2.	Los Angeles, CA	3,838,011
3.	Chicago, IL	2,828,914
4.	Houston, TX	2,261,537
5.	Phoenix, AZ	1,598,320
6.	Philadelphia, PA	1,443,335
7.	San Antonio, TX	1,359,895
8.	San Diego, CA	1,267,078
9.	Dallas, TX	1,251,894
10.	San Jose, CA	952,454
11.	Detroit, MI	914,852
12.	Jacksonville, FL	814,861
13.	Indianapolis, IN	798,234
14.	San Francisco, CA	769,256
15.	Austin, TX	761,628
16.	Columbus, OH	751,711
17.	Fort Worth, TX	711,797
18.	Charlotte, NC	691,870
19.	Memphis, TN	672,463
20.	Baltimore, MD	636,279
21.	El Paso, TX	614,103
22.	Milwaukee, WI	603,175
23.	Seattle, WA	601,269
24.	Boston, MA	601,265
25.	Nashville, TN	597,847
26.	Denver, CO	597,369
27.	Washington, DC	591,226
28.	Las Vegas, NV	567,370
29.	Louisville, KY	558,329
30.	Portland, OR	555,565
31.	Oklahoma City, OK	554,050
32.	Atlanta, GA	537,729
33.	Tucson, AZ	530,084
34.	Albuquerque, NM	529,486
35.	Fresno, CA	475,523
36.	Sacramento, CA	464,350
37.	Long Beach, CA	464,054
38.	Mesa, AZ	458,176
39.	Kansas City, MO	452,782
40.	Virginia Beach, VA	433,128
41.	Cleveland, OH	432,141
42.	Omaha, NE	429,741
43.	Miami, FL	422,245
44.	Oakland, CA	403,130
45.	Raleigh, NC	393,007
46.	Tulsa, OK	384,370
47.	Colorado Springs, CO	378,513
48.	Minneapolis, MN	378,012
49.	Honolulu, HI	375,691
50.	Arlington, TX	375,277

*2008 World Book estimates based on data from the U.S. Census Bureau.

50 LARGEST METROPOLITAN AREAS IN THE UNITED STATES

Rank	Metropolitan area*	Population†
1.	New York–Northern New Jersey–Long Island, NY-NJ	18,844,311
2.	Los Angeles–Long Beach–Santa Ana, CA	12,881,624
3.	Chicago–Naperville–Joliet, IL-IN-WI	9,578,405
4.	Dallas–Fort Worth–Arlington, TX	6,311,130
5.	Philadelphia–Camden–Wilmington, PA-NJ-DE-MD	5,844,959
6.	Houston–Sugar Land–Baytown, TX	5,779,050
7.	Atlanta–Sandy Springs–Marietta, GA	5,450,010
8.	Miami–Fort Lauderdale–Pompano Beach, FL	5,444,192
9.	Washington–Arlington–Alexandria, DC-VA-MD-WV	5,358,220
10.	Boston–Cambridge–Quincy, MA-NH	4,492,583
11.	Detroit–Warren–Livonia, MI	4,455,051
12.	Phoenix–Mesa–Scottsdale, AZ	4,349,800
13.	San Francisco–Oakland–Fremont, CA	4,224,949
14.	Riverside–San Bernardino–Ontario, CA	4,197,442
15.	Seattle–Tacoma–Bellevue, WA	3,358,512
16.	Minneapolis–St. Paul–Bloomington, MN-WI	3,241,564
17.	San Diego–Carlsbad–San Marcos, CA	2,987,019
18.	St. Louis, MO–IL	2,818,251
19.	Tampa–St. Petersburg–Clearwater, FL	2,773,925
20.	Baltimore–Towson, MD	2,677,912
21.	Denver–Aurora, CO	2,512,273
22.	Pittsburgh, PA	2,344,412
23.	Portland–Vancouver–Beaverton, OR-WA	2,215,680
24.	Cincinnati–Middletown, OH-KY-IN	2,150,374
25.	Sacramento–Arden-Arcade–Roseville, CA	2,118,701
26.	Orlando–Kissimmee, FL	2,092,365
27.	Cleveland–Elyria–Mentor, OH	2,085,620
28.	San Antonio, TX	2,042,046
29.	Kansas City, MO-KS	2,007,042
30.	Las Vegas–Paradise, NV	1,906,395
31.	San Jose–Sunnyvale–Santa Clara, CA	1,826,434
32.	Columbus, OH	1,773,994
33.	Indianapolis–Carmel, IN	1,720,223
34.	Charlotte–Gastonia–Concord, NC–SC	1,718,140
35.	Virginia Beach–Norfolk–Newport News, VA-NC	1,663,798
36.	Austin-Round Rock, TX	1,663,667
37.	Providence–New Bedford–Fall River, RI-MA	1,595,235
38.	Nashville–Davidson–Murfreesboro–Franklin, TN	1,558,905
39.	Milwaukee–Waukesha–West Allis, WI	1,548,468
40.	Jacksonville, FL	1,328,196
41.	Memphis, TN-MS-AR	1,293,142
42.	Louisville/Jefferson County, KY–IN	1,245,478
43.	Richmond, VA	1,233,198
44.	Oklahoma City, OK	1,210,730
45.	Hartford–West Hartford–East Hartford, CT	1,193,124
46.	Salt Lake City, UT	1,128,102
47.	Buffalo–Niagara Falls, NY	1,120,992
48.	Birmingham–Hoover, AL	1,117,790
49.	Raleigh–Cary, NC	1,096,567
50.	New Orleans–Metairie–Kenner, LA	1,071,854

*The U.S. Census Bureau defines a metropolitan area as a large population nucleus with adjacent communities having a high degree of economic and social integration.

†2008 World Book estimates based on data from the U.S. Census Bureau and other sources.

50 LARGEST URBAN CENTERS IN THE WORLD

Rank	Urban center*	Population
1.	Tokyo, Japan	35,939,000
2.	Mumbai, India	19,672,000
3.	Mexico City, Mexico	19,334,000
4.	São Paulo, Brazil	19,320,000
5.	New York City, U.S.	19,293,000
6.	Delhi, India	16,583,000
7.	Shanghai, China	15,515,000
8.	Kolkata, India	15,302,000
9.	Dhaka, Bangladesh	14,292,000
10.	Buenos Aires, Argentina	12,980,000
11.	Karachi, Pakistan	12,723,000
12.	Los Angeles, U.S.	12,675,000
13.	Cairo, Egypt	12,288,000
14.	Rio de Janeiro, Brazil	12,025,000
15.	Beijing, China	11,519,000
16.	Manila, Philippines	11,471,000
17.	Osaka, Japan	11,321,000
18.	Moscow, Russia	10,479,000
19.	Istanbul, Turkey	10,354,000
20.	Lagos, Nigeria	10,154,000
21.	Paris, France	9,935,000
22.	Seoul, South Korea	9,774,000
23.	Jakarta, Indonesia	9,520,000
24.	Guangzhou, China	9,224,000
25.	Chicago, U.S.	9,131,000
26.	Kinshasa, Congo	8,587,000
27.	London, U.K.	8,587,000
28.	Lima, Peru	8,242,000
29.	Bogotá, Colombia	8,107,000
30.	Tehran, Iran	8,100,000
31.	Shenzhen, China	7,922,000
32.	Wuhan, China	7,448,000
33.	Chennai, India	7,421,000
34.	Tianjin, China	7,378,000
35.	Hong Kong, China	7,344,000
36.	Bengaluru, India	7,064,000
37.	Lahore, Pakistan	6,909,000
38.	Taipei, Taiwan	6,904,000
39.	Bangkok, Thailand	6,847,000
40.	Chongqing, China	6,621,000
41.	Hyderabad, India	6,621,000
42.	Santiago, Chile	5,822,000
43.	Belo Horizonte, Brazil	5,802,000
44.	Baghdad, Iraq	5,768,000
45.	Madrid, Spain	5,690,000
46.	Miami, U.S.	5,688,000
47.	Ahmadabad, India	5,594,000
48.	Philadelphia, U.S.	5,582,000
49.	Ho Chi Minh City, Vietnam	5,579,000
50.	Toronto, Canada	5,359,000

Source: 2008 estimates based on data from the United Nations and other official government sources.

*The United Nations defines an urban center as a city surrounded by a continuous built-up area having a high population density.

Violent crime in Chicago received national attention in April, when 38 individuals—13 of whom were public school students—were shot or stabbed during one weekend. Nine of these individuals died. Statistics released in May revealed that for the first quarter of 2008 the murder rate in Chicago increased by 9 percent and the violent crime rate by 6 percent, compared with the same period in 2007.

Police blamed the surge in violence on a combination of gang rivalries, gun proliferation, and warm weather. Some criminologists said they were puzzled by the violence because Chicago was one of only two large cities (the other being Washington, D.C.) in which the ownership of handguns was banned.

D.C. gun ban overturned. The U.S. Supreme Court, in a 5-to-4 vote in June 2008, struck down a Washington, D.C., ban on handgun ownership. In making the landmark decision, the court ruled—for the first time—that the Second Amendment to the Constitution of the United States guarantees that individuals have the right to own guns for self-defense.

The court's ruling left the legality of Chicago's gun ban in doubt. After the ruling, the Illinois State Rifle Association, the major gun owners' advocacy organization in Illinois, filed a lawsuit in federal court to overturn the Chicago gun ban.

Carbon footprints. Most of the U.S. cities with large *carbon footprints* are in areas in which coal-fired power plants provide energy or in which urban sprawl has led to long commutes. That was the conclusion of a study reported in May by the Brookings Institution, a Washington, D.C.-based organization that studies economic, governmental, and international issues. The term "carbon footprint" refers to the amount of carbon dioxide produced by human activities, mainly the burning of *fossil fuels* (coal, oil, natural gas). Scientists blame carbon dioxide released into the atmosphere for global warming.

The study, based on an analysis of residential energy consumption and highway transportation, found that the U.S. metropolitan area with the largest carbon footprint was Lexington-Fayette, Kentucky. Metropolitan areas with the next largest carbon footprints were—in consecutive order—Indianapolis, Indiana; Cincinnati-Middletown (in Ohio, Kentucky, and Indiana); Toledo, Ohio; Louisville, Kentucky; Nashville-Davidson-Murfreesboro, Tennessee; St. Louis, Missouri; Oklahoma City, Oklahoma; Harrisburg-Carlisle, Pennsylvania; and Knoxville, Tennessee.

■ Alfred J. Smuskiewicz

See also **Banking: A Special Report; Chicago; Dallas; Houston; Los Angeles; New York City; Philadelphia; Washington, D.C.**

Classical music. The global economic crisis in 2008 had a harmful impact on classical music, a fragile corner of the nonprofit economy that depends as much on donations as on ticket sales. Orchestras and opera companies cut costs by eliminating rehearsals and canceling performances, scaling back health insurance for employees, and searching for new ways to tighten their belts without damaging their artistic products.

Loud music and hearing loss. Turn down the volume of MP3 players or risk permanent hearing loss. That was the warning from scientists with the European Union in an October report that reinforced findings of previous studies. The scientists reported that from 2.5 million to 10 million people in Europe could suffer permanent hearing loss from listening to MP3 players at unsafe volumes—more than 89 decibels—for more than one hour daily for at least five years.

Mozart and Beethoven discoveries. In September, music scholars announced the discovery of a previously unknown piece of music handwritten by composer Wolfgang Amadeus Mozart (1756-1791). The preliminary draft, found in a library in Nantes, France, contained only the melodic line, with no harmony or instrumentation.

Also in September, musicology professor Peter McCallum of the University of Sydney in Australia announced the discovery of a previously unknown *bagatelle* (short piano piece) believed to be the last work composed by Ludwig van Beethoven (1770-1827). McCallum found the composition as he was examining Beethoven's sketchbook in the state library in Berlin, Germany.

New operas. The San Francisco Opera performed the world premiere of *The Bonesetter's Daughter,* composed by Stewart Wallace to a libretto by Amy Tan, in September. The opera, based on Tan's 2001 novel, tells the story of a troubled Chinese-American woman who, escorted by a ghost, travels into her immigrant mother's past. Steven Sloane conducted the operatic premiere.

In May 2008, the Lyric Opera of Kansas City (Missouri) gave the world premiere of *John Brown,* with music and libretto by Kirke Mechem. The title figure was an *abolitionist* (person advocating an end to slavery) who some historians believe helped spark the American Civil War (1861-1865) and lead the way for the civil rights movement of the 1960's in the United States.

Jake Heggie's *Last Acts* had its world premiere by the Houston Grand Opera in February 2008. The musical play in three acts was based on an unpublished play by Terrence McNally, with music by Heggie and lyrics by Gene Scheer. It is the story of an actress, her two adult children, and their struggle to know and love one another.

Lee Hoiby's *This Is the Rill Speaking* had its world premiere by the ensemble American Opera Projects, in association with Purchase (New York) College Opera, in April. The one-act opera is set to a libretto by Mark Shulgasser based on a play by Lanford Wilson about a small rural U.S. town.

New orchestral and choral works. James Levine, music director of the Boston Symphony Orchestra, conducted the orchestra in the world premieres of two symphonies by U.S. composers in 2008. William Bolcom's Symphony No. 8 was premiered in February, and John Harbison's Symphony No. 5, in April. Bolcom's symphony included a vocal component based on the writings of English poet William Blake (1757-1827). Harbison's symphony included text from poems about the ancient Greek myths of Orpheus and Eurydice.

In October, the Juilliard Orchestra, under conductor James Conlon, performed the world premiere of Ellen Taaffe Zwilich's Symphony No. 5 at Carnegie Hall in New York City. The Pulitzer Prize-winning Zwilich was the first woman composer to have earned a doctorate degree from the Juilliard School of Music in New York City.

Marin Alsop led the Cabrillo Festival Orchestra in the world premiere of Christopher Rouse's Concerto for Orchestra in August at the Cabrillo Festival of Contemporary Music in Santa Cruz, California. The world premiere of Joseph Schwantner's *Chasing Light...* was given by the Reno Chamber Orchestra in September at the University of Nevada in Reno.

Bernard Rands's *chains like the sea* had its world premiere in October by the New York Philharmonic, in honor of the composer's 75th birthday. Lorin Maazel conducted the performance. Lawrence Siegel's *Kaddish: Music of Remembrance and Hope* received its first performance in November in Minneapolis, Minnesota, by the VocalEssence chorus and soloists, under conductor Philip Brunelle.

In April, Chinese pianist Lang Lang performed the world premiere of Piano Concerto by the Chinese composer Tan Dun. Leonard Slatkin conducted the New York Philharmonic in the performance. Another Chinese-born composer, Bright Sheng, was on hand in October for the first performance of his Harp Concerto, played by harpist Yolanda Kondonassis with the San Diego Symphony, with Jahja Ling conducting.

August 4, 1964, an evening-long oratorio by U.S. composer Steven Stucky, had its world premiere in September 2008 by the Dallas Symphony Orchestra, with Jaap van Zweden conducting. Set to a libretto by Gene Scheer, the vocal symphony is based on the events of the title date, when U.S. President Lyndon B. Johnson announced that Vietnamese forces had attacked a U.S. ship in the Gulf of Tonkin, leading to a Congressional resolution justifying U.S. involvement in the Vietnam War (1957-1975).

Richard Wagner's *Parsifal*, produced at the Bayreuth Festival in Germany in July, was staged as a metaphor of German history by director Stefan Herheim. To illustrate the decadence of the Weimar Republic (1918-1933), Herheim has the character Klingsor dress in women's underwear and stockings.

GRAMMY AWARD WINNERS IN 2008

Classical Album, *Tower: Made in America;* Nashville Symphony Orchestra; Leonard Slatkin, conductor; Tim Handley, producer

Orchestral Performance, *Tower: Made in America;* Nashville Symphony Orchestra; Leonard Slatkin, conductor

Opera Recording, *Humperdinck: Hansel & Gretel;* New London Children's Choir and Philharmonia Orchestra of London; Sir Charles Mackerras, conductor; Jennifer Larmore, Rebecca Evans, and Jane Henschel, soloists; Brian Couzens, producer

Choral Performance, *Brahms: Ein Deutsches Requiem;* Rundfunkchor Berlin and Berliner Philharmoniker; Simon Rattle, conductor

Instrumental Soloist with Orchestra, *Barber/Korngold/Walton: Violin Concertos;* Vancouver Symphony Orchestra; Bramwell Tovey, conductor; James Ehnes, violin

Instrumental Soloist without Orchestra, *Beethoven Sonatas, Vol. 3;* Garrick Ohlsson, piano

Chamber Music Performance, *Strange Imaginary Animals;* eighth blackbird

Small Ensemble Performance, *Stravinsky: Apollo, Concerto in D; Prokofiev: 20 Visions Fugitives;* Moscow Soloists; Yuri Bashmet, conductor

Classical Vocal Performance, *Lorraine Hunt Lieberson Sings Peter Lieberson: Neruda Songs;* Lorraine Hunt Lieberson, mezzo-soprano

Classical Contemporary Composition, *Tower: Made in America;* Joan Tower, composer

Classical Crossover Album, *A Love Supreme: The Legacy of John Coltrane;* Turtle Island Quartet

Violin Concerto, by Christopher Theofanidis, was given its world premiere in October by soloist Sarah Chang, with Andris Nelsons leading the Pittsburgh Symphony Orchestra. Michael Daugherty's *Troyjam,* for narrator and orchestra, was given its first performance in May at the John F. Kennedy Center for the Performing Arts in Washington, D.C. Leonard Slatkin conducted the National Symphony Orchestra in the performance.

Also in May, U.S. composer Kevin Puts's Piano Concerto had its world premiere by the Los Angeles Chamber Orchestra. Jeffrey Kahane conducted the orchestra from the piano.

Deaths. Henry Brant, the Pulitzer Prize-winning U.S. composer known for his "spatial" music, in which performers are dispersed throughout the concert hall, died in April at age 94. In July, Norman Dello Joio, one of the most prolific popular U.S. classical music composers, died at age 95. Donald Erb, one of the most widely performed U.S. composers of his generation, died in August at age 81. Giuseppe di Stefano, celebrated as one of the greatest operatic tenors of the 1900's, died in March 2008 at age 86.   ■ John von Rhein

See also **Popular music.**

Clothing. See Fashion.

Coal. See Energy supply.

Colombia. In 2008, President Álvaro Uribe Vélez maintained the highest approval rating—more than 80 percent—of any Latin American chief executive. Murder and kidnapping rates have declined during his two terms, and the government's 50-year war against well-armed rebel forces appeared to be winding down.

Dramatic hostage rescue. On July 2, Colombian commandos freed 15 hostages who had been held by the Revolutionary Armed Forces of Colombia (FARC), a rebel group long at war with the Colombian government. Among those freed were Íngrid Betancourt, kidnapped in 2002 when campaigning for the Colombian presidency, and three American civilian contractors. The Americans were captured after their drug surveillance flight crashed in rebel territory in 2003. Eleven Colombian soldiers and police officers were also rescued.

In 2008, FARC's infrastructure was in disarray following the death from natural causes of Manuel Marulanda, the movement's leader since 1964, and the killing of his principal deputy, Raúl Reyes, in a government attack. A third top FARC commander, Gerardo Aguilar Ramírez, was captured during the hostage rescue.

March for Freedom and Peace. The joy inspired by the freeing of the captives was dampened by concern for those still held by FARC militants. On July 20, more than 1 million Colombians, clad in white, marked their country's Independence Day by taking to the streets, chanting "Free them now!" More than 700 people were believed to still be in FARC hands, including roughly 25 political figures.

Military murders. An investigation in October 2008 discovered that the Colombian military had been killing innocent civilians to inflate body counts of dead rebels and criminals. It was found that poor civilians were being randomly collected, dressed as rebels, and shot. Since 2002, there were more than 500 suspected cases leading to the deaths of 1,015 people. General Mario Montoya, the supreme army commander, resigned on Nov. 4, 2008, following the dismissal of 27 other members of the military. More than 2,300 state and military officials were under investigation for the killings. Colombia's human rights record was already under scrutiny as part of a Colombian Supreme Court investigation into the government's ties to right-wing paramilitary groups linked to drug trafficking, murder, and kidnapping.   ■ Nathan A. Haverstock

See also **Latin America**.

Commonwealth of Independent States.
See Armenia; Azerbaijan; Belarus; Georgia; Kazakhstan; Kyrgyzstan; Russia; Uzbekistan; Ukraine.

Comoros. See Africa.

American Keith Stansell arrives at Lackland Air Force Base, Texas, on July 2, 2008, after five years of captivity with rebels in Colombia. Stansell was one of 15 people freed by the Colombian military in a daring rescue operation.

Computer. Computer technology branched out in multiple directions in 2008. A huge military supercomputer reached an important milestone in computing speed. Conversely, companies released small, lightweight laptop computers, called "netbooks," that were designed for greater portability rather than greater computing power.

Macbook Air. In January, Apple Inc. of Cupertino, California, released an ultra-thin laptop computer, the Macbook Air. The computer weighs only three pounds (1.36 kilograms) and can fit easily in a manila envelope. But it lacks a feature standard on most laptop computers—an optical disc drive for watching DVD's and installing software. The standard Macbook Air model costs about $1,800, several hundred dollars more than Apple's regular Macbook laptops.

New netbooks. Computer makers released several new netbook laptop computers in 2008. They included the Mini-Note by Palo Alto, California-based Hewlett-Packard, and the Aspire, manufactured by Taiwan-based Acer Inc. Like the MacBook Air, netbooks are small, lightweight laptop computers designed with a focus on portability and Internet use. The netbooks are much less expensive than Apple's laptop but have fewer features and less computing speed.

With price tags as low as $300, companies marketed netbooks as cheap gateways to the Internet and useful Web programs. Many programs that once had to be installed on computers—such as word processors and video games—are now available on Web sites. Netbooks also take advantage of the ability to store data, photos, and other documents on Internet servers rather than on a computer's hard drive. Some larger computer companies worried that netbook sales could threaten their business model, which relies on selling powerful, expensive computers.

Petaflop record. In June 2008, a military supercomputer made history as the first machine capable of performing one petaflop—that is, a thousand trillion—calculations per second. The $133-million computer, called Roadrunner, uses 12,960 chips, including chips originally designed for Sony's Playstation 3 video game console. Many of its chips can perform separate calculations at the same time. Hour for hour, the machine uses about as much energy as does a shopping center.

The military plans to use Roadrunner to perform calculations involving military weapons. For example, the machine's computing power could accurately simulate extremely complex nuclear explosions down to minute details. Scientists have requested the opportunity to use Roadrunner to help model problems involving climate change before the military begins its calculations.

■ Daniel Kenis

Congo (Brazzaville). See Africa.

Congo (Kinshasa). The Democratic Republic of Congo (DRC) remained politically unstable in 2008. President Joseph Kabila faced ongoing opposition from rebels and ill-disciplined army units, mainly in the mineral-rich eastern provinces of North and South Kivu. In November, the United Nations (UN) Security Council voted to expand its mission (known by the acronym MONUC) in Congo from 17,000 to 20,000 peacekeepers.

Broken cease-fire. In the hope of establishing permanent peace in the DRC's turbulent east, UN and Western diplomats brokered a deal on Jan. 23, 2008, between Kabila's government and more than 20 rival rebel groups, including one led by renegade army general Laurent Nkunda. As with similar deals signed since the end of the civil war in 2002, the 2008 cease-fire failed to hold. Subsequent clashes involving various armed groups competing for power and influence in eastern DRC resulted in large numbers of killings and rapes. In 2008, the UN estimated that over 1 million people had been displaced in North and South Kivu, including those who had fled previous phases of fighting. More than 3 million people died during the civil war (1998–2002), mostly from conflict-related hunger and disease.

Ugandan rebels known as the Lord's Resistance Army staged multiple raids on villages in northeastern Congo in late December, killing nearly 190 people. The raids were carried out after DRC and Uganda launched a joint offensive on December 14 to flush the rebels out of bases in Congo's Garamba National Park.

At the root of the 2008 clashes was the presence of Hutu militias in the DRC. These militias had carried out the 1994 genocide of Tutsis in Rwanda and subsequently fled to eastern DRC. They are bitter enemies of Nkunda, a Congolese Tutsi.

Bemba arrested. Jean-Pierre Bemba, the former vice president of the DRC who was defeated by Joseph Kabila in the 2006 presidential election, was arrested in Belgium on May 24, 2008. He was accused by the International Criminal Court (ICC) of leading Congolese rebels in a campaign of rape and torture in neighboring Central African Republic in 2002 and 2003.

UN investigation. On Aug. 12, 2008, UN Secretary-General Ban Ki-moon said that he was "deeply troubled" by a UN report claiming that some Indian peacekeepers may have engaged in sexual exploitation and abuse of local women in North Kivu. Earlier in April, a BBC television investigation claimed that the UN had covered up evidence of arms sales to DRC rebels and trafficking in gold and ivory by Indian and Pakistani UN troops.

■ Simon Baynham

See also **Africa; Disasters; United Nations.**

Congress of the United States.

The Democrats increased their majorities in both houses of Congress in the November 2008 elections. During the year, Congress passed three major bills intended to help bolster the faltering U.S. economy.

Elections were held on November 4 for all 435 seats in the House of Representatives and for 35 seats in the 100-seat Senate. The Democrats won 257 House seats—a pickup of 21 seats—compared with the Republicans' 178. The Democrats also picked up at least 7 Senate seats, thus raising their majority to at least 58 seats (including the seats of 2 independents who caucused with them) compared with at least 41 for the Republicans. One Senate race, in Minnesota, remained undecided at the end of 2008. The new Congress was scheduled to take office on Jan. 6, 2009.

Many political analysts attributed the Democrats' success to public dissatisfaction with the Republican administration of President George W. Bush. In the months leading up to the election, that dissatisfaction had been amplified by anxiety over the nation's worst financial crisis in decades. The Democrats also benefited from the popularity of the Democratic presidential candidate, U.S. Senator Barack Obama of Illinois, who was elected on Nov. 4, 2008, over his Republican opponent, U.S. Senator John McCain of Arizona.

In Alaska, Anchorage Mayor Mark Begich (D.) narrowly defeated U.S. Senator Ted Stevens (R.), ending Stevens's 40-year Senate career. Just eight days before the election, Stevens had been convicted by a federal jury on seven felony counts of making false statements on Senate financial disclosure forms. The jury found Stevens guilty of violating federal ethics laws by knowingly failing to report more than $250,000 in home improvements and other gifts that he had received from an oil services firm and its chief executive officer.

At least three other Republican Senate incumbents were also ousted by Democratic challengers. In New Hampshire, former Governor Jeanne Shaheen (D.) unseated U.S. Senator John Sununu (R.) to become the state's first woman U.S. senator. Sununu had defeated Shaheen in the 2002 Senate race. In North Carolina, Kay Hagan (D.), a state senator, upset U.S. Senator Elizabeth Dole (R.). In Oregon, Jeff Merkley (D.), speaker of the state House, beat U.S. Senator Gordon Smith (R.) in a close race.

In addition, Democrats won three races for Senate seats being left open by retiring Republicans. In Colorado, U.S. Representative Mark Udall (D.) defeated former U.S. Representative Bob Schaffer (R.) for the seat being vacated by U.S. Senator Wayne Allard. In New Mexico, U.S. Representative Tom Udall (D.) beat U.S. Representative Steve Pearce (R.) for the seat being vacated

by U.S. Senator Pete Domenici. (The two Udalls are cousins.) In Virginia, former Governor Mark Warner (D.) beat former Governor Jim Gilmore (R.) for the seat being vacated by U.S. Senator John Warner. (The two Warners are not related.)

In Kentucky, U.S. Senate Minority Leader Mitch McConnell (R.) survived a stiff challenge from millionaire businessman Bruce Lunsford (D.). In Georgia, U.S. Senator Saxby Chambliss (R.) defeated Jim Martin (D.), a former state representative, in a December 2 runoff election after neither man received 50 percent of the vote on November 4. In Louisiana, U.S. Senator Mary Landrieu (D.) held onto her seat despite a strong bid by State Treasurer John Kennedy (R.).

In Minnesota, officials were still recounting ballots and resolving legal disputes in late December to determine the winner of an extremely close Senate race. After the initial counting of returns, U.S. Senator Norm Coleman (R.) led Al Franken (D.), a former comedian and writer for TV's "Saturday Night Live," by only about 200 votes out of 2.9 million cast.

In House races, Democratic challengers defeated 14 Republican incumbents, including Chris Shays (R., Connecticut), who lost to businessman Jim Himes (D.). Himes's win made New England's House delegation entirely Democratic. New York City Councilman Michael McMahon (D.) won an open House seat in Staten Island, making New York City's House delegation entirely Democratic. Five Democratic incumbents lost, including William Jefferson (D., Louisiana), who was awaiting trial on federal corruption charges, including bribery. Jefferson lost in a delayed election on December 6 to lawyer Anh "Joseph" Cao (R.), the first Vietnamese American elected to Congress.

The economy. Congress spent much of 2008 debating how to reinvigorate the struggling U.S. economy. Americans faced falling home values and rising home foreclosure rates; high prices for fuel and food; increasing unemployment; and a crisis in financial and credit markets that led to the failure or take-over of several major investment banks and commercial banks.

Early in the year, Congress passed a bipartisan economic stimulus bill that provided $168 billion in tax relief to consumers and businesses. President Bush signed the bill on February 13. Under the bill, most Americans in 2008 received income tax rebates of up to $600 for individuals and up to $1,200 for couples. The bill also allowed businesses to write off a larger portion of their equipment purchases.

In the first half of 2008, legislators batted around proposals to bolster the housing market but could not reach agreement on a plan. Then, in July, Treasury Secretary Henry Paulson announced that the government needed immediate

MEMBERS OF THE UNITED STATES HOUSE OF REPRESENTATIVES

The House of Representatives of the second session of the 111th Congress consisted of 257 Democrats and 178 Republicans (not including representatives from American Samoa, the District of Columbia, Guam, the Northern Mariana Islands, Puerto Rico, and the Virgin Islands) when it convened on Jan. 6, 2009. This table shows congressional district, legislator, and party affiliation. Asterisk (*) denotes those who served in the 110th Congress; dagger (†) denotes "at large."

Alabama
1. Jo Bonner, R.*
2. Bobby Bright, D.
3. Mike Rogers, R.*
4. Robert Aderholt, R.*
5. Parker Griffith, D.
6. Spencer Bachus, R.*
7. Artur Davis, D.*

Alaska
†Donald E. Young, R.*

Arizona
1. Ann Kirkpatrick, D.
2. Trent Franks, R.*
3. John Shadegg, R.*
4. Ed Pastor, D.*
5. Harry Mitchell, D.*
6. Jeff Flake, R.*
7. Raúl Grijalva, D.*
8. Gabrielle Giffords, D.*

Arkansas
1. Marion Berry, D.*
2. Vic Snyder, D.*
3. John Boozman, R.*
4. Mike Ross, D.*

California
1. Mike Thompson, D.*
2. Wally Herger, R.*
3. Dan Lungren, R.*
4. Tom McClintock, R.
5. Doris Matsui, D.*
6. Lynn Woolsey, D.*
7. George Miller, D.*
8. Nancy Pelosi, D.*
9. Barbara Lee, D.*
10. Ellen Tauscher, D.*
11. Jerry McNerney, D.*
12. Jackie Speier, D.*
13. Pete Stark, D.*
14. Anna Eshoo, D.*
15. Mike Honda, D.*
16. Zoe Lofgren, D.*
17. Sam Farr, D.*
18. Dennis Cardoza, D.*
19. George Radanovich, R.*
20. Jim Costa, D.*
21. Devin Nunes, R.*
22. Kevin McCarthy, R.*
23. Lois Capps, D.*
24. Elton Gallegly, R.*
25. Howard McKeon, R.*
26. David Dreier, R.*
27. Brad Sherman, D.*
28. Howard Berman, D.*
29. Adam Schiff, D.*
30. Henry Waxman, D.*
31. Xavier Becerra, D.*
32. Hilda Solis, D.*††
33. Diane Watson, D.*
34. Lucille Roybal-Allard, D.*
35. Maxine Waters, D.*
36. Jane Harman, D.*
37. Laura Richardson, D.*
38. Grace Napolitano, D.*
39. Linda Sánchez, D.*
40. Ed Royce, R.*
41. Jerry Lewis, R.*
42. Gary Miller, R.*
43. Joe Baca, D.*
44. Ken Calvert, R.*
45. Mary Bono Mack, R.*
46. Dana Rohrabacher, R.*
47. Loretta Sanchez, D.*
48. John Campbell, R.*
49. Darrell Issa, R.*
50. Brian Bilbray, R.*
51. Bob Filner, D.*
52. Duncan Hunter, R.*
53. Susan Davis, D.*

Colorado
1. Diana DeGette, D.*
2. Jared Polis, D.
3. John Salazar, D.*
4. Betsy Markey, D.
5. Doug Lamborn, R.*
6. Mike Coffman, R.
7. Ed Perlmutter, D.*

Connecticut
1. John Larson, D.*
2. Joe Courtney, D.*
3. Rosa DeLauro, D.*
4. Jim Himes, D.
5. Christopher Murphy, D.*

Delaware
†Michael Castle, R.*

Florida
1. Jeff Miller, R.*
2. Allen Boyd, D.*
3. Corrine Brown, D.*
4. Ander Crenshaw, R.*
5. Virginia Brown-Waite, R.*
6. Clifford Stearns, R.*
7. John Mica, R.*
8. Alan Grayson, D.
9. Gus Bilirakis, R.*
10. C. W. Bill Young, R.*
11. Kathy Castor, D.*
12. Adam Putnam, R.*
13. Vern Buchanan, R.*
14. Connie Mack, R.*
15. Bill Posey, R.
16. Tom Rooney, R.
17. Kendrick Meek, D.*
18. Ileana Ros-Lehtinen, R.*
19. Robert Wexler, D.*
20. Debbie Wasserman Schultz, D.*
21. Lincoln Diaz-Balart, R.*
22. Ron Klein, D.*
23. Alcee Hastings, D.*
24. Suzanne Kosmas, D.
25. Mario Diaz-Balart, R.*

Georgia
1. Jack Kingston, R.*
2. Sanford Bishop, Jr., D.*
3. Lynn Westmoreland, R.*
4. Hank Johnson, D.*
5. John Lewis, D.*
6. Tom Price, R.*
7. John Linder, R.*
8. Jim Marshall, D.*
9. Nathan Deal, R.*
10. Paul Broun, R.*
11. Phil Gingrey, R.*
12. John Barrow, D.*
13. David Scott, D.*

Hawaii
1. Neil Abercrombie, D.*
2. Mazie K. Hirono, D.*

Idaho
1. Walt Minnick, D.
2. Mike Simpson, R.*

Illinois
1. Bobby Rush, D.*
2. Jesse Jackson, Jr., D.*
3. Daniel Lipinski, D.*
4. Luis Gutierrez, D.*
5. vacant
6. Peter J. Roskam, R.*
7. Danny Davis, D.*
8. Melissa Bean, D.*
9. Jan Schakowsky, D.*
10. Mark Kirk, R.*
11. Debbie Halvorson, D.
12. Jerry Costello, D.*
13. Judy Biggert, R.*
14. Bill Foster, D.
15. Timothy Johnson, R.*
16. Donald Manzullo, R.*
17. Phil Hare, D.*
18. Aaron Schock, R.
19. John Shimkus, R.*

Indiana
1. Peter Visclosky, D.*
2. Joe Donnelly, D.*
3. Mark Souder, R.*
4. Steve Buyer, R.*
5. Dan Burton, R.*
6. Mike Pence, R.*
7. André Carson, D.
8. Brad Ellsworth, D.*
9. Baron P. Hill, D.*

Iowa
1. Bruce Braley, D.*
2. David Loebsack, D.*
3. Leonard Boswell, D.*
4. Thomas Latham, R.*
5. Steve King, R.*

Kansas
1. Jerry Moran, R.*
2. Lynn Jenkins, R.

3. Dennis Moore, D.*
4. Todd Tiahrt, R.*

Kentucky
1. Edward Whitfield, R.*
2. Brett Guthrie, R.
3. John Yarmuth, D.*
4. Geoff Davis, R.*
5. Harold (Hal) Rogers, R.*
6. Ben Chandler, D.*

Louisiana
1. Steve Scalise, R.
2. Anh "Joseph" Cao, R.
3. Charles Melancon, D.*
4. John Fleming, R.
5. Rodney Alexander, R.*
6. Bill Cassidy, R.
7. Charles Boustany, Jr., R.*

Maine
1. Chellie Pingree, D.
2. Michael Michaud, D.*

Maryland
1. Frank Kratovil, Jr., D.
2. C. A. Ruppersberger, D.*
3. John Sarbanes, D.*
4. Donna Edwards, D.
5. Steny Hoyer, D.*
6. Roscoe Bartlett, R.*
7. Elijah Cummings, D.*
8. Chris Van Hollen, D.*

Massachusetts
1. John Olver, D.*
2. Richard Neal, D.*
3. James McGovern, D.*
4. Barney Frank, D.*
5. Niki Tsongas, D.*
6. John Tierney, D.*
7. Edward Markey, D.*
8. Michael Capuano, D.*
9. Stephen Lynch, D.*
10. William Delahunt, D.*

Michigan
1. Bart Stupak, D.*
2. Peter Hoekstra, R.*
3. Vernon Ehlers, R.*
4. Dave Camp, R.*
5. Dale Kildee, D.*
6. Fred Upton, R.*
7. Mark Schauer, D.
8. Mike Rogers, R.*
9. Gary Peters, D.
10. Candice Miller, R.*
11. Thaddeus McCotter, R.*
12. Sander Levin, D.*
13. Carolyn Cheeks Kilpatrick, D.*
14. John Conyers, Jr., D.*
15. John Dingell, D.*

Minnesota
1. Timothy Walz, D.*
2. John Kline, R.*

††Appointed to positions in the Obama Cabinet or administration.

3. Eric Paulsen, R.
4. Betty McCollum, D.*
5. Keith Ellison, D.*
6. Michele Bachmann, R.*
7. Collin Peterson, D.*
8. James Oberstar, D.*

Mississippi
1. Travis Childers, D.
2. Bennie Thompson, D.*
3. Gregg Harper, R.
4. Gene Taylor, D.*

Missouri
1. William Clay, D.*
2. Todd Akin, R.*
3. Russ Carnahan, D.*
4. Ike Skelton, D.*
5. Emanuel Cleaver II, D.*
6. Samuel Graves, R.*
7. Roy Blunt, R.*
8. Jo Ann Emerson, R.*
9. Blaine Luetkemeyer, R.

Montana
†Dennis Rehberg, R.*

Nebraska
1. Jeff Fortenberry, R.*
2. Lee Terry, R.*
3. Adrian Smith, R.*

Nevada
1. Shelley Berkley, D.*
2. Dean Heller, R.*
3. Dina Titus, D.

New Hampshire
1. Carol Shea-Porter, D.*
2. Paul Hodes, D.*

New Jersey
1. Robert Andrews, D.*
2. Frank LoBiondo, R.*
3. John Adler, D.
4. Christopher Smith, R.*
5. Scott Garrett, R.*
6. Frank Pallone, Jr., D.*
7. Leonard Lance, R.
8. William Pascrell, Jr., D.*
9. Steven Rothman, D.*
10. Donald Payne, D.*
11. Rodney Frelinghuysen, R.*
12. Rush Holt, D.*
13. Albio Sires, D.*

New Mexico
1. Martin Heinrich, D.
2. Harry Teague, D.
3. Ben Luján, D.

New York
1. Tim Bishop, D.*
2. Steve Israel, D.*
3. Peter King, R.*
4. Carolyn McCarthy, D.*
5. Gary Ackerman, D.*
6. Gregory Meeks, D.*
7. Joseph Crowley, D.*
8. Jerrold Nadler, D.*
9. Anthony Weiner, D.*
10. Edolphus Towns, D.*
11. Yvette Clarke, D.*
12. Nydia Velázquez, D.*
13. Michael McMahon, D.

14. Carolyn Maloney, D.*
15. Charles Rangel, D.*
16. José Serrano, D.*
17. Eliot Engel, D.*
18. Nita Lowey, D.*
19. John Hall, D.*
20. Kirsten Gillibrand, D.*
21. Paul Tonko, D.
22. Maurice Hinchey, D.*
23. John McHugh, R.*
24. Michael Arcuri, D.*
25. Daniel Maffei, D.
26. Christopher Lee, R.
27. Brian Higgins, D.*
28. Louise McIntosh
    Slaughter, D.*
29. Eric Massa, D.

North Carolina
1. G. K. Butterfield, D.*
2. Bob Etheridge, D.*
3. Walter Jones, Jr., R.*
4. David Price, D.*
5. Virginia Foxx, R.*
6. Howard Coble, R.*
7. Mike McIntyre, D.*
8. Larry Kissell, D.
9. Sue Myrick, R.*
10. Patrick McHenry, R.*
11. Heath Shuler, D.*
12. Melvin Watt, D.*
13. Brad Miller, D.*

North Dakota
†Earl Pomeroy, D.*

Ohio
1. Steve Driehaus, D.
2. Jean Schmidt, R.*
3. Michael Turner, R.*
4. Jim Jordan, R.*
5. Robert Latta, R.*
6. Charles Wilson, D.*
7. Steve Austria, R.
8. John Boehner, R.*
9. Marcy Kaptur, D.*
10. Dennis Kucinich, D.*
11. Marcia Fudge, D.
12. Pat Tiberi, R.*
13. Betty Sutton, D.*
14. Steven LaTourette, R.*
15. Mary Jo Kilroy, D.
16. John Boccieri, D.
17. Timothy Ryan, D.*
18. Zachary Space, D.*

Oklahoma
1. John Sullivan, R.*
2. Dan Boren, D.*
3. Frank Lucas, R.*
4. Tom Cole, R.*
5. Mary Fallin, R.*

Oregon
1. David Wu, D.*
2. Greg Walden, R.*
3. Earl Blumenauer, D.*
4. Peter DeFazio, D.*
5. Kurt Schrader, D.

Pennsylvania
1. Robert Brady, D.*

2. Chaka Fattah, D.*
3. Kathy Dahlkemper, D.
4. Jason Altmire, D.*
5. Glenn Thompson, R.
6. Jim Gerlach, R.*
7. Joe Sestak, D.*
8. Patrick Murphy, D.*
9. Bill Shuster, R.*
10. Christopher Carney, D.*
11. Paul Kanjorski, D.*
12. John Murtha, D.*
13. Allyson Schwartz, D.*
14. Michael Doyle, D.*
15. Charles Dent, R.*
16. Joseph Pitts, R.*
17. Tim Holden, D.*
18. Tim Murphy, R.*
19. Todd Platts, R.*

Rhode Island
1. Patrick Kennedy, D.*
2. James Langevin, D.*

South Carolina
1. Henry Brown, Jr., R.*
2. Joe Wilson, R.*
3. J. Gresham Barrett, R.*
4. Bob Inglis, R.*
5. John Spratt, Jr., D.*
6. James Clyburn, D.*

South Dakota
†Stephanie Herseth
  Sandlin, D.*

Tennessee
1. David Roe, R.
2. John J. Duncan, Jr., R.*
3. Zach Wamp, R.*
4. Lincoln Davis, D.*
5. Jim Cooper, D.*
6. Bart Gordon, D.*
7. Marsha Blackburn, R.*
8. John Tanner, D.*
9. Steve Cohen, D.*

Texas
1. Louis Gohmert, R.*
2. Ted Poe, R.*
3. Sam Johnson, R.*
4. Ralph M. Hall, R.*
5. Jeb Hensarling, R.*
6. Joe Barton, R.*
7. John Culberson, R.*
8. Kevin Brady, R.*
9. Al Green, D.*
10. Michael McCaul, R.*
11. K. Michael Conaway, R.*
12. Kay Granger, R.*
13. Mac Thornberry, R.*
14. Ron Paul, R.*
15. Rubén Hinojosa, D.*
16. Silvestre Reyes, D.*
17. Chet Edwards, D.*
18. Sheila Jackson-Lee, D.*
19. Randy Neugebauer, R.*
20. Charlie Gonzalez, D.*
21. Lamar Smith, R.*
22. Pete Olson, R.
23. Ciro Rodriguez, D.*
24. Kenny Marchant, R.*

25. Lloyd Doggett, D.*
26. Michael Burgess, R.*
27. Solomon Ortiz, D.*
28. Henry Cuellar, D.*
29. Gene Green, D.*
30. Eddie Bernice Johnson, D.*
31. John Carter, R.*
32. Pete Sessions, R.*

Utah
1. Rob Bishop, R.*
2. Jim Matheson, D.*
3. Jason Chaffetz, R.

Vermont
†Peter Welch, D.*

Virginia
1. Robert Wittman, R.*
2. Glenn Nye, D.
3. Robert Scott, D.*
4. J. Randy Forbes, R.*
5. Tom Perriello, D.
6. Robert Goodlatte, R.*
7. Eric Cantor, R.*
8. James Moran, Jr., D.*
9. Rick Boucher, D.*
10. Frank Wolf, R.*
11. Gerry Connolly, D.

Washington
1. Jay Inslee, D.*
2. Rick Larsen, D.*
3. Brian Baird, D.*
4. Doc Hastings, R.*
5. Cathy McMorris Rodgers, R.*
6. Norman Dicks, D.*
7. Jim McDermott, D.*
8. Dave Reichert, R.*
9. Adam Smith, D.*

West Virginia
1. Alan Mollohan, D.*
2. Shelley Moore Capito, R.*
3. Nick Rahall II, D.*

Wisconsin
1. Paul Ryan, R.*
2. Tammy Baldwin, D.*
3. Ron Kind, D.*
4. Gwen Moore, D.*
5. James Sensenbrenner, Jr., R.*
6. Thomas Petri, R.*
7. David Obey, D.*
8. Steve Kagen, D.*

Wyoming
†Cynthia Lummis, R.

Nonvoting representatives
American Samoa
Eni F. H. Faleomavaega, D.*
District of Columbia
Eleanor Holmes Norton, D.*
Guam
Madeleine Bordallo, D.*
Northern Mariana Islands
Gregorio "Kilili" Camacho Sablan, I.
Puerto Rico
Pedro Pierluisi, D.
Virgin Islands
Donna Christensen, D.*

MEMBERS OF THE UNITED STATES SENATE

The Senate of the first session of the 111th Congress consisted of 55 Democrats, 42 Republicans, 2 Independents, and 1 vacancy when it convened on Jan. 6, 2009. The first date in each listing shows when the senator's term began. The second date shows when the senator's term expires.

STATE	TERM
Alabama	
Richard C. Shelby, R.	1987-2011
Jeff Sessions, R.	1997-2015
Alaska	
Mark Begich, D.	2009-2015
Lisa Murkowski, R.	2002-2011
Arizona	
John McCain III, R.	1987-2011
Jon Kyl, R.	1995-2013
Arkansas	
Blanche Lambert Lincoln, D.	1999-2011
Mark Pryor, D.	2003-2015
California	
Dianne Feinstein, D.	1992-2013
Barbara Boxer, D.	1993-2009
Colorado	
Mark Udall, D.	2009-2015
Ken Salazar, D.*	2005-2011
Connecticut	
Christopher J. Dodd, D.	1981-2011
Joseph I. Lieberman, I.	1989-2013
Delaware	
Ted Kaufman, D.	2009-2011
Thomas Carper, D.	2001-2013
Florida	
Bill Nelson, D.	2001-2013
Mel Martinez, R.	2005-2011
Georgia	
Saxby Chambliss, R.	2003-2015
Johnny Isakson, R.	2005-2011
Hawaii	
Daniel K. Inouye, D.	1963-2011
Daniel K. Akaka, D.	1990-2013
Idaho	
Jim Risch, R.	2009-2015
Mike Crapo, R.	1999-2011
Illinois	
Richard J. Durbin, D.	1997-2015
[vacant]	
Indiana	
Richard G. Lugar, R.	1977-2013
Evan Bayh, D.	1999-2011
Iowa	
Charles E. Grassley, R.	1981-2011
Tom Harkin, D.	1985-2015
Kansas	
Sam Brownback, R.	1996-2011
Pat Roberts, R.	1997-2015
Kentucky	
Mitch McConnell, R.	1985-2015
Jim Bunning, R.	1999-2011

STATE	TERM
Louisiana	
Mary L. Landrieu, D.	1997-2015
David Vitter, R.	2005-2011
Maine	
Olympia Snowe, R.	1995-2013
Susan M. Collins, R.	1997-2015
Maryland	
Benjamin L. Cardin, D.	2007-2013
Barbara A. Mikulski, D.	1987-2011
Massachusetts	
Edward M. Kennedy, D.	1962-2013
John F. Kerry, D.	1985-2015
Michigan	
Carl Levin, D.	1979-2015
Debbie Stabenow, D.	2001-2013
Minnesota	
Amy Klobuchar, D.	2007-2013
undetermined in 2008	
Mississippi	
Thad Cochran, R.	1978-2015
Roger Wicker, R.	2008-2013
Missouri	
Christopher S. (Kit) Bond, R.	1987-2011
Claire C. McCaskill, D.	2007-2013
Montana	
Max Baucus, D.	1978-2015
Jon Tester, D.	2007-2013
Nebraska	
Mike Johanns, R.	2009-2015
Ben Nelson, D.	2001-2013
Nevada	
Harry M. Reid, D.	1987-2011
John Ensign, R.	2001-2013
New Hampshire	
Judd Gregg, R.	1993-2011
Jeanne Shaheen, D.	2009-2015
New Jersey	
Robert Menendez, D.	2006-2013
Frank R. Lautenberg, D.	2003-2015
New Mexico	
Tom Udall, D.	2009-2015
Jeff Bingaman, D.	1983-2013
New York	
Charles E. Schumer, D.	1999-2011
Hillary Rodham Clinton, D.*	2001-2013
North Carolina	
Kay Hagan, D.	2009-2015
Richard Burr, R.	2005-2011
North Dakota	
Kent Conrad, D.	1987-2013
Byron L. Dorgan, D.	1992-2011

STATE	TERM
Ohio	
Sherrod Brown, D.	2007-2013
George V. Voinovich, R.	1999-2011
Oklahoma	
James M. Inhofe, R.	1994-2015
Tom Coburn, R.	2005-2011
Oregon	
Ron Wyden, D.	1996-2011
Jeff Merkley, D.	2009-2015
Pennsylvania	
Arlen Specter, R.	1981-2011
Bob Casey, Jr., D.	2007-2013
Rhode Island	
Jack Reed, D.	1997-2015
Sheldon Whitehouse, D.	2007-2013
South Carolina	
Lindsey Graham, R.	2003-2015
Jim DeMint, R.	2005-2011
South Dakota	
Tim Johnson, D.	1997-2015
John Thune, R.	2005-2011
Tennessee	
Bob Corker, R.	2007-2013
Lamar Alexander, R.	2003-2015
Texas	
Kay Bailey Hutchison, R.	1993-2013
John Cornyn, R.	2003-2015
Utah	
Orrin G. Hatch, R.	1977-2013
Robert F. Bennett, R.	1993-2011
Vermont	
Patrick J. Leahy, D.	1975-2011
Bernie Sanders, I.	2007-2013
Virginia	
Mark Warner, D.	2009-2015
Jim Webb, D.	2007-2013
Washington	
Patty Murray, D.	1993-2011
Maria Cantwell, D.	2001-2013
West Virginia	
Robert C. Byrd, D.	1959-2013
John D. Rockefeller IV, D.	1985-2015
Wisconsin	
Herbert Kohl, D.	1989-2013
Russell D. Feingold, D.	1993-2011
Wyoming	
John Barrasso, R.	2007-2013
Mike Enzi, R.	1997-2015

*Appointed to positions in the Obama Cabinet.

authority to stabilize the giant mortgage finance companies Fannie Mae and Freddie Mac. These two companies held or guaranteed about $5 trillion worth of the $12 trillion in outstanding mortgages on U.S. houses. Their stock prices had sunk that month because of investor fears about their financial condition. Congress added Fannie and Freddie rescue provisions to a mortgage relief bill it had been considering and quickly sent the bill to President Bush, who signed it on July 30. The bill gave the Treasury Department authority to lend new money to Fannie and Freddie and to buy assets from them, including their mortgage holdings and shares of their stock. A new agency was created to strengthen oversight over the companies. In addition, the bill included a variety of housing aid provisions, including authorization for the Federal Housing Administration to insure $300 billion worth of home loans. This provision was designed to help homeowners who were at risk of foreclosure to replace their adjustable-rate mortgages with fixed-rate, government-insured mortgages. At the time the bill was enacted, Paulson said he did not think that the Fannie and Freddie rescue authority would have to be exercised. However, the housing market continued to deteriorate, and on September 7, the two companies were placed under full government control.

In mid-September, turmoil erupted on Wall Street. One major investment banking firm, Lehman Brothers, declared bankruptcy; another one, Merrill Lynch, was acquired by Bank of America; and an insurance giant, American International Group (AIG), was bailed out by the U.S. Federal Reserve System. The financial crisis stemmed from the housing crisis because many financial institutions had invested heavily in securities backed by mortgages. In an attempt to contain the ripple effect of the financial instability, President Bush urged Congress to pass legislation to give the Treasury Department the authority to buy up to $700 billion worth of troubled assets from financial institutions. Congressional negotiators met with Bush administration officials for several days in late September to hammer out the details of the plan. The legislation that emerged had bipartisan support but also faced significant opposition. Many lawmakers argued that taxpayer money should not be used to bail out Wall Street executives who had made bad investment decisions. Several Republicans objected to the huge government intervention on grounds that it violated free-market principles. This opposition led the House to reject the rescue measure on September 29, prompting a huge decline in stock markets. On October 1, the Senate packaged the rescue measure with several other provisions—including extensions of numerous expiring tax breaks and an increase in federal insurance for bank deposits—and passed it. The House reversed itself on October 3 and approved the Senate package, and President Bush signed the bill later that day. The $700-billion rescue package, called the Troubled Asset Relief Program (TARP), was originally pitched as a plan to buy up financial firms' hard-to-sell mortgage-backed assets. However, the legislation gave the Treasury Department broad discretionary powers, and by the end of 2008, TARP funds had mostly been used to make direct capital injections into financial firms by buying stock in them.

Late in the year, the automakers General Motors, Ford, and Chrysler found themselves facing severe financial difficulties. In September, Congress had appropriated $7.5 billion to guarantee $25 billion in loans for the automakers to help them upgrade their factories for the production of fuel-efficient vehicles. The automakers returned to Congress in November and December to plead for further federal aid. On December 10, the House passed a $14-billion emergency loan package aimed at helping the automakers stave off bankruptcy. However, the next day, the bill failed to clear the Senate and was scuttled.

In the face of rising unemployment, Congress enacted two extensions of unemployment benefits in 2008. The first one, signed by President Bush on June 30, provided 13 extra weeks of benefits to people who had exhausted their 26 weeks of regular benefits. The second extension, signed by the president on November 21, provided another 7 to 13 weeks of benefits, with more weeks in states with unemployment rates of at least 6 percent.

Energy policy debates cropped up repeatedly in Congress during 2008, particularly during the first half of the year, when oil prices rose to more than $140 a barrel and gasoline prices shot up above $4 a gallon. Most proposals, including an effort to limit speculation in energy commodities markets, stalled in the face of partisan disagreement. However, Congress did renew $16.9 billion in tax credits for renewable energy, attaching the provisions to the financial rescue bill that President Bush signed on October 3. Congress also allowed a 27-year-old ban on oil drilling off the Atlantic and Pacific coasts to expire on October 1. The energy discussions in Congress subsided in the second half of the year as oil and gasoline prices plummeted and as lawmakers turned their attention to the financial crisis.

Other legislation. In July, Congress enacted a controversial bill overhauling the Foreign Intelligence Surveillance Act. The bill expanded the government's eavesdropping powers in terrorism cases and granted immunity to telecommunications companies that had participated in a secret National Security Agency warrantless wiretapping program. In June, Congress provided $162 billion for the wars in Iraq and Afghanistan. In September, Congress approved a $630-billion stopgap spending bill for the 2009 fiscal year, which began on Oct. 1, 2008. The bill provided increased, full-year funding for the Defense, Homeland Security, and Veterans Affairs departments but left funding for other agencies at fiscal 2008 levels through March 6, 2009. Congress also passed legislation in 2008 that expanded the reach of the Americans with Disabilities Act; required insurers to provide mental health coverage comparable to the coverage available for physical ailments; provided increased educational benefits for veterans; reauthorized Amtrak, the national passenger rail system; reauthorized the Higher Education Act and boosted financial aid for college students; renewed federal farm programs for five years; and banned employers and health insurers from discriminating on the basis of genetic information. ■ Mike Lewis

See also **Agriculture; Automobile; Bank: A Special Report; Cabinet, U.S.; Democratic Party; Disability; Education; Elections: A Special Report; Health care issues; Labor and employment; Republican Party; Safety; Taxation; Telecommunications; Transportation; United States, Government of the; United States, Government of the: A Special Report; United States, President of the.**

Conservation. Scientists issued stark warnings about endangered species in 2008, though encouraging news on some species offered hope.

Mass mammal loss. Half the world's mammals are declining and at least one-quarter are endangered, according to a report from the Switzerland-based conservation group International Union for Conservation of Nature (IUCN). The report is the most thorough survey of mammals since 1996, drawing on research by 1,800 scientists in more than 130 countries. It warned that monkeys and other primates are especially vulnerable. Nearly 80 percent of primates in Asia are endangered, mostly due to hunting and deforestation. Dolphins and other sea mammals are also under threat from pollution and fishing nets.

Apart from the special report, the IUCN maintains a "Red List" describing the conservation status of more than 40,000 species. The updated list found that nearly 40 percent of these species are threatened with extinction. One-third of the species that make coral reefs are threatened, as are one-third of frogs and other amphibians. Many scientists believe that people may be causing the first mass extinction of species since the dinosaurs disappeared 65 million years ago.

Preserving diversity. Representatives from 191 countries met in Bonn, Germany, in May 2008 for the United Nations Convention on Biological Diversity. Participants noted that 16 years after the convention was established at the Earth Summit in Rio de Janeiro, Brazil, extinction is still reducing the variety of living things. Environmental destruction and extinctions cost the world economy as much as $4.8 trillion a year, according to a report given at the meeting. Representatives discussed the profits wealthier nations make by exploiting the biological wealth of poor nations. Members agreed to develop a plan to help poorer nations benefit more from their natural resources. The convention previously set the goal of achieving a "significant reduction" in extinctions by 2010.

Good gorilla news. In August 2008, the Wildlife Conservation Society, a New York-based conservation group, announced that researchers had discovered more than twice as many western lowland gorillas living in central Africa than was estimated previously. The survey found about 125,000 gorillas living in remote northern areas of Congo (Kinshasa). The areas surveyed cover 18,000 square miles (47,000 square kilometers) of dense forest and a swampy region that biologists nicknamed the "green abyss." Scientists had thought that hunting, war, and disease had reduced gorilla numbers to a total of 50,000. Despite the encouraging news, scientists warned that serious threats to gorilla survival remain. These threats include the Ebola virus and hunting by people.

Western lowland gorillas are by far the most numerous kind of this animal. Mountain gorillas, by contrast, number fewer than 1,000 animals in the wild. In February, Congo (Kinshasa), Rwanda, and Uganda agreed to coordinate their efforts to save mountain gorillas, which have been hit hard by poaching and a series of brutal wars in the region. The project will discourage poaching by promoting ecotourism and by boosting the incomes of local villagers.

Leatherback comeback. In June, leatherback sea turtles returned to a Texas beach they had not used in decades. Leatherbacks are the world's largest turtles, reaching up to 8 feet (2.4 meters) long and weighing up to 2,000 pounds (907 kilograms). They spend their lives in the ocean but crawl onto beaches to lay eggs. A park biologist in Texas confirmed the first nesting of leatherbacks there since the 1930's.

Leatherback numbers have plunged in recent years, particularly in the Pacific Ocean. The beaches at Terengganu, in Malaysia, teemed with leatherback nests in the 1960's. Wildlife officials confirmed only three nests there in 2008, though this was an improvement over 2007, when no leatherbacks nested there. People eat leatherback flesh and eggs, and the animals are often caught unintentionally in fishing nets. The IUCN, which lists leatherbacks as critically endangered, has urged that certain areas of the Pacific Ocean be closed to commercial fishing when the turtles migrate.

Disappearing devils. Australia declared Tasmanian devils endangered in May 2008. Tasmanian devil numbers have fallen by more than half in the last decade, due to a rare, contagious cancer.

Polar bears. The U.S. Fish and Wildlife Service (FWS) declared polar bears "threatened" under the Endangered Species Act in May. Three years of lawsuits preceded the classification. About 20,000 polar bears survive, but their numbers are in decline as Arctic sea ice shrinks due to global warming. Polar bears need sea ice to hunt seals, and scientists have found the bodies of polar bears that starved to death. Other bears have drowned trying to swim to distant ice. The FWS report on protecting polar bears warned that they may be extinct by 2050.

Beluga whales. The U.S. government also declared that a population of Alaskan beluga whales is endangered. About half the population of the relatively small, whitish whales in Cook Inlet, near Anchorage, have been lost over the last decade.

Salmon collapse. The salmon fishery in the American Northwest collapsed in 2008, spurring the U.S. government to ban commercial salmon fishing there in May. For the second year in a row, only a fraction of the expected number of salmon returned to the Sacramento River in northern California to breed. Scientists are uncertain what caused the collapse.

Madagascar's riches. France pledged $20 million in 2008 to preserve wildlife in Madagascar. Madagascar has been isolated from the rest of Africa for millions of years, and 98 percent of its mammals, 92 percent of its reptiles, and 80 percent of its plants live nowhere else. Many species have become endangered as people have cut down the island's forests. The money will go to a $50-million World Wildlife Federation trust fund.

Homeless pandas. The deadly earthquake that struck southwestern China in May 2008 damaged or destroyed more than 80 percent of the area where wild giant pandas live, according to the Chinese government. Nearly 90 percent of all wild pandas live in the region. Forty-nine nature reserves were damaged, including the giant panda

In 2008, the polar bear became the first species classified as threatened under the Endangered Species Act because of climate change. Shrinking sea ice brought about by global warming has caused polar bear numbers to dwindle to about 20,000.

center at the Wolong Nature Reserve. Fortunately, only one panda was killed by the quake.

Wolves in court. United States federal courts found that the FWS improperly removed gray wolves from the endangered list in 2007. The courts issued injunctions restoring federal protection to gray wolves in the Rocky Mountain and Great Lakes regions. In October 2008, the FWS reopened its effort to remove federal protection for the wolves. ■ Edward Ricciuti

See also **Biology; China; Disasters; Global warming; Ocean; Zoos.**

Costa Rica. See Latin America.
Côte d'Ivoire. See Africa.

The Colorado, long essential to agriculture in the Southwest, has become increasingly vital to the region's fast-growing cities— at a time of prolonged drought.

The Colorado River:
Lifeline of the Southwest

By Edward Ricciuti

The Colorado River has played such a vital role in the development of the American Southwest that it is often referred to as that region's "lifeblood." In the rain-poor Southwest, growth has been limited not by land, which is plentiful, but by water, which is not. In fact, for much of the Southwest, the Colorado River is the only reliable major source of water.

Colorado River water has transformed desert and other dry areas into cities, farmland, and ranches. Historically, most of the water supplied by the river and its extensive system of tributaries—at least 80 percent—has gone to farmers and livestock producers. Colorado water irrigates about

3.5 million acres (1.4 million hectares) of agricultural land. Since the mid-1900's, however, Colorado River water has become increasingly important to cities and towns in the Southwest, one of the fastest-growing regions of the United States. In 2008, it supplied more than 25 million people with drinking water, relatively few of whom lived directly along the river.

By the early 2000's, public officials and water management experts openly worried about the future of the Colorado River and the states that depend on it. Urban areas that have thrived because of the river now pose a serious threat to its health. Rising demand is only part of the problem, however. Since the late 1990's, Colorado, along with much of the West, has suffered from the worst drought to hit the region in more than 100 years. In addition, scientists warned that rising global temperatures could drastically reduce the snowfall in the Rockies. Melting snow running off the mountains in the spring and early summer is the source of about 96 percent of the river's water.

Worst of all, scientific studies of the Colorado's average flow over the past 1,200 years have revealed that modern plans to manage the water supply are haunted by a serious mistake made just before the Southwest

The Grand Canyon was created over the past 6 million years mainly by the turbulent flow of the Colorado River. Described as "the most sublime of earthly spectacles," the canyon displays 2 billion years of geologic history in its walls, which may rise 1 mile (1.6 kilometers) above the river.

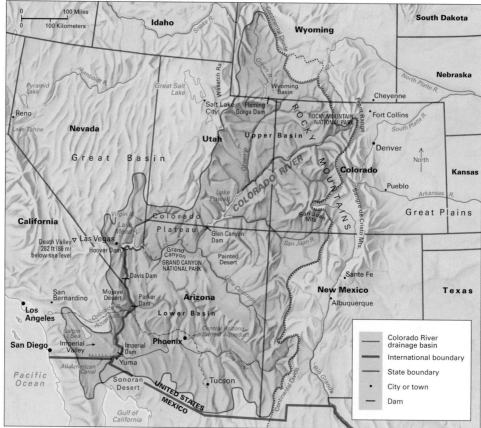

The Colorado River and its many tributaries drain about 250,000 square miles (650,000 square kilometers) of the western United States and Mexico. As the river flows from the Rocky Mountains to the Gulf of California, it descends about 10,000 feet (3,048 meters).

began experiencing its wildfire growth. In the 1920's, delegates from the seven states in the Colorado River *basin* (drainage area) and the U.S. government created a plan to tame the flood-prone river and divide up its water. The planners based the water allotments for various regions on measurements of the river's flow taken at that time. However, the water levels that the planners considered "normal" were actually abnormally high, because previous decades in the late 1800's and early 1900's were unusually wet in the Colorado basin.

Now, in the 2000's, it is increasingly clear that the Colorado cannot supply the amount of water the planners believed it could. Many public officials and water-use experts fear that the competition for the Colorado's water could become increasingly fierce among urban areas, farmers and ranchers, wildlife habitats, and recreational interests.

West to the sea

The Colorado River and its extensive system of tributaries drain a vast region about 250,000 square miles (650,000 square kilometers) in area. The Colorado basin includes parts of Arizona, California, Colorado, Nevada, New Mexico, Utah, and Wyoming, and a small part of Mexico. The river itself begins in the Rocky Mountains, at La Poudre Pass Lake

The author:
Edward Ricciuti is a free-lance writer.

in Colorado. From there, it flows mainly southwest across 1,360 miles (2,189 kilometers) of the United States and 90 miles (145 kilometers) of Mexico.

Before the river was harnessed in the early 1900's, it emptied into the Gulf of California, just south of the United States-Mexico border. However, so much of the Colorado's water is now dammed and diverted that, except in very wet years, it vanishes in the sands of the Sonoran Desert several miles above its original mouth. The Colorado River Delta, a major wetland habitat, now receives only about 25 percent of the water that flowed through it 100 years ago.

More water is diverted from the Colorado basin than from any other river system in the United States. In fact, the Colorado is one of the most controlled rivers in the world. Nearly every drop of water flowing through it and its tributaries is allotted under a complex network of laws, compacts, court decisions, and contracts collectively known as "The Law of the River." The river provides water to the seven basin states as well as small areas of western Texas and Idaho, Mexico, and Native American tribal lands. To regulate and channel this water, the Bureau of Reclamation, an agency of the U.S. Department of the Interior, operates a network of 479 dams, 58 reservoirs, and 5 major canal systems.

Historically, southern California has been the river's major recipient. Without the Colorado, the fertile Imperial Valley in southeastern California would quickly return to the desert it was in the early 1900's. The Imperial Valley, which covers more than 500,000 acres (202,000 hectares), is one of the nation's major sources of produce, ranging from tomatoes to dates. It is fed by water diverted from the Colorado through a canal system that includes the All-American Canal, the largest irrigation canal in the world. The Colorado also supplies water to Los Angeles, San Diego, San Bernardino, and, in fact, most of urbanized

Farms in California's Imperial Valley and elsewhere in the Southwest use at least 80 percent of the water diverted from the Colorado River. The Imperial Valley, a major source of vegetables for U.S. consumers, uses about half of the water allotted to the upper half of the Colorado basin, about 978 trillion gallons (3,700 trillion liters) annually.

EXPLORING THE COLORADO RIVER

In 1869, John Wesley Powell, a geologist, biologist, and explorer, led the first expedition of white men to travel in boats down the Colorado River through the Grand Canyon. At that time, the Colorado was the only unnavigated, unmapped river system in the United States. Powell's record of the difficult journey, *The Exploration of the Colorado River of the West,* was published in 1875 as a report to the Smithsonian Institution in Washington, D.C. During the expedition, Powell recorded information about the terrain and the plant and animal life along the river. He also studied the cultures of the Indian tribes he met along the way.

Members of the Powell expedition navigate one of the many rapids on the Colorado River, in an illustration based on photographs taken by crew member John K. Hillers.

"All winter long snow falls on its mountain-crested rim, filling the gorges, half burying the forests, and covering the crags and peaks ... When the summer sun comes this snow melts and tumbles down the mountain sides in millions of cascades. A million cascade brooks unite to form a thousand torrent creeks; a thousand torrent creeks unite to form half a hundred rivers beset with cataracts; half a hundred roaring rivers unite to form the Colorado, which rolls, a mad, turbid stream, into the Gulf of California."

....From The Exploration of the Colorado River and Its Canyons (1875)

By John Wesley Powell

The Colorado River originates at La Poudre Pass Lake (above) in the Rocky Mountains of Colorado. Near the historic mouth of the river (left), a kayak sits mired at low tide in the mudflats that cover much of the Colorado River Delta. Little of the river reaches its historic mouth near the Gulf of California because so much of the water is diverted for farms and cities in the Southwest.

southern California. The population in this area—more than 23 million in 2008—was expected to grow to 65 million by 2030. California's vast irrigated cropland, plus its high urban water usage, has made it endlessly thirsty for the Colorado's water, often to the displeasure of other states.

Population boom in the desert

The river is equally important to other urban areas in the Southwest. In recent decades, some of the driest areas of the United States have also been among those with the greatest growth in population. Cities and their suburbs have sprawled far into the desert. Low-cost land and warm winters have brought vast numbers of people into landscapes once populated by the sidewinder and scorpion. Generators at dams along the river also provide hydroelectric power for homes and industry in many parts of this vast region. Abundant electric power also made air conditioning widespread, contributing to the boom times in the desert.

THE SOUTHWEST'S SOARING POPULATION

	1958	2008
California	14,337,000	36,846,000
Arizona	1,140,000	6,516,000
Nevada	267,000	2,640,000

Source: World Book estimates based on data from the U.S. Census Bureau.

The flow of the Colorado River varies naturally over time. Since 1999, however, water levels have dropped significantly every year except in 2005 because of lower-than-normal snow- and rainfall.

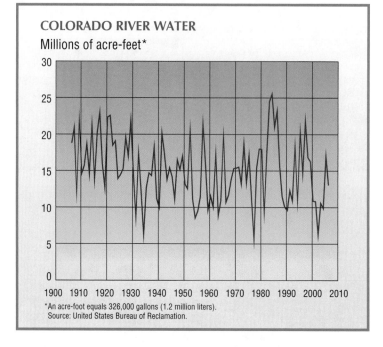

COLORADO RIVER WATER
Millions of acre-feet*

*An acre-foot equals 326,000 gallons (1.2 million liters).
Source: United States Bureau of Reclamation.

Pipelines carry the Colorado's water to Phoenix, Tucson, and other cities in Arizona. The population of Maricopa County, which includes Phoenix, has grown at an annual rate of more than 17 percent since 2000. That translates to a net increase of almost 300 people a day. Population estimates predict that within a few years, the Phoenix and Tucson metropolitan areas, now 120 miles (193 kilometers), apart will merge.

The situation is similar in other parts of the Southwest. Las Vegas exists because of water from the Colorado. In 1980, the population of Clark County, Nevada, which includes Las Vegas, was less than 500,000. Today, the county has four times as many people. Subdivisions now stand in the shadow of Red Rock Canyon, a wilderness preserve outside of Las Vegas that only a few years ago was a half hour's drive from the nearest suburbs. Water consumption in the county doubled between 1985 and 2000.

Since 2002, Las Vegas and other towns covered by the Southern Nevada Water Authority (SNWA) have reduced the area's total water consumption by about 20 percent. One of the chief conservation methods is a program that pays residents to replace their water-hungry turf with low-water plants. The SNWA is also attempting to build a pipeline to carry water from eastern Nevada to the southern part of the state, though this plan is highly controversial.

Water from the Colorado River is also diverted eastward, particularly to the fast-growing cities and towns along the eastern face of the Rocky Mountains in Colorado. Known as the Front Range Urban Corridor, this population belt extends from Pueblo to Denver and Fort Collins and across the Wyoming border to Cheyenne. Drier than the western

slopes of the Rockies, the Front Range is also far more populous. By 2007, 4.2 million people lived on the Front Range, up 13 percent from 2000. As the population on the Front Range has grown, it has sucked up an increasing amount of water from the Colorado drainage basin. Historically, agricultural interests in western Colorado had to share only a small portion of their water with urban areas on the other side of the mountains, but that situation has changed. The Front Range now gets half of its drinking water from the Colorado River.

Badger Creek Rapid in Marble Canyon, Arizona, is one of a number of areas of fast-moving water that have survived on the heavily dammed Colorado River.

Taming the river

Native Americans have used water from the Colorado to irrigate their crops for hundreds of years. Efforts to siphon large amounts of water from the river and its tributaries, however, began when U.S. settlers entered the region. As early as 1854, water was diverted for irrigation at Blacks Fork, a tributary of the Colorado in Wyoming.

Before it was dammed, the flow of the Colorado River was erratic. Water flowing down the river could drop to a comparative trickle or swell to a raging flood, depending on the weather. Periodic flooding because of snowmelt in the spring or thunderstorms in the summer damaged agriculture and other activities in its basin and also wasted precious water. Falling water levels because of droughts created hardships for the region's farmers and ranchers.

The dams that were built to tame the Colorado in the 1900's were designed to store and channel water for agriculture, residential use, and industry; to produce electric power; and, importantly, to control floods. The two most important dams on the river are the Hoover Dam, a national landmark finished in 1935, and the Glen Canyon Dam,

Hoover Dam, completed in 1935, blocked the flow of the Colorado River near the Arizona-Nevada border to create Lake Mead. The dam and reservoir were designed to control flooding along the river, provide water for farms in Arizona and Colorado, and generate hydroelectric power.

Fast-growing towns around Phoenix, Arizona, and other areas of the Southwest have increased the demand for water from the Colorado River. By 2030, the population of the area served by the river was expected to grow from 25 million to more than 65 million.

completed in 1963. Glen Canyon Dam, which is about 650 miles (1,000 kilometers) southwest of Denver, is in Arizona, but its large reservoir, Lake Powell, lies mostly in Utah. Hoover Dam is about 25 miles (40 kilometers) southeast of Las Vegas and about 250 miles (400 kilometers) downstream from the Glen Canyon Dam. It impounds Lake Mead. At about 115 miles (185 kilometers) long and 589 feet (180 meters) deep, Lake Mead is the largest artificially created lake and reservoir in the United States.

Controlling the southward flow of the Colorado from Lake Powell to Lake Mead is the key to managing what are known as the Upper Basin and the Lower Basin. Under the 1922 Colorado River Compact, the Colorado basin was split geographically, into upper (northern) and lower (southern) halves. The dividing line was at Lees Ferry, near Page, Arizona, just south of the Utah border. The states in the Upper Basin include Colorado, New Mexico, Utah, and Wyoming; the Lower Basin includes Arizona, California, and Nevada.

According to the compact, both basins were entitled to 7.5 million acre-feet of water per year. (An acre-foot is the amount of water needed to cover 1 acre to a depth of 1 foot, equal to about 326,000 gallons [1.2 million liters], enough water for a family of four for one year.) In actuality, however, the Upper Basin was required to deliver 75 million acre-feet of water to the Lower Basin during each 10-year period. Because the flow of the river varies from year to year, depending on snowpack and rainfall, the Upper Basin states sometimes had difficulty meeting that requirement. In addition, conflict over water allotments among the states within each basin arose immediately, particularly between Arizona and California. In fact, Arizona did not ratify the Colorado River Compact until 1944.

Disputes over water allotments continued even after the construction of the Glen Canyon Dam in 1963. That project was designed to enable the Upper Basin states to store water for their own use while meeting their obligation to the Lower Basin. However, at times Lake Powell, impounded by the dam, still served as a water storage bank for Lake Mead. If reserves in Lake Powell rose during wet years, they could be removed during times of drought to serve the Lower Basin, rather than maintained for use in the Upper Basin.

Historic meeting
The drought in the Southwest that began in 1999 spurred the need for a new agreement. Water levels in Lake Mead and Lake Powell had reached historic lows. By 2005, Lake Powell was down to one-third of its

Las Vegas and other fast-growing towns in southern Nevada get about 90 percent of their water from Lake Mead, though Nevada is entitled to only about 2 percent of the Colorado's annual flow. Despite major water conservation efforts, the Lake Mead reservoir was only about half full in 2008.

capacity and 145 feet (44 meters) below capacity. By 2003, Lake Mead was slightly fuller—at two-thirds of its capacity—but only because of water released from Lake Powell. Marinas and other recreational facilities that had been at water's edge were high and dry. Facilities for ferry service had to be picked up and moved lower down the lake's slopes.

In December 2007, U.S. Secretary of the Interior Dirk Kempthorne signed what he called a "historic" agreement intended to promote increased cooperation among the seven states in the basin. In place until 2026, the agreement is designed "to meet the challenges of the current eight-year drought in the basin and, potentially, low-water conditions caused by continued drought or other causes in the future." Among those "other causes" could be a severe decrease in meltwater from a dwindling snowpack in the Rockies.

The new plan ensures that Lake Powell and Lake Mead are managed to rise and fall together in both dry and wet years, so that Powell will not be excessively drained to keep Mead full. For the first time, Lower Basin states will have to cut back on water if Lake Mead drops to a critical point; both areas of the basin will share the risks of drought. The agreement also set up a framework allowing cities in the Lower Basin to buy water from farmers who let their fields go fallow in dry years.

There have been spurts of recovery from the drought. A slightly wetter-than-normal winter in 2007 filled Lake Powell to its highest level in six years during the summer of 2008. Although the lake rose by 45 feet (14 meters), it was still only 63 percent full. With Powell filling, managers released more water than planned into Lake Mead. As a result, Mead fell by only about half of the 12 feet (4 meters) water managers had predicted. Still, Lake Mead remained only about half full. Meanwhile, the drought showed no sign of abating.

Drought as a fact of life

Even in years with sufficient rain, the annual flow of water in the Colorado River is much less than that of many other rivers with similar watersheds. The Columbia River in the Pacific Northwest, for example, drains a basin about the same size as the Colorado's but carries about 12 times as much water. The Colorado's annual flow is only 1 percent of the Mississippi River's. The average flow at Lees Ferry in the 1920's was from 16 million to 17 million acre-feet. However, the measurements were made during a prolonged rainy period that had raised the flow to an unusually high level. Although the annual average flow in some years dropped to 13.5 million acre-feet, the 1922 Colorado Compact was based on the higher estimate.

Evidence is mounting that there is no such thing as an average or normal flow in the Colorado—and that long, periodic droughts are the rule rather than the exception. "No single year will ever be normal," states the Bureau of Reclamation. There are wet periods and, commonly, spells of drought, some long, some short. Three droughts lasting from 4 to 11 years occurred in the 1900's. According to the U.S. Geological Survey (USGS), long-term cycles of cooling and warming in the Pacific Ocean, not yet fully understood, may influence precipitation in the Colorado basin.

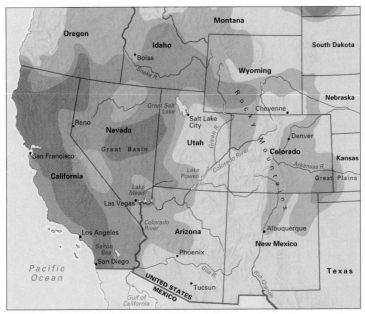

In 2008, a prolonged drought continued to affect much of the Colorado River basin. The drought was the area's worst in more than 500 years, according to some scientific studies.

Drought conditions in the southwestern United States in late 2008

Areas with severe drought conditions

Areas with moderate drought conditions

Areas near or at drought conditions

Areas without drought conditions

0	200 Miles
0	200 Kilometers

Source: National Drought Mitigation Center, University of Nebraska-Lincoln.

A line of white mineral deposits, known as the "bathtub ring," in Lake Powell, the reservoir for the Glen Canyon Dam, became in the early 2000's a symbol of the drought plaguing the Southwest. In 2008, water levels in the lake rebounded somewhat because higher-than-normal snowmelt from the Rocky Mountains increased the water flow of the Colorado River.

Cactus and other desert plants decorate a garden in Scottsdale, Arizona. Scottsdale is one of a number of Southwestern cities that pay residents to replace grassy turf with low-water-use landscaping.

A scientific study of annual tree rings, which are thick or thin depending on rainfall, shows that the Colorado region has experienced many cycles of drought since the end of the 1400's. Released in 2007 by the National Academies, a scientific advisory group to the U.S. government, the study suggests that some of these droughts lasted for decades. The report warned that similar droughts are likely to occur in the future and "may be longer and more severe because of a regional warming trend that shows no signs of dissipating. Coping with water shortages is becoming more difficult because of rapid population growth, and technology and conservation will not provide a panacea for dealing with limited water supplies in the long run." The Academies report added that a recipe for disaster is in the works: "limited water supplies, rapidly increasing populations, warmer regional temperatures and the specter of recurrent drought." It predicted a future of continued conflict among water users.

Other reports also painted a similarly bleak picture. A briefing on the impact of climate change on the Colorado River for members of Congress by the USGS in 2008 warned of substantial water supply shortages. Another study group led by the U.S. Department of Agriculture warned of a decreasing snowpack and earlier runoff. Rapid, early melting of the snowpack can trigger sudden floods, wasting water and causing damage along rivers.

In October, Colorado Governor Bill Ritter sponsored a conference on managing drought and climate risk in Denver. The goal of the meeting was to bring together officials from a variety of state agencies involved in water issues to discuss challenges posed by global warming. Conferees noted some scientific predictions that, with rising temperatures and less mountain snow, rainfall rather than snowfall would be the main source of the region's water. Governor Ritter noted, "… the present and future reliability of its [Colorado basin's] water resources face the combined effects of increased growth, changing landscapes and climate change. Climate change, together with natural variability and increasing demand, may lead to … drought conditions rarely or never observed in the historic record."

Is there a solution?

Many water experts believe that conservation may be the only workable way to cope with the problem of supply and demand in the Colorado basin. Among the methods discussed have been using wastewater for agricultural irrigation, relying more on water-saving drip irrigation, planting more drought-resistant crops, and ending wasteful landscaping practices—such as trying to grow New England lawns in the desert. Water conservation alone without measures to control development, however, may not work, at least according to the report by the National Academies. "Technology and conservation measures are useful and necessary for stretching existing water supplies but any gains in water supply will be eventually absorbed by the growing population."

The new agreement on managing the Colorado's water expires in 2026. Many experts believe that given the urgent nature of the water problem, at least a partial solution must be found long before then to avert disaster.

Courts in 2008 legalized gay marriage in two states, ruled in favor of a fundamentalist Mormon sect in Texas, and convicted a United States senator and a big-city mayor of felonies.

Gay marriage. On May 15, the California Supreme Court ruled 4 to 3 that the state Constitution guaranteed gay couples the right to marry. The decision voided state laws that had limited marriage to opposite-sex couples. Local officials in California began issuing marriage licenses to same-sex couples on June 16. But on November 4, voters approved a state ballot initiative to amend the Constitution to recognize only marriage between a man and a woman. About 18,000 gay couples had wed in California prior to the initiative's passage, and it was unclear whether their marriages would be allowed to stand. On November 19, the California Supreme Court agreed to review the legality of the initiative.

On October 10, the Connecticut Supreme Court voted 4 to 3 to strike down the state's ban on gay marriage as unconstitutional. The court ruled that the state's civil union law, intended to give gay couples the same basic rights as married couples, was an inadequate substitute for marriage rights. Local officials in Connecticut began issuing marriage licenses to same-sex couples on November 12. Massachusetts was the only other state where gay marriage was legal in 2008.

YFZ Ranch case. In April 2008, Texas state police and child welfare officials removed more than 400 children from the Yearning for Zion (YFZ) Ranch near Eldorado, Texas. The YFZ Ranch is owned by the Fundamentalist Church of Jesus Christ of Latter-Day Saints (FLDS), a sect that practices polygamy. The officials removed the children because of sexual abuse concerns, including concerns that underage girls were being forced to marry and have sexual relations with much older men. However, on May 22, a Texas appeals court ruled that the state acted improperly in removing the children because it had failed to show that they were in immediate danger. On May 29, the Texas Supreme Court upheld the lower court's ruling. Nearly all of the children were returned to their parents in June. By the end of 2008, most of the child welfare cases involving the FLDS children had been dropped, but criminal charges related to underage and polygamous marriages had been brought against some FLDS members.

Politicians convicted. On October 27, a U.S. District Court jury in Washington, D.C., convicted U.S. Senator Ted Stevens (R., Alaska) on seven felony counts of making false statements on Senate financial disclosure forms. The jury found Stevens guilty of violating federal ethics laws by knowingly failing to report more than $250,000 in home improvements and other gifts that he had received from an oil services company and its chief executive officer. Despite the conviction, Stevens continued his Senate reelection bid. But

Anchorage Mayor Mark Begich narrowly defeated Stevens in the November 4 election.

On September 4, in a Michigan circuit court, Kwame Kilpatrick, the Democratic mayor of Detroit, pleaded guilty to two felony charges of obstruction of justice and pleaded no contest to one felony charge of assaulting a police officer. He had faced other charges, including perjury, but they were dropped as part of plea deals. The obstruction-of-justice charges stemmed from his efforts to cover up an extramarital affair with his former chief of staff. He had lied about the affair, under oath, during a whistle-blower case brought by police officers who claimed they were fired for investigating wrongdoing by the mayor's staff. Kilpatrick was sentenced to four months in jail and ordered to pay the city $1 million in restitution. He resigned as mayor on September 18 and began his jail sentence on October 28.

Guantánamo terrorism cases. On June 5, five alleged high-level members of the terrorist network al-Qa`ida were arraigned before a U.S. military commission at Guantánamo Bay, Cuba. The men, all Guantánamo detainees, each faced 2,973 charges of murder, one for each victim of the Sept. 11, 2001, attacks against the United States. The most prominent defendant was Khalid Shaikh Mohammed, a Pakistani believed to be the mastermind behind the attacks.

Two Guantánamo detainees were convicted in 2008 in the first trials held under the 2006 Military Commissions Act. (A third detainee, David Hicks, was convicted in 2007 in a plea deal before trial.) On Aug. 6, 2008, a military jury convicted Salim Hamdan, a Yemeni and a former driver for al-Qa`ida leader Osama bin Laden, of giving material support to al-Qa`ida. The jury acquitted Hamdan of conspiracy to commit terrorist acts. He was sentenced to 5 ½ years in prison, with credit for the 5 years he had already served. On November 25, the U.S. military returned Hamdan to Yemen, where he served the last month of his sentence. On October 31, a military jury convicted Ali Hamza al-Bahlul, a Yemeni and a former al-Qa`ida propaganda chief, of conspiracy, solicitation to commit murder, and providing material support for terrorism. He was sentenced to life in prison.

Detention rulings. On June 12, the U.S. Supreme Court ruled that Guantánamo prisoners were entitled to habeas corpus—that is, the right to challenge their detention in federal court. Judges began to hear Guantánamo habeas corpus cases later in 2008. On October 7, a U.S. District Court judge in Washington, D.C., ordered that 17 Chinese Uygurs be released from Guantánamo and allowed to enter the United States. The government had already cleared the Uygurs for release but did not want to return them to China, where they would likely be persecuted,

and could not find other countries willing to take them. The government also did not want to allow the Uygurs into the United States and thus appealed the judge's order. On October 20, a three-judge panel of the U.S. Court of Appeals for the District of Columbia voted to allow the government to continue holding the Uygurs at Guantánamo pending resolution of their case.

On November 20, in another habeas corpus case, a U.S. District Court judge in Washington, D.C., ordered the release of five Algerians from Guantánamo, saying that the government's evidence for holding them was weak. The judge ruled that a sixth Algerian should not be released because he was a worker for al-Qa`ida.

On July 15, the U.S. Court of Appeals for the Fourth Circuit upheld the U.S. government's authority to indefinitely detain a U.S. resident as an "enemy combatant." The decision came in the case of Ali Saleh Kahlah al-Marri, a Qatari being held in a U.S. military prison in South Carolina. Al-Marri had been arrested at his Illinois residence in 2001 and designated an "enemy combatant" in 2003. The decision overturned a 2007 ruling by a three-judge panel of the court. On Dec. 5, 2008, the U.S. Supreme Court announced that it would review Marri's case.   ■ Mike Lewis

See also **Crime; Human rights; Supreme Court of the United States.**

Cricket.
United States billionaire Sir Allen Stanford in 2008 sponsored a deal with the England and Wales Cricket Board for an annual "winner take all," $20-million Twenty20 challenge between England and the Stanford Superstars in Antigua (West Indies). The controversial event, which ended on November 2 with an easy Superstars win over England, was another sign that cash and quick-fire Twenty20 were challenging the traditions of cricket.

Indian Premier League. The success of the Indian Premier League (IPL) strengthened the position of the Board of Control for Cricket in India (BCCI) in world cricket. Eight franchises lured world stars for the IPL Twenty20 tournament in April and May in India. Mahendra Singh Dhoni of Chennai Super Kings was the highest-paid player ($1.5 million). Rajasthan Royals, led by Australian Shane Warne, beat Kings in the final.

Test cricket. In 2008 tests, England twice beat New Zealand, 2-1 at home and 2-0 in New Zealand, but lost 1-2 to South Africa. Michael Vaughan resigned the captaincy to Kevin Pietersen. South Africa also beat West Indies 2-1, and Bangladesh 2-0. Against Bangladesh, South Africa's opening batsmen Neil McKenzie (226) and Graeme Smith (232) hit 415 to break a first-wicket record for test matches that had lasted since 1956.

India and South Africa, vying with Australia for

the number-one spot, fought a close test in April 2008, tying their first match and then winning one match each. West Indies also leveled with Sri Lanka, which gained its first test win in the Caribbean, thanks to the leading wicket-taker Muttiah Muralitharan. Sri Lanka also beat India 2-1. Australia recorded a 16th consecutive win during their 2-1 win over India but lost 0-2 in India at year-end, when India also beat England (X-X). During the 2-0 victory over West Indies, Australian captain Ricky Ponting passed 10,000 runs in test matches, the seventh player in cricket history to do so.

ODI's. New Zealand beat Bangladesh 3-0 with a stunning batting blitz by Brendon McCullum (80 not out in 28 balls in the final game) Zealand came out a 3-1 winner in both of their 2008 ODI tussles against England. England ODI captain Paul Collingwood stepped down in favor of Kevin Pietersen, who secured a 4-0 win over South Africa.

India beat Sri Lanka 3-2 and thrashed England 5-0. Pakistan was starved of international cricket at home because of security concerns, which led to the postponement of the International Cricket Council Champions Trophy scheduled for September. But the Pakistanis cruised to 5-0 wins over Zimbabwe and Bangladesh, with batter Salman Butt amassing a record-breaking 451 runs against Bangladesh. South Africa won over West Indies (5-0) and Bangladesh (3-0). West Indies beat Sri Lanka 2-0 but lost 0-5 to Australia, which easily topped Bangladesh.

Twenty20. Twenty20 produced enthusiastic crowds and innovative techniques. England's Kevin Pietersen startled the New Zealand opposition and fans by changing his batting stance from right-handed to left-handed mid-play. Brendon McCullum (New Zealand) hit a world's record 158 in the IPL. The Twenty20 World Cup was scheduled for England in 2009.

English cricket. Durham won the 2008 County Championship. Warwickshire won Division Two, Middlesex the Twenty20 Cup, and Essex the Friends Provident Trophy. South African Martin van Jaarsveld, playing for Kent against Surrey, hit two 100's and took 5 wickets in an inning. This all-round feat had been done just once before, by Sri Lanka's Mahela Jayawardene, in 1997. In a Friends Provident Trophy match, Essex batsman Ravi Bopara scored 201 not out, only the seventh player to score a one-day 200.

Women's cricket. In an ODI series, England beat New Zealand 3-1. By beating Australia, England retained the coveted Ashes honor. The series was Australia's first home defeat in 36 years. Preparation for the 2009 ICC Women's World Cup in Australia included England wins over West Indies and South Africa. ■ Brian Williams

See also **Australia; India; United Kingdom.**

Crime. The number of violent crimes in the United States decreased in 2007 after increasing for two straight years, reported the Federal Bureau of Investigation (FBI) in September 2008. The FBI's annual "Crime in the United States" report includes data from more than 17,700 U.S. law enforcement agencies on the violent crimes of murder and nonnegligent manslaughter, forcible rape, robbery, and aggravated assault, as well as the property crimes of burglary, larceny-theft, motor vehicle theft, and arson.

According to the FBI report, the more than 1.4 million violent crimes in 2007 represented a decline of 0.7 percent compared with 2006. All four violent crimes in the report decreased in number—forcible rape rates by 2.5 percent; murders and nonnegligent manslaughters by 0.6 percent; aggravated assaults by 0.6 percent; and robberies by 0.5 percent.

The report noted that more than 9.8 million property crimes occurred in the United States in 2007, representing a decrease of 1.4 percent compared with 2006. This was the fifth straight year of property crime decreases. The number of motor vehicle thefts decreased by 8.1 percent; larceny-thefts by 0.6 percent; and burglaries by 0.2 percent.

The FBI estimated that law enforcement agencies across the United States made 14.2 million arrests in 2007, excluding arrests for traffic offenses. This number compared with 14.4 million arrests in 2006.

Hate crimes. Law enforcement agencies in the United States reported 7,624 incidents of hate crimes, representing 9,006 separate criminal offenses, to the FBI in 2007. These numbers were contained in the FBI's "Hate Crimes Statistics 2007" report, released in October 2008. The FBI defines a hate crime as a crime motivated by bias against a particular race, religion, sexual orientation, ethnicity/national origin, or disability.

According to the report, 52 percent of the victims of U.S. hate crimes in 2007 were targeted because of their race; 17 percent because of their religious beliefs; 16 percent because of their sexual orientation; and 14 percent because of their ethnicity or national origin. Property destruction or damage accounted for 32 percent of all reported hate crime offenses; personal intimidation, for 29 percent; simple assault, for 12 percent; and aggravated assault, for 8 percent.

Anthrax attacks. As federal prosecutors were preparing to charge Bruce E. Ivins with murder in connection with the anthrax terrorist attacks that killed 5 people and injured at least 17 others in late 2001, Ivins, a microbiologist at the U.S. Army laboratory at Ft. Detrick, Maryland, committed suicide in July 2008. Ivins, who reportedly had a history of psychiatric problems, had been under surveillance by the FBI for many months in connection with the crimes.

The anthrax attacks took place within weeks of the Sept. 11, 2001, airplane terrorist attacks on the United States. Letters containing anthrax spores (inactive forms of the *Bacillus anthracis* bacterium) were mailed to several government and media addresses in the United States. The deadly bacteria became active when the spores were inhaled or entered the victims' bodies through other means. The incidents led to one of the largest criminal investigations in U.S. history.

Largest child custody battle. The Texas Supreme Court ruled in May 2008 that state authorities had no right to remove more than 400 children from the Yearning for Zion Ranch in western Texas in April. The compound was operated by a religious sect that practiced polygyny, in which one man is married to several women. Officials with the Texas Department of Family and Protective Services had argued that the children were in immediate danger of sexual or physical abuse, because the sect sanctioned marriage between underage girls and men. The high court, however, ruled that state officials failed to present evidence of such danger.

Fraud. By September 2008, U.S. financial institutions had received more than 62,000 reports of suspicious mortgage activity during fiscal year 2008 (Nov. 1, 2007-Oct. 31, 2008). According to the FBI, this number represented a record rate of mortgage fraud complaints, totaling as much as $6 billion.

Mortgage fraud includes any scheme by a mortgage applicant or other party to misstate, misrepresent, or omit information relied upon by an underwriter or lender to fund, purchase, or insure a mortgage loan. The mortgage fraud problem was part of the larger mortgage market crisis that threatened the stability of the U.S. and world economies in 2008. This crisis prompted the U.S. Congress to pass a multibillion-dollar rescue package for the financial industry in October.

In December, federal prosecutors indicted Bernard L. Madoff, director of New York City-based Bernard Madoff Investment Securities LLC, on charges of fraud. Through his company, he allegedly ran an elaborate Ponzi scheme, cheating a number of wealthy clients and charities out of as much as $50 billion. A Ponzi scheme, named for 1920's scam artist Charles Ponzi, involves making investors believe they are receiving profits from successful financial dealings when they are actually being paid with money from other investors. When investment money stops coming in, the scheme collapses. According to authorities, Madoff apparently ran the operation for decades.   ■ Alfred J. Smuskiewicz

See also **Bank: A Special Report; Courts; Prison.**

Croatia. A series of high-profile murders in 2008 in Zagreb, Croatia's capital, prompted the government of Prime Minister Ivo Sanader to launch a concerted attack on organized crime in October. The anticrime initiative gained greater urgency when leaders of the European Union (EU) warned Croatia's leaders in November that the crime wave, if unchecked, could hinder the country's prospects for admittance to the European association.

Violent crime. On October 6, a gunman shot and killed Ivana Hodak, the daughter of a prominent lawyer, in her Zagreb home. The lawyer, Zvonimir Hodak, had been defending a high-ranking former official of the Croatian Defense Ministry charged with embezzlement in a criminal court case.

On October 23, a car bomb killed Ivo Pukanic, the owner and editor-in-chief of the *Nacional*, a major Croatian newspaper, in downtown Zagreb. A colleague of Pukanic's was also killed in the car blast.

Croatian crime experts suspected that the two incidents, as well as other gangland-style murders in Croatia during 2008, were the work of operatives hired by a network of organized criminals active across the Balkans. In the case of Ivo Pukanic, the *Nacional* had exposed links between organized crime and prominent individuals, and Pukanic had received death threats for months.

Government response. As Croatian police, working closely with law enforcement officials of neighboring Serbia and Bosnia-Herzegovina, rounded up suspects to be indicted for the Hodak and the Pukanic murders, the Croatian government launched several initiatives to fight crime. Prime Minister Sanader dismissed and replaced his government's ministers of the interior and justice, as well as the national police chief. Sanader's government also established the National Office for Suppressing Corruption and Organized Crime—an anticrime unit dubbed "the Croatian FBI."

Foreign policy. The Sanader government's policy of encouraging Croatian integration into European institutions paid dividends in 2008. In April, NATO invited Croatia, along with Albania, to join the defense alliance as full members in 2009. On Nov. 5, 2008, the European Commission, the executive arm of the EU, issued a "road map" for Croatia's eventual accession to the EU, coupled with an admonition for Croatia to fight organized crime vigorously. The EU road map is an action list for a candidate nation to complete just before achieving full membership. EU officials projected that, barring failure to complete the road map, Croatia could join the EU in 2010 or early 2011.   ■ Sharon L. Wolchik

See also **Europe.**

Cuba. On Feb. 19, 2008, an ailing Fidel Castro Ruz, 81, resigned as president of Cuba. In power since 1959, Castro was succeeded by his brother Raúl, 76, who became acting president after Fidel fell seriously ill in July 2006. During 2008, Raúl Castro introduced small changes designed to make life easier under the Communist dictatorship. For example, Cubans were permitted to stay at luxury hotels and resorts, once reserved only for foreign tourists. People could also legally buy computers, DVD players, plasma televisions, and cell phones.

Agricultural reform. To energize a struggling agricultural sector, Cuban authorities turned to private farmers and cooperatives in April to increase food production. The objective was to bring under cultivation an estimated 55 percent of Cuba's arable land that was fallow. Much of this potentially fertile land was on state-controlled farms, where managers had failed to plant crops on more than two-thirds of their holdings.

Also, landless Cubans were able to acquire at no cost parcels of about 33 acres (13 hectares) each, which they could farm for 10 years without government interference. They were also provided with free seed, fertilizer, and tools. The new farmers would be allowed to renew their concessions for another 10 years and could increase their holdings to 100 acres (40 hectares).

Private agricultural cooperatives and agribusinesses were able to own larger tracts of land on 25-year renewable terms. "What we need is production, no matter where it comes from," said Gilberto Zayas, one of the program's administrators. He noted that Cuba needed thousands more farmers to reduce the estimated $2 billion spent on imported food in 2008.

Devastating tropical storms. A series of tropical storms in 2008 wreaked havoc on the Cuban economy. Authorities braced for a food crisis lasting at least six months following the loss of 30 percent of the island's crops. Damage from the storms was estimated at about $5 billion. This figure included damage to about 450,000 residences that left 200,000 people homeless. As Hurricane Ike bore down on the island in September, authorities oversaw the orderly evacuation of an estimated 2.6 million people, or 23 percent of the country's total population.

Russian ties. In August, Russian Prime Minister Vladimir Putin announced plans to restore closer ties with Cuba. Prior to its collapse in 1991, the former Soviet Union was an important supplier of oil, arms, and grain to Cuba. The renewed cooperation was hoped to improve Cuban energy, agriculture, and health services, while reasserting Russian influence in the Caribbean.

■ Nathan A. Haverstock

See also **Latin America; Weather.**

Cyprus. See Middle East.

Czech Republic. The center-right government of Prime Minister Mirek Topolanek experienced political setbacks in 2008. In October, local elections and elections to the upper chamber of the Czech parliament produced big gains for the main opposition party, the Social Democrats. Also in October, Topolanek's government survived a no-confidence vote by a narrow margin. The stability of the Czech government was of particular concern to the European Union (EU), since the Czech leadership was to hold the rotating EU presidency in the first half of 2009.

In part, Topolanek's governing coalition was losing popular support, analysts noted, because of its advocacy of an antimissile system proposed by the United States for installation in the Czech Republic and Poland. Polls revealed that a majority of Czech citizens were against the proposal. In July, Czech officials signed an agreement with U.S. officials for the antimissile installation, but as of late 2008, the Czech parliament had not ratified the accord.

The Czech economy slowed its pace of growth in 2008. The *gross domestic product* (GDP)—the value of all goods and services produced in a country in a year—grew at a rate of 4.6 percent in 2008, down from 6.5 percent in 2007.

■ Sharon L. Wolchik

See also **Europe.**

Dallas. The Dallas School District laid off 375 teachers on Oct. 16, 2008, as part of a cost-cutting program meant to close part of a projected $84-million deficit. The district earlier had to dismiss a number of employees, including counselors, clerks, and assistant principals. Superintendent Michael Hinojosa stated on September 10 that the district had failed to budget for 750 teachers that were hired for the Dallas Achieves educational reform effort. The school district remained solvent only because it had $120 million in reserves.

AT&T moves to Dallas. AT&T announced on June 26 that it was moving its headquarters from San Antonio to Dallas. AT&T officials said the relocation will help the telecom company's growth prospects. Dallas's central location, major airport, skilled work force, and low business costs have made it a top choice for corporate relocations.

Doors open to hurricane victims. In September, Dallas provided shelter for thousands of evacuees from the Texas Gulf Coast fleeing Hurricane Ike. The city opened the Dallas Convention Center, Loos Field House, and two recreation centers to shelter those left homeless by the storm. In late August, Dallas handled more than 1,000 evacuees from Hurricane Gustav.

Cotton Bowl expanded. A $57-million expansion of the Cotton Bowl near downtown Dallas was unveiled in September. The stadium in

Fair Park was expanded to 92,000 seats, making it the ninth largest stadium in the United States. The renovation also includes a 16,000-square-foot (1,485-square-meter) media center. The Cotton Bowl is the site of the annual football rivalry between the University of Oklahoma and the University of Texas. State Fair officials hope the expansion will attract more major football games.

Convention hotel controversy. A petition drive was launched in September 2008 to force a voter referendum on a proposed convention hotel in downtown Dallas. The City Council approved $42 million for acquisition of land for the hotel in May. A City Council committee recommended that the city build the hotel, at a cost of $450 million to $500 million, and have a major hotelier operate it. Convention business in Dallas is declining in part because there is no hotel connected to the convention center. In October, opponents submitted enough signatures to force a public vote on the hotel in May 2009.

Mavericks coach dismissed. Two years after he was named National Basketball Association (NBA) Coach of the Year, Dallas Mavericks Coach Avery Johnson was fired on April 30, 2008. Johnson had the highest winning percentage in franchise history, but he failed to get the Mavericks past the first round of the play-offs for two years after taking them to the NBA finals in 2006. Rick Carlisle was named as Johnson's replacement.

State-of-the-art homeless center opens. The Bridge, a $21-million center for the homeless, addicted, and mentally ill, opened on May 20, 2008, in downtown Dallas. The center is designed to rehabilitate the city's homeless population, which officials estimate may be as high as 7,000.

Corruption. Former City Council member James Fantroy was found guilty on February 28 of embezzling more than $20,000 from Paul Quinn College. He was sentenced in May to one month in prison and ordered to pay a fine. The judge had offered to suspend the prison sentence in exchange for a public apology, but Fantroy refused. Fantroy died on October 26 following a long battle with kidney cancer.

TV special on county jail opposed. County Commissioners and Dallas County Sheriff Lupe Valdez clashed in June over plans for the Discovery Channel to film a TV special in the county jail. Commissioners said the sheriff could not allow film crews in the jail without their permission. Sheriff Valdez disagreed. The Dallas County Jail has failed five straight state inspections and is under a federal court order to improve conditions for prisoners. A Discovery Channel crew had begun filming in the jail but withdrew on July 2 when a temporary restraining order was issued to block the sheriff's actions.   ■ Henry Tatum

See also **City; Weather.**

Dance. Several milestones were honored by three of the major ballet companies of the United States in 2008: the San Francisco Ballet, the American Ballet Theatre (ABT), and the New York City Ballet.

San Francisco Ballet turns 75. Founded in 1933, the San Francisco company is the oldest professional group in the United States. To celebrate its 75th anniversary, artistic director Helgi Tomasson invited 10 choreographers to create new works, all of which premiered within the first three nights of the company's New Works Festival, which ran from April 22 to May 6. Participating choreographers included such luminaries as Paul Taylor, Mark Morris, and Christopher Wheeldon; and such home-grown talent as Val Caniparoli, Yuri Possokhov, and Julia Adam. With each choreographer given total artistic freedom, the content of the ballets varied widely.

The company extended its celebration into autumn. In September, October, and November, it brought some of its premieres to the Harris Theater in Chicago; the New York City Center; the Orange County Performing Arts Center in Costa Mesa, California; and the Kennedy Center for the Performing Arts in Washington, D.C.

American Ballet Theatre tribute. Antony Tudor (1908-1987), considered one of the great choreographers of the 1900's, was especially esteemed for developing the psychological ballet. Yet his work is rarely performed, even by ABT, the company with which Tudor spent much of his career after leaving his native United Kingdom for New York City in 1939. To mark the 100th anniversary of Tudor's birth, ABT presented five of his ballets and part of a sixth: *Jardin aux Lilas* (1936), *Judgment of Paris* (1938), *Pillar of Fire* (1942), *Continuo* (1971), *The Leaves Are Fading* (1975), and the pas de deux from his *Romeo and Juliet* (1943). Tudor's *Romeo and Juliet* has largely been forgotten, but it is considered one of his most poetic ballets. It also exemplifies his originality; the score for Tudor's ballet was by the British composer Frederick Delius, rather than the more familiar score by Sergei Prokofiev. The Tudor tribute took place on October 31 at the New York City Center.

Tribute at New York City Ballet. The 90th anniversary of Jerome Robbins's birth was the occasion for a season-long retrospective from April 29 to June 29 by the New York City Ballet. The retrospective was centered on the company's home, the New York State Theater at the Lincoln Center for the Performing Arts in New York City. Although more famous for his work on Broadway, Robbins spent the bulk of his career with the City Ballet, where he worked alongside George Balanchine. The retrospective on Robbins included 33 of his ballets, ranging from *Fancy*

Free, which premiered in 1944, to Robbins's last ballet, *Brandenburg,* which premiered in 1997. During the retrospective, on June 18, a well-known principal dancer at City Ballet, Damian Woetzel, retired from performance. Woetzel danced three Robbins ballets as a farewell, *Fancy Free, Rubies,* and *Prodigal Son.*

The other important event of the City Ballet's spring season was the premiere, on May 29, 2008, of *Concerto DSCH,* to music by Dimitri Shostakovich and choreography by Alexei Ratmansky. Critics praised the ballet's verve and originality. In a surprise move in September, Ratmansky, who had been expected to join City Ballet as resident choreographer, announced that he would instead join City Ballet's rival ABT as artist-in-residence in 2009.

Mark Morris Dance Group. The most noteworthy premiere by Mark Morris was his version of *Romeo and Juliet,* first seen on July 4, 2008, at Bard College in Annandale-on-Hudson, New York. Morris's *Romeo & Juliet, On Motifs of Shakespeare* uses the original Prokofiev score dating from 1935, which musicologist Simon Morrison of Princeton University in New Jersey found in a Russian archive. The score is around 20 minutes longer than the standard version used to accompany most other versions of the ballet. What makes the 1935 score radical, however, is

the composer's libretto: Romeo and Juliet live happily ever after. Prokofiev was pressured to make changes to his original score and libretto to see the work performed, as the Soviets had barred production of the original work as it was written. Morris added his own new bit, as well—Tybalt and Mercutio are danced by women. As can be imagined, this Romeo and Juliet drew strong reactions from critics.

New works by Tharp. Unlike Morris, Twyla Tharp does not have her own company, but her free-lance career flourished this year. Inspired by Miami's bustling club life, *Nightspot,* the ballet Tharp created for the Miami City Ballet, bowed March 28 in the company's home city. With music by Elvis Costello, *Nightspot* represented a crossroads of Latin and pop music sensibilities and personality types.

Tharp made another foray into the commercial music scene by commissioning Danny Elfman to compose his first score for a ballet. Elfman has written scores for nearly 50 films, including *Batman* (1989), *Good Will Hunting* (1997), and *Spider-Man* (2002). The result of the collaboration between Tharp and Elfman, *Rabbit and Rogue,* was first seen on June 3, 2008, during ABT's two-month season at the Metropolitan Opera House in New York City. Tharp cast the ballet for ABT's two superstars, Ethan Stiefel and

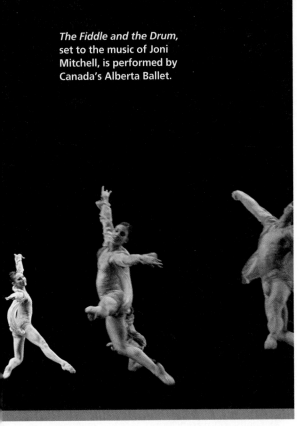

The Fiddle and the Drum, set to the music of Joni Mitchell, is performed by Canada's Alberta Ballet.

Herman Cornejo, with Stiefel playing the rogue and Cornejo the rabbit. Their characters had a competitive but humorous relationship that easily lent itself to being a wry comment on ABT's backstage life. Tharp's other two premieres were presented by Seattle's Pacific Northwest Ballet. Debuting on September 25 at the Marion Oliver McCaw Hall, the two new pieces were seen as a study in contrast. *Opus 111,* danced to a Brahms string quartet, conveyed the serenity of the countryside. *Afternoon Ball,* with music by Vladimir Martynov, portrayed the degeneracy of city life.

Joffrey's new space. At long last, the Joffrey Ballet found a permanent home in Chicago, its home base since 1995. In September 2008, the company, under its new director, Ashley Wheater, acquired space in a building in Chicago's theater district. The studios in the new building had glass walls that allowed passersby to watch the dancers rehearse.

Deaths. Several major figures in dance died in 2008. On October 6, Nadia Nerina, once a dancer in London's Royal Ballet, died at age 80. Gerald Arpino, cofounder and choreographer of the Joffrey Ballet, died on October 29, at 85. And dance critic Clive Barnes, who had reviewed for *The Times* in London and for *The New York Times* and the *Post* in New York City, died at age 81, on November 19. ■ Nancy Goldner

DEATHS

in 2008 included those listed below, who were Americans unless otherwise indicated.

Adams, Edie (Elizabeth Edith Enke) (1927–October 15), actress and singer who was most famously the comedy foil of her late husband, Ernie Kovacs, and the sexy spokesperson for Muriel cigars.

Alexy II (Alexei Mikhailovich Rudiger) (1929–December 5), Estonian-born patriarch of the Russian Orthodox Church who became a powerful influence in Russian society by revitalizing the church after the fall of Communism.

Arnold, Eddy (1918–May 8), singer whose run of 57 consecutive Top 10 hits and sale of 80 million records helped transform country music from a regional to a national genre.

Arpino, Gerald (1923–October 29), Joffrey Ballet cofounder and choreographer whose very American and sometimes controversial dances updated and popularized ballet.

Asinof, Eliot (1919–June 10), minor league baseball player turned author who wrote *Eight Men Out* (1963), about the 1919 Black Sox Scandal.

Attardi, Giuseppe (1923–April 5), Italian-born geneticist who was instrumental in uncov-

Eddy Arnold, singer

ering the function of mitochondrial DNA and how its linked mutations affect aging.

Ayd, Frank J., Jr. (1920–March 17), psychiatrist who pioneered the use of Thorazine and reserpine on people with schizophrenia, which resulted in the new medical field of psychopharmacology.

Barnes, Clive (1927–November 19), influential British critic who reviewed dance in London and dance and theater in New York.

Berger, Frank (1913–March 18), Czech-born American physician who invented the first mass-market psychiatric drug, Miltown.

Blackwell, Richard (Richard Sylvan Selzer) (1922–October 19), designer whose acidic annual "worst dressed list" made his fashion company, Mr. Blackwell, a household name.

Blakeslee, Donald (1917–September 3), highly decorated World War II fighter pilot who commanded the first U.S. squadron to reach Berlin and who is believed to have flown more missions than any other American pilot.

Bowman, Christopher (1967–January 10), child actor and former figure skating champion who was dubbed "Bowman the Showman."

Brinkman, Eddie (1941–September 30), record-setting shortstop who played in the majors for 15 seasons before becoming a scout and coach for the Chicago White Sox.

Brunious, John (1940–February 12), jazz trumpeter who as leader of the Preservation Hall Jazz Band devoted his career to the music of New Orleans.

Buckley, William F., Jr. (1925–February 27), articulate and witty columnist, editor, novelist, and television talk show host who was the founding father of the modern American conservative movement.

Burk, Joe (1914-January 13), rowing champion who won the James E. Sullivan Award for best U.S. amateur athlete of the year and who was a member of the U.S. Rowing Hall of Fame.

Butz, Earl (1909–February 2), Agriculture Department secretary in the Nixon and Ford administrations who was famously forced to resign in 1976 for making a racist joke.

Cachao (Israel López) (1918-March 22), Grammy Award-winning Cuban musician, bassist, and composer who was credited with creating the mambo.

Carlin, George (1937–June 22), comedian and actor whose masterful wordplay and biting antiestablishment humor made him unique in the field of standup comedy.

Carr, Herman (1924-April 9), physicist who pioneered magnetic resonance imaging.

Carruth, Hayden (1921–September 29), poet whom critics described as intellectually ambitious for his wide-ranging works.

Charisse, Cyd (Tula Ellice Finklea) (1921?–June 17), beautiful, lithe dancer who is best remembered for her sensual dance sequences opposite Gene Kelly in *Singin' in the Rain* (1952) and opposite Fred Astaire in *The Band Wagon* (1953) and *Silk Stockings* (1957).

Christodoulos (Christodoulos Paraskevaides) (1939–January 28), archbishop of the Orthodox Church of Greece who is credited with easing centuries of tensions with the Roman Catholic Church by receiving Pope John Paul II in 2001.

Clarke, Sir Arthur C. (1917–March 19), British-born author of more than 100 works, often dealing with space travel and the idea that humanity's destiny lay outside the confines of Earth. See **Portrait** at **Literature**.

Colledge, Cecilia (1920–April 12), world champion British figure skater who executed the first double jump in women's competition and invented the camel and layback spins and the one-foot axel jump.

Collins, Dottie (1923–August 12), star pitcher for the All-American Girls Professional Baseball League in the 1940's whose efforts to launch a woman's professional baseball exhibit at the Baseball Hall of Fame culminated in the 1992 film *A League of Their Own*.

Cornioley, Pearl Witherington (1914–February 24), English-born French resistance leader who parachuted into occupied France during World War II and eventually was in command of 3,000 underground fighters.

William F. Buckley, Jr., editor

Court, Hazel (1926–April 15), English actress who became a cult figure known as the "scream queen" for her appearances in Roger Corman's *Premature Burial* (1962) and *The Masque of the Red Death* (1964) and other horror movies.

Crichton, Michael (1942–November 4), author of such enormously popular novels as *The Andromeda Strain* (1969) and *Jurassic Park* (1990). Crichton also created the hit TV series "ER."

Daniel, Margaret Truman (1924–January 29), author of Washington, D.C.-based murder mysteries who also wrote best-selling biographies of her parents, Harry and Bess Truman.

Dassin, Jules (1911–March 31), blacklisted movie director—*Naked City* (1948), *Rififi* (1955), and *Never on Sunday* (1960)—who was considered a master of film noir.

Cyd Charisse, dancer

DeBakey, Michael E. (Michel Dabaghi) (1908–July 11), world-famous heart surgeon who successfully implanted the first assisting heart and won fame for his contributions to techniques used to replace damaged blood vessels, including the coronary bypass operation.

Dello Joio, Norman (1913–July 24), composer who won the 1957 Pulitzer Prize in music for his *Meditations on Ecclesiastes* (1957) for orchestra.

Diddley, Bo (Otha Ellas Bates McDaniel) (1928–June 2), influential musician who was one of the founders of rock 'n' roll and who gave the music its characteristic rhythm. See **Portrait** at **Popular music.**

Di Stefano, Giuseppe (1921–March 3), Italian tenor whose rich voice and dramatic personality made him a major figure in opera in the 1950's and 1960's.

Dith Pran (1942–March 30) Cambodian-born photojournalist (he became a U.S. citizen) whose terrifying experiences under the Khmer Rouge regime were re-created in the Academy Award-winning 1984 film *The Killing Fields.*

Dulles, Avery (1918–December 12), scholar and teacher who was the only American theologian ever appointed to the College of Cardinals. Avery Dulles was the son of John Foster Dulles, secretary of state from 1953 to 1959.

Dunham, Madelyn (1922–November 3), grandmother who died two days before the man she helped raise, Barack Obama, was elected president of the United States.

Faraz, Ahmed (1931–August 25), Pakistani poet who was modern Urdu poetry's foremost figure.

Farber, Manny (1917–August 18), painter and film critic whose idiosyncratic vision, taste, and style made him a unique voice in film criticism.

Felker, Clay (1925–July 1), editor who created *New York,* a new kind of magazine that spawned dozens of similar city magazines.

Felt, W. Mark (1913-December 18), former associate director of the FBI who was journalists Woodward and Bernstein's "Deep Throat" source during the Watergate scandal.

Ferrer, Mel (1917–June 2), actor who appeared in more than 100 films, played opposite his then-wife Audrey Hepburn in *War and Peace* (1956), and directed her in *Green Mansions* (1959) and *Wait Until Dark* (1967).

Fischer, Bobby (1943–January 17), eccentric chess master whose world championship win in 1972 over Russian champion Boris Spassky made Fischer a Cold War hero.

Foch, Nina (Nina Consuelo Maud Fock) (1924–December 5), Dutch-born actress and acting coach who most famously played the pharaoh's daughter who adopts Moses in *The Ten Commandments* (1956).

Folkman, Judah (1933–January 14), cancer researcher who pioneered the concept that tumors can be kept in check by blocking their blood supply, changing the course of modern medicine.

Judah Folkman, scientist

Ford, Alan (1923–November 3), athlete who was the first swimmer to break 50 seconds in the 100-yard freestyle, a record he held for eight years.

Froehlich, Edwina (1915–June 8), breast-feeding advocate who was one of the founders of La Leche League International.

Furth, George (George Schweinfurth) (1932–August 11), actor and playwright who won a Tony and Drama Desk award for the book of *Company,* the 1970 Broadway musical with music and lyrics by Stephen Sondheim.

Gajdusek, Daniel Carleton (1923–December 11), physician and medical researcher who shared the 1976 Nobel Prize in physiology or medicine for discoveries about the origin and spread of infectious diseases.

Garland, Beverly (1926–December 5), B-movie actress who made her film debut in the noir classic *D.O.* (1950) and who played Fred McMurray's second wife on the long-running TV comedy "My Three Sons."

Getty, Estelle (1923–July 22), actress who played "the mother" in the Broadway production of *Torch Song Trilogy* (1981) and most famously Sophia on the TV show "The Golden Girls" (1985-1992).

Giardello, Joey (1930-September 2), boxer who was a former world middleweight champion and a member of the International Boxing Hall of Fame and the World Boxing Hall of Fame.

Gibson, Jack (1929–May 9), Australian Rugby League coach, player, and commentator who was named best Australian Rugby League coach of all time by the Australian Rugby League and National Rugby League.

Gibson, William (1914–November 25), Tony Award-winning playwright best known for *The Miracle Worker*.

Giroux, Robert (1914–September 5), Farrar, Straus and Giroux publishing house partner who served as editor to some of the great writers of his time, including T. S. Eliot, Bernard Malamud, Flannery O'Connor, and Susan Sontag.

Estelle Getty, actress (left) with other Golden Girls

Goodman, Dody (Dolores Goodman) (1914?–June 22), zany comedian who played the spacey matriarch on the soap opera "Mary Hartman, Mary Hartman."

Grant, Johnny (1923–January 9), "honorary mayor of Hollywood" who presided over more than 500 Hollywood Walk of Fame inductions.

Griffin, Johnny (1928–July 25), tenor saxophonist whom critics considered one of the most talented jazz musicians of his generation.

Gunsalus, Irwin C. (1912–October 25), biochemist who discovered lipoic acid, one of the active forms of vitamin B_6, which is an effective treatment for chronic liver disease.

Gygax, Gary (1938–March 4), writer of fantasy books, including the Greyhawk series, who co-created Dungeons & Dragons, the fantasy game that is credited with launching the role-playing phenomenon. See **Portrait** at **Toys and games.**

Harel, Yossi (Yossef Hamburger) (1918–April 26), Israeli commando and spy who sailed *Exodus 1947*, the ship carrying Jews attempting to enter Palestine, into Haifa harbor in the face of British opposition.

Harrison, Gilbert (1915–January 3), editor and publisher of *The New Republic* from 1953 until 1974 who was an influential figure in liberal politics of the era.

Hartford, Huntington, II (1911–May 19), eccentric A&P grocery chain heir who went through much of his fortune sponsoring various failed projects, most famously the Gallery of Modern Art launched in 1964.

Isaac Hayes, musician

Hayes, Isaac (1942–August 10), singer, song-writer, and actor who won an Academy Award for "Theme from Shaft" and who was the voice of Chef on "South Park."

Healey, Jeff (1966–March 2), Canadian blues-rock guitarist, singer, and songwriter who hit platinum in the late 1980's with the album *See the Light*.

Helms, Jesse (1921–July 4), North Carolina conservative who during his 30 years in the U.S. Senate denounced civil rights, gay rights, foreign aid, and modern art.

Herlie, Eileen (Eileen Herlihy) (1918–October 8), Scottish-born actress who played Myrtle Fargate on "All My Children" for some 30 years.

Heston, Charlton (John Charlton Carter) (1923–April 5), iconic movie actor who will forever be associated with such bigger-than-life roles as Moses in *The Ten Commandments* (1956), the title role in *Ben-Hur* (1959), Michelangelo in *The Agony and the Ecstasy* (1965), and a talking human being in *Planet of the Apes* (1968).

Hill, Phil (1927–August 28), auto racing legend who in 1958 was the first American to win the 24-hour race at Le Mans.

Hillary, Sir Edmund (1919–January 11), New Zealander explorer who in 1953 became a hero and world famous as one of the first two people to successfully climb Mount Everest and return. See **Portrait** at **New Zealand.**

Hillerman, Tony (1925–October 26), author of a highly popular and critically acclaimed series of mysteries that feature two Navajo Tribal Police detectives.

Hinckley, Gordon B. (1910–January 27), president of the Church of Jesus Christ of Latter-day Saints who oversaw the expansion of the church from 9 million to 13 million members.

Hofmann, Albert (1906–April 29), Swiss chemist who discovered LSD and accidentally licked a trace from his fingertip, taking the world's first acid trip.

Holmes, Tommy (1917–April 14), Boston Braves outfielder who in June and July 1945 hit in 37 consecutive games, setting a record that stood until 1978.

Hua Guofeng (1921-August 20), chairman of the Chinese Communist Party from 1976 to 1981 who also served as premier, China's top government post, from 1976 to 1980.

Hubbard, Freddie (1938-December 29), jazz musician who was one of the foremost hard-bop trumpeters of his generation.

Hurwicz, Leonid (1917–June 24), Russian-born economist who won the 2007 Nobel Prize in economics for his theory explaining how both buyers and sellers can maximize gains.

Ichikawa, Kon (1915–February 13), Japanese director who made two acclaimed antiwar films, *The Burmese Harp* (1956) and *Fires on the Plain* (1959).

Immonen, Riitta (1918–August 24), Finnish fashion designer and columnist who cofounded the Finnish textile and clothing company Marimekko.

Jastrow, Robert (1925–February 8), former head of NASA's Goddard Institute for Space Studies who made regular appearances on

Charlton Heston, actor

television as a highly accessible guide to science, space, and space technology.

Jeter, Bob (1937–November 20), All-Pro cornerback who played with the Green Bay Packers when the team won the 1965 NFL championship and the first two Super Bowls, in 1967 and 1968.

Johnson, Van (1916–December 12), popular movie actor of the 1940's and early 1950's who most often played the "boy next door" opposite such stars as June Allyson, Lana Turner, and Esther Williams.

Johnston, Ollie (1912–April 14), the last of the "nine old men" Disney illustrators. Johnston animated the dwarfs in *Snow White and the Seven Dwarfs* (1937) and created Thumper in *Bambi* (1942).

Heath Ledger, actor

Jordan, Hamilton (1944–May 20), political strategist who helped Jimmy Carter win the presidency and served as his chief of staff.

Kantrowitz, Adrian (1918-November 14), heart surgeon who performed the first pediatric heart transplant, which was also the first human heart transplant in the United States.

Keyes, Evelyn (1916–July 4), actress who played Suellen O'Hara in *Gone With the Wind* (1939) and most famously had relationships with or married a string of famous men, including John Huston, Mike Todd, and Artie Shaw.

Kitt, Eartha (Eartha Mae Keith) (1927–December 25), singer and performer who purred her way through Broadway and movie musicals, television, including the campy "Batman," and nightclubs for some 60 years.

Knerr, Richard (1925–January 14), Wham-O cofounder who with partner Arthur "Spud" Melin invented the Hula Hoop, SuperBall, and Silly String and marketed Frisbee.

Korman, Harvey (1927–May 29), comedian who played Carol Burnett's second banana for 10 seasons of "The Carol Burnett Show."

LaFontaine, Don (1940–September 1), master of the voice-over whose rich baritone graced more than 5,000 movie trailers and at least 35,000 commercials, earning him the title "the voice of God."

Lamb, Willis, Jr. (1913–May 15), scientist who was awarded the 1955 Nobel Prize in physics for the Lamb Shift—his discovery that different energy levels exist among electrons in hydrogen atoms.

Lantos, Tom (Tamás Péter Lantos) (1928–February 11), Hungarian-born member of the U.S. House of Representatives (D., California) and chairman of the House Foreign Affairs Committee. Lantos was the only Holocaust survivor to ever serve in Congress.

Lederberg, Joshua (1925–February 2), biologist who at the age of 33 was awarded the Nobel Prize for his pioneering study of genetic recombination in bacteria. A founder of the field of molecular biology, Lederberg also demonstrated that an organism's genetic material could be manipulated.

Ledger, Heath (1979–January 22), Australian actor whose career skyrocketed from *10 Things I Hate About You* (1999) and *The Patriot* (2000) to *Brokeback Mountain* (2005), for which he was nominated for an Academy Award for best actor, and *The Dark Knight* (2008).

Leigh, Dorian (Dorian Leigh Parker) (1917–July 7), one of the most photographed models of the 1940's and 1950's who was the sister of supermodel Suzie Parker and at least partially on whom Truman Capote based his *Breakfast at Tiffany's* character Holly Golightly.

Leonard, John (1939–November 5), influential literary critic who championed the early works and careers of Toni Morrison, Gabriel García Márquez, and Kurt Vonnegut, who once described Leonard as "the smartest man who ever lived."

Lorenz, Edward Norton (1917–April 16), mathematician who pioneered chaos theory and coined the term "butterfly effect."

Love, Kermit (1916–June 21), ballet costumer who most famously created Sesame Street's Big Bird, Oscar the Grouch, Cookie Monster, and Kermit the Frog.

Loving, Mildred (Mildred Delores Jeter Loving) (1939-May 2), black civil rights activist whose marriage to a white man led to a landmark U.S. Supreme Court ruling that overturned state bans on interracial marriage.

Mac, Bernie (Bernard Jeffrey McCullough) (1957–August 9), stellar stand-up comedian who appeared in more than 15 films, including *Ocean's Eleven* (2001) and its sequels, and had his own TV series, "The Bernie Mac Show," from 2001 to 2006.

Maharishi Mahesh Yogi (Mahesh Srivastava) (1917–February 5), Beatles' Indian guru who introduced transcendental meditation to the West.

Maheu, Robert (1917–August 4), FBI and CIA operative who became the public face of Howard Hughes after the eccentric billionaire withdrew from public view.

Makeba, Miriam (1932–November 10), highly distinctive South African singer whose dazzling international career and political activism (she was banished from apartheid South Africa for several years) earned her the title "Mama Africa."

Martin, Del (Dorothy Taliaferro) (1921–August 27), early activist in the gay, lesbian, bisexual, and transgendered rights movement who cofounded the first U.S. lesbian organization and the first lesbian newspaper.

Martin, Dick (1922–May 24), comedian who, with partner Dan Rowan, presided over "Rowan and Martin's Laugh-In," a late 1960's television phenomenon that made stars of the hosts as well as Goldie Hawn and Lily Tomlin.

Mcdonald, Gregory (1937–September 7), award-winning author of more than 26 books, including the best-selling Fletch mystery novels.

McKay, Jim (James McManus) (1921–June 7), sportscaster who traveled some 5 million miles to cover more than 100 sports as host of ABC's "Wide World of Sports," for which he penned "The thrill of victory and the agony of defeat."

McKusick, Victor (1921–July 22), physician who pioneered the connection of diseases to specific genes, creating the field of medical genetics.

Metzenbaum, Howard (1917–March 12), U.S. senator (D., Ohio) who most famously used his encyclopedic knowledge of Senate rules to block special interest legislation for private industry.

Minghella, Anthony (1954–March 18), British filmmaker—*The Talented Mr. Ripley* (1999) and *Cold Mountain* (2003)—who received the 1996 Academy Award for best direction for *The English Patient.*

Mitchell, Mitch (John Mitchell) (1947–November 12), English drummer who was the last sur-

viving member of the legendary Jimi Hendrix Experience of the 1960's.

Mohammed, W. Deen (Wallace Dean Muhammad) (1933–September 9), imam of the Muslim American Community, formerly the Nation of Islam, the largest of the black Muslim organizations.

Mondavi, Robert (1913–May 16), vintner whose innovations and marketing techniques put California's Napa Valley and the American wine industry on the map.

Morse, Barry (Herbert Morse) (1918–February 2), British-born Canadian actor who most famously played Lieutenant Philip Gerard, the detective who chased Richard Kimble, on "The Fugitive."

Mott, Stewart (1937–June 12), General Motors heir and philanthropist who supported the promotion of abortion reform, civil and gay rights, gun control, and peace.

Murcer, Bobby (1946–July 12), All-Star outfielder who both played for the New York Yankees and was the team's long-time broadcaster.

Mwanawasa, Levy (1948–August 19), president of Zambia who attempted to rout out corruption and reform the country's economics.

Narz, Jack (1922–October 15), unknowing TV host of "Dotto," one of the rigged game shows of the 1950's, and later the long-time host of "Concentration."

Nerina, Nadia (Nadine Judd) (1927–October 6), South African-born dancer who was London's Royal Ballet prima ballerina in the 1950's and 1960's and for whom choreographer Frederick Ashton created *La Fille Mal Gardée,* one of the world's most popular ballets.

Eartha Kitt, singer

Suzanne Pleshette, actress

Netsch, Walter A. (1920–June 15), architect and former Skidmore, Owings & Merrill partner who designed the modern classic Inland Steel Building in Chicago and the U.S. Air Force Academy campus, including the Cadet Chapel, in Colorado Springs.

Nettleton, Lois (1927–January 18), actress who appeared in hundreds of television programs—from classic episodes of "The Twilight Zone," in the 1950's and 1960's, to "The Mary Tyler Moore Show" in the 1970's, "The Golden Girls" in the 1980's, and "Seinfeld" in the 1990's.

Newman, Paul (1925–September 26), Academy Award-winning superstar whose decades-long career included such hits as *Cat on a Hot Tin Roof* (1958), *Hud* (1963), *Butch Cassidy and the Sundance Kid* (1969), and *The Sting* (1973).

Odetta (Odetta Holmes) (1930–December 2), influential blues, folk, and gospel singer and actress who became the voice of the civil rights movement of the 1960's and 1970's.

Page, Anita (Anita Pomares) (1910–September 6), silent screen actress who may have been the last surviving star of the silent era.

Page, Bettie (1923–December 11), 1950's pinup queen whose titillating but strangely innocent images made her a cult figure among 21st-century aficionados and the subject of the 2005 film *The Notorious Bettie Page*.

Palade, George (1912–October 7), Romanian-born biologist whose research into the inner workings of cells laid the foundation for the field of cell biology and earned him a Nobel Prize in 1974.

Pappas, Ike (Icarus Nestor Pappas) (1933–August 31), CBS news correspondent who covered the Vietnam War, the assassination of Martin Luther King, Jr., and most famously, the murder of Lee Harvey Oswald, from whom Pappas happened to be standing at arm's length.

Pausch, Randy (1960–July 25), computer science professor and *World Book* contributor who chronicled his battle with pancreatic cancer in a speech that became known as the "Last Lecture," which when published became a *New York Times* best seller.

Peale, Ruth Stafford (1906–February 6), author, editor, and speaker who launched the magazine *Guideposts* after cofounding the inspirational organization Guideposts with her husband, Norman Vincent Peale.

Pinter, Harold (1930–December 24), British playwright who was awarded the 2005 Nobel Prize for literature for his more than 30 plays, including such masterworks as *The Birthday Party, The Caretaker, The Homecoming*, and *Betrayal*.

Pleshette, Suzanne (1937–January 19), actress who appeared in Alfred Hitchcock's *The Birds* (1963) and hundreds of TV episodes but was best known as Emily Hartley, Bob's disarmingly honest wife on "The Bob Newhart Show."

Podres, Johnny (1932–January 13), baseball player who pitched a shutout in Game 7 of the 1955 World Series, giving the Brooklyn

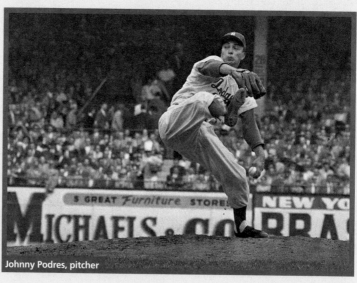

Johnny Podres, pitcher

Dodgers their only series championship.

Pollack, Sydney (1934–May 26), actor, producer, and director— *They Shoot Horses, Don't They?* (1969), *The Way We Were* (1973), *Tootsie* (1982)—who won Academy Awards for both producing and directing *Out of Africa* (1985).

Rauschenberg, Robert (Milton Ernest Rauschenberg) (1925– May 12), prolific painter, printmaker, sculptor, and photographer who was one of the most influential American artists of the second half of the 20th century.

Reaney, James (1926–June 11), Canadian poet and playwright who sought to express the allegorical patterns behind the sights, sounds, and customs of rural Ontario.

Robert Rauschenberg, artist

Reed, Jerry (Jerry Reed Hubbard) (1937–September 1), country music singer who had dozens of Top 40 hits and actor who appeared in three "Smokey and the Bandit" films.

Reiner, Estelle (1914–October 25), inspiration for the Laura Petrie character on "The Dick Van Dyke Show," which her husband Carl Reiner created and produced and often wrote, and film extra who delivered the famous line, "I'll have what she's having," in *When Harry Met Sally* (1989), which her son Rob Reiner directed.

Rescigno, Nicola (1916–August 4), opera conductor who helped found the Lyric Opera of Chicago in 1952 and the Dallas Opera in 1957.

Richmond, Julius (1916–July 27), pediatrician and public health advocate who, as the first national director of Project Head Start, shaped the program and who, as surgeon general, issued the first official report that declared that "overwhelming proof" existed that tobacco causes lung cancer.

Robbe-Grillet, Alain (1922–February 18), French author of the novels *Les Gommes* (1953) and *Le Voyeur* (1955) and the screenplay *Last Year in Marienbad* (1961) who was the most prominent of the "New Novelists," who in the mid-1950's broke with traditional literary elements.

Rosenman, Leonard (1924–March 4), film composer who is credited with introducing avant-garde music to Hollywood in *East of Eden* (1955) and *Rebel Without a Cause* (1955) and who won Academy Awards for *Barry Lyndon* (1975) and *Bound for Glory* (1976).

Tim Russert, TV moderator

Russert, Tim (1950–June 13), NBC Washington Bureau chief who, as moderator of "Meet the Press" for 16 years, was the dean of the Sunday morning television political journalists.

Saint Laurent, Yves (1936–June 1), Algerian-born French fashion designer who was considered one of the most influential couturiers of the second half of the 20th century and who forever changed the industry by branching from haute couture into ready-to-wear. See **Portrait** at **Fashion.**

Scheider, Roy (1932–February 10), actor who was nominated for Academy Awards for *The French Connection* (1971) and for *All That Jazz* (1979) but who was best known for playing a beach resort cop in *Jaws* (1975).

Schnellbacher, Otto (1923–March 10), Univer-

Alexander Solzhenitsyn, novelist

sity of Kansas star athlete who went on to play both professional basketball and football.

Schreckengost, Viktor (1906–January 26), artist and industrial designer who co-created the first cab-over-engine truck and designed iconic children's pedal cars and wagons, the molded metal lawn chair, and the riding lawn mower.

Scofield, Paul (David Scofield) (1922–March 19), renowned British stage actor who earned critical acclaim for his *Hamlet* and *King Lear* and worldwide fame for his portrayal of Sir Thomas More in *A Man for All Seasons,* for which he won the 1966 Academy Award for best actor.

Seamans, Robert (1918–June 28), MIT aeronautics professor who joined NASA in 1960 and as deputy administrator played a key role in putting a man on the moon.

Sills, Paul (1927–June 2), father of improvisational sketch comedy and story theater who cofounded Chicago's Second City troupe from which "Saturday Night Live" sprang.

Simplot, J. R. (1909–May 25), billionaire entrepreneur who among other profitable enterprises invented the frozen French fry.

Smith, Mike (1943–Februay 28), lead singer for The Dave Clark Five, whose 1960's hits included "Glad All Over," "Catch Us If You Can," and "Over and Over."

Snow, Tony (1955-July 12), news anchor and Fox News commentator who served as a speechwriter in the administration of President George Herbert Walker Bush and as press secretary for President George W. Bush from 2006 to 2007.

Solzhenitsyn, Alexander (1918–August 3), Russian novelist whose imprisonment in a labor camp inspired *A Day in the Life of Ivan Denisovich* (1962), which elevated him to worldwide fame. He was awarded the 1970 Nobel Prize in literature. See also **Literature.**

Stafford, Jo (1917–July 16), singer of jazz and traditional pop standards who enjoyed great popularity from the 1930's into the 1960's.

Stendahl, Krister (1921–April 15), Swedish Lutheran bishop and former dean of the Harvard Divinity School who preached unity and tolerance.

Stevens, Dave (1955–March 10), illustrator and comic book artist who created the Rocketeer.

Stewart, John (1939–January 19), onetime member of the Kingston Trio who wrote "Daydream Believer" for the Monkees as well as hits for Rosanne Cash and Joan Baez and recorded the critically acclaimed solo album *California Bloodlines* (1969).

Stubbs, Levi (Levi Stubbles) (1936–October 17), lead singer for the Four Tops whose 1960's hits included "Baby I Need Your Loving," "I Can't Help Myself," and "Bernadette."

Stuhlinger, Ernst (1913–May 25), German-born scientist who played a key role in the development of rockets that propelled American astronauts to the moon.

Suharto (1921–January 27), general and president of Indonesia whose more-than-30-year rule (1967-1998) is often considered one of the most brutal and corrupt dictatorships of the 1900's.

Sumac, Yma (Zoila Augusta Emperatriz Chávarri del Castillo) (1922?–November 1), Peruvian-born soprano, known as the "Nightingale of the Andes," whose four-octave voice, bird calls, wild animal imitations, elaborate costumes, and claim of being an Inca princess made her a singing sensation of the 1950's.

Teicher, Lou (1924–August 3), pianist who was half of the piano act Ferrante & Teicher that had two enormous hit singles in 1960, "Theme from *The Apartment*" and "Theme from *Exodus,*" and went on to sell millions of albums.

Templeton, Sir John (1912–July 8), mutual fund pioneer, and philanthropist who in 1973 established the Templeton Prize for progress in religion.

Terkel, Studs (Louis Terkel) (1912–October 31),

radio and TV personality and Pulitzer Prize-winning author who, using his talents as an interviewer, became the preeminent oral historian of the common man and woman in America during the 1900's.

Tilly, Charles (1929–April 29), sociologist who wrote extensively on the relationship between society and politics.

Tresh, Tom (1937–October 15), Yankees shortstop and left fielder who played on three World Series teams and was the American League rookie of the year in 1962.

Tudor, Tasha (Starling Burgess) (1915–June 18), writer and illustrator of children's literature whose *Mother Goose* (1944) and *1 Is One* (1956) were named Caldecott Honor Books.

Tuwhare, Hone (1922–January 16), Maori author who was New Zealand's most honored and prolific poet.

Utzon, Jørn (1918–November 29), Danish architect who designed the Sydney (Australia) Opera House, one of the architectural masterpieces of the 1900's.

Von Bülow, Sunny (Martha Crawford von Bülow) (1932–December 6), heiress who was in an insulin-induced coma for 28 years and whose husband, Claus, was tried twice on charges of attempting to murder her.

Wallace, David Foster (1962–September 12), novelist of enormous range, originality, and depth whose *The Broom of the System* (1986) and *Infinite Jest* (1996) were met with wide critical acclaim. See also **Literature.**

Wasserman, Dale (1914–December 21), playwright who wrote the Broadway hits *One Flew Over the Cuckoo's Nest* and *Man of La Mancha.*

Weller, Thomas Huckle (1915–August 23), research biologist who shared the 1954 Nobel Prize in physiology or medicine for growing poliomyelitis viruses on tissues of human embryos outside the body.

Wells, Henrietta Bell (1912–February 27), the last surviving member, and the only female member, of the 1930 Wiley College debate team that particpated in the first interracial college debate in the United States.

Wexler, Jerry (1917–August 15), *Billboard* magazine reporter who coined the term "rhythm

Studs Terkel, interviewer and writer

and blues" and record producer who greatly popularized the genre by promoting Ray Charles, Aretha Franklin, and Wilson Pickett.

Weyrich, Paul (1942–December 18), conservative strategist who helped found the Heritage Foundation and propel the right-wing takeover of the Republican Party in the 1980's and 1990's.

Wheeler, John A. (1911–April 13), physicist and teacher who helped forge the theory of nuclear fission and coined the term "black hole."

White, Dwight "Mad Dog" (1949–June 6), "steel certain" defense end who helped the Pittsburgh Steelers capture four Super Bowl titles in the 1970's.

Whitney, Phyllis (1903–February 8), author of 73 titles—romantic mysteries, children's mysteries, and young-adult novels—that sold more than 50 million copies in paperback alone.

Widmark, Richard (1914–March 24), veteran actor who appeared in more than 70 films, including *Kiss of Death* (1947), which made him an instant star; John Ford's revisionist Western *Cheyenne Autumn* (1963); and *Madigan* (1968), a role he reprised in a 1970's television series.

Winston, Stan (1946–June 15), make-up artist and special effects wizard who received Academy Awards for his work on *Aliens* (1986), *Terminator 2: Judgment Day* (1991), and *Jurassic Park* (1993).

Wright, Richard (1943–September 15), founding member of and dominant musical force in Pink Floyd, the British rock band known for the hit albums *Dark Side of the Moon* and *The Wall.*

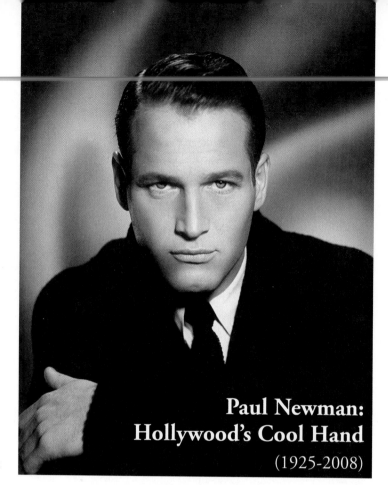

Paul Newman:
Hollywood's Cool Hand
(1925-2008)

By Shawn Brennan

P aul Newman was a classic American motion-picture star who radiated "cool." His cinematic stature was matched only by his colorful off-screen reputation as a maverick and a humanitarian. Newman first captivated Hollywood with his handsome looks and sparkling blue eyes, but he won over both critics and audiences worldwide with his talent and charisma. He touched the inner rebel in his audience, playing memorable characters from Butch Cassidy to Hud, from "Fast Eddie" to "Cool Hand" Luke. He was an Academy Award winner, a devoted partner in one of the most enduring marriages in show business, a professional race car driver, a political activist, and a successful entrepreneur who donated all of his profits to charity. Newman once advised young actors, "Make sure you live life, which means don't do things where you court celebrity, and give something positive back to our society." The 83-year-old actor died on Sept. 26, 2008, after a long and larger-than-life career that bore out that philosophy.

From Cleveland to Hollywood

Paul Leonard Newman was born in Cleveland on Jan. 26, 1925. His father, Arthur Samuel Newman, was the owner of a successful sporting goods store. Paul's mother, Theresa, worked in his father's store while raising Paul and his older brother Arthur, Jr. As his business prospered, Arthur, Sr., moved his family to the affluent neighboring suburb of Shaker

Heights, where the boys grew up. The young Paul was bright and had a talent for sports. He also showed an early interest in the theater, which his mother encouraged. Paul made his acting debut at age 7, as the court jester in a school production of *Robin Hood*.

After graduating from Shaker Heights High School in 1943, Newman briefly attended Ohio University in Athens but was expelled for unruly behavior. He then served three years in the United States Naval Air Corps as a radio operator during World War II (1939-1945). In 1946, he won an athletic scholarship to Kenyon College in Gambier, Ohio. Newman played college football until an incident at a local bar landed him in jail and he was kicked off the team. He turned his attention to drama and appeared in several college and summer-stock productions before graduating from Kenyon in 1949 with a bachelor's degree in English.

In 1949, Newman moved to Chicago, where he worked with the Woodstock Players and met the actress Jacqueline "Jackie" Witte. They were married later that year. In 1950, the couple had a son, Scott. Newman's father died that same year, leaving Paul to run the store. Newman chose to risk the security of the successful Cleveland business to pursue his dream of acting. He sold his share in the business to his brother and moved his family to New Haven, Connecticut, to enroll in the graduate drama program at Yale University. In 1952, Newman moved the family to New York City where he studied at the Actors Studio under the distinguished acting teacher Lee Strasberg. In 1953, Newman made his Broadway debut in William Inge's Pulitzer Prize-winning play *Picnic*. He was spotted by Warner Brothers executives, who signed him to a motion-picture contract. The couple had a daughter, Susan, in 1953. Another daughter, Stephanie, was born in 1954, the same year that Newman graduated from Yale.

In 1954, Newman also made his film debut in the Biblical epic *The Silver Chalice*, for which he received terrible reviews. He was so embarrassed by his performance that a dozen years later, when the film was scheduled to be broadcast on television, he took out a full-page ad in the Hollywood trade paper *Variety* apologizing for his performance and urging people not to watch the broadcast. Newman reveled in ridiculing the film for the rest of his life. He returned to the stage in *The Desperate Hours* and did some television work before redeeming himself in his next film, *Somebody Up There Likes Me* (1956). His portrayal of boxer Rocky Graziano drew rave reviews from critics. Several other successful films followed in the late 1950's. Newman received his first Academy Award nomination for best actor for his performance as Brick Pollitt opposite Elizabeth Taylor in the 1958 film adaptation of the Tennessee Williams play *Cat on a Hot Tin Roof*.

A Hollywood love story

In 1958, Newman won a best actor award at the Cannes Film Festival for his performance in *The Long, Hot Summer*, based on stories by William Faulkner. Newman's co-star in the film, Joanne Woodward, had won an Oscar that year for her performance as a woman with multiple personalities in *The Three Faces of Eve*. Newman met Woodward when she was an understudy for the lead role in *Picnic* on Broadway. They fell

The author:
Shawn Brennan is a World Book subject editor.

Newman starred with his wife Joanne Woodward in the drama *From the Terrace* (1960). The couple appeared in 10 films together.

in love while filming *The Long, Hot Summer.* His wife Jackie granted Newman a divorce in 1958, and Newman and Woodward were married soon after. Eschewing the Hollywood lifestyle, the couple moved to Westport, Connecticut, where they raised three daughters: Elinor "Nell" Teresa, born in 1959; Melissa "Lissy" Stewart, born in 1961; and Claire "Clea" Olivia, born in 1965.

Newman and Woodward starred in 10 films together. Newman also directed three films starring his wife: *Rachel, Rachel* (1968), which received an Oscar nomination for best picture; *The Effect of Gamma Rays on Man-in-the-Moon Marigolds* (1972), which also starred his daughter Nell; and *The Glass Menagerie* (1987), based on the play by Tennessee Williams. Woodward was married to Newman until his death. When asked about his notable marital fidelity, Newman famously responded, "I have steak at home; why go out for hamburger?"

American icon

Newman reached superstar status in the 1960's, beginning with *The Hustler* (1961). He received his second Oscar nomination for his portrayal of Eddie Felson, an arrogant small-time pool hustler who challenges the legendary "Minnesota Fats," played by Jackie Gleason, to a high-stakes match. Newman received another Oscar nomination for his performance as a reckless young man who tarnishes everything he touches in the Western *Hud* (1963), based on the novel by Larry McMurtry. Newman received his fourth nomination for *Cool Hand Luke* (1967), in which he played Luke Jackson, a prisoner in a Southern chain gang who becomes a hero among his fellow inmates when he refuses to buckle under authority. Newman co-starred with Robert Redford in the immensely popular *Butch Cassidy and the Sundance Kid* (1969), based on the exploits of the historical Western outlaws. The film made Redford a star and initiated a long-time friendship with Newman. The two teamed up again in another huge hit, the 1930's crime comedy *The Sting* (1973). The film won an Oscar for best picture.

Newman explored a variety of roles in the 1970's in films ranging from the title character in the Western *The Life and Times of Judge Roy Bean* (1972), to the architect of a doomed skyscraper in the popular disaster film *The Towering Inferno* (1974), to the coach of a minor-league hockey team of thugs in the cult classic comedy *Slap Shot* (1977). In the 1980's, Newman received Oscar nominations for his performance as the son of an Irish mob boss who fights to restore his reputation in *Absence of Malice* (1981) and for his portrayal of an alcoholic ambulance chaser who redeems himself by taking a medical malpractice case to trial in *The Verdict* (1982).

Newman received nine Academy Award nominations during his career. In 1986, he was awarded an honorary Oscar "in recognition of his many and memorable and compelling screen performances and for his personal integrity and dedication to his craft." The following year, Newman won a best actor Oscar when he reprised the role of Eddie Felson as an aging pool shark in *The Color of Money,* co-starring Tom Cruise.

Newman continued to deliver fine performances well into his senior years, earning nominations for his portrayals of a ne'er-do-well approaching retirement age in the drama *Nobody's Fool* (1994) and an Irish American organized crime boss in the Depression-era *Road to Perdition* (2002).

Living life; giving back

Newman became interested in automobile racing while training for the 1969 film *Winning,* in which he starred as a professional race car driver. Newman's first professional race was in 1972. He won several national championships as a driver in Sports Car Club of America road racing. In 1982, he became co-owner of the Newman-Haas racing team. His team won several championships in open-wheel IndyCar racing. In 1995, at the age of 70, Newman became the oldest driver to be part of a winning team in a major sanctioned race when he won in his class at the 24 Hours of Daytona.

Newman and Woodward were also among Hollywood's most politically active couples. They campaigned for many liberal causes and political candidates. In 1978, President Jimmy Carter appointed Newman as a U.S. delegate to the U.N. Conference on Nuclear Disarmament.

In 1982, with writer A. E. Hotchner, Newman founded "Newman's Own," a successful line of food products. The brand began with a homemade salad dressing that Newman and Hotchner had prepared and given to friends as gifts. The dressing's enthusiastic reception led Newman and Hotchner to sell the dressing commercially. The brand has since expanded to include pasta sauce, lemonade, popcorn, salsa, wine, and other products. Newman established a policy that all proceeds from the sale of the company's products after taxes would be donated to charity. By 2008, the company had donated more than $250 million to thousands of charities. Newman once quipped that he was embarrassed to discover that his salad dressing had grossed more than his movies. In 1994, Newman received the Academy's Jean Hersholt Humanitarian Award for his charity work.

Reflecting upon his life, Newman said, "I'd like to be remembered as a guy who tried—who tried to be part of his times, tried to help people communicate with one another, tried to find some decency in his own life, tried to extend himself as a human being. Someone who isn't complacent, who doesn't cop out." There is no question that Newman not only tried—but succeeded magnificently.

Newman and Robert Redford became one of Hollywood's most famous duos when they starred together as outlaws in the Western *Butch Cassidy and the Sundance Kid* (1969).

Democratic Party.

The Democratic Party made sweeping gains in the elections of Nov. 4, 2008, in what political experts called a referendum on the eight years of the policies of Republican President George W. Bush. The election took place during an economic crisis, at a time when polls indicated that more than 80 percent of voters felt the country was on the "wrong track."

Presidential election. Senator Barack Obama (D., Illinois) defeated Senator John McCain (R., Arizona) on November 4, taking 365 electoral votes, compared with 173 for McCain. Obama also won the popular vote with 67.1 million votes, compared with 58.4 million for McCain. A total of 125 million people voted in the election.

Nominating contests. Obama's victory in the race for the Democratic nomination was the culmination of a series of caucus and primary contests lasting from January through June.

Senator Hillary Clinton (D., New York) had entered the race as the frontrunner for the nomination. Months before the primaries began, Clinton secured more than 100 endorsements from elected and appointed Democratic officials called *superdelegates*. Other candidates included U.S. Senators Joe Biden of Delaware and Christopher Dodd of Connecticut, New Mexico Governor Bill Richardson, former Senators John Edwards of North Carolina and Mike Gravel of Alaska, and U.S. Representative Dennis Kucinich of Ohio.

Democratic officials in both Florida and Michigan incurred the wrath of the national party after moving their states' primaries ahead of February 5, in violation of party rules. In 2007, the Democratic National Committee (DNC) voted to bar both states' delegates from the national convention.

The 2008 nominating contests began in Iowa on January 3. Obama scored a surprise win, but Clinton defeated him in New Hampshire's primary a few days later. After February 5, "Super Tuesday," when more than 20 states held caucuses or primaries, Clinton and Obama were virtually tied. But Obama wrapped up the month with a series of victories. Despite strong showings for Clinton in future contests in Ohio, Texas, and Pennsylvania, Obama's February run built up a lead in delegates he would not relinquish. On May 31, the DNC voted to seat all of Michigan and Florida's delegates at the national convention, but with half-a-vote each. In June, Obama reached the necessary total of delegates to secure the nomination.

Democratic National Convention. On August 23, Obama chose Senator Joe Biden as his vice presidential running mate. In Denver on August 28, Democrats formally nominated Obama as their presidential candidate.

U.S. Senate. The Democrats gained 7 seats in November, holding a 58-to-41 majority, including the two independent senators who generally align themselves with Democrats. The winner of the Norm Coleman (R., Minnesota)-Al Franken race was yet to be determined at year's end. New Senate Democrats included Mark Begich of Alaska, Kay Hagan of North Carolina, Jeff Merkley of Oregon, Jeanne Shaheen of New Hampshire, Mark Udall of Colorado and his cousin Tom Udall of New Mexico, and Mark Warner of Virginia.

House of Representatives. The party also built on advances it had made in the 2006 congressional elections, attaining a 257-to-178 majority. Victories in the 2008 congressional and presidential races marked the first time since 1994 that Democrats held the presidency and controlled both houses of Congress.

Gubernatorial races. Democrats won 7 of 11 races for governor in November 2008. Only one governorship—Missouri's—switched parties. In that race, Missouri Attorney General Jay Nixon, a Democrat, defeated U.S. Representative Kenny Hulshof in the race to succeed Governor Matt Blunt, who had decided not to seek reelection. After the election, Democrats held 29 governorships compared with 21 for Republicans.

Also in November, voters reelected Democratic Governors Christine Gregoire of Washington, John Lynch of New Hampshire, Joe Manchin of West Virginia, and Brian Schweitzer of Montana. Lieutenant Governor Beverly Perdue of North Carolina and State Treasurer Jack Markell of Delaware won open races to succeed Democratic governors stepping down because of term limits.

Scandals. New York Governor Eliot Spitzer resigned on March 17 after it was revealed he had patronized a high-priced prostitution ring under investigation by the federal government. Lieutenant Governor David A. Paterson replaced Spitzer, becoming the state's first African American governor.

Federal prosecutors on December 8 charged Illinois Governor Rod Blagojevich with corruption. Prosecutors accused Blagojevich of trying to sell President-elect Obama's Senate seat "for financial and personal benefits for himself and his wife."

Fund-raising. The Democratic National Committee, Democratic Senatorial Campaign Committee, and Democratic Congressional Campaign Committee raised a combined $462.4 million in the election cycle dating from Jan. 1, 2007, to mid-October 2008, according to the Federal Election Commission. Their Republican counterparts, the Republican National Committee, Republican Senatorial Committee, and National Republican Congressional Committee, raised $518.8 million through the same period. ■ Ken Shenkman

See also **Congress of the United States; Elections: A Special Report; People in the news** (Joe Biden, Michelle Obama); **Republican Party; State government; United States, Government of the.**

Denmark. In 2008, Prime Minister Anders Fogh Rasmussen's minority Liberal-Conservative coalition party retained its narrow parliamentary majority only with the support of the anti-immigrant Danish People's Party. Many Danes speculated that Rasmussen would not serve to the end of his term (2011) but would use his prestige to become the first permanent president of the European Council, the supreme political body of the European Union (EU, Europe's main economic bloc), or the Secretary-General of the North Atlantic Treaty Organization (NATO, the West's main defense alliance). In addition to a great deal of foreign travel, the prime minister initiated an international commission to create jobs in Africa and ensured that Denmark will host the United Nations summit on climate change in 2009.

European integration. Rasmussen focused in 2008 on integrating Denmark more fully into the EU. Although a long-time member, Denmark does not use the euro and retains the right to "opt out" of cooperation in foreign policy and judicial affairs. Changing the terms of integration would require a national referendum. In June, Rasmussen raised the possibility of such a vote. However, he postponed the idea after Irish voters rejected the EU reform treaty and after the European Court of Justice (the EU's highest court) ruled against restrictive immigration laws similar to Denmark's.

Immigration and integration. The government's restrictive immigration policy continued in 2008 to be driven by the need for support in Parliament from the Danish People's Party. In May, the party's leader, Pia Kjaersgaard, initiated a campaign to prohibit judges from wearing Islamic headscarves in court. The government responded by proposing a new law to ban the wearing of all religious symbols by judges. In February, leading Danish newspapers reprinted a cartoon depicting the Muslim prophet Muhammad that in 2006 led to anti-Danish protests throughout the Muslim world. The papers reprinted the cartoon in support of "free speech" after Danish police arrested several suspects who had allegedly plotted to assassinate the cartoonist. The republication led to more anti-Danish protests, including a car bombing at the Danish embassy in Pakistan.

Greenland. Voters in Greenland, a territory of Denmark, strongly favored greater autonomy in a referendum held in November 2008. Greenland was granted control over justice and police affairs, some control over foreign affairs, and the rights to potential Arctic resources.

Economy. EU economists forecast that Denmark's *gross domestic product* (GDP, the value of all goods and services produced in a country in a year) would increase by only 0.7 percent in 2008.

■ Jeffrey Kopstein
See also **Bank: A Special Report; Europe; Pakistan.**

Disability. On Oct. 3, 2008, United States President George W. Bush signed a new law requiring insurance plans to provide equal coverage for mental and physical illnesses. Most plans currently provide greater coverage for such physical illnesses as cancer and heart disease than for mental illnesses such as autism and depression. The new law was to go into effect on Jan. 1, 2010.

Defining disability. In September 2008, the U.S. Congress passed a new law that more broadly defines disability under the 1990 Americans with Disabilities Act (ADA) and overturns a number of Supreme Court rulings. With the passage of the ADA Amendments Act, such impairments as diabetes, heart disease, and cancer may be considered disabilities, and individuals with such conditions are to be protected from job discrimination.

The 1990 law contains language to the effect that people are protected from job discrimination if they have physical and mental impairments that "substantially limit" their ability to be hired for or to perform a particular job. The courts interpreted this wording to mean that only people who are truly disabled are entitled to protection under the law. According to the courts, people whose impairment or medical condition could be treated with such aids as medication, artificial limbs, or hearing aids, or people who were in remission from such diseases as cancer, are not eligible. Such an interpretation led to situations in which an individual was considered too impaired to perform the duties of a particular job but not impaired enough to be protected under the ADA.

Expanding the ADA. In May 2008, the Bush administration proposed new regulations that would give people with disabilities greater access to public spaces. The rules update the implementation of the ADA and call for such improvements as greater access to playground equipment for children in wheelchairs and the installation of lifts or ramps in courthouses. Public comment on the proposed rules was to continue throughout 2008.

Blade Runner. In May, Oscar Pistorius, a South African double amputee, was cleared by the Court of Arbitration for Sport in Lausanne, Switzerland, to compete in the 2008 Summer Olympic Games. Pistorius, whose legs were amputated as an infant because of a birth defect, is known as "Blade Runner" because he runs on J-shaped carbon-fiber blades. The Monaco-based International Association of Athletics Federations, the governing body for track and field sports, had ruled that the prosthetics give Pistorius an advantage over able-bodied athletes and thus disqualify him from competing against them. Despite the clearance, Pistorius was unable to participate in the Games because he failed to qualify. In the Paralympic Games in August, Pistorius won the 100-, 200-, and 400-meter sprints in his class. ■ Kristina Vaicikonis

Disasters. The deadliest disaster of 2008 was a cyclone in Myanmar (also known as Burma) that left 138,000 people dead or missing. Disasters that resulted in major loss of life include the following:

Aircraft crashes

February 21—Venezuela. A twin-engine, turbo-prop commercial airliner en route from Mérida, Venezuela, to Caracas, the capital, crashes in a remote region in western Venezuela, killing all 46 people aboard. Flying at 12,000 feet (4,000 meters), the ATR 42-300 flies into the side of a mountain.

August 20—Spain. Spanair Flight 5022 crashes during take-off from Madrid-Barajas Airport in Madrid, the capital, killing 154 people. The plane was en route to the Canary Islands carrying 172 passengers and crew members.

August 24—Kyrgyzstan. An Itek Air Boeing 737 carrying 90 passengers and crew members crashes as it attempts an emergency landing immediately after take-off from Bishkek, the capital. Sixty-eight people are killed and more than a dozen others are injured. The flight was bound for Tehran, Iran.

September 14—Russia. An Aeroflot Boeing 737 jet preparing to land in Perm, in central Russia, bursts into flames, explodes, and crashes, killing all 88 passengers and crew members aboard. The flight originated in Moscow, the capital.

Earthquakes

February 3—Central Africa. At least 39 people are killed and more than 600 others are injured in Rwanda and Congo (Kinshasa) when an earthquake of magnitude 6 strikes central Africa's Great Lakes region. The epicenter of the quake was in Congo (Kinshasa's) Bukavu province, near the Rwanda border.

May 12—China. A 7.9-magnitude earthquake kills nearly 70,000 people, injures nearly 300,000 others, and leaves 18,000 people missing. The quake was centered 55 miles (89 kilometers) northwest of Chengdu, the capital of Sichuan, and affected more than half the country's provinces.

August 30—China. At least 41 people are killed when an earthquake of magnitude 6.1 strikes near the town of Panzhihua in Sichuan province, near the border with Yunnan province. Nearly 600 others are injured during the original tremor and more than 400 aftershocks.

October 5—Kyrgyzstan. Nearly 60 people are killed and 50 others are injured when an earthquake of 6.3 magnitude strikes the southern province of Osh, near the country's border with China.

October 29—Pakistan. At least 215 people are killed when an earthquake of 6.4 magnitude strikes about 45 miles (70 kilometers) north of Quetta in the Baluchistan Province of southwestern Pakistan. Hundreds of huts in the area are destroyed, leaving some 15,000 people homeless.

The survivor of a major earthquake in China's Sichuan province examines the remains of his house in May 2008. The 7.9-magnitude quake killed nearly 70,000 people, injured nearly 300,000 others, and left 18,000 people missing.

Explosions and fires

January 7—South Korea. At least 40 people are killed and 10 others are injured in a warehouse fire in the city of Icheon, 50 miles (80 kilometers) south of Seoul, the capital. Fire officials speculate that flammable vapors from materials being used by the workers may have ignited, triggering a chain of explosions.

September 10—Southern Africa. Government officials report that at least 89 people died and thousands of others were displaced by wildfires that swept across Mozambique, South Africa, and Swaziland the previous week. The fires, which appear to have been triggered by high temperatures, were spread by strong winds.

Mine disaster

March 28—Tanzania. At least 65 miners are killed when heavy rains trigger flooding that causes a tanzanite mine to collapse. The mine is about 25 miles (40 kilometers) southeast of Arusha in northeastern Tanzania.

Shipwrecks

March 31—Nigeria. At least 40 people—including the bride—are killed when a dugout boat carrying a wedding party capsizes in Nigeria's north central Kano state. The travelers were escorting the bride from the Bagwai district to the village of Badau in the northwest.

May 12—Bangladesh. As many as 125 people are presumed dead when a ferry carrying 150 passengers sinks in the Ghorautura River about 113 miles (180 kilometers) northeast of Dhaka, the capital, during a storm. Twenty-five people survive.

June 7—Libya. At least 40 people are dead and more than 100 others are missing when a boat carrying illegal immigrants from Libya to Italy capsizes in the Mediterranean Sea, about 60 miles (100 kilometers) west of Tripoli. The migrants were originally from Bangladesh, Egypt, Somalia, and Tunisia.

June 21—Philippines. A ferry overturns about 1 mile (1.6 kilometers) off Sibuyan Island as Typhoon Fengshen strikes the Philippines. Of 850 passengers and crew members, only 57 survive. Nearly 500 people on land also die in the storm.

July 22—Congo (Kinshasa). At least 42 people are killed and more than 100 others are missing as a boat overloaded with more than 180 passengers strikes a rock and sinks in the remote Oubangui River at the border between Congo (Kinshasa) and the Central African Republic.

November 4—Philippines. At least 42 people are killed when an inter-island ferry carrying some 120 commuters overturns off the island of Masbate. The ferry was struck by sudden strong winds, though the sky was clear.

Storms and floods

February 13—China. The Chinese government reports that more than 100 people are dead in the most severe winter storms to hit China in some 50 years. The storms have destroyed some 350,000 homes, cut power to entire villages, and forced the evacuation of more than 825,000 people from central, eastern, and southern China since January 10.

February 5—Mid-southern United States. Tornadoes strike Alabama, Arkansas, Kentucky, Mississippi, and Tennessee from February 4 to February 6, killing 57 people and injuring at least 100 others.

February 11—Bolivia. President Evo Morales declares a natural disaster as more than 50 people are killed and some 40,000 others are left homeless in the country's eastern lowlands because of flooding. The province of Beni is the hardest hit.

March 19—Midwestern United States. At least 17 people are dead and several others are missing after days of heavy rain cause flooding in Arkansas, Illinois, Indiana, Kentucky, Missouri, and Ohio.

Some areas report as much as 12 inches (30 centimeters) of rain that, in addition to melting snow, brought rivers well above flood stage.

May 2—Myanmar. Nearly 85,000 people are killed and more than 53,000 others are missing as Cyclone Nargis deluges southwestern Myanmar's delta region with 20 inches (50 centimeters) of rain. A storm surge 12 feet (3.7 meters) high accompanied the downpour.

May 10—United States. Multiple tornadoes leave at least 23 people dead and more than 150 others injured in Georgia, Missouri, and Oklahoma. One of the tornadoes is accompanied by winds of 175 miles (280 kilometers) per hour.

May 25—Midwestern United States. Nine people are killed in Iowa and Minnesota and at least 50 others are injured as more than 100 tornadoes are reported across the Midwest during the Memorial Day weekend.

June 17—China. State authorities report that at least 112 people are dead and nearly 1.3 million others have been evacuated as the worst floods in 50 years ravage the Pearl River Delta.

August 8—Vietnam. Tropical storm Kammuri sweeps through northwest Vietnam, causing floods and landslides that leave at least 100 people dead and more than 50 others missing.

August 24—Southern United States. Eleven people in Florida and one person in Georgia are killed as Tropical Storm Fay makes landfall in Florida four times before carrying heavy rain into Alabama and Mississippi. Fay caused at least 50 deaths in Haiti and Cuba before reaching Florida.

September 1—Haiti. Hurricane Hanna strikes Haiti with heavy rains, causing flooding and landslides that kill at least 529 people. The port city of Gonaives is particularly hard hit. Hanna made landfall at the South Carolina-North Carolina border on September 6, causing 7 additional deaths in the United States.

September 8—China. At least 276 people are killed when a dam holding back waste from an illegal mine is weakened by rain and collapses, sending a wall of mud and rocks onto houses and a market below. The landslide occurred near Linfen City in the central province of Shanxi.

September 22—India. National disaster officials report that more than 2,300 people throughout India have been killed in floods caused by monsoon rains since the monsoon season began in June.

September 28—Vietnam. Government authorities report that at least 32 people have died in flash floods and landslides caused by heavy rains brought by Typhoon Hagupit. The typhoon killed at least 8 people in the Philippines and 17 in China earlier in the week.

November 2—Vietnam. State media report that at least 92 people have been killed over the past week as floods engulfed northern and central Vietnam. Most of Hanoi, the capital, was submerged under 3 feet (1 meter) of water.

Train wrecks

April 28—China. At least 70 people are killed and more than 420 others are injured when two passenger trains collide at Zibo in eastern China's Shandong province. A train traveling from Beijing to the resort town of Qingdao derailed, striking a train en route from Yantai to Xuzhou.

September 12—California. Twenty-five people are killed and more than 130 others are injured as a passenger train carrying commuters and a freight train crash head-on northwest of Los Angeles. According to a spokesperson for the commuter train line Metrolink, an engineer on the passenger train failed to heed a signal to stop.

Other disasters

April 26—Morocco. At least 55 people are killed and dozens of others are injured when fire races through a mattress factory in Casablanca.

May 15—Nigeria. A road grader strikes an oil pipeline causing an explosion and fire that spreads to a nearby school and homes. More than 100 people are killed and dozens of others are injured.

August 3—India. Thousands of pilgrims stampede on a remote mountain path en route to a Hindu temple about 100 miles (160 kilometers) from the Himalayan town of Shimla, causing the deaths of 145 people and injuring dozens of others.

August 27—Malta. At least 70 African migrants drown about 40 miles (70 kilometers) off Malta as they attempt to cross the Mediterranean Sea.

September 6—Egypt. At least 61 people are killed and dozens of others are injured when large boulders fall from the cliffs of Muqattam onto the Duwayqa district of Cairo below. The boulders, each weighing some 77 tons (70 metric tons), completely obliterate a 6-story residential building.

September 30—India. At least 224 people are killed and dozens of others are injured in a stampede among some 25,000 pilgrims in Jodhpur, in India's western Rajasthan state. The pilgrims were approaching the Chamunda Devi temple along a steep, narrow path when a wall collapsed, sparking the stampede.

November 7—Haiti. A school building in Petionville collapses during a celebration, causing the deaths of at least 92 teachers, schoolchildren, and their families.

December 2—Zimbabwe. Representatives of the World Health Organization, an agency of the United Nations, report that at least 473 people have died during the past month in a cholera epidemic. Zimbabwe's ongoing political and economic crisis has caused the collapse of the country's sanitation system and water shortages. By mid-December, 800 people had died. ■ Kristina Vaicikonis

See also **China; Haiti; India; Myanmar; Pakistan; Weather.**

Drought. See Weather.

Drug abuse. An estimated 19.9 million Americans aged 12 or older were *current* (within the past month) users of illegal drugs, 126.8 million were current drinkers of alcohol, and 70.9 million were tobacco users in 2007, according to the National Survey on Drug Use and Health (NSDUH), released in September 2008. The NSDUH is an annual survey by the United States Substance Abuse and Mental Health Services Administration.

Illegal drugs. The 8-percent rate of current overall illegal drug use reported in the 2007 NSDUH was similar to the rates reported each year since 2002. In addition, marijuana was once again the most commonly used illegal drug, with 5.8 percent of Americans using it in 2007.

The 2007 NSDUH reported substantial declines in the use of illegal drugs among youth. For Americans between the ages of 12 and 17, current illegal drug use fell from a rate of 11.6 percent in 2002 to 9.5 percent in 2007. This decrease included reductions in the use of nearly all types of illegal drugs in this age category. Among young adults between the ages of 18 and 25, the rate of cocaine use decreased from 2.2 percent to 1.7 percent from 2006 to 2007, while the rate of methamphetamine use dropped from 0.6 percent to 0.4 percent.

However, the NSDUH results showed drug use

increases in certain drug and age categories. Current nonmedical use of prescription pain relievers by adults aged 18 to 25 increased from 4.1 percent in 2002 to 4.6 percent in 2007. During this same period, overall current illegal drug use by adults aged 55 to 59 more than doubled, from 1.9 percent to 4.1 percent.

Alcohol. The 2007 NSDUH showed that 51.1 percent of Americans were current drinkers of alcohol, similar to the 50.9 percent reported for 2006. The rate of Americans participating in *binge drinking* (having five or more drinks on the same occasion) during the past month was 23.3 percent in 2007, while the rate of Americans who were *heavy drinkers* (having five or more drinks on the same occasion on five or more days) during the past month was 6.9 percent. These rates were similar to those reported for 2006. Americans between the ages of 12 and 17 used alcohol at a rate of 15.9 percent in 2007, compared with 17.6 percent in 2002.

Tobacco. According to the 2007 NSDUH, 28.6 percent of Americans were current users of a tobacco product (cigarettes, smokeless tobacco, cigars, or pipe tobacco)—a decrease from the 29.6 percent reported for 2006. Among Americans aged 12 to 17, the rate of current cigarette use was 9.8 percent in 2007, compared with 13 percent in 2002. ■ Alfred J. Smuskiewicz

Drugs. Some of the 93 reported deaths tentatively linked to the blood-thinning medication heparin from January 2007 to March 2008 were, in fact, caused by a contaminant in the drug, reported the United States Food and Drug Administration (FDA) in July 2008. The report was part of an ongoing investigation into problems with heparin products, most of them sold by Baxter International of Deerfield, Illinois, which obtained the drug's raw ingredients from a processing facility in China. Heparin is widely used to prevent blood clots during kidney dialysis, heart surgery, and other medical procedures.

Reports of heparin-related deaths led Baxter to issue a recall of the drug in February. The FDA investigation revealed that batches of Baxter's heparin were contaminated with a chemical impurity that could cause severe allergic reactions. The investigation concluded, however, that 25 of the reported deaths were caused by factors unrelated to heparin use.

Actor highlights drug errors. More public attention was drawn to heparin in May, when actor Dennis Quaid testified before the U.S. Congress regarding the near fatal experiences of his twin children with the drug. Quaid described how the newborn twins almost died in 2007 after hospital staff gave them adult-level doses of heparin (1,000 times the normal dose of heparin for an infant) while treating them for *Staphylococcus* infections. According to Quaid, the mistake happened because the pill bottles made by Baxter were virtually identical for the child-strength heparin and the adult-strength heparin.

Quaid, who was in the process of suing Baxter for the mix-up, urged members of Congress to reject a proposal that would shield pharmaceutical companies against certain consumer lawsuits.

Avandia deception? The British-based pharmaceutical company GlaxoSmithKline failed to properly disclose to the FDA all required information on studies of rosiglitazone (sold under the brand name Avandia) from 2001 to 2007. The FDA made that announcement in April 2008. A study published in May 2007 linked rosiglitazone to an increased risk of heart attack in patients with diabetes—causing sales of the popular diabetes drug to plummet. After publication of this study, the FDA required a strict warning label about this risk to be placed on the drug.

GlaxoSmithKline denied that it had withheld safety-related information about rosiglitazone from the FDA. Furthermore, the company continued to dispute the May 2007 study linking rosiglitazone to heart attacks.

Hormone replacement risks. Although most of the risks of hormone replacement therapy (HRT) using Prempro (a combination of synthetic estrogens and progesterone) vanish by 2 ½ years after women stop HRT, some risks remain. That conclusion was reported in March 2008 based on a new analysis of data from the Women's Health Initiative (WHI), a U.S. government-funded research project involving 16,000 women.

Researchers with the WHI reported in 2002 that Prempro, sold by Wyeth Pharmaceuticals of Collegeville, Pennsylvania, increased women's risks of heart attack, stroke, blood clots, and breast cancer. The new analysis followed up with the women for 29 months after they quit using Prempro. The researchers found that the increased risks of heart attack, stroke, and blood clots were reduced by the end of this period. However, the risk of breast cancer remained high—as did the risks of other types of cancer.

Expensive equals effective? If patients believe that the drugs they are taking are expensive, the drugs may actually be more effective, according to a study published in March 2008 by researchers at the Massachusetts Institute of Technology in Cambridge. The higher price of a drug apparently gives patients the impression of the drug's probable greater effectiveness, and this, in turn, leads to a beneficial therapeutic effect, according to the researchers.

The MIT team administered electric shocks to the wrists of 82 subjects before and after giving the subjects "pain-relief" pills. Half the subjects were informed that the pills cost $2.50 each. The other half were told that the pills cost 10 cents each. In reality, all the subjects were given identical *placebos* (dummy pills). Eighty-five percent of the subjects given "expensive" pills reported pain relief; only 61 percent of the subjects given "cheap" pills reported pain relief.

Americans on chronic meds. In 2007, for the first time, more than half (51 percent) of Americans with health insurance were using prescription drugs for *chronic* (long-term) health problems. This conclusion, reported in May 2008, was based on data gathered by Medco Health Solutions, Inc., of Franklin Lakes, New Jersey, which manages prescription drug programs.

The report noted that the prescription medications most widely used by adults were taken for high blood pressure, high cholesterol, and depression. The prescription drugs used most often by children were for asthma, allergies, and attention-deficit/hyperactivity disorder.

The researchers attributed the increasing use of drugs for chronic conditions to growing rates of heart disease, obesity, and diabetes among Americans—as well as to advertising by pharmaceutical companies.   ■ Alfred J. Smuskiewicz

See also **AIDS; Drug abuse; Health care issues; Medicine; Mental health; Public health.**

East Timor. See Asia.

Eastern Orthodox Churches. The
world's Orthodox churches moved toward greater cooperation and unity in 2008. Representatives of the 14 *autocephalous* (independent) Orthodox churches met in Istanbul, Turkey, for a historic gathering from October 10 to 12. In a joint statement, the church leaders pledged "to safeguard the unity of the Orthodox Church" and to resolve divisions "with a spirit of love and peace." Ecumenical Patriarch Bartholomew of Constantinople organized the meeting to mark 2,000 years since the birth of Saint Paul, one of the most important leader of early Christianity who founded congregations throughout Asia Minor and southeastern Europe.

Roman Catholic relations. On March 6 in Rome, Ecumenical Patriarch Bartholomew spoke at the Pontifical Oriental Institute, a Roman Catholic educational center devoted to studies of Eastern Christianity, and met with Pope Benedict XVI. The two religious leaders met again in Rome on June 28 and 29 and inaugurated a year devoted to Saint Paul. Patriarch Bartholomew also addressed the Roman Catholic bishops in Rome on October 18.

New leaders were elected by several Orthodox churches in 2008. On February 7, the Holy Synod of the Autocephalous Orthodox Church of Greece elected Metropolitan Ieronymos of Thebes and Livadia as its *primate* (head of the entire church). Ieronymos succeeded Archbishop Christodoulos of Athens and All Greece, who had died on January 28.

On May 12, the Russian Orthodox Church Outside Russia elected Metropolitan Hilarion, archbishop of the Diocese of Australia and New Zealand, as its new head, called first hierarch. Hilarion succeeded Metropolitan Laurus, who had died on March 16.

The 15th All American Council of the Orthodox Church in America (OCA), with about 600 delegates, met in Pittsburgh from November 10 to 13. The council elected Bishop Jonah of Fort Worth, Texas, to become Archbishop of Washington and New York and Metropolitan of All America and Canada. Jonah succeeded Metropolitan Herman in the position. Metropolitan Herman had retired on September 4 after a special investigative committee of the OCA recommended that he and several others be disciplined for mishandling a financial scandal.

Death. Patriarch Alexy II of Moscow and All Russia, the head of the Russian Orthodox Church, died at age 79 on December 5. He presided over the extensive rebuilding of the Church of Russia following the collapse of communism and decades of state persecution. Bishops will elect a new patriarch at a meeting scheduled for late January 2009.   ■ Thomas FitzGerald

Economics, United States. Commer-
cial activity and industrial output across the United States slowed substantially during 2008, as long-term problems in financial markets came to a head. These problems brought the flow of credit on which business and industry depend to an abrupt halt in September and October. Businesses rely heavily on credit availability, particularly money markets, which are venues for short-term investment, to fund their operating expenses. These expenses include, among others, purchase of materials, payroll, and customer loans.

Before the autumn financial crisis, the U.S. economy was in recession and had been for nearly a year, according to economists with the National Bureau of Economic Research, an organization specializing in the study of economics. However, the recession deepened sharply in the second half of 2008, with monthly job losses mounting to 533,000 in November, making that month the worst for negative job growth since December 1974. Overall, the U.S. economy lost 2 million jobs in 2008, with unemployment soaring to 6.7 percent by the third quarter (July–September). As the autumn economic crisis deepened, economists predicted a long and deep recession with further hemorrhaging of jobs.

Economic historians noted that the credit breakdowns that overwhelmed financial markets in the autumn set off the worst financial panic since the 1929 stock market crash that triggered the Great Depression. That economic cataclysm threw millions out of work and drove down the value of goods and property through much of the 1930's.

In late 2007 and in 2008, the crisis emerged as a result of mushrooming mortgage *defaults* (failure to make promised payments) in the United States. Debt obligations from the nation's overheated, loosely regulated mortgage market of the mid-2000's had been translated into securities that were avidly purchased by global investors. The scale of defaults emerging in 2007 and 2008 shattered confidence in the U.S. mortgage-backed securities, which infected the entire financial system. These problems began to show up in early 2008 with the failure of a string of U.S. financial institutions. Panic soon spread beyond the financial sector, triggering periodic sell-offs on the New York Stock Exchange and other world stock exchanges.

As the financial crisis expanded and spread offshore, some economists warned that unless the situation were well managed by governments and central banks, the global economy might slide into another 1930's-style depression. Other economists argued that this grim scenario was too pessimistic, especially after authorities of many nations acted in concert to cut interest rates and inject cash into

money markets. Among such measures was the so-called $700-billion "bailout" of U.S. financial markets by the administration of President George W. Bush and Congress in October 2008.

In the first half of the year, the U.S. economy seemingly had dodged several threats. Statistics released by the U.S. Department of Commerce (DOC) showed that economic growth had virtually stalled in the fourth quarter (October–December) of 2007. In response, the U.S. Federal Reserve System (the Fed), the nation's central bank network, cut the federal funds rate several times in the first half of 2008 and then again in October and December. These actions cumulatively lowered the rate from 4.25 to from 0.25 to 0 percent. (The federal funds rate is the interest rate the Fed charges for overnight loans between commercial banks.)

In February, the U.S. Congress, alarmed by the threat of recession, passed a $168-billion stimulus bill that funded tax-rebate checks for most households. The DOC later reported that the economy grew a mild 0.9 percent in the first quarter (January–March) and then 2.8 percent in the second quarter (April–June), when the stimulus checks boosted consumer spending.

Fuel price pressure. During the first half of 2008, prices for gasoline and other oil-based fuels soared, pulling more money out of households

SELECTED KEY U.S. ECONOMIC INDICATORS

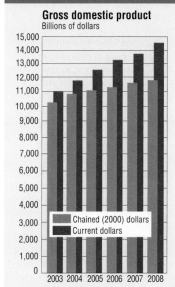

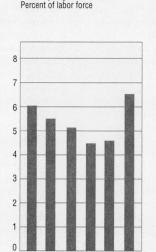

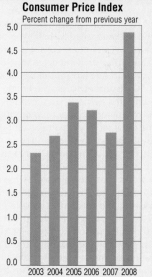

Sources: U.S. Department of Commerce and U.S. Department of Labor, except 2008 figures, which are estimates from The Conference Board.

The gross domestic product (GDP) measures the value in current prices of all goods and services produced within a country in a year. Many economists believe the GDP is an accurate measure of the nation's total economic performance. Chained dollars show the amount adjusted for inflation. The unemployment rate is the percentage of the total labor force that is unemployed and actively seeking work. The Consumer Price Index measures inflation by showing the change in prices of selected goods and services consumed by urban families and individuals.

and businesses at a time of falling real estate values, weak wage growth, and slow business activity. As the price of oil mounted to a high of $147 a barrel in July, the national average price of gasoline spiked to $4.11, the U.S. Energy Information Administration reported. This price surge squeezed consumers' discretionary spending.

Soaring jet fuel costs, coupled with weak demand, wreaked havoc on the airline industry in 2008. Within the space of about four weeks between mid-February and mid-March, five U.S.-based airlines filed for bankruptcy or shut down operations. They included Honolulu-based Aloha Airlines; Indianapolis-based ATA; Columbus, Ohio-based Skybus Airlines; Denver-based Frontier Airlines; and Purchase, New York-based EOS Airlines. Many surviving U.S. airlines cut flights in 2008 to minimize their losses.

The trucking industry also struggled to cope with spiraling fuel costs. In April, trucking groups urged President Bush to release oil from the U.S. Strategic Petroleum Reserve (SPR) to ease tight market supplies and price pressures. Bush responded that he would tap the SPR only in a national emergency or in response to supply disruptions.

Consumer prices. Pushed by fuel and food prices, consumer prices that had been flat in February increased 0.6 percent in May; they then surged 1.1 percent in June and 0.8 percent in July. Fed officials expected the steep increases to level off, but they refrained from cutting interest rates over the summer months to avoid applying inflationary pressure to the economy.

After July, however, oil prices reversed course and declined steadily, falling to below $50 per barrel in December. Consumer prices reflected the slide, either showing no change or declining slightly in August, September, and October.

Consumer jitters. The timing of the crash in money markets, with its inevitable negative impact on consumer confidence, prompted worries that the retail sector would take a hit during the pre-Christmas holiday shopping season. For many retailers, the period between Thanksgiving and Christmas is a make-or-break time for annual profit margins. Statistics released by the DOC showed a 3.1-percent drop in consumer spending in the third quarter, and economists speculated that consumer reluctance could carry over into the holiday season. Economists reasoned, moreover, that retailers' worries about end-of-year sales could prompt them to cut restocking of goods for 2009, injecting yet another negative feedback into the economy.

The industrial sector. Weakening consumer demand in 2008 began to act as a brake on factory production. Especially hard-hit was the U.S. auto industry, though foreign auto manufacturers experienced declines in sales worldwide. For the cash-strapped Big Three—Chrysler LLC of Auburn Hills, Michigan; Ford Motor Company of Dearborn, Michigan; and General Motors (GM) Corporation of Detroit—prospects were so grim that the companies' heads appeared before Congress in November asking for a multibillion-dollar bailout. On December 19, President Bush extended a $17.4-billion short-term loan to General Motors and Chrysler to tide them over until March 2009. Ford had only asked for a loan guarantee in case of an emergency.

Overall factory activity, as measured by the purchasing manager's index (PMI) compiled by the Tempe, Arizona-based Institute for Supply Management (ISM), trended downward in 2008—marginally in the first three quarters and then steeply in the fourth quarter. The index slipped from 50.7 in January to 48.3 in February and remained around these levels through August. (A reading of 50 delineates the boundary between expansion and contraction in the factory sector.)

In September, the financial crisis emerged full-blown, eroding investor and consumer confidence. ISM's PMI metric reflected these developments, with factory activity measuring 43.5 in September, 38.9 in October, and 37.3 in November. ■ John D. Boyd

See also **Bank: A Special Report; Economics, World; Energy supply: A Special Report; United States, Government of the: A Special Report.**

Economics, World.
Much of the developed world entered economic recession in 2008 or seemed poised to do so in 2009, as global growth in output of goods and services declined steeply, especially in late 2008. The giant United States economy was already in recession at the beginning of 2008, according to economists with the National Bureau of Economic Research (NBER), an organization specializing in the study of economics. Consumer demand in the United States stimulates economic growth across the globe, and the U.S. downturn implied trouble for much of the global economy, analysts said.

The fundamental cause of the world's economic woes was the globalization of a financial crisis that extinguished normal flows of credit on which most economic activity depends. In addition, volatile prices for petroleum and other *commodities* (unprocessed basic goods) interfered with economic growth. In the first half of 2008, oil prices surged, constraining economic activity on a broad scale. In the second half, oil prices fell steeply, helping consumers but posing threats to countries that rely on oil export income.

Financial crisis. The crisis that overtook the world's financial sector in late 2008, strangling credit sources for business and industry, had its roots in the United States. In the mid-2000's, the overheated U.S. mortgage market attracted global investors. The investors did not invest directly in U.S. mortgages, but rather in *securities* (derived investments) created from pools of the mortgages. These securities promised attractive returns with apparently low risk. However, much of the commerce in U.S. mortgages had taken place largely in the absence of regulation, and many mortgage holders eventually found themselves overextended. As a result, the rate of mortgage *defaults* (failure to make promised payments) soared in 2007 and 2008, shaking the confidence of holders of U.S. mortgage-backed securities. This loss of confidence spread like a virus through world financial markets; eventually, banks and other financial institutions that had large holdings of the securities—now dubbed "toxic"—found themselves in financial trouble.

A succession of failures or near failures of major financial institutions in 2008 triggered panic on the world's stock exchanges and prompted governments to intervene on an unprecedented scale. Governments of the United States, the United Kingdom, Switzerland, and other nations expended vast sums buying stakes in troubled banks, in effect reversing long-standing free market economic policies. Many governments also bought up toxic securities, and their central banks injected cash into financial systems.

Countries with especially vulnerable banking systems fared the worst. In Iceland, the cascading failures of the country's three major banks in October led to the collapse of the country's currency, the krona, on world currency markets, leaving the country essentially bankrupt.

Fuel prices. For the first seven months of 2008, prices for petroleum-based fuels skyrocketed, regularly setting new record highs and transferring wealth from energy-consuming nations to energy-exporting nations. The fuel price surge cramped businesses, consumers, and government agencies alike. The resulting inflation, moreover, limited the ability of central banks to cut interest rates to spur growth.

From January to July, petroleum prices more than doubled, reaching a peak of $147 per barrel on July 11. As supply began to outpace demand, however, prices began to retreat; then they plummeted after the financial crisis deepened in the third quarter (July–September). By December, the per-barrel price of oil dipped below $50—the lowest level in three years. As 2008 came to a close, the world's major oil exporting nations faced shrinking export income.

World economic survey. The global economy grew by over 5 percent in 2006 and 2007. However, economists with the International Monetary Fund (IMF) projected only 3.7-percent global economic growth in 2008 and 2-percent growth in 2009. (The IMF is a United Nations–affiliated organization that provides short-term credit to member nations.)

The U.S. economy slipped into recession in late 2007, according to NBER economists. The recession intensified with accelerating job losses in late 2008 due to the effects of the deepening financial crisis. Officials of the United Kingdom (U.K.) reported that the U.K. economy had contracted by 0.5 percent during third quarter 2008. IMF economists projected that in 2009 the U.S. economy would contract by 0.7 percent and the U.K. economy, by 1.3 percent.

Recession in Germany in late 2008 helped drag the eurozone, the member states of the European Union (EU) using the euro currency, into its first area-wide recession since adoption of the euro in 1999. France, Italy, and Spain—all eurozone countries—entered recession in 2008 or were expected to do so in early 2009.

In November 2008, Japan's government reported that the country experienced negative growth in the third quarter. The report, the second in succession indicating contraction, confirmed that the Japanese economy—the world's second-largest—was officially in recession.

Developing countries, including the Asian giants China and India, felt the global economic squeeze as well in the second half of 2008. China's fast-paced growth in 2007 of nearly 12 percent would likely slow to less than 10 percent in 2008 and perhaps dip below 9 percent in 2009, IMF economists projected. Other economists predicted an even steeper decline in growth. One measure of China's economic slowdown in 2008, analysts noted, was a falloff in electric power production in October, the first such monthly decline since 2005.

China's economic boom of recent years had been stoked by global demand for manufactured goods, particularly from the giant U.S. economy. As the United States slid into recession and consumer demand contracted, orders for China's products fell off steeply. As the global financial crisis deepened in the autumn, the Chinese government funded a domestic economic stimulus package of nearly $600 billion, the largest in its history. Sociologists, meanwhile, speculated that a sustained economic downturn in China could dislocate millions of boomtown migrants who, if furloughed, might return to their impoverished home villages.

Economic growth in India slowed in 2008 to less than 8 percent, compared with 10 percent in 2006 and 2007. Economists with the IMF predicted that growth would fall to 6 percent in 2009. ■ John D. Boyd

See also **Bank: A Special Report; Economics, United States; Energy supply: A Special Report; United States, Government of the: A Special Report.**

Ecuador. On Sept. 28, 2008, voters in Ecuador strongly approved a new Constitution backed by President Rafael Correa Delgado. The new Constitution enhanced the powers of the president and permitted Correa to seek a second consecutive four-year term. It also guaranteed all Ecuadoreans free education through college, eliminated mandatory military service, and provided pensions for stay-at-home mothers and unregistered small business owners.

Seizure of private companies. On July 8, Ecuadorean authorities seized 195 businesses in an effort to recover debts resulting from the 1998 failure of Filanbanco, one of Ecuador's largest banks. The businesses were all once controlled by William and Roberto Isaias. The brothers had operated Filanbanco and, after its failure, fled to the United States to escape fraud charges.

Border conflict. On March 1, 2008, the Colombian military attacked a guerrilla camp in Ecuador, killing several members of the terrorist group FARC, which had long waged a civil war against the Colombian government. Ecuador saw the attack as a violation of its sovereignty and massed troops at the border with Colombia. The dispute was peacefully resolved March 7.

◼ Nathan A. Haverstock

See also **Latin America**.

Education. In 2008, the United States marked the 25th anniversary of the landmark education report *A Nation at Risk* (1983). The National Commission on Excellence in Education had reported in *A Nation at Risk* that U.S. students lagged far behind students in many other industrialized nations. The report warned of a "rising tide of mediocrity" in American schools that would endanger the nation's competitiveness around the world. It set off a series of reform efforts that led to the standards and accountability movement of today.

No Child Left Behind. The centerpiece of the standards and accountability movement is the federal No Child Left Behind Act of 2001. The act, often referred to as NCLB, calls for student testing in public schools from kindergarten through grade 12 and holds schools accountable for student progress.

Many education experts credit NCLB with bringing greater attention to the needs of struggling learners and underserved populations of students. But the law continued to draw criticism in 2008 for narrowing the curriculum with its focus on testing in mathematics, reading, and science. Studies showed a significant increase in time devoted to reading and math instruction and a shift away from other subjects, such as social studies, art, and music.

Congress failed to reauthorize NCLB in 2008, meaning that the law remained in effect without Congress making any changes. With reauthorization postponed, the U.S. Department of Education enlisted a panel of experts to recommend regulatory changes, which do not need congressional approval. The department appointed a National Technical Advisory Panel in August to make suggestions on standards, assessments, and accountability requirements, such as how to determine whether a school has made adequate progress toward meeting educational goals. The panel includes state assessment directors, test designers, and other experts.

Under NCLB, schools that fail to make adequate yearly progress (AYP) may have to pay for tutoring for their students and take other actions to improve achievement. If test scores for a particular school fail to show adequate progress for five years, the school must undergo radical changes called "restructuring." NCLB allows several restructuring options, including turning the school over to the state or to a private management company, replacing much of the school's staff, or any other major action that will significantly change how the school is run.

The Center on Education Policy, an independent, nonprofit research organization based in Washington, D.C., reported in September an increase in the number of schools being restructured under NCLB. The report studied schools in five states—California, Georgia, Maryland, Michigan, and Ohio. Nearly 3,600 schools in the five states were designated as needing restructuring during the 2007-2008 school year, a 56 percent increase over the previous year.

The Department of Education continued to introduce more flexibility into how schools are held accountable under NCLB. In July 2008, the department approved six states—Florida, Georgia, Illinois, Indiana, Maryland, and Ohio—to participate in a pilot program called *differentiated accountability*. The program is designed to allow states to distinguish between schools that come close to meeting requirements and those that need more significant reform.

Graduation rates. A record number of students—more than 3.3 million—earned a high school diploma in 2008, according to federal estimates. About three-fourths of the nation's 9th graders completed high school within four years, according to the latest data, from the 2004-2005 school year.

NCLB requires states to report their high school graduation rates to the federal government. But the act allows the states to set their own formulas for calculating how many students graduate from high school within four years and how many drop out. As a result, some states understated the number of dropouts, federal officials said. In 2005, the National Governors Association (NGA), made up of the governors of the 50 states, agreed to a common formula for calculating graduation rates. The Education Department in October 2008 announced new rules requiring all states to use the NGA formula by 2011.

Paying for college. College costs increased in every category for the 2008-2009 school year, according to an annual survey by the College Board. The College Board is a not-for-profit association, based in New York City, whose members are schools, colleges, universities, and other educational organizations. Tuition and fees at public four-year colleges rose 6.4 percent for in-state students, to an average of $6,585. Tuition and fees at private four-year colleges averaged $25,143, an increase of 5.9 percent.

Congress passed two measures in 2008 to help make higher education more affordable. In response to a credit crunch, Congress passed the Ensuring Continued Access to Student Loans Act in May. The act assured the availability of federal student loans for college and raised limits on the loans. In August, Congress approved the Higher Education Opportunity Act. The act makes it easier to apply for certain types of student financial aid. It also requires that colleges with the greatest cost increases submit reports to the Department of Education explaining why costs have increased and what steps they will take to keep tuition and fees down.

SAT's and ACT's. The use of the ACT and SAT exams in the college admission process continued to draw scrutiny in 2008. More colleges and universities made it optional for applicants to submit their scores. Some critics also raised questions about the validity of the scores in predicting students' success.

A national commission recommended in September 2008 that colleges and universities consider dropping the tests as a requirement for entry. The National Association for College Admission Counseling, an organization of educational counselors based in Arlington, Virginia, convened the panel. The commission, made up of college admissions personnel and high school guidance counselors, said that institutions should give greater consideration to the difficulty of the high school curriculum and how well students mastered it, rather than to standardized tests.

The College Board, which owns the SAT, announced a new policy that allows students to withhold their lowest scores from college admissions offices. Beginning in March 2009, students may take the exam multiple times and submit only their best score, rather than all scores.

■ Kathleen Kennedy Manzo

Egypt. The Egyptian government continued to crackdown on political opposition during 2008. In August, an Egyptian court sentenced, in absentia, Egyptian-American sociologist and human rights activist Saad Edin Ibrahim to two years in prison. Ibrahim, who was living in self-imposed exile in the United States, was convicted of tarnishing Egypt's reputation by writing prodemocracy articles in the international press. In an article published in *The Washington Post* in 2007, Ibrahim called for the United States to cut its yearly aid of $1.3 billion to Egypt as a form of pressure to induce democratic reform.

Facebook rebellion. A youth movement mobilized by the online social network Facebook organized a nationwide strike on April 6, 2008, in protest of soaring prices and low wages and in support of textile workers in Al-Mahalla al-Kubra, in northern Egypt. Clashes between striking textile workers and police led to the deaths of at least two people and the wounding of dozens more. Egyptian authorities detained more than 300 demonstrators during the strike.

The youth movement, which became known as the April 6 Movement, continued to be politically active throughout 2008. After attending a symposium organized by the liberal democratic al-Ghad Party on July 23, approximately 26 members of the April 6 Movement were jailed.

Israel-Hamas cease-fire. After weeks of intensive negotiations, Egyptian officials in June successfully brokered a cease-fire between Israel and Hamas, the militant Palestinian organization that controlled the Gaza Strip. The cease-fire, which went into effect on June 19, ended rocket attacks against Israel by Hamas fighters in Gaza and Israeli military strikes against Hamas.

Muslim attacks on Copts. Egypt's community of Copts, Christians who trace their lineage to the ancient Egyptians, called on Egyptian President Hosni Mubarak to provide greater protection for them after a number of attacks by Muslims in 2008. On May 31, a group of local Muslims attacked the Abu Fana Monastery, near the city of al-Minya in southern Egypt. One Muslim assailant was killed and four Copts, including two monks, were wounded in the fighting. On October 3, in the village of al-Tayaba in al-Minya province, a Muslim attack led to the death of a Copt and to the wounding of several Copts and Muslims.

"Queens of Egypt," an exhibition featuring 150 relics and statues from ancient Egypt, with a focus on Egyptian queens, princesses, and goddesses, opened in July in Monte Carlo in Monaco. First Lady Suzanne Mubarak of Egypt and Prince Albert of Monaco were on hand for the opening.

■ Marius Deeb

See also **Israel; Middle East.**

2008 Election:

A PIVOTAL CHOICE

With the United States in the grips of a crippling financial crisis and fighting two wars overseas, voters on November 4 chose Democratic Senator Barack Obama of Illinois to take the country in a new direction.

By Ken Shenkman

On Nov. 4, 2008, American voters were asked to make a choice between presidential candidates representing "change" and "experience." Perhaps never before had such a choice appeared so sharply defined. Democratic Senator Barack Obama of Illinois, the first African American candidate nominated by a major party, became the first person of color elected to the presidency. Obama faced Republican Senator John McCain of Arizona, who, at 72, was the oldest candidate to make a first run for the office. McCain's surprise pick for running mate, Alaska Governor Sarah Palin, became the first woman nominated for vice president on the Republican ticket.

Obama, backed by one of the most disciplined and well-organized campaigns in presidential history, defeated McCain by 53 percent to 46 percent, with a margin of about 8 million votes. With Obama's victory, the Democrats, who had captured Congress in the 2006 elections, gained control of both the executive and legislative branches of the federal government for the first time since 1994.

The election itself set records. In addition to raising an unprecedented amount of money for a political campaign, Obama ran the first campaign in which digital media played an integral role. Voter turnout, which included a record number of early voters, was the largest for any presidential campaign. Some experts estimated that 25 percent of the 125 million people who went to the polls took advantage of extended early voting days or cast absentee ballots.

Obama and his fellow Democrats benefited from a national mood that had turned against Republican President George W. Bush. More than 80 percent of Americans said the country was headed in the "wrong direction," according to opinion polls. From the outset of the presidential campaign, Obama worked to link McCain to President Bush, whose public approval ratings had fallen to record levels, and to Bush's legacy of rising health care and energy costs and the costly and unpopular wars in Iraq and Afghanistan. During the later stages of the campaign, the U.S. economy—rocked by the worst financial crisis since the Great Depression of the 1930's—emphatically emerged as the top issue with voters. Democrats tied McCain to efforts to deregulate the financial markets whose meltdown led to soaring home foreclosure rates, massive bank failures, a crashing stock market, and dramatic drops in the value of Americans' retirement accounts.

The competitors

In 2008, for the first time since 1952, a sitting president or vice president did not campaign for the nomination. The wide-open contest drew interest from a number of prominent figures from both major parties.

Senators Barack Obama of Illinois and Hillary Clinton of New York participate in 1 of more than 20 debates held by contenders for the Democratic presidential nomination. Both candidates tallied about 18 million votes in primary contests that began in January. By June, Obama had enough delegates to secure the nomination.

ELECTIONS ■ A Special Report

Senator Hillary Clinton of New York was the leading candidate for the 2008 Democratic nomination. Clinton, a former U.S. first lady, held double-digit leads over her Democratic opponents, including Obama, in nearly all national polls throughout 2007. Clinton also secured early commitments from a large number of elected and appointed party officials, known as superdelegates, authorized to vote for the nominee at the 2008 Democratic National Convention in Denver.

Obama, a first-term senator from Illinois, was a compelling if relatively inexperienced entry into the Democratic field. Obama, who ran on a platform of "change" and bipartisan cooperation, had leaped to national fame on the strength of his keynote address touting the "politics of hope" at the 2004 Democratic National Convention in Boston. Rounding out the Democratic field were former U.S. Senator John Edwards of North Carolina, the 2004 vice presidential running mate of Senator John Kerry (D., Massachusetts); Senators Joe Biden of Delaware and Christopher Dodd of Connecticut; former Senator Mike Gravel of Alaska; Representative Dennis Kucinich of Ohio; Governor Bill Richardson of New Mexico; and former Governor Tom Vilsack of Iowa. The candidates competed in more than 20 debates from April 2007 to April 2008.

Former New York City Mayor Rudy Giuliani ranked as the favorite for the 2008 Republican nomination in many opinion polls throughout 2007. His positions on taxes, national security, and crime won him support from many leading party figures. However, his liberal positions on such social issues as abortion and gay rights cost him support from the socially conservative base of the Republican Party.

Arizona Senator John McCain was also considered a strong candidate. He spent more than five years in a North Vietnamese prison camp after his jet-bomber was shot down in 1967, during the Vietnam

The author:
Ken Shenkman covers the United States for *World Book.*

War (1957-1975). He was known for his appeal with independent voters, largely on his record of bucking his party with his "maverick" stands on such issues as campaign finance and immigration reform.

Mitt Romney had a strong record as a business executive. He had taken liberal positions on a number of social issues while governing left-leaning Massachusetts, however. During the campaign, Romney claimed he had undergone a change of heart on the issues of abortion and gay marriage. But such "flip-flops" and Romney's Mormon faith made many social conservatives wary.

Minister and former Arkansas Governor Mike Huckabee held positions that appealed to social conservatives, but his populist positions on taxes and government spending drew opposition from antitax groups. United States Representative Ron Paul of Texas ran an alternative Republican campaign that received the backing of libertarian-minded voters for his opposition to the Iraq War, the "war on drugs," and the federal income tax.

Other Republican candidates included actor and former Senator Fred Thompson of Tennessee, Senator Sam Brownback of Kansas, former Virginia Governor Jim Gilmore, activist Alan Keyes of Maryland, former Wisconsin Governor Tommy Thompson, and Representatives Duncan Hunter of California and Tom Tancredo of Colorado.

Battle for the nomination

In 2007, many states scheduled their nominating contests earlier than usual in an effort to gain greater influence over the process. More than 20 states—including California, Georgia, Illinois, New Jersey, and New York—scheduled primaries or caucuses for "Super Tuesday," Feb. 5, 2008. A caucus is a gathering of individuals to nominate candidates for office.

Some states scheduled their contests for earlier than Super Tuesday, violating national party rules. In 2007, the Democratic National Committee (DNC) voted to bar Florida and Michigan delegates from the national convention unless those states reversed their decisions to hold primaries in January 2008. Also in 2007, the Republican National Committee (RNC) voted to strip five states—Florida, Michigan, New Hampshire, South Carolina, and Wyoming—of half their delegates to the national convention because they scheduled their primaries for January 2008.

Voting for presidential nominees began in Iowa on January 3. Obama surprised many political experts by winning that state's Democratic caucuses with 38 percent of the vote, followed by Edwards with 30 percent and Clinton with 29 percent. Obama emerged from the contests with momentum and appeared to lead in the polls for the next primary, in New Hampshire. Clinton defied predictions, however, winning that state's contest on January 8. Michigan held the next primary on January 15. In deference to the DNC ban, Obama and others had removed their names from the state's ballot in 2007. Clinton, the only major contender on the ballot, finished first with 55 percent of the vote.

Obama won the South Carolina primary on January 26. Florida held its primary on January 29. Neither candidate had campaigned in the state, and Clinton outpolled Obama, 50 to 33 percent. Edwards withdrew from the race on January 30, and the nomination fight was left to Obama and Clinton.

On Super Tuesday, February 5, Clinton won primaries in California, Massachusetts, New York, and a number of smaller states. Obama took more states overall, generally by larger margins. He scored primary wins in such states as Georgia, Illinois, and Missouri, and caucus victories in several other states. The candidates ended the day roughly tied in elected delegates, though Clinton still held a significant lead in pledged superdelegates.

Clinton and her staff had predicted in 2007 that the race would be wrapped up by Super Tuesday, and they made little effort to win in caucus states. In contrast, Obama and his staff had planned for a long, close race, registering thousands of new voters and setting up campaign offices in places most Democrats had long neglected, including North Carolina. In the two weeks following Super Tuesday, Obama collected 11 straight victories, including caucuses in Hawaii and Maine and primaries in Maryland, Virginia, and Wisconsin. He now held a 120-delegate lead. Clinton's campaign manager resigned on Feb. 10, 2008.

Clinton won primaries in Ohio and Texas on March 4. Despite her strong showing, however, she barely blunted Obama's lead.

In mid-March, Obama faced questions about Jeremiah A. Wright, Jr., his former pastor at a mainly African American church in Chicago. Inflammatory sermons by Wright surfaced on video-sharing Web sites and drew heavy media attention. On March 18, in a Philadelphia speech, Obama spoke of his mixed racial identity and asked Americans for their help to put aside racial resentments and to focus instead on shared goals, including better health care and educational opportunities.

Clinton next won Pennsylvania's April 22 primary by about 10 points, but again she gained little ground on Obama. Some Obama supporters suggested that Clinton drop out of the race for the good of the party, an offer she adamantly refused. Some Clinton backers said the suggestions

Social conservatives, who make up the base of the Republican Party, flocked by the thousands to Republican campaign events to see Alaska Governor Sarah Palin, chosen by presidential nominee John McCain as his running mate.

were sexist and accused the media of being biased in their coverage of her campaign. Clinton rallied supporters with the reminder that she was "trying to break the highest and hardest glass ceiling," a reference to gender as a traditional barrier to women's career advancement.

The candidates split the remaining contests. On May 31, the DNC voted to seat all of Michigan and Florida's delegates at the national convention, but each delegate would have only half a vote. In early June, Obama gained enough delegates to secure the Democratic nomination.

The Republican field clashed in more than a dozen debates in 2007, leading up to the Iowa caucuses on Jan. 3, 2008. Huckabee captured a commanding 34 percent of the vote. Romney finished second with 25 percent. On January 8, McCain revived his campaign with a victory in New Hampshire.

McCain and Romney split the other contests leading up to the Florida primary on January 29. McCain outpolled Romney, 36 to 31 percent. At that point, McCain had not received more than 38 percent of the vote in any primary, but he began to build a daunting lead in delegates. Giuliani, who had staked his campaign on winning Florida, finished a distant third. He dropped out of the race the next day.

On Super Tuesday, February 5, McCain took many of the day's biggest prizes, including California, Illinois, and New York. Romney followed with victories in seven states, including Massachusetts and the majority-Mormon state of Utah. Huckabee, meanwhile, won his home state of Arkansas and four other states. The day established McCain as the race's clear leader, but the results revealed a continued weakness of the Arizona senator among socially conservative voters. Romney suspended his campaign on February 7.

McCain and Huckabee each won states on February 9. From that point, McCain did not lose another race, locking up the nomination after a sweep of states on March 4. Huckabee then dropped out of the race.

In the months that followed, McCain embarked on a series of week-long "biography" and "poverty" tours, highlighting his history of public service and visiting economically depressed areas in such states as Alabama, Kentucky, Louisiana, and Ohio. His campaign slogan was "Country First."

Senator Joe Biden (above left), flanked by Barack Obama, acknowledges his nomination for vice president before cheering supporters at the Democratic National Convention in Denver in August. Obama chose Biden in part for his foreign policy expertise and his appeal to working-class voters.

The conventions

On August 28, at the Democratic National Convention in Denver, delegates nominated Obama for president. For his acceptance speech,

Senators John McCain of Arizona (right) and Barack Obama clashed in three nationally televised debates in September and October. During the debates, McCain sought to portray Obama as inexperienced. Obama tried to link McCain with the widely unpopular policies of President George W. Bush.

Obama spoke at Invesco Field before 84,000 people. On August 23, Obama notified supporters by cell-phone text message that he had chosen Senator Joe Biden as his running mate.

The Republican National Convention in Saint Paul, Minnesota, opened on September 1 with a shortened schedule. McCain had delayed the convention because Hurricane Gustav was expected to make a violent landfall on the Gulf Coast, parts of which had not recovered from devastation caused by Hurricane Katrina in 2005. On Aug. 29, 2008, McCain surprised many political experts by announcing that he had selected Sarah Palin, the 44-year-old governor of Alaska, as his running mate. McCain accepted the Republican nomination on September 4.

Public opinion polls indicated that McCain's choice of Palin had energized the Republicans' conservative base. However, in the few television interviews Palin granted, she stumbled over a number of questions. Clips from her interview with CBS News anchor Katie Couric spread rapidly via the Internet, and many Americans began to question Palin's qualifications to be "a heartbeat away" from the presidency.

The debates

The presidential candidates competed in a series of three nationally televised debates. The first, held on September 26 at the University of Mississippi in Oxford, focused on foreign policy and economic matters. The second debate, held on October 7 at Belmont University in Nashville, was notable for its "town-hall" format. The third took place on October 15 at Hofstra University in Hempstead, New York. Opinion polls generally agreed that Obama won all three debates. The vice presidential candidates also participated in a debate held on October 2 at Washington University in St. Louis.

During the debates and in campaign events, Obama and McCain presented sharply contrasting views on a number of topics, including foreign policy, taxes, and energy. Obama favored a timetable for withdrawing troops from Iraq and said the United States should not be afraid to negotiate with its enemies. McCain rejected a timetable and said Obama's approach to negotiations was naïve. On taxes, Obama planned to increase some taxes on corporations and the wealthy while cutting rates for 95 percent of taxpayers. McCain, whose approach to tax policy largely mirrored that of President Bush, said Obama's plan would stifle economic growth. Both candidates pledged to reduce the nation's dependence on foreign oil, but they differed on the steps needed to achieve such a goal. The GOP ticket was vocal in its support for expanding domestic oil production, made evident by the rallying cry, "Drill, baby, drill!"

The general campaign

The McCain-Palin ticket surged ahead in national polls in the weeks after the Republican convention, but Obama and Biden retook the lead in mid-September. Commentators gave Obama high marks for his even temperament during the debates and for his response to the economic crisis. Up against a charismatic candidate, questions about Palin, and an economic collapse that had occurred under the Republicans' watch, McCain's campaign became increasingly negative. It also began to focus on tax issues and highlight an Ohio tradesman nicknamed "Joe the Plumber" as an example of one who would benefit from McCain's tax plan. In the final weeks of the campaign, Obama's huge fund-raising advantage allowed him to outspend McCain by large margins on TV ads.

The 2008 election was also noteworthy for the increasing importance of the Internet as a source of news. Polls showed that in 2008 one-third of Americans used the Internet for election coverage, up from one-tenth in 2004. Many Web sites offered access to politically oriented video clips.

The expanded role of digital media was an important development during the 2008 campaign. Millions of people watched election-related videos online (below left). The selection of Joe Biden as Obama's running mate was announced to supporters via text-message (below).

Popular votes

State	Obama	McCain
Alabama	811,764	1,264,879
Alaska	122,485	192,631
Arizona	948,648	1,132,560
Arkansas	418,049	632,672
California	7,612,947	4,618,041
Colorado	1,216,793	1,020,135
Connecticut	994,320	627,688
Delaware	255,394	152,356
District of Columbia	210,403	14,821
Florida	4,143,957	3,939,380
Georgia	1,843,452	2,048,244
Hawaii	324,918	120,309
Idaho	235,219	400,989
Illinois	3,319,237	1,981,158
Indiana	1,367,503	1,341,667
Iowa	818,240	677,508
Kansas	499,979	685,541
Kentucky	751,515	1,050,599
Louisiana	780,981	1,147,603
Maine	421,484	296,195
Maryland	1,612,692	956,663
Massachusetts	1,894,067	1,105,908
Michigan	2,867,680	2,044,405
Minnesota	1,573,354	1,275,409
Mississippi	520,864	687,266
Missouri	1,442,180	1,445,812
Montana	229,725	241,816
Nebraska	329,132	448,801
Nevada	531,884	411,988
New Hampshire	384,591	316,937
New Jersey	2,085,051	1,545,495
New Mexico	464,458	343,820
New York	4,363,386	2,576,360
North Carolina	2,123,390	2,109,698
North Dakota	141,113	168,523
Ohio	2,708,685	2,501,855
Oklahoma	502,294	959,745
Oregon	978,605	699,673
Pennsylvania	3,192,316	2,586,496
Rhode Island	296,547	165,389
South Carolina	862,042	1,034,500
South Dakota	170,886	203,019
Tennessee	1,093,213	1,487,564
Texas	3,521,164	4,467,748
Utah	301,771	555,497
Vermont	219,105	98,791
Virginia	1,958,370	1,726,053
Washington	1,548,654	1,098,072
West Virginia	301,438	394,278
Wisconsin	1,670,474	1,258,181
Wyoming	80,496	160,639
U.S. Total	67,066,915	58,421,377

These clips, created by news organizations, bloggers, amateur enthusiasts, and the campaigns themselves, were viewed and circulated online at unprecedented levels. The concept of "viral video"—the rapid spreading of clips via e-mail, blog postings, and video-sharing Web sites—was not a new one, but the excitement and tenor of the election year's contests brought the phenomenon to the forefront of the political arena. Some pundits labeled the contest the "first YouTube presidential election," after the video-sharing site that was created in 2005. Candidates moved to take advantage of the trend, hoping to have their videos—and messages—go "viral." Obama's staff also used advantages in online organizing and volunteer enthusiasm to set up a sophisticated get-out-the-vote operation.

The 2008 election was particularly notable for shattering all previous political fund-raising records. Obama raised huge sums of money with the help of small donations from hundreds of thousands of supporters through his Web site. Obama's fund-raising juggernaut continued to roll after the senator opted out of the public campaign finance system and its spending limits, reversing a campaign pledge in the process. All told, Obama raised well over $700 million during the fight for the nomination and the presidency. McCain accepted $84 million of public financing for the general election. Advertisements by the RNC, however, helped mitigate some of McCain's funding disadvantages.

How Americans voted

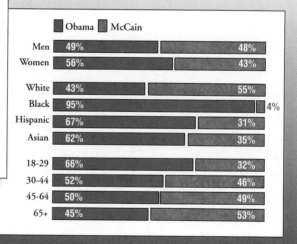

Obama ■ McCain

	Obama	McCain
Men	49%	48%
Women	56%	43%
White	43%	55%
Black	95%	4%
Hispanic	67%	31%
Asian	62%	35%
18-29	66%	32%
30-44	52%	46%
45-64	50%	49%
65+	45%	53%

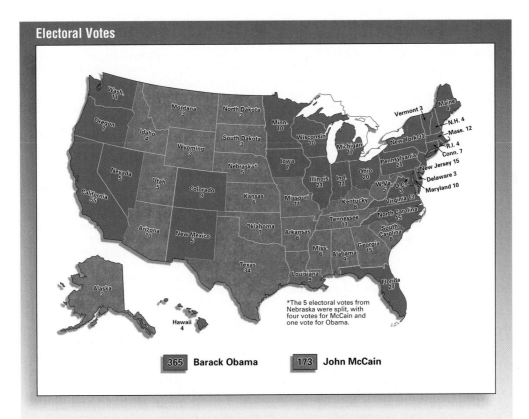

*The 5 electoral votes from Nebraska were split, with four votes for McCain and one vote for Obama.

365 Barack Obama   **173** John McCain

On Election Day, November 4, Obama won 365 electoral votes, while McCain finished with 173 electoral votes. The Illinois senator expanded the Democratic map, capturing the District of Columbia and 28 states. These included all the states Democratic presidential candidate John Kerry carried in 2004 and pick-ups of nine states won by President Bush: Colorado, Florida, Indiana, Iowa, Nevada, New Mexico, North Carolina, Ohio, and Virginia.

Many political commentators called McCain's concession speech one of the most gracious in history. Before a subdued crowd of supporters in Phoenix, McCain said, "I urge all Americans who supported me to join me in not just congratulating him [Obama], but offering our next president our good will and earnest effort to find ways to come together to find the necessary compromises to bridge our differences and help restore our prosperity, defend our security in a dangerous world, and leave our children and grandchildren a stronger, better country than we inherited."

The new president-elect acknowledged his victory at an outdoor rally in Chicago's Grant Park before a huge crowd—estimates varied from 125,000 to half a million. Looking somber, he said, "This victory alone is not the change we seek — it is only the chance for us to make that change. And that cannot happen if we go back to the way things were. ... This is our time ... to reclaim the American Dream and reaffirm that fundamental truth that out of many, we are one; that while we breathe, we hope, and where we are met with cynicism, and doubt, and those who tell us that we can't, we will respond with that timeless creed that sums up the spirit of a people: Yes, we can."

Electronics. In 2008, the United States government urged consumers to act environmentally friendly by recycling cell phones. Several companies made important breakthroughs in electronic technology, including work on an extremely thin type of light and a tiny memory component. New electronic games in 2008 simulated the evolution of organisms and civilizations, as well as the performance of rock music.

Recycling cell phones. In January 2008, the U.S. Environmental Protection Agency (EPA) began a $175,000 public education campaign urging people to recycle cell phones. Cell phones, like many other electronic products, contain harmful metals and other chemicals that can threaten the environment if not properly disposed of. About 150 million Americans owned cell phones in 2008, so the environmental effect of throwing them away is considerable. The EPA's campaign drew attention to drop-off centers for old cell phones, where they can be redistributed to charities or stripped of working parts. In addition, major U.S. cell phone providers accept old cell phones at their stores.

Organic LED lights. Several companies made breakthroughs in organic light-emitting diode (OLED) technology in 2008. OLED's are energy-efficient chemical lights that can be cheaply produced and attached to super-thin, flexible bases. The OLED's light up when electric current passes through their base.

In January, Tokyo-based Sony Corporation began selling a small OLED television in the United States. The $2,500 television, called the XEL-1, has a screen only 1.7 inches (3 millimeters) thick. It also featured extremely deep colors.

In March 2008, New York City-based General Electric "printed" OLED lights on a bendable plastic sheet, much like the way newspapers are printed on rolls of paper. The company hoped that the production process would lead to cheaper and innovative new uses for the lights.

Memristor. In May 2008, Hewlett-Packard Company, a computer technology firm in Palo Alto, California, announced it had built a working *memristor* (also called a memory resistor). A memristor can "remember" the amount of electric charge flowing through it, making it potentially useful for data storage in computers, artificial intelligence, and other technologies. Company researchers created memristor-based circuits as small as 15 nanometers. A nanometer is 1 billionth of a meter—only slightly larger than a single atom. Memristors could allow engineers to shrink electronic devices to microscopic sizes.

Video games evolve—and rock out. In September 2008, Electronic Arts of Redwood City, California, released *Spore*, a computer game that simulates the evolution of life and civilizations. The game puts players in control of a single-celled organism that is struggling to eat and avoid being eaten. As the organism grows larger, the player can control its evolution into a large, fantastic creature. The game then shifts its focus to tribes, cities, and whole civilizations of such creatures. Eventually, the player directs this civilization's expansion to other planets. *Spore*'s designer, Will Wright, is famous for his other open-ended simulation games, including *SimCity* and *The Sims.*

Several new music games were also released in 2008. In September, Electronic Arts released *Rock Band 2*. In October, Activision, a game company based in Santa Monica, California, released *Guitar Hero World Tour*. The games allow people to play along with popular rock songs on plastic guitars and drum sets. They also feature karaoke gameplay with a microphone.

Both games come with dozens of songs, ranging from classic rock and heavy metal to newer indie and emo bands. The games also allow players to buy other songs and download them from the Internet. By exposing a younger audience to older bands from the 1970's and 1980's, the Rock Band and Guitar Hero series have helped bring profits to the struggling music business. They have also become an effective way for new bands to gain exposure and make money. ■ Daniel Kenis

See also **Computers; Telecommunications.**

Employment. See Economics; Labor.

El Salvador. A 2008 study revealed that El Salvador had the highest murder rate in the world for people ages 15 to 24. Tough new laws and repeated crackdowns have failed to stem the flood of drug-related gang warfare. Since 2004, more than 14,000 people have been killed in El Salvador, mostly in the capital, San Salvador. Cases of extortion, car-jackings and thefts, assault, rape, and robbery were also on the rise. Due in large part to escalating crime, presidential candidate Mauricio Funes of the Farabundo Martí National Liberation Front led all voting polls in the run-up to 2009 national elections. Opposing Funes was Rodrigo Ávila of the Nationalist Republican Alliance (Arena), the governing party in El Salvador since 1989. Funes's candidacy was further buoyed by anger over rising food and fuel prices, as well as the resignation of the national police chief after two of his aides were linked to drug traffickers.

Monument to the war dead. In March 2008, 3,169 names were added to the 30,000 names already on the Monument to Memory and Truth, a memorial to the dead and missing in the Salvadoran Civil War (1980-1992). The war claimed more than 75,000 lives.

■ Nathan A. Haverstock

See also **Agriculture: A Special Report; Latin America.**

Electric power. See Energy supply.

Energy supply. World energy markets were in turmoil in 2008. Supplies were ample, yet fuel and other energy prices surged to record levels in the first six months of the year. Prices then plunged in the second half of 2008 as a global financial crisis erupted and demand dwindled.

Oil and gasoline. Crude oil, from which gasoline is processed, reached a record high of $147 a barrel in July. Analysts predicted that crude oil would keep rising to above $200 a barrel, but by December, the barrel price had fallen below $45. (An oil barrel holds 42 gallons [159 liters], and fuels priced by the gallon followed similar pricing patterns.) The average retail price of gasoline topped a record $4 a gallon in July, but by December the average price was below $1.80. Reacting to escalating prices amid an economic recession, consumers reduced energy use, reducing demand.

The United States consumed nearly one out of every four barrels of oil in the world in 2008, yet U.S. petroleum consumption fell by 1.2 million barrels per day to less than 20 million barrels per day—the biggest decline since 1980. Petroleum production in the United States fell as well, 130,000 barrels per day less than the 2007 average. New oil platforms in the Gulf of Mexico were expected to come on stream in 2009 and increase domestic production for the first time since 1991.

The world's oil supplies increased in the wake of shrinking demand. Prior to mid-2008, the rapid rise in consumption, particularly in India and China, had siphoned off the world's surplus oil and had raised concern over possible shortages. A combination of supply worries and a speculative rush by investors into oil markets triggered the price run-ups of 2007 and early 2008.

The International Energy Agency (IEA), the Paris-based energy watchdog for the industrialized nations, forecast that global demand for oil—which grew slightly in 2008 to 86.2 million barrels a day—will average only 86.5 million barrels a day in 2009. "World oil demand is set to continue to expand through to 2030 on current trends, albeit more slowly than over the past two decades," the IEA said in its 2008 World Energy Outlook. Overall trends, the outlook stated, were unchanged. The use of fossil fuels—oil, gas, and coal—continued and will continue to dominate, especially in emerging economies, ever-increasing global emissions of carbon dioxide.

OPEC cuts production. The decline in oil prices in the latter half of 2008 was the steepest drop since 1981, raising concerns among the member states of the Organization of the Petroleum Exporting Countries (OPEC), a permanent intergovernmental organization with headquarters in Vienna. OPEC provides 40 percent of the world's oil. In November and December 2008,

OPEC began a series of emergency meetings to try to prop up the price of oil by reducing output. The price target was above $75 a barrel. But several OPEC members already suffering economically, such as Venezuela and Iran, were unlikely to cut production. Nigerian oil officials maintained that their country already was pumping below its OPEC quota because of militant attacks on its oil infrastructure. Ecuador, the smallest producer in the group at 500,000 barrels a day, may default on hundreds of millions of dollars of debt, forcing it out of OPEC after being reinstated in 2007 following a 15-year hiatus. OPEC president Chakib Khelil estimated that the price collapse had cost the cartel's 13-member nations a total of $700 billion.

To cope with shrinking demand, OPEC cut oil production by 1.5 million barrels per day on November 1 and by 2.2 million barrels per day on December 17 as Iranian Oil Minister Gholam Hossein Nozari had recommended.

In the major oil-consuming nations, spikes in energy costs renewed focus on fuel-efficient vehicles and on the development of such renewable energy supplies as wind, water, and sunlight. But cheaper fossil fuel energy once again sapped these efforts, shelving several planned projects.

For consumers, however, the reversed course in energy prices was welcome news indeed. In addition to the reduced burdens on U.S. household budgets, the nation as a whole saved money as the cost of oil went down. The United States imported up to 60 percent of its oil needs and sent vast sums of money to the countries that produce the petroleum.

Non-OPEC oil supplies suffered in 2008 from disruptions in Mexico, the North Sea, and Russia. However, supplies grew in Azerbaijan, Brazil, and the United States. Overall, non-OPEC production declined by 310,000 barrels per day in 2008.

Natural gas. Natural gas consumption, which is more weather-driven than oil, rose by 0.5 percent in 2008. The Energy Information Administration—a section of the U.S. Department of Energy—predicted no increase in consumption for 2009 but foresaw a rise in production as offshore facilities damaged in 2008 by Hurricanes Gustav and Ike resumed service.

Coal. In 2008, production and consumption remained flat, but U.S. coal exports soared 40 percent after supply disruptions in Australia, South Africa, and China. With normal supply conditions, exports will fall dramatically in 2009.

■ James Tanner

See also **Economics, United States.**

Engineering. See Building and Construction.

England. See United Kingdom.

Economic Crisis:

The Oil Price Surge

By Mike Lewis

In 2008, $140-a-barrel oil and $4-a-gallon gasoline became a reality, putting a major strain on consumers and the U.S. economy.

In 2008, for the first time in history, the price of crude oil reached, and then surpassed, $100 a barrel. It rose to $147.27 on July 11—an all-time high, even after adjustment for inflation. Also, the average retail price of regular unleaded gasoline in the United States reached $4 a gallon for the first time ever. It hit $4.11—also an all-time inflation-adjusted record—on July 17, according to the motorist group AAA and the Oil Price Information Service, a private source for petroleum pricing and news.

Throughout the 1990's, per-barrel oil prices hovered in the $10-to-$40 range, and the average per-gallon price at the gas pump never exceeded $1.40. But in the early 2000's, oil prices climbed up—way up. Prices rose above $40 a barrel in 2004 and then kept rising, though there were many oscillations. In the first half of 2008, $100-a-barrel oil put a major strain on motorists, shippers, farmers, airlines, and other oil-dependent consumers and businesses. Then, in the second half of the year, both oil and gasoline prices plunged (again, with oscillations). By early December, the price of oil was below $50 a barrel, and the average U.S. price of gasoline was below $2 a gallon.

What happened? Why did oil prices rise so dramatically—and then fall so dramatically? What were the economic effects? What did politicians, pundits, and economists propose be done about the price of oil? And in 2008, what did the future appear to hold?

Reasons for price changes

Economists and other experts offered a variety of explanations for the huge price run-ups of the early 2000's. There also was no shortage of disagreements about the relative importance of the likely causes. Many analysts said that the rising prices were mostly the result of simple economics—the fundamental forces of supply and demand. A number of observers pointed to weakness in the value of the U.S. dollar as a contributing factor. In addition, there was much debate about whether speculation in oil futures markets might be pushing up prices.

One culprit often fingered by ordinary Americans, and their elected officials, was private oil company greed. Angry rhetoric was often aimed at the private oil giants with the famous brand names: the U.S.-based ExxonMobil, Chevron, and ConocoPhillips, and the Europe-based BP, Royal Dutch Shell, and Total. In a July 2008 CNN/Opinion Research poll, 68 percent of Americans pointed to U.S. oil firms as a major cause of high gasoline prices. (Poll respondents also named other causes—for example, 65 percent cited overseas oil producers, 57 percent cited oil market speculators, and 56 percent cited rising worldwide demand.)

Many economists, however, believed that the public's tendency to scapegoat private oil firms was misguided. Private companies, these experts claimed, had little power to influence the price of oil, largely because they controlled only a small fraction of the world's oil reserves. The vast majority of oil reserves were controlled not by private firms, but by companies run by oil-rich national governments. Some of the largest government-run companies were in Saudi Arabia, Iran, Iraq, other Persian Gulf countries, Russia, Venezuela, Nigeria, and Mexico. In the early 2000's, 13 countries belonged to the Organization of the Petroleum Exporting Countries (OPEC), an intergovernmental association whose members depend heavily on oil exports. The journalist Vijay V. Vaitheeswaran, writing in *Foreign Policy* magazine in 2007, explained that "... a conspiratorial cabal does meet regularly behind closed doors to rig prices and supply. However, that cabal is not Big Oil. It is OPEC. ... The Western firms are price takers, not price setters."

Demand and supply

The global economy grew by about 5 percent per year from 2004 to 2007. Most of this growth was in developing countries, notably China and India. With economic growth came growth in the demand for energy. Worldwide oil consumption rose nearly 4 percent between 2004 and 2007. In many developing countries, demand for oil was partly driven by government subsidies and other administrative measures that kept the domestic prices of fuel artificially low. The New York City-based

The author:
Mike Lewis is a Associate Manager of *The World Book Encyclopedia.*

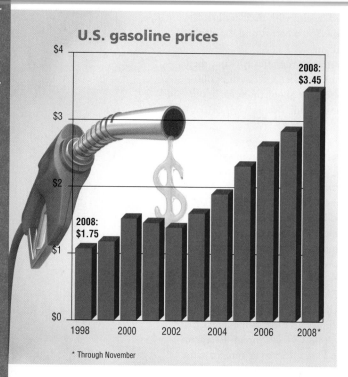

U.S. gasoline prices

2008: $3.45

2008: $1.75

$4
$3
$2
$1
$0

1998   2000   2002   2004   2006   2008*

* Through November

Annual nationwide average retail price per gallon of gasoline (all grades) in the United States. Gasoline prices differ, often drastically, in different regions of the country and at different times of the year.

financial services firm Morgan Stanley estimated that in early 2008, half of the world's people enjoyed fuel subsidies.

Oil production, however, did not grow substantially in response to rising demand. From 2005 to 2008, oil production growth in non-OPEC countries slowed to levels well below historical averages, and OPEC countries did not increase their output enough to fill the gap. In addition, from 2003 to 2008, the world capacity for surplus oil production was usually below 2 million barrels per day, compared with an average capacity of 3.9 million barrels per day from 1996 to 2002, according to the U.S. Energy Information Administration (EIA), an agency of the U.S. Department of Energy. Furthermore, inventories of crude oil and petroleum products in the United States and other developed countries fluctuated significantly in the early 2000's. These inventories were at record lows in 2003, then relatively high in 2006 and early 2007, then somewhat low in early 2008, according to the EIA and the International Energy Agency (IEA), an intergovernmental organization of about 30 developed countries. Also, there were dozens of oil supply disruptions in the early 2000's, caused by power failures, worker strikes, pipeline leaks and explosions, hurricanes and other natural disasters, saboteurs, and civil wars. Significant supply disruptions were caused by the war in Iraq and by militant activity against oil producers in Nigeria.

It should be noted that there was much uncertainty in the demand and supply data from such agencies as the EIA and the IEA. Developing countries were often unable or unwilling to provide reliable data on oil consumption or stockpiling. OPEC countries often did not reliably report their oil output and usually did not divulge when new fields would begin production or how quickly existing fields were declining.

Refineries

Oil refinery problems magnified concerns about fuel supplies. In the United States, oil refineries often operated at near capacity in the early 2000's to meet demand. Also, not all refineries could process all different kinds of crude oil, and not all refineries could produce all the various gasoline blends needed to comply with clean-air regulations in different parts of the country. Therefore, refinery shutdowns—such as those in September 2008 in the Gulf Coast because of Hurricane Ike—caused significant fuel price increases because of the inability to shift refinery work elsewhere. Oil companies also claimed that it was too difficult to build new refineries because of the high cost of construction and of compliance with strict environmental regulations. No new U.S. refineries had been built since 1976.

There were also growing fears about the future of world oil supplies. Some analysts believed that the world had already reached, or would soon reach, the period of "peak oil." Peak oil refers to the notion of the world's oil production hitting a peak and then declining. More optimistic analysts were hopeful that technology would make it increasingly possible to locate new sources of oil and extend the life of existing sources. These experts looked toward the possibility of extracting oil from such substances as tar sands, coal, and shale.

In mid-2008, Saudi Arabia—the most important OPEC member—agreed to modestly increase its output. Around the same time, some developing countries reduced fuel subsidies to ease the strain on their government budgets. These measures played a role in pushing oil prices down after July. However, according to many analysts, the main cause of the price decline was a decline in demand in rich countries, as consumers began to reduce their spending. In November, Saudi Arabia and other OPEC members began to cut their oil output.

The sharp jump in oil prices in the early 2000's coincided with a decline in the value of the U.S. dollar against other leading currencies. Worldwide, oil is priced and traded in U.S. dollars. A weak dollar against the euro gave Europeans relatively more purchasing power and partially contributed to demand for oil in Europe. In addition, the windfall profits of oil producers were partly offset by the fact that their income was in the form of a weak currency, thus dampening their incentive to greatly raise output. Also, the weak dollar encouraged financial investors to move away from investments in the currency in favor of investments in commodities, especially oil. In the second half of 2008, the value of the dollar rose significantly, coinciding with the drop in oil prices.

Speculation

The oil prices that are reported in the news are actually the prices of oil traded in futures markets. In a futures market, participants trade contracts that obligate them to buy or sell a commodity at an agreed-upon price at an agreed-upon date in the future. The purpose of a futures contract is to manage risk. Airlines might buy futures contracts to protect themselves from rising fuel prices. Oil companies might sell futures contracts to protect themselves from falling fuel prices.

From 2004 to 2008, activity in crude oil futures markets greatly increased. The number of outstanding contracts, known as *open interest,* more than tripled during this period, and the number of traders doubled. Much of the growth in open interest was among *speculators*—that is, traders whose objective was to achieve profits by betting on price movements. Often the speculators were

investment banks or similar entities that were investing in futures markets on behalf of pension funds, wealthy individuals, or other clients. Some observers argued that the large inflow of speculative investment into crude oil futures markets was creating an artificial appearance of high demand and forcing prices higher.

An interagency task force headed by the Commodity Futures Trading Commission (CFTC), an independent U.S. agency, issued a report in July 2008 on speculative activity in crude oil futures. The task force's preliminary conclusion was that speculation was not systematically propelling oil prices upward. According to the report, changes in speculative traders' positions were occurring in response to price changes, rather than in advance of price changes. In addition, there was no indication of any rise in oil stockpiles during the periods of rising prices. Such a rise would be expected if speculators were behind the price increases. The CFTC did, however, begin an investigation in December 2007 of crude oil trading, storage, and transportation, with the purpose of determining whether illegal market manipulation was occurring. It should be noted that a large portion of the world's futures market activity was not subject to CFTC oversight, thus limiting the agency's ability to make a conclusive assessment about either speculative or manipulative activity.

Effects of costly oil

In the first half of 2008, the high price of oil hit American consumers in a number of ways. Soaring prices for automobile fuel were the most obvious. Americans spent an increasingly larger share of their income on fuel. High oil prices also caused Americans to pay more for their food—in part because of the higher costs of transporting the food and in part because corn was being diverted from the food supply to make ethanol fuel. Skyrocketing food prices were an even more serious problem in the world's less developed countries. Oil prices also fueled worries in early 2008 that the U.S. economy would, officially, enter into recession. Many analysts believed that the drop in oil prices after July was mainly the result of reduced consumer spending in the United States and other developed countries.

The industrial economy suffered greatly as a result of rising oil prices. In the early 2000's, the "Big Three" U.S. automakers—General Motors, Ford, and

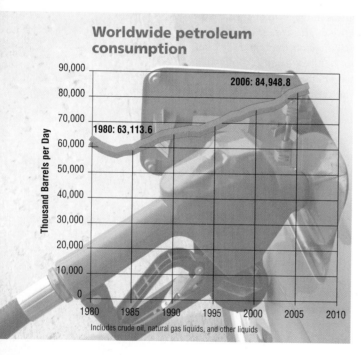

Worldwide petroleum consumption

2006: 84,948.8

1980: 63,113.6

Thousand Barrels per Day

90,000
80,000
70,000
60,000
50,000
40,000
30,000
20,000
10,000
0

1980 1985 1990 1995 2000 2005 2010

Includes crude oil, natural gas liquids, and other liquids

Chrysler—generally produced vehicles that were not particularly energy-efficient, including large numbers of expensive, gas-guzzling sport utility vehicles and pickup trucks. But $4-a-gallon gasoline shifted car buyers' appetites toward smaller, more fuel-efficient vehicles. Furthermore, falling home prices caused many people to postpone buying new vehicles. GM's sales of cars and light trucks in the first 11 months of 2008 were down 22 percent compared with the same period a year earlier; Ford's sales declined 20 percent; and Chrysler's sales dropped 28 percent. Transportation companies also suffered. Worldwide, more than 25 airlines went bankrupt in 2008.

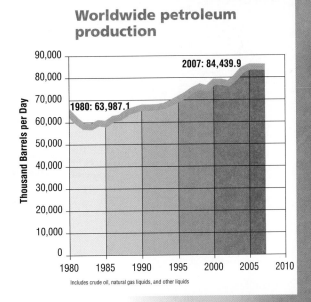

Worldwide petroleum production

2007: 84,439.9

1980: 63,987.1

Thousand Barrels per Day

Includes crude oil, natural gas liquids, and other liquids

It took a while for fuel consumption in developed countries to fall in response to high prices. In the United States, consumption did not start to decline until 2007. In the first nine months of 2008, Americans drove 3.5 percent fewer miles than they did in the first nine months of 2007. Once consumption had dropped, however, there were some positive effects. Reduced driving meant fewer traffic deaths. In addition, high oil prices began to produce the market incentives for more investment in alternative energy development.

The future

United States politicians offered many proposals in response to skyrocketing oil prices, especially given that 2008 was an election year. Some politicians called for releasing oil from the country's Strategic Petroleum Reserve, a stockpile intended for use in emergencies. Others wanted to crack down on oil market speculation or repeal tax breaks for oil companies. The Democratic presidential candidate, Senator Barack Obama of Illinois, favored imposing a "windfall tax" on oil firms' profits and using the proceeds to give taxpayers an "energy rebate." The Republican presidential candidate, Senator John McCain of Arizona, proposed a suspension of the federal gasoline tax in the summer months. All of these ideas had their critics. *The Economist* magazine argued that Obama's windfall tax would have the likely effect of diverting investment in oil production away from the United States, and that McCain's "gas tax holiday" would simply encourage people to drive more, pushing up prices while reducing government revenues. (After oil prices fell and after he won the presidential election, Obama shelved the windfall tax idea.)

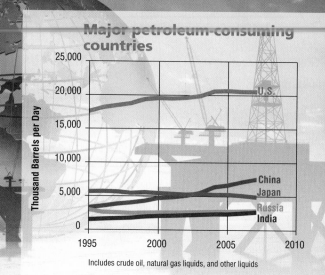

Major petroleum-consuming countries

Thousand Barrels per Day

25,000

20,000 — U.S.

15,000

10,000

5,000 — China / Japan / Russia / India

0

1995   2000   2005   2010

Includes crude oil, natural gas liquids, and other liquids

Many politicians called for increases in domestic oil drilling, either in offshore waters, or in a portion of the Arctic National Wildlife Refuge (ANWR) in Alaska, or both. Officials of the U.S. government estimated in early 2008 that there were about 18 billion barrels of oil in offshore areas not already open to drilling. Supporters of more drilling argued that an increase in oil supply would help bring down prices. Opponents of the idea argued that it would take at least 10 years to recover oil from any new drilling sites and that the amount of oil would probably be too small, and too expensive to recover, to make much difference in prices. Supporters and opponents of both offshore and ANWR drilling also argued over the degree to which such drilling might endanger the environment. After much midyear debate in 2008, Congress allowed a ban on offshore drilling to lapse on October 1.

Some people, such as *The New York Times* pundit Thomas Friedman, suggested that the goal should be not to lower oil prices, but to keep them artificially high using taxes. If the market price of oil dropped below a certain level, taxes would kick in to make U.S. users pay the target amount. The intent would be to reduce U.S. fuel consumption, which would in turn cut carbon dioxide emissions; reduce the need to use the U.S. military to ensure global oil commerce; encourage investment in alternative energy development; and reduce the flow of money to such "petro-dictatorships" as Iran, Russia, and Venezuela.

By the end of 2008, with oil prices well below their midyear highs, the outlook for future price changes remained murky. There was much debate about the future of oil supplies and whether the world had reached the period of peak oil. Most analysts expected the demand for oil to continue to rise in China and other developing countries, but it was unclear whether that increase would be large enough to offset a drop in consumption in the rich world, especially with the looming threat of a global recession. See **Bank: A Special Report; U. S., Government of the: A Special Report.**

Environmental pollution. Dead zones posed a growing threat to the world's oceans in 2008. In addition, pollution threatened the 2008 Summer Olympic Games in Beijing, and new regulations were enacted while others faltered.

Dead zones. The dead zone in the Gulf of Mexico narrowly missed setting a new record for size in 2008. Dead zones are areas of the ocean with little or no life. They are caused chiefly by agricultural fertilizer that washes into coastal waters from rivers. Just as fertilizer helps plants to grow on land, it helps algae to grow in the sea. If enough fertilizer reaches the ocean, it can cause an explosive growth of algae called an *algal bloom*. Algae that are not eaten eventually die and fall into deeper waters, where bacteria use oxygen in the water to feed on the dead algae. As oxygen levels drop, most creatures that live at the bottom cannot survive. Each summer, low oxygen levels wipe out fish and such *invertebrates* (animals lacking backbones) as lobsters from huge areas of the sea, leaving little behind but microscopic life. Unfortunately, many dead zones occur in areas that were once prime fishing grounds.

The dead zone in the Gulf of Mexico in 2008 was surpassed in size only in 2002. The gulf dead zone measured about 8,000 square miles (20,720 square kilometers), roughly the size of New Jersey. The dead zone has more than doubled in size in the last 20 years. Scientists believe that hurricane activity in 2008 prevented the dead zone from growing larger than it did in 2002.

Meanwhile, an August 2008 study published in the journal *Science* found that there are now more than 400 dead zones around the world. Taken together, the dead zones cover about 95,000 square miles (246,000 square kilometers), roughly the size of New Zealand. The number of dead zones is up from about 300 in 1995. In fact, the number of dead zones has approximately doubled each decade since the 1960's.

China greens for gold. An algal bloom threatened to entangle sailers competing in the Summer Olympics in China. The algae covered about 5,000 square miles (12,950 square kilometers) of water in the Yellow Sea. Algal blooms and dead zones are common in China's coastal waters, where rivers loaded with fertilizers and raw sewage empty into the sea. By July, the Chinese had deployed 20,000 people and 1,000 boats to dispose of the algae. This effort had removed more than 700,000 tons (635,000 metric tons) of algae by the time the Games began in August.

Removing algae was only one of many steps Chinese officials took in a $20-billion effort to clean up the environment around Beijing for the Games. The largest concern was air pollution. Beijing suffers from some of the worst air pollu-

A volunteer removes algae from the bay at Qingdao, China, in July in preparation for sailing events at the 2008 Summer Olympic Games. In all, the Chinese cleaned more than 700,000 tons (635,000 metric tons) of algae from the shoreline.

tion in the world. By 2008, 20 of the world's 30 most air-polluted cities were in China, according to the World Bank, a United Nations affiliate.

Chinese officials took drastic measures to reduce air pollution for the Olympics. They temporarily closed hundreds of factories around Beijing and halted most building construction. They also banned half of Beijing's 3.5 million cars from the road during the games. These efforts produced marked improvements in Beijing's air quality, but despite protests from environmentalists, the restrictions were lifted in September.

Oil spills, offshore drills. The United States Supreme Court in June further reduced $2.5 billion in punitive damages imposed on the energy company Exxon in connection with the *Exxon Valdez* oil spill of 1989. In that disaster, an oil tanker spilled 11 million gallons (42 million liters) of crude oil into the Alaskan wilderness. The oil spill killed thousands of birds, fish, and other animals. A jury ordered $5 billion in damages to punish Exxon for negligence. A federal court later cut the award by half, and the Supreme Court ordered lower courts to further reduce the amount. In August 2008, Exxon settled the case for $383 million.

A collision between two ships spilled nearly 280,000 gallons (1 million liters) of heavy fuel oil into the Mississippi River near New Orleans in July. The river was closed for six days while crews cleaned up the spill.

Hurricane Ike destroyed 52 offshore oil platforms when it struck the Gulf of Mexico in September 2008, though there was only one offshore oil spill of about 8,400 gallons (32,000 liters). Ike devastated oil tanks and pipelines in Texas and Louisiana, however, spilling about 500,000 gallons (1.9 million liters) into the Gulf.

Muzzling motors. The U.S. Environmental Protection Agency (EPA) issued new rules regulating exhaust from lawn mowers and motorboats in September. Under the new rules, manufacturers were ordered to reduce the smog-forming emissions given off by lawn equipment by 35 percent by 2011. For motorboats, such emissions were to be cut by 70 percent. Manufacturers may have to add catalytic converters to their equipment to meet the new standards, which could boost prices. The EPA predicted that the changes would save 300 lives each year through reduced air pollution.

Another set of regulations from the EPA was thrown out by a federal appeals court in July 2008. The Clean Air Interstate Rule would have required 28 mostly eastern states to reduce the amount of soot and smog-forming chemicals pumped into the air. Such air pollution comes chiefly from power plants, especially those that burn coal. The EPA predicted that the regulation would prevent 17,000 premature deaths each year. The regulation was considered the Bush administration's sig-

nature clean-air policy. The courts ruled, however, that the EPA had overstepped its authority.

The EPA issued new restrictions on releasing lead into the atmosphere in October. Exposure to lead can cause severe health problems, especially in children. The new limit on lead is 10 times as strict as the previous limit.

Deadly breath. Scientists continued to explore the health effects of air pollution in 2008. A January study in the journal *Circulation Research* found that the tiniest particles in automobile exhaust do the most damage to arteries. Such particles are only $\frac{1}{1,000}$ as wide as a human hair, or about 180 nanometers. The EPA does not regulate these tiny particles, which are able to pass from the lungs to the blood. Inside arteries, the particles interfere with *high density lipoprotein,* often called *good cholesterol.* The result is hardening and blockage of the arteries, which can cause heart attacks and strokes.

A May study in the journal *Annals of Neurology* found that even low levels of fine particles in the air can increase the risk of stroke. An August study in the *Journal of the American College of Cardiology* found that air pollution has both short-term and long-term effects on health. People who were already suffering from heart disease are at the greatest risk, according to the study.

Children are especially vulnerable to air pollution, according to a June study in the *Journal of Respiratory and Critical Care Medicine.* The study found that children who live close to major highways are more likely to develop asthma, allergies, and other lung problems. A September report in the *Journal of Environmental Planning and Management* found that one in three public schools in the United States is less than ¼ mile (400 meters) from such a highway.

Toxic spill. A toxic river of coal sludge that broke through a retention wall at a power plant in eastern Tennessee on December 22 damaged about 15 homes, killed hundreds of fish, and threatened water supplies for millions of people. Officials from the Tennessee Valley Authority (TVA), which operates the coal-fired plant, estimated that 5.4 million cubic yards (4.1 million cubic liters) of fly ash, a byproduct of coal incineration, coated at least 300 acres (120 hectares) to a depth of up to 6 feet (1.8 meters). Some of the sludge, which contained mercury and other heavy metals, flowed into the Emory River and other tributaries of the Tennessee River. Initial reports indicated elevated levels of some pollutants in water supplies. The plant is about 40 miles (64 kilometers) west of Knoxville. ■ Brian Johnson

See also **Conservation; Global Warming.**

Equatorial Guinea. See Africa.

Eritrea. See Africa.

Ethiopia. See Africa.

EUROPE

The nations of Europe struggled in 2008 with the economic slowdown that struck the rest of the world. At the same time, Slovenia and France, which held the rotating six-month presidency of the European Union (EU, Europe's main political and economic organization), took steps to advance needed reforms within the bloc.

Slovenia's presidency. In the first half of the year, Slovenia—the first post-Communist nation to hold the presidency of the EU—shifted the bloc's attention to the western Balkans, hoping to stabilize the region and promote membership for more of the nations that once made up Yugoslavia. Slovenia also encouraged the ratification of the EU reform treaty—also known as the Lisbon Treaty—which was signed in December 2007. The agreement, which must be ratified by all 27 EU members to go into effect, is designed to streamline decision making and to create new permanent positions of president and foreign minister. In addition, Slovenia worked on climate change and energy issues.

The French presidency. In the second half of 2008, French President Nicolas Sarkozy followed an ambitious agenda that focused on immigration reform, energy, the environment, and defense. Most of his attention, however, was devoted to persuading the members that had not yet ratified the Lisbon Treaty to do so. Beginning in October, the EU turned much of its attention to dealing with the global economic crisis. EU members disagreed over the size and scope of their response.

By the end of 2008, jockeying had begun for positions in a new European Commission (the executive branch of the EU). The commission's five-year term was set to expire in October 2009. (Each EU member appoints a commissioner; the European Council appoints the commission president; and the European Parliament confirms all of the appointments.) Commission President José Manuel Barroso of Portugal, a politician from the center-right, indicated in 2008 his desire for a second term. Several other commissioners also indicated a wish to remain in office. Their ambitions were challenged by center-left members of the European Parliament. In addition to party politics,

Russian tanks pause in the village of Dzhaba in Georgia's breakaway republic of South Ossetia on August 9. Russia intervened in a conflict between Georgia and South Ossetia, invading Georgian territory and launching air strikes inside Georgia. Hundreds of soldiers and civilians were killed in the fighting. A secessionist government backed by Russia took over South Ossetia.

FACTS IN BRIEF ON EUROPEAN COUNTRIES

Country	Population	Government	Monetary unit*	Foreign trade (million U.S.$) Exports[†]	Imports[†]
Albania	3,187,000	President Bamir Topi; Prime Minister Sali Berisha	lek (82.33 = $1)	1,076	3,999
Andorra	79,000	Co-sovereigns bishop of Urgel, Spain, and the president of France; Head of Government Albert Pintat Santolària	euro (0.68 = $1)	149	1,879
Austria	8,221,000	President Heinz Fischer; Chancellor Alfred Gusenbauer	euro (0.68 = $1)	162,100	160,300
Belarus	9,615,000	President Aleksandr Lukashenko; Prime Minister Sergei Sidorsky	ruble (2,111.00 = $1)	24,470	28,320
Belgium	10,490,000	King Albert II; Prime Minister Herman Van Rompuy	euro (0.68 = $1)	322,200	323,200
Bosnia-Herzegovina	3,923,000	Chairman of the Presidency Haris Silajdzic; Prime Minister Nikola Spiric	marka (1.33 = $1)	4,243	9,947
Bulgaria	7,549,000	President Georgi Parvanov; Prime Minister Sergei Stanishev	lev (1.33 = $1)	18,440	28,670
Croatia	4,392,000	President Stjepan Mesic; Prime Minister Ivo Sanader	kuna (4.85 = $1)	12,620	25,990
Czech Republic	10,205,000	President Václav Klaus; Prime Minister Mirek Topolánek	koruna (16.36 = $1)	122,300	116,600
Denmark	5,463,000	Queen Margrethe II; Prime Minister Anders Fogh Rasmussen	krone (5.08 = $1)	101,200	102,000
Estonia	1,334,000	President Toomas Hendrik Ilves; Prime Minister Andrus Ansip	kroon (10.66 = $1)	11,080	14,750
Finland	5,285,000	President Tarja Halonen; Prime Minister Matti Vanhanen	euro (0.68 = $1)	89,910	78,050
France	61,225,000	President Nicolas Sarkozy; Prime Minister François Fillon	euro (0.68 = $1)	546,000	600,900
Germany	82,414,000	President Horst Köhler; Chancellor Angela Merkel	euro (0.68 = $1)	1,354,000	1,075,000
Greece	11,128,000	President Carolos Papoulias; Prime Minister Kostas Karamanlis	euro (0.68 = $1)	23,910	80,790
Hungary	10,020,000	President László Sólyom; Prime Minister Ferenc Gyurcsány	forint (160.63 = $1)	87,770	86,880
Iceland	300,000	President Ólafur Ragnar Grímsson; Prime Minister Geir H. Haarde	krona (82.75 = $1)	4,793	6,181
Ireland	4,269,000	President Mary McAleese; Prime Minister Brian Cowen	euro (0.68 = $1)	115,500	84,760
Italy	58,818,000	President Giorgio Napolitano; Prime Minister Silvio Berlusconi	euro (0.68 = $1)	502,400	498,100
Kosovo	2,161,000	President Fatmir Sejdiu; Prime Minister Hashim Thaçi	euro (0.68 = $1)	148	not available
Latvia	2,267,000	President Valdis Zatlers; Prime Minister Ivars Godmanis	lat (0.48 = $1)	8,143	14,820
Liechtenstein	36,000	Prince Hans-Adam II; Prime Minister Otmar Hasler	Liechtenstein franc (1.16 = $1)	2,470	917

*Exchange rates as of Sept. 30, 2008.　　　　　　　　　　　　　　　　　　[†]Latest available data.

the composition of the commission also depended on ratification of the Lisbon Treaty. The post of external relations commissioner, for example, would be replaced by that of foreign minister.

Lisbon Treaty. On June 13, Irish voters rejected the Lisbon Treaty in a national referendum. (Ireland was the only EU member that held a referendum on the issue; other nations allowed their legislature

and executive to make the decision.) EU leaders immediately declared that ratification should continue in other member nations and that a second referendum could be held in Ireland at a later date. By December, 25 members had ratified the treaty. Besides Ireland, the Czech Republic had also failed to ratify the pact. Czech President Václav Klaus claimed that some sections of the treaty violated

Country	Population	Government	Monetary unit*	Foreign trade (million U.S.$)	
				Exports[†]	Imports[†]
Lithuania	3,374,000	President Valdas Adamkus; Prime Minister Andrius Kubilius	litas (2.35 = $1)	17,180	22,800
Luxembourg	469,000	Grand Duke Henri; Prime Minister Jean-Claude Juncker	euro (0.68 = $1)	18,420	23,130
Macedonia	2,048,000	President Branko Crvenkovski; Prime Minister Nikola Gruevski	denar (41.35 = $1)	3,350	4,977
Malta	409,000	President Eddie Fenech Adami; Prime Minister Lawrence Gonzi	euro (0.68 = $1)	3,238	4,541
Moldova	3,982,000	President Vladimir Voronin; Prime Minister Vasile Tarlev	leu (9.64 = $1)	1,361	3,677
Monaco	34,000	Prince Albert II; Minister of State Jean-Paul Proust	euro (0.68 = $1)	716	916
Montenegro	629,000	President Filip Vujanovic; Prime Minister Milo Djukanovic	euro (0.68 = $1)	171	602
Netherlands	16,513,000	Queen Beatrix; Prime Minister Jan Peter Balkenende	euro (0.68 = $1)	456,800	406,300
Norway	4,671,000	King Harald V; Prime Minister Jens Stoltenberg	krone (5.38 = $1)	140,300	77,240
Poland	38,077,000	President Lech Kaczynski; Prime Minister Donald Tusk	zloty (2.27 = $1)	144,600	160,200
Portugal	10,678,000	President Aníbal Cavaco Silva; Prime Minister José Sócrates	euro (0.68 = $1)	51,500	75,300
Romania	21,517,000	President Traian Basescu; Prime Minister Calin Popescu-Tariceanu	new leu (2.41 = $1)	40,320	64,540
Russia	141,358,000	President Dmitry Medvedev; Prime Minister Vladimir Putin	ruble (24.65 = $1)	355,500	223,400
San Marino	29,000	2 captains-regent appointed by Grand Council every 6 months	euro (0.68 = $1)	1,291	2,035
Serbia	7,358,000	President Boris Tadic; Prime Minister Vojislav Kostunica	new dinar (52.01 = $1)	8,824	18,350
Slovakia	5,395,000	President Ivan Gasparovic; Prime Minister Robert Fico	koruna (20.62 = $1)	57,530	58,400
Slovenia	2,001,000	President Danilo Türk; Prime Minister Janez Jansa	euro (0.68 = $1)	27,060	29,390
Spain	44,687,000	King Juan Carlos I; Prime Minister José Luis Rodríguez Zapatero	euro (0.68 = $1)	256,700	380,200
Sweden	9,179,000	King Carl XVI Gustaf; Prime Minister Fredrik Reinfeldt	krona (6.40 = $1)	170,100	151,400
Switzerland	7,542,000	President Pascal Couchepin	franc (1.10 = $1)	200,100	187,100
Turkey	74,824,000	President Abdullah Gül; Prime Minister Recep Tayyip Erdogan	new lira (1.19 = $1)	115,300	162,000
Ukraine	46,060,000	President Viktor Yushchenko; Prime Minister Yulia Tymoshenko	hryvnia (4.61 = $1)	49,840	60,410
United Kingdom	60,590,000	Queen Elizabeth II; Prime Minister Gordon Brown	pound (0.55 = $1)	442,200	621,400

the nation's sovereignty and referred the matter to the country's constitutional court. In November, the court ruled that the sections were not unconstitutional. The Czech Parliament was to vote on the treaty in February 2009.

The legislatures of two other nations—Germany and Poland—ratified the treaty. However, the presidents of both countries refused to sign it until, in Germany's case, a constitutional court responded to a challenge to the treaty and, in Poland's case, Ireland overturned its "no" vote. At an EU summit meeting on Dec. 12, 2008, Irish Prime Minister Brian Cowen agreed to hold a second referendum on the treaty in 2009, after EU leaders agreed to concessions in response to the concerns of Irish voters.

Economic crisis. Most of the nations of Europe initially responded to the global economic crisis by making individual decisions about bailing out national banks and guaranteeing deposits. In November, French President Sarkozy attempted to negotiate a more unified response. He called for a global financial summit, which took place in Washington, D.C., on November 14 and 15. Leaders of the Group of 20, the world's major industrialized nations and largest developing countries, discussed reforms emphasizing greater transparency and more strenuous regulation of the financial sector.

Later in the month, the European Commission introduced a plan for EU members that included tax cuts, funding for infrastructure and job training, and incentives to boost green technologies in the construction and automobile sectors. The commission also announced a stimulus package, which called for 200 billion euros ($260 billion) of spending—an average 1.5 percent of each member's *gross domestic product* (GDP). (The GDP is the value of all goods and services produced in a country in a year.) The commission gave EU members that use the common currency, the euro, permission to temporarily depart from budgetary discipline and run deficits that exceed the EU's target of 3 percent of GDP. At the EU summit meeting in December, the economic stimulus plan won unanimous support.

Also in December, the European Central Bank cut the cost of borrowing by a record 0.75 percent to its main lending rate. The cut followed two 0.5-percent cuts in October and November that were intended to stimulate private investment.

Environment and energy. EU environment ministers met in December 2008 to finalize an agreement on a new climate and energy package for the bloc. In 2007, EU members had agreed on a goal known as the 20-20-20 plan, which called for the EU to cut carbon dioxide emissions by 20 percent and to increase renewable energy to 20 percent of energy consumption by 2020. The core of the agreement was a carbon emissions trading system, whereby the rights to pollute and emit greenhouse gases are purchased and traded by industry using a system of credits. Because only about 8.5 percent of the EU's energy came from renewable resources in 2008, achieving the goal was expected to be an expensive task.

East European members, including Poland and Hungary, which depend on coal for much of their energy, demanded a free allocation of permits for their power generation sectors to help them reach the goal. Germany and Italy expressed concern that such subsidies would be costly for them and would make their own energy-intensive industries less competitive. By the end of the summit, however, the leaders of both eastern and western European nations agreed to a plan that offered compensation for the former and loopholes for the latter.

Enlargement. After admitting Bulgaria and Romania in 2007, EU populations and governments grew wary of accepting more new members. The newer member states were poorer and more prone to high-level corruption than the older West European members. In July 2008, the European Commission suspended almost 800 million euros ($1 billion) in aid to Bulgaria over corruption and fraud concerns. Nevertheless, on December 15, the former Yugoslav republic of Montenegro formally submitted its application to join the EU. The EU was to evaluate the request before allowing Montenegro to become a candidate for membership.

Although Turkey has been a candidate to join the EU since 1999 and began accession negotiations in 2005, progress toward membership remained slow in 2008. According to a report issued by the European Commission in November, Turkey made no move toward normalizing relations and permitting trade with the Republic of Cyprus. (Cyprus has been divided since 1974 into the Republic of Cyprus and the Turkish Republic of Northern Cyprus. The Republic of Cyprus is controlled by Cypriots of Greek origin. That government is recognized by all countries except Turkey. The Turkish Republic of Northern Cyprus is controlled by Cypriots of Turkish origin. Their government is recognized by Turkey alone.) The Commission also declared that Turkey still has much to do in fighting corruption and organized crime and ensuring total civilian control over the military.

Croatia, which has also been negotiating to join the EU since 2005, was deemed by the European Commission in 2008 to have made significant progress toward membership. According to a November report, negotiations could be completed by the end of 2009 for entry in 2010 or 2011. However, the commission noted that improvement is still needed in such areas as judicial reform, the fight against corruption, the return of refugees displaced during the Balkan wars of the 1990's, and cooperation with the United Nations (UN) International Criminal tribunal for the former Yugoslavia at The Hague, the Netherlands.

In May 2008, the European Commission approved Slovakia's application to join the eurozone, the group of EU and other European nations that use the euro as a common currency. Slovakia met strict requirements for joining the group of 15 nations, including restricting interest rates, budget deficits, and inflation.

Immigration. In October, the EU adopted a common immigration policy proposed by French President Nicolas Sarkozy. The agreement called on members to attract highly skilled workers and help them integrate into their new nation; expel illegal immigrants; strengthen border controls; standardize asylum practices; and work with countries from which large numbers of people migrate.

Foreign affairs. Relations between the EU and Russia worsened in August 2008, after Russia invaded Georgia's breakaway province of South Ossetia. Negotiations on such issues as energy security and economic and political cooperation were broken off while the French EU presidency under Nicolas Sarkozy spearheaded talks on Russia's withdrawal from Georgia. The talks were resumed in December, despite disagreements among EU members over whether Russia, by withdrawing from Georgia proper but not from South Ossetia, had complied with the EU-brokered peace accord. Some EU members considered it vitally important to renew contacts with Russia, from which the EU imports more than one-fourth of its natural gas.

China canceled its December summit with the EU after Sarkozy announced plans to meet with the Dalai Lama, the exiled spiritual leader of Tibet. (China has occupied Tibet since 1950.) Human rights concerns came to the fore in EU-China relations during the 2008 Summer Olympic Games in Beijing in August. Many EU leaders stayed away from the opening ceremonies after Chinese troops shot Tibetan protesters. Relations were further frayed when China executed a biochemist whose daughters are Austrian citizens on charges that he had passed secrets to Taiwan.

Controversy surrounded the EU's police and justice mission to Kosovo, which began in December 2008, when several thousand ethnic Albanians protested against the deployment. (The former province of Serbia, which declared its independence in February, has a population composed of 90 percent ethnic Albanians and 8 percent Serbs.) The protesters worried that the EU mission, which was approved by the UN Security Council on the condition that it not take a stand on Kosovo's disputed declaration of independence, would not respect Kosovar sovereignty.

The UN also called on the EU to take on a stronger military role in peacekeeping in Congo (Kinshasa), where fighting that broke out in August between Tutsi rebels and government forces had created a humanitarian crisis. EU leaders divided on the issue. Belgium supported the proposed mission and Germany opposed it, suggesting greater support for UN troops already in the region instead.

Economy. All of the nations of Europe were affected by the global economic crisis, with advanced economies experiencing the sharpest slowdown in growth. EU economists forecast that GDP growth for the bloc would fall from 2.9 percent in 2007 to 1.4 percent in 2008.

■ Jeffrey Kopstein

See also **Bank: A Special Report; Congo (Kinshasa); Economics, World; Global warming; United Nations;** various European country articles.

European Union. See Europe.
Farm and farming. See Agriculture.

Fashion. In 2008, the state of economy—battered by a mortgage crisis, a credit crisis, and rising costs and unemployment—reduced the amount of money available for clothing. Early in the year, many doubted that fashion sales would be affected by the economic downturn. By fall of 2008, however, retailers from Target to Saks were all reporting sales much lower than they had forecast earlier in the year. Even sales of luxury items, thought to be recession proof, decreased, as wealthy consumers found the value of both their homes and their stock portfolios declining.

Politics and fashion became entwined in 2008. In France, a former model turned singer-songwriter married that nation's president in February. Carla Bruni-Sarkozy, new bride of president Nicolas Sarkozy, had worked as a supermodel in the 1990's. During state visits, the press extensively covered her glamorous clothing, which was often designed by the Dior fashion house.

Michelle Obama, wife of U.S. President-elect Barack Obama, also drew attention for her sense of style. Her wardrobe featured simple, classic clothing, such as sheath dresses. With her signature pearl necklace and her hair in a flip, the effect harkened back to the early 1960's and so was sometimes compared with the style of first lady Jacqueline Kennedy. Mrs. Obama's wardrobe featured some designer clothing—she especially favored Chicago designer Maria Pinto—but some of her clothing was purchased off-the-rack.

Style also created some negative publicity. Vice presidential candidate Sarah Palin, the governor of Alaska who shared the Republican ticket with Arizona Senator John McCain, was criticized for her look. Palin, a former beauty-pageant contestant, looked very stylish in her designer clothing, but she was faulted once the press reported that the Republican National Committee had footed the bill for her wardrobe at a cost of some $150,000 plus another $150,000 for the services of stylists. The committee stated it had donated Palin's wardrobe to charity after the campaign.

Trends. Popular items in 2008 included anything in plaid; chunky jewelry; long, narrow scarves; ruffled blouses; ankle-length summer dresses; trench coats; and high-heeled shoes.

Shoes, in fact, provided the most varied fashion possibilities for the year. Boots above the knee were popular, but so were brightly colored versions of the British Wellington boot. Ballet flats were a craze, but so were shoes with stiletto heels and a hidden platform at the front. Open-toed shoes were worn in all seasons, sometimes with tights, which had once been against the rules of fashion. It all made for an interesting year for feet. ■ Bernadine Morris

Fiji. See Pacific Islands.

Yves Saint Laurent
Fashions Fade, Style Is Eternal

Yves Saint Laurent, an Algerian-born French fashion designer, was considered by many to be the last of the great Parisian couturiers. He died in Paris on June 1, 2008, at the age of 71.

Saint Laurent was born Yves Henri Donat Mathieu-Saint-Laurent on Aug. 1, 1936, in Oran, Algeria (while Algeria was still a department of France). Saint Laurent's prominent family lived in a villa on the Mediterranean Sea. As a child, Saint Laurent became fascinated by theater, especially theatrical costumes, which led him to an interest in fashion. By the time he was a teenager, he was designing clothing for his mother.

At 17, Saint Laurent went to Paris to study fashion design, but he became bored and quit. Shortly after leaving school, he won a design competition with his sketch of a dress. When Christian Dior was shown Saint Laurent's sketches, he took him on as his assistant. Dior died unexpectedly in 1957, and at 21, Saint Laurent was named head designer of the House of Dior. Saint Laurent's first Dior collection, in the spring of 1958, made him a star. This so-called "Trapeze" collection featured garments narrow at the shoulders and wide at the hem. In that same year, he met Pierre Bergé, who was to be Saint Laurent's personal partner for around two decades and his business partner and manager for life.

In 1960, Saint Laurent had a difficult year. In July, his show featured beatnik-inspired fashions, such as turtlenecks and leather jackets. This look would eventually become popular, but at the time it was not well received. In September, he was drafted to serve in the French army in Algeria, in that country's war of independence. The military was impossible for Saint Laurent, and within three weeks he had a breakdown and was sent to a mental hospital. In later years, Saint Laurent linked his problems with depression to that time. The House of Dior promoted Saint Laurent's assistant to head designer. When Saint Laurent was released from the hospital, he had no job. He sued Dior for damages and, with the money won in the judgment, opened his own fashion house in 1961.

Groundbreaking designs by Saint Laurent included a shift dress from 1965, based on the black-lined squares of the Dutch painter Piet Mondrian; and a line of peasant-style clothing from 1976, known as the Russian collection. Other fashion innovations included his emphasis on pants for women, and his simple black suit for women, based upon the tuxedo, known in France as *le smoking*. He opened his first ready-to-wear shop in 1966, the first of more than 100 such stores. The rest of Paris couture soon followed, and thus began the trend for designers to create a line of clothing—especially sportswear—for women to buy off-the-rack. His firm eventually became a pioneer of fashion licensing, with Saint Laurent's name on everything from perfume to accessories.

A retrospective of Saint Laurent's designs was held at the Costume Institute of the Metropolitan Museum of Art in 1983. Saint Laurent retired in 2002, but his influence in the design world was likely to continue long after his death.

■ Christine Sullivan

Finland. Finland's four-party, center-right coalition led by Prime Minister Matti Vanhanen suffered a setback in 2008, when it was revealed that at least two dozen members of parliament had broken the law by not revealing sources of money donated by supporters. International agencies have rated Finland as one of the least corrupt countries in the world, and the nation's political leaders were concerned that the scandal would lower the country's ranking. In addition, polls indicated the public's concern that the interests of wealthy lobbyists would carry more weight than those of ordinary citizens. Legal analysts pointed to an ambiguity in the law, which requires that the sources of funding be reported but stipulates no punishment for those failing to do so. In May, the leaders of Finland's main political parties set a limit on campaign contributions to members of parliament and moved to impose sanctions for noncompliance with the reporting requirement.

Vanhanen also faced criticism of his private life in 2008 over a former girlfriend's publication of an account of their relationship in 2007. The prime minister had sued the book's publisher for invasion of privacy, arguing that public figures are nevertheless entitled to a private life. In March 2008, the court dismissed the charges.

Relations with Russia. In April, Russia doubled the export duties on its raw timber to support its own wood-processing industry and indicated it would raise the fees again before 2009. The wood issue is highly sensitive in Finland, where the papermaking industry accounts for 10 percent of the country's *gross domestic product* (GDP, the value of all goods and services produced in a country in a year). In June 2008, Finland threatened to respond by imposing road transit fees on goods shipped to Russia through its territory. In addition, José Manuel Barroso, the principal leader of the European Union (EU, Europe's main economic bloc), indicated that imposition of the duties may hinder Russia's entry into the World Trade Organization and prevent deeper cooperation between Russia and the EU. In November, Russian Prime Minister Vladimir Putin postponed the tariffs.

In the wake of Russia's August incursion into Georgia, Finland considered joining the North Atlantic Treaty Organization (NATO, the West's main military alliance), of which it is not a member. In March, Finland had taken an intermediate step and announced that it would participate in future operations of NATO's rapid reaction force.

School shooting. Finns were shocked in September when a student in a vocational school in Kauhajoki, in western Finland, shot and killed 10 classmates before taking his own life. The student had been questioned by police the day before about a violent video he had posted on the Internet. In November 2007, an 18-year-old student had killed eight classmates before committing suicide after a similar posting on the Web.

Nobel Prize. Former Finnish President Martti Ahtisaari won the Nobel Peace Prize in 2008 for his work as a mediator in international conflicts over the past three decades.

Economy. Finland's high-tech economy suffered during the global economic crisis. EU economists forecast the GDP would grow by only 2.4 percent in 2008, compared with 4.5 percent in 2007. ■ Jeffrey Kopstein

See also **Europe; Nobel Prizes.**

Fire. See **Disasters.**

Flood. See **Disasters.**

Food. Safety concerns were among the most important food-related issues throughout the world in 2008. A salmonella outbreak first reported in New Mexico in mid-April became the largest food-borne outbreak (in terms of number of confirmed cases) in the United States in 10 years. According to the U.S. Centers for Disease Control and Prevention (CDC) in Atlanta, a rare strain of the bacterium *Salmonella saintpaul* sickened more than 1,400 people in 43 states, the District of Columbia, and Canada and may have contributed to 2 deaths.

At first, the outbreak was attributed to fresh tomatoes. On June 7, the CDC recommended that consumers avoid raw red plum, red round, and red Roma tomatoes. In July, investigators announced that they had discovered the bacteria on fresh jalapeño peppers traced to a farm in Mexico. Infected serrano peppers were also found on a neighboring farm. However, according to the CDC, tomatoes could not be ruled out as a source of the infection. By the end of August, the outbreak appeared to have ended.

Canadian cold cuts. An outbreak of a food-borne illness called listeriosis, caused by the bacterium *Listeria monocytogenes,* caused the deaths of at least 18 people in Canada and sickened dozens of others in 2008. The outbreak began in July and was traced to luncheon meats from a single plant in Toronto belonging to Maple Leaf Foods, one of the country's largest food processors. In August, Maple Leaf Foods recalled more than 200 products. The case caused particular concern because of the length of time that elapsed before Canadian public health authorities realized there was a connection between the first two reported cases of the illness. Yet more time passed before the findings were confirmed and the recall begun.

Chinese melamine scandal. An international scandal erupted in early September 2008 after reports were released that some infant formulas produced in China were tainted with melamine. Melamine is an industrial chemical

A law enforcement officer observes as workers at a dairy in Wuhan, in central China, dispose of tainted milk. At least four children in China died and thousands of others were sickened in 2008 when a number of dairies added the industrial chemical melamine to milk to make it appear to contain more protein.

used in the production of coatings, laminates, wood adhesives, ceiling tiles, and flame retardants. Ingesting the substance can cause kidney stones and other ailments. In 2007, melamine used in the manufacture of cat and dog food in China sickened and killed thousands of pets in the United States.

By October 2008, it had become clear that milk and other dairy products, as well as eggs and such foods as chocolate that are made with dairy products, were also tainted. At least 4 infants in China died and more than 52,000 others were sickened after ingesting milk-based formula and milk containing melamine.

An investigation showed that at least 22 Chinese dairy plants had added melamine to watered-down milk products to make the products appear to contain higher levels of protein. Dairy products were pulled from shelves in China, and more than a dozen Southeast Asian and African nations banned the importation of Chinese dairy products. According to a representative of the World Health Organization, an agency of the United Nations, the crisis of confidence among Chinese consumers in their nation's food quality system would be difficult to overcome.

COOL new law. In September 2008, a new COOL (for "country-of-origin labeling") law went into effect. The law requires that by March 30, 2009, retailers label the source of raw beef, veal, lamb, pork, chicken, goat, wild and farm-raised fish and shellfish, fresh or frozen fruits and vegetables, peanuts, pecans, macadamia nuts, and whole ginseng. Previously, only seafood was required to carry such a label. Advocates of the law hoped that it would allow consumers to avoid foods from nations with weak food safety records.

U.S. food safety campaign. Throughout 2008, the U.S. Food and Drug Administration (FDA) continued to enact changes outlined in its Food Protection Plan, released in November 2007. The purpose of the plan is to improve the country's food safety program.

In August 2008, the agency allowed produce sellers to begin irradiating certain kinds of greens to prevent the spread of some bacteria that cause food-borne illnesses. Processors can use radiation on spinach and iceberg lettuce to kill *Escherichia coli, Salmonella,* and *Listeria.* Irradiation does not kill viruses. Nevertheless, consumer safety advocates agreed that it is a safe practice and may reduce outbreaks of illness, particularly among people with weakened immune systems.

In November, the agency began to establish offices in countries that export food to the United States. China became the first country with such an office when a facility opened in Beijing. The agency hoped that inspectors in foreign offices could monitor food exports before they entered the United States.

■ Kristina Vaicikonis

See also **China; Public health; Safety.**

THE 2008 COLLEGE FOOTBALL SEASON

NATIONAL CHAMPIONS

NCAA BCS	Florida	24	Oklahoma	14
NCAA FCS	Richmond	24	Montana	7
NCAA Div. II	Minnesota (Duluth)	21	N.W. Missouri State	14
NCAA Div. III	Mount Union	31	Wisc. (Whitewater)	26
NAIA	Sioux Falls (S.D.)	23	Carroll College	7

BOWL CHAMPIONSHIP SERIES (BCS) GAMES

BOWL	RESULT			
Rose	Southern California	38	Penn State	24
Orange	Virginia Tech	20	Cincinnati	7
Fiesta	Texas	24	Ohio State	21
Sugar	Utah	31	Alabama	17

OTHER BOWL GAMES

BOWL	RESULT			
Alamo	Missouri	30	Northwestern	23
Armed Forces	Houston	34	Air Force	28
Capital One	Georgia	24	Michigan State	12
Car Care	West Virginia	31	North Carolina	30
Champs Sports	Florida State	42	Wisconsin	13
Chick-fil-A	Louisiana State	38	Georgia Tech	3
Cotton	Mississippi	47	Texas Tech	34
EagleBank	Wake Forest	29	Navy	19
Emerald	California	24	Miami	17
GMAC	Tulsa	45	Ball State	13
Gator	Nebraska	26	Clemson	21
Hawaii	Notre Dame	49	Hawaii	21
Holiday	Oregon	42	Oklahoma State	31
Humanitarian	Maryland	42	Nevada	35
Independence	Louisiana Tech.	17	Northern Illinois	10
Insight	Kansas	42	Minnestoa	21
International	Connecticut	38	Buffalo	20
Las Vegas	Arizona	31	Brigham Young	21
Liberty	Kentucky	25	East Carolina	19
Motor City	Florida Atlantic	24	Central Michigan	21
Music City	Vanderbilt	16	Boston College	14
New Mexico	Colorado State	40	Fresno State	35
New Orleans	Southern Miss.	30	Troy	27
Outback	Iowa	31	South Carolina	10
Papa Johns.com	Rutgers	29	No. Carolina State	23
Poinsettia	Texas Christian	17	Boise State	16
St. Petersburg	South Florida	41	Memphis	14
Sun	Oregon State	3	Pittsburgh	0
Texas	Rice	38	Western Michigan	14

CONFERENCE CHAMPIONS

NCAA FOOTBALL BOWL SUBDIVISION (FBS)

CONFERENCE	SCHOOL
Atlantic Coast	Virginia Tech
Big 12	Oklahoma
Big East	Cincinnati
Big Ten	Ohio State and Penn State (tie)
Conference USA	East Carolina
Independents	Navy
Mid-American	Buffalo
Mountain West	Utah
Pacific 10	USC
Southeastern	Florida
Sun Belt	Troy
Western Athletic	Boise State

NCAA FOOTBALL CHAMPIONSHIP SUBDIVISION (FCS)

CONFERENCE	SCHOOL
Big Sky	Montana
Big South	Liberty
Colonial	James Madison
Great West	California Polytechnic
Independents	Bryant
Ivy League	Brown and Harvard (tie)
Mid-Eastern	South Carolina State
Missouri Valley	Northern Iowa and Southern Illinois (tie)
Northeast	Albany
Ohio Valley	Eastern Kentucky
Patriot	Colgate
Pioneer	Jacksonville
Southern	Appalachian State
Southland	Central Arkansas
Southwestern	Grambling State

ALL-AMERICAN TEAM (FBS)

(as chosen by the Associated Press)

OFFENSE
Quarterback—Sam Bradford, Oklahoma
Running backs—Shonn Greene, Iowa;
  MiQuale Lewis, Ball State
Wide receivers—Michael Crabtree, Texas Tech;
  Jarrett Dillard, Rice
Tight end—Chase Coffman, Missouri
Center—A.Q. Shipley, Penn State
Other linemen—Andre Smith, Alabama; Duke Robinson,
  Oklahoma; Michael Oher, Mississippi; Max Unger, Oregon
Place-kicker—Graham Gano, Florida State
Kick returns—Perrish Cox, Oklahoma State

DEFENSE
Linemen—Aaron Maybin, Penn State; Brian Orakpo, Texas;
  Jerry Hughes, TCU; Terrence Cody, Alabama;
Linebackers—Scott McKillop, Pittsburgh; Rey Maualuga,
  Southern California; Brandon Spikes, Florida
Backs—Alphonso Smith, Wake Forest; Eric Berry, Ten-
  nessee;
  Taylor Mays, Southern California; Malcolm Jenkins, Ohio
  State
Punter—Pat McAfee, West Virginia
Punt return—Brandon James, Florida

PLAYER AWARDS
Heisman Trophy (best player)—Sam Bradford, Oklahoma
Bednarik Trophy (best defensive player)—Rey Maualuga,
Southern California

Football. In a battle between college foot-ball's top two offenses, the University of Florida Gators defeated the University of Oklahoma Sooners in a surprisingly low-scoring affair, 24-14, in Miami on Jan. 8, 2009, in the Bowl Championship Series (BCS) title game for its second national championship in three seasons.

Unlike in recent years, there were few complaints about the teams selected for the championship match-up. Florida, led by quarterback Tim Tebow, bounced back from a single loss to steamroll through its final nine games. The Gators averaged more than 49 points a game. They then won the Southeastern Conference title game over top-ranked Alabama 31-20.

Oklahoma also had lost only once, a 45-35 loss to the University of Texas in October, and the Sooners scored a record 702 points over the season. They scored 60 or more points in five straight games. The only controversy occurred when Oklahoma was selected over Texas to play in the Big 12 Conference title game against Missouri. Texas, Oklahoma, and Texas Tech all finished the season tied in conference play, and BCS standings were used as a tiebreaker. Although Texas had beaten Oklahoma, they came in second since they lost to Texas Tech, who was throttled by Oklahoma.

In the National Football League (NFL), the New York Giants scored one of the greatest upsets of all time in Super Bowl XLII, defeating the New England Patriots 17-14 on Feb. 3, 2008, in Glendale, Arizona. The loss denied the previously unbeaten Patriots the chance to be the first team ever to go 19-0 in NFL history. Giants quarterback Eli Manning won the Super Bowl Most Valuable Player (MVP) award.

The 2008 NFL season. The New England Patriots suffered the loss of their star quarterback, Tom Brady, to a season-ending injury in the first quarter of the first game of the 2008 season—a 17-0 victory over the Kansas City Chiefs. Brady had started 128 consecutive games. Backup quarterback Matt Cassell, who had not started a football game since high school, replaced Brady and led the team to an impressive 11-5 record. But the Patriots lost the division title to the Miami Dolphins and did not make the play-offs.

The loss of Tom Brady by New England, combined with early losses by the Indianapolis Colts, created a void at the top of the powerful American Football Conference (AFC). The void was filled by the Tennessee Titans, who opened the season with 10 straight wins, and the Pittsburgh Steelers, who finished 12-4. The Miami Dolphins also accomplished one of the biggest turn-arounds in NFL history. They won their division and made the play-offs with an 11-5 record after finishing 1-15 the previous season.

The New York Jets acquired Brett Favre, the NFL's all-time leader in passing yards and touchdown passes, from the Green Bay Packers in 2008. Favre had announced his retirement in a tearful press conference in March, but he soon began to have second thoughts. However, the Packers had moved forward with their new starting quarterback, Aaron Rodgers. In early August, the Packers dealt Favre to the New York Jets, who finished 4-12 the previous season. The Jets finished 9-7, did not make the play-offs and their coach was fired after the season.

Among the biggest surprises were the Arizona Cardinals, who won the NFC West for their first division title since 1975 and first play-off since 1998. The 2008 season was only the second winning season for the Cardinals in the last 24 years.

The Detroit Lions set a record for futility in 2008 by going 0-16, the worst team record in NFL history. The Lions were the first team to have a winless season since 1976, when the Tampa Bay Buccaneers finished 0-14 as an expansion team. No team has gone winless since the NFL expanded the regular season to 16 games in 1978.

Personal conduct problems. The 2008 NFL season was marred by several violations of the league's personal conduct policy by several high-profile players. Dallas Cowboys cornerback Adam "Pacman" Jones was suspended indefinitely on October 14 by NFL Commissioner Roger Goodell, following a fight in a Dallas hotel. The Tennessee Titans had traded Jones to Dallas in the off-season after he had incurred several suspensions for personal conduct following arrests. Jones was reinstated in time for his team's December 7 loss against the Pittsburgh Steelers, but was released by the team after the season.

New York Giants wide receiver Plaxico Burress accidentally shot himself in the leg with a handgun while at a New York City night club in late November. He was suspended by the NFL for the remainder of the season and play-offs. Burress also faced criminal charges for illegal possession of a gun.

Super Bowl XLII. The New York Giants upset the New England Patriots' bid to become just the second NFL team to go unbeaten for an entire season and play-offs. Only the 1972 Miami Dolphins (17-0) have accomplished that feat. In the game, the Patriots took a 14-10 lead in the closing minutes. But Giants quarterback Eli Manning led the Giants on a 12-play, 83-yard drive that culminated in a 13-yard touchdown pass to wide receiver Plaxico Burress with a mere 35 seconds left in the game. The Giants blitzing defense sacked Brady five times.

2007-2008 NFL play-offs. In the AFC wild-card play-offs, the Jacksonville Jaguars upset the Pittsburgh Steelers 31-29 on Jan. 5, 2008, in Pittsburgh. The San Diego Chargers beat the Tennessee Titans 17-6 on January 6 in San Diego. The New England Patriots eliminated visiting Jacksonville 31-20 the following week while San Diego upset the Indianapolis Colts 28-24 on January 12 in Indianapolis. The Patriots improved their record to 18-0 in the season by defeating the Chargers 21-12 in the AFC title game in Foxborough, Massachusetts, on January 20.

In the NFC wild-card play-offs, the Seattle Seahawks beat the visiting Washington Redskins 35-14 on January 5, and the New York Giants won 24-14 over the Tampa Bay Buccaneers the next day in Tampa. On January 12, the Green Bay Packers routed Seattle 42-20 in Green Bay, Wisconsin, and the Giants edged their rivals, the Dal-

2008 NATIONAL FOOTBALL LEAGUE FINAL STANDINGS

AMERICAN CONFERENCE

North Division

	W.	L.	T.	Pct.
Pittsburgh Steelers*	12	4	0	.750
Baltimore Ravens*	11	5	0	.688
Cincinnati Bengals	4	11	1	.281
Cleveland Browns	4	12	0	.250

East Division

	W.	L.	T.	Pct.
Miami Dolphins*	11	5	0	.688
New England Patriots	11	5	0	.688
N.Y. Jets	9	7	0	.563
Buffalo Bills	7	9	0	.438

South Division

	W.	L.	T.	Pct.
Tennessee Titans*	13	3	0	.813
Indianapolis Colts*	12	4	0	.750
Houston Texans	8	8	0	.500
Jacksonville Jaguars	5	11	0	.313

West Division

	W.	L.	T.	Pct.
San Diego Chargers*	8	8	0	.500
Denver Broncos	8	8	0	.500
Oakland Raiders	5	11	0	.313
Kansas City Chiefs	2	14	0	.125

*Made play-offs

NATIONAL CONFERENCE

North Division

	W.	L.	T.	Pct.
Minnestoa Vikings*	10	6	0	.625
Chicago Bears	9	7	0	.563
Green Bay Packers	6	10	0	.375
Detroit Lions	0	16	0	.000

East Division

	W.	L.	T.	Pct.
New York Giants*	12	4	0	.750
Philadelphia Eagles*	9	6	1	.594
Dallas Cowboys	9	7	0	.563
Washington Redskins	8	8	0	.500

South Division

	W.	L.	T.	Pct.
Carolina Panthers*	12	4	0	.750
Atlanta Falcons*	11	5	0	.688
Tampa Bay Buccaneers	9	7	0	.563
New Orleans Saints	8	8	0	.500

West Division

	W.	L.	T.	Pct.
Arizona Cardinals*	9	7	0	.563
San Francisco 49ers	7	9	0	.438
Seattle Seahawks	4	12	0	.250
St. Louis Rams	2	14	0	.125

*Made play-offs

TEAM STATISTICS

Leading offenses	Plays	Yards per game
Denver	1,019	395.8
Houston	1,019	382.1
New England	1,095	365.4
San Diego	924	349.0
Miami	965	345.6

Leading defenses	Avg. points against	Yards per game
Pittsburgh	13.9	237.2
Baltimore	15.2	261.1
Tennessee	14.6	293.6
New England	19.3	309.0
Indianapolis	18.6	310.9

TEAM STATISTICS

Leading offenses	Plays	Yards per game
New Orleans	1,047	410.7
Arizona	998	365.8
Atlanta	1,011	361.2
New York	1,021	355.9
Green Bay	1,012	351.1

Leading defenses	Avg. points against	Yards per game
Philadelphia	18.1	274.3
Washington	18.5	288.8
New York	18.4	292.0
Minnesota	20.8	292.4
Dallas	22.8	294.3

INDIVIDUAL STATISTICS

Leading scorers, TD's	TD's	Rush	Rec.	Ret.
Thomas Jones, New York	15	13	2	0
LenDale White, Tennessee	15	15	0	0
Maurice Jones-Drew, Jacksonville	14	12	2	0
LaDainian Tomlinson, San Diego	12	11	1	0

Leading kickers	PAT made/att.	FG made/att.	Longest FG	Pts.
S. Gostkowski, New England	40/40	36/40	50	148
Phil Dawson, Cleveland	18/18	30/36	56	108
Rian Lindell, Buffalo	34/34	30/38	53	124
Rob Bironas, Tennessee	40/40	29/33	51	127

Leading quarterbacks	Att.	Comp.	Yds.	TD's	Ints.
Jay Cutler, Denver	616	384	4,526	25	18
Philip Rivers, San Diego	478	312	4,009	34	11
Peyton Manning, Indianapolis	555	371	4,002	27	12
Matt Cassel, New England	516	327	3,693	21	11
Chad Pennington, Miami	476	321	3,653	19	7

Leading receivers	Passes caught	Rec. yards	Avg. gain	TD's
Andre Johnson, Houston	115	1,575	13.7	8
Brandon Marshall, Denver	104	1,265	12.2	6
Wes Welker, New England	111	1,165	10.4	3
Reggie Wayne, Indianapolis	82	1,145	14.0	6

Leading rushers	Rushes	Yards	Avg.	TD's
Thomas Jones, New York	290	1,312	4.5	13
Steve Slaton, Houston	268	1,282	4.8	9
Chris Johnson, Tennessee	251	1,228	4.9	9
LaDainian Tomlinson, San Diego	292	1,110	3.8	11

Leading punters	Punts	Yards	Avg.	Longest
Shane Lechler, Oakland	90	4,391	48.8	70
Brett Kern, Denver	46	2,149	46.7	64
Mike Scifres, San Diego	51	2,332	45.7	67
Dave Zastudil, Cleveland	75	3,410	45.5	65

INDIVIDUAL STATISTICS

Leading scorers, TD's	TD's	Rush	Rec.	Ret.
DeAngelo Williams, Carolina	20	18	2	0
Michael Turner, Atlanta	17	17	0	0
Brandon Jacobs, New York	15	15	0	0
Brian Westbrook, Philadelphia	14	9	5	0

Leading kickers	PAT made/att.	FG made/att.	Longest FG	Pts.
John Carney, New York	38/38	35/38	51	143
David Akers, Philadelphia	45/45	33/40	51	144
Matt Bryant, Tampa Bay	35/36	32/38	49	131
Josh Brown, St. Louis	19/19	31/36	54	112

Leading quarterbacks	Att.	Comp.	Yds.	TD's	Ints.
Drew Brees, New Orleans	635	413	5,069	34	17
Kurt Warner, Arizona	598	401	4,583	30	14
Aaron Rodgers, Green Bay	536	341	4,038	28	13
Donovan McNabb, Philadelphia	571	345	3,916	23	11
Tony Romo, Dallas	450	276	3,448	26	14

Leading receivers	Passes caught	Rec. yards	Avg. gain	TD's
Larry Fitzgerald, Arizona	96	1,431	14.9	12
Steve Smith, Carolina	78	1,421	18.2	6
Roddy White, Atlanta	88	1,382	15.7	7
Calvin Johnson, Detroit	78	1,331	17.1	12

Leading rushers	Rushes	Yards	Avg.	TD's
Adrian Peterson, Minnesota	363	1,760	4.8	10
Michael Turner, Atlanta	376	1,699	4.5	17
DeAngelo Williams, Carolina	273	1,515	5.5	18
Clinton Portis, Washington	342	1,487	4.3	9

Leading punters	Punts	Yards	Avg.	Longest
Donnie Jones, St. Louis	82	4,100	50.0	68
Andy Lee, San Francisco	66	3,155	47.8	82
Chris Kluwe, Minnesota	73	3,473	47.6	63
Jon Ryan, Seattle	78	3,557	45.6	63

las Cowboys, 21-17 on January 13 in Dallas. On January 20, the Giants won for the third straight time on the road in the play-offs, beating Green Bay 23-20 in overtime.

Colleges. On Jan. 8, 2009, Florida rode a strong defensive effort to defeat Oklahoma to win the BCS National Championship. Florida twice stopped Oklahoma inside the 10-yard line and blocked a field goal. Both quarterbacks, Tebow and Heisman Trophy winner Sam Bradford of Oklahoma, threw a pair of interceptions, but Tebow was named the game's Most Outstanding Player after rushing for 109 yards and completing 18 of 30 passes for 231 yards, including the decisive 4-yard toss to David Nelson with 3:07 to play.

In the other BCS bowls, the University of Southern California defeated Penn State University 38-24 in the Rose Bowl on January 1. Virginia Tech defeated Cincinnati, 20-7, in the Orange Bowl. The University of Utah finished the season 12-0, and the team was ranked sixth in the final BCS standings. The ranking earned the Utes a spot in the Sugar Bowl, where they soundly defeated Alabama 31-17 on January 2. On January 5, the University of Texas defeated Ohio State by 24-21 in the Fiesta Bowl.

Down year for Big Blue. The University of Michigan suffered its worst season in its 129-year history, finishing 3-9 under new coach Rich Rodriguez. The Wolverines lost the most games in a season in school history, missed a bowl trip for the first time in 34 years, and had their first losing season in 41 years. In its season-ending game with archrival Ohio State, Michigan lost by 35 points, the biggest margin in 40 years.

Heisman Trophy. University of Oklahoma quarterback Sam Bradford was awarded the 2008 Heisman Trophy on December 13. Bradford beat out the previous winner, University of Florida's Tim Tebow, and University of Texas quarterback Colt McCoy. He was the fifth Oklahoma player ever to win the Heisman Trophy.

Notable deaths. Gene Upshaw, 63, a Hall of Fame offensive lineman with the Oakland Raiders and executive director of the NFL Players Association, died on Aug. 20, 2008, just days after he was diagnosed with pancreatic cancer. Upshaw was drafted by the Raiders in 1967 and played for 15 seasons. Samuel "Sammy" Baugh, 94, a legendary quarterback for the Washington Redskins from 1937 to 1952 died in December. Baugh was one of 16 charter members inducted into the Professional Football Hall of Fame in 1963.

Canadian Football League. The Calgary Stampeders beat the Montreal Alouettes 22-14 on Nov. 23, 2008, for the Grey Cup title. It was Calgary's sixth Grey Cup, but the first since 2001.

■ Michael Kates

France. President Nicolas Sarkozy in the first part of 2008 became better known for his whirlwind romance and marriage in February to former supermodel Carla Bruni than for the high-energy policy initiatives with which he began his presidency in 2007. Polls indicated, however, that his high-profile personal life hurt his approval rating.

After his ruling center-right party performed poorly in municipal elections in March 2008, Sarkozy returned to his agenda of reforming France's economy and labor market. In June, the government sent a bill to Parliament that changed the way trade unions are represented in labor negotiations. In effect, the bill also dismantled France's traditional 35-hour work week by allowing companies to negotiate with employees the number of hours in excess of 35 they will work. The bill, which passed in July, was less ambitious than expected and did little to change the overall tax burden for the economy.

Sarkozy's educational reforms, begun in 2007, brought both improvements and controversy in 2008. New regulations gave public universities more autonomy. The universities were allowed, for the first time, to raise money from private sources and to recruit professors at competitive salaries. However, plans to cut the number of teachers in public primary and secondary schools to decrease the number of civil servants on the government payroll generated strikes and demonstrations. Plans to change the number of semesters from three to two and to cut classroom hours met with resistance as well. Sarkozy postponed the plans in December after strikes by secondary school students threatened to become violent.

Sarkozy's main opposition, the Socialist Party, remained divided in 2008. After party leader Francois Hollande stepped down in November, a dispute broke out over the vote for a new leader. Martine Aubry, the mayor of Lille and the initiator of the 35-hour work week, won the election—by a razor-thin margin—over Ségolène Royal, who challenged the result. A party commission declared Aubry the winner on November 26.

Economic policy. Although France's economy was resilient in early 2008, by autumn, the global economic downturn forced Sarkozy to change course. The Société Générale, one of France's largest banks, was rocked by scandal when it was revealed in January that a trader had lost $7.14 billion in bank funds by taking unauthorized bets on investments linked to European markets. In the face of a global financial crisis, the French national statistics office forecast in October that the economy would go into recession. The government immediately launched plans to help French companies remain globally competitive. In November, France became the first large economy to provide state-backed credit insurance to companies left without coverage because of fears of bankruptcy. In December, Sarkozy unveiled a $33-billion stimulus plan that included help for the auto and construction industries.

Foreign policy. In July 2008, France assumed the rotating, six-month presidency of the European Union (EU—Europe's main political and economic bloc). The position propelled Sarkozy onto the global stage. In June, he unveiled France's first full defense review in 14 years. The document called for a smaller—but better-equipped—military. It also provided for France's reintegration into the command structure of the North Atlantic Treaty Organization (NATO—the West's main military alliance) in 2009. France had withdrawn its forces from NATO in 1966, though it remained a member of the alliance politically.

In July 2008, France led the EU in launching the Union for the Mediterranean at a meeting in Paris. Sarkozy's plan for the organization was to draw several EU and non-EU neighbors that border the Mediterranean Sea into a closer relationship as an alternative to full EU membership. In the face of resistance from Germany and other EU members who suspected that the new bloc would primarily serve French interests, would split the EU, and would divert resources from other projects, Sarkozy's plan was scaled back.

In August and September, Sarkozy spearheaded negotiations with Russia following its invasion of two breakaway republics of neighboring Georgia.

France's relations with the United States improved in 2008. In April, Sarkozy announced an increase in the number of French soldiers serving in the NATO-led mission in Afghanistan. He faced criticism for this move in August when 10 French soldiers were killed in Afghanistan. Also in support of U.S. policy, France teamed up with the United Kingdom in October in stepping up pressure on Iran to comply with United Nations resolutions on its nuclear program.

In October, Sarkozy convinced U.S. President George W. Bush to hold a summit of the Group of 20, the leaders of the world's major industrialized and developing countries. At the meeting in November, the leaders agreed on the need for new regulatory measures. However, they provided few specific guidelines for change.

Economy. France narrowly avoided recession in 2008, posting a growth rate for the third quarter (July-September) of 0.1 percent. However, EU economists forecast that the global economic crisis would take the country into recession in 2009.

■ Jeffrey Kopstein

See also **Bank: A Special Report; Europe.**

Gabon. See Africa.

Gambia. See Africa.

Gas and gasoline. See Energy supply.

Genetic engineering. See Biology; Medicine.

French President Nicolas Sarkozy visits the pyramids at Giza, west of Cairo, Egypt, with Italian model Carla Bruni, who became his wife in February. Sarkozy's approval rating plunged in early 2008, as French voters claimed that his flamboyant lifestyle was preventing him from addressing serious economic issues.

Geology. A 7.9-magnitude earthquake struck the Sichuan Province of China on May 12, 2008, killing nearly 70,000 people and injuring nearly 300,000 others. Many of the dead and injured were in the provincial capital of Chengdu.

Geologists noted that the fundamental cause of the earthquake was sudden movement in a fault that is part of the boundary between the Indian-Australian and Eurasian tectonic plates, which are among 30 slabs that make up the outer shell of Earth. These two plates began pushing against each other approximately 50 million years ago, forming the Himalaya and the Plateau of Tibet. Scientists with the United States Geological Survey (USGS) stated that the Sichuan earthquake brought other major faults in the region closer to failure. The USGS estimated the probability within the next 10 years of another regional earthquake of at least magnitude 6 to be 57 percent to 71 percent.

People reported feeling the Sichuan earthquake as far away as Vietnam, Pakistan, and Thailand. In China, numerous buildings collapsed, including a chemical plant that released toxic liquid ammonia after it was damaged. The earthquake also resulted in numerous large landslides across rivers, creating swelling "barrier lakes" that posed flooding threats to millions of people. Chinese engineers used heavy moving equipment and dynamite to drain the barrier lakes.

After the earthquake, scientists used the radar system on Italy's COSMO-SkyMed satellite to assess ground deformation as much as 50 miles (80 kilometers) away from the epicenter (the point on the surface directly above the quake's center). This information was used to help direct rescue missions.

Life below Earth's surface. Further proof that life can survive in conditions previously thought to be uninhabitable came in June, when researchers at Pennsylvania State University in University Park reported finding living bacteria in ice deep below Earth's surface. These bacteria were the latest example of microorganisms known as extremophiles, which thrive in extreme conditions, such as crushing pressure or freezing or nearly boiling temperatures.

Microbiologist Jennifer Loveland-Curtze of Penn State led a team that discovered the bacteria in a *core* (cylindrical sample) of ice drilled out of the Greenland ice sheet. The researchers found living microbes, which they named *Chryseobacterium greenlandensis,* in a section of the core that had been locked in glacial ice for 120,000 years and that had been buried 1.8 miles (2.9 kilometers) below the surface. Proving that the microbes were still alive, Loveland-Curtze grew them in her laboratory by incubating them in a cold, low-nutrient, oxygen-free solution.

In May, biogeologist R. John Parkes of Cardiff University in Wales reported finding extremophile microorganisms living at temperatures near the boiling point, between 140 °F and 212 °F (60 °C and 100 °C), in muddy sediment approximately 1 mile (1.6 kilometers) below the sea floor of the Atlantic Ocean. Parkes determined that the sediment, off the coast of Newfoundland, was 111 million years old. Parkes classified the microbes as archaea, which are single-celled, bacteria-like organisms. The archaea were discovered at depths nearly twice that of microbes previously found below the sea floor.

Parkes said that the archaea he found might survive by *metabolizing* (chemically altering) methane, a natural gas. According to Parkes, the discovery of life in such extreme conditions increased the likelihood that microbes might live on other planets, such as Mars.

Runaway greenhouse effect. During the past 500 million years, there have been five major mass extinctions, in which most species of plants and animals disappeared. The greatest mass extinction occurred at the end of the Permian Period, approximately 251 million years ago, when as much as 96 percent of all species died out. In April, geologist Alexei V. Ivanov of the Russian Academy of Sciences in Moscow published results indicating that the main cause of this Permian-Triassic (P-T) extinction was a "runaway greenhouse effect," in which the climate warmed substantially. This warming, according to Ivanov, was caused by the release into the atmosphere of vast amounts of carbon dioxide and methane during an enormous outpouring of volcanic lava. Carbon dioxide and methane are greenhouse gases, which warm Earth's surface by trapping heat like the roof of a greenhouse.

Ivanov reached his conclusion by producing the most accurate measurements to date of the extent of the Siberian Traps, preserved fields of ancient lava in western Siberia that date from the time of the P-T extinction. According to the measurements, the Siberian Traps have an extent of 2.8 million square miles (7.3 square kilometers) and a volume of approximately 960,000 cubic miles (4 million cubic kilometers). These measurements revealed that the Siberian Traps are larger than previously believed, suggesting, in turn, that the greenhouse effect during the P-T extinction was greater than previously thought.

In August, the National Science Foundation launched an international project to further study the Siberian Traps. This five-year project, led by geologist Linda Elkins-Tanton of the Massachusetts Institute of Technology in Cambridge, involved 28 scientists from seven countries.

■ Henry T. Mullins

See also **Biology; China; Disasters.**

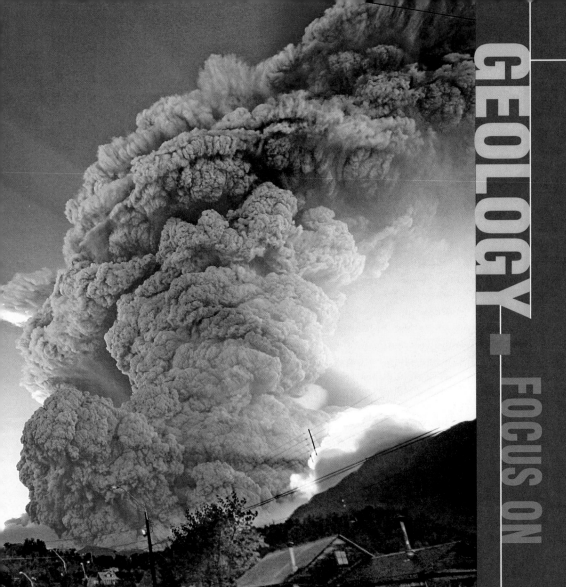

A thick cloud of smoke, steam, and ash released by the volcanic eruption on May 6 rises high over the town of Chaitén, Chile, which is 6.2 miles (10 kilometers) from the volcano. The plume eventually rose as high as 55,000 feet (16,800 meters) and drifted eastward over the Andes Mountains into Argentina.

The Chaitén volcano in southern Chile erupted in May 2008 for the first time in approximately 9,000 years.

Bolts of lightning dramatically highlight an electrical storm above and around Chaitén volcano on May 2. The storm was sparked by a cloud of hot ash as it rose through the cooler air. This temperature difference resulted in a movement of *electrons* (negatively charged particles), which acted like a *capacitor* (storage device) to cause the huge electrical discharges.

A mudflow cuts a twisting course through the town of Chaitén on June 3. The mudflow, which drained into the nearby Chaitén River, was caused by heavy rains carrying ash from the volcano. The eruption, combined with the flooding, destroyed many properties and led to the evacuation of thousands of people.

Georgia experienced a tumultuous year in 2008. The victories of incumbent President Mikheil Saakashvili in January presidential elections and of his ruling United National Movement in May parliamentary elections led to massive opposition protests. In August, the Georgian government's attempt to reassert control over the breakaway province of South Ossetia sparked armed conflict with Russia.

Elections. Georgia held early presidential elections on January 5. Saakashvili had called the snap election after street protests by the opposition led him to declare a state of emergency the previous November. The Central Election Commission declared Saakashvili the winner with 53.5 percent of the vote. His closest challenger, opposition leader Levan Gachechiladze, took 25.7 percent. Badri Patarkatsishvili, another Saakashvili critic and a key instigator of the November 2007 demonstrations, received 7.1 percent. Gachechiladze insisted that Saakashvili had rigged the election results and thousands of his supporters protested in the capital city of Tbilisi on Jan. 6, 2008. Election observers from the Organization for Security and Co-operation in Europe (OSCE) criticized the election for ballot-box stuffing, instances of multiple voting, and other irregularities.

Saakashvili's United National Movement won a strong majority of seats in parliamentary elections on May 21, taking 59.2 percent of the vote. The United Opposition bloc trailed with only 17.7 percent. The Christian Democrats and the Labor Party also cleared the 7-percent threshold for parliamentary representation, earning 8.7 and 7.4 percent of the vote, respectively. The OSCE gave a generally positive assessment of the election but noted further instances of ballot-box stuffing and other irregularities. The announcement of the results triggered another large opposition rally in front of the parliament building in Tbilisi, and the United Opposition bloc boycotted the opening session of parliament on June 7.

Conflict with Russia. Tensions rose between the Russian and Georgian governments in early 2008 over the breakaway Georgian provinces of Abkhazia and South Ossetia, both of which have large populations of Russian citizens. In response to Kosovo's *secession* (withdrawal) from Serbia and its recognition by the West in February, the Russian government moved to increase its ties with the two provinces. On March 28, Saakashvili offered greater autonomy to Abkhazia, but the republic's president, Sergei Bagapsh, repeated demands for full independence.

On August 7, as relations deteriorated, the Georgian military shelled the South Ossetian capital of Tskhinvali. Saakashvili claimed that Georgia did so in response to Russian and South Ossetian military provocations. Russian armed forces responded by occupying Tskhinvali and sending troops into undisputed Georgian territory, including the strategically located cities of Gori and Poti. The Russian government also formally recognized the independence of Abkhazia and South Ossetia on August 26.

The Georgian government broke diplomatic relations with Russia in response on August 29, and Russia immediately reciprocated. The United States government vigorously supported its ally Saakashvili and condemned Russia for employing disproportionate force in the conflict. European Union (EU) president and French leader Nicolas Sarkozy successfully negotiated a settlement that required the Russian military to pull back to pre-conflict positions and placed EU peacekeepers in a 4-mile (7-kilometer) buffer zone around the Abkhaz and South Ossetian borders.

In the aftermath of the conflict, Saakashvili dismissed Prime Minister Lado Gurgenidze and Zaza Gogava, his military chief of staff. The clash over the breakaway regions weakened Saakashvili's political position by undermining Georgia's efforts to join the North Atlantic Treaty Organization (NATO). The fight also demonstrated that the Georgian military could not compete with Russia's armed forces and gave Russia greater influence in Abkhazia and South Ossetia.   ■ Juliet Johnson

See also **Europe; Russia.**

Germany. The "grand coalition" government of Chancellor Angela Merkel—comprised of the Christian Democratic Union (CDU) and the Social Democratic Party (SPD)—remained in power in 2008. However, the coalition's ability to govern was increasingly questioned as Merkel, of the CDU, and Vice Chancellor and Foreign Minister Frank-Walter Steinmeier, of the SPD, prepared to face each other as their party's respective candidates for chancellor in national elections slated for September 2009. The government's plan to eliminate the budget deficit by 2011 had to be put aside in fall 2008, as Germany fell into recession during the global financial crisis.

Initially, German Finance Minister Peer Steinbrück viewed the financial crisis as primarily an "American problem." In early November, the government propped up several of the country's largest banks—including the second largest bank, Commerzbank—with a loan guarantee package of $630 billion. As the "problem" began to affect the global economy, the European Central Bank pressured Germany—the largest economy in the European Union (EU)—to enact a large fiscal stimulus package. (The EU is Europe's main political and economic organization.) The government, however, was reluctant to run up large new deficits, and neither coalition partner wanted to anger voters before the upcoming election. Nevertheless, on December 5, parliament passed a $29-billion stimulus package that included tax breaks on new cars and credit assistance for struggling businesses.

Changing party landscape. The inability of the grand coalition to take a strong lead during turbulent times seemed to discredit both parties in the eyes of voters and resulted in losses in several state elections during 2008. In Bavaria, the long-dominant, right-of-center Christian Social Union (the sister party of the CDU) performed poorly, losing its absolute majority for the first time in 46 years. The opposition SPD also lost votes, garnering a mere 18.6 percent. In Hesse, the locally dominant CDU, after running a campaign critical of foreigners, lost to the SPD, which nevertheless failed to win a majority of the votes. Negotiations with the Greens and the Left Party (comprised of former East German Communists and disgruntled West German Social Democrats) to form an SPD minority government collapsed; new elections were scheduled for January 2009. In elections in Lower Saxony in 2008, the SPD received only 30 percent of the vote, its worst performance since World War II (1939-1945).

According to political observers, such results suggest a significant change in Germany's political landscape, with smaller parties gaining in popularity at the expense of the larger, traditional parties. Although Angela Merkel retained her popularity as chancellor during 2008 and was to be the CDU's candidate in 2009, the SPD fell into disarray. After surveys showed that less than a fifth of the German public backs the party, SPD leader Kurt Beck resigned. He was replaced with Foreign Minister and SPD candidate for chancellor Frank-Walter Steinmeier. The Social Democrats found themselves caught between their participation as junior partner in the federal government, where they get little credit for the government's accomplishments, and criticism from the Left Party that the SPD has shifted away from its working class origins. The SPD has hesitated to work with the Left Party in forming governments at the state level and refused to do so at the federal level. The CDU, for its part, has been exploring the possibility of new coalition partners, especially the Greens, with whom it governs Hamburg.

Foreign policy. In 2008, Germany often replaced France as the United States's most difficult ally. To stabilize the government of Afghanistan, the German government contributed over 4,500 soldiers to the mission of the North Atlantic Treaty Organization (NATO—the main security alliance of the West). However, Germany refused to allow its troops to engage in combat by keeping them out of the dangerous southern part of Afghanistan. German public opinion favored abandoning the mission altogether.

Regarding Iran, Germany worked with the United States and other United Nations Security Council members to pressure the Islamic republic to comply with Security Council resolutions to ensure that its nuclear energy program is not a weapons program. Germany's leaders hesitated, however, to join other Western countries in calling for tougher economic sanctions. As the West's biggest exporter to Iran, Germany has economic interests in sustaining trade relations.

At the NATO summit in April, Germany resisted the U.S.-led initiative to more quickly grant membership in the organization to Ukraine and Georgia. German officials maintained that such a move would needlessly anger the Russians, who still resented the expansion of NATO into former allies in Eastern Europe. When Russia sent its army into a breakaway region of Georgia in August, Germany maintained that both sides shared blame, though most countries in the West condemned the invasion. Experts maintain that Germany's attitudes on these issues reflect its dependence on Russia for more than a third of its oil and natural gas.

Economy. Because of the global economic crisis, EU economists forecast that Germany's economy would grow by only 1.7 percent in 2008, compared with 2.5 percent in 2007. ■ Jeffrey Kopstein

See also **Economics, World; Europe; Georgia**.

Ghana. See Africa.

Global warming. Sea ice in the Arctic Ocean narrowly missed setting a record for minimum coverage in summer 2008. In September, the National Snow and Ice Data Center (NSIDC) reported that the summer ice cover was the second lowest since satellites began monitoring the area in 1979. In 2008, the ice exceeded 2007 levels—the lowest ever recorded—by only 9.4 percent. The 2008 summer ice cover was also 34 percent smaller than the average from 1979 to 2000. The NSIDC is a scientific information management organization affiliated with the University of Colorado at Boulder.

Scientists at the NSIDC also reported in March 2008 that perennial ice covered less than 30 percent of the Arctic Ocean during the previous winter. The long-term average extent for this old, thick ice, which lasts through the summer, is from 50 to 60 percent. Because thinner ice melts more rapidly than perennial ice, the decline of perennial ice raises the chances of a larger summer ice melt.

Permafrost. Reduced ice cover is causing *permafrost* (permanently frozen soil) in the Arctic to thaw more quickly than expected, according to a June analysis. Much of the permafrost in the Arctic has been frozen for thousands of years, but it may melt as the Arctic warms. The study found that the warming rate tripled over land during periods when sea ice was melting rapidly.

Several studies in 2008 warned that thawing permafrost could release vast quantities of greenhouse gases into the atmosphere. A September study in the journal *Bioscience* more than doubled previous estimates of the carbon stored in permafrost. The study found that permafrost holds 1.8 trillion tons (1.6 trillion metric tons) of carbon, about twice as much the gas as there is in the atmosphere. Up to 80 percent of this carbon could be released during thawing, the study warned.

Scientists also worried that thawing permafrost may release huge amounts of methane, which is a more potent greenhouse gas than carbon dioxide. However, much uncertainty remained among scientists on how quickly permafrost may thaw and on how much greenhouse gas the thawing permafrost may release.

Pause in rising temperatures. In June, temperature readings of the lower part of the tropical atmosphere showed the fifth-lowest level in the past 30 years. The measurements were made using satellite data by scientists at the University of Alabama in Huntsville and at Remote Sensing Systems, a company in Santa Rosa, California. According to the scientists, the findings suggest that though average global surface temperatures remained at high levels, the recent surge of global warming that began in the 1970's paused in 2008. The reason for and likely duration of this decline remained unknown.

Ocean temperatures. While surface air temperatures have been among the hottest on record in the past five years, data from over 3,100 buoys deployed in the world's oceans indicate that the heat content of the water has declined slightly during the same period. The Argo drifting buoys, operated by scientists from 27 countries, continuously measure temperature to a depth of 6,500 feet (2,000 meters). These measurements allow scientists to calculate the quantity of heat in the upper ocean. Because the vast majority of the solar energy that reaches Earth's atmosphere is stored in the ocean, accurately measuring the warmth of the ocean is a key to understanding patterns of long-term global warming and cooling.

The lack of warming observed by the buoys is a mystery to the scientists involved in analyzing the data. They speculated that heat may be escaping to outer space or being stored deeper in the ocean. Josh Willis of NASA's Jet Propulsion Laboratory (JPL) in Pasadena, California, stressed that, "Global warming doesn't mean that every year will be warmer than the last."

In early 2008, a pattern of sea-surface temperatures known as the Pacific Decadal Oscillation (PDO) shifted to a cold phase, according to JPL researchers. Scientists believe the PDO affects Pacific and Atlantic hurricane activity, the occurrence of droughts and flooding around the Pacific basin, agricultural growing seasons, and global temperature patterns. The cold phase of the PDO is characterized by a large pool of cooler-than-normal water that extends from the Gulf of Alaska along the west coast of North America to the tropical central Pacific.

Phases of the PDO can last as long as 20 to 30 years. The current warm phase began in 1977. In contrast, other Pacific Ocean temperature patterns, including El Niño and La Niña, occur every 3 to 7 years and last from about 6 to 18 months.

Some climatologists believe that the warm phase of the PDO contributed to the rise in global temperatures that occurred during the second half of the 1900's. The cold phase may limit global warming over the next decade, scientists speculated. However, they stressed that a cold-phase PDO would not change long-term predictions for global warming.

G-8 agreement. In July 2008, leaders of the Group of 8 (G-8) countries pledged to reduce emissions of heat-trapping greenhouse gases by 50 percent by 2050. The G-8 consists of the most developed economies in the world, including Japan. Environmentalists criticized the reduction level promised by the G-8 governments as well as the lengthy deadline.   ■ Fred Gadomski

See also **Conservation.**

Golf. Tiger Woods captured just one major in 2008. However, his triumph at the United States Open in a stunning play-off was considered by many to be among his greatest achievements.

After finishing second at the Masters, Woods underwent left knee surgery for an injury suffered while running in fall 2007 and sat out for two months before returning for the U.S. Open on June 16, 2008, in San Diego. Playing in obvious pain and limping, Woods moved ahead in the third round, then gave up the lead on the final Sunday, only to force an 18-hole play-off round on Monday. Woods's two-putt par on the 19th hole of the play-off gave him his 14th career major.

Two days after his victory, Woods revealed he had been playing with a double stress fracture of his left tibia suffered while rehabilitating from his knee surgery. He underwent surgery to repair his left knee and sat out the rest of the 2008 season.

Men's professional golf. Vijay Singh won the Professional Golfers' Association (PGA) Tour's FedEx Cup, a four-tournament play-off at the end of the season to determine the points leader. He collected a $10-million annuity.

Trevor Immelman captured the Masters on April 13 in Augusta, Georgia, leading from beginning to end and finishing with an 8-under 280. His victory over Woods was his first major.

Padraig Harrington fought through a painful

wrist injury to outduel Australian Greg Norman and win the British Open on July 20 in Southport, England. Harrington, of Ireland, finished at 3-over 283, four shots ahead of Ian Polter. Norman fell to third on the final round. The 53-year-old Norman thus failed to become the oldest major winner in history. Harrington then won the final major of the season, the PGA Championship, on August 10 in Bloomfield Township, Michigan. Harrington, trailing by three shots, shot a 4-under on the final day for a two-shot victory.

Ryder Cup. The United States defeated a heavily favored European team 16 ½ points to 11 ½ points at the Valhalla Country Club in Louisville, Kentucky, on September 19-21. The victory returned the cup to the United States for the first time since 1999.

LPGA. Annika Sorenstam retired at the end of the 2008 season. Sorenstam won 10 majors and 72 events on the Ladies Professional Golf Association (LPGA) tour. Mexico's Lorena Ochoa captured the first major of 2008 with a convincing five-stroke victory at the Kraft Nabisco Championship in Rancho Mirage, California, on April 6. Ochoa, who won three of the season's first four events, won with an 11-under 277.

Yani Tseng of Taiwan started the run of Asian women winning majors at the LPGA Championship on June 8. Tseng, a rookie on the LPGA circuit, captured the tournament in Havre de Grace, Maryland, on the fourth play-off hole to beat Maria Hjorth. The two had tied at 12-under 276. Inbee Park, 19, of South Korea became the youngest U.S. Women's Open champion on June 29 with a 9-under 283. The four-stroke victory in Edina, Minnesota, was her first on the LPGA tour. On August 3, Ji-Yai Shin of South Korea captured the final major, the Women's British Open, with an 18-under 270 in Sunningdale, England. She beat Tseng by three shots.

Champions Tour. On the tour for men more than 50 years old, Jay Haas won his second Senior PGA Championship in three years with a one-shot victory in Rochester, New York. Bruce Vaughn captured the Senior British Open on July 27, sinking a 20-foot (1.5-meter) putt on the first play-off hole to beat John Cook in Troon, Scotland. Eduardo Romero cruised to the U.S. Senior Open title on August 3 in Colorado Springs, Colorado, earning a four-shot victory with a 6-under 274.

Fred Funk finished with a 19-under 269 to win The Tradition, on August 17 in Sunriver, Oregon, by three strokes. In the final major of the year—the Senior Players Championship in Timonium, Maryland, on October 12—D. A. Weibring won, defeating Funk by one stroke. ■ Michael Kates

See also **Sports**.

Great Britain. See **United Kingdom**.

Greece. Prime Minister Kostas Karamanlis's center-right New Democracy government ruled with a mere two-seat majority in 2008. Karamanlis's party was weakened by internal dissent but faced an equally divided opposition in the Panhellenic Socialist Party (PASOK). In March, despite wide-scale union protests, Karamanlis's government pushed through changes in public administration and a pension reform package designed to decrease corruption and encourage people to work longer. However, the government's narrow majority made it difficult to implement the proposed changes.

Corruption. The New Democracy government confronted allegations in January that senior officials in the culture ministry were bribed to turn a blind eye to property developers' plans for construction on culturally protected sites. In July, a Greek prosecutor filed charges in a case in which the German electronics firm Siemens was accused of contributing money to Greek officials through offshore companies to seal contracts supplying security equipment for the 2004 Olympic Games in Athens. Also in July 2008, the chief of Greece's antimoney-laundering unit was dismissed after the judiciary would not back his probe into a scandal involving overpayment for government bonds by a state pension fund.

Riots broke out in Athens on December 6, after a police bullet killed a 15-year-old student who was taking part in an anarchist-led demon-

Protesters hang giant banners before the Parthenon in Athens on December 17. The weeks of demonstrations—the most violent and widespread in Greece in decades—were sparked when a teenager was killed by a police bullet in Athens on December 6.

stration. Violent unrest shook the country for weeks. The demonstrators torched government buildings, police stations, and hundreds of businesses. Karamanlis was unwilling to impose such tough measures as curfews in fear of inciting greater violence. In addition, police were unable to restore order by pursuing the demonstrators onto university campuses because they were prohibited by a decades-old law from doing so.

The protests soon evolved into an expression of disapproval of the government's economic, social, and educational policies. Political analysts maintained that successive governments had failed to address the concerns of young people, from the poor quality of education provided by highly politicized universities to the absence of good jobs for those who complete their studies. Opposition politicians called for Karamanlis to resign.

Economy. Despite the global economic crisis, Karamanlis's government passed a belt-tightening budget in December to try to reduce the country's high debt. European Union economists forecast that Greece's economic growth would decline from 4.0 percent in 2007 to 3.1 percent in 2008.   ■ Jeffrey Kopstein

See also **Europe**.

Grenada. See Latin America; West Indies.

Guatemala. On Jan. 14, 2008, Álvaro Colom Caballeros of the National Union of Hope party was sworn in as president. Colom, a social democrat, was Guatemala's first left-of-center chief executive since 1954. He defeated the right-wing retired general, Pérez Molina, in a tight election. Colom was best known for his efforts to bring home 40,000 refugees who had been displaced during the country's 36-year civil war, which ended in 1996.

Guatemala had one of Latin America's highest murder rates and was a major transit route for the cocaine trade. Colom pledged to fight crime and poverty by creating jobs and improving education and health care. His vice president, Rafael Espada, was once a cardiac surgeon at the Methodist DeBakey Heart Center in Houston.

Ex-president extradited. In October 2008, former Guatemalan president Alfonso Portillo was extradited from Mexico to face longstanding corruption charges in his native country. Upon the end of his presidency in 2004, Portillo fled Guatemala after being charged with embezzling more than $15 million in public funds.
■ Nathan A. Haverstock

See also **Latin America**.

Guinea. See Africa.

Guinea-Bissau. See Africa.

Guyana. See Latin America.

Haiti. Two tropical storms and two hurricanes devastated Haiti in 2008, killing at least 800 people. The storms destroyed 60 percent of the nation's agriculture and washed away roads, bridges, and homes. Haiti's infrastructure was so badly damaged it often took weeks to reach stranded Haitians with supplies.

Schools collapse. On November 7, 92 people died when a high school collapsed near the capital, Port-au-Prince. The hillside school was built with little structural steel or cement and had partially collapsed in 2000. The owner of the church school was arrested. On Nov. 12, 2008, a second school collapsed in the city, but most of the children were at recess, and no one was killed.

Political stalemate broken. Haitian lawmakers ratified the selection of Michèle Pierre-Louis as prime minister on July 31, after three months of political deadlock. She faced the daunting task of calming tensions following bloody food riots that led to her predecessor's ouster in April. Seven people were killed in the riots, including a member of the United Nations peacekeeping force stationed in Haiti. The price of rice, beans, and fruit had gone up 50 percent since 2007.   ■ Nathan A. Haverstock

See also **Disasters; Food: A Special Report; Latin America; West Indies**.

Harness racing. See Horse racing.

Health care issues. The United States presidential campaign and various state initiatives dominated health care issues in 2008. Arizona Senator John McCain, the Republican candidate for president, supported extending coverage to more Americans through tax credits and encouraging individuals to purchase their own insurance; he also sought to end tax benefits for employers who offer coverage to employees. Illinois Senator Barack Obama, the Democratic nominee, supported a broader role for government in extending coverage, stronger regulation of private insurers, and required coverage of all children.

Obama appointments. After winning the election on November 4, President-elect Obama nominated former Senator Tom Daschle (D., South Dakota) to be secretary of the U. S. Department of Health and Human Services and director of the new White House Office of Health Reform. Obama also named health policy analyst Jeanne Lambrew as deputy director of the new agency.

State elections. Washington state voters approved legalizing "physician-assisted suicide" in the November elections. The initiative allows Washington physicians to prescribe fatal doses of various pharmaceuticals for terminally ill patients. Arizona voters defeated a ballot measure that would have prevented the establishment of a government-run universal insurance system.

Voters in Michigan approved the use of marijuana for certain medical conditions, the 13th state to do so. Michigan voters also approved stem-cell research, which previously had been heavily restricted. (The discovery and isolation of embryonic stem cells in 1998 led to debate over whether it is moral to use cells taken from human embryos for research. The embryos are destroyed in the process of isolating the stem cells, which many people consider wrong; other people believe that the potential medical benefits of stem cells justify their use.)

Congressional actions. In May, U.S. President George W. Bush signed a measure protecting people from losing their jobs or health insurance because they are at genetic risk of certain diseases. In July, Congress overrode President Bush's veto of a bill designed to prevent cuts in payments to physicians by the Medicare program, which pays some health care costs for persons over age 65 and for other groups.

In October, Congress passed a law requiring private insurers to treat mental illness the same as other conditions. In the past, insurers had provided less coverage for mental diseases than for physical ailments.

After the election, Senator Max Baucus (D., Montana), chairman of the Senate Finance Committee, announced a plan for universal coverage and greater efficiency in health care. Senator Edward Kennedy (D., Massachusetts), a longtime proponent of universal coverage, gave up his seat on the Senate Judiciary Committee to concentrate on health care reform as chairman of the Senate Health, Education, Labor, and Pensions Committee.

Children's health insurance. In 2007, President Bush had signed a temporary extension of the State Children's Health Insurance Program (SCHIP) to last through March 2009; SCHIP was designed as a federal/state partnership, similar to Medicaid—which covers health costs for very poor and disabled people—with the goal of expanding health insurance to children whose families earn too much money to be eligible for Medicaid but not enough money to purchase private insurance. Its extension beyond March 2009 was expected to be a high priority for the incoming Congress.

State programs. In 2008, Massachusetts continued to develop its universal health care coverage program, which required all state citizens to have health insurance. (The state provides subsidies to people who are unable to afford private health insurance.) As of October, 439,000 previously uninsured people had obtained insurance since the program was begun in 2006. However, high costs threatened continued progress. New Jersey implemented the first phase of a universal coverage program, which required coverage of all children. In California, the state Assembly passed a universal coverage proposal, but the Senate voted it down. As state budgets tightened in the 2008 recession, many states cut Medicaid benefits.

Uninsured decline. In August, the U.S. Census Bureau announced that 45.7 million Americans lacked health insurance in 2007, a slight drop from 2006. Analysts cited increased state health care coverage for the decline. Texas had the highest rate—24.8 percent—of uninsured residents; Massachusetts had the lowest rate—7.9 percent.

Food and Drug Administration (FDA). The embattled FDA, which is charged with ensuring the safety of foods and medications in the United States, had a challenging year in 2008. An outbreak of food poisoning caused by *Salmonella* bacteria sickened more than 1,400 people; it eventually was linked to vegetables grown and packed in Mexico. Batches of the drug heparin were found to be tainted in 2008, killing at least 19 people. The contamination came from an ingredient manufactured in China. As a result, the FDA in November opened inspection offices in China. In October, eight FDA scientists, in a letter to Congress, accused the agency of sloppy oversight and misconduct.   ■ Emily Friedman

See also **Drugs; Food; Medicine; Public health.**

Hobbies. See **Toys and games.**

NATIONAL HOCKEY LEAGUE STANDINGS

WESTERN CONFERENCE

Central Division

	W.	L.	OTW.†	OTL.††	Pts.
Detroit Red Wings*	54	21	7	7	115
Nashville Predators*	41	32	8	9	91
Chicago Blackhawks	40	34	9	8	88
Columbus Blue Jackets	34	36	5	12	80
St. Louis Blues	33	36	4	13	79

Northwest Division

Minnesota Wild*	44	28	9	8	98
Colorado Avalanche*	44	31	11	7	95
Calgary Flames*	42	30	6	10	94
Edmonton Oilers	41	35	19	6	88
Vancouver Canucks	39	33	10	10	88

Pacific Division

San Jose Sharks*	49	23	9	10	108
Anaheim Ducks*	47	27	12	8	102
Dallas Stars*	45	30	8	7	97
Phoenix Coyotes	38	37	9	7	83
Los Angeles Kings	32	43	7	7	71

EASTERN CONFERENCE

Northeast Division

	W.	L.	OTW.	OTL.	Pts.
Montreal Canadiens*	47	25	10	10	104
Ottawa Senators*	43	31	6	8	94
Boston Bruins*	41	29	9	12	94
Buffalo Sabres	39	31	9	12	90
Toronto Maple Leafs	36	35	8	11	83

Atlantic Division

Pittsburgh Penguins*	47	27	8	8	102
New Jersey Devils*	46	29	15	7	99
New York Rangers*	42	27	12	13	97
Philadelphia Flyers*	42	29	6	11	95
New York Islanders	35	38	10	9	79

Southeast Division

Washington Capitals*	43	31	11	8	94
Carolina Hurricanes	43	33	7	6	92
Florida Panthers	38	35	9	9	85
Atlanta Thrashers	34	40	15	8	76
Tampa Bay Lightning	31	42	4	9	71

*Made play-offs   †Overtime wins   ††Overtime losses

STANLEY CUP CHAMPIONS—Detroit Red Wings
(defeated Pittsburgh Penguins, 4 games to 2)

LEADING SCORERS	Games	Goals	Assists	Pts.
Patrick Kane, Chicago	82	21	51	72
Scott Gomez, New York R	81	16	54	70
Zach Parise, New Jersey	81	32	33	65
Dustin Brown, Los Angeles	78	33	27	60
Brian Rolston, Minnesota	81	31	28	59

LEADING GOALIES (26 or more games)	Games	Goals against	Avg.
Ryan Miller, Buffalo	76	197	2.64
Tim Thomas, Boston	57	136	2.44
Rick Dipietro, New York I	63	174	2.82
Ty Conklin, Pittsburgh	33	78	2.51

AWARDS

Adams Award (coach of the year)—Bruce Boudreau, Washington

Calder Trophy (best rookie)—Patrick Kane, Chicago

Clancy Trophy (leadership)—Vincent Lecavalier, Tampa Bay

Conn Smythe Trophy (Most Valuable Player in Stanley Cup)— Henrik Zetterberg, Detroit

Hart Trophy (Most Valuable Player)—Alex Ovechkin, Washington

Jennings Trophy (goalkeeper[s] for team with fewest goals against)—Chris Osgood and Dominik Hasek, Detroit

Lady Byng Trophy (sportsmanship)—Pavel Datsyuk, Detroit

Masterton Trophy (perseverance, dedication to hockey)— Jason Blake, Toronto

Norris Trophy (best defenseman)—Nicklas Lidstrom, Detroit

Pearson Award (best player as voted by NHL players)— Alex Ovechkin, Washington

Ross Trophy (leading scorer)—Alex Ovechkin, Washington

Selke Trophy (best defensive forward)—Pavel Datsyuk, Detroit

Vezina Trophy (best goalkeeper)—Martin Brodeur, New Jersey

Hockey. In the National Hockey League (NHL) in 2008, the Detroit Red Wings captured their fourth Stanley Cup in 11 years by beating the Pittsburgh Penguins 3-2 on June 4 in Pittsburgh. Swedish players made a huge impact for Detroit, which had its best regular season on record. Defenseman Nicklas Lidstrom became the first European captain of a Stanley Cup champion team. Henrik Zetterberg, who had a goal and assist in the Cup clincher and 27 play-off points, won the Conn Smythe Trophy as the play-off's Most Valuable Player.

Play-offs. Detroit made it to the Stanley Cup Finals by defeating the Dallas Stars 4 games to 2 in the Western Conference Finals. Detroit had swept Colorado in the conference semifinals and slipped past Nashville 4 games to 2. Dallas eliminated defending champion Anaheim in the first round. Pittsburgh swept Ottawa in the first round, eliminated the New York Rangers 4 games to 1 in the Eastern Conference semifinals, and beat Philadelphia 4 games to 1 in the conference Finals.

In the Stanley Cup Finals, Detroit captured the first two games at home by a 7-0 cumulative margin but lost Game 3 at Pittsburgh. Detroit won Game 4 and appeared poised to close out the series on June 2 leading 3-2 late in the final minute of Game 5 in Detroit. But the Penguins scored with 34.3 seconds left and then won the game in triple overtime to stay alive. The Red Wings jumped out to a 3-1 lead in the decisive Game 6, but the Penguins scored with 1:27 to play and nearly tied the game in the final second.

Regular season. In the Western Conference, the Red Wings was the only team to have more than 49 wins, finishing with 54 and a league-best 115 points to win the Central Division and secure home ice advantage. San Jose won 49 games and had 108 points to win the Pacific. Minnesota, with 44 wins and 98 points, won the Northwest. In the Eastern Conference, Montreal and Pittsburgh each had 47 wins, but the Canadiens took the top seed and the Northeast Division with 104 points. Pittsburgh won the Atlantic with 102 points, and Washington won 43 games and had 94 points to capture the Southeast.

World championships. Russia beat Canada 5-4 in overtime in Quebec City, Canada, on May 18 to win its first championship since 1993. The United States upset Canada 4-3 in Harbin, China, on April 12, 2008, for its second women's world championship.

Colleges. After finishing second the last two years, Boston College captured its third men's National Collegiate Athletic Association title with a 4-1 win over Notre Dame on April 12 in Denver. The University of Minnesota (Duluth) women's team defeated the University of Wisconsin (Madison) 4-1 on March 22 in Duluth.   ■ Michael Kates

Honduras. See Latin America.

Horse racing.
Thoroughbred racing in 2008 looked like it would have its first Triple Crown winner since Affirmed claimed the title in 1978. But after dominating performances in the first two of the Triple Crown races in 2008—winning by about five lengths in both the Kentucky Derby and the Preakness Stakes—Big Brown faltered in the Belmont Stakes. He finished last after a nail dislodged and his rear right shoe worked itself loose.

With his victory on September 27 in the Jockey Club Gold Cup in Elmont, New York, Curlin became the first North American horse to break the $10-million mark. The 4-year-old colt's 11th victory in 15 races earned him $450,000 and pushed his career earnings to $10,246,800. Cigar held the previous mark of $9,999,815, set in 1996.

In harness racing, Enough Talk became the first trotter to break 1 minute, 50 seconds when he ran 1:49.3 on Oct. 11, 2008, in New Kent, Virginia, in the Patriot Invitational.

Three-year-olds. On May 3, jockey Kent Desormeaux won his third Kentucky Derby, riding favorite Big Brown to victory. Big Brown was the seventh undefeated horse to win the Kentucky Derby. Filly Eight Belles, who finished second, broke both front ankles shortly after finishing the race and was euthanized on the track. In the Preakness Stakes on May 17 at Baltimore's Pimlico Race Course, Big Brown coasted to a 5 ¼-length victory. But at the 140th running of the Belmont Stakes on June 7 in Elmont, a stunned crowd of 94,476 watched 38-to-1 shot Da'Tara win the race.

International racing. Curlin captured the $6-million World Cup on March 29 in Dubai, United Arab Emirates, by a record-setting 7 ¾

Big Brown, ridden by jockey Kent Desormeaux, captures a first-place finish at the Preakness Stakes at the Pimlico Race Track in Baltimore on May 17, 2008, winning by about five lengths. Big Brown also won the Kentucky Derby but finished last in the third race of the Triple Crown, the Belmont Stakes, after a nail dislodged and his rear right shoe became loose.

MAJOR HORSE RACES OF 2008

THOROUGHBRED RACING

Race	Winner	Value to Winner
Belmont Stakes	Da' Tara	$600,000
Blue Grass Stakes	Monba	$465,000
Breeders' Cup Classic	Raven's Pass	$2,700,000
Breeders' Cup Ladies' Classic	Zenyatta	$1,080,000
Breeders' Cup Mile	Goldikova	$1,080,000
Breeders' Cup Dirt Mile	Albertus Maximus	$540,000
Breeders' Cup Sprint	Midnight Lute	$1,080,000
Breeders' Cup Turf	Conduit	$1,620,000
Breeders' Cup Turf Sprint	Desert Code	$540,000
Breeders' Cup Marathon	Muhannak	$270,000
Breeders' Cup Filly & Mare Sprint	Ventura	$540,000
Breeders' Cup Filly & Mare Turf	Forever Together	$1,080,000
Breeders' Cup Fillies Turf	Maram	$540,000
Breeders' Cup Juvenile	Midshipman	$1,080,000
Breeders' Cup Juvenile Fillies	Stardom Bound	$1,080,000
Breeders' Cup Juvenile Turf	Donativum	$540,000
Canadian International Stakes	Marsh Side	$1,200,000
Epsom Derby (United Kingdom)	New Approach	£802,444
Dubai World Cup (United Arab Emirates)	Curlin	$3,500,000
Haskell Invitational Stakes	Big Brown	$600,000
Hollywood Gold Cup Stakes	Mast Track	$450,000
Irish Derby (Ireland)	Frozen Fire	€843,000
Jockey Club Gold Cup	Curlin	$450,000
Kentucky Derby	Big Brown	$1,400,000
Kentucky Oaks	Proud Spell	$300,000
King George VI and Queen Elizabeth Diamond Stakes (United Kingdom)	Duke of Marmalade	£450,000
Lane's End Stakes	Adriano	$300,000
Melbourne Cup	Viewed	$2,100,000 ($3,300,000 Australian)
Oaklawn Handicap	Tiago	$300,000
Pacific Classic Stakes	Go Between	$600,000
Preakness Stakes	Big Brown	$600,000
Prix de l'Arc de Triomphe (France)	Zarkava	€2,285,600
Santa Anita Derby	Colonel John	$450,000
Santa Anita Handicap	Heatseeker	$600,000
Stephen Foster Handicap	Curlin	$589,000
Travers Stakes	Colonel John	$600,000
Woodbine Mile (Canada)	Rahy's Attorney	$600,000

HARNESS RACING

Race	Winner	Value to Winner
Cane Pace	Art Official	$196,425
Hambletonian	Deweycheatumnhowe	$750,000
Kentucky Futurity	Deweycheatumnhowe	$342,000
Little Brown Jug	Shadow Play	$255,768
Meadowlands Pace	Art Official	$550,000
Messenger Stakes	Somebeach-somewhere	$325,000
Woodrow Wilson	Major In Art	$175,000
Yonkers Trot	Napoleon	$302,927

€ = euro (European Union dollar)

lengths. Sun Classique won the $5 million Dubai Sheema Classic by 2 ¾ lengths over Viva Pataca.

In European racing, Irish horse New Approach won the Epsom Derby on June 7, giving jockey Kevin Manning his first win in England's most prestigious race. Frozen Fire gave trainer Aidan O'Brien his third straight Irish Derby championship at the Curragh Racecourse in Kildare with his victory on June 29. Zarkava won the Prix de l'Arc de Triomphe on October 5 in Paris. Viewed captured the Melbourne Cup on November 4 in Melbourne, Australia, winning in a photo finish.

Harness. Napoleon won the first leg of the trotting triple crown, the Yonkers Trot, on June 28. Deweycheatumnhowe became the first unbeaten winner of the $1.5 million-Hambletonian, posting his 15th straight win at that August 2 race. The horse captured the final leg, the Kentucky Futurity, on October 4. In the pacing triple crown, Art Official captured the Cane Pace on September 1; Shadow Play won the Little Brown Jug on September 18; and Somebeachsomewhere won the Messenger Stakes on October 25. ■ Michael Kates

Hospital. See Health care issues.
Housing. See Building and construction.

Houston. Hurricane Ike dealt a catastrophic blow to the Houston area after making landfall near Galveston on Sept. 13, 2008, drowning the upper Texas coast and battering inland areas with hurricane-force winds. By directly striking the Gulf Coast's most populous area, Ike became one of the costliest hurricanes ever to hit the United States. The storm, which at one point spanned nearly 500 miles (800 kilometers), caused billions of dollars of damage.

Although below major-hurricane status as a Category-2 storm on the Saffir-Simpson scale, Ike produced a massive 10-to-15-foot (3-to-5-meter) storm surge that inundated Galveston Island and Bolivar Peninsula, which lie between Houston and the Gulf of Mexico. The storm killed more than 70 people—including more than 35 in Texas—and flooded about 100,000 homes.

Some of Houston's skyscrapers, including the 75-story JPMorgan Chase Tower, sustained damage when windows were blown out. The high winds also damaged several retractable-roof panels of Reliant Stadium, home of the Houston Texans of the National Football League. The damage forced the team to play all of its games with the roof open during the 2008 season.

Democratic gains in Harris County. Senator Barack Obama (D., Illinois) received nearly 20,000 more votes than Arizona Senator John McCain in Harris County in elections on November 4. Obama's tally marked the first time since

Lyndon B. Johnson's 1964 election that a Democratic presidential candidate won the popular vote in the county. Voters in 2008 also swept 20 Republican state district judges out of the civil and criminal court houses, ending the near-total dominance that Republicans exercised over the county's judicial system since 1994. Most countywide offices remained in the hands of the Republican incumbents, however. Republican Judge Pat Lykos, for example, narrowly defeated her Democratic challenger, former Houston Police Chief C. O. "Brad" Bradford, for the district attorney position in November.

Scandals harm Republicans. Harris County Republicans were battered by scandals throughout 2008. In February, Harris County District Attorney Chuck Rosenthal resigned, citing a combination of prescription drugs that had impaired his judgment. He stepped down three months after it came to light that he had deleted more than 2,500 e-mails that had been subpoenaed in connection with a federal civil rights lawsuit.

In April, a federal judge ordered Rosenthal to pay $18,900 in sanctions after finding him in contempt of court for deleting the e-mails. Also contributing to Rosenthal's downfall was a federal court's release of some of his other e-mails, the content of which included sexually explicit images and allegedly racist content.

Other Republican officeholders also faced trouble in 2008. Sheriff Tommy Thomas came under scrutiny after the death of more than 140 inmates in the Harris County jail system since 2001 triggered a U.S. Department of Justice investigation. Following the court's release of Rosenthal's controversial e-mails, Thomas and his staff tried to delete about 750,000 e-mails, investigators said. The messages were preserved, however, and an investigation revealed that the communications included a number of racial slurs by deputies. Thomas lost his 2008 reelection bid to challenger Adrian Garcia by more than 140,000 votes.

Houston surgeon dies. The city mourned the death of one of its most respected citizens when Michael E. DeBakey, a famed heart surgeon, died on July 11 at the age of 99. For his contributions to Houston's medical center and bringing general acclaim to the region, city officials afforded DeBakey the unprecedented honor of lying in repose at City Hall.

Considered the father of modern heart surgery, DeBakey was credited by some as the greatest surgeon of the 1900's. He invented dozens of procedures and devices used to repair hearts and arteries. Under DeBakey's watch, Baylor College of Medicine grew from a nondescript medical school into one that consistently ranks among the country's 10 best. ■ Eric Berger

See also **Election: A Special Report.**

Human rights. The United States Department of State issued its annual report on international human rights on March 11, 2008. According to the report, countries with unaccountable authoritarian rulers were the most systematic human rights violators. The report singled out North Korea, Myanmar, Iran, Syria, Zimbabwe, Cuba, Belarus, Uzbekistan, Eritrea, and Sudan as having the worst human rights records in 2007. China was also cited as having a poor record. The report acknowledged the international and domestic criticism directed at the United States for its own human rights record, particularly regarding actions taken in its fight against terrorism.

On Jan. 16, 2008, Freedom House, a nongovernmental organization based in Washington, D.C., issued its annual report on political rights and civil liberties worldwide. The report rated 90 countries as "free," 60 countries as "partly free," and 43 countries as "not free." The lowest-rated countries in the "not free" category were Cuba, Libya, Myanmar, North Korea, Somalia, Sudan, Turkmenistan, and Uzbekistan.

Karadzic. On July 21, Serbian authorities captured Radovan Karadzic, the Bosnian Serb leader during the 1992-1995 war in Bosnia-Herzegovina and one of the world's most wanted fugitives. He was sent to the International Criminal Tribunal for the former Yugoslavia in The Hague, the Netherlands, on July 30, 2008, and arraigned the next day on 11 charges of genocide, complicity in genocide, crimes against humanity, and war crimes. He was accused of organizing the 1995 massacre of more than 7,000 Bosniaks (Bosnian Muslims) in Srebrenica. He was also accused of running concentration camps in Bosnia.

Bashir. On July 14, 2008, the prosecutor at the International Criminal Court (ICC) in The Hague filed 10 charges of genocide, crimes against humanity, and war crimes against Sudanese President Umar Hassan al-Bashir and asked for an arrest warrant. Bashir was alleged to have masterminded a genocide campaign involving the widespread murder, forcible transfer, torture, and rape of members of three ethnic groups in Sudan's Darfur region. Members of the groups had begun a rebellion in 2003, prompting government forces and government-backed militias to begin attacking Darfurians. The violence was still in process in 2008. Bashir became the first sitting head of state to be targeted by the ICC.

Bagosora. On December 18, the International Criminal Tribunal for Rwanda in Arusha, Tanzania, convicted Colonel Theoneste Bagosora and two other former Rwandan military officers of genocide, crimes against humanity, and war crimes in connection with the 1994 massacre of 800,000 Rwandans, mostly Tutsi. The three men were sentenced to life in prison. ■ Mike Lewis

Hungary. International institutions including the International Monetary Fund (IMF), the World Bank, and the European Union (EU) contributed more than $25 billion in loans to Hungary in October 2008 after the Hungarian currency, the forint, declined sharply against world currencies. (The IMF is an international organization that provides short-term credit to member nations; the World Bank provides loans to governments for development projects.) Economists had speculated that if the forint were allowed to go into free fall, Hungary's entire financial structure might collapse, just as Iceland's had done weeks before.

The Hungarian economy, burdened by excessive budget deficits, has performed poorly since the mid-2000's. The country's *gross domestic product* (GDP)—the value of all goods and services produced in a country in a year—grew by only 1.3 percent in 2007 and 2.0 percent in 2008.

Politics. The governing coalition of Prime Minister Ferenc Gyurcsany remained in power in 2008 but suffered major political setbacks. In March, Hungarian voters overwhelmingly rejected the government's reforms involving increased fees for doctor visits, hospital stays, and university tuition—all part of an austerity program intended to reign in Hungary's outsized deficit. The referendum had been called by Gyurcsany's political opponents in parliament.

Following the referendum, Prime Minister Gyurcsany dismissed his government's health minister, a member of the Liberal Party, a partner in his governing coalition. As a result, Liberal members of parliament (MP's) withdrew from the government. However, Liberal MP's continued to support the government on critical votes in parliament, such as confidence motions.

Relations between Hungary and Slovakia, Hungary's northern neighbor, remained tense in 2008. The crux of the tension was the status of Slovakia's large Hungarian minority. The Hungarian government claimed that since Slovak Prime minister Robert Fico came to power in 2006 with the ultranationalist Slovak National Party in his governing coalition, the situation of Slovakia's Hungarian minority had deteriorated.

An incident in a southern Slovak town in November 2008 inflamed public opinion in Hungary. Violence between Slovak and Hungarian fans at a soccer match resulted in forceful intervention by Slovak police and scores of injuries to spectators. In Budapest, Hungary's capital, demonstrators burned the Slovak flag in front of the Slovak embassy. The Hungarian government called on Slovak officials to investigate the police response to determine if it was "proportional" to the violence.   ■ Sharon L. Wolchik

See also **Europe; Iceland; Slovakia.**

Ice skating. Jeff Buttle in 2008 became the first Canadian man to win a world title in more than a decade at the World Championships. Japan's Mao Asada captured her first world title. The American skaters struggled to win just one medal, with Johnny Weir's bronze saving the Americans from coming home empty-handed for the first time since 1994.

World Championships. In Göteborg, Sweden, Asada fell on the opening triple axel of her long program on March 20, 2008, but collected herself to land the rest of her jumps. She finished with a score of 185.56 points. Carolina Kostner of Italy finished second. South Korea's Yu-Na Kim took the bronze for the second straight year.

In the men's competition, Buttle's performances came under criticism because he did not attempt a quad—four-revolution jump—even though it is a regular part of most men's programs. The judges did not seem to mind, as Buttle won the gold on March 22 with 245.17 points, nearly 14 points ahead of defending champion Brian Joubert of France. Weir was third.

German skaters won both world titles in pairs. On March 19, Aliona Savchenko and Robin Szolkowy took the gold in the pairs competition. Two days later, Isabelle Delobel and Olivier Schoenfelder captured their first ice dancing title.

United States Championships. Evan Lysacek won his second straight national title in the men's competition in St. Paul, Minnesota, in late January, despite finishing tied with Johnny Weir at 244.77 points. Lysacek was awarded the gold because he won the free skate, which is the tie-breaker, and Weir had to settle for silver. Stephen Carriere took the bronze.

In the women's competition, Mirai Nagasu, who turned 15 in April 2008, became the second youngest woman to win the title. Rachael Flatt, also 15, finished second. Neither was eligible to compete at the world championships because skaters had to be 15 by July 1, 2007, to qualify. Ashley Wagner finished third. Tanith Belbin and Ben Agosto won their fifth straight ice dancing crown and Keauna McLaughlin and Rockne Brubaker won the pairs title.

European championships. Czech Tomas Verner captured his first European championship, largely on the strength of his short program in Zagreb, Croatia, on Jan. 24, 2008. Stephane Lambiel of Switzerland was second, and Joubert was third. Defending champion Carolina Kostner became the first Italian woman to win two European titles, topping Switzerland's Sarah Meier. Finland's Laura Lepisto was third. Russia's Oksana Domnina and Maxim Shabalin won the ice dancing title, and Germany's Savchenko and Szolkowy won the pairs title.
     ■ Michael Kates

Iceland in 2008 became the first national casualty of the worldwide credit crisis as the country's banks failed and its currency collapsed—all within the space of 10 days in early October. Iceland's financial troubles sent shock waves across Europe and triggered severe contraction of the economy.

The first crack appears. Iceland's three main banks greatly expanded their operations into the international market during the 2000's and became highly dependent on international credit flows. In 2008, the global tightening of credit severely strained these banks.

In late September, one of Iceland's big-three banks, Glitnir, found itself with insufficient cash to meet its obligations. Iceland's government responded by nationalizing Glitnir—that is, buying ownership shares in the bank. Days later, Landsbanki, another big bank, failed and was nationalized, followed by Kaupthing, Iceland's largest bank.

Currency collapse. Iceland's currency, the krona, began to slide against world currencies in the summer of 2008. As Iceland's banking industry unraveled in late September and early October, the krona went into free fall. By October 9, when trading of the currency was suspended on international markets, the krona had lost about two-thirds of its value.

Hardship. Effects of the financial meltdown were felt almost immediately by Iceland's population. Iceland, an island nation in the North Atlantic Ocean, is home to about 313,000 people. Most food and petroleum must be imported into the country, as well as many manufactured goods. With the collapse of the krona, these goods suddenly became far more expensive—and obtainable only in foreign currencies. Iceland's government actively sought loans from the international community to shore up its banks and, more immediately, to pay for imports needed by Iceland's people. The collapse of the krona also fueled inflation, which mounted to an annual rate of 16 percent in October and was likely to rise to 25 percent in 2009, experts said.

Businesses throughout Iceland quickly discovered that they were unable to obtain stocks of goods from abroad using their krona reserves. Many businesses downsized operations and cut staff. Economists estimated that Iceland's economy would contract by 10 percent during 2009.

Loan. In October, the International Monetary Fund (IMF)—a United Nations affiliate that provides short-term credit to member nations—loaned $2.1 billion to Iceland. Economists estimated, however, that Iceland would ultimately need at least $6 billion to recover from its financial crisis.   ■ Robert N. Knight

See also **Bank: A Special Report; Economics, World; Europe; U.S. Government: A Special Report.**

Immigration. The United States government strengthened its enforcement efforts against illegal immigration in fiscal year (FY) 2008 (Oct. 1, 2007-Sept. 30, 2008). Congress did not tackle the issue of immigration reform in 2008.

Enforcement. The number of deportations, arrests, and workplace investigations carried out by U.S. Immigration and Customs Enforcement (ICE), an agency of the U.S. Department of Homeland Security, reached record levels in FY 2008. ICE returned nearly 350,000 illegal aliens to their native countries, up from about 290,000 in FY 2007. During workplace raids in FY 2008, ICE made about 1,100 criminal arrests (up from about 860 in FY 2007) and took more than 5,100 illegal aliens into custody (up from about 4,100 in FY 2007).

The two largest FY 2008 workplace raids took place at the Agriprocessors kosher meat-packing plant in Postville, Iowa, on May 12 and at an electrical transformer factory operated by Howard Industries in its home city of Laurel, Mississippi, on August 25. Authorities detained nearly 400 suspected undocumented workers in Iowa and nearly 600 such workers in Mississippi. In Iowa, about 300 workers were convicted and sentenced later in May on federal criminal charges of document fraud. Previously, most illegal aliens detained in workplace raids had simply been deported. Many people criticized the Iowa proceedings, saying

Federal agents escort Sholom Rubashkin (right), former head of Agriprocessors kosher meat-packing plant in Iowa, into court on Oct. 30, 2008. He was charged with employing hundreds of illegal immigrants and with 9,000 child-labor law violations.

that their speediness raised the risk of error and that many of the defendants were uneducated Spanish speakers who did not understand the charges. In the Mississippi raid—the largest single-workplace immigration raid in U.S. history—fewer than 10 workers were charged criminally. Government officials denied that the lower number was a response to the earlier criticism.

State laws. In December, the National Conference of State Legislatures reported that in 2008, 41 states had enacted 205 immigration-related laws and resolutions. (In 2007, 240 immigration measures had been enacted in 46 states.) Many of the 2008 laws set eligibility requirements for driver's licenses, imposed sanctions on employers of undocumented workers, or dealt with immigrant detention by law enforcement agencies.

Slowdown. According to U.S. census figures issued on September 23, the growth in the U.S. immigrant population slowed significantly in 2007. The foreign-born population grew by about 511,000 in 2007, compared with an average growth of about 1 million a year from 2000 to 2006. Observers suggested that the sluggish economy, plus the federal crackdown on illegal immigration, might be reducing the flow of foreigners into the United States. The estimated foreign-born population in 2007 was 38.1 million, or 12.6 percent of the overall population.   ■ Mike Lewis

India in 2008 was shaken by violence. The worst attack began on November 26, when heavily armed militants launched attacks at a railway station, a popular restaurant, a Jewish center, and two luxury hotels in Mumbai, formerly known as Bombay. The attacks left at least 170 people dead, including nine militants killed by Indian commandos. Security forces brought the wave of violence to a halt on November 29. The slowness of Indian security forces to react was widely criticized. Home Minister Shivraj Patil and other officials resigned in the wake of the attacks.

Indian officials said the terrorists were from Lashkar-e-Taiba, a terrorist group based in Pakistan. Its goal had been to break India's control on the Srinagar region of Jammu and Kashmir, a Himalayan state whose ownership is disputed by India and Pakistan. Despite the Pakistani government's denial of any involvement with the terrorists, the violence brought the two nuclear-armed nations to their angriest confrontation since 2001.

Bombings had plagued India for years. Bombs attached to parked bicycles killed about 60 people in the tourist city of Jaipur in May 2008. On July 26, a series of about 20 bombs in the city of Ahmadabad left at least 45 people dead. On September 13, a series of bombs killed 21 people in New Delhi, the capital. On October 30, 86 people were killed by a coordinated series of bombings in four towns in the northeastern state of Assam.

A little-known group, the Indian Mujahedeen, claimed responsibility for the Ahmadabad bombings, which they said were in revenge for the 2002 killing of at least 1,000 Muslims by Hindu mobs there. The group also claimed responsibility for the Jaipur and New Delhi attacks.

The Assam attacks were blamed on separatists belonging to the indigenous Bodo tribe. The National Democratic Front of Bodoland, which wants an independent Bodo homeland, denied responsibility for the attacks. In August, violence between Bodo tribespeople and Muslim migrants in Assam left more than 50 people dead.

Christians in rural eastern India were attacked by Hindus beginning in August, with at least 20 people killed and dozens of churches burned. The Hindus blamed Christians for the death of a Hindu priest, though police blamed Maoist guerrillas. Hard-line Hindu organizations had in recent years tried to eliminate Christians in their midst.

In Jammu and Kashmir, violence erupted over a decision by the Indian Kashmir government in May to allocate 98 acres (40 hectares) of land for use by pilgrims to a Hindu shrine. Majority Muslims in the area protested, leading to weeks of rioting in which more than 30 people died. The government revoked the allocation, leading angry Hindus to block traffic into Muslim areas.

On October 21, the first trade traffic in more

Fires rage through the Taj Mahal Palace & Tower Hotel in Mumbai, India, on Nov. 29, 2008. Indian commandos stormed the building after militants took hostages there during a three-day terrorist attack that left more than 170 people dead.

debate, the coalition won a confidence motion on the agreement, 275 to 256 votes. India agreed to separate its civil and military nuclear facilities, with civil ones to be supervised by the International Atomic Energy Agency. The U.S. Congress approved the deal on October 1.

Politics. The Indian political struggle over the agreement, coupled with anger over the slowness of security forces to react to the Mumbai terrorism, left cloudy prospects for parliamentary elections due by May 2009. The Hindu-nationalist Bharatiya Janata Party (BJP), which lost power in 2004, showed signs in 2008 of a resurgence. In May, the BJP took power in southern Karnataka state, the center of India's booming electronics industry.

Inflation and other economic problems loomed as political issues in 2008, despite rapid economic growth. In August, inflation rose above 12 percent, the highest point in more than a decade. In June, the government raised fuel prices to limit losses suffered by government-owned fuel companies. This touched off angry protests in a nation where an estimated 260 million people live below the poverty line.

Officials ordered banks to excuse or discount loans to some 43 million farmers by June 30. The government planned to repay the banks over four years by increasing its already high deficit spending. Critics noted

than 60 years began between the Indian and Pakistani parts of Kashmir. Trucks began carrying produce across the border on two days each week.

Nuclear agreement. On Oct. 10, 2008, India and the United States signed a Civilian Nuclear Cooperation Agreement under which the United States would supply India with fuel for nuclear power plants. The agreement was a victory for India's Prime Minister Manmohan Singh. Indian Communists, who had supported the coalition government led by Singh's Congress Party, opposed nuclear cooperation with the United States. Without Communist support, Congress leaders put together a new coalition with small parties. On July 22, after two days of strenuous

that the poorest farmers most in need of financial relief were unable to deal with banks because they tended to borrow from village moneylenders, who were not covered under the plan. Experts estimate that some 10,000 Indian farmers commit suicide each year, many because they are unable to repay loans from these high-interest lenders.

Lunar orbiter. On October 22, India launched its first spacecraft to orbit the moon. The craft was scheduled to orbit the moon for two years, photographing the surface. Scientists intended to use the photographs to produce a three-dimensional atlas of the moon. ■ Henry S. Bradsher

See also **Asia; Disasters; Pakistan; Space exploration; Terrorism.**

Indian, American. A lawsuit against the United States government on behalf of nearly 500,000 Indians continued in 2008. The suit, brought in 1996 by Elouise Cobell of the Montana Blackfeet tribe, charged that since 1887, the U.S. Department of the Interior had mishandled more than $100 billion in trust funds administered by the department for individual Indians. The funds contain royalties from leasing rights for mining, oil and gas extraction, timber, and grazing on Indian lands.

On Jan. 30, 2008, Judge James Robertson of the U.S. District Court for the District of Columbia ruled that the Interior Department had "unreasonably delayed" its accounting of the amount owed to the Indians. He also concluded that "completion of the required accounting is an impossible task." Instead, the judge ordered that a trial begin on June 9 to determine the amount to be awarded to the Indians as compensation for the underpayments.

In March 2007, the government had proposed settling the case for $7 billion. Later, government trustees claimed that the money lost from the accounts was less than $500 million. During the June 2008 trial, Cobell argued that $48 billion had been lost due to mismanagement. On August 7, Robertson ruled that the government was liable for $455.6 million. Both Cobell and the government appealed the ruling.

Achievement scores. The U.S. Department of Education released in May 2008 the results of reading and mathematics tests that American Indian (AI) and Alaska Native (AN) students took as part of the National Assessment of Educational Progress (also called "the Nation's Report Card"). The tests, administered in 2007 to a sample group of more than 10,000 fourth- and eighth-grade students in both public and Bureau of Indian Education schools, compared the students' results with those recorded in similar tests in 2005.

According to the results, there was no significant change in the average test scores of AI and AN students from 2005 to 2007. However, a higher percentage of fourth graders (25 percent) scored in the "at or above proficient" category in mathematics in 2007 than did in 2005 (21 percent). Among non-American Indian or Alaska Native students, 40 percent of fourth-graders scored "at or above proficient" in mathematics. In both reading and mathematics, at both the fourth- and eighth-grade levels, AI/AN students consistently scored lower than white and Asian/Pacific Islander students; about the same as Hispanic students; and higher than black students. In both grades, AI/AN students attending public schools scored higher than AI/AN students in Bureau of Indian Education schools.

Piestewa Peak. A name change enacted by an Arizona state panel in 2003 to honor the first known Native American woman to be killed in combat as a member of the U.S. military was made official in 2008. The U.S. Board on Geographic Names voted 11 to 2 to change the name of Squaw Peak in Phoenix to Piestewa Peak in honor of U.S. Army Private First Class Lori Piestewa. Piestewa, a Hopi-Hispanic mother of two, was the first female soldier to die in the war in Iraq. She was killed on March 23, 2003, when the convoy in which she was traveling was ambushed southeast of Baghdad, the capital.

Canadian government apology. Prime Minister Stephen Harper on June 11, 2008, formally apologized to native Canadians on behalf of the Canadian government. In the early 1900's, the government had forced some 150,000 Indian, Inuit, and *Métis* (of mixed white and Indian ancestry) children into residential schools. The practice of taking native children ages 7 to 16 from their parents and sending them to residential schools began in 1920 to force their assimilation. The schools, where children were punished for speaking their own language or practicing their own religion, were closed in the 1970's, in the face of widespread evidence that children had been physically and sexually abused. Assembly of First Nations National Chief Phil Fontaine responded to the apology, asserting "This day will help us to put that pain behind us." ■ Kristina Vaicikonis

Indonesia. The government of Indonesia announced in March 2008 that the number of people living in poverty had dropped to 15.4 percent of the population from 16.7 percent in 2004. During the same period, unemployment had decreased, and the price of rice had fallen, said officials. Exports of such commodities as palm oil, rubber, and natural gas had contributed to the fastest economic growth in a decade in 2007. However, growth slowed to an 18-month low of 6.1 percent in the third quarter of 2008, down from 6.4 percent in the second.

President Susilo Bambang Yudhoyono said in his state of the nation speech on August 15 that decreasing oil prices would enable the government to slash its subsidy costs. He outlined plans to convert power stations from oil to coal, encourage use of nonsubsidized fuel, and extend energy-saving programs. Yudhoyono also increased pay for civil servants by 15 percent and raised spending on health, education, and infrastructure. These steps were widely seen as preparation for presidential elections scheduled for 2009. Polls showed his popularity decreasing throughout 2008.

Oil. Once an exporter of oil, Indonesia announced on May 28 that it would withdraw from the Organization of the Petroleum Exporting Countries (OPEC) when its membership expired in late 2008. Indonesia's oil production had dropped as demand surged, turning the country into a net importer. As international oil prices soared in May, the government could not afford to raise subsidies enough to keep domestic retail prices stable, and fuel prices rose 30 percent in 2008.

Religion. Hard-line Islamic groups in 2008 continued to agitate against a minority Muslim sect, Ahmadiyah, whose followers believe, contrary to mainstream Islamic teachings, that Muhammad was not the last prophet of Islam. Facing pressure from members of the mainstream Islamic majority, Yudhoyono issued a decree on June 9 that Ahmadiyah followers could not spread their religion and called for a halt to most of the group's activities. Human rights groups argued that the decree in effect banned the group in a nation whose constitution guarantees freedom of worship.

Terrorism. On November 9, Indonesia executed three Islamic militants convicted of the 2002 bombing of nightclubs on the resort island of Bali. Some 202 people died in the attack.

Suharto, an army leader who took power in Indonesia in 1966 and ruled as a dictator until 1998, died on Jan. 27, 2008, at the age of 86. Honored for presiding over economic growth but criticized for brutality and corruption, Suharto evaded trial for corruption in his last years by pleading ill health.   ■ Henry S. Bradsher

See also **Asia; Energy supply: A Special Report.**

International trade. Commerce in

goods and services among nations slowed markedly in 2008, especially in the second half of the year, as chaos in financial markets set off economic contractions in major importing regions. Even before then, global trade had slowed due to weakened consumer demand in the United States, the world's largest import market, and due to soaring prices for *commodities* (such physical substances as oil, metals, or grain). The rise in commodity prices forced global consumers to trim discretionary spending, affecting commerce in manufactured goods and services.

According to estimates by the International Monetary Fund (IMF), the volume of world trade expanded by 4.6 percent in 2008. In 2007, global trade had expanded by 7.2 percent and in 2006, by 9.3 percent. (The IMF is a United Nations organization that provides short-term credit to member nations.)

In December 2008, the World Bank—an international organization that provides loans to governments and private firms for development projects—predicted that during 2009, the volume of world trade would decrease by 2.1 percent. Not since 1982 had global trade volume contracted by so much in one year.

U.S. trade shifts. The U.S. Department of Commerce (DOC) reported in October 2008 that

the U.S. trade deficit—the shortfall in value between goods and services sent abroad and those brought into the United States—reached $478 billion for the first eight months of 2008, up slightly from the $471 billion reported at that point in 2007. Analysts noted, however, that the nature of that deficit was shifting in ways that were altering trade flows around the world; U.S. exports grew faster than imports, placing strains on trading partners that relied heavily on their own export trade with the United States.

In the first eight months of 2008, the value of U.S. exports rose nearly 18 percent, at a time when the U.S. dollar was exceptionally weak against many other currencies, thus making U.S. goods cheaper in foreign markets. In the same period, the value of imports rose about 13 percent; economists attributed much of this increase to fast-rising petroleum prices.

However, with the steep decline in petroleum prices and the global economic slowdown after mid-2008, the flow of imported goods into the United States subsided significantly. The DOC reported a $5-billion decline in imports from July to August, and analysts predicted steeper declines to come.

Trade leaders. In 2008, Canada retained its rank as the largest U.S. trading partner, for both exports and imports, and Mexico was the third largest U.S. supplier of imports. The trading structure created by the North American Free Trade Agreement (NAFTA) spurred trade among North America's three largest countries in 2008 as it had since the pact's implementation in 1994.

The second largest U.S. trading partner in 2008 (as in 2007) was China, a giant supplier of manufactured goods to consumer nations. In the first eight months of 2008, China sold $217 billion of goods to the United States but bought only $50 billion in U.S. products, leaving a bilateral deficit of $168 billion. China buys large amounts of debt of the United States and other wealthy nations, in effect using export profits to lend consumer nations money to buy its goods.

In the year ending in August 2008, Germany, a leading producer of factory goods, accumulated a merchandise trade surplus—that is, goods only—of $280 billion. Close behind was China with a $258-billion surplus. Russia amassed a $200-billion surplus, mainly on exports from its huge oil and gas sector. In the same period, Saudi Arabia, the world's largest oil exporter, racked up a $151-billion surplus.

Price distortions. Volatile commodity prices rose rapidly in the first half of 2008, then slid in the second half. Fast-growing economies of developing nations such as China and India stoked prices for coal, metals, and other input materials. Record hikes in oil prices through midsummer applied upward price pressure to a wide array of other goods, including food. Spiking prices introduced short-term distortions into trade patterns: exporters of oil and other commodities raked in large profits; importers incurred major and unexpected costs for necessities such as oil and grain.

In mid-July, oil prices peaked at $147 a barrel and then began to ebb steadily. By then, the U.S. dollar had reversed its downward trend, removing some price pressure on the petroleum market, which uses the dollar for pricing. At the same time, the global economic slowdown was beginning to make itself felt in a variety of economic sectors. By August, prices for a number of other commodities were posting sizable one-month declines—but still were up sharply from 2007.

The global financial crisis that erupted in September 2008 prompted economists to predict recessions—possibly severe—in the United States, the United Kingdom, and other Western countries in 2009. The crisis was spurred by a succession of failures of U.S. banks and investment firms. The implications of contracting major economies on international trade flows seemed obvious, prompting economists to revise sharply downward the trade forecasts made earlier in the year.   ■ John D. Boyd

See also **Bank: A Special Report; Economics, U.S. & World; U.S. Government: A Special Report.**

Internet. The Internet had a profound effect on the United States presidential election in 2008. Online donations made up a major part of fundraising for political campaigns, especially those of the alternative Republican candidate, Ron Paul, and the Democratic nominee, Barack Obama.

Obama's campaign also made extensive use of the Internet's social networking capabilities. Obama's Web site, much like such sites as Facebook and MySpace, allowed his supporters to join groups and send messages to each other. Obama's Web site also enabled his supporters to easily organize meetings and fund-raisers and make phone calls on behalf of the campaign.

The Internet also negatively affected political campaigns, in the form of false rumors about candidates spread through e-mails and *blogs* (online diaries). In June, Obama's campaign set up a Web site—http://fightthesmears.com—designed to disprove specific rumors about him.

In September, a college student broke into Republican vice presidential candidate Sarah Palin's personal e-mail account on Yahoo. A Web site called Wikileaks published some of its contents. As governor of Alaska, Palin had an official government e-mail account, but she occasionally used her personal e-mail account for state business. The student, who faced charges, used publicly available information to figure out

answers to Palin's security questions on Yahoo.

Internet radio troubles. In June, U.S. officials made an important ruling affecting Internet radio companies. Such companies include Pandora, based in Oakland, California; last.fm, based in London; and Live 365, based in Foster City, California. The ruling forces such companies to pay the recording industry 0.007 cents each time they play a song over the Internet. Record labels, represented by the Recording Industry Association of America (RIAA) in Washington, D.C., own the copyrights to many of the songs broadcast on Internet radio stations.

Internet radio companies, like traditional radio companies, sell advertisements to finance their operation. However, traditional radio companies have never had to pay a fee each time they play a song on-air. Such radio stations often benefit record labels by broadcasting their music to a wide audience. Internet radio stations had hoped the same idea would apply to them and that they would only have to pay a portion of their advertising revenue to record labels instead of a per-song charge. Some Internet radio companies feared that the ruling would put them out of business.

Online ad deals. In June 2008, Sunnyvale, California-based Yahoo! Inc. and its competitor, Mountain View, California-based Google Inc., reached a deal allowing Google to sell its advertisements on Yahoo's Web sites. Both companies run popular online search engines—that is, programs that help users find Web pages—and sell ads that appear alongside the search results.

But in November, the Yahoo-Google deal fell apart after Google pulled out amid concerns about violation of antitrust laws. Antitrust laws prevent companies from getting too large and threatening competition that is essential to the marketplace. Because Yahoo and Google are two of the largest sellers of online ads, some experts and government officials worried that the deal would give the companies too much power to control ad prices and prevent competition in the online advertising market.

Victory for net neutrality. In July, the head of the U.S. Federal Communications Commission (FCC) moved to punish Philadelphia-based Comcast Corporation for preventing open access to the Internet. Comcast, the largest U.S. cable company, had slowed or blocked Internet traffic for customers who were using a certain kind of file-sharing program. According to FCC rules, Internet providers such as Comcast must provide "open and accessible" networks, and Comcast's actions violated that principle.

The FCC's move satisfied supporters of a principle called "net neutrality," which holds that all data traffic on the Internet should be treated equally. Opponents of net neutrality believe that Internet providers, such as Comcast, should have the right to charge more for, or restrict access to, certain kinds of data traveling through their networks. Supporters argue that such practices undermine the democratic nature of the Internet and could lead to censorship.

Google Chrome. In September 2008, Google Inc. released a new Web browser, called Chrome, for Windows computers. Web browsers are computer programs that allow people to view Web pages and navigate the Internet. Other Web browsers include Microsoft's Internet Explorer, Apple's Safari, and Mozilla's Firefox.

Google's new browser has a simpler layout than other popular browsers. It was also designed from the ground up to take advantage of advanced features of modern Web pages, such as video players, games, and word processors. In addition, Chrome provides sophisticated protection against Web sites that contain dangerous programs or that cause browsers to stop working.

Chrome, like Firefox, is an open-source browser—that is, its computer code is "open" for anyone to see. Google hoped to motivate other Web developers to innovate by freely sharing its code for Chrome. ■ Daniel Kenis

See also **Computer; Election: A Special Report; Telecommunications.**

Iran. International economic pressure continued to be exerted on Iran in 2008 to try to force the Islamic Republic to halt its enrichment of uranium for use as nuclear fuel. In January, United States officials pressured institutions in some Arab Gulf countries, including Ahli United Bank of Bahrain, to stop doing business with Iran. In addition, a number of banks in France continued refusing to issue letters of credit for trade with Iran—a policy that began in late 2007. The Iranian government circumvented these restrictions by opening lines of credit that were settled in euros rather than dollars to attract investment and business back to Iran.

New centrifuges. The United Nations (UN) International Atomic Energy Agency reported in February 2008 that Iran had experimented with a new generation of centrifuges capable of producing uranium fuel for either nuclear power plants or nuclear weapons. Iranian officials dismissed the report, insisting that their program focused exclusively on the peaceful use of nuclear energy. In April, however, Iran's president, Mahmoud Ahmadinejad, announced that his country had 6,000 new centrifuges capable of enriching uranium five times faster than its old centrifuges.

United Nations sanctions. The UN Security Council imposed new sanctions on Iran in March because of that country's refusal to stop enrich-

ing uranium. The sanctions included inspection of cargo going into and out of Iranian ports to search for prohibited equipment that could be used to build nuclear weapons. The sanctions also included the monitoring of Iranian financial institutions, travel bans, and the freezing of assets involved in the building of uranium-enriching centrifuges.

Geneva meeting. In July, U.S. Undersecretary of State William J. Burns attended a meeting in Switzerland with Iranian officials to discuss Iran's nuclear plans. Representatives from the four other permanent members of the UN Security Council—China, France, Russia, and the United Kingdom—plus Germany and European Union foreign policy chief Javier Solana also attended. The negotiators requested that Iran provide specific answers regarding halting its uranium enrichment program. Rather than provide these answers, however, Iranian officials proposed more talks after UN sanctions were lifted.

Turkmenistan cut off natural gas supplies to Iran in January, claiming technical problems. However, energy analysts speculated that the two countries were haggling over price. As a result, Iranian officials halted Iran's natural gas exports to Turkey to meet its own domestic demand for gas. ■ Mary-Jane Deeb

See also **Middle East; Turkey; United Nations.**

Iraq. A spokesman for United States General David H. Petraeus, commander of the Multinational Force in Iraq, reported in January 2008 that the senior leadership of Iran had kept its promise to not send any more weapons to insur-

gents in Iraq. The spokesman also stated that there had been a 60-percent decline in violence in Iraq during the previous six months, including reductions in the use of improvised explosive devices to attack U.S. and Iraqi forces and Iraqi civilians.

Surge successes. General Petraeus appeared before the U.S. Congress in April to testify about the progress of the war in Iraq. He reported that the level of violence and the number of civilian deaths continued to decline substantially. The general attributed this improvement to a number of factors, especially the increase in the number of U.S. forces fighting in Iraq as part of the so-called "surge," as well as the addition during the previous 16 months of more than 133,000 Iraqi soldiers and police to the Iraqi Security Forces. The expanded security forces, which totaled about 540,000 individuals, were able to deal serious blows to al-Qa`ida (the global Islamic terrorist organization) and other extremist elements that had been creating havoc in Iraq.

General Petraeus also described the emergence of Iraqi volunteers from both the Sunni and Shi`ah communities as the "Sons of Iraq" organization. The 91,000 volunteers worked with U.S. forces to protect their communities by helping the troops locate weapons caches and explosive devices and secure roads and infrastructure.

Following General Petraeus's report to Congress, U.S. President George W. Bush announced that there would be no further reduction in U.S. force levels in Iraq during his presidency. He argued that the surge had saved innumerable lives, though he acknowledged that the security situation remained precarious in Iraq. President Bush added that a pullout of U.S. forces would empower al-Qa`ida and increase the territorial and political ambitions of Iran in the region, thus threatening U.S. interests and security. President Bush also announced that U.S. troops would be deployed for only one year at a time in Iraq, and off-duty troops would stay home for at least a year before being redeployed to Iraq.

U.S. troop presence extended. The Iraqi parliament approved a plan in November to allow U.S. forces to remain in Iraq for three additional years beyond the expiration of their United Nations mandate in December 2008. The approved extension followed months of contentious negotiations between U.S. officials and the Iraqi administration of Prime Minister Nouri al-Maliki. The support of the prime minister's Cabinet came after the top Shi`ah cleric, Grand Ayatollah Ali al-Sistani, reviewed and approved the agreement.

Australian withdrawal. For Australia, the war in Iraq came to an end on June 1, when the Australian Defence Force in southern Iraq officially handed over its commitment to U.S. forces and lowered the Australian flag over Camp Terendak. The 550 Australian soldiers of

On December 14, an Iraqi journalist shouts "This is a good-bye kiss" and hurls his shoes at U.S. President George W. Bush's head (a grave insult in the Arab world) during a press conference in Baghdad. Earlier, President Bush had declared that the Iraq War "has not been easy, but it has been necessary for American security, Iraqi hope, and world peace."

Overwatch Battle Group-West who had been headquartered at the camp left Iraq a few days earlier. The withdrawal of Australian combat troops from Iraq, which Australian officials had negotiated with U.S. officials, fulfilled an election promise of the new prime minister of Australia, Kevin Rudd.

Basra banditry. In late March, six months after British forces gave up control of the large southeastern Iraqi city of Basra, Prime Minister Maliki ordered an attack on the Basra militias of Shi`ah cleric Muqtada al-Sadr. Experts in Iraqi affairs noted that the attack appeared to be prompted by the disorderly conduct of the Shi`ah militias, which had resorted to banditry and smuggling, creating chaos in the city. The week-long battle between the Iraqi military forces and the militias left hundreds dead. A cease-fire was established after al-Sadr called for his forces "to cooperate with the government to achieve security."

Turkish attack. Two battalions of about 10,000 troops from Turkey entered northern Iraq in February in pursuit of rebels belonging to the Kurdistan Workers Party (PKK), a group seeking to establish a self-governing homeland for the Kurdish people of southwestern Asia. This cross-border movement was a major offensive by Turkey to hunt down PKK rebels and destroy their camps. Iraqi officials called upon Turkish authorities to respect Iraq's territorial sovereignty, and the U.S. government urged Turkey to limit its attacks to specific PKK targets.

The Turkish offensive lasted six days. The number of casualties could not be accurately accounted for, because neither the Turks nor the Kurds reported the numbers of their dead and wounded after the Turkish troops pulled out.

Iraq-Iran relations. In early March, President Mahmoud Ahmadinejad of Iran made the first visit to Iraq by an Iranian head of state since the end of the Iran-Iraq War (1980-1988). He received a warm welcome from Iraq's president, Jalal Talabani, who sought Iranian assistance in strengthening Iraq's security against Turkey, which Iraqi officials viewed as a threat because of Turkish military incursions against the Kurds. Many Iraqi Kurdish leaders had developed strong ties with Iranians during years of exile in Iran when Saddam Hussein was the leader of Iraq.

King Abdullah II of Jordan visited Iraq in August 2008, becoming the first Arab head of state to visit that country since U.S.-led forces ousted Saddam Hussein in 2003. The king met with Prime Minister Maliki and members of Maliki's Cabinet to discuss security cooperation and economic relations. The discussion included the renewal of an oil agreement between the two countries, ensuring that Jordan would continue purchasing oil from Iraq at a discounted rate. The leaders also discussed the more than 700,000 Iraqi refugees who were living in Jordan. King Abdullah expressed his desire to see the refugees return to their homes in Iraq.

Hoshyar Zebari, Iraq's foreign minister, described the meeting as a "breakthrough" that showed that Iraq was returning to some form of normalcy and stability in international relations.

Opium production. In Diyala province, northeast of the Iraqi capital, Baghdad, farmers increasingly planted poppies to produce opium in 2008. Iraqi farmers resorted to planting the narcotic because they could no longer subsist by growing traditional crops as a result of a lack of government assistance and competition from cheap fruit and vegetable imports from neighboring countries. With the assistance of Afghan opium growers and funding from drug smugglers who plied their trade from Afghanistan, Iraqi farmers produced large quantities of opium for sale throughout the Arabian Peninsula. ■ Mary-Jane Deeb

See also **Armed forces; Iran; Middle East; Turkey; United Nations; Year in brief.**

Ireland. In 2008, Bertie Ahern, who had served as Ireland's prime minister (*taoiseach*) since 1997, resigned and was replaced by his finance minister and deputy prime minister, Brian Cowen. Ahern, who was leader of the Fianna Fáil party, had been the subject of a corruption inquiry following allegations that he had improperly accepted loans from businessmen in 1993 and 1994, when he was finance minister. In April 2008, Ahern announced that he would resign. He was admired for his role in the peace settlement in Northern Ireland and for presiding over more than a decade of prosperity. Cowen took over as Fianna Fáil leader and became the new taoiseach on May 7. He governed in a coalition with the Green Party, the Progressive Democrats, and several independents.

Lisbon Treaty. In June, the Irish people voted in a referendum to reject the Lisbon Treaty to reform the structure of the European Union (EU, Europe's main economic bloc). Unlike other EU members, Ireland's Constitution required it to hold a referendum on the issue. The result was a crisis for the future organization of the bloc. Political analysts cited the complexity of the treaty as one reason for the negative vote, as well as fears that it might lead to a loss of control over such issues as the legality of abortion and same-sex marriage in Ireland. At a summit meeting of EU leaders in December, Cowen agreed to hold another referendum in 2009, after EU officials promised Ireland additional safeguards to protect its sovereignty.

Recession. Having earned the label "Celtic Tiger" for its prosperity over the previous decade, Ireland fell into a recession in 2008. The recession was caused by a decline in homebuilding and consumer spending and deepened because of the global financial crisis, the rise in oil and food prices, and the strength of the euro, the common currency used by some EU nations. Unemployment increased from 5 percent in January to 7.8 percent in November.

In September, following a collapse in bank share prices, Finance Minister Brian Lenihan tried to maintain confidence in the Irish banking sector by guaranteeing all deposits. The plan, which cost 400 billion euros ($558 billion), angered Ireland's EU partners, as international deposits flowed into Irish banks, making other European banks less competitive.

Budget. The budget released by the government in October caused public criticism and a loss of confidence in its ability to deal with the recession. Lenihan reported that the deficit for 2009 would be 6.5 percent of *gross domestic product* (GDP, the total of all goods and services produced in a year), twice the amount allowed for EU countries that use the euro.   ■ Rohan McWilliam

See also **Europe; Northern Ireland.**

Islam. For many Muslims around the world, one of the most striking events of 2008 was the election in the United States of Barack Obama, a president with Muslim heritage. Obama is a Christian, but his father, Barack Hussein Obama, Sr., was a Muslim from Kenya. Polls showed that more than 10 percent of people in the United States believed Obama to be a Muslim.

Former Secretary of State Colin L. Powell responded to the question of whether Obama was a Muslim. Powell said, "Well, the correct answer is, he is not a Muslim, he's a Christian. He's always been a Christian. But the really right answer is, what if he is? Is there something wrong with being a Muslim in this country? The answer's no, that's not America."

Al-Qa`ida, an organization that supports the activities of Muslim extremists, responded to Obama's election with an attack that many people viewed as racist. Al-Qa`ida's deputy leader, Ayman al-Zawahiri, accused Obama of betraying his race and his father's Muslim heritage. Zawahiri referred to Obama and to Powell and Condoleezza Rice, the nation's two African American secretaries of state, as "house slaves," a demeaning term for blacks who do the bidding of whites.

The role of women. In June, Turkey's Constitutional Court overturned a constitutional amendment that would have prohibited discrimination against women in education based on their dress. The amendment would have lifted a ban on the wearing of headscarves at universities. However, the Turkish government has an official policy of *laicism* (the exclusion of religion from government and political affairs). It has restricted many traditional religious practices, including the wearing of headscarves. The lifting of the ban on headscarves set off large public protests before the Constitutional Court overturned the amendment.

Egypt's grand mufti, the nation's top expert on Islamic law, issued a formal *fatwa* (opinion on religious law) stating that there was no Islamic legal objection to a woman serving as a muezzin. The muezzin calls the faithful to prayer five times a day. The Supreme Fatwa Council of al-Azhar University in Cairo, Egypt's highest Islamic legal body, confirmed the ruling but added some conditions. The woman must be needed for the job and must need the work; it must not interfere with her household duties; and her husband must agree to her undertaking this duty. Other scholars, including some in Saudi Arabia, disputed the idea that a woman may issue the call to prayer because that role "inevitably requires that she mix in assemblies of men." An Egyptian woman applied formally for a position as a muezzin, but her application has not yet been acted upon.

In France, an appeals court in November overturned a ruling that *annulled* (canceled) the marriage of a Muslim couple. The husband had requested the annulment because, on the wedding night, he discovered that his bride was not a virgin, as she had claimed to be. He cited a French civil law that allowed for the dissolution of the marriage if one of the parties lacked "the essential qualities."

In Morocco, a fatwa approving marriage for young girls stirred debate and public outrage. The fatwa, issued in September by the Moroccan legal expert Mohammed Maghraoui, said that girls as young as 9 years old might marry because such marriages tend to be successful. Morocco's High Council of Ulemas, a panel of legal experts, condemned the marriage of underage girls.

Morocco's King Mohammed VI, in his role as "Commander of the Faithful," ordered a series of religious reforms to place the clergy under tighter control. Among other changes, preachers now must receive certification from the country's Ministry of Islamic Affairs.

Minaret controversy. In Switzerland, right-wing parties collected enough signatures to force a referendum on banning minarets, the towers attached to mosques from which the muezzin calls worshippers. The government opposed the referendum, as did all major Swiss church organizations. But the Swiss Constitution provides that

A couple wrapped in the Israeli flag are among spectators watching a laser show during festivities in Jerusalem in May marking the 60th anniversary of the establishment of the nation of Israel. Other celebratory events included fireworks, air force flyovers, and a huge party for anyone born on May 14, Israel's Independence Day.

a referendum (direct vote of citizens) must take place if 100,000 signatures are gathered, and the organizers say they have met that requirement. No date has been set for the vote.

Burial of terrorists refused. A Muslim cemetery in Mumbai, India, refused to bury the bodies of nine terrorists who were killed during attacks on the city in November. At least 10 gunmen killed more than 170 people in attacks that targeted two luxury hotels, the city's main train station, a hospital, and a Jewish center. The Jama Masjid Trust, which controls the Badakabrastan graveyard in Mumbai, said it would not bury the dead terrorists because they were not true followers of Islam. The trust's action made it unlikely that any Muslim cemetery in Mumbai would bury the terrorists.

The Deoband Dar al-Ulum, an influential Islamic academy in Deoband, India, issued a formal statement in February saying, "There is no place for terrorism in Islam." Thousands of *madrasahs* (seminaries) in South Asia are affiliated with the Deoband academy.

The name Muhammad became the second most popular boy's name in the United Kingdom in 2007, according to the British Office for National Statistics. it was expected to reach the number-one ranking by 2008. ■ A. Kevin Reinhart

See also **India; Terrorism; Turkey.**

Israel. In January 2008, United States President George W. Bush made his first visit to Israel since becoming president in 2001. He expressed his hope that a final peace agreement between the Israelis and Palestinians could be achieved within a year. President Bush offered his assistance and that of the U.S. government in the difficult peace negotiations that lie ahead.

Peace talks lead to trouble. Negotiations between the Israelis and Palestinians began on Jan. 14, 2008. Core issues between the two sides included the questions of whether Jerusalem would be divided into sectors under Israeli and Palestinian control, whether Palestinian refugees and their descendants would be allowed to return to their homes, the future of Israeli settlements in Palestinian areas, and the borders of an eventual Palestinian state. Israel's minister of strategic affairs, Avigdor Lieberman, resigned from the Cabinet in protest against the negotiations with the Palestinians. Furthermore, Lieberman withdrew his party, the ultranationalist Yisrael Beiteinu, from the governing coalition. This withdrawal decreased the parliamentary majority that supported Prime Minister Ehud Olmert from 78 to 67 of 120 seats.

Hamas, a Palestinian militant Islamic organization, expressed its opposition to the peace negotiations by increasing its rocket attacks against

Israeli towns close to the Gaza Strip. Hamas had seized control of the Gaza Strip from the moderate Palestinian Authority in June 2007. These attacks were met with Israeli military retaliation, resulting in the deaths of hundreds of Palestinians, including both militants and civilians. The Palestinian Authority, headed by President Mahmoud Abbas, blamed Hamas for the Israeli offensive against the Gaza Strip.

Prime Minister Olmert and President Abbas met in April and May 2008 in anticipation of President Bush's second visit to Israel to push forward the peace process. President Bush visited Israel from May 14 to May 16, though the main purpose of the visit was to commemorate the 60th anniversary of the establishment of Israel.

Although the Israeli and Palestinian negotiation teams—led by, respectively, Israeli Foreign Minister Tzipi Livni and former Palestinian Prime Minister Ahmad Quray—met several times in 2008, both sides expressed decreasing optimism about reaching a final peace agreement by the end of the year.

Attack on Jerusalem school. In the first major attack in Jerusalem in more than four years, a Palestinian gunman killed eight students and wounded nine others inside a Jewish seminary on March 6. A Hamas spokesman praised the attack as "heroic." However, Palestinian President Abbas issued a statement condemning "all attacks that target civilians, whether they are Palestinian or Israeli."

Israel-Hamas truce. A truce between Israel and Hamas, brokered by Egypt, went into effect on June 18. Nevertheless, violations of the truce occurred on both sides. Violence escalated dramatically in late December, after the cease-fire expired, with Hamas militants firing numerous rockets and mortar rounds into Israel and Israeli forces conducting military strikes into Gaza.

Winograd Commission report. After about 17 months of investigation, the Winograd Commission in January produced a 617-page report on the July-to-August 2006 war between Israel and Hezbollah, a militant Islamic group based in southern Lebanon. The expert members of the commission, headed by former judge Eliyahu Winograd, found "great and grave faults" in the decisions made at the time by Israeli Cabinet and military officials. Although the Israeli army—the strongest army in the Middle East—fought only a few thousand paramilitary fighters, the war was inconclusive and led to the deaths of more than 160 Israeli soldiers and civilians, as well as more than 1,200 Lebanese, most of them civilians.

Israel-Hezbollah prisoner exchange. In July 2008, after two years of German-mediated negotiations, Hezbollah returned the remains of two Israeli soldiers captured in the 2006 war, in exchange for five prisoners and the remains of 200 Lebanese and Palestinians held by Israel. The returned Hezbollah prisoners were the last held by Israel.

Olmert resignation. Prime Minister Olmert revealed in July 2008 that he planned to submit his resignation to Israeli President Shimon Peres in September, after primary elections to select a new leader of the Kadima Party. Prime Minister Olmert was under police investigation regarding illegal funds he had allegedly accepted from U.S. millionaire financier Morris Talansky over a 13-year period, when Olmert was mayor of Jerusalem and a Cabinet minister. Foreign Minister Livni announced her intention of running for the Kadima Party leadership to replace Olmert.

Livni won the primary elections, held on September 17, with 43 percent of the vote, compared with 42 percent for her main opponent, Minister of Transportation Shaul Mofaz. However, Livni informed President Peres in October that her negotiations with the various political parties to form a new government had failed. President Peres then called for new elections to be held in February 2009. Until a new government could be formed, Israeli law required that Prime Minister Olmert remain in power.

■ Marius Deeb

See also **Judaism; Lebanon; Middle East**.

Italy. Prime Minister Romano Prodi's 20-month-long, center-left government, made up of nine political parties, collapsed on Jan. 24, 2008, after losing a vote of confidence in the Senate, the upper house of Parliament. Prodi had improved public finances, lowering the country's budget deficit. However, he had also introduced hefty tax increases, which led to several of his coalition parties to withdraw their support. In addition, his government was dogged by outrage over tens of thousands of tons of trash that lay uncollected and unprocessed in Campagnia, the region around Naples, for nearly a month, and that Spain had surpassed Italy in per capita economic output.

In the general election on April 13 and 14, a coalition of right-wing parties led by Silvio Berlusconi's People of Freedom won a strong majority in both houses of Parliament. Berlusconi's opponent, Walter Veltroni, leader of the center-left Democratic Party, was unable to shed the image of disorganization and incompetence from Prodi's tenure and could not convince voters that he had fully broken with his own Communist past.

The flamboyant Berlusconi had previously been prime minister for nine months in 1994 and 1995 and for a five-year term from 2001 to 2006. His partners in 2008 included a stronger group of rightist, regional, and formerly neofascist parties. Voters in 2008 elected candidates representing only 6 political parties to the new parliament, compared with 20 parties in the Parliament during Prodi's term. Political observers noted that the elimination of numerous tiny parties would make it easier for Berlusconi to govern.

Politics of scandal. Berlusconi's large parliamentary majority opened the possibility of significant reforms of Italy's public administration, tax collection, and public education systems. Instead, the government concentrated on reigning in the judiciary. Political experts and opposition politicians maintained that restrictions on wiretapping and the delay of criminal cases enshrined in new legislation had more to do with preventing investigators from prosecuting Berlusconi for bribery and releasing transcripts of politically compromising telephone conversations with a female colleague than with improving the administration of justice.

Immigration and the EU. In its first cabinet meeting in May, Berlusconi's government introduced tough measures to stem illegal immigration and expel unwanted foreigners. The measures included the imprisonment of illegal immigrants for up to four years and the expulsion of citizens of the European Union (EU—Europe's main political and economic bloc) who could not prove that they have the means to support themselves. Such policies were aimed particularly at Romanian Roma (also called Gypsies), an estimated 50,000 of whom had moved to Italy since Romania joined the EU in 2007 and who are widely viewed as contributing to a rise in crime. In July 2008, Berlusconi's government also announced plans to fingerprint Roma—including children—for purposes of identification, because many Roma do not have identification documents.

The EU Parliament condemned the measures and stated that EU members are not allowed to expel EU citizens to other member nations nor are nations allowed to set minimum income requirements for residency. In September, however, the European Commission (which proposes legislation for the EU and oversees its treaties) ruled that the fingerprinting campaign was legal in that its purpose was "identifying persons who cannot be identified in any other way" rather than a collection of "data based on ethnic origin or religion."

Global economic crisis. In November, the EU called on its members to provide a stimulus package of 200 billion euros ($260 billion) to help Europe recover from the global economic crisis. Berlusconi's government announced a package for Italy of 80 billion euros ($100 billion). However, critics noted that this amount included only 5 billion euros ($7 billion) of new spending; the remainder consisted of EU funds previously allocated to Italy. Berlusconi claimed that Italy's large public debt precluded him from matching the large stimulus packages put forward by France and

Germany. The government also had no plans to recapitalize the country's banks. According to Berlusconi, Italy's banks are among the healthiest in Europe because they refused to take on the types of risky investments that American and European banks did. Italy's largest trade union held a one-day strike on December 12 to protest the small size of the stimulus package.

Foreign policy. Berlusconi, a strong ally of the United States in the run-up to the 2003 invasion of Iraq, refused to follow the U.S. lead in condemning Russia following Russia's invasion of Georgia and two breakaway Georgian provinces in August 2008. Italy further advocated a quick resumption of EU-Russian trade talks and assured Russia that it would be invited to the first Group of 8 meeting in 2009, when Italy assumes the presidency of the group of eight major industrialized nations. Critics pointed to the strong energy relationship between Russia and Italy, especially Italy's stake in the planned South Stream pipeline that is to transport Russian natural gas across the Black Sea.

Economy. EU economists forecast a strong downturn in Italy's economic growth, slowing from 1.5 percent in 2007 to 0 percent in 2008.

◼ Jeffrey Kopstein

See also **Europe.**

Ivory Coast. See Côte d'Ivoire in **Africa.**

Jamaica. See **Latin America; West Indies.**

Japan. On Sept. 24, 2008, Taro Aso became Japan's fourth prime minister in two years. The grandson of a prime minister, Aso had served as foreign minister in two earlier governments. He held the key job of secretary-general of the majority Liberal Democratic Party (LDP) under his predecessor as prime minister, Yasuo Fukuda.

Junichiro Koizumi stepped down in September 2006 after five years as a popular prime minister and was replaced by Shinzo Abe, also the grandson of a prime minister. After tumult and public embarrassments, Abe quit a year later. Fukuda, the son of a prime minister, took the job on Sept. 25, 2007. He abruptly resigned on Sept. 1, 2008.

Fukuda started 2008 with plans to overcome labor market discrimination against women and the elderly, improve the status of increasing numbers of workers with only temporary jobs, reduce governmental deficits, and help consumers. He soon ran into trouble, mainly from the Democratic Party of Japan (DPJ), which controlled the upper house of parliament. The LDP dominated the more powerful lower house that chooses prime ministers.

Tax struggle. The DPJ tried to block several of Fukuda's legislative actions. One was the renewal of a 30-year-old tax on gasoline earmarked for the road construction industry, which is closely tied to the LDP. This tie had resulted, critics said, in unnecessary roads, bridges, and tunnels being built. In March, the DPJ blocked the tax renewal in the upper house, but in April Fukuda used the LDP's two-thirds majority in the lower house to override the upper house vote.

Fukuda's approval rating fell to about 20 percent after the government introduced a new health care policy in April that raised premiums for the approximately 13 million Japanese over 75 years old, a group that usually supported the LDP.

Censure. Based on the unpopularity of this policy and other issues, the DPJ pushed a nonbinding motion through the upper house on June 11 censuring Fukuda. The DPJ hoped to force Fukuda into dissolving the lower house of parliament and calling a general election.

Instead, Fukuda shuffled his cabinet and the LDP leadership on August 1 in an effort to win more support. He replaced 13 of 17 ministers, and he promised reforms at an autumn session of parliament. Facing fights within the LDP as well as with the DPJ, however, Fukuda resigned.

Instead of the usual LDP backroom choice of a successor, five party leaders sought the prime minister's post. Among contenders was the first woman to contest the LDP leadership, former Defense Minister Yuriko Koike.

Cabinet. Aso won 351 of 525 LDP votes for prime minister. He named a cabinet that included people with limited reputations, including a son and a grandson of prime ministers. He also named the youngest cabinet minister since World War II (1939-1945), 34-year-old Yuko Obuchi, the daughter of another prime minister.

Economy. Aso faced the worldwide financial crisis after Japan's economy slowed early in 2008. Economic growth declined to just 1 percent as the prices of imports, especially oil, rose faster than exports. By midyear, the unemployment rate had edged close to a two-year high at 4.1 percent. Economists became concerned about a possible recession when statistics showed a small decline in national output from April to June. On August 29, Fukuda's cabinet announced a stimulus package of tax cuts, fuel

Japanese Prime Minister Taro Aso reviews troops during Japan's annual Self-Defense Forces Day in October 2008. Aso became prime minister after his predecessor, Yasuo Fukuda, resigned on September 1.

subsidies, and loans to small companies.

By the time Aso took office in September, Japan's unemployment rate had reached a two-year high of 4.2 percent, and the country's debt stood at 170 percent of its *gross domestic product* (GDP). (GDP is the total amount of goods and services produced in a country in a year.) On November 17, officials announced that Japan had entered a recession. In December, government officials announced that industrial production had plummeted by 8.1 percent in November, marking the largest such drop since Japan began measuring production statistics in 1953.

Foreign relations. Japan reached agreement with China on June 18, 2008, on natural gas under a disputed area of the East China Sea. The agreement allowed Japanese companies to invest in the gas and share profits from Chinese development. Cooperation in the gas fields did not, however, resolve the boundary issue.

Chinese President Hu Jintao on May 6 began the first state visit to Japan in a decade. Prime Minister Abe had begun a series of visits to China in 2006 after years of chilly relations. China was angered by Japanese officials visiting Yasukuni, a shrine honoring soldiers, including those who had fought in China in World War II. Prime Minister Koizumi had made annual visits to the shrine, but his successors had stayed away, helping ties with China.

The conflict in Afghanistan reverberated in Japanese politics. Since 2001, a Japanese refueling vessel and a destroyer had been deployed in the Indian Ocean to support Western warships engaged in operations in Afghanistan. The mission was suspended in November 2007 after the DPJ gained control of parliament's upper house. On Jan. 11, 2008, the lower house overrode DPJ opposition to resume refueling.

On November 28, officials announced that Japan would cease flying supply missions from Kuwait to Western forces in Iraq by the end of 2008. On December 17, the last of the supply planes that Japan had deployed in 2004 left Kuwait. Both the Afghanistan and Iraq missions were controversial in Japan, with some critics saying they violated the nation's pacifist constitution.

Ainu. Parliament voted on June 6, 2008, to recognize the Ainu ethnic group on the northern island of Hokkaido as "an indigenous people possessing a unique language, religion, and culture." This set the stage for reversing a century of discrimination in a country where the national self-image included racial and cultural unity. Popular culture had refused to acknowledge that any race predated the Japanese on their islands, and the Ainu were left in scorned poverty. Scientists are not certain about the ancestry of the Ainu, and their language has not been clearly classified.

Earthquakes. Japan was rocked by two significant earthquakes during 2008. On June 14, at least 12 people were killed by a 7.2-magnitude earthquake 250 miles (400 kilometers) northeast of the capital, Tokyo. The same area was shaken again on July 24, when a 6.8-magnitude quake injured an estimated 90 people.

Accident. On February 19, a Japanese destroyer rammed a small fishing vessel, cutting it in half. The two fishermen on the boat were not found. The defense ministry reported that the destroyer crew had been alerted to the presence of the small boat at least 12 minutes before the accident. ■ Henry S. Bradsher

See also **Afghanistan; Asia; China.**

Jordan. King Abdullah II made a historic visit to Iraq in August 2008, becoming the first Arab head of state to visit that nation since United States-led forces ousted Iraqi President Saddam Hussein in 2003. King Abdullah expressed his willingness to assist in Iraq's ongoing efforts at improving reconstruction, security, and stability, emphasizing the need for "a comprehensive national reconciliation." Iraqi Prime Minister Nouri Kamel al-Maliki thanked King Abdullah for his support of Iraq and its elected government.

King Abdullah made two visits to the United States in 2008, on March 4 and April 24, to meet with President George W. Bush. A third meeting with President Bush occurred on May 18 at the World Economic Forum on the Middle East in Sharm al-Sheikh, Egypt. The peace process between Israel and the Palestinians was the major topic discussed in all three meetings. The Jordanian monarch stressed the importance of continued U.S. support for Israeli-Palestinian negotiations aimed at resolving remaining "final status" issues, which would lead to the establishment of an independent Palestinian state. King Abdullah also met frequently in 2008 with Israeli Prime Minister Ehud Olmert and Palestinian President Mahmoud Abbas to advance the peace process. ■ Marius Deeb

See also **Iraq; Israel; Middle East.**

Judaism. An economic crisis that began in the United States in late 2007 shook first the American Jewish community, then the Jewish community worldwide in 2008. Lehman Brothers Holdings Inc., a global financial services company headquartered in New York City, filed for bankruptcy in September. Many other financial institutions suffered large losses, and stock markets in many countries plunged. The economic downturn damaged the livelihoods of many thousands of Jews who worked in the financial industry. The crisis also raised fears of renewed anti-Semitism. Some Web sites charged that Jews were responsible for the economic woes.

United States. The historic U.S. presidential election engaged the attention of the American Jewish community in 2008. In the spirited Democratic primary campaign, Senator Hillary Rodham Clinton of New York received greater support from Jews than did Senator Barack Obama of Illinois. Some Jews questioned Obama's support for Israel. A number of Obama's associates were known to be strong critics of Israel. They included Obama's former pastor, Jeremiah A. Wright, Jr.; and Palestinian scholar Rashid Khalidi, who taught at the University of Chicago when Obama did.

In April, former President Jimmy Carter met with a representative of the militant Palestinian organization Hamas. Obama criticized Carter's visit, saying he would not talk to Hamas until it recognized Israel and renounced terrorism.

On June 4, the day after Obama clinched the Democratic nomination, he spoke to the American Israel Public Affairs Committee, a pro-Israel lobbying group. Obama expressed strong support for Israel. He said that Jerusalem should remain the capital of Israel and "remain undivided." The next day, a campaign adviser explained that Obama would not rule out Palestinian control over parts of the city. The adviser called Jerusalem "a final status issue," which meant that its status must be negotiated between Israelis and Palestinians.

The campaign stimulated increased political involvement among American Jews. In April, Jeremy Ben-Ami, a former senior domestic policy adviser to President Bill Clinton, and other leading Jews formed a new lobbying group called J Street. J Street described itself as the "political arm of the pro-Israel, pro-peace movement." Obama supporters, with the help of comedian Sarah Silverman, organized a movement called the Great Schlep. The Great Schlep encouraged young Jews to visit grandparents in the swing state of Florida, where both parties had a chance of winning, and urge the grandparents to vote for Obama.

Exit polls showed that Obama, who won the election, captured about 78 percent of the Jewish vote. Jews voted for the Democratic presidential candidates by similar margins in 2000 and 2004.

On May 12, 2008, U.S. Immigration and Customs Enforcement raided the Agriprocessors kosher meat-packing plant in Postville, Iowa. Immigration officials arrested 389 undocumented workers during the raid. Agriprocessors was one of the nation's largest kosher meat producers. On November 4, Agriprocessors filed for bankruptcy and shut its Iowa plant, creating a nationwide shortage of kosher meat.

Israel celebrated its 60th birthday in 2008 amidst political uncertainty. Reported peace negotiations with Syria yielded no results. In June, Israel and Hamas agreed to a six-month truce in the Gaza Strip; however, fighting resumed in December. Israel and Hamas had repeatedly attacked each other since Hamas seized Gaza in June 2007.

In September 2008, Israel's Prime Minister Ehud Olmert resigned while facing a corruption investigation. Tzipi Livni, Olmert's foreign minister, was elected to succeed Olmert as head of the ruling Kadima party. But she proved unable to form a new government coalition, and so new elections were scheduled for February 2009. Olmert will remain as prime minister until then.

■ Jonathan D. Sarna and Jonathan J. Golden
See also **Immigration; Israel; Middle East.**

Kampuchea. See Cambodia.
Kazakhstan. See Asia.

Kenya. In January and February 2008, ethnic violence over the bitterly disputed victory of Mwai Kibaki in the Dec. 27, 2007, presidential election resulted in the deaths of at least 1,200 people and displaced some 350,000 others. The poll was widely regarded as rigged, an assessment admitted as true by Kenya's electoral commission chief, Samuel Kivuitu, during an investigation in August 2008.

Most of the fighting involved members of President Kibaki's majority Kikuyu tribe and protesters from main opposition leader Raila Odinga's Luo tribe, Kenya's second largest ethnic group. The hostilities brought a host of simmering grievances to the fore—relating to poverty, inequality, and disputes over land ownership—which acted as triggers for Kenya's deep-rooted tribalism. In one incident on January 29, army helicopters fired machine guns to disperse mobs in the tourist town of Naivasha, 40 miles (64 kilometers) northwest of the capital, Nairobi. The rival gangs had been attacking each other with machetes, clubs, and bows and arrows.

Surprise agreement. However, on February 28, former United Nations Secretary-General Kofi Annan mediated a peace deal to end the crisis, Kenya's worst since its independence from the United Kingdom in 1963. The largely unexpected breakthrough involved splitting Kenya's Cabinet posts roughly evenly between Kibaki's coalition Party of National Unity (PNU) and Odinga's Orange Democratic Movement (ODM). The deal also created the post of prime minister, to be held by Odinga.

Despite disputes about the precise powers of the prime minister, Odinga was sworn into office with the rest of the Cabinet on April 12. In theory, the power-sharing formula gave Odinga and his party an equal share in running the country. But analysts cautioned that the pact was only a first step, and not a solution, to long-standing ethnic tensions over land and political power.

Economy. The riots and unrest that followed the disputed election results had severe economic repercussions for Kenya's economy in 2008, especially in the country's vital tourist industry. Kenya's post-election violence scared away visitors, negatively affecting hotel and game park bookings, and thus employment.

"Witch" killings. In May, 86 people were arrested in the western Kisii district of Kenya in connection with the burning to death of eight women and three men between the ages of 80 and 96 who had been accused of being witches. The area had seen similar attacks in the past when individuals suspected of sorcery were killed or shunned.   ■ Simon Baynham
See also **Africa.**

Kiribati. See Pacific Islands.

Korea, North.

Korea, North. After years of difficult negotiations, North Korea in 2008 reached a new agreement to halt work that might contribute to making nuclear weapons. The Communist state had promised China, Japan, Russia, South Korea, and the United States that by the end of 2007 it would disable its main nuclear reactor at Yongbyon and provide complete details of its nuclear program in return for aid. Inspectors reported that the reactor had been shut down in July 2008, but by December the government had failed to provide any details about its nuclear program.

Progress. In May 2008, North Korea delivered 18,000 pages of material on its nuclear program to U.S. officials before turning over a full declaration on June 26. On June 27, the cooling tower at the main Yongbyon reactor was demolished. However, North Korean officials requested further aid before dismantling the country's weapons-grade plutonium production facilities.

On August 26, a state news agency reported that the dismantling had halted because the United States had not removed North Korea from its list of countries that promote terrorism. United States officials claimed that they would leave North Korea on the list until they were able to verify the claims of the declaration. North Korea responded by beginning to reassemble the Yongbyon plant. On October 11, the United States announced that it had removed North Korea from the terrorism list. North Korean officials then said it would resume dismantling and allowed United Nations inspectors to reenter the reactor site.

Kim Jong-il's health was the source of much speculation in 2008. The 66-year-old leader failed to appear at a military parade on September 9 marking the 60th anniversary of the North Korean nation. American intelligence officials believed Kim to be seriously ill, possibly having suffered a stroke; South Korean intelligence suggested that he was recovering from surgery. North Korea asserted that Kim was healthy, and in October released photos of him purportedly at a sporting event. Some observers noted that the photos were undated and that they proved nothing. His 2008 disappearance was not the first time Kim had stayed out of public view long enough to stir speculation about his health.

Famine. Devastating floods and cuts in food aid from China and South Korea forced the government to admit in 2008 that it was facing a food crisis and to appeal for aid. In 2006, the government had insisted that it did not need food aid. An estimated 500,000 North Koreans died in famines in the 1990's. The United Nations World Food Program warned of famine and quickly began expanded emergency aid.

■ Henry S. Bradsher

See also **Asia; Korea, South.**

Firefighters battle a blaze at Seoul's Great South Gate, one of South Korea's greatest cultural treasures, on February 10. Destroyed by the fire, the gate, completed in 1398, was one of the city's few structures that survived the Japanese occupation (1905-1945) and the Korean War (1950-1953).

Korea, South.

Korea, South. Lee Myung-bak was sworn in as president of South Korea on Feb. 25, 2008, after winning a landslide victory in elections two months earlier. Lee was a former mayor of the capital, Seoul, and a construction company executive known as "The Bulldozer" for his forceful personality. He pledged to revive the nation's economy, work economically with North Korea if it abandoned its nuclear weapons program, and improve relations with the United States, which keeps troops in South Korea to help protect the nation from North Korea. Lee's conservative Grand National Party won 153 out of 299 seats in National Assembly elections held on April 9.

Protests. In April, the government lifted a ban on importing beef from the United States. The ban was imposed in 2003 after bovine spongiform encephalopathy (BSE), or "mad

cow disease," was reported in the United States. South Korea had imported an estimated $800 million of American beef annually. The lifting of the ban was based on new quarantine and inspection rules.

Protests against the suspension of the ban for fear of BSE quickly broadened into complaints over policies on education, the economy, and other issues. On June 10, 2008, an estimated 100,000 people staged a candlelight demonstration in support of retaining the ban. After the government formally lifted the ban on June 26, the protests turned violent. Hundreds of police and civilians were injured. Lee fired his agriculture, education, and health ministers in July in response to the protesters.

Economy. South Korea's economy was hit hard by worldwide financial problems in late 2008. During his presidential campaign, Lee advocated deregulation and increased corporate investment in an effort to raise economic growth to 7 percent a year. However, inflation of consumer prices surged to a seven-year high of 4.9 percent in May, making the possibility of meeting his goal unlikely.

By October, both the value of the South Korean currency, the won, and Seoul's stock market had fallen sharply amid international turmoil. In November, the nation's central bank lowered its interest rate to 4 percent, the lowest level since mid-2006, to combat the economic difficulties.

Fire. One of South Korea's most treasured landmarks, the Great South Gate in Seoul, was destroyed by fire on Feb. 10, 2008. A 69-year-old man upset by a land dispute said he started the fire that destroyed the 600-year-old wooden structure. The gate, which served as

Seoul's main entrance after the city became Korea's capital in 1394, was one of the only historic buildings in the city to survive both the Japanese occupation of South Korea (1910-1945) and the Korean War (1950-1953).

■ Henry S. Bradsher
See also **Asia; Korea, North; People in the News** (Lee Myung-bak).

Kosovo declared independence from Serbia on Feb. 17, 2008. Although the government of Serbia strenuously protested Kosovo's action, nations including the United States, the United Kingdom, France, and Germany recognized Kosovo's independence. Russia, China, and some other nations refused to recognize Kosovo.

Kosovo, historically a province of Serbia, is home to a large ethnic Albanian majority and an ethnic Serb minority. In the late 1990's, ethnic Albanian rebels began an insurgency against Serbian authorities, who had been directed by the government of Slobodan Milosevic to carry out repressive measures against the province's Albanian population. A Serbian army invaded the province in March 1999, driving thousands of ethnic Albanians from their homes. The North Atlantic Treaty Organization (NATO) responded with air strikes, and Serbia (then called Yugoslavia) withdrew its forces in June 1999.

Since 1999, Kosovo had been protected by NATO troops and governed by United Nations officials. These organizations continued providing assistance after independence. The new Kosovo faced challenges of building a stable government and economy and of integrating its ethnic Serb minority. ■ Sharon L. Wolchik
See also **Europe; Serbia.**

Kuwait. See Middle East.

Kyrgyzstan. See Asia.

Labor and employment. The United States economy lost about 2 million jobs in 2008 as the nation slid into recession. In autumn, global financial markets seized up, with lending at all levels coming to an unforeseen sudden halt. By late 2008, economists were predicting a long and deep recession and further job loss.

At the beginning of 2008, U.S. employment measured 146.2 million, according to the U.S. Bureau of Labor Statistics (BLS), an agency of the Department of Labor (DOL). Late in the year it stood at 144.3 million. BLS data show that the U.S. unemployment rate rose from 4.7 percent at the end of 2007 to 6.7 percent at the end of 2008. BLS statistics indicated that the year's jobless rates among men ranged from 4.4 percent at the start of the year to 6.5 percent at the end; for women,

from 4.2 percent at the start to 5.5 percent at the end; and for teenagers, from 18 percent at the start to 20.4 percent at the end of the year.

The number of people filing for first-time unemployment benefits rose to a seasonally adjusted 586,000 for the week ending December 20. The higher-than-expected number of claims was the highest since November 1982.

The unemployment rate of white workers was 4.4 percent at the start of 2008; by year's end, it was 6.1 percent. African American workers' jobless rate was 9.2 percent in January and 11.2 percent at year's end. For Hispanic workers, the jobless rate ranged from 6.3 percent at the start of 2008 to 8.6 percent at year's end.

Compensation (wages, salaries, and benefits) for civilian workers rose 2.9 percent in the 12 months ending in the third quarter of 2008, compared with a 3.3-percent increase for the same period a year earlier, according to the BLS Employment Cost Index. Wages rose 3.1 percent during the 2007–2008 period, while benefits rose 2.6 percent. The average hourly wage for clerical and nonsupervisory workers was $18.17, compared with $17.57 a year earlier.

Industrial relations continued to be troubled by disputes over sharing health care costs between companies and workers, labor analysts observed in 2008. The problem was growing in urgency because some competitors of American companies do not fund health care as part of their direct labor costs and, therefore, have a built-in competitive advantage. For similar reasons, pension costs were a source of contention for management and labor as well.

Steel industry. Clinching negotiations that began in midspring, the United Steelworkers Union and United States Steel Corporation of Pittsburgh, Pennsylvania, reached agreement in September on a new contract covering 16,000 steelworkers. The agreement, which was overwhelmingly approved by union members, provided a $6,000 "ratification" bonus to each member, a $1 hourly increase in the first year, and 4-percent pay hikes in each of the remaining three years of the four-year contract.

In autumn, the United Steelworkers also reached agreement on a four-year contract with Luxembourg-based ArcelorMittal, covering 14,000 workers in 14 states; and with Cleveland-Cliffs Iron Company of Cleveland, Ohio, covering another 2,300 workers in two states. Both agreements mirrored the terms the union reached earlier with United States Steel.

Communications industry. In August, Verizon Communications Inc. of New York City reached agreement on new three-year contracts with the Communication Workers of America and the International Brotherhood of

Electrical Workers. The contracts, which covered 65,000 Verizon workers in 10 northeastern and mid-Atlantic states and the District of Columbia, provided a 10.5-percent wage increase over a three-year term. Verizon agreed to contribute a fixed amount for each year of service to cover future retirees' health care costs. Members of the unions approved the agreement in September.

Also in August, Qwest Communications International Inc. of Denver reached a tentative three-year agreement with the Communication Workers of America (CWA) covering about 20,000 workers in 13 states. In late September, however, CWA members rejected the plan. Qwest and CWA returned to the negotiating table and came up with a revised agreement on October 10, which the union rank and file approved. The new contract expanded wage provisions—embracing a 12.5-percent increase over three years—but retained increases in premiums to be paid by workers for their health care.

Entertainment industry. Over the 2007-2008 television and radio season, labor and management were confronted with the need to conclude several major collective bargaining agreements to maintain continuous output of movies, television, and radio. The sticking point in all of the bargaining was how to share revenues from "new media," such as DVD's and the Internet.

In January 2008, the Alliance of Motion Picture and Television Producers (AMPTP), the negotiating organization for the Hollywood studios, concluded an agreement with the Directors Guild of America (DGA), which provided a general framework for sharing revenue from the use of original programs on the new media. In February, the Writers' Guild of America (WGA) approved a similar agreement, ending a 100-day strike that began on Nov. 5, 2007. Analysts rated the walkout the most costly in entertainment industry history. In May 2008, the Association of Film, Television, and Radio Artists (AFTRA) and the AMPTP reached agreement on a new contract containing similar provisions for sharing revenue from new media.

Despite the successful conclusion of agreements with other Hollywood "talent" unions, bargaining between AMPTP and the Screen Actors' Guild (SAG) deadlocked. In November, a federal mediator overseeing the negotiations declared that there was no use in continuing the talks. Entertainment industry insiders speculated that union leaders would next poll the SAG membership for authorization to strike.

In July, the Actors Equity Association (AEA) and the Broadway League (BL) reached agreement on a new 39-month contract. (AEA represents stage actors and stage managers; BL represents producers and theater owners in New York City.) The contract provided an 11.25-percent increase in actors' and stage managers' compensation and stipulated how recorded shows could be used over the Internet and in publicity releases.

Food industry. In April, members of the United Food and Commercial Workers Union (UFCW) ratified a four-year agreement with The Kroger Company of Cincinnati, covering over 11,000 workers in northern Kentucky and southern Indiana. The contract provided wage increases ranging from 90 cents to $3 an hour and left workers' health care arrangements unchanged. It required Kroger to increase contributions to workers' pensions by 40 percent.

On September 30, the UFCW reached agreements with two grocery chains in Cleveland. These agreements covered 8,700 workers.

Aerospace industry. On August 28, the Boeing Company of Chicago presented its "best and final" offer to the International Association of Machinists (IAM) to unlock deadlocked negotiations over a new three-year contract. The union rejected the offer, however, and workers struck Boeing on September 6.

Boeing and union representatives agreed on October 8 to resume negotiations and agreed

CHANGES IN THE UNITED STATES LABOR FORCE

	2007	2008*
Civilian labor force	153,306,000	155,038,000
Total employment	146,016,000	144,958,000
Unemployment	7,291,000	10,080,000
Unemployment rate	4.8%	6.5%

Change in weekly earnings of production and nonsupervisory workers (nonfarm business sector)		
Current dollars	3.8%	3.5%
Constant (1982) dollars	0.1%	-0.4%

| Change in output per employee hour (nonfarm business sector) | 1.5% | 2.0% |

*All 2008 data are through the third quarter of 2008 (preliminary data).
Source: *World Book* estimates based on data from the U.S. Bureau of Labor Statistics.

on a new contract later that month. IAM members ratified the agreement on November 1. The contract, expanded to four-year coverage, provided 15-percent pay increases and bonuses totaling $8,000 over the four years. In another concession by Boeing, the contract left arrangements for workers' contributions to health insurance premiums unchanged.

Airline industry. In October, the U.S. Justice Department approved the merger of Minneapolis-based Northwest Airlines and Atlanta-based Delta Airlines. The unions potentially affected by the merger—the International Association of Machinists and the Association of Flight Attendants—vowed to protect the jobs and pay members. At congressional hearings in April, representatives of the two merging airlines promised lawmakers that they would not close hub airports or lay off workers.

Health industry. In October, Catholic Healthcare West of San Francisco reached an agreement with the Service Employees International Union's United Healthcare Workers-West, representing 14,000 workers in 33 California health care facilities. The four-year agreement provided an average cumulative wage increase of 26 percent.

Trucking industry. In August, members of the International Brotherhood of Teamsters rejected a three-year contract that union representatives had negotiated with the National Automobile Transporters Labor Division (NATLD). In the talks, the Teamsters represented truck drivers and the NATLD, transportation companies that deliver new cars from U.S. ports to dealerships. The negotiating units returned to the bargaining table and on September 19 reached a second tentative agreement. According to this agreement, wages would be frozen for the first two years only of the three-year contract; also, new hires' wage rates would not be reduced as proposed in the August agreement. Teamsters approved the deal in October.

Automobile industry. In late 2008, executives of the three major U.S. auto manufacturers—Chrysler LLC of Auburn Hills, Michigan; Ford Motor Company of Dearborn, Michigan; and General Motors (GM) Corporation of Detroit—appeared before Congress to request billions in bailout funds for the ailing industry. All three companies suffered big losses in 2008, and GM and Chrysler reported that their cash reserves were nearly exhausted. Congressional negotiators, recognizing that the fate of the "Big Three" would have profound implications for the future of the millions of workers associated with U.S. automobile manufacturing sought to craft a package in which all industry segments, including the workers and the United Automobile Workers Union, would play their part. A $14-billion bailout plan was passed by the House of Representatives in December but died in the Senate over Republican demands for greater union concessions. On December 18, President George W. Bush announced that he was making a $17.4-billion short-term loan package available to the Big Three. He called on labor to agree to wage and work rules competitive with those of foreign automakers by the end of 2009; he also called for the elimination of the "jobs bank," which gave laid-off workers long-term supplementary pay. However, the UAW had already agreed to suspend the program earlier in December.

Unions. In 2007, there were 15.67 million members in U.S. labor unions—12.1 percent of all wage and salary workers, according to the most recent available data from the BLS. In 2006, union members made up 12 percent of the work force. The 2007 data revealed that, within the private sector, some 29.4 percent of workers in the utilities industry were unionized. Running a close second and third were the transportation industry (22.3 percent) and the telecommunications industry (20.8 percent). In the public sector, nearly 40 percent of workers at all levels of government were union members.

Federal government. On Sept. 25, 2008, President Bush signed the Americans with Disabilities Amendments Act (ADAA) of 2008. The ADAA revised the original 1990 Americans with Disabilities Act (ADA) in light of several U.S. Supreme Court decisions that had restricted application of the law to a degree not envisioned by many of ADA's original proponents.

On May 21, 2008, President Bush signed the Genetic Information Nondiscrimination Act. It bars employers from discriminating against employees on the basis of their genetic profiles and prohibits genetic discrimination by insurance companies and health care organizations.

International employment. In the second half of 2008, rates of unemployment increased in nearly all of the world's developed nations, due in part to the credit crisis that engulfed financial markets. By the third quarter, unemployment in the United States spiked to 6.7 percent. Unemployment in the Eurozone, the 15 member nations of the European Union (EU) that use the euro currency, rose to 7.5 percent. Unemployment in Japan in mid-2008 was 4 percent and in the United Kingdom, 5.8 percent.

■ Robert W. Fisher

See also **Bank: A Special Report; Disability; Economics; U.S. Government: A Special Report.**

Labrador. See Canadian provinces.

Laos. See Asia.

LATIN AMERICA

Major nations in Latin America, including Argentina, Brazil, Chile, Mexico, and Venezuela, demonstrated remarkable resilience in the face of the economic turmoil that rocked world financial markets in 2008. Fortunately for them, the crisis occurred following a decade-long boom in the value of the region's exports of petroleum, raw materials, and agricultural commodities.

Drawing on growing demand for their raw materials and commodities in Asia, particularly in China, several nations in Latin America continued to rack up sizable trade surpluses and swell their hard-currency reserves. By the time the 2008 global financial crisis began, prudent governments had set aside large percentages of these fiscal windfalls—tens of billions of dollars in several instances—against a future economic downturn. Brazil in 2008 had more than $200 billion in reserves following one of the longest periods of growth the Latin American region had ever known.

South American Union. On May 23, the leaders of all 12 South American nations established the Union of South American Nations (UNASUR). The group, modeled on the European Union, was to work toward the eventual adoption of a common currency and the coordination of regional energy, immigration, and communication policies.

UNASUR members were invited to join the Bank of the South, headquartered in Caracas, Venezuela. The bank was created in 2007 as an

A Pataxó Hã-Hã-Hãe Indian in traditional headdress and body paint carries legal documents to a hearing before the Supreme Federal Court of Brazil in Brasília, the capital, on Sept. 24, 2008. The Pataxó petitioned to recover thousands of acres of ancestral land given to farmers by the government in the 1960's and 1970's.

alternative to the World Bank and International Monetary Fund, both United Nations-affiliated lending agencies. Venezuela's President Hugo Chávez and several of the leaders of the bank's other charter members (Argentina, Bolivia, Brazil, Ecuador, Paraguay, and Uruguay) believed that the agencies were dominated—often to the detriment of Latin American countries—by the United States government. The bank's initial capital of $10 billion was provided largely by Chávez.

Brazil a world power. In 2008, several of Latin America's government-controlled corporate giants, often decried in the U.S. business media as forms of socialism, racked up record profits. These included most of the region's largest producers of natural gas, petroleum, and such raw materials as copper and iron ore.

Brazil's Companhia Vale do Rio Doce (VALE), the world's second largest mining company, drew on its earnings to embark on a $59-billion, five-year investment program to finance future expansion. VALE also placed a $1.6-billion order for the construction of vessels in China to be used exclusively to carry iron ore—of which VALE was the world's largest producer—to markets in Asia. However, the company proved susceptible to the economic times as slumping demand for iron ore caused VALE to reduce production by 9 percent in October and cut 1,300 jobs in December. A further 5,500 workers were idled with pay to slow production and 1,200 others were reassigned.

In contrast, Embraer, a Brazilian manufacturer of midsized commercial jet aircraft. Embraer, the world's fourth largest aircraft maker, had seen its sales double in value in the previous decade. In 2008, the company was on target to deliver 200 jets. As of midyear, Embraer had $20.6 billion in orders on its books, including $6 billion for executive jets.

Thanks to growing exports of manufactured goods and raw materials, Brazil accounted for 37 percent of Latin America's total wealth in 2008. It also was ranked during the year among the world's major emerging market economies, alongside China, India, and Russia. Brazil's boom in international commerce and huge, recently discovered offshore oil reserves continued to generate enormous wealth. By 2008, Brazil had more than 220,000 millionaires.

Rise of the middle class. Through outlays of unprecedented size in social programs, the Brazilian government also managed to reduce the gap between the rich and poor. For the first time in the populous country's history, the number of Brazilians classified as middle class in 2008 exceeded the number of people living in poverty.

Amid an explosion in the availability of credit, the number of Brazilians taking out mortgages to buy homes—up 72 percent in 2007—continued to rise. The same was true of the number of people financing new vehicles, up 45 percent in 2007 for total sales of 2.46 million vehicles. In 2008, the upward trend continued, as the terms for loans became more favorable for borrowers and repayment periods lengthened.

Waning U.S. influence. During 2008, the economic importance of the United States in the region decreased as Latin American nations opened up new markets in Europe and Asia. President Chávez of Venezuela struck deals with Chinese leaders that were expected to lead to billions of dollars of new investment in Venezuela and a quadrupling of the oil it supplied China.

Chávez signed agreements with Russia aimed at further reducing the role of American companies in Venezuela. Under these agreements, for example, U.S. and international oil companies, whose assets Chávez seized or brought under Venezuelan government control in 2006 and 2007, were to be replaced by Russian natural gas and oil giants to exploit the vast energy resources of the Orinoco Basin.

Protests over higher prices. The role of the United States continued to be of paramount importance to many smaller, less affluent Latin American nations, whose fortunes were still closely tied to the U.S. economy. Gasoline that topped $5 per gallon and a 15-percent increase in the cost of food sparked sporadic protests in Central America and elsewhere in the region.

To ease the situation, at least temporarily, some governments imposed price controls or subsidized sales of basic foodstuffs. Others encouraged citizens, as an act of patriotism, to plant home gardens. In April, officials in Guyana began distributing free seeds, fertilizer, and hand farming tools to families in rural areas. This was meant to help offset the impact of skyrocketing prices for chicken and rice, which had increased by 50 percent and 80 percent, respectively, in the previous year, according to President Bharrat Jagdeo.

With the possible exception of Haiti, nowhere was the shortage of food more dire than in Cuba, which lost 30 percent of its standing crops to the devastation caused by tropical storms in 2008. In their wake, Cuban authorities rushed to put in place a program for farm reform announced earlier in the year and leased unused state-controlled lands to farmers in the private sector.

Alternative forms of energy. In energy-poor nations, the rush was also on in 2008 to reduce their dependency on costly oil imports that sapped the strength of the economy. The newly elected government of Guatemala, for example, sought private funding for projects to

FACTS IN BRIEF ON LATIN AMERICA

Country	Population	Government	Monetary unit[†]	Foreign trade (million U.S.$) Exports[††]	Imports[††]
Antigua and Barbuda	84,000	Governor General Louisse Lake-Tack; Prime Minister Baldwin Spencer	XCD dollar (2.70 = $1)	84	523
Argentina	39,746,000	President Cristina Fernández de Kirchner	peso (3.03 = $1)	55,780	42,530
Bahamas	336,000	Governor General Arthur Hanna; Prime Minister Hubert Ingraham	dollar (1.00 = $1)	674	2,401
Barbados	282,000	Governor General Sir Clifford Straughn Husbands; Prime Minister David Thompson	dollar (2.02 = $1)	385	1,586
Belize	312,000	Governor General Sir Colville Young, Sr.; Prime Minister Dean Barrow	dollar (2.00 = $1)	429	642
Bolivia	9,764,000	President Evo Morales	boliviano (6.97 = $1)	4,490	3,249
Brazil	193,540,000	President Luiz Inácio Lula da Silva	real (1.62 = $1)	160,600	120,600
Chile	16,763,000	President Michelle Bachelet	peso (519.80 = $1)	67,640	43,990
Colombia	43,127,000	President Álvaro Uribe Vélez	peso (1,894.30 = $1)	30,580	31,170
Costa Rica	4,550,000	President Óscar Arias Sánchez	colón (553.45 = $1)	9,268	12,260
Cuba	11,371,000	President Raúl Castro	peso (0.93 = $1)	3,734	10,080
Dominica	80,000	President Nicholas Liverpool; Prime Minister Roosevelt Skerrit	XCD dollar (2.70 = $1)	94	296
Dominican Republic	9,290,000	President Leonel Fernández Reyna	peso (34.79 = $1)	7,237	13,820
Ecuador	13,832,000	President Rafael Correa	U.S. dollar	14,370	12,760
El Salvador	7,218,000	President Elías Antonio Saca	colón (8.75 = $1) U.S. dollar	4,035	8,108
Grenada	106,000	Governor General Daniel Williams; Prime Minister Keith Mitchell	XCD dollar (2.70 = $1)	38	343
Guatemala	13,532,000	President Álvaro Colom	quetzal (7.43 = $1)	6,940	12,620
Guyana	753,000	President Bharrat Jagdeo Prime Minister Samuel Hinds	dollar (200.30 = $1)	683	1,006
Haiti	9,037,000	President Réne Préval; Prime Minister Michèle Pierre-Louis	gourde (38.95 = $1)	522	1,734
Honduras	7,691,000	President Manuel Zelaya	lempira (18.95 = $1)	5,594	8,556
Jamaica	2,695,000	Governor General Kenneth Hall; Prime Minister Bruce Golding	dollar (72.25 = $1)	2,331	5,784
Mexico	110,915,000	President Felipe Calderón Hinojosa	peso (10.15 = $1)	271,900	281,900
Nicaragua	5,458,000	President Daniel Ortega	gold cordoba (19.49 = $1)	2,313	4,078
Panama	3,394,000	President Martín Torrijos Espino	balboa (1.00 = $1)	9,312	12,620
Paraguay	6,352,000	President Fernando Lugo Méndez	guarani (3,970.00 = $1)	5,463	6,094
Peru	29,180,000	President Alan García Pérez	new sol (2.96 = $1)	27,960	19,600
Puerto Rico	3,959,000	Governor Luis G. Fortuño*	U.S. dollar	46,900	29,100
St. Kitts and Nevis	44,000	Governor General Cuthbert Montraville Sebastian; Prime Minister Denzil Douglas	XCD dollar (2.70 = $1)	84	383
St. Lucia	172,000	Governor General Pearlette Louisy; Prime Minister Stephenson King	XCD dollar (2.70 = $1)	288	791
St. Vincent and the Grenadines	121,000	Governor General Sir Frederick Nathaniel Ballantyne; Prime Minister Ralph E. Gonsalves	XCD dollar (2.70 = $1)	193	578
Suriname	458,000	President Runaldo Ronald Venetiaan	dollar (2.75 = $1)	1,391	1,297
Trinidad and Tobago	1,316,000	President George Maxwell Richards; Prime Minister Patrick Manning	dollar (6.20 = $1)	13,390	7,670
Uruguay	3,370,000	President Tabaré Ramón Vázquez Rosas	peso (19.25 = $1)	5,063	5,554
Venezuela	28,112,000	President Hugo Chávez Frías	new bolívar (2.15 = $1)	69,170	45,460

*Elected Nov. 4, 2008; due to take office on Jan. 2, 2009.
[†]Exchange rates as of Sept. 30, 2008.

[††]Latest available data.

expand and diversify the nation's sources of power and reduce the amount of electric power produced by oil to just 1 percent by 2022. In Nicaragua, authorities invited foreign companies to develop the proven geothermal sources of energy within the string of volcanoes that dot the nation's landscape.

In Chile, the Grupo Enhol, a renewable energy conglomerate based in Spain, announced in early August a $1-billion investment to construct what was to be Latin America's largest wind farm. The Spanish company planned to install 243 windmills on a 25,000-acre (110,000-hectare) tract of land called the Parque Talinay, located in the hills near Coquimbo. The windmills were expected to add 500 megawatts to Chile's central electric-power grid by 2011, power needed to develop newly discovered copper deposits in the region.

Elections and new constitutions. In 2008, elections in the Dominican Republic brought President Leonel Fernández a third consecutive term. Raised in New York City, the popular leader warned Dominicans at his inauguration in mid-August of hard times ahead because of the "deteriorating global economy."

In Grenada, Tillman Thomas, a veteran law-maker, became prime minister in 2008 following an upset victory over a party that had held power for 13 years. He pledged better management of the tiny nation's economy, which suffered sub-stantial damage from severe tropical storms in 2008. In Guatemala, Álvaro Colom, a socialist and civil engineer by profession, became his country's first left-of-center president in 53 years.

In Paraguay, there was another such turnover, when Fernando Armindo Lugo Méndez, 56, of the Patriotic Alliance for Change was sworn in for a five-year term as president on August 15. The stunning upset victory by Lugo, a former Roman Catholic bishop, marked the end of 62 years of rule by the Colorado Party. At his inauguration, Lugo, who was much admired for his work with the poor, addressed the crowd in both Spanish and Guarani, a language spoken commonly by Paraguayan Indians. He pledged to improve their economic standing by mounting a program of agricultural reform. To finance this ambition in a country where just 1 percent of the population owned 77 percent of the farmable land in 2008, he vowed to increase Paraguay's share of the revenues generated by the Itaipú Dam, owned by Paraguay and Brazil. The current accord on rev-enues from the world's largest hydroelectric facil-ity was due to expire in 2010.

Two Andean nations sought to redress long-standing social inequalities by writing new con-stitutions. Ecuadorean voters approved by a wide margin a constitution drafted by a national assembly and supported by their popular leader,

President Rafael Correa, on Sept. 28, 2008. Under the new constitution, all Ecuadoreans were guar-anteed a free education through college. Stay-at-home mothers, as well as those working in unregistered businesses in the informal econ-omy, became eligible for government-paid retirement pensions.

In Bolivia, another progressive president, Evo Morales, sought to enhance the standing of the country's long-downtrodden *indigenous* (native) majority through a similar course of action. The Bolivian Congress set Jan. 25, 2009, as the date for a national referendum on the new constitu-tion. If approved, Bolivia would hold national elections on Dec. 6, 2009, with Morales eligible to seek just one more five-year term.

Tribe photographed. In May 2008, news media around the world carried photographs of what was described as one of the world's last "uncontacted" tribes. The photos were taken near the border between Brazil and Peru by a low-flying airplane operated by Survival Interna-tional, a nonprofit organization based in London whose mission is to help tribal peoples to "defend their lives, protect their lands, and determine their own futures." The tribe was said to be previously unknown to outsiders. Photo-graphs showed Indians painted bright red, about to shoot arrows from their drawn bows at the overhead aircraft.

It was later revealed that the tribe had been known since 1910 and that the story was a pub-licity stunt by Survival International to bring attention to the more than 60 tribes in Brazil whose way of life was being threatened by deforestation and contacts with outsiders. Since 2000, more than 93,000 square miles (150,000 square kilometers) of rain forest have been cleared in the Brazilian Amazon.

Russian naval power. In November and December 2008, Russian naval vessels conducted joint exercises with the Venezuelan navy. The maneuvers coincided with a four-nation tour by Russian President Dmitry Medvedev, who sought to increase Russian influence in Latin America.

Map of violence. A November 2008 study showed that Latin America had the highest mur-der rates in the world for people ages 15 to 24. Data from 83 countries showed the chance of being murdered in Latin America was 30 times greater than in Europe. The study blamed Latin America's history of armed conflicts and a preva-lence of gangs and drug trafficking. El Salvador had the highest youth murder rate, at 92 per 100,000 people.   ■ Nathan A. Haverstock

See also **Food: A Special Report**; various Latin American country articles.

Latvia. See Europe.

Law. See **Civil rights; Courts; Crime; Prison.**

Lebanon. On May 6, 2008, Lebanon's Cabinet fired Brigadier General Wafiq Shuqayr, the security chief of Beirut International Airport in Lebanon's capital, because he allowed the pro-Syria opposition group Hezbollah to set up spy cameras for monitoring flights into and out of the airport. The Cabinet also asked Lebanon's army to dismantle Hezbollah's secure telecommunications network because it posed a threat to national security.

Hezbollah and Amal, another pro-Syria group, used these decisions as a pretext to wage war against forces aligned with the anti-Syria "Cedar Revolution" leaders Saad al-Hariri and Walid Jumblat in Beirut and Mount Lebanon. The Cedar Revolution leaders called for the army to restore order in the two Lebanese cities. After several days of fighting—and more than 40 deaths—the Cabinet reversed its decision to fire Shuqayr.

Doha agreement. In an attempt to resolve Lebanon's long-time political crisis, Emir Hamad bin Khalifa al-Thani, the leader of Qatar, convened the Lebanese Dialogue Conference in Doha, Qatar's capital, on May 16. Conference attendees represented all 14 major political parties and parliamentary blocs in Lebanon. An agreement reached on May 21 specified that General Michel Suleiman, the popular commander of Lebanon's army, be elected president and that the pro-Syria opposition be given 11 ministries in the 30-member Cabinet. In return, Hezbollah and its allies ended their sit-in that had been blocking downtown Beirut since December 2006 and accepted a prohibition on the use of weapons to resolve political disputes.

New president. The Doha agreement led to the May 25, 2008, election by the National Assembly (parliament) of General Suleiman as the new president of Lebanon. Until the agreement was reached, Nabih Birri, the pro-Syria speaker of the Chamber of Deputies, had prevented the National Assembly from convening to vote for president. Suleiman received 118 of 127 parliamentary votes cast. Prime Minister Fouad Siniora formed the government's new Cabinet in July.

President Suleiman made an official state visit to Syria in August. During his visit, he reached an agreement with Syria's president, Bashar al-Assad, to form committees for the demarcation of borders between the two countries, to establish formal diplomatic ties, and to open embassies in each other's capital cities.

Terrorist attacks. A number of terrorist attacks attributed by experts to Syria occurred in Lebanon in 2008. On January 25, a car bomb in a Beirut suburb killed Captain Wissam Eid, director of the intelligence unit in Lebanon's Internal Security Forces. Eid had been instrumental in uncovering the secret cells of the terrorist organization Fatah al-Islam, as well as in investigating cell phone communications that led to the assassination of former Prime Minister Rafik al-Hariri in February 2005.

On Aug. 13, 2008, the day President Suleiman arrived in Syria, a bomb exploded in the northern Lebanese port city of Tripoli. The explosion killed at least 18 people, most of them members of the Lebanese army. Some political observers construed the attack as a warning by pro-Syria forces to Suleiman and the army. On August 28, Hezbollah fighters in southern Lebanon attacked a Lebanese army helicopter, killing an air force officer.

On September 29—after a visit by Suleiman to the United States, which included a request for military aid for the Lebanese army—another bomb was detonated in Tripoli. That attack killed six people, including four soldiers.

International tribunal. United Nations Secretary-General Ban Ki-moon announced in November that an international tribunal to prosecute those responsible for political killings in Lebanon would begin work in March 2009. The focus of the tribunal was to be the 2005 murder of former Prime Minister al-Hariri. ■ Marius Deeb

See also **Middle East; Syria.**

Lesotho. See Africa.

Liberia. See Africa.

Library. Violent weather played havoc on a number of library systems in the United States in 2008, though the damage was not nearly as devastating as that caused by hurricanes Katrina and Rita in 2005. In September 2008, Hurricane Ike hit the Gulf coast of Louisiana and eastern Texas. The Rosenberg Library in Galveston, Texas, suffered the most damage, when a storm surge inundated the collection that was housed on the first floor. In Cedar Rapids, Iowa, the city library was all but wiped out when heavy June rains made the nearby Cedar River overflow and flood most of the buildings in the downtown area. Repairs to the Cedar Rapids Public Library were expected to take up to three years. In the interim, people were to use the city's only branch, which is located in an unaffected part of the city.

Funding woes. Because most public libraries in the United States are supported by taxes, the 2008 financial crisis hit many libraries. Donors that libraries relied on to fund such extras as reading clubs and after-school tutoring either began reducing how much they gave or stopped donating altogether. State and local governments cut library funding as well, because officials could not collect as much in property taxes or sales taxes as the plunge in home sales spread to sales of cars and other expensive items.

Library budget problems caused crises around

the country. Officials in a number of communities tried to lower government expenses by closing neighborhood or downtown libraries. Protesters were successful in forcing officials to keep libraries open in Long Beach, California; Memphis, Tennessee; and Hartford, Connecticut. In other places, people brainstormed ways to save their libraries. Volunteers in Josephine County, Oregon, formed an organization to raise enough money to restart public library service. They hoped to have at least one of the county's four libraries open by the end of the year, after having gone for more than a year with no libraries at all. The county had closed the libraries in April 2007 because of lack of funds. In suburban Detroit, the trustees of the cash-starved Macomb County Library in 2008 agreed to let Wayne State University lease its building and become its manager. The university benefited from the arrangement because students studying library and information science would be able to get on-the-job training.

Popularity. Ironically, more people flocked to their public libraries even as the libraries were looking for enough money to stay open. A database created by the Gannett News Service, using federal research and state statistics for U.S. communities of 10,000 or more people, showed that 10 percent more people visited libraries in 2006 than did in 2002. The database also showed that libraries loaned 9 percent more titles during that same period. According to an American Library Association survey, 99 percent of public libraries in the United States offered Internet access by 2008; and in 73 percent of selected cities and towns, the public library was the only place to access online services for free.

Privacy. On July 10, 2008, U.S. President George W. Bush signed into law an act that amended the Foreign Intelligence Surveillance Act. The amendments allow the government to secretly read e-mails and intercept telephone calls that U.S. citizens send and receive at libraries and elsewhere. The American Civil Liberties Union and other citizens' watch groups sued the federal government, claiming that the law was unconstitutional under the Fourth Amendment.

Freedom of speech. Censorship became a hot topic during the 2008 presidential election, after Alaska Governor Sarah Palin was nominated as the Republican vice-presidential candidate. Public opinion became critical of Palin when the media claimed she had asked the librarian of the Wasilla (Alaska) Public Library how books could be banned from the collection in 1996 while Palin was serving as the city's mayor. However, city officials said the allegations were unfounded.

■ Beverly Goldberg

See also **Bank: A Special Report; Weather.**

Libya assumed the presidency of the United Nations (UN) Security Council on Jan. 1, 2008. The UN General Assembly had elected Libya to the 15-member Security Council in October 2007 for a two-year term. The Security Council presidency, which is held for one month, rotates among member countries in alphabetical order.

United States relations. In January 2008, Foreign Minister Abdel-Rahman Shalqam became the highest-ranking Libyan government official to visit Washington, D.C., since the 1970's. Shalqam signed a number of educational and technical exchange agreements with U.S. officials.

In October 2008, Libya made payments of $1.8 billion to a fund for families of victims of terrorist attacks in which Libyan agents were implicated—the Pan Am Flight 103 bombing over Lockerbie, Scotland, in 1988 and the La Belle discotheque bombing in 1980 in what was then West Berlin, West Germany. The payments cleared the way for the November 2008 approval by the U.S. Senate of diplomat Gene Cretz as the first U.S. ambassador to be stationed in Libya in 36 years.

Natural gas exploration. Officials with the Libyan government-owned National Oil Company announced in February 2008 that they had signed natural gas exploration and production-sharing agreements with Royal Dutch Shell of the Netherlands, Occidental Petroleum of Los Angeles, and Liwa, a petroleum company based in the United Arab Emirates. Libyan officials planned to substantially increase Libya's production of natural gas and to make Libya a major exporter of natural gas to the European Union.

Russian contracts. President Vladimir Putin of Russia visited Libya in April, the first such visit by a Russian or Soviet head of state since 1985. Putin agreed to write off Libya's $4.5-billion debt to Russia in exchange for a number of military and civilian contracts between the two countries. Putin and his delegation signed 10 trade, investment, and other agreements with their Libyan counterparts, the largest of which was a $3.4-billion contract to build a railway between the Libyan cities of Sirte and Benghazi.

"King of kings." More than 200 kings and other tribal leaders from several African countries met in Benghazi in August 2008 and bestowed the title of "king of kings" on Libyan leader Mu'ammar al-Qadhafi. Qadhafi, in turn, urged the visiting leaders to support his vision of a united Africa with one currency, one army, and one African passport that would allow Africans to travel and work anywhere on the continent. Qadhafi also urged the creation of a grassroots movement throughout Africa that would work toward achieving those goals. ■ Mary-Jane Deeb

See also **Africa; United Nations.**

Liechtenstein. See Europe.

Literature. Two literary giants died in 2008. Alexander Solzhenitsyn, a Soviet dissident, died in Moscow on August 3 at age 89. Solzhenitsyn's work *The Gulag Archipelago* (1973-1975) exposed the repression of Stalin's regime and, specifically, the labor camps Stalin had devised for criminals and political prisoners. The book led to Solzhenitsyn's expulsion from the Soviet Union; he returned home in 1994, after the fall of the Soviet system.

American author David Foster Wallace—a novelist, short-story writer, essayist, and journalist—committed suicide on Sept. 12, 2008, at age 46. Wallace, whose best-known work was perhaps the novel *Infinite Jest* (1996), had been called a "prose magician" and "one of his generation's pre-eminent talents" by *The New York Times.*

Pulitzer Prize. The 2008 Pulitzer Prize for Fiction, granted "for distinguished fiction by an American author, preferably dealing with American life," was awarded to Dominican-born American author Junot Díaz for his debut novel, *The Brief Wondrous Life of Oscar Wao.* Oscar is a Dominican-American misfit hoping to be "the Dominican Tolkien." The book negotiates Oscar's family history in the Dominican Republic during the political reign of Rafael Trujillo and in present-day New Jersey. Although this was a first novel, Díaz had previously published *Drown,* a short-story collection, in 1996.

The finalists for the Pulitzer for Fiction were Denis Johnson, for his Vietnam saga, *Tree of Smoke;* and Lore Segal, for her collection of related short stories, *Shakespeare's Kitchen,* which narrated the activities of a Connecticut think tank.

A genius grant. The John D. and Catherine T. MacArthur Foundation, a Chicago-based grant-making body, awarded one of its 2008 fellowships—colloquially known as "genius grants"—to a fiction writer, 31-year-old Nigerian-American Chimamanda Adichie. Her works included *Purple Hibiscus* (2003), winner of the 2005 Commonwealth Writers' Prize for Best First Book, and *Half of a Yellow Sun* (2006). The book was described by the MacArthur Foundation as a novel that "unflinchingly portrays the horror and destruction of the civil war following the establishment of the Republic of Biafra" and that was "enlightening audiences both in her homeland and around the world."

PEN/Faulkner Award. Kate Christensen's novel *The Great Man* won the 2008 PEN/Faulkner award for fiction. The title referred to a recently deceased painter, but it was deliberately misleading, as the novel actually followed the story of three women in his life—a wife, a mistress, and

Salman Rushdie displays the medal he was awarded for "services to literature" when knighted by Queen Elizabeth II at Buckingham Palace in June. Several Muslim nations protested the honor. Rushdie's 1988 novel *The Satanic Verses* has been condemned by Iranian Ayatollah Khomeini, who issued a *fatwa* (religious edict) that threatened Rushdie's life.

Arthur C. Clarke:
Scientific Rapture

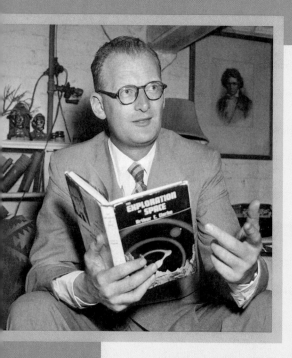

Arthur C. Clarke was less interested in human beings than in human destiny. As the world's most famous science fiction author, Clarke published hundreds of essays and more than 100 books. He was an inexhaustible champion of space exploration, who described communications satellites many years before people could reach space. An asteroid, a dinosaur, and even one of Earth's orbits are all named in Clarke's honor. He died at age 90, on March 19, 2008.

Clarke was born on Dec. 16, 1917, in Somerset County, in the United Kingdom. At 13, he built a telescope and began to build small rockets. He became an avid fan of science fiction. He soon joined the British Interplanetary Society, a group that promoted space exploration. He was twice chairman of the society.

During World War II (1939-1945), Clarke was an officer with the Royal Air Force, helping to develop radar technology. Legend has it that when Clarke and fellow space enthusiasts heard a V-2 rocket from Germany roaring overhead, they stood and applauded the coming space age.

In 1945, Clarke described in detail how "extra-terrestrial relays" could route communications from an orbit of 22,300 miles (35,888 kilometers). This is precisely the orbit communications satellites used when they were launched 20 years later. The orbit Clarke described now bears his name, though he was typically modest about his contribution. "My early disclosure may have advanced the cause of space communications by about 15 minutes," he quipped.

Clarke published his first science fiction story in 1945, and his first novel, *Childhood's End,* followed in 1953. In the coming decades, he wrote many novels, including *2001: A Space Odyssey* (1968), *Rendezvous with Rama* (1973), and *The Fountains of Paradise* (1979). Clarke won the Hugo and Nebula awards, as well as every major honor in science fiction. His awards and mementos eventually filled up an entire room, which he jokingly called the "Ego Chamber."

Clarke delighted in scientific realism, and his novels include detailed descriptions of visionary technology, from generation ships to space elevators. Clarke's great limitation as a writer was that his characters resemble the anonymous engineers of the space age, men whose feelings about their families seem secondary to their passion for a perfect orbital insertion. Clarke himself was married only briefly, and it is telling that his most memorable character was HAL, the serene but murderous computer from *2001*.

Clarke wrote that "any sufficiently advanced technology is indistinguishable from magic," and most of the aliens he imagined are indistinguishable from gods. Indeed, many of Clarke's novels end in a sort of scientific rapture, in which people take their rightful place among the alien gods. Consider the end of *2001*, for example, when the Star Child comes to Earth to announce a new age. This secular mysticism allowed Clarke to explore biblical questions even as he respected scientific laws.

Clarke died in Sri Lanka, where he settled in 1956 to pursue his love of scuba diving. Before his death, Clarke arranged for a rocket to carry a lock of his hair into space. He certainly earned his place there. ■ Brian Johnson

a sister. One judge, Molly Giles, called the book "intelligent, consistently entertaining, and original."

Other literature in 2008. It was a fruitful year for well-established writers as well. The Indian-British author Salman Rushdie published his 10th novel, *The Enchantress of Florence,* a blending of history and fantasy, about which Christopher Hitchens wrote, "the worlds of illusion and enchantment seem to collapse in upon themselves, leaving a rich compost of legend and myth for successor generations."

Something to Tell You, the sixth novel by the British novelist Hanif Kureishi, depicted a psychoanalyst's amusing and tragic struggles with middle age; Kureishi's countryman David Lodge, best known for his academic satires *Changing Places* (1975) and *Small World* (1984), achieved similar comic effects with a middle-aged linguistics professor in *Deaf Sentence.*

Jhumpa Lahiri, an American author of Indian descent and the author of the Pulitzer Prize-winning short-story collection *Interpreter of Maladies* (1999) and the novel *The Namesake* (2003), returned in 2008 with a collection of interrelated short stories called *Unaccustomed Earth.* Many of these stories dealt with pronounced cultural differences, as well as with the travails and pleasures of assimilation; all of them examined the difficulties of simple human interaction. Michiko Kakutani in *The New York Times* observed that the first-generation Indian-Americans in Lahiri's stories have "grown up translating the mysteries of the United States for their relatives, they are fluent navigators of both Bengali and American culture but completely at home in neither; they always experience themselves as standing slightly apart, given more to melancholy observation than wholehearted participation."

Toni Morrison, a Nobel laureate and author of eight previous novels, took readers to America in the late 1600's in *A Mercy,* which examined slavery and the many tragedies it engendered. Marilynne Robinson's third novel, *Home,* returned to the setting of her Pulitzer Prize-winning *Gilead* (2004), a small Iowa town in the 1950's, and used the same characters to tell a new story of family and reconciliation. James Wood in *The New Yorker* called it "magnificently moving" and "richly pondered."

John Updike's 27th novel, *The Widows of Eastwick,* was a sequel to his 1984 classic, *The Witches of Eastwick,* and followed his supernatural trio of women, now old and lonely, back to Eastwick, Rhode Island. It was described in *Library Journal* as "an unsatisfying rumination on the loss of sexual vitality and death," and *Publishers Weekly* called it "a tepid sequel." Tobias Wolff's *Our Story Begins: New and Selected Stories* was released to universal acclaim, with the *Washington Post* calling it a "towering monument of a book," *The New York Times* describing Wolff's voice as "unfailingly authentic," and the *Houston Chronicle* comparing him to Chekhov. The book included 10 new stories.

Philip Roth's 25th novel, *Indignation,* took place during the Korean War (1950-1953) and concerned a young man leaving his Newark, New Jersey, home for Winesburg College in Ohio, in part to escape his overprotective father. Dealing with sexual awakening and coming of age, the book was well received by a variety of critics.

Library of America published another Roth volume in 2008. *Philip Roth: Novels and Other Narratives 1986–1991* was made up of *The Counterlife* (1986), *The Facts* (1988), *Deception* (1990), and *Patrimony* (1991). This edition was the fifth in the Library of America's series of Roth's works.

The Library of America also released two volumes of William Maxwell's work, in honor of the author's centenary. *William Maxwell: Early Novels and Stories* included *Bright Center of Heaven* (1934), *They Came Like Swallows* (1937), *The Folded Leaf* (1945), and *Time Will Darken It* (1948). *William Maxwell: Later Novels and Stories* included *The Château* (1961) and *So Long, See You Tomorrow* (1980). Maxwell, an editor at *The New Yorker* from 1936 to 1976 (with a few periods away from the magazine) and a contributor until 1999, devoted his fiction primarily to semiautobiographical reflections on childhood, family, and life in the Midwest.

Big-city fiction. Two critically acclaimed novels set in New York City were published in 2008. The first, by Irish-born author Joseph O'Neill, took the Sept. 11, 2001, terrorist attacks on the United States as its thematic backdrop. *Netherland,* O'Neill's third novel, follows the marital difficulties and resulting self-discovery of Hans van den Broek, a banker from the Netherlands. Hans becomes involved in a cricket club made up of immigrants, and he learns about the American Dream from the perspective of America's outsiders, after his wife and child return to London following the September 11 terrorist attacks. Richard Price's *Lush Life,* set in Manhattan's Lower East Side, was the novelist's eighth work. The setting, an area of both urban decay and gentrification, is the scene of a street murder when these two sides collide.

The Lazarus Project, by Bosnian-American Aleksandar Hemon, looked at another American city, in another era: Chicago in the early 1900's. The novel was based upon a true story—the killing of a young Jewish immigrant named Lazarus Averbuch in 1908 by George Shippy, Chicago's chief of police. Shippy claimed self-defense for the killing and stated that Averbuch was an anarchist who had come to his home to kill him. The action of the novel takes place in the present, as a Bosnian-American writer attempts to uncover the truth about the crime.

Washington, D.C., came in for novelistic criticism and satire in 2008. Curtis Sittenfeld, the author of *Prep* (2005) and *Man of My Dreams* (2006), published *American Wife*, an account of the life of the fictional First Lady Alice Blackwell, whom the author admittedly modeled on First Lady Laura Bush. Sittenfeld called her book "a labor of love," adding, "I sincerely admire Laura Bush. But I understand that people may see it as peculiar and inappropriate." In *Supreme Courtship*, the latest comic offering from Christopher Buckley, a fictional president who keeps finding his nominees to the Supreme Court blocked decides to shake things up by picking a television-courtroom personality in the style of the judge on the reality-television program "Judge Judy."

Bolaño's masterpiece translated. The last novel by the late Chilean novelist Roberto Bolaño, *2666*, was translated into English in 2008. The novel had been published posthumously in Spanish in 2004. Hailed by a number of American and European critics as the writer's masterpiece, *2666* is epic in size and scope, connecting the works of a mysterious German novelist to a series of unsolved murders in a Mexican border town resembling Ciudad Juárez, itself the site of hundreds of unsolved murders of women during over the last 15 years. Bolaño, who garnered many accolades with the 2007 translation of his 1998 novel *Los detectives salvajes*, titled *The Savage Detectives*, had been compared favorably to the Colombian novelist Gabriel Garcia Márquez.

Crimes and spies. Several notable novels were published in the crime and espionage genres in 2008. Lee Child produced his 12th "Jack Reacher" novel, *Nothing to Lose*, and James Lee Burke released the 17th installment of his "Dave Robicheaux" series, *Swan Peak*. Alan Furst, the author of a number of celebrated espionage novels, including 2006's *The Foreign Correspondent*, released *The Spies of Warsaw* in 2008. Set in Poland in 1937, the book concerned the attempts of a Franco-Polish spy network to outsmart its German enemies.

The world of crime and mystery writing lost two great authors in 2008. Gregory McDonald, creator of the best-selling "Fletch" series, died on September 7, and James Crumley, a hard-boiled mystery writer and the author of the acclaimed thriller *The Last Good Kiss* (1978), died on September 17.   ■ Stefan Beck

See also **Literature for children; Nobel Prizes; Poetry; Pulitzer Prizes.**

Literature for children. Picture books remained a strong draw in 2008. Middle-grade readers enjoyed new themes in fiction, and popular fantasy series continued to grow. Some of the outstanding books of 2008 included the following:

Picture books. *Ten Little Fingers and Ten Little Toes* by Mem Fox, illustrated by Helen Oxenbury (Harcourt). This simple counting book celebrates what unites children all around the world: 10 little fingers, 10 little toes, and someone to count with a kiss. Ages 2 to 5.

Dinosaur vs. Bedtime by Bob Shea (Hyperion). A small, fiery-red dinosaur challenges opponents all day long with a "Roar!" until sleepiness conquers all. Ages 3 to 6.

Old Bear by Kevin Henkes (Greenwillow). As Old Bear heads into hibernation, his memories of all the seasons make for vivid dreams. And when he awakens, he sees again, in Henkes's bountifully colored landscape, the joy of spring. Ages 3 to 6.

Jibberwillies at Night by Rachel Vail, illustrated by Yumi Heo (Scholastic). Katie calls herself "a really happy kid," and she is, all day long. "But sometimes the JIBBERWILLIES come." She and her Mom campaign against the critters, which are tough, but not invincible. Ages 3 to 7.

The Day Leo Said I Hate You by Robie H. Harris, illustrated by Molly Bang (Little, Brown). One day, when too many "NO's" from Mommy drive Leo over the edge, Leo says what he shouldn't. He and Mom—who "bellowed" and "hollered" because she was so upset—find a way back to each other. Ages 3 to 7.

Sourpuss and Sweetie Pie by Norton Juster, illustrated by Chris Raschka (Michael di Capua Books). Many grandparents will recognize the dual personalities—loving and crabby—of this little child, wrapped up in the bright expressionistic swipes of Raschka's pictures. Ages 3 to 5.

Traction Man Meets Turbo Dog by Mini Grey (Knopf). Traction Man is the brave and true hero of the kitchen world, coming to the rescue of his beloved companion, Scrubbing Brush, who has been banished to the trash bin as "unhygienic." Ages 4 to 8.

A Couple of Boys Have the Best Week Ever by Marla Frazee (Harcourt). Eamon and his best friend spend a week with Eamon's grandparents while attending nature camp. The text describes the week from the adults' point of view, but the pictures, in a funny counterpoint, show where the boys find the real fun. Ages 4 to 8.

Garmann's Summer by Stian Hole (Eerdmans). At the end of summer, Garmann's aunts always come to visit, and this year, he shares with them his fears about starting school. They, unexpectedly, share their fears as well.

This translation of the 2007 prizewinner from the Bologna Children's Book Fair brilliantly examines the fears that all of us have at times. Ages 4 to 8.

Fiction. *My One Hundred Adventures* by Polly Horvath (Schwartz & Wade). Jane is 12 and lives a quiet life with her poet mother and siblings year-round "by the sea." Couldn't something special happen this year? And it does, as she takes unexpected balloon rides with a budding faith healer, is bribed into babysitting by a duplicitous neighbor, and sees her mother receiving mysterious visitors. Ages 8 to 12.

Diary of a Wimpy Kid: Rodrick Rules by Jeff Kinney (Amulet). Greg has a lot to record in this sequel to Kinney's 2007 print version of his Web comic. The middle school student deals with a blackmailing brother, the terrors of a talent show, and a family Thanksgiving. Ages 9 to 12.

Savvy by Ingrid Law (Dial). Beaumont family children, on their 13th birthday, are revealed to have a special power, a "savvy," often not yet under control. Mibs's birthday gift proves a useful "savvy" on a road trip to reach her hospitalized father. Delicate language, great humor. Ages 9-14.

The Astonishing Life of Octavian Nothing, Traitor to the Nation, Volume II: The Kingdom on the Waves by M. T. Anderson (Candlewick). Anderson completes his riveting account of the American Revolution from the viewpoint of a teenaged slave. Octavian and his former teacher, Dr. Trefusis, escape to join the British side, where slaves are promised post-war freedom. Octavian learns more about his mother, who "taught herself the tale she needed to tell, truth or no" and

Brian Selznick's *The Invention of Hugo Cabret*, published in 2007, was awarded the American Library Association's Caldecott Medal for "the most distinguished American picture book" in 2008. The 526-page book was the first novel to win the illustrator's award.

about the emptiness of some political promises. Ages 13 to 16.

Fantasy. *The Tales of Beedle the Bard* by J. K. Rowling (Scholastic). Various themes from the Harry Potter series are brought back to life in these five tales. Rowling originally released the stories in an edition of seven handwritten copies in 2007. Ages 10 and up.

Emmy and the Home for Troubled Girls by Lynne Jonell, illustrated by Jonathan Bean (Holt). In this sequel to *Emmy and the Incredible Shrinking Rat,* the evil nanny, Miss Barmy, is now rodent-sized but just as nasty. She's hiding little girls (previously shrunk) in a dollhouse named "The Home for Troubled Girls." Emmy Addison, working both in rodent and human sizes, thwarts Miss Barmy's aims. Ages 9 to 12.

The Hunger Games by Suzanne Collins (Scholastic). What if reality shows were real and death came for everyone but the winner? Katniss Everdeen doesn't look like a likely winner in these games, set in a desolate future America. But when her little sister is chosen to fight to the death, 16-year-old Katniss takes her place. Ages 12 to 15.

Brisingr by Christopher Paolini (Knopf). In the third book of the Inheritance Cycle, Eragon, reunited with his cousin Roran, struggles to inspire the revolutionary forces—human beings, elves, dwarves, and others—to defeat the evil King Galbatorix. Features mid-air dragon-rider combat and secrets and schemes galore. Ages 12 to 15.

Breaking Dawn by Stephenie Meyer (Little, Brown). Bella, a small-town girl from Washington state, loves Edward, a vampire who feeds on animals instead of people. She herself is beloved by Jacob, a werewolf. Meyer brings her Twilight Saga to a decidedly gory—but witty—conclusion with book four of the series. Ages 12 to 16.

Informational books. *We Are the Ship, The Story of Negro League Baseball* by Kadir Nelson (Hyperion). An anonymous player remembers the days of the Negro League, from the 1920's until after Jackie Robinson broke the color barrier and entered the majors. Nelson gives a good sense of how styles of play and public personalities were responses to exclusion, drawing readers in with his striking, full-page paintings. Ages 7 to 10.

Wanda Gág: The Girl Who Loved to Draw by Deborah Kogan Ray (Viking). Many children who have loved Gág's *Millions of Cats* now have a chance to understand the life behind those pictures. Gág grew up in the early 1900's in a family that loved and supported art but was often poor. The pictures show her determination and the Minnesota world that shaped her. Ages 7 to 10.

Mars and the Search for Life by Elaine Scott (Clarion). Scott's story of our explorations of Mars encompasses the Galileo space probe, the way the planet was portrayed in comic books of the 1900's, and launches planned in 2020. The text never hurries over the explanations of why scientists think and work as they do. Ages 10 to 13.

The Way We Work by David Macaulay (Houghton Mifflin). Human bodies are the "we" in this encyclopedic work. Teeth, brain, eyes, digestion, and more, Macaulay's detailed drawings help us see how we manage to get it all done. Ages 10 to 15.

Awards. The 2008 Newbery Medal was awarded to Laura Amy Schlitz for *Good Masters, Sweet Ladies! Voices from a Medieval Village.* The award is given by the American Library Association (ALA) for the "most distinguished contribution to American literature for children" published the previous year. The ALA's Caldecott Medal for "the most distinguished American picture book" was awarded to Brian Selznick for *The Invention of Hugo Cabret,* the first novel to win the illustrator's award. The Michael L. Printz Award, for excellence in literature for young adults, went to Geraldine McCaughrean for *The White Darkness.* ■ Mary Harris Russell

See also **Literature.**

Lithuania. Former Prime Minister Andrius Kubilius's center-right Homeland Union party triumphed in Lithuania's October 2008 parliamentary elections, ousting the ruling center-left coalition led by Prime Minister Gediminas Kirkilas's Social Democratic Party. Kirkilas's government had faced strong criticism for its ineffective responses to rising inflation and an economic slowdown.

Party-list voting determines 70 seats in Lithuania's 141-seat parliament, with the remainder decided through single-mandate district elections. In an October 13 election that decided the party-list seats, Homeland Union won 19.7 percent of the vote; television producer Arunas Valinskas's National Resurrection Party won 15.1 percent; and the Order and Justice party of former President Rolandas Paksas took 12.7 percent. The ruling Social Democrats came in fourth with 11.7 percent. After runoff elections on October 26 that determined the winners of most single-mandate districts, Homeland Union formed a 79-seat center-right coalition with National Resurrection, the Liberal Union, and the Liberal and Center Union. The Social Democrats held 26 seats.

Parliament chose the National Resurrection Party's Valinskas as its new speaker on November 18 and Homeland Union's Kubilius as Prime Minister on November 27. ■ Juliet Johnson

See also **Europe.**

Los Angeles and the surrounding region of southern California rode out 2008's economic storm better than many areas because of a diversified business and industrial base. However, high fuel and food prices, the mortgage meltdown, strikes, layoffs, and crime-fighting presented challenges for the region—Los Angeles, Orange, Riverside, San Bernardino, and Ventura counties.

City budget. On May 19, the Los Angeles City Council approved Mayor Antonio Villaraigosa's $7-billion budget—a $193-million increase—as budget experts warned that the city faced a short-fall of nearly $400 million the next fiscal year. To finance the hiring of 1,000 officers by 2010 to supplement the existing 10,000-person police force, the council unanimously voted to hike fees by at least $98 million, forcing the public to pay more for trash removal, parking, and park maintenance.

Labor. A three-month strike in late 2007 and early 2008 by the Writers Guild of America cost the Los Angeles economy $1.5 billion in lost jobs, wages, and spending, the Los Angeles Economic Development Corporation estimated. Screen Actors Guild (SAG) members worked without a contract after their contract expired on June 30. Negotiations with the studios stalled over how actors are to be paid for work distributed on the Internet and other new media. To plan for a possible actors' strike, studios revamped their lineups to wrapup shooting early for 2009 releases.

Transportation. Los Angeles International Airport (LAX) lost at least 15 long-haul flights in 2008. The cuts were a setback to airport officials seeking to boost international traffic to offset cutbacks in domestic flights. Foreign carriers pointed to high fuel costs and slowing international demand. The reduction in flights could lead to a loss of $9 billion in tourism-related revenue in the region, according to Los Angeles Economic Development Corporation officials.

Weak demand for new automobiles led to a huge backlog of imported cars at the Los Angeles/Long Beach ports, the nation's largest containerized shipping complex. Long Beach officials reported a 12-percent drop in containerized imports from 2007 to 2008.

Housing. Three southern California-based *subprime* mortgage lenders came under federal investigation in 2008. Subprime mortgages are offered to customers with below-standard credit histories or documentation. Countrywide, a unit of Countrywide Financial Corporation of Calabasas, avoided financial collapse by being bought by Bank of America Corporation of Charlotte, North Carolina, in a deal that closed on July 1. IndyMac Federal Bank of Pasadena was seized by federal regulators on July 11. New Century Financial Corporation of Irvine was also under investigation in 2008 by a federal grand jury in Los Angeles. The company went bankrupt in early 2007.

Housing experts reported in October 2008 that repossessed properties accounted for more than half of all residential properties sold in southern California that month. According to DataQuick Information Systems, home sales in October increased by about 70 percent and prices fell by 30 percent compared with October 2007.

Disasters. A Los Angeles Metrolink commuter train collided with a Union Pacific freight train on Sept. 12, 2008, leaving 25 people dead. In mid-November, three separate wildfires burned in Los Angeles, Orange, and Santa Barbara counties, destroying about 1,000 residences.

Broad patronage. The Los Angeles County Museum of Art opened the new $60-million Broad Contemporary Art Museum on Wilshire Boulevard in February. The museum was designed by Italian architect Renzo Piano and funded by billionaire arts patron Eli Broad. In late December, Broad's foundation pledged $30 million for a bailout of the financially strapped Museum of Contemporary Art in Los Angeles. Broad offered to match the first $15 million raised by the museum's trustees and to donate $3 million per year for exhibits over the next five years .   ■ Margaret A. Kilgore

See also **Bank: A Special Report; City; Labor and employment.**

Luxembourg. See Europe.

Macedonia. Parliamentary elections held in June 2008 returned a majority for Prime Minister Nikola Gruevski's center-right VMRO-DPMNE party. In the election, the Democratic Union for Integration (DUI) outpolled the Democratic Party of Albanians (DPA)—both are ethnic Albanian parties—leading Gruevski to invite the DUI to replace the DPA in his governing coalition. Macedonia's population is about 75 percent Slavic and 25 percent ethnic Albanian. Its governing arrangements date from a 2001 agreement that ended a civil war between the two groups.

Violence at or near polling places marred the conduct of the June 2008 elections in several Albanian-majority towns and drew international criticism. Macedonian authorities subsequently conducted re-votes in some affected districts.

Macedonia's campaign for European integration received a blow in April, when Greek delegates at the North Atlantic Treaty Organization (NATO) summit in Bucharest, Romania, vetoed membership for Macedonia. The Greek government objected to the use by the former Yugoslav republic of the name "Macedonia," which historically has identified a region of Greece. NATO officials urged Greece and Macedonia to resolve the dispute.   ■ Sharon L. Wolchik

See also **Europe.**

Madagascar. See Africa.

Rolling Stone magazine was published in a new format in 2008. Jann Wenner, publisher and cofounder of the magazine, hoped that reducing the trim size to a standard 8 by 11 inches (20 by 28 centimeters) would increase sales at newsstands.

Magazine. Sales of magazines at newsstands for the first half of 2008 dropped by more than 6 percent, according to the Schaumburg, Illinois-based Audit Bureau of Circulations (ABC), an organization that tracks figures for media sales and circulation. Subscriptions were down for the same period according to ABC but not by such a large amount. Sales of magazines in nearly every category followed these trends.

Election effects. Magazines capitalized on whatever they could to capture readers in an economic downturn. The tremendous voter interest in the 2008 presidential campaign meant that coverage, and especially covers, frequently featured one or both of the presidential candidates. And, though conservatives complained, far more magazines ran feature stories and covers of Democrat Barack Obama than of Republican John McCain. This was not to be wondered at, as a *USA Today*/Gallup poll reported favorable ratings for Obama to be 68 percent, while 50 percent had such a view of McCain. Obama sold magazines, and, therefore, he appeared on the covers of many publications, including *Time, Newsweek, GQ, Vanity Fair, Rolling Stone,* and others. Entertainment magazines, such as *Us* and *People,* ran stories and covers of Obama and his family almost weekly in November and found that these covers sold magazines as well or sometimes better than covers with high-profile entertainers and socialites.

The times are a-changing. After more than 40 years, the format of *Rolling Stone* changed with its Oct. 30, 2008, issue. The magazine's size was reduced from a format of 10 by 12 inches (25 by 30 centimeters) to the standard magazine size of around 8 by 11 inches (20 by 28 centimeters). Although *Rolling Stone*'s paid circulation in 2008 was as high as it has ever been, at 1.4 million, its sales at newsstands had declined. Publisher Jann Wenner hoped the change in format would improve the magazine's marketability.

Change on the right. A venerable magazine of conservative American politics, the *National Review,* lost its founder in 2008. Conservative icon William F. Buckley, Jr., founded the *National Review* in 1955 and was a contributor until his death on Feb. 27, 2008. He was credited with reinvigorating conservative political philosophy in the United States. In October 2008, Buckley's son, Christopher, a well-known novelist, resigned his post writing the back-page column for the *National Review.* Christopher Buckley offered his resignation after endorsing the Democratic candidate Barack Obama. For the first time in more than 50 years, no Buckley would be associated with the magazine. ■ Christine Sullivan

Malawi. See Africa.

Malaysia. The National Front coalition that had ruled Malaysia since its 1957 independence suffered a setback in general elections on March 8, 2008. The number of coalition seats in parliament fell from 199 to 140, though it retained a simple majority. The coalition's major member, the United Malays National Organization, fell from 109 seats to 79. Coalition partners also lost seats as ethnic groups turned against policies favoring the Malay majority. Opposition parties won control of an unprecedented 5 of Malaysia's 13 states. The setback was widely blamed on Prime Minister Abdullah bin Ahmad Badawi, who had failed to push through promised political reforms. He announced in October that he would resign in March 2009.

Anwar Ibrahim, Malaysia's most prominent opposition politician, returned to parliament in an Aug. 26, 2008, by-election. He attempted to bring down Abdullah's government by convincing supporters of the ruling coalition to defect, but his efforts were unsuccessful.

Inflation hit 8.5 percent in mid-2008, the country's highest in almost 27 years. The steep rise was partially due to high food, fuel, and electricity prices. ■ Henry S. Bradsher

See also **Asia; Food: A Special Report.**

Manitoba. See **Canadian provinces.**

Marshall Islands. See **Pacific Islands.**

Mauritius. See **Africa.**

Medicine. Life expectancy is declining for women in many parts of the United States—particularly in rural and low-income areas in the Deep South, Appalachia, and the Lower Midwest—according to survey results released in April 2008 by physician Christopher J. L. Murray of the University of Washington in Seattle and colleagues at Harvard School of Public Health in Boston, Massachusetts. The researchers noted that the decline was likely related to increases among women in such unhealthy behaviors as smoking, poor diet, and lack of exercise.

Premature birth problems. Individuals who are born prematurely (before 38 weeks of pregnancy) are more likely to die during childhood and—if they survive to adulthood—less likely to have their own children than are other individuals. Those were the conclusions drawn in March 2008 from a statistical analysis by physician Geeta Swamy of Duke University Medical School in Durham, North Carolina, and colleagues.

The researchers concluded that for boys born between 22 and 27 weeks of pregnancy, the risk of death between ages 1 and 6 was about five times greater than normal. This risk increased to seven times greater than normal between ages 7 and 13. For girls born between 22 and 27 weeks of pregnancy, the risk of death between ages 1 and 6 was almost 10 times greater than normal,

but there was no increased death risk for girls between ages 7 and 13.

The analysts found that premature boys who survived into adulthood were 76 percent less likely than normal to have children. Premature girls who survived into adulthood were 67 percent less likely than normal to have children. The researchers attributed the lower reproduction rates to increased medical and socioeconomic problems among these individuals.

Predicting stroke risk. Improved methods of predicting risk of stroke were reported in February at a conference sponsored by the American Stroke Association of Dallas. The new risk assessment methods were based on three studies.

One study, led by researchers at the University of Missouri Medical School in Columbia, described how *mammograms* (X-ray images used to detect breast cancer) can show calcium deposits in breast arteries. Such deposits increase stroke risk. Another study, led by investigators at the University of Miami in Florida, found that a test of blood sugar-to-insulin ratio—commonly used with patients who have diabetes—can also be used to assess stroke risk in patients without diabetes. The third study, by scientists at Columbia University in New York City, concluded that the risk of stroke was greater among elderly persons who nap frequently during the day, compared with elderly persons who nap less often.

Sleep apnea reduces survival. Individuals with sleep apnea are two to four times as likely to die from any cause than are individuals without the disorder, reported researchers with an 18-year, 1,500-subject study called the Wisconsin Sleep Cohort in August. According to the researchers, sleep apnea—in which breathing repeatedly pauses during sleep, leading to sleep disruption—gradually and dangerously erodes the health of people with the condition.

Vision for the blind. Four people with a rare form of hereditary blindness obtained substantial improvements in their vision after receiving gene therapy, two teams of physicians reported in April. In the gene therapy, the physicians injected the healthy versions of genes into the eyes of patients, via a disabled virus that delivered the genes into eye cells. The healthy genes performed functions that were left undone by faulty genes that cause Leber congenital amaurosis, a type of visual impairment that often progresses from difficulty seeing in dim light to complete blindness. Physicians at the University of Pennsylvania Medical School in Philadelphia and University College London in the United Kingdom reported that, after the procedure, patients could see well in dim light. ■ Alfred J. Smuskiewicz

See also **AIDS; Drugs; Health care issues; Mental health; Public health.**

Mental health. Several rare genetic *mutations* (changes) increase the risk of schizophrenia, according to a March 2008 report by a team of researchers led by psychiatrist Jack McClellan of the University of Washington in Seattle. The researchers said that the mutations—deletions or duplications of certain segments of *deoxyribonucleic acid* (DNA, the molecule that makes up genes)—cause disruptions in brain development.

McClellan's team analyzed the DNA of more than 150 people with schizophrenia, which is characterized by hallucinations, delusions, and disorganized thinking. The team compared this DNA with the DNA of 268 people without schizophrenia. The analysis revealed that various mutations occurred three to four times more often in individuals with schizophrenia than in those without schizophrenia.

The scientists concluded that specific schizophrenia-related mutations are likely to vary depending on the individual. They added that the identification of the mutations in a patient would allow physicians to prescribe the most effective medications for that patient.

Facing up to autism. The brains of adults with autism have an abnormally low level of *neuron* (nerve cell) connections in regions involved in processing social and emotional information—including information for recognizing faces. So reported a group of researchers led by radiologist Elizabeth Aylward of the University of Washington Autism Center in Seattle in June.

Autism, which appears in childhood and persists throughout life, is characterized by a limited ability to communicate and interact with other people. Aylward's team used magnetic resonance imaging (MRI) to compare brain activity in subjects who had autism with brain activity in subjects who did not have autism. The MRI images were made while the subjects were shown pictures of faces and told to press a button if they were shown the same face more than once.

The MRI's revealed that in subjects with autism, there appeared to be only weak connections between the fusiform area (which is involved in face recognition) and adjacent areas of the limbic system (which processes social and emotional information).

Autism mutations. The understanding of autism was further advanced in July, when researchers at Harvard University in Cambridge, Massachusetts, announced that they had identified several previously unknown genetic mutations in patients with the disease. The findings indicated that different individuals have different sets of mutations that cause autism.

St. John's wort worthless? Researchers reported in June that they found no evidence that St. John's wort (*Hypericum perforatum*) is effective in treating children with attention-deficit/hyperactivity disorder (ADHD), a condition characterized by inattentiveness and restlessness. Investigators led by physician Wendy Weber of Bastyr University in Kenmore, Washington, administered St. John's wort to 27 children with ADHD and a *placebo* (inactive substance) to 27 other children with ADHD for eight weeks. After then comparing the two groups of children for inattentiveness and other ADHD characteristics, the researchers found no statistically significant differences in ADHD characteristics between the children who received St. John's wort and those who received placebos.

Vets needing help. In the most comprehensive study to date of United States veterans of the wars in Afghanistan and Iraq, researchers concluded in April that nearly one in five of the veterans in those conflicts suffers from severe depression or post-traumatic stress disorder. Moreover, according to the Rand Corporation, a policy research organization in Santa Monica, California, many veterans fail to get adequate treatment for their mental health problems.

In May, the U.S. Army reported that soldiers committed suicide in 2007 at the highest rate since such records began to be kept in 1980.

■ Alfred J. Smuskiewicz

See also **Drugs; Medicine.**

Mexico. On Sept.1, 2008, President Felipe Calderón Hinojosa acknowledged that "public insecurity" was his country's "biggest problem." He blamed the surge in violence on the "disintegration of public and government [law enforcement] institutions," which, he said, were simply "overwhelmed" by internal problems as well as by crime. It was a painful admission of failure by a leader who had declared war on drug traffickers.

Since taking office in December 2006, Calderón had deployed nearly 30,000 soldiers and federal police to combat the drug trade, only to find that crimes were often abetted by corruption within his own forces. By late 2008, around 7,700 people had been killed—many of them innocents purposely targeted or simply caught in the crossfire.

Candlelight vigil against crime. On August 31, hundreds of thousands of Mexicans protested against crime at candlelight vigils in public plazas around the nation. Clad in white, many of them carried photos of slain loved ones.

Among the dead was a 14-year-old boy, Fernando Martí, whose decomposed body, along with that of his driver, was found stuffed in the trunk of a car after his father, a wealthy businessman, had paid hundreds of thousands of dollars in ransom for his release. Suspicion for the murders fell on a gang headed by Sergio Ortiz, a former police detective in Mexico City, the capital. Ortiz was detained along with four other suspects in September.

Drug traffickers retaliate. During 2008, Mexico's drug cartels went on the offensive, battling against their pursuers and among themselves. In bloody shoot-outs and assassinations, the mobsters went beyond small arms and gangland tactics, fighting desperately to maintain their estimated $23 billion in annual profits. They used improvised explosive devices, tortured and beheaded their victims, and posted grisly videos of executions on the Internet. Mutilated corpses were displayed as messages and warnings. Mass graves containing dozens of bodies were found in several locations. Cartel members even outgunned government forces in pitched battles, firing AK-47 assault rifles bought at gun shows in the United States and smuggled across the border.

Independence Day massacre. On September 15, eight people were killed and more than 100 were injured when drug gangs lobbed grenades into a crowd in the main plaza of Morelia, in the state of Michoacán. Thousands of people had gathered to celebrate the eve of the anniversary of the 1810 rebellion that led to Mexico's independence. President Calderón, who grew up in Morelia, asked the people to "remain united in the face of those who want to divide us."

Operation Clean House. On Oct. 27, 2008, five members of the attorney general's organized crime unit were arrested. They were accused of taking monthly payments of up to $450,000 from drug cartels in exchange for information on antinarcotics efforts. More than 30 others were under investigation. Victor Gerardo Garay, the acting federal police commissioner, resigned on November 1 amid accusations that he was working with drug cartels. Two other top police officials were arrested later in the month on similar charges.

Mérida Initiative. On June 26, the United States Senate approved a $400-million aid package for training, equipment, and intelligence to fight the illicit drug trade in Mexico. But Mexicans remained skeptical. A 2008 survey by the nonprofit Citizens Institute for Crime Studies in Mexico City reported that 86 percent of Mexicans had little or no trust in their local police departments.

Minister dead. On November 4, Interior Minister Juan Camilo Mouriño, 37, and 13 others were killed in an airplane crash in Mexico City. Mouriño was Mexico's second leading politician and a close friend of President Calderón. Government officials called the crash an accident.

■ Nathan A. Haverstock

See also **Drug abuse; Latin America.**

Micronesia, Federated States of.

See **Pacific Islands.**

Police in Mexico City salute three of the hundreds of officers killed in 2008 during a largely unsuccessful nationwide crackdown on drug traffickers. Drug-related murders in Mexico more than doubled in 2008.

MIDDLE EAST

Some progress was achieved in addressing political conflicts in certain countries in the Middle East in 2008. In other countries, prospects for finding solutions to conflicts remained dismal. In Lebanon, the election of a new president occurred after the anti-Syria "Cedar Revolution" majority and the pro-Syria minority reached an agreement. Despite the agreement, Syria-sponsored terrorist activities continued unabated in Lebanon. Iraqis witnessed an improvement in the level of violence in their country in 2008 as a result of the United States troop "surge" and a new policy of cooperation with Sunni tribes.

A political crisis erupted in Israel in 2008 with corruption charges leveled against Prime Minister Ehud Olmert. The conflict in the Darfur region of Sudan continued and led to the indictment of Sudan's president by the International Criminal Court (ICC) at The Hague in the Netherlands.

Agreement follows violence in Lebanon. Lebanon's Cabinet decided in May 2008 to replace the security chief of Beirut International Airport, in the capital of Lebanon, because he allowed the pro-Syria militant group Hezbollah to set up spy cameras to monitor flights. The Cabinet also moved to dismantle Hezbollah's telecommunications network. Hezbollah and Amal, another militant group, responded by attacking Cedar Revolution forces in Beirut and Mount Lebanon. The fighting lasted for a week, resulting in more than 40 deaths. Cedar Revolution leaders finally brought the violence to an end by calling up the Lebanese army to restore order.

The ruler of Qatar, Emir Hamad bin Khalifa al-Thani, mediated the crisis in Lebanon by convening a conference on May 16 in Doha, Qatar's capital, which leaders of all of Lebanon's major political parties and parliamentary blocs attended. An agreement, reached on May 21, led to the election of the popular commander of the Lebanese army, General Michel Suleiman, as president of Lebanon. In addition, the pro-Syria opposition was given 11 ministries in the 30-member Cabinet. Following this agreement, Hezbollah and its allies ended the sit-in in downtown Beirut that they began in December 2006. They also accepted a prohibition on the use of weapons to resolve political conflicts.

Syria-sponsored terrorism continues. On Jan. 25, 2008, a car bomb was detonated in a Beirut suburb, killing Captain Wissam Eid, director of the intelligence unit in Lebanon's Internal Security Forces. Many political observers attributed this murder to Syria. Captain Eid had played an important role in uncovering the secret cells of the terrorist organization Fatah al-Islam and in deciphering cell phone communications that led to the assassination of former Lebanese Prime Minister Rafik al-Hariri in 2005.

On Aug. 13, 2008, the day President Suleiman arrived on an official visit to Syria, a bomb exploded in the northern Lebanese city of Tripoli, killing at least 18 people. Most of the victims were members of the Lebanese army. Some political observers speculated that this attack was a veiled warning by Syria and its allies to the Lebanese army and to President Suleiman.

Trouble in Syria. Events in Lebanon in 2008 led to the snubbing of Syrian President Bashar al-Assad by major Arab leaders, who boycotted the Arab League Summit held in Damascus, the capital of Syria, in March. President Hosni Mubarak of Egypt, King Abdullah of Saudi Arabia, King Abdullah II of Jordan, and representatives from Lebanon refused to participate in the summit because Syria, through its proxies in Lebanon, had prevented the convening of the Lebanese parliament to elect a new president.

Two leading Hezbollah operatives were assassinated in Syria in 2008, most likely—according to experts in Syrian affairs—because they knew too much about Syria's interconnection with Hezbollah and involvement in terrorist attacks. In February, Imad Mughniyeh, mastermind behind numerous Hezbollah terrorist operations that caused the deaths of hundreds of Western nationals, was assassinated by a car bombing in Damascus. Experts said President Assad may have had Mughniyeh murdered to prevent him from cooperating with an international tribunal investigating Syria's terrorist activities. In August, General Muhammad Suleiman was assassinated by a sniper at a seaside resort in Syria. He had reportedly been a "right-hand man" of President Assad and a liaison officer to Hezbollah with close ties to Mughniyeh.

Surge success in Iraq. General David H. Petraeus, U.S. commander of the Multinational Force in Iraq, testified before the U.S. Congress in April, pointing out that there had been a considerable decrease in the number of civilian deaths in Iraq within the previous six months, as well as a decline in the level of violence in that conflict-torn country. General Petraeus

Palestinians from the Gaza Strip pass into Egypt through a damaged section of a border wall in January. Palestinians blew holes into the wall with explosives to allow Gaza residents to cross into Egypt to buy food, fuel, and other supplies, which had become scarce because of an Israeli blockade. Israel objected to Hamas militants' control over the territory.

FACTS IN BRIEF ON MIDDLE EASTERN COUNTRIES

Country	Population	Government	Monetary unit*	Foreign trade (million U.S.$) Exports[†]	Imports[†]
Bahrain	722,000	King Hamad bin Isa Al-Khalifa; Prime Minister Khalifa bin Salman Al-Khalifa	dinar (0.38 = $1)	13,790	10,930
Cyprus	853,000	President Demetris Christofias; (Turkish Republic of Northern Cyprus: President Mehmet Ali Talat)	euro (0.68 = $1)	1,495 (includes Northern Cyprus)	7,840
Egypt	77,243,000	President Mohammed Hosni Mubarak; Prime Minister Ahmed Nazif	pound (5.37= $1)	24,450	44,950
Iran	72,048,000	Supreme Leader Ayatollah Ali Khamenei; President Mahmoud Ahmadinejad	rial (8,229.00 = $1)	88,260	53,880
Iraq	30,958,000	President Jalal Talabani; Prime Minister Nouri Kamel al-Maliki	dinar (1,177.00 = $1)	38,140	25,670
Israel	7,250,000	President Shimon Peres; Prime Minister Ehud Olmert	shekel (3.58 = $1)	50,370	55,790
Jordan	5,816,000	King Abdullah II; Prime Minister Nadir al-Dahabi	dinar (0.71 = $1)	5,700	12,020
Kuwait	2,895,000	Emir Sabah al-Ahmad al-Jabir al-Sabah; Prime Minister Nasser Muhammad al-Ahmad al-Sabah	dinar (0.27 = $1)	63,720	20,640
Lebanon	3,894,000	President Michel Suleiman; Prime Minister Fouad Siniora	pound (1,500.00 = $1)	4,077	11,930
Oman	2,705,000	Sultan and Prime Minister Qaboos bin Said	rial (0.39 = $1)	23,100	11,000
Qatar	841,000	Emir Hamad bin Khalifa al-Thani; Prime Minister Hamad bin Jassim bin Jabr al-Thani	riyal (3.64 = $1)	42,020	19,860
Saudi Arabia	26,362,000	King and Prime Minister Abdullah ibn Abd al-Aziz Al Saud	riyal (3.75 = $1)	226,700	82,640
Sudan	39,076,000	President Umar Hassan Ahmad al-Bashir	pound (2.09 = $1)	8,879	7,722
Syria	20,423,000	President Bashar al-Assad; Prime Minister Mohammed Naji al-Otari	pound (46.20 = $1)	11,140	10,500
Turkey	74,824,000	President Abdullah Gül; Prime Minister Recep Tayyip Erdogan	new lira (1.19 = $1)	115,300	162,000
United Arab Emirates	4,724,000	President Khalifa bin Zayed al-Nahyan; Prime Minister Mohammad bin Rashid al-Maktum	dirham (3.67 = $1)	178,900	116,600
Yemen	23,054,000	President Ali Abdullah Saleh; Prime Minister Ali Muhammad Mujawwar	rial (199.00 = $1)	7,311	6,735

*Exchange rates as of Sept. 30, 2008.　　　　　　　　[†]Latest available data.

attributed these improvements to the increase in the number of U.S. troops, commonly referred to as the "surge," and to cooperation with tribal leaders from both the Sunni and Shi`ah communities. According to the general, these leaders were instrumental in the formation of local forces made up of some 91,000 volunteers, who—with the expanded Iraqi army and security forces—dealt serious blows to the terrorist operations of al-Qa`ida in Iraq.

In November, the Iraqi parliament approved an agreement to allow U.S. forces to remain in Iraq until the end of 2011—three years after the expiration of their United Nations (UN) mandate.

Two important visits by leaders of neighboring countries in 2008 signaled that Iraq had returned to normal diplomatic relations in the Middle East region. President Mahmoud Ahmadinejad of Iran visited Iraq in March. Iraqi

President Jalal Talabani regarded Iran as a counterbalance to Turkey, which Iraqi officials viewed as a threat because of frequent Turkish military incursions into northern Iraq to attack Kurdish militants. King Abdullah II of Jordan visited Iraq in August. The king was the first Arab head of state to visit Iraq since U.S.-led forces deposed Iraqi dictator Saddam Hussein in 2003.

Hezbollah and Hamas in Israel. The Winograd Commission, headed by former judge Eliyahu Winograd, issued its report on the Israeli-Hezbollah war of July-to-August 2006 in January 2008. The report pointed out "great and grave faults" in the decisions made by both the Israeli Cabinet and the Israeli military during the war. The results of the brief conflict were inconclusive. The war also claimed the lives of more than 160 Israeli soldiers and civilians, despite the fact that the Israeli army fought against only a few thousand paramilitary fighters.

Israeli-Palestinian peace negotiations in 2008 about the core issues—concerning the final status of Jerusalem, Israeli settlements, Palestinian refugees, and borders of a Palestinian state—led to the resignation of the Israeli Cabinet's minister of strategic affairs, Avigdor Lieberman, in January. Lieberman, who represented the ultranationalist Yisrael Beiteinu Party, strongly opposed the peace negotiations. He also withdrew Yisrael Beiteinu from the governing coalition.

On the Palestinian side, the militant organization Hamas demonstrated its opposition to the peace negotiations by increasing its rocket attacks against Israeli towns near the Gaza Strip. Hamas had seized control of the Gaza Strip in 2007 from the moderate Palestinian Authority, headed by Palestinian President Mahmoud Abbas. Egyptian officials brokered a cease-fire between Israel and Hamas in June 2008. Nevertheless, both sides committed violations of this cease-fire during the rest of the year. Violence escalated dramatically in late December, after the cease-fire expired. Israeli airstrikes on Hamas security compounds in Gaza left hundreds dead.

Despite frequent meetings between Israeli and Palestinian officials in 2008—including Israeli Prime Minister Olmert and Palestinian President Abbas and teams headed by Israeli Foreign Minister Tzipi Livni and former Palestinian Prime Minister Ahmad Quray—little progress was made. No final-status peace agreement was reached by the end of 2008.

Olmert scandal. Prime Minister Olmert was subjected to a number of police interrogations in 2008 involving allegations that he had received funds illegally from U.S. financier Morris Talansky. Olmert announced in July that he would resign from the leadership of the Kadima Party after a primary election. The September primary was won by Foreign Minister Tzipi Livni. However, as prime minister-designate, Livni was unable to put together a new Israeli Cabinet from the various Israeli political parties. Therefore, Israeli President Shimon Peres scheduled new parliamentary elections for February 2009. Prime Minister Olmert remained in power at the end of 2008.

Conflict in Darfur. Three rebel groups in Chad armed by the government of Sudan attacked the palace of Chadian President Idriss Déby in N'Djamena, the capital of Chad, in February. The attack was an unsuccessful attempt to topple President Déby from power, which was prompted by his support of Sudanese rebels in the violence-plagued Darfur region of Sudan. In retaliation for the attack in N'Djamena, 3,000 rebels from Darfur headed by fighters with the Justice and Equality Movement attacked Khartoum, the capital of Sudan, in May. However, Sudanese government forces successfully beat back the rebels.

The ICC indicted President Umar Hassan Ahmad al-Bashir of Sudan in July. The ICC prosecutor, Luis Moreno-Ocampo, charged President Bashir with 10 counts of mass crimes, including three counts of genocide. In the genocide counts, President Bashir was accused of conducting the "ethnic cleansing" of three tribes in Darfur by using a rebel insurgency that was under his control to murder, rape, and deport members of these tribes.

Terrorism and faith in Saudi Arabia. Authorities in Saudi Arabia indicted 991 people in October on charges of participating in more than 30 terrorist operations in the kingdom since May 2003. The authorities also noted that Saudi security forces had prevented more than 160 other terrorist attacks during that time.

Saudi King Abdullah was responsible for initiating two interfaith conferences in 2008, signaling that Saudi Arabia was becoming more open and tolerant toward religions other than Islam. The first conference was held in Madrid, capital of Spain, in July, with more than 300 political and cultural leaders from 50 countries attending. The second conference was held at UN headquarters in New York City in November, with more than a dozen world leaders participating. King Abdullah co-chaired the UN conference. ■ Marius Deeb

See also **Africa; Armed forces; Terrorism; United Nations; United States, Government of the;** various Middle East country articles.

Mining. See **Energy supply.**

Moldova. See **Europe.**

Monaco. See **Europe.**

Mongolia. See **Asia.**

Montenegro. Milo Djukanovic, the architect of Montenegro's 2006 independence from Serbia, returned to politics as prime minister and head of the ruling Democratic Party of Socialists in February 2008. Djukanovic had retired from politics in late 2006, leaving his close ally Zeljko Stranovic in charge as prime minister; Stranovic announced his resignation in January 2008 because of poor health. In April, Montenegrin voters elected Filip Vujanovic, a Djukanovic ally, as president. The two leaders pressed for Montenegro's rapid integration into the North Atlantic Treaty Organization (NATO) and the European Union.

In March, Prime Minister Djukanovic traveled to Bari, Italy, to answer Italian prosecutors' questions about his alleged past involvement in a cigarette smuggling operation. In 2003, prosecutors in Naples had issued an arrest warrant for Djukanovic, but an Italian judge invalidated the warrant because of the Montenegrin's diplomatic immunity as a government leader.

In October 2008, Montenegro recognized the independence of Kosovo, the Albanian-majority former province of Serbia. Kosovo declared independence on February 17, despite strenuous Serbian protests. Serbia retaliated against Montenegro by expelling its ambassador from Belgrade, the Serbian capital.   ■ Sharon L. Wolchik

See also **Europe; Kosovo; Serbia.**

Montreal. Busker-turned-billionaire Guy Laliberté, creator of the Montreal-based Cirque du Soleil, sold one-fifth of the international touring circus company in 2008 to one of the world's most powerful investment groups. (A busker is someone who performs informally in public places for money.) Laliberté said in an August 6 announcement that private equity investor Istithmar World Capital and real estate developer Nakheel—both units of Dubai World, a government-owned holding company in the United Arab Emirates—had each acquired a 10-percent stake in his entertainment empire as part of what he called a strategic partnership rather than the start of a take-over.

"I'm still the captain of the boat," Laliberté said. "This is not a sale to raise funds because we're in excellent financial health." He founded Cirque du Soleil in 1984 while still a street performer. The unconventional circus had 10 permanent and 7 touring shows worldwide in 2008.

Crime. Two tobacco firms, Montreal-based Imperial Tobacco Canada and Toronto-based Rothmans Benson & Hedges, agreed on July 31, 2008, to pay criminal and civil fines of more than $1.1 billion after pleading guilty to aiding the smuggling of contraband cigarettes between the United States and Canada in the 1980's and 1990's. (All monetary figures are in Canadian dollars.) The smuggling defrauded Canadian governments of

billions of dollars in unpaid taxes. The charges followed an eight-year investigation by the Royal Canadian Mounted Police. Federal Revenue Minister Gordon O'Connor told a news conference that the fines were the largest in Canadian history.

On Jan. 28, 2008, Vincent Lacroix, founder and former chief executive of the now-bankrupt Montreal mutual fund firm Norbourg Asset Management, was sentenced to 12 years in prison and fined $255,000. Lacroix, who had swindled 9,200 investors of $115 million over a five-year period, was found guilty on Dec. 11, 2007, of 51 Quebec Securities Act violations. On June 18, 2008, he was charged with 200 further counts of fraud, conspiracy to defraud, conspiracy to commit forgery, fabricating documents, and money laundering.

According to a coroner's report released on September 4, Kimveer Gill—the 25-year-old gunman who killed a female student and wounded 16 other students at Montreal's Dawson College on Sept. 13, 2006, before taking his own life—had planned his attack for April 20, the seventh anniversary of the Columbine High School massacre in Colorado. His timetable changed because the gun he ordered had not yet arrived. Also, Gill wrote in his journal that he was prepared to kill his parents had they found out about his plan.

Business. Montreal-based Bombardier Inc., the world's third-largest civil aircraft maker, on July 13, 2008, launched its long-awaited CSeries jet project. It was expected to generate up to 3,500 direct jobs for the Montreal region over the next 20 years. The firm aimed to capture half of the market for 100- to 149-seat fuel-efficient planes.

Chantal Petitclerc, a Montreal wheelchair racer, retired from Paralympic competition after sweeping all five of her events at the 2008 Paralympic Games in Beijing in September, mirroring her achievement at the 2004 Paralympics in Athens, Greece. She increased her career Paralympic medal count to 14 gold medals and 21 overall. A paraplegic since she was 13, Petitclerc planned to focus on marathon and road racing after her retirement from track racing.

Royal wedding. Peter Phillips, grandson of Queem Elizabeth II of the United Kingdom, married Montreal commoner Autumn Kelly on May 17, 2008, at Windsor Castle in the United Kingdom. One British tabloid newspaper described the marriage as "blue blood meets blue collar." The couple, both 30, met at the 2003 Canadian Grand Prix in Montreal. Phillips was a sponsorship manager with the racing team BMW Williams, and Kelly was working in the BMW hospitality suite. Phillips is the only son of Princess Anne and her former husband, Captain Mark Phillips.

■ Mike King

See also **Canada; Canadian provinces.**
Morocco. See Africa.

Motion pictures. A Hollywood writers' strike stretched into the new year, and a summer blockbuster broke box-office records in 2008. Higher ticket prices made up for lower theater attendance in an uncertain economy.

Strike settlement. The first Hollywood writers' strike in 20 years was settled on February 12 after a 100-day contract stand-off between the Writers Guild of America and the Alliance of Motion Picture and Television Producers. Television and film writers wanted more money when films and TV shows were sold on such Internet sites as Apple Inc.'s iTunes Store, based in Cupertino, California. Among the contract's renegotiated terms was an annual pay hike ranging from 3 to 3.5 percent for writers. Some 50,000 film and television workers were out of work during the strike, which cost the Los Angeles economy an estimated $1.5 billion.

Notable early 2008 films. The monster movie *Cloverfield* was the most successful January release ever, earning $40 million in its opening weekend and becoming the first film of the year to gross over $100 million. *In Bruges,* the critically acclaimed directorial film debut of Irish theater writer and director Martin McDonagh, premiered at the Sundance Film Festival in January. The crime comedy, which was also written by McDonagh, starred Brendan Gleeson and Colin Farrell as two Irish hit men who hide out in Belgium after a contract killing goes bad. In February, the 3-D Walt Disney Pictures release *Hannah Montana & Miley Cyrus: Best of Both Worlds Concert* became the highest-grossing concert film and the highest-grossing 3-D movie in history. The turnout prompted Disney to extend indefinitely the run of the film, which was initially to play for a week.

The summer of the superhero began with the early May release of *Iron Man,* starring Robert Downey, Jr., as the Marvel Comics armor-suited superhero and his alter ego, the playboy industrialist Tony Stark. It was the year's first film to earn more than $300 million at the domestic box office. *The Incredible Hulk,* also based on a Marvel Comics character, was a hit at the box office when it was released in June. Starring Edward Norton in the title role, the film earned $55 million in its first week in U.S. theaters.

The sudden death of Heath Ledger in January heightened anticipation for the July release of the Batman sequel *The Dark Knight,* in which Ledger portrayed Batman's nemesis, the Joker. The film took in a record $155 million in its first weekend and went on to become the second-highest grossing film of all time. Many critics predicted a posthumous Oscar win for Ledger's comically sinister performance.

The comic book-inspired *Hellboy II: The Golden Army,* released in July, was a critical and box-office success. The film was a sequel to *Hellboy* (2004),

which was also directed by Guillermo del Toro and also starred Ron Perlman as the title character.

An antidote to the season's bumper crop of superhero films came in the form of *Hancock,* starring Will Smith as a reluctant and reckless alcoholic anti-superhero. Released the first week of July 2008, the film grossed $227 million domestically for the season.

Other notable summer films. In May, Harrison Ford starred in *Indiana Jones and the Kingdom of the Crystal Skull,* reprising the title character nearly 20 years after the release of the last film in the series. The film earned $127 million at the domestic box office in its opening weekend. Also opening in May was *Sex and the City,* the feature-film adaptation of the HBO television series of the same name. Although the romantic comedy received mixed reviews from critics, it was a commercial success, earning $152 million at the box office for the season.

Mamma Mia!, based on the hit Broadway musical and starring Meryl Streep, opened on the same day as *The Dark Knight,* at number two. The two films' combined box-office earnings helped Hollywood set an overall record of $253 million for a three-day weekend. Another of the summer's most popular releases was the horror-adventure sequel *The Mummy: Tomb of the Dragon Emperor.* It earned $40 million in its opening weekend.

Kids' flicks. Several 2008 films fared well with children and critics, as well as at the box office. *Horton Hears a Who!,* based on the book by Dr. Seuss and featuring the voice of Jim Carrey, earned $45 million after its opening in March. The fantasy adventure *The Chronicles of Narnia: Prince Caspian* brought in $55 million at the box office in its opening in May. The DreamWorks animated comedy *Kung Fu Panda,* featuring the voice of Jack Black, earned $60 million after its opening in June. Also opening in June was the Pixar animated science-fiction film *WALL•E,* which earned $63 million during its first weekend. The DreamWorks animated sequel *Madagascar: Escape 2 Africa* also earned $63 million when it opened in November—more than its 2005 predecessor, *Madagascar.*

Film festival buzz fueled interest in a number of pictures released in U.S. theaters later in 2008. *Elegy,* based on a novel by Philip Roth, premiered at the Berlin Film Festival in February. The romantic drama starred Ben Kingsley as an older professor who seduces one of his former students, played by Penélope Cruz. Both actors were praised for their performances in the film.

The four-hour movie *Che,* directed by Steven Soderbergh, generated excitement on its premiere at the Cannes International Film Festival in May. Benicio del Toro won a unanimous best actor

Daniel Day-Lewis (right) won a best actor Oscar for his performance as Daniel Plainview, a charismatic but ruthless California oil prospector in the early 1900's in *There Will Be Blood*. Dillon Freasier starred as Plainview's adopted son H. W. The film was based on a 1927 novel by Upton Sinclair.

Literary adaptations and a biographical picture won Academy Awards in 2008.

Josh Brolin starred as a Texas hunter stalked by a psychopathic killer in *No Country for Old Men*, based on the 2005 novel by Cormac McCarthy. The film won four Oscars, including one for best picture.

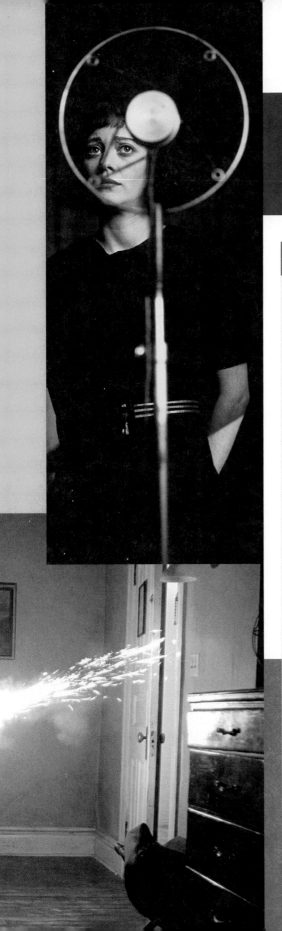

Marion Cotillard received the Academy Award for best actress for her portrayal of the legendary French singer Edith Piaf in *La Vie en Rose*. It was the first time an Oscar was awarded for a French-language role.

ACADEMY AWARD WINNERS IN 2008

The following winners of the 2007 Academy Awards were announced in February 2008:

Best Picture: *No Country for Old Men*

Best Actor: Daniel Day-Lewis, *There Will Be Blood*

Best Actress: Marion Cotillard, *La Vie en Rose*

Best Supporting Actor: Javier Bardem, *No Country for Old Men*

Best Supporting Actress: Tilda Swinton, *Michael Clayton*

Best Director: Joel and Ethan Coen, *No Country for Old Men*

Best Original Screenplay: Diablo Cody, *Juno*

Best Screenplay Adaptation: Joel and Ethan Coen, *No Country for Old Men*

Best Animated Feature: *Ratatouille*

Best Cinematography: Robert Elswit, *There Will Be Blood*

Best Film Editing: Christopher Rouse, *The Bourne Ultimatum*

Best Original Score: Dario Marianelli, *Atonement*

Best Original Song: "Falling Slowly" from *Once*

Best Foreign-Language Film: *The Counterfeiters* (Austria)

Best Art Direction: Dante Ferretti and Francesca Lo Schiavo, *Sweeney Todd*

Best Costume Design: Alexandra Byrne, *Elizabeth: The Golden Age*

Best Sound Mixing: Scott Millan, David Parker, and Kirk Francis, *The Bourne Ultimatum*

Best Sound Editing: Karen Baker Landers and Per Hallberg, *The Bourne Ultimatum*

Best Makeup: Didier Lavergne and Jan Archibald, *La Vie en Rose*

Best Visual Effects: Michael Fink, Bill Westenhofer, Ben Morris, and Trevor Wood, *The Golden Compass*

Best Animated Short Film: *Peter & the Wolf*

Best Live-Action Short Film: *Le Mozart des Pickpockets* (The Mozart of Pickpockets)

Best Feature Documentary: *Taxi to the Dark Side*

Best Short Subject Documentary: *Freeheld*

award for his portrayal of the Argentine revolutionary Ernesto "Che" Guevara.

Also premiering at Cannes was Woody Allen's romantic comedy *Vicky Cristina Barcelona.* Set in Spain, the film starred Javier Bardem as a painter who tries to seduce two young American women. The film received favorable reviews, with critics singling out Penélope Cruz for her fiery performance as the painter's passionate and volatile ex-wife.

Joel and Ethan Coen garnered attention at the Venice Film Festival in August with the premiere of their screwball comedy *Burn After Reading.* Brad Pitt and Frances McDormand starred as fitness instructors who stumble across a CIA agent's memoirs. George Clooney portrayed an oafish federal marshal who is having an affair with the agent's wife. The film, which also starred John Malkovich and Tilda Swinton, received a positive response from critics and audiences.

The surprise winner of the Golden Lion, the Venice Film Festival's best-film award, was *The Wrestler,* directed by Darren Aronofsky. It starred Mickey Rourke as a washed-up professional wrestler trying to make a comeback.

Premiering at the Toronto International Film Festival in September was *Slumdog Millionaire,* co-directed by Danny Boyle and India's Loveleen Tandan. The comedy-romance, which won the festival's people's choice award, is the story of an orphaned Indian teenager who becomes a contestant on the Hindi version of "Who Wants to Be a Millionaire?" Also premiering at the festival was Spike Lee's *Miracle at St. Anna,* based on the true story of four African American soldiers who were trapped in a village in Tuscany, Italy, during World War II (1939-1945). The film was viewed by some as Lee's response to Clint Eastwood's 2006 films about the war, *Flags of Our Fathers* and *Letters from Iwo Jima.* Lee had been publicly critical of Eastwood for failing to include any African Americans in the two films. Lee's film angered Italy's surviving partisans, who criticized the depiction of one of the fighters as a traitor who worked secretly with the Nazis.

Politically themed films began to hit theaters in the months leading up to the 2008 U.S. presidential election. The comedy *Swing Vote,* released in August, starred Kevin Costner as a politically apathetic, alcoholic single father whose vote would decide the presidential election. *An American Carol,* a comedy spoof of Charles Dickens's *A Christmas Carol,* was released in October. The controversial film starred Kevin Farley as Michael Malone, a parody of political documentary filmmaker Michael Moore. The film, which also starred Jon Voight, Kelsey Grammer, and Dennis Hopper, was considered a box-office flop. One of the year's most talked-about films was Oliver Stone's *W.,* based on the life and presidency of President George W.

Bush. Josh Brolin received favorable reviews for his manic portrayal of the president.

Notable fall and year-end releases. In October 2008, *High School Musical 3: Senior Year*—the first in the series of Disney television films to be released in theaters—broke the record for the largest opening for a musical and was the first film since *The Dark Knight* to top both the domestic and worldwide box office. Ralph Fiennes and Keira Knightley were praised for their portrayals of the Duke and Duchess of Devonshire in the period drama *The Duchess,* based on Amanda Foreman's best-selling 1998 biography. Clint Eastwood's Prohibition-Era thriller *Changeling* received respectable critical and box-office reception. Based on a true story, the film starred Angelina Jolie as a mother who recognizes that the boy returned to her by police after a kidnapping is not her son.

Daniel Craig was back in November as agent 007 in the 22nd James Bond film, *Quantum of Solace.* It earned more than $67 million in its opening weekend—more than any other Bond film. The teen vampire film *Twilight,* based on a popular book, sold out at many theaters before it opened in late November. The film earned more than $70 million in its first weekend. *Australia,* starring Nicole Kidman and Hugh Jackman, opened the day before Thanksgiving to slow U.S. box-office sales. Called "the Australian *Gone With the Wind,*" the three-hour epic, directed by Baz Luhrmann, tells the story of the bombing of Darwin, Australia, by Japanese forces during World War II.

Frost/Nixon, directed by Ron Howard, opened in theaters in early December. The film was adapted from the hit Broadway play based on a series of 1977 televised interviews between British talk show host David Frost and former President Richard M. Nixon. It starred original cast members Frank Langella in his Tony Award-winning role as Nixon and Michael Sheen as Frost. Opening the same day in wide release was *Milk,* directed by Gus Van Sant. Sean Penn received positive reviews for his portrayal of Harvey Milk, the openly gay California politician who was assassinated in 1978.

The 2008 Christmas Day release of *The Curious Case of Benjamin Button,* starring Brad Pitt, Cate Blanchett, and Tilda Swinton, was anxiously awaited by audiences. The mystery-drama was based on a 1922 short story by the American author F. Scott Fitzgerald about a man who ages backward. Two other anxiously awaited 2008 films opened the following day: the historical thriller *Valkyrie,* starring Tom Cruise, based on the true story of a plot by German army officers to assassinate Adolf Hitler; and *Revolutionary Road,* in which Leonardo DiCaprio was reunited with his *Titanic* (1997) co-star Kate Winslet. Based on the novel by Richard Yates, the drama is the story of a young suburban couple in the mid-1950's struggling to come to terms with their personal problems while trying to raise their two children.

Foreign films. The Brazilian crime drama *Elite Squad,* directed by José Padilha, was the winner of numerous international film festival awards in 2008. The movie is a semifictional account of the BOPE, the Special Police Operations Battalion of the Rio de Janeiro Military Police. The French film *The Class,* directed by Laurent Cantet, was the unanimous winner of the Palme d'Or at Cannes. Based on a best-selling 2006 autobiographical novel by François Bégaudeau, the drama follows a year in the life of a French teacher working in a tough, multicultural Paris middle school.

Another notable festival film was the animated feature *Waltz with Bashir,* directed by Israel's Ari Folman, about former Israeli soldiers coming to terms with their war experiences in Lebanon in the early 1980's. Critics also praised the French drama *A Christmas Tale,* written and directed by Arnaud Desplechin, starring Catherine Deneuve as the matriarch of a dysfunctional family who has been diagnosed with cancer.

■ Shawn Brennan

See also **Labor and employment; People in the news** (Joel and Ethan Coen; Marion Cotillard; Daniel Day-Lewis); **Television.**

Mozambique. See Africa.
Music. See Classical music; Popular music.

Myanmar.
A cyclone that hit Myanmar (also called Burma) in May 2008 sparked crisis as well as controversy about the government's reaction to the disaster. Cyclone Nargis hit southwestern Myanmar on May 2, continuing through the following day. The storm left more than 138,000 people dead and missing and caused an estimated $4 billion in additional damage and losses.

Response. The *junta* (military government) that had presided over Myanmar since it took power in 1962 was slow to react to the storm's devastation. While initially doing little itself, the junta refused to let many foreign aid workers into the Irrawaddy River delta areas where entire villages were swept away and some 2 million survivors were left without food or clean water.

The junta had long tried to hide the poverty to which it had reduced Myanmar. International affairs experts believed that the junta's fear of foreign interference made them reject many offers of aid for cyclone victims. United States Secretary of Defense Robert Gates accused the junta of "criminal neglect" of its citizens in its slow response.

Little of the first relief supplies flown by foreign countries to the commercial capital, Yangon, was distributed where it was needed. Private citizens distributed supplies to devastated areas. Buddhist monks, whose substantial monasteries had survived the storm, sheltered and fed many of the survivors.

Amid intense international criticism, the junta finally allowed some foreign organizations to help. The cyclone hit just before the planting of the annual rice crop, leaving fields temporarily ruined, and a representative from the United Nations (UN) World Food Program estimated that the country might require rice imports for a full year. On Sept. 24, 2008, the UN Food and Agriculture Organization reported that 97 percent of damaged rice fields had been replanted.

Critics of the junta accused government officials of selling supplies needed for relief work, including gasoline and construction materials, at black market prices. In August, the UN reported that about $1.5 million in aid money had been lost as a result of Myanmar's foreign exchange controls that benefited the government.

Constitution. The junta held a referendum in most of the nation on May 10, and in cyclone-hit areas two weeks later, on a new constitution that it had been working on for 14 years. It claimed overwhelming approval for the document, which perpetuated military control. Critics called the results fraudulent, accusing officials of marking ballots for many people.   ■ Henry S. Bradsher

See also **Asia; Disasters; Weather.**

Namibia. See Africa.
Nauru. See Pacific Islands.

Nepal.
A new national assembly voted on May 28, 2008, to abolish Nepal's 239-year-old monarchy and make the Himalayan nation a republic.

Gyanendra Bir Bikram Shah Dev had succeeded his murdered brother in 2001 as king, a role regarded by many of Nepal's Hindu majority as an incarnation of the Hindu deity Lord Vishnu. Gyanendra seized absolute power in 2005 but was forced by public protests a year later to relinquish it. He handed his crown and scepter to the government on June 11, 2008, returning to his pre-2001 role as a private businessman. Gyanendra was forced to move from the royal palace, which the new government turned into a museum.

Election. Some 60 percent of Nepal's 17.6 million eligible voters cast assembly ballots on April 10, 2008, after political campaigning marked by violence. Election observers from the European Union said voting occurred in a "general atmosphere of fear and intimidation." Most of the campaign violence was blamed on the Communist Party of Nepal (Maoist) and its Young Communist League. Advocating an end to the monarchy, land reforms, and other changes, the Maoists had fought a 10-year guerrilla war in which an estimated 13,000 people died. It agreed with parliament in November 2006 on a cease-fire and election of the assembly to write a new constitution.

had created the ragged Maoist army that mercilessly ravaged government supporters in the underdeveloped, impoverished nation during the decade of civil war. The Congress Party voted against his becoming prime minister, accusing the Maoists of election brutality and failing to return private property seized by guerrillas.

The 2006 peace agreement called for merging some 30,000 Maoist guerrillas into the Nepalese army. After the Maoists took power in 2008, they invited other armed rebel groups to join government negotiations headed by Peace and Reconstruction Minister Janardan Sharma, a former guerrilla leader.

◾ Henry S. Bradsher
See also **Asia.**

Blood streams down the face of a Tibetan monk beaten by police during a pro-Tibet rally in Kathmandu, Nepal, on March 17, 2008. Monks also led protests within Tibet against Chinese control, which Tibet's exiled Dalai Lama continued to oppose.

The Maoists won 220 out of 601 assembly seats. The Nepali Congress party, which had been criticized for its inefficient rule during the 1990's, won 110 seats, and the United Marxist-Leninist Party (UML) won 103. The remaining seats went to smaller parties.

Forming a government. On July 22, 2008, after much political wrangling, the assembly elected Ram Baran Yadav of the Congress Party to the largely ceremonial post of Nepal's president. He defeated a Maoist candidate 308 to 282.

Finally, on August 15, the assembly chose the Maoist leader, Pushpa Kamal Dahal, for the key post of prime minister. Dahal is better known as Prachanda, which means "the fierce one." He

Netherlands. The governing center-right, three-party coalition under Prime Minister Jan Peter Balkenende disagreed over policy in 2008. The main challenges early in the year came from the right-wing Proud of the Netherlands and Freedom parties, which criticized the government's policies on immigration and freedom of speech. The coalition grew increasingly shaky in July, after the minister for employment, Piet Hein Donner, announced a plan for raising the retirement age to 70 only a month after a governmental commission recommended raising it to 67.

Culture and Islam. In February, a controversy erupted over an anti-Islamic documentary film sponsored by a member of parliament, Geert Wilders. The film, *Fitna*, depicts the Muslim religion as an extremist ideology. Wilders used the film's release to promote the agenda of his anti-immigrant Freedom Party.

Lisbon Treaty. In July, the Dutch parliament ratified the Lisbon Treaty of the European Union (EU—Europe's main economic bloc). The treaty, designed to streamline decision making in the EU, resembled the constitutional treaty. That document was rejected in a nationwide referendum in 2005 because most Dutch citizens believed it transferred too much power to EU bureaucrats. The government suspected that the Lisbon Treaty would also be rejected if it were subject to a popular vote, so the question was put before parliament instead.

Foreign policy. In November 2008, Dutch Foreign Minister Maxime Verhagen announced that the Netherlands would withdraw its 1,700 troops from Afghanistan by the end of 2010. The troops had been sent as part of the NATO (North Atlantic Treaty Organization)-led International Security Assistance Force. The Dutch forces played a leading role in the southern Uruzgan province. However, the mission caused controversy at home. Other European nations were reluctant to share the burden of combat, and the militant Islamic Taliban forces grew in strength during 2008.

Economy. Despite a banking system that had weathered the storm surrounding the subprime mortgage crisis, by the end of 2008 the Netherlands succumbed to the general trend of the eurozone. EU economists forecast that the country's *gross domestic product* (GDP—the value of all goods and services produced in a country in a year) would fall to 2.3 percent in 2008, from 3.5 percent in 2007. In its 2009 draft budget, released in September 2008, the government included incentives for those who choose to work beyond the age of 62, the average retirement age in the Netherlands, in an effort to keep more people working longer.   ■ Jeffrey Kopstein

See also **Afghanistan; Bank: A Special Report; Europe.**

New Brunswick. See **Canadian provinces.**

New York City. Mayor Michael R. Bloomberg set off a furious legal battle when he announced plans on Oct. 2, 2008, to run for a third term when his present term expires in 2009—in spite of a City Charter law restricting sitting mayors to two terms.

The city has had three three-term mayors in modern times—Fiorello H. LaGuardia, Robert F. Wagner, and Edward I. Koch—but in 1993 and again in 1996 voters amended the City Charter to limit officeholders to two terms. The mayor himself expressed support in the past for term limits.

Bloomberg, a Democrat turned Republican turned independent, is one of the nation's wealthiest individuals and enormously popular with constituents. He cited the economic downturn for his change of mind. "Given the events of recent weeks and given the enormous challenges we face, I don't want to walk away from a city I feel I can help lead through these tough times," Bloomberg explained. He said that it was too late to hold a referendum on the issue before the Nov. 3, 2009, election, but he said he would support a referendum a year after the mayoral election.

On Oct. 23, 2008, over angry dissent from some members, the City Council voted 29 to 22 to approve the mayor's term-limits change, bypassing a referendum, and clearing the way for many

A temporary waterfall, part of Danish-Icelandic artist Olafur Eliasson's installation "The New York City Waterfalls," cascades beneath the Brooklyn Bridge. Four man-made waterfalls enlivened the East River from June 26 to October 13.

councilmen as well to seek election for an extra four years.

Hard times on Wall Street took a toll on the city's economy in 2008. Economic turmoil caused by a 5,000-point drop in the stock market, the bankruptcy of investment bank Lehman Brothers, and industry layoffs could cause New York state to lose 40,000 private sector jobs and $3 billion in tax revenues over the next two years, according to a report from state Controller Thomas DiNapoli.

Governor Eliot Spitzer resigned on March 17 in a stunning downfall for a former crusading state attorney general and so-called "sheriff of Wall Street." Spitzer had won the governorship in 2006 with a record 69 percent of the vote. Spitzer admitted patronizing a high-priced prostitution service in Washington, D.C., a month earlier. Experts said his real crime appeared to have been breaking up his transactions into small amounts, knowingly circumventing a federal law requiring the reporting of any transfer over $10,000. Spitzer, who returned to his father's New York City real estate agency, was not charged with a crime.

Spitzer was succeeded by Lieutenant Governor David Paterson. Paterson became the state's first African-American governor and the nation's first legally blind governor.

Sports facilities. Yankee Stadium, home to the New York Yankees since 1923, and Shea Stadium, home to the New York Mets since 1964, both closed for good in September 2008 after disappointing baseball seasons. The fields will be replaced by stadiums under construction next door.

The Yanks shared the Polo Grounds with the New York baseball Giants until the early 1920's, when the Giants, alarmed by the popularity of slugger Babe Ruth, forced the club to build a stadium in the Bronx just across the Harlem River. It became known as "The House that Ruth Built." At Yankee Stadium, the Yankees won a record 26 world championships. The new $1.6-billion stadium will open in April 2009.

The Mets also played their first two seasons at the historic Polo Grounds before moving into their own stadium, named for William A. Shea, an attorney credited with returning National League baseball to New York City in 1962. The Dodgers and Giants had bolted from the city to the West Coast four years earlier. The Mets were slated to move into the $800-million Citi Field in 2009.

Shea Stadium was also the scene of a historic concert by the Beatles on Aug. 15, 1965, with "Beatlemania" at its height. In the stadium's last concerts, Billy Joel played a two-night engagement, July 16 and 18, 2008. It included an appearance by former Beatle Paul McCartney, who closed the second show with an emotional rendition of the Beatles classic, "Let It Be." ■ Owen Moritz

See also **Bank: A Special Report; City.**

New Zealand. A center-right government led by the National Party was elected on Nov. 8, 2008, ending the nine-year administration of Helen Clark, New Zealand's first elected female prime minister. Conceding defeat, Clark resigned as leader of the Labour Party. National Party head John Key became prime minister. The National Party secured 58 of the 122 seats in Parliament and coalition arrangements with three minor parties secured them a further 11 seats. National's negotiations balanced the right-wing ACT Party's five seats against an equal number held by the left-of-center Maori Party. New Zealand operates under a proportional representation system in which voters elect a territorial constituency candidate and, separately, select a party from which further "list" representatives may be drawn. The proportion of the nationwide vote won by a party determines the total number of seats it will hold in Parliament.

National had fought the campaign on issues of law and order, education standards, health care, and taxation. Much of Labour's campaign had been personal attacks on Key's trustworthiness. Experts cited the world economic crisis and a desire for change after three terms of Labour-led coalitions as reasons for the Nationals' victory.

Trade. Clark had been a strong advocate of free trade agreements and, on April 7, New Zealand became the first developed country to sign such an agreement with China. The free trade agreement was set to eliminate tariffs on some 96 percent of New Zealand's exports to China by 2019. A free trade agreement with the United States, which New Zealand had sought for more than a decade, advanced on Sept. 22, 2008, with the announcement that the United States would enter negotiations to join the so-called Trans-Pacific Agreement. The agreement is a free trade pact joining Brunei, Chile, New Zealand, and Singapore.

Economy. On November 13, outgoing Finance Minister Michael Cullen revealed a worsening economic forecast. The world financial crisis turned government cash surpluses of the past decade into budget deficits projected to be $5.9 billion in 2008-2009, up from the $3.5 billion that had previously been forecast. (All amounts are in New Zealand dollars.) Economic growth in 2008 was projected at less than 0.2 percent. Unemployment hit its highest level since December 2003, rising 4.2 percent in September 2008. Unemployment was projected to hit 5.7 percent by 2010. The New Zealand government in 2008 moved to guarantee bank deposits and interbank loans during the credit crisis. ■ Gavin Ellis

See also **Bank: A Special Report; Pacific Islands.**

Newfoundland and Labrador. See Canadian provinces.

Sir Edmund Hillary:
Conqueror of Everest

Tenzing Norgay (left) and Edmund Hillary

Sir Edmund Hillary, a New Zealand bee-keeper who became renowned as one of the greatest adventurers of modern times, died on Jan. 11, 2008. In 1953, Hillary and Tenzing Norgay, a Sherpa tribesman from Nepal, thrilled the world by becoming the first two men to climb to the summit of Mount Everest, Earth's highest mountain, and then return.

The perilous journey, which seven previous expeditions had failed to complete, brought Hillary many honors, including a knighthood, and made his name famous. But he often seemed less impressed by the achievement than the many people who flocked to his public appearances and lectures. In 2003, on the 50th anniversary of his Everest climb, he described himself as an "average bloke" and "an enthusiastic mountaineer of modest abilities." Although Hillary climbed other peaks in the Himalaya, landed a plane at the North Pole, and trekked across Antarctica, he was proudest of his long career of public service, especially his work on behalf of the people of Nepal.

Edmund Percival Hillary was born on July 20, 1919, in Auckland, New Zealand. His strict, religious parents operated a commercial honey bee farm, where Edmund helped out. In fact, for most of his life, he listed his occupation as "beekeeper." Tall, gangling, and shy, Hillary discovered mountain climbing at 16 and soon relished the activity for the freedom it offered.

After serving in New Zealand's air force during World War II (1939-1945), he joined a local climbing club and began scaling his country's many mountains. In 1950, he moved on to the Swiss Alps and began planning an assault on Everest. His pioneering climb to the top of Everest in 1953 followed several reconnaissance expeditions on the mountain. He described his experience—marked by howling winds, treacherous crevasses, and a terrifying slip—in *High Adventure* (1955), one of the 13 books he wrote about his life.

In 1960, Hillary led a climbing expedition, which was sponsored by Chicago-based World Book, to Mount Makalu I, another peak in the Himalaya. Conducted mainly to explore the human ability to adjust to high altitudes, the expedition also searched for evidence of the Yeti, a hairy beast sometimes known as the Abominable Snowman. In an article for the 1962 *World Book Year Book,* he wrote, "We reached a definite conclusion that the yeti was a myth created from an accumulation of blue-bear sightings, melted tracks of foxes and wolves, snow leopard cries, and the natural superstition of simple mountain people."

In the years after he climbed Everest, Hillary also devoted himself to public service. He supported environmental causes and established a foundation committed to humanitarian work on behalf of the Nepalese people. "My life is not so much stepping on top of a peak that has never been stepped on before, or traveling to the South Pole, but, rather, the building of schools and medical clinics for the very worthy people of the Himalayas," he said. In 2003, Nepal made Hillary an honorary citizen. He also served as New Zealand's ambassador to India, Bangladesh, and Nepal from 1985 to 1988 and as president of New Zealand's Peace Corps. "I am a lucky man," he told an interviewer after climbing Everest. "I have had a dream and it has come true, and that is not a thing that happens often to men." ■ Barbara A. Mayes

NEWS BYTES

Selected news from 2008:

On a wing and a prayer. On September 26, Swiss adventurer Yves Rossy became the first person to fly a home-built "jetpack" across the English Channel. The former military pilot's custom device, which reportedly cost more than $285,000 to develop and build, consisted of a single carbon composite wing carrying four kerosene-powered turbines. He wore a flame-retardant suit to protect himself from the heat of the engines.

After leaping from an airplane more than 8,800 feet (2,680 meters) above Calais, France, Rossy ignited the turbines. Rossy's device had no steering controls; the pilot controlled the direction of his flight by moving his body as he flew at speeds of up to 186 miles (300 kilometers) per hour. Less than 10 minutes after his flight began, Rossy was 22 miles (35.4 kilometers) away, over Dover, in the United Kingdom. He looped above a crowd of spectators before deploying a parachute and landing safely.

Aksum obelisk unveiled. In September, Ethiopia celebrated the restoration of the Aksum obelisk, one of the country's greatest historical treasures. The 1,700-year-old, 78-foot (24-meter)

monument commemorates Ethiopia's adoption of Christianity in the mid-300's under King Ezana and is viewed as a symbol of national identity by most Ethiopians.

The obelisk had lain in pieces for centuries before Italian troops, then occupying Ethiopia, shipped the obelisk to Rome in 1937 to celebrate dictator Benito Mussolini's 15th year in power. It stood near Rome's Circus Maximus until it was dismantled in 2003 due to damage it had suffered in a lightning strike. It was returned to Ethiopia in 2005. In September 2008, the restored obelisk was finally unveiled in front of a crowd of tens of thousands of people, including the president and prime minister of Ethiopia.

Tourists in September 2008 contemplate the newly restored "The Battle of Gettysburg," a *cyclorama* (epic picture on the wall of a circular room) at the Gettysburg Museum in Pennsylvania. The 377-foot- (115-meter-) wide painting, which dates from 1884, depicts the 1863 Battle of Gettysburg, a major turning point in the American Civil War (1861-1865).

Junk raft. Over the summer, two men sailed from California to Hawaii on a pile of junk. Marcus Eriksen of the Long Beach, California-based non-profit Algalita Marine Research Foundation, along with fellow "eco-mariner" Joel Paschal, built a vessel called JUNK out of 15,000 plastic bottles that served as pontoons; 20 sailboat masts that formed the vessel's deck; 5,000 plastic bags woven into rope; and the fuselage of a Cessna 310 airplane, which they used as a cabin. The purpose of their voyage was to bring attention to plastic pollution in the ocean and protest against wasteful "single-use plastics" that, the researchers noted, usually wind up in the ocean. They set sail from Long Beach, California, on June 1. Leaving the Long Beach area proved a challenge, after a series of storms left JUNK badly damaged. They repaired the raft and continued their voyage.

Over the three months it took the men to

A portrait of the Austrian composer Wolfgang Amadeus Mozart dating from about 1783 is displayed shortly after being authenticated in March 2008. The painting is one of only four known Mozart portraits dating from the period between 1781 and the composer's death in 1791.

sail to Honolulu, Hawaii, they spent an average of three hours per day repairing and maintaining the raft. The pair stayed in contact with the mainland with a solar-powered satellite telephone, which also allowed them to post information about their voyage to the Internet on an almost daily basis. On August 27, the pair arrived in Hawaii. They were surprised and dismayed to note that, after three months at sea, none of the 15,000 plastic bottles showed much wear, which, they noted, proved their durability. Many such bottles currently pollute the ocean.

A long-delayed pardon. The city council of Florence, Italy, voted in June to revoke the ruling that sent medieval poet Dante Alighieri into exile. Alighieri, best known for the epic poem *The Divine Comedy,* was active in Florentine politics in the late 1200's. He became involved in a dispute between two groups, the Guelphs and the Ghibellines, who were fighting for control of the province of Tuscany. A political group within the Guelphs who were hostile toward Dante gained control of Florence in 1301 and the following year voted

What My Dad Gave Me, a sculpture on display at Rockefeller Center in New York City in June and July, mirrors the iconic GE Building behind it. American artist Chris Burden created the 65-foot- (20-meter-) tall sculpture out of stainless steel parts modeled on the original Erector set, a toy consisting of small metal girders that could be used to build miniature structures and machines.

dealing primarily in brass and bronze. At an auction in the 1930's or 1940's, he bought a 5 ½-inch (14-centimeter) intricately designed metal cup featuring the two-faced ancient Roman god Janus, shown with braided hair adorned with snake ornaments. He passed it down to his grandson John Webber, who put the cup in a box under a bed and forgot about it.

In 2007, Webber rediscovered the cup when he moved to a new house and realized that it was neither brass nor bronze. He sent the cup to the British Museum in London, where experts said they had never seen anything like it. Webber then sent the cup to a laboratory, where analysis yielded a surprising discovery— the cup was made of a single piece of 22-carat gold dated to about 400 to 300 B.C., probably from the Achaemenid Empire of ancient Persia. Webber, 70, sold the cup at an auction, with the winning bid at $100,000.

At auction in 2008: In August, a copy of The Beatles's original 1962 management contract was auctioned by London's specialty auction house The Fame Bureau for $426,000. The document was signed by all four Beatles—George Harrison, John Lennon, Paul McCartney, and Richard Starkey, better known as Ringo Starr— as well as manager Brian Epstein. In July 2008, the iconic bass drum head from the cover of the band's 1967 album *Sgt. Pepper's Lonely Hearts Club Band* sold for $1.07 million.

to banish the poet from Florence for the rest of his life, condemning him to death if he returned. Dante lived the rest of his life in exile and died in the northern Italian city of Ravenna in 1321.

Some city councilors in 2008 voted against the revocation, calling it meaningless in the modern world. Some opponents claimed that Dante's poetry was made great by his exile and suffering and, therefore, pardoning him was unnecessary. *The Divine Comedy* and many of Dante's other works were composed entirely while the poet was in exile.

One man's trash. A cup left by a junk dealer to his grandson was revealed in 2008 to be an ancient Persian artifact. William Sparks, who was a "rag and bone man" in the southwestern United Kingdom, ran a scrap metal business

In June 2008, the writing desk and chair used by Charles Dickens when he wrote the novel *Great Expectations* in 1860 and 1861 sold for more than $850,000. The money raised by the auction went to the Great Ormond Street Hospital for Children in London. Dickens was a friend of the hospital's founder.

A gold-encrusted dagger once owned by Shah Jahan, the Mughal emperor who built the Taj Mahal, sold in April 2008 for $3.3 million. Inscriptions on the blade of the dagger suggest that it was made as a gift for Shah Jahan in 1630, only two years into his reign. He ruled the Mughal empire from 1628 to 1666.

A 1935 Alfa Romeo 2300 Pescara Spyder custom built for Italian dictator Benito Mussolini was auctioned for $1.1 million in March 2008, setting a record for that model. The car is featured in films and photographs of Mussolini, who is shown waving to crowds from the passenger seat. In 1936, Mussolini's chauffeur, a former test driver for Alfa Romeo, drove the car in the Mille Miglia, a 1,000-mile (1,600-kilometer) endurance race.

 S. Thomas Richardson

The Hula Hoop turned 50 in 2008. Arthur "Spud" Melin (left) and Richard Knerr founded Wham-O Inc. in 1958 to produce and distribute the hollow plastic hoops, which they based on a rattan hoop toy that was somewhat popular in Australia. The Hula Hoop quickly became a nation-wide craze.

Uno the beagle beat two poodles to win Best in Show at the famed Westminster Kennel Club Dog Show in New York City on Feb. 12, 2008. Although the beagle was the only dog consistently listed among the most popular dogs in the United States for nearly 100 years, it had never won Best in Show. Uno enjoyed a busy reign, meeting with First Lady Laura Bush and riding in Macy's annual Thanksgiving Day Parade in New York City.

Newspaper. The circulation of print newspapers in the United States dropped significantly in 2008. The independent Audit Bureau of Circulations in Schaumburg, Illinois, reported an average 4.6-percent drop in weekday circulation for April through September, compared with the same period in 2007. Sunday circulation fell an average of 4.8 percent. Increased Internet usage, along with some publishers' decisions to stop delivering newspapers to less profitable customers, contributed to the decline in print readership.

On December 16, the *Detroit Free Press* and *The Detroit News* announced that beginning in March 2009 they will offer only three days of home delivery a week. Subscribers will receive papers on Thursdays, Fridays, and Sundays, which are the most profitable in terms of ad revenue.

Large newspaper publishers, including Gannett Company, Inc., in McLean, Virginia; The New York Times Company in New York City; and The McClatchy Company in Sacramento, California, also reported falling revenues, as advertisers moved their ads to the Internet and as the U.S. economy suffered from a global credit crisis.

Suspended publications. *The New York Sun,* a conservative newspaper founded in 2002, stopped publishing in late September 2008. The newspaper, printed five days a week, could not raise enough capital to continue operating. In October, the 100-year-old *Christian Science Monitor* announced plans to limit its print production to a weekly edition, beginning in April 2009, and to focus its resources on its Web site. The newspaper's print circulation had fallen by more than 65 percent over the last 20 years.

Tribune Group shakeup. Financial difficulties led the Tribune Group, in Chicago, to file for Chapter 11 bankruptcy in December 2008. The Tribune faced a debt of $13 billion, nearly double the amount of its $7.6 billion dollars in assets. The company announced that it would continue operating while working to restructure its debt. In July, the Tribune had cut about a fifth of the staff at three of its newspapers—*The Morning Call* of Allentown, Pennsylvania; the *Orlando Sentinel* of Orlando, Florida; and the *Sun-Sentinel* of Fort Lauderdale, Florida.

In May, Cablevision Systems Corporation in Bethpage, New York, acquired from the Tribune Group a 97-percent share of the Newsday Media Group, which publishes *Newsday,* a daily newspaper serving Long Island. Tribune kept a 3-percent stake. Cablevision's share of Newsday Media Group cost $632 million.

Associated Press to be dropped. In 2008, a number of newspapers announced plans to stop using the Associated Press (AP) news service. Users expressed a need to cut expenses or dissatisfaction with the rate structure. ■ Dawn Krajcik

Nicaragua. On Nov. 9, 2008, the ruling, left-wing Sandinista National Liberation Front party claimed victory in 105 of 146 mayoral races in Nicaragua amid credible allegations that some of the elections had been rigged. The opposition Constitutionalist Liberal Party charged that President Daniel Ortega's action in barring international observers from monitoring the elections had prompted widespread vote fraud and intimidation. In Managua, the capital, two people were killed in post-election violence.

In August, the Polaris Geothermal Corporation of Toronto, Canada, announced a $96-million investment to triple its production at a geothermal field on the slopes of the Momotombo volcano near the city of León. The Nicaraguan government also invited bids from foreign companies to develop geothermal energy from the San Cristóbal volcano in the northwestern part of the country.

On September 16, Father Miguel d'Escoto Brockmann, a Nicaraguan diplomat, delivered his first speech as president of the United Nations General Assembly. The 75-year-old priest did not mince words: "The state of our world today is deplorable, inexcusable and, therefore, shameful." ■ Nathan A. Haverstock

See also **Latin America.**

Niger. See Africa.

Nigeria. On Aug. 20, 2008, President Umaru Yar'Adua announced a major shake-up in Nigeria's military. The chief of the defense staff and the three service heads of the army, navy, and air force were all retired and replaced. Analysts speculated that the government was unhappy with the way the armed forces had handled unrest in the oil-rich Niger Delta—a crisis that Yar'Adua had promised to address when he gained office in May 2007.

Delta disturbances. During 2008, members of the rebel group called the Movement for the Emancipation of the Niger Delta (MEND) stepped up their attacks on the region's oil facilities. On June 19, gunmen in powerboats assaulted a giant deepwater production vessel floating 75 miles (120 kilometers) off the coast, forcing Royal Dutch Shell to shut it down with a loss of 200,000 barrels a day. On July 17, an attack on an oil pipeline owned by Italian firm Eni S.p.A. cost Nigeria another 50,000 barrels per day. These and other acts of sabotage reduced Nigeria's oil production by about a quarter in 2008.

The nation ranked as the world's eighth largest oil exporter and the largest in sub-Saharan Africa. Oil revenues provide more than 80 percent of Nigeria's government revenue. But MEND and other militant groups say that very little of this wealth has been used to ease poverty in the delta. Foreign correspondents claimed that some attacks were the work of criminal gangs, who made money from ransom payments and stealing oil.

Political developments. On February 26, a judicial panel ended months of uncertainty over the fate of President Yar'Adua when it dismissed a case calling for a rerun of the April 2007 presidential election on the grounds of fraud and violence. The prospect of a rerun had raised concerns about political stability in Africa's most populous nation.

A few days earlier, another Nigerian tribunal annulled the election of David Mark, the president of the Senate. He had been chosen as a senator for Benue state in disputed gubernatorial elections held in April 2007. The case was seen as causing further political uncertainty because, under the federal constitution, Mark would take over as president if Yar'Adua and the vice president were ever forced to step down.

Justice system condemned. On Feb. 26, 2008, London-based human-rights organization Amnesty International released a detailed report on Nigeria's criminal justice system that criticized the country for its systematic violation of prisoners' rights. The report found that at least 65 percent of inmates had never been convicted of any crime and that torture was widely used by police to force confessions. ■ Simon Baynham

See also **Africa; Energy supply: A Special Report.**

Nobel Prizes in literature, peace,

economic sciences, and the sciences were awarded in October 2008 by the Norwegian Storting (parliament) in Oslo and by the Karolinska Institute, the Royal Swedish Academy of Sciences, and the Swedish Academy of Literature, all in Stockholm. Each prize was worth about $1.4 million.

The 2008 Nobel Prize in literature went to French writer Jean-Marie Gustave Le Clézio, a major figure in European literature. Le Clézio's writings, which reflect experimental styles, often portray conflicts between the modern technological world and more traditional cultures. He was described by the Swedish Academy as an "author of new departures, poetic adventure and sensual ecstasy, explorer of a humanity beyond and below the reigning civilization." Le Clézio gained fame with his first novel, *The Interrogation* (1963). His many other novels include *The Giants* (1973), *Onitsha* (1991), *The Prospector* (1993), and *The Wandering Star* (2004). He has also written short stories, essays, personal reflections, and children's literature.

The 2008 Peace Prize was awarded to Martti Ahtisaari of Finland, a diplomat and peacemaker, for "his important efforts, on several continents and over more than three decades, to resolve international conflicts. These efforts have contributed to a more peaceful world and to 'frater-

nity between nations' in Alfred Nobel's spirit." Ahtisaari, who served as president of Finland from 1994 to 2000, has been actively involved in peace efforts in various regions of Africa, Asia, and Europe since the late 1970's. He played a key role in helping the southwest African country of Namibia negotiate its independence from South Africa in 1990. In the early 2000's, Ahtisaari founded the Crisis Management Initiative, an independent organization dedicated to peace preservation and conflict resolution. During this time, he also served as a special United Nations envoy to help resolve Kosovo's long-standing conflict with Serbia.

The 2008 Nobel Prize in economic sciences was won by Paul Krugman, a professor of economics and international affairs at Princeton University in Princeton, New Jersey, for a new theory explaining patterns of international trade. He also writes for *The New York Times,* where he has frequently criticized the economic policies of United States President George W. Bush.

Krugman was recognized for research analyzing such issues as the reasons nations produce and trade certain commodities and how urbanization and globalization affect international trade. Krugman's theory "clarifies why worldwide trade is in fact dominated by countries which not only have similar conditions, but also trade in similar products—for instance, [exporting and importing] cars. This kind of trade enables specialization and large-scale production, which result in lower prices and a greater diversity of commodities."

The 2008 Nobel Prize in physiology or medicine was awarded to three European scientists for their discoveries of two viruses that cause severe diseases. Harald Zur Hausen, a German scientist who worked at the German Cancer Research Center in Heidelberg, discovered in the 1980's that the human papillomavirus (HPV) causes cervical cancer in women. His finding eventually led to the development of vaccines to help prevent what is the second most common cancer among women.

French scientists Françoise Barré-Sinoussi and Luc Montagnier, both of the Pasteur Institute in Paris, discovered in the mid-1980's that AIDS is caused by the human immunodeficiency virus. Montagnier is also director of the nonprofit World Foundation for AIDS Research and Prevention in Paris. The identification of the AIDS virus led to the development of methods to diagnose infected patients and to screen blood products as well as to screen antiviral drugs that have "substantially decreased spread of the disease and dramatically increased life expectancy among treated patients."

The 2008 Nobel Prize in physics went to Japanese-born American physicist Yoichiro Nambu of the University of Chicago and to Japanese scientists Toshihide Maskawa of Kyoto University and

Makoto Kobayashi of the High Energy Accelerator Research Organization in Tsukuba, both in Japan. Nambu won for his explanation of broken symmetry, an important property of *subatomic particles* (particles of matter smaller than atoms). Maskawa and Kobayashi identified the particles that must exist for Nambu's theory to work. The work of the three scientists helped in the development of the Standard Model, the leading fundamental theory of physics that describes all known subatomic particles and their interactions.

The 2008 Nobel Prize in chemistry was awarded to Japanese-born American scientist Osamu Shimomura of the Marine Biological Laboratory in Woods Hole and Boston University Medical School, both in Massachusetts; Martin Chalfie of Columbia University in New York City; and Roger Y. Tsien of the University of California, San Diego. The men were honored for their work with the green fluorescent protein (GFP), a molecule found in jellyfish that glows when exposed to ultraviolet light. An invaluable tool in biochemical research, GFP can be linked to other proteins, "tagging" them so they can be viewed under a microscope. Using GFP, researchers have been able to observe such previously invisible processes as the development of nerve cells in the brain and the spread of cancer cells. ■ Barbara A. Mayes

See also **Literature; Physics.**

Northern Ireland.
The power-sharing Assembly in Northern Ireland continued to function in 2008, as did the peace process. The province of the United Kingdom (U.K.) has been divided by violence between the Protestant majority, who seek to maintain the union with the U.K., and the Roman Catholic minority, who want the province to become part of the Republic of Ireland.

The six counties of Ulster formed the province of Northern Ireland in 1920. The rest of Ireland gained independence from the U.K. in 1921. Violence broke out in 1969 between Protestant Unionists and Catholic groups. The Catholics were represented by the political party Sinn Féin, which had links to a paramilitary organization called the Irish Republican Army (IRA). In 1969, the British government deployed troops to keep the peace. However, the two sides agreed to a cease-fire in the Good Friday Agreement of 1998. After a previous government collapsed over mutual suspicion in 2003, a power-sharing national Assembly was created in 2007. That year, most British troops withdrew, and direct rule by the U.K. ended.

Paisley. In 2008, the Reverend Ian Paisley retired. As leader of the Democratic Unionist Party (DUP), he had become first minister for Northern Ireland in 2007. Paisley, who had founded the party in 1971, was noted for his resistance to any settlement with Catholic nationalists in the province. He

had, however, agreed as part of the peace process to form a government in 2007 with Martin McGuiness of Sinn Féin as deputy first minister.

Paisley stepped down as party leader on May 31, 2008, and was replaced by the deputy leader of the DUP, Peter Robinson. Robinson was elected first minister by the National Assembly on June 5. Sinn Féin and the DUP resolved a long-running dispute about policing when a Justice department with both Catholic and Protestant input was created in November to oversee the police and the courts.

Nationalists and the IRA. Concern remained about nationalist splinter groups, such as the "Real IRA," which had broken away from the IRA when the latter accepted the cease-fire in 1998 and agreed to decommission its weapons. In February 2008, police in Northern Ireland reinstated checks on vehicles entering the province after concerns that the Real IRA might be continuing terrorist activities. Officials were also concerned about a new nationalist organization, the Army of Ireland, which has opposed the peace process.

In September, however, the Independent Monitoring Commission (IMC), which evaluates the status of paramilitary groups, reported that there is no evidence that the IRA is currently engaged in terrorist activities. The IMC said that the group is solely a political organization. ■ Rohan McWilliam

See also **Ireland; United Kingdom.**

Norway.
The three-party government consisting of the Labor Party, the Socialist Left Party, and the Center Party under Prime Minister Jens Stoltenberg faced several challenges in 2008. Nevertheless, the coalition was expected to survive until the next national election in 2009.

Pension reform. In March and April 2008, the government continued a reform of the country's retirement and pension systems begun in 2005. The new system was to be phased in beginning in 2010. All parties agreed on the general retirement age of 67 (with incentives to stay on the job until 70) and a clear link between the size of the pension and the value of a lifetime's work. Differences arose, however, between the parties and trade unions over the introduction of an early retirement package at age 62. Some leading politicians and economists maintained that such an option would induce people to leave the work force early and place an unsustainable burden on the nation's resources.

Church and state. In April 2008, all seven of Norway's political parties agreed to amend the Constitution to loosen the ties between church and state. Under the agreement, the Evangelical Lutheran Church will no longer be the official state church. Although the church will continue to receive state funds, other faiths will receive such funding as well. The change to the Constitution was expected to take place in 2012.

Energy and environment. Early in 2008, the government presented a plan for reducing Norway's greenhouse gas emissions, with the intention of making the country *carbon-neutral* (making no net contribution to the planet's carbon footprint) by 2030. Because the country is one of Europe's main producers of oil and natural gas, Norwegian parties wanted to present an environmentally friendly image. The plan would put Norway 20 years ahead of its previously stated goal of 2050.

Russia's increasing willingness to use its energy resources as a source of power in the region raised Norway's profile in 2008. In November, after Russian Prime Minister Vladimir Putin threatened to cancel a pipeline to carry natural gas to Western Europe under the Baltic Sea, Stoltenberg reassured Europe that Norway could serve as an alternative supply source.

The Norwegian economy contracted in 2008, as part of the worldwide economic crisis. Economists forecast that Norway's *gross domestic product* (the value of all goods and services produced in a country in a year) would fall from 3.7 percent in 2007 to 2.5 percent in 2008. ■ Jeffrey Kopstein

See also **Europe.**

Nova Scotia. See Canadian provinces.
Nuclear energy. See Energy supply.
Nunavut. See Canadian territories.
Nutrition. See Food.

Ocean.
There were more signs in 2008 that ocean life is in decline, from jellyfish swarms to endangered coral. Yet, scientists also found life thriving in places long assumed to be barren.

Jellyfish jam-up. Enormous swarms of stinging jellyfish clogged coastlines around the Mediterranean in the summer, from Israel to Gibraltar. More than 19,000 people were stung in one coastal region of Spain alone. Jellyfish swarms are a growing problem around the world, with masses washing ashore in Australia, Japan, New England, and South Africa. The stings are intensely painful or even deadly in rare cases.

Most scientists blame the problem on global warming, overfishing, and pollution. Warmer waters help jellyfish to grow and reproduce more quickly. Fish that eat jellyfish or compete with them for food, such as tuna and sharks, have been overfished throughout the oceans. Pollution can reduce levels of oxygen in the water, a condition in which jellyfish thrive. Fish that hunt jellyfish are driven away by low levels of oxygen, but such low levels have little impact on jellyfish.

New reefs, fresh peril. Researchers with Conservation International of Arlington, Virginia, announced in July the discovery of vast coral reefs off the coast of Brazil. The reefs roughly double the size of one of the Atlantic Ocean's largest and richest reef systems, the Abrolhos Bank. The reefs were not found earlier because they are at a greater depth than is typical. This depth has helped protect the reefs from overfishing. In some places, the reefs harbor 30 times as many fish as would be found on most shallower reefs.

The Switzerland-based International Union for Conservation of Nature reported in July that one-third of reef-building corals face extinction. Coral reefs are threatened by global warming, invasive species, overfishing, and pollution. Reefs support many species found nowhere else.

Benthic bounty. The ocean floor is rich with microscopic life, according to a May report in the science journal *Nature.* Conditions on the ocean floor, at depths of 2 miles (3.2 kilometers) or more, are extreme. Scientists had long thought that life was scarce at these depths because of high pressure, lack of food, and total darkness.

To their surprise, the authors of the study found thousands of times as much microscopic life on the ocean floor as in the water above. Life on the bottom appears to be as diverse as life in farm soil, according to the scientists from the University of Southern California in Los Angeles. Most bacteria on the bottom are new to science. Researchers believe the bacteria get their energy from chemical reactions in the rocks of the ocean floor.

Remarkably, there may be even more life in the rocks *beneath* the ocean floor. An August study in *Nature* found a wealth of life hundreds of feet below the ocean floor. Researchers from the University of Bremen, Germany, suggested that a staggering 90 billion tons (82 billion metric tons) of microscopic life occupies 48 million cubic miles (200 million cubic kilometers) of buried mud. These figures suggest that about half of all microscopic cells on Earth live buried in the ocean mud. These buried cells store 1/10 as much carbon as all tropical rain forests. The study found that a kind of microscopic life called *archaea* dominates the depths. Archaea thrive in conditions deadly to most forms of life.

Scientists filmed fish at depths of nearly 5 miles (8 kilometers) for the first time in September. The pale snailfish observed by scientists at the University of Aberdeen in Scotland were highly active and appear to live in groups, though pressure at this depth is equivalent to that created by 1,600 elephants standing on the roof of a car.

Motion of the ocean. On June 20, NASA launched a satellite that promises to improve ocean and climate models. The Ocean Surface Topography Mission/Jason 2 satellite carries instruments that measure oceanic surface height every 10 days. These measurements will allow better mapping of ocean currents and tides. Ocean currents have an important but poorly understood impact on global climate. ■ Brian Johnson

See also **Biology; Conservation.**

THE 2008 SUMMER GAMES

The world's top athletes gathered in Beijing in August 2008 to compete in the XXIX Olympiad of the modern era.

ARCHERY

Men's individual
GOLD   Viktor Ruban, Ukraine
SILVER   Park Kyung-Mo, South Korea
BRONZE   Bair Badenov, Russia

Men's team
GOLD   South Korea**
SILVER   Italy
BRONZE   China

Women's individual
GOLD   Zhang Juan Juan, China
SILVER   Park Sung-Hyun, South Korea
BRONZE   Yun Ok-Hee, South Korea

Women's team
GOLD   South Korea
SILVER   China
BRONZE   France

BASEBALL

GOLD   South Korea
SILVER   Cuba
BRONZE   United States

BASKETBALL

Men
GOLD   United States
SILVER   Spain
BRONZE   Argentina

Women
GOLD   United States
SILVER   Australia
BRONZE   Russia

BEACH VOLLEYBALL

Men
GOLD   Philip Dalhausser and Todd Rogers, United States
SILVER   Marcio Araujo and Fabio Magalhaes, Brazil
BRONZE   Ricardo Santos and Emanuel Rego, Brazil

Women
GOLD   Kerri Walsh and Misty May-Treanor, United States
SILVER   Wang Jie and Tian Jia, China
BRONZE   Xue Chen and Zhang Xi, China

BADMINTON

Men's singles
GOLD   Lin Dan, China
SILVER   Chong Wei Lee, Malaysia
BRONZE   Chen Jin, China

Men's doubles
GOLD   Markis Kido and Hendra Setiawan, Indonesia
SILVER   Fu Haifeng and Cai Yun, China
BRONZE   Lee Jaejin and Hwang Jiman, South Korea

Women's singles
GOLD   Zhang Ning, China
SILVER   Xie Xingfang, China
BRONZE   Maria Kristin Yulianti, Indonesia

Women's doubles
GOLD   Yu Yang and Du Jing, China
SILVER   Lee Hyojung and Lee Kyungwon, South Korea
BRONZE   Zhang Yawen and Wei Yili, China

Mixed doubles
GOLD   Lee Yongdae and Lee Hyojung, South Korea
SILVER   Nova Widianto and Liliyana, Indonesia
BRONZE   He Hanbin and Yu Yang, China

Badminton gold medalist Zhang Ning, of China

BOXING

Light flyweight 106 lbs. (48 kg)
GOLD   Zou Shiming, China
SILVER   Serdamba Purevdorj, Mongolia
BRONZE   Paddy Barnes, Ireland, and Yampier Hernandez G, Cuba

Flyweight 112 lbs. (51kg)
GOLD   Somjit Jongjohor, Thailand
SILVER   Andris Laffita Hernandez, Cuba
BRONZE   Vincenzo Picardi, Italy, and Georgy Balakshin, Russia

Bantamweight 119 lbs. (54 kg)
GOLD   Badar-Uugan Enkhbat, Mongolia
SILVER   Yankiel Leon Alarcon, Cuba
BRONZE   Veaceslav Gojan, Moldova, and Bruno Julie, Mauritius

Featherweight 126 lbs. (57kg)
GOLD   Vasyl Lomachenko, Ukraine
SILVER   Khedafi Djelkhir, France
BRONZE   Yakup Kilic, Turkey, and Shahin Imranov, Azerbaijan

Lightweight 132 lbs. (60 kg)
GOLD   Alexey Tishchenko, Russia
SILVER   Daouda Sow, France
BRONZE   Hrachik Javakhyan, Armenia, and Yordenis Ugas, Cuba

Light Welterweight 141 lbs. (64kg)
GOLD   Felix Diaz, Dominican Republic
SILVER   Manus Boonjumnong, Thailanda
BRONZE   Alexis Vastine, France, and Roniel Iglesias Sotolongo, Cuba

Welterweight 152 lbs. (69kg)
GOLD   Bakhyt Sarsekbayev, Kazakhstan
SILVER   Carlos Banteaux Suarez, Cuba
BRONZE   Kim Jungjoo, South Korea, and Hanati Silamu, China

Middleweight 165 lbs. (75kg)
GOLD   James Degale, United Kingdom
SILVER   Emilio Correa Bayeaux, Cuba
BRONZE   Darren John Sutherland, Ireland, and Vijender Kumar, India

Light Heavyweight 179 lbs. (81 kg)
GOLD   Zhang Xiaoping, China
SILVER   Kenny Egan, Ireland
BRONZE   Yerkebulan Shynaliyev, Kazakhstan, and Tony Jeffries, United Kingdom

Heavyweight 201 lbs. (91 kg)
GOLD   Rakhim Chakhkiev, Russia
SILVER   Clemente Russo, Italy
BRONZE   Osmai Acosta Duarte, Cuba, and Deontay Wilder, United States

Super Heavyweight Over 201 lbs. (Over 91 kg)
GOLD   Roberto Cammarelle, Italy
SILVER   Zhang Zhilei, China
BRONZE   David Price, United Kingdom, and Vyacheslav Glazkov, Ukraine

CANOE-KAYAK

MEN'S
SLALOM RACING
Canoe singles
GOLD   Michal Martikan, Slovakia
SILVER   David Florence, United Kingdom
BRONZE   Robin Bell, Australia

Canoe doubles
GOLD   Pavol Hochschorner and Peter Hochschorner, Slovakia
SILVER   Jaroslav Volf and Ondrej Stepanek, Czech Republic
BRONZE   Mikhail Kuznetsov and Dmitry Larionov, Russia

Kayak singles
GOLD   Alexander Grimm, Germany
SILVER   Fabien Lefevre, France
BRONZE   Benjamin Boukpeti, Togo

MEN'S
FLATWATER
500-meter kayak singles
GOLD   Ken Wallace, Australia
SILVER   Adam van Koeverden, Canada
BRONZE   Tim Brabants, United Kingdom

500-meter canoe singles
GOLD   Maxim Opalev, Russia
SILVER   David Cal, Spain
BRONZE   Iurii Cheban, Ukraine

500-meter kayak doubles
GOLD   Saul Craviotto and Carlos Perez, Spain
SILVER   Ronald Rauhe and Tim Wieskotter, Germany
BRONZE   Raman Piatrushenka and Vadzim Makhneu, Belarus

500-meter canoe doubles
GOLD   Meng Guanliang and Yang Wenjun, China
SILVER   Sergey Ulegin and Alexander Kostoglod, Russia
BRONZE   Christian Gille and Thomasz Wylenzek, Germany

1,000-meter kayak singles
GOLD   Tim Brabants, United Kingdom
SILVER   Eirik Veraas Larsen, Norway
BRONZE   Ken Wallace, Australia

1,000-meter canoe singles
GOLD   Attila Sandor Vajda, Hungary
SILVER   David Cal, Spain
BRONZE   Thomas Hall, Canada

1,000-meter kayak doubles
GOLD   Martin Hollstein and Andreas Ihle, Germany
SILVER   Kim Wraae Knudsen and Rene Holten Poulsen, Denmark
BRONZE   Andrea Facchin and Antonio M. Scaduto, Italy

1,000-meter canoe doubles
GOLD   Andrei Bahdanovich and Aliaksandr Bahdanovich, Belarus
SILVER   Christian Gille and Thomasz Wylenzek, Germany
BRONZE   Gyorgy Kozmann and Tamas Kiss, Hungary

1,000-meter kayak fours
GOLD   Belarus
SILVER   Slovakia
BRONZE   Germany

* World record
** Olympic record

CANOE-KAYAK, CONTINUED

WOMEN'S
SLALOM RACING
Kayak singles
GOLD   Elena Kaliska, Slovakia
SILVER acqueline Lawrence, Australia
BRONZE Violetta Oblinger Peters, Austria

WOMEN'S
FLATWATER
500-meter kayak singles
GOLD   Inna Osypenko-Radomska,
    Ukraine
SILVER Josefa Idem, Italy
BRONZE Katrin Wagner-Augustin,
    Germany

500-meter kayak doubles
GOLD   Katalin Kovacs and Natasa
    Janic, Hungary
SILVER Beata Mikolajczyk and Aneta
    Konieczna, Poland
BRONZE Marie Delattre and Anne-
    Laure Viard, France

500-meter kayak fours
GOLD   Germany
SILVER Hungary
BRONZE Australia

CYCLING

MEN
BMX
Men's BMX
GOLD   Maris Strombergs, Latvia
SILVER Mike Day, United States
BRONZE Donny Robinson,
    United States

ROAD
Men's road race
GOLD   Samuel Sanchez, Spain
SILVER Davide Rebellin, Italy
BRONZE Fabian Cancellara,
    Switzerland

Men's individual time trial
GOLD   Fabian Cancellara,
    Switzerland
SILVER Gustav Larsson, Sweden
BRONZE Levi Leipheimer,
    United States

TRACK
Madison sprint
GOLD   Juan Esteban Curuchet and
    Walter Fernando Perez,
    Argentina
SILVER Joan Llaneras and Antonio
    Tauler, Spain
BRONZE Mikhail Ignatyev and Alexei
    Markov, Russia

Keirin sprint
GOLD   Chris Hoy, United Kingdom
SILVER Ross Edgar, United Kingdom
BRONZE Kiyofumi Nagai, Japan

Men's sprint
GOLD   Chris Hoy, United Kingdom
SILVER Jason Kenny, United
    Kingdom
BRONZE Mickael Bourgain, France

Team sprint
GOLD   United Kingdom
SILVER France
BRONZE Germany

Individual pursuit
GOLD   Bradley Wiggins, United
    Kingdom
SILVER Hayden Roulston, New
    Zealand
BRONZE Steven Burke, United
    Kingdom

Team pursuit
GOLD   United Kingdom*
SILVER Denmark
BRONZE New Zealand

Points race
GOLD   Joan Llaneras, Spain
SILVER Roger Kluge, Germany
BRONZE Chris Newton,
    United Kingdom

MOUNTAIN BIKE
Mountain bike
GOLD   Julien Absalon, France
SILVER Jean-Christophe Peraud,
    France
BRONZE Nino Schurter, Switzerland

WOMEN
BMX
Women's BMX
GOLD   Anne-Caroline Chausson,
    France
SILVER Laetitia le Corguille, France
BRONZE Jill Kintner, United States

ROAD
Women's road race
GOLD   Nicole Cooke, United Kingdom
SILVER Emma Johansson, Sweden
BRONZE Tatiana Guderzo, Italy

Women's Individual time trial
GOLD   Kristin Armstrong,
    United States
SILVER Emma Pooley,
    United Kingdom
BRONZE Karin Thurig, Switzerland

TRACK
Sprint
GOLD   Victoria Pendleton,
    United Kingdom
SILVER Anna Meares, Australia
BRONZE Guo Shuang, China

Individual pursuit
GOLD   Rebecca Romero,
    United Kingdom
SILVER Wendy Houvenaghel,
    United Kingdom
BRONZE Lesya Kalitovska, Ukraine

Points race
GOLD   Marianne Vos, Netherlands
SILVER Yoanka Gonzalez, Cuba
BRONZE Leire Olaberria, Spain

MOUNTAIN BIKE
Mountain bike
GOLD   Sabine Spitz, Germany
SILVER Maja Wloszczowska, Poland
BRONZE Irina Kalentyeva, Russia

BMX cyclist Anne-
Caroline Chausson,
of France

* World record
** Olympic record

DIVING

Men's 3-meter springboard
GOLD   He Chong, China
SILVER   Alexandre Despatie, Canada
BRONZE   Qin Kai, China

Men's 10-meter platform
GOLD   Matthew Mitcham, Australia
SILVER   Zhou Luxin, China
BRONZE   Gleb Galperin, Russia

Men's synchronized 3-meter springboard
GOLD   Wang Feng and Qin Kai, China
SILVER   Dmitry Sautin and Yuriy Kunakov, Russia
BRONZE   Illya Kvasha and Oleksiy Prygorov, Ukraine

Men's synchronized 10-meter platform
GOLD   Lin Yue and Huo Liang, China
SILVER   Patrick Hausding and Sascha Klein, Germany
BRONZE   Gleb Galperin and Dmitriy Dobroskok, Russia

Women's 3-meter springboard
GOLD   Guo Jingjing, China
SILVER   Julia Pakhalina, Russia
BRONZE   Wu Minxia, China

Women's 10-meter platform
GOLD   Chen Ruolin, China
SILVER   Emilie Heymans, Canada
BRONZE   Wang Xin, China

Women's synchronized 3-meter springboard
GOLD   Guo Jingjing and Wu Minxia, China
SILVER   Julia Pakhalina and Anastasia Pozdnyakova, Russia
BRONZE   Ditte Kotzian and Heike Fischer, Germany

Women's synchronized 10-meter platform
GOLD   Wang Xin and Chen Ruolin, China
SILVER   Briony Cole and Melissa Wu, Australia
BRONZE   Paola Espinosa and Tatiana Ortiz, Mexico

FENCING

INDIVIDUAL EVENTS

Men's epee
GOLD   Matteo Tagliariol, Italy
SILVER   Fabrice Jeannet, France
BRONZE   Jose Luis Abajo, Spain

Men's foil
GOLD   Benjamin Kleibrink, Germany
SILVER   Yuki Ota, Japan
BRONZE   Salvatore Sanzo, Italy

Men's sabre
GOLD   Zhong Man, China
SILVER   Nicolas Lopez, France
BRONZE   Mihai Covaliu, Romania

Women's epee
GOLD   Britta Heidemann, Germany
SILVER   Ana Maria Branza, Romania
BRONZE   Ildiko Mincza-Nebald, Hungary

Women's foil
GOLD   Maria Vezzali, Italy
SILVER   Nam Hyunhee, South Korea
BRONZE   Margherita Granbassi, Italy

Women's sabre
GOLD   Mariel Zagunis, United States
SILVER   Sada Jacobson, United States
BRONZE   Becca Ward, United States

TEAM EVENTS

Men's epee
GOLD   France
SILVER   Poland
BRONZE   Italy

Men's sabre
GOLD   France
SILVER   United States
BRONZE   Italy

Women's foil
GOLD   Russia
SILVER   United States
BRONZE   Italy

Women's sabre
GOLD   Ukraine
SILVER   China
BRONZE   United States

EQUESTRIAN

INDIVIDUAL EVENTS

Jumping
GOLD   Eric Lamaze, Canada
SILVER   Rolf-Goran Bengtsson, Sweden
BRONZE   Beezie Madden, United States

Dressage
GOLD   Anky van Grunsven, Netherlands
SILVER   Isabell Werth, Germany
BRONZE   Heike Kemmer, Germany

Eventing
GOLD   Hinrich Romeike, Germany
SILVER   Gina Miles, United States
BRONZE   Kristina Cook, United Kingdom

TEAM EVENTS

Jumping
GOLD   United States
SILVER   Canada
BRONZE   Norway

Dressage
GOLD   Germany
SILVER   Netherlands
BRONZE   Denmark

Eventing
GOLD   Germany
SILVER   Australia
BRONZE   United Kingdom

FIELD HOCKEY

Men
GOLD   Germany
SILVER   Spain
BRONZE   Austria

Women
GOLD   Netherlands
SILVER   China
BRONZE   Argentina

GYMNASTICS

MEN

Team
GOLD	China
SILVER	Japan
BRONZE	United States

All-around
GOLD	Yang Wei, China
SILVER	Kohei Uchimura, Japan
BRONZE	Benoit Caranobe, France

Floor exercise
GOLD	Zhou Kai, China
SILVER	Gervasio Deferr, Spain
BRONZE	Anton Golotsutskov, Russia

Pommel horse
GOLD	Xiao Qin, China
SILVER	Filip Ude, Croatia
BRONZE	Louis Smith, United Kingdom

Rings
GOLD	Cheng Yibing, China
SILVER	Yang Wei, China
BRONZE	Oleksandr Vorobiov, Ukraine

Vault
GOLD	Leszek Blanik, Poland
SILVER	Thomas Bouhail, France
BRONZE	Anton Golotsutskov, Russia

Parallel bars
GOLD	Li Xiaopeng, China
SILVER	Yoo Wonchul, South Korea
BRONZE	Anton Fokin, Uzbekistan

Horizontal bar
GOLD	Zhou Kai, China
SILVER	Jonathan Horton, United States
BRONZE	Fabian Hambuechen, Germany

Trampoline
GOLD	Lu Chunlong, China
SILVER	Jason Burnett, Canada
BRONZE	Dong Dong, China

WOMEN

Team
GOLD	China
SILVER	United States
BRONZE	Romania

All-around
GOLD	Nastia Liukin, United States
SILVER	Shawn Johnson, United States
BRONZE	Yang Yilin, China

Vault
GOLD	Hong Un Jong, North Korea
SILVER	Oksana Chusovitina, Germany
BRONZE	Cheng Fei, China

Uneven parallel bars
GOLD	He Kexin, China
SILVER	Nastia Liukin, United States
BRONZE	Yang Yilin, China

Balance beam
GOLD	Shawn Johnson, United States
SILVER	Nastia Liukin, United States
BRONZE	Cheng Fei, China

Floor exercise
GOLD	Sandra Izbasa, Romania
SILVER	Shawn Johnson, United States
BRONZE	Nastia Liukin, United States

Trampoline
GOLD	He Wenna, China
SILVER	Karen Cockburn, Canada
BRONZE	Ekaterina Khilko, Uzbekistan

JUDO

MEN

Extra lightweight 132 lbs. (60 kg)
GOLD	Choi Minho, Korea
SILVER	Ludwig Paischer, Austria
BRONZE	Rishod Sobirov, Uzbekistan, and Ruben Houkes, Netherlands

Half-lightweight 146 lbs. (66 kg)
GOLD	Masato Uchishiba, Japan
SILVER	Benjamin Darbelet, France
BRONZE	Yordanis Arencibia, Cuba, and Pak Chol Min, North Korea

Lightweight 161 lbs. (73 kg)
GOLD	Elnur Mammadli, Azerbaijan
SILVER	Wang Kichun, South Korea
BRONZE	Rasul Boqiev, Tajikistan, and Leandro Guilheiro, Brazil

Half-middleweight 179 lbs. (81 kg)
GOLD	Ole Bischof, Germany
SILVER	Kim Jaebum, South Korea
BRONZE	Tiago Camilo, Brazil, and Roman Gontiuk, Ukraine

Middleweight 198 lbs. (90 kg)
GOLD	Irakli Tsirekidze, Georgia
SILVER	Amar Benikhleff, Algeria
BRONZE	Hesham Mesbah, Egypt, and Sergei Aschwanden, Switzerland

Half-heavyweight 220 lbs. (100 kg)
GOLD	Tuvshinbayar Naidan, Mongolia
SILVER	Askhat Zhitkeyev, Kazakhstan
BRONZE	Movlud Miraliyev, Azerbaijan, and Henk Grol, Netherlands

Heavyweight over 220 lbs. (100 kg)
GOLD	Satoshi Ishii, Japan
SILVER	Abdullo Tangriev, Uzbekistan
BRONZE	Oscar Brayson, Cuba, and Teddy Riner, France

MODERN PENTATHLON

MEN
GOLD	Andrey Moiseev, Russia
SILVER	Edvinas Krungolcas, Lithuania
BRONZE	Andrejus Zadneprovskis, Lithuania

WOMEN
GOLD	Lena Schoneborn, Germany
SILVER	Heather Fell, United Kingdom
BRONZE	Victoria Tereshuk, Ukraine

Gymnast Leszek Blanik, of Poland

RHYTHMIC GYMNASTICS

INDIVIDUAL
GOLD	Evgeniya Kanaeva, Russia
SILVER	Inna Zhukova, Belarus
BRONZE	Anna Bessonova, Ukraine

TEAM
GOLD	Russia
SILVER	China
BRONZE	Belarus

WOMEN

Extra lightweight 106 lbs. (48 kg)
GOLD   Alina Alexandra Dumitru, Romania
SILVER   Yanet Bermoy, Cuba
BRONZE   Paula Belen Pareto, Argentina, and Ryoko Tani, Japan

Half-lightweight 115 lbs. (52 kg)
GOLD   Xian Dongmei, China
SILVER   An Kum Ae, North Korea
BRONZE   Soraya Haddad, Algeria, and Misato Nakamura, Japan

Lightweight 126 lbs. (57 kg)
GOLD   Giulia Quintavalle, Italy
SILVER   Deborah Gravenstijn, Netherlands
BRONZE   Ketleyn Quadros, Brazil, and Xu Yan, China

Half-middleweight 139 lbs. (63 kg)
GOLD   Ayumi Tanimoto, Japan
SILVER   Lucie Decosse, France
BRONZE   Elisabeth Willeboordse, Netherlands, and
          Won Ok Im, North Korea

Middleweight 154 lbs. (70 kg)
GOLD   Masae Ueno, Japan
SILVER   Anaysi Hernandez, Cuba
BRONZE   Ronda Rousey, United States, and Edith Bosch,
          Netherlands

Half-heavyweight 172 lbs. (78 kg)
GOLD   Yang Xiuli, China
SILVER   Yalennis Castillo, Cuba
BRONZE   Jeong Gyeongmi, South Korea, and Stephanie
          Possamai, France

Heavyweight over 172 lbs. (78 kg)
GOLD   Tong Wen, China
SILVER   Maki Tsukada, Japan
BRONZE   Lucija Polavder, Slovenia, and Idalys Ortiz, Cuba

SAILING

OPEN

49er dinghy sailing
GOLD   Warrer Jonas and Martin Kirketerp Ibsen, Denmark
SILVER   Iker Martinez de Lizarduy and Xabier Fernandez, Spain
BRONZE   Jan Peter Peckolt and Hannes Peckolt, Germany

Laser
GOLD   Paul Goodison, United Kingdom
SILVER   Vasilij Zbogar, Slovenia
BRONZE   Diego Romero, Italy

Tornado
GOLD   Fernando Echavarri and Anton Paz, Spain
SILVER   Darren Bundock and Glenn Ashby, Australia
BRONZE   Santiago Lange and Carlos Espinola, Argentina

MEN

Finn
GOLD   Ben Ainslie, Great Britain
SILVER   Zach Railey, United States
BRONZE   Guillaume Florent, France

470
GOLD   Nathan Wilmot and Malcolm Page, Australia
SILVER   Nick Rogers and Joe Glanfield, United Kingdom
BRONZE   Nicolas Charbonnier and Olivier Bausset, France

Star
GOLD   Iain Percy and Andrew Simpson, United Kingdom
SILVER   Robert Scheidt and Bruno Prada, Brazil
BRONZE   Fredrik Loof and Anders Ekstrom, Sweden

ROWING

MEN

Single sculls
GOLD   Olaf Tufte, Norway
SILVER   Ondrei Synek, Czech Republic
BRONZE   Mahe Drysdale, New Zealand

Double sculls
GOLD   David Crawshay and Scott Brennan, Australia
SILVER   Tonu Endrekson and Juri Jaanson, Estonia
BRONZE   Matthew Wells and Stephen Rowbotham,
          United Kingdom

Lightweight double sculls
GOLD   Zac Purchase and Mark Hunter, United Kingdom
SILVER   Dimitrios Mougios and Vasileios Polymeros, Greece
BRONZE   Mads Reinholdt Rasmussen and Rasmus Nicholai Quist
          Hansen, Denmark

Quadruple sculls
GOLD   Poland
SILVER   Italy
BRONZE   France

Pairs
GOLD   Drew Ginn and Duncan Free, Australia
SILVER   David Calder and Scott Frandsen, Canada
BRONZE   Nathan Twaddle and George Bridgewater, New Zealand

Fours
GOLD   United Kingdom
SILVER   Australia
BRONZE   France

Lightweight fours
GOLD   Denmark
SILVER   Poland
BRONZE   Canada

Eights
GOLD   Canada
SILVER   United Kingdom
BRONZE   United States

WOMEN

Single sculls
GOLD   Rumyana Neykova, Bulgaria
SILVER   Michelle Guerette, United States
BRONZE   Ekaterina Karsten, Belarus

Double sculls
GOLD   Georgina Evers-Swindell and
          Caroline Evers-Swindell, New Zealand
SILVER   Annekatrin Thiele and Christiane Huth, Germany
BRONZE   Elise Laverick and Anna Bebington, United Kingdom

Lightweight double sculls
GOLD   Kirsten van der Kolk and Marit van Eupen,
          Netherlands
SILVER   Sanna Sten and Minna Nieminen, Finland
BRONZE   Melanie Kok and Tracy Cameron, Canada

Quadruple sculls
GOLD   China
SILVER   United Kingdom
BRONZE   Germany

Pairs
GOLD   Georgeta Andrunache and Viorica Susanu, Romania
SILVER   Wu You and Gao Yulan, China
BRONZE   Yuliya Bichyk and Natallia Helakh, Belarus

Eights
GOLD   United States
SILVER   Netherlands
BRONZE   Romania

* World record
** Olympic record

SAILING, CONTINUED

RS:X
GOLD	Tom Ashley, New Zealand
SILVER	Julien Bontemps, France
BRONZE	Shahar Zubari, Israel

WOMEN
Europe
GOLD	Anna Tunnicliffe, United States
SILVER	Gintare Volungeviciute, Lithuania
BRONZE	Xu Lijia, China

470
GOLD	Elise Rechichi and Tessa Parkinson, Australia
SILVER	Marcelien de Koning and Lobke Berkhout, Netherlands
BRONZE	Fernanda Oliveira and Isabel Swan, Brazil

Yngling
GOLD	United Kingdom
SILVER	Netherlands
BRONZE	Greece

RS:X
GOLD	Yin Jian, China
SILVER	Alessandra Sensini, Italy
BRONZE	Bryony Shaw, United Kingdom

Swimmer Michael Phelps, of the United States, who won a record eight gold medals

SHOOTING

RIFLE
Men's 10-meter air
GOLD	Abhinav Bindra, India
SILVER	Zhu Qinan, China
BRONZE	Henri Hakkinen, Finland

Men's 50-meter prone
GOLD	Artur Ayvazian, Ukraine
SILVER	Matthew Emmons, United States
BRONZE	Warren Potent, Australia

Men's 50-meter 3 position
GOLD	Qiu Jian, China
SILVER	Jury Sukhorukov, Ukraine
BRONZE	Rajmond Debevec, Slovenia

Women's 10-meter air
GOLD	Katerina Emmons, Czech Republic
SILVER	Lioubov Galkina, Russia
BRONZE	Snjezana Pejcic, Croatia

Women's 50-meter 3 position
GOLD	Du Li, China**
SILVER	Katerina Emmons, Czech Republic
BRONZE	Eglis Yaima Cruz, Cuba

PISTOL
Men's 10-meter air
GOLD	Pang Wei, China
SILVER	Jin Jong Oh, South Korea
BRONZE	Jason Turner, United States

Men's 50-meter
GOLD	Jin Jong Oh, South Korea
SILVER	Tan Zongliang, China
BRONZE	Vladimir Isakov, Russia

Men's 25-meter rapid fire
GOLD	Oleksandr Petriv, Ukraine**
SILVER	Ralf Schumann, Germany
BRONZE	Christian Reitz, Germany

Women's 10-meter air
GOLD	Guo Wenjun, China**
SILVER	Natalia Paderina, Russia
BRONZE	Nino Salukvadze, Georgia

Women's 25-meter
GOLD	Chen Ying, China**
SILVER	Gundegmaa Otryad, Mongolia
BRONZE	Munkhbayar Dorjsuren, Germany

SHOTGUN
Men's trap
GOLD	David Kostelecky, Czech Republic**
SILVER	Giovanni Pellielo, Italy
BRONZE	Alexey Alipov, Russia

Men's double trap
GOLD	Walton Eller, United States**
SILVER	Francesco D'Aniello, Italy
BRONZE	Hu Binyuan, China

Men's skeet
GOLD	Vincent Hancock, United States
SILVER	Tore Brevold, Norway
BRONZE	Anthony Terras, France

Women's trap
GOLD	Satu Makela-Nummela, Finland**
SILVER	Zuzana Stefecekova, Slovakia
BRONZE	Corey Cogdell, United States

Women's skeet
GOLD	Chiara Cainero, Italy
SILVER	Kimberly Rhode, United States
BRONZE	Christine Brinker, Germany

SOCCER

MEN
GOLD	Argentina
SILVER	Nigeria
BRONZE	Brazil

Women
GOLD	United States
SILVER	Brazil
BRONZE	Germany

SOFTBALL
GOLD	Japan
SILVER	United States
BRONZE	Australia

* World record
** Olympic record

SWIMMING

MEN

Men's 50-meter freestyle
GOLD	Cesar Cielo Filho, Brazil	:21.30**
SILVER	Amaury Leveaux, France	
BRONZE	Alain Bernard, France	

Men's 100-meter freestyle
GOLD	Alain Bernard, France	:47.21
SILVER	Eamon Sullivan, Australia	
BRONZE	Cesar Cielo Filho, Brazil, and Jason Lezak, United States	

Men's 200-meter freestyle
GOLD	Michael Phelps, United States	1:42.96*
SILVER	Park Taehwan, South Korea	
BRONZE	Peter Vanderkaay, United States	

Men's 400-meter freestyle
GOLD	Park Taehwan, South Korea	3:41.86
SILVER	Zhang Lin, China	
BRONZE	Larsen Jensen, United States	

Men's 1,500-meter freestyle
GOLD	Oussama Mellouli, Tunisia	14:40.84
SILVER	Grant Hackett, Australia	
BRONZE	Ryan Cochrane, Canada	

Men's 100-meter backstroke
GOLD	Aaron Peirsol, United States	:52.54*
SILVER	Matt Grevers, United States	
BRONZE	Hayden Stoeckel, Australia, and Arkady Vyatchanin, Russia	

Men's 200-meter backstroke
GOLD	Ryan Lochte, United States	1:53.94*
SILVER	Aaron Peirsol, United States	
BRONZE	Arkady Vyatchanin, Russia	

Men's 100-meter breaststroke
GOLD	Kosuke Kitajima, Japan	:58.91*
SILVER	Alexander Dale Oen, Norway	
BRONZE	Hugues Duboscq, France	

Men's 200-meter breaststroke
GOLD	Kosuke Kitajima, Japan	2:07.64**
SILVER	Brenton Rickard, Australia	
BRONZE	Hugues Duboscq, France	

Men's 100-meter butterfly
GOLD	Michael Phelps, United States	:50.58**
SILVER	Milorad Cavic, Serbia	
BRONZE	Andrew Lauterstein, Australia	

Men's 200-meter butterfly
GOLD	Michael Phelps, United States	1:52.03*
SILVER	Laszlo Cseh, Hungary	
BRONZE	Takeshi Matsuda, Japan	

Men's 200-meter individual medley
GOLD	Michael Phelps, United States	1:54.23*
SILVER	Laszlo Cseh, Hungary	
BRONZE	Ryan Lochte, United States	

Men's 400-meter individual medley
GOLD	Michael Phelps, United States	4:03.84*
SILVER	Laszlo Cseh, Hungary	
BRONZE	Ryan Lochte, United States	

Men's 4x100-meter freestyle relay
GOLD	United States	3:08.24*
SILVER	France	
BRONZE	Australia	

Men's 4x200-meter freestyle relay
GOLD	United States	6:58.56*
SILVER	Russia	
BRONZE	Australia	

Men's 4x100-meter medley relay
GOLD	United States	3:29.34*
SILVER	Australia	
BRONZE	Japan	

Men's 10-kilometer marathon
GOLD	Maarten van der Weijden, Netherlands	1:51:51.6
SILVER	David Davies, United Kingdom	
BRONZE	Thomas Lurz, Germany	

WOMEN

50-meter freestyle
GOLD	Britta Steffen, Germany	:24.06**
SILVER	Dara Torres, United States	
BRONZE	Cate Campbell, Australia	

100-meter freestyle
GOLD	Britta Steffen, Germany	:53.12**
SILVER	Lisbeth Trickett, Australia	
BRONZE	Natalie Coughlin, United States	

200-meter freestyle
GOLD	Federica Pellegrini, Italy	1:54.82*
SILVER	Sara Isakovic, Slovenia	
BRONZE	Pang Jiaying, China	

400-meter freestyle
GOLD	Rebecca Adlington, United Kingdom	4:03.22
SILVER	Katie Hoff, United States	
BRONZE	Joanne Jackson, United Kingdom	

800-meter freestyle
GOLD	Rebecca Adlington, United Kingdom	8:14.10*
SILVER	Alessia Filippi, Italy	
BRONZE	Lotte Friis, Denmark	

100-meter backstroke
GOLD	Natalie Coughlin, United States	:58.96
SILVER	Kirsty Coventry, Zimbabwe	
BRONZE	Margaret Hoelzer, United States	

200-meter backstroke
GOLD	Kirsty Coventry, Zimbabwe	2:05.24*
SILVER	Margaret Hoelzer, United States	
BRONZE	Reiko Nakamura, Japan	

100-meter breaststroke
GOLD	Leisel Jones, Australia	1:05.17**
SILVER	Rebecca Soni, United States	
BRONZE	Mirna Jukic, Austria	

200-meter breaststroke
GOLD	Rebecca Soni, United States	2:20.22*
SILVER	Leisel Jones, Australia	
BRONZE	Sara Nordenstam, Norway	

100-meter butterfly
GOLD	Lisbeth Trickett, Australia	:56.73
SILVER	Christine Magnuson, United States	
BRONZE	Jessicah Schipper, Australia	

200-meter butterfly
GOLD	Liu Zige, China	2:04.18*
SILVER	Jiao Liuyang, China	
BRONZE	Jessicah Schipper, Australia	

200-meter individual medley
GOLD	Stephanie Rice, Australia	2:08.45*
SILVER	Kirsty Coventry, Zimbabwe	
BRONZE	Natalie Coughlin, United States	

400-meter individual medley
GOLD	Stephanie Rice, Australia	4:29.45*
SILVER	Kirsty Coventry, Zimbabwe	
BRONZE	Katie Hoff, United States	

4x100-meter freestyle relay
GOLD	Netherlands	3:33.76**
SILVER	United States	
BRONZE	Australia	

4x200-meter freestyle relay
GOLD	Australia	7:44.31*
SILVER	China	
BRONZE	United States	

4x100-meter medley relay
GOLD	Australia	3:52.69*
SILVER	United States	
BRONZE	China	

Women's 10-kilometer marathon
GOLD	Australia	1:59:27.7
SILVER	Keri-Anne Payne, United Kingdom	
BRONZE	Cassandra Patten, United Kingdom	

SYNCHRONIZED SWIMMING

TEAM
GOLD   Russia
SILVER Spain
BRONZE China
DUET
GOLD   Anastasia Davydova and Anastasia Ermakova, Russia
SILVER Andrea Fuentes and Gemma Mengual, Spain
BRONZE Saho Harada and Emiko Suzuki, Japan

TEAM HANDBALL

MEN
GOLD   France
SILVER Iceland
BRONZE Spain

WOMEN
GOLD   Norway
SILVER Russia
BRONZE South Korea

TABLE TENNIS

Men's singles
GOLD   Ma Lin, China
SILVER Wang Hao, China
BRONZE Wang Liqin, China
Men's team
GOLD   China
SILVER Germany
BRONZE South Korea
Women's singles
GOLD   Zhang Yining, China
SILVER Wang Nan, China
BRONZE Guo Yue, China
Women's team
GOLD   China
SILVER Singapore
BRONZE South Korea

TENNIS

Men's singles
GOLD   Rafael Nadal, Spain
SILVER Fernando Gonzalez, Chile
BRONZE Novak Djokovic, Serbia
Men's doubles
GOLD   Roger Federer and Stanislas Wawrinka, Switzerland
SILVER Simon Aspelin and Thomas Johansson, Sweden
BRONZE Bob Bryan and Mike Bryan, United States
Women's singles
GOLD   Elena Dementieva, Russia
SILVER Dinara Safina, Russia
BRONZE Vera Zvonareva, Russia
Women's doubles
GOLD   Serena Williams and Venus Williams, United States
SILVER Anabel Medina Garrigues and Virginia Ruano Pascual, Spain
BRONZE Yan Zi and Zheng Jie, China

TAEKWONDO

MEN'S
Under 128 lbs. (58 kg)
GOLD   Guillermo Perez, Mexico
SILVER Yulis Gabriel Mercedes, Dominican Republic
BRONZE Chu Mu-Yen, Taiwan, and Rohullah Nikpai, Afghanistan
Under 150 lbs. (68 kg)
GOLD   Son Taejin, South Korea
SILVER Mark Lopez, United States
BRONZE Sung Yu-Chi, Taiwan, and Servet Tazegul, Turkey
Under 176 lbs. (80 kg)
GOLD   Hadi Saei, Iran
SILVER Mauro Sarmiento, Italy
BRONZE Steven Lopez, United States, and Zhu Guo, China
Over 176 lbs. (80 kg)
GOLD   Cha Dongmin, South Korea
SILVER Alexandros Nikolaidis, Greece
BRONZE Arman Chilmanov, Kazakhstan, and Chika Yagazie Chukwumerije, Nigeria

WOMEN'S
Under 108 lbs. (49 kg)
GOLD   Wu Jingyu, China
SILVER Buttree Puedpong, Thailand
BRONZE Dalia Contreras Rivero, Venezuela, and Daynellis Montejo, Cuba
Under 126 lbs. (57 kg)
GOLD   Lim Sujeong, South Korea
SILVER Azize Tanrikulu, Turkey
BRONZE Diana Lopez, United States, and Martina Zubcic, Croatia
Under 148 lbs. (67 kg)
GOLD   Hwang Kyungseon, South Korea
SILVER Karine Sergerie, Canada
BRONZE Gwladys Patience Epangue, France, and Sandra Saric, Croatia
Over 148 lbs. (67 kg)
GOLD   Maria del Rosario Espinoza, Mexico
SILVER Nina Solheim, Norway
BRONZE Natalia Falavigna, Brazil, and Sarah Stevenson, United Kingdom

Runner Usain Bolt of Jamaica

* World Record
** Olympic Record

TRACK AND FIELD

MEN

100 meters
GOLD	Usain Bolt, Jamaica	:9.69*
SILVER	Richard Thompson, Trinidad and Tobago	
BRONZE	Walter Dix, United States	

200 meters
GOLD	Usain Bolt, Jamaica	:19.30*
SILVER	Shawn Crawford, United States	
BRONZE	Walter Dix, United States	

400 meters
GOLD	LaShawn Merritt, United States	:43.75
SILVER	Jeremy Wariner, United States	
BRONZE	David Neville, United States	

800 meters
GOLD	Wilfred Bungei, Kenya	1:44.65
SILVER	Ismail Ahmed Ismail, Sudan	
BRONZE	Alfred Kirwa Yego, Kenya	

1,500 meters
GOLD	Rashid Ramzi, Bahrain	3:32.94
SILVER	Asbel Kipruto Kiprop, Kenya	
BRONZE	Nicholas Willis, New Zealand	

5,000 meters
GOLD	Kenenisa Bekele, Ethiopia	12:57.82**
SILVER	Eliud Kipchoge, Kenya	
BRONZE	Edwin Cheruiyot Soi, Kenya	

10,000 meters
GOLD	Kenenisa Bekele, Ethiopia	27:01.17**
SILVER	Sileshi Sihine, Ethiopia	
BRONZE	Micah Kogo, Kenya	

Marathon
GOLD	Samuel Kamau Wansiru, Kenya	2:06:32**
SILVER	Jaouad Gharib, Morocco	
BRONZE	Tsegay Kebede, Ethiopia	

110-meter hurdles
GOLD	Dayron Robles, Cuba	:12.93
SILVER	David Payne, United States	
BRONZE	David Oliver, United States	

400-meter hurdles
GOLD	Angelo Taylor, United States	:47.25
SILVER	Kerron Clement, United States	
Bronze	Bershawn Jackson, United States	

3000-meter steeplechase
GOLD	Brimin Kiprop Kipruto, Kenya	8:05.81
SILVER	Mahiedine Mekhissi-B., France	
BRONZE	Richard Kipkemboi Mateelong, Kenya	

20-kilometer walk
GOLD	Valeriy Borchin, Russia	1:19:01
SILVER	Jefferson Perez, Ecuador	
BRONZE	Jared Tallent, Australia	

50-kilometer walk
GOLD	Alex Schwazer, Italy	3:37:09**
SILVER	Jared Tallent, Australia	
BRONZE	Denis Nizhegorodov, Russia	

4x100-meter relay
GOLD	Jamaica	:37.10*
SILVER	Trinidad and Tobago	
BRONZE	Japan	

4x400-meter relay
GOLD	United States	2:55.39**
SILVER	Bahamas	
BRONZE	Russia	

High jump
GOLD	Andrey Silnov, Russia	7 ft. 9 in. (2.36 m)
SILVER	Germaine Mason, United Kingdom	
BRONZE	Yaroslav Rybakov, Russia	

Pole vault
GOLD	Steve Hooker, Australia	19 ft. 6 ½ in. (5.96 m)**
SILVER	Evgeny Lukyanenko, Russia	
BRONZE	Denys Yurchenko, Ukraine	

Long jump
GOLD	Irving Jahir Saladino Aranda, Panama	27 ft. 4 ½ in. (8.34 m)
SILVER	Khotso Mokoena, South Africa	
BRONZE	Ibrahim Camejo, Cuba	

Triple jump
GOLD	Nelson Evora, Portugal	57 ft. 11 ½ in. (17.67 m)
SILVER	Phillips Idowu, United Kingdom	
BRONZE	Leevan Sands, Bahamas	

Shot-put
GOLD	Tomasz Majewski, Poland	70 ft. 7 in. (21.51 m)
SILVER	Christian Cantwell, United States	
BRONZE	Andrei Mikhnevich, Belarus	

Discus
GOLD	Gerd Kanter, Estonia	225 ft. 9 ½ in. (68.82 m)
SILVER	Piotr Malachowski, Poland	
BRONZE	Virgilijus Alekna, Lithuania	

Hammer
GOLD	Primoz Kozmus, Slovenia	269 ft. 1 in. (82.02 m)
SILVER	Vadim Devyatovskiy, Belarus†	
BRONZE	Ivan Tsikhan, Belarus†	

Javelin
GOLD	Andreas Thorkildsen, Norway	297 ft. 1¾ in. (90.57 m)**
SILVER	Ainars Kovals, Latvia	
BRONZE	Tero Pitkamaki, Finland	

Decathlon
GOLD	Bryan Clay, United States	8,791 pts.
SILVER	Andrei Krauchanka, Belarus	
BRONZE	Leonel Suarez, Cuba	

WOMEN

100 meters
GOLD	Shelly-Ann Fraser, Jamaica	:10.78
SILVER	Sherone Simpson, Jamaica	
BRONZE	Kerron Stewart, Jamaica	

200 meters
GOLD	Veronica Campbell-Brown, Jamaica	:21.74
SILVER	Allyson Felix, United States	
BRONZE	Kerron Stewart, Jamaica	

400 meters
GOLD	Christine Ohuruogu, United Kingdom	:49.62
SILVER	Shericka Williams, Jamaica	
BRONZE	Sanya Richards, United States	

800 meters
GOLD	Pamela Jelimo, Kenya	1:54.87
SILVER	Janeth Jepkosqei Busienei, Kenya	
BRONZE	Hasna Benhassi, Morocco	

1,500 meters
GOLD	Nancy Jebet Langat, Kenya	4:00.23
SILVER	Iryna Lishchynska, Ukraine	
BRONZE	Nataliya Tobias, Ukraine	

5,000 meters
GOLD	Tirunesh Dibaba, Ethiopia	15:41.40
SILVER	Elvan Abeylegesse, Turkey	
BRONZE	Meseret Defar, Ethiopia	

† Stripped of medals after testing positive for drugs

TRACK AND FIELD, CONTINUED

10,000 meters
GOLD	Tirunesh Dibaba, Ethiopia	29:54.66**
SILVER	Elvan Abeylegesse, Turkey	
BRONZE	Shalane Flanagan, United States	

Marathon
GOLD	Constantina Tomescu, Romania	2:26:44
SILVER	Catherine Ndereba, Kenya	
BRONZE	Zhou Chunxiu, China	

Women 100-meter hurdles
GOLD	Dawn Harper, United States	:12.54
SILVER	Sally McLellan, Australia	
BRONZE	Priscilla Lopes-Schliep, Canada	

Women 400-meter hurdles
GOLD	Melaine Walker, Jamaica	:52.64**
SILVER	Sheena Tosta, United States	
BRONZE	Tasha Danvers, United Kingdom	

3,000-meter steeplechase
GOLD	Gulnara Galkina-Samitova, Russia	8:58.81*
SILVER	Eunice Jepkorir, Kenya	
BRONZE	Ekaterina Volkova, Russia	

20-kilometer walk
GOLD	Olga Kaniskina, Russia	1:26:31**
SILVER	Kjersti Tysse Platzer, Norway	
BRONZE	Elisa Rigaudo, Italy	

4x100-meter relay
GOLD	Russia	:42.31
SILVER	Belgium	
BRONZE	Nigeria	

4x400-meter relay
GOLD	United States	3:18.54
SILVER	Russia	
BRONZE	Jamaica	

High jump
GOLD	Tia Hellebaut, Belgium	6 ft. 8¾ in. (2.05 m)
SILVER	Blanka Vlasic, Croatia	
BRONZE	Anna Chicherova, Russia	

Pole vault
GOLD	Elena Isinbaeva, Russia	16 ft. 7 in. (5.05 m)*
SILVER	Jennifer Stuczynski, United States	
BRONZE	Svetlana Feofanova, Russia	

Long jump
GOLD	Maurren Higa Maggi, Brazil	23 ft. 1 in. (7.04 m)
SILVER	Tatyana Lebedeva, Russia	
BRONZE	Blessing Okagbare, Nigeria	

Triple jump
GOLD	Francoise Mbango Etone, Cameroon	50 ft. 6 in. (15.39 m)**
SILVER	Tatyana Lebedeva, Russia	
BRONZE	Hrysopiyi Devetzi, Greece	

Shot-put
GOLD	Valerie Vili, New Zealand	67 ft. 5 ½ in. (20.56 m)
SILVER	Natallia Mikhnevich, Belarus	
BRONZE	Nadzeya Ostapchuk, Belarus	

Discus
GOLD	Stephanie Brown Trafton, United States	212 ft. 5 in. (64.74 m)
SILVER	Yarelys Barrios, Cuba	
BRONZE	Olena Antonova, Ukraine	

Hammer
GOLD	Aksana Miankova, Belarus	250 ft. 5 ½ in. (76.34 m)**
SILVER	Yipsi Moreno, Cuba	
BRONZE	Zhang Wenxiu, China	

Javelin
GOLD	Barbora Spotakova, Czech Republic	234 ft. 3 ¾ in. (71.42 m)*
SILVER	Maria Abakumova, Russia	
BRONZE	Christina Obergfoll, Germany	

Heptathlon
GOLD	Nataliia Dobrynska, Ukraine	6,591 pts.
SILVER	Hyleas Fountain, United States	
BRONZE	Tatiana Chernova, Russia	

TRIATHLON

Men
GOLD	Jan Frodeno, Germany
SILVER	Simon Whitfield, Canada
BRONZE	Bevan Docherty, New Zealand

Women
GOLD	Emma Snowsill, Australia
SILVER	Vanessa Fernandes, Portugal
BRONZE	Emma Moffatt, Australia

VOLLEYBALL

Men		**Women**	
GOLD	United States	GOLD	Brazil
SILVER	Brazil	SILVER	United States
BRONZE	Russia	BRONZE	China

WATER POLO

Men's		**Women's**	
GOLD	Hungary	GOLD	Netherlands
SILVER	United States	SILVER	United States
BRONZE	Serbia	BRONZE	Australia

WEIGHTLIFTING[†]

MEN

123 lbs. (56 kg)
GOLD	Long Qingguan, China	644 lbs (292 kg)
SILVER	Anh Tuan Hoang, Vietnam	
BRONZE	Eko Yuli Irawan, Indonesia	

137 lbs. (62 kg)
GOLD	Zhang Xiangxiang, China	703 lbs (319 kg)
SILVER	Diego Salazar, Colombia	
BRONZE	Triyatno, Indonesia	

152 lbs. (69 kg)
GOLD	Liao Hui, China	767 lbs (348 kg)
SILVER	Vencelas Dabaya-Tientcheu, France	
BRONZE	Tigran Martirosyan, Armenia	

170 lbs. (77 kg)
GOLD	Sa Jaehyouk, South Korea	807 lbs (366 kg))
SILVER	Li Hongli, China	
BRONZE	Gevorg Davtyan, Armenia	

187 lbs. (85 kg)
GOLD	Lu Yong, China	869 lbs (394 kg)
SILVER	Andrei Rybakou, Belarus*	869 lbs (394 kg)
BRONZE	Tigran Varban Martirosyan, Armenia	

207 lbs. (94 kg)
GOLD	Ilya Ilin, Kazakhstan	895 lbs (406 kg)
SILVER	Szymon Kolecki, Poland	
BRONZE	Khadzhimurat Akkaev, Russia	

231 lbs. (105 kg)
GOLD	Andrei Aramnau, Belarus*	961 lbs (436 kg)
SILVER	Dmitriy Klokov, Russia	
BRONZE	Dmitry Lapikov, Russia	

Over 231 lbs. (Over 105 kg)
GOLD	Matthias Steiner, Germany	1,016 lbs (461 kg)
SILVER	Evgeny Chigishev, Russia	
BRONZE	Viktors Scerbatihs, Latvia	

WRESTLING

MEN'S FREESTYLE
121 lbs. (55 kg)
GOLD	Henry Cejudo, United States
SILVER	Tomohiro Matsunaga, Japan
BRONZE	Besik Kudukhov, Russia, and Radoslav Velikov, Bulgaria

132 lbs. (60 kg)
GOLD	Mavlet Batirov, Russia
SILVER	Vasyl Fedoryshyn, Ukraine
BRONZE	Seyedmorad Mohammadi, Iran, and Kenichi Yumoto, Japan

146 lbs. (66 kg)
GOLD	Ramazan Sahin, Turkey
SILVER	Andriy Stadnik, Ukraine
BRONZE	Sushil Kumar, India, and Otar Tushishvili, Georgia

163 lbs. (74 kg)
GOLD	Buvaysa Saytiev, Russia
SILVER	Soslan Tigiev, Uzbekistan
BRONZE	Murad Gaidarov, Belarus, and Kiril Terziev, Bulgaria

185 lbs. (84 kg)
GOLD	Revazi Mindorashvili, Georgia
SILVER	Yusup Abdusalomov, Tajikistan
BRONZE	Taras Danko, Ukraine, and Georgy Ketoev, Russia

212 lbs. (96 kg)
GOLD	Shirvani Muradov, Russia
SILVER	Taimuraz Tigiyev, Kazakhstan
BRONZE	Khetaq Gazyumov, Azerbaijan, and George Gogshelidze, Georgia

265 lbs. (120 kg)
GOLD	Artur Taymazov, Uzbekistan
SILVER	Bakhtiyar Akhmedov, Russia
BRONZE	David Musulbes, Slovakia, and Marid Mutalimov, Kazakhstan

MEN'S GRECO-ROMAN
121 lbs. (55 kg)
GOLD	Nazyr Mankiev, Russia
SILVER	Rovshan Bayramov, Azerbaijan
BRONZE	Roman Amoyan, Armenia, and Park Eun-Chul, South Korea

132 lbs. (60 kg)
GOLD	Islam-Beka Albiev, Russia
SILVER	Vitaliy Rahimov, Azerbaijan
BRONZE	Nurbakyt Tengizbayev, Kazakhstan, and Ruslan Tiumenbaev, Kyrgyzstan

146 lbs. (66 kg)
GOLD	Steeve Guenot, France
SILVER	Kanatbek Begaliev, Kyrgyzstan
BRONZE	Mikhail Siamionau, Belarus, and Armen Vardanyan, Ukraine

163 lbs. (74 kg)
GOLD	Manuchar Kvirkelia, Georgia
SILVER	Chang Yongxiang, China
BRONZE	Christophe Guenot, France, and Yavor Yanakiev, Bulgaria

185 lbs. (84 kg)
GOLD	Andrea Minguzzi, Italy
SILVER	Zoltan Fodor, Hungary
BRONZE	Nazmi Avluca, Turkey

212 lbs. (96 kg)
GOLD	Aslanbek Khushtov, Russia
SILVER	Mirko Englich, Germany
BRONZE	Asset Mambetov, Kazakhstan, and Adam Wheeler, United States

265 lbs. (120 kg)
GOLD	Mijain Lopez, Cuba
SILVER	Khasan Baroev, Russia
BRONZE	Mindaugas Mizgaitis, Lithuania, and Yuri Patrikeev, Armenia

WOMEN'S FREESTYLE
106 lbs. (48 kg)
GOLD	Carol Huynh, Canada
SILVER	Chiharu Icho, Japan
BRONZE	Irini Merleni, Ukraine, and Mariya Stadnik, Azerbaijan

121 lbs. (55 kg)
GOLD	Saori Yoshida, Japan
SILVER	Alena Kartashova, Russia
BRONZE	Anna Gomis, France

139 lbs. (63 kg)
GOLD	Kaori Icho, Japan
SILVER	Sara McMann, United States
BRONZE	Randi Miller, United States, and Yelena Shalygina, Kazakhstan

159 lbs. (72 kg)
GOLD	Wang Jiao, China
SILVER	Stanka Zlateva, Bulgaria
BRONZE	Kyoko Hamaguchi, Japan, and Agnieszka Wieszczek, Poland

WOMEN
106 lbs. (48 kg)
GOLD	Chen Xiexia, China**	467 lbs (212 kg)
SILVER	Sibel Ozkan, Turkey	
BRONZE	Chen Wei-Ling, Taiwan	

117 lbs. (53 kg)
GOLD	P. Jaroenrattanatarakoon, Thailand	487 lbs (221 kg)
SILVER	Yoon Jinhee, South Korea	
BRONZE	Nastassia Novikava, Belarus	

128 lbs. (58 kg)
GOLD	Chen Yanqing, China**	538 lbs (244 kg)
SILVER	Marina Shainova, Russia	
BRONZE	O Jong Ae, North Korea	

139 lbs. (63 kg)
GOLD	Pak Hyon Suk, North Korea	531 lbs (241 kg)
SILVER	Irina Nekrassova, Kazakhstan	
BRONZE	Lu Ying-Chi, Taiwan	

152 lbs. (69 kg)
GOLD	Liu Chunhong, China*	631 lbs (286 kg)
SILVER	Oxana Slivenko, Russia	
BRONZE	Natalya Davydova, Ukraine	

165 lbs. (75 kg)
GOLD	Cao Lei, China**	622 lbs (282 kg)
SILVER	Alla Vazhenina, Kazakhstan	
BRONZE	Nadezda Evstyukhina, Russia	

Over 165 lbs. (Over 75 kg)
GOLD	Jang Miran, South Korea*	719 lbs (326 kg)
SILVER	Olha Korobka, Ukraine	
BRONZE	Mariya Grabovetskaya, Kazakhstan	

† Weight is total of two lifts: (1) snatch and (2) clean and jerk.

* World record
** Olympic record

Pacific Islands. In 2008, voters in Vanuatu chose a new Parliament, the Marshall Islands Parliament elected a new president, and a king was crowned in Tonga. Papua New Guinea moved toward developing its sago industry, and Kiribati expanded the size of a major marine reserve. (Sago is a starch found in the center of various tropical palm trees.)

The Pacific Islands Forum held its 39th meeting in Niue in August. Forum membership includes representatives of all the independent island nations plus Australia and New Zealand. Fiji was the focus of much discussion. Pacific leaders expressed concern that Frank Bainimarama, who has led Fiji since taking over in a 2006 *coup* (overthrow), might not live up to his commitment to hold national elections in March 2009. Forum officials threatened to expel Fiji from the organization if Bainimarama postponed elections.

Vanuatu. On Sept. 2, 2008, more than 300 candidates vied for seats in Vanuatu's 52-member Parliament. Edward Natapei of the Vanua'aku Party was chosen as prime minister to lead a coalition government. Natapei appointed his predecessor as prime minister, Ham Lini, as his deputy.

Tonga. King George Tupou V was crowned on August 1. The 60-year-old monarch soon began a tour of the more distant islands in his kingdom. King George promised to pay close attention to the increasing pressure for more democracy in a political system that heavily favors nobility. Preparation for events leading up to the coronation was budgeted at about $2.5 million, an amount that was heavily criticized by some opposition politicians.

Kiribati. In January, the government of Kiribati doubled the size of the Phoenix Islands Protected Area (PIPA), which conserves one of Earth's last intact oceanic coral ecosystems. PIPA consists of eight coral atolls and two submerged reef systems in a region of abundant marine and bird life. The protected area, which covers about 158,000 square miles (410,000 square kilometers), is nearly uninhabited by human beings, but includes underwater mountains and other deep-sea habitat. It is now the world's largest marine protected area.

King George Tupou V of Tonga is formally crowned on Aug. 1, 2008. Before his coronation, the king, an absolute monarch, promised to institute democratic reforms.

FACTS IN BRIEF ON PACIFIC ISLAND COUNTRIES

Country	Population	Government	Monetary unit*	Foreign trade (million U.S.$) Exports†	Imports†
Fiji	876,000	President Ratu Josefa Iloilovatu Uluivuda; Interim Prime Minister Frank Bainimarama	dollar (1.59 = $1)	1,202	3,120
Kiribati	106,000	President Anote Tong	Australian dollar (1.17 = $1)	17	62
Marshall Islands	68,000	President Litokwa Tomeing	U.S. dollar	9	55
Micronesia, Federated States of	112,000	President Emanuel Mori	U.S. dollar	14	133
Nauru	15,000	President Marcus Stephen	Australian dollar (1.17 = $1)	0.06	20
New Zealand	4,188,000	Governor General Anand Satyanand; Prime Minister John Key	dollar (1.43 = $1)	27,350	29,060
Palau	21,000	President Tommy Esang Remengesau, Jr.	U.S. dollar	6	107
Papua New Guinea	6,253,000	Governor General Sir Paulius Matane; Prime Minister Sir Michael Somare	kina (2.49 = $1)	4,686	2,629
Samoa	187,000	Head of State Tuiatua Tupua Tamasese Efi; Prime Minister Tuila'epa Sailele Malielegaoi	tala (2.39 = $1)	131	324
Solomon Islands	510,000	Governor General Nathaniel Waena; Prime Minister Derek Sikua	dollar (7.14 = $1)	237	256
Tonga	107,000	King George Tupou V; Prime Minister Feleti Sevele	pa'anga (1.85 = $1)	22	139
Tuvalu	11,000	Governor General Filoimea Telito; Prime Minister Apisai Ielemia	Australian dollar (1.17 = $1)	1	13
Vanuatu	223,000	President Kalkot Mataskelekele; Prime Minister Edward Natapei	vatu (96.69 = $1)	40	156

*Exchange rates as of Sept. 30, 2008. †Latest available data.

Solomon Islands. The Regional Assistance Mission to Solomon Islands (RAMSI) marked the fifth year of its mission to establish order in the Solomons in the aftermath of severe civil strife. RAMSI is a multinational force led by Australia. Its anniversary was celebrated with a function on Parliament premises on September 5 that was attended by RAMSI's participating foreign officials, Prime Minister Derek Sikua, officials from the Pacific Islands Forum, and other dignitaries. Prime Minister Sikua credited RAMSI with bringing peace and economic stability to the Solomons. However, some opposition politicians questioned the need for continuing intervention.

Fiji. In September 2008, medical authorities in Fiji reported an outbreak of dengue fever. By October, nearly 2,000 cases of the mosquito-borne illness had been diagnosed in Fiji. The World Health Organization warned of a possible pandemic of dengue in the Pacific, as American Samoa, Palau, and other Pacific nations also recorded more cases.

Papua New Guinea (PNG) and Malaysia in July signed an agreement to develop the sago industry in PNG. Sago is a staple food in PNG and elsewhere in the region. The agreement calls for a 50,000-acre (20,000-hectare) plantation to be established in Wewak, in northern PNG. Papua New Guinea will produce the sago and process it into flour before exporting it to Malaysia in an agreement expected to benefit both nations.

Marshall Islands. On January 7, the Parliament of the Marshall Islands elected opposition leader Litokwa Tomeing as the country's president. Tomeing and other politicians expressed displeasure with the country's long-standing

Compact of Free Association with the United States, which gave the United States continued use of a missile testing range in the Marshalls in return for economic and military assistance. Tomeing also expressed interest in forging diplomatic ties with China, which could cause tension with the United States. ■ Eugene Ogan

See also **Australia; New Zealand.**

Painting. See Art.

Pakistan. Threatened with impeachment by Parliament, President Pervez Musharraf resigned on Aug. 18, 2008. Musharraf had run Pakistan since 1999, when as army chief he ousted Prime Minister Nawaz Sharif, head of the Pakistan Muslim League-Nawaz (PML-N). On Sept. 6, 2008, Asif Ali Zardari was elected to succeed Musharraf. Zardari had led the Pakistani People's Party (PPP) since the Dec. 27, 2007, assassination of his wife, former Prime Minister Benazir Bhutto.

Musharraf began to lose his grip on power in the Feb. 18, 2008, elections for the lower house of Parliament. The PPP won 121 seats and the PML-N won 91. Musharraf's supporters won only 54 seats.

Musharraf had passed command of the army to General Ashfaq Pervez Kayani in November 2007. In February 2008, Kayani ordered army officers to withdraw from governmental jobs. With the army no longer voicing support for him after the election, Musharraf lost effective power in the face of a coalition between Zardari and Sharif.

On August 25, Sharif withdrew his party from the coalition, frustrated with the PPP's refusal to reinstate judges Musharraf had fired in 2007. Nonetheless, Zardari won the presidential election, despite public doubts about his record. A businessman who entered

politics because of his wife, Zardari spent 11 years in jail on corruption charges. Many of the charges were eventually dropped.

Islamic militants of the Afghan Taliban and the international al-Qa`ida terrorist organization strengthened their grip on Pakistan's border with Afghanistan in 2008. In addition, militants and domestic Islamic extremists extended their influence into new areas. In Swat, a formerly peaceful

Supporters of former Pakistani Prime Minister Nawaz Sharif gather near a poster of Sharif to celebrate the resignation of President Pervez Musharraf on Aug. 18, 2008. Musharraf led a military coup that ousted Sharif's government in 1999.

northern resort valley, extremists challenged the government and defied army attempts to regain control of the area.

Pakistan's government reduced security operations in tribal areas under an agreement for traditional tribal leaders to curtail militants' activities. However, militants took advantage of the lessened pressure to gain new strength. The government later began arming tribal militias allied against the Taliban. An army offensive beginning in August was claimed to have killed more than 1,500 militants in Bajaur, a tribal border area.

Militants in 2008 recruited and trained local and foreign fighters for attacks against government and Western forces in Afghanistan. In response to militant attacks into Afghanistan from Pakistan, United States forces made aerial missile attacks on suspected militant hideouts in Pakistan and made commando raids across the border. These cross-border attacks, some of which reportedly killed civilians and Pakistani government troops in addition to targeted militants, angered the Pakistani government. Prime Minister Yousaf Raza Gilani said the attacks were undermining his government's fight against terrorism and were stoking anti-American sentiment.

American officials, including the senior officer in Afghanistan, accused Pakistan's Directorate for Inter-Services Intelligence (ISI), a secret service agency, of supporting the Taliban. Some U.S. officials suspected ISI agents of defying government policy by backing Afghan militants, whom the ISI had supported before 2001. Pakistan's foreign minister, Shah Mahmood Qureshi, announced on Nov. 23, 2008, that the ISI's political wing had been "made inactive." International affairs experts had long believed that the ISI had held a great deal of control over Pakistan's government, even apparently having held final say on government job appointments.

Terrorism spread inside Pakistan in 2008. Swat was one of several regions where government buildings were bombed. A suicide bomber killed at least six people in a June 2 attack on the Danish embassy in Islamabad, the capital. A newspaper in Denmark had published cartoons angering Muslims. Al-Qa`ida in Afghanistan claimed responsibility for the attack.

Other bombings targeted police and ISI agents. On August 21, suicide bombers killed at least 64 people outside Pakistan's main weapons factory in the northern city of Wah. A bomb on September 20 killed at least 40 people at an Islamabad hotel.

On November 26, groups of gunmen believed to be members of a Pakistani-based terrorist group attacked hotels, restaurants, and other sites that catered primarily to American and British tourists in Mumbai, India's financial capital. Indian police brought the attacks to an end on November 29,

after more than 170 people had died. Pakistan's government denied having a hand in the attacks.

Economy. Inflation hit 25 percent in late 2008, as the value of the Pakistani currency, the rupee, plummeted on world markets and foreign exchange reserves fell. Food shortages created public unrest and poverty remained widespread.

Shaukat Tarin, Zardari's finance adviser, struggled to strengthen an economy burdened with heavy bills for its armed forces and for food, fertilizer, and fuel imports. He hoped to cut a budget deficit of over 7 percent of the gross domestic product, the total value of goods and services produced in a country in a year. Pakistan unsuccessfully sought large loans from Saudi Arabia and China before turning to the International Monetary Fund (IMF), a United Nations affiliate that usually sets stiff requirements for domestic economic reforms in return for lending money to nations. On November 25, the IMF approved a $7.6-billion loan to stabilize the country's economy.

Earthquake. An earthquake shook mountainous southwest Pakistan on Oct. 29, 2008, killing at least 215 people and leaving an estimated 15,000 others homeless. ■ Henry S. Bradsher

See also **Asia; Denmark; Disasters; India; Terrorism.**

Palau. See Pacific Islands.

Paleontology.
Sauropod dinosaurs, which include some of the largest land animals that ever lived, may have gotten so big because they had many bird-like characteristics, according to a report in the Oct. 10, 2008, issue of the journal *Science.* In the report, paleontologists P. Martin Sander of the University of Bonn, Germany, and Marcus Clauss of the University of Zurich, Switzerland, surmise that certain physical characteristics of species rather than environmental condition favor the development of large bodies. Many of the characteristics that favor the evolution of large body size among dinosaurs are typical of birds and other animals. Characteristics that limit body size are more typical of mammals.

The sauropod dinosaurs, such as the giant *Brachiosaurus*, thrived from the Late Triassic Period, about 200 million years ago, until the end of the Cretaceous Period, about 65 million years ago. Over 120 species are known from fossils throughout the world. Nearly all sauropods were large—more than twice the size of the largest modern land mammals, with a long neck, a small head, a long tail, and a huge, deep chest and stomach. Their vast bulk may have made adult sauropods largely immune to attacks by other animals that may have instead preyed upon their young.

Several factors helped these dinosaurs reach such enormous size. The sauropods laid eggs

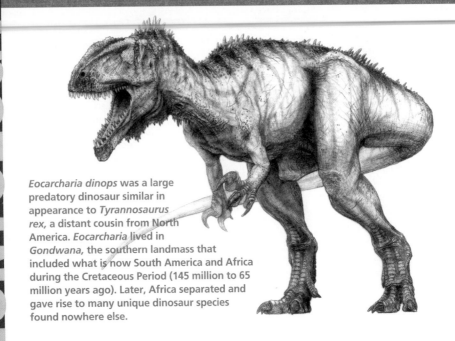

Eocarcharia dinops was a large predatory dinosaur similar in appearance to *Tyrannosaurus rex*, a distant cousin from North America. *Eocarcharia* lived in *Gondwana*, the southern landmass that included what is now South America and Africa during the Cretaceous Period (145 million to 65 million years ago). Later, Africa separated and gave rise to many unique dinosaur species found nowhere else.

In 2008, paleontologists described two new species of meat-eating dinosaurs that provide a rare look into an ancient African ecosystem of predators and scavengers.

University of Chicago paleontologist Paul Sereno excavates the 110 million-year-old fossils of a dinosaur in Niger, Africa. In 2008, Sereno and his team published descriptions of two new species of meat-eating dinosaurs from the Sahara Desert site.

Eocarcharia dinops (fierce-eyed dawn shark) was named for the large ridge of bone over the eyes that gave the dinosaur an intimidating glare. The bony brows may have been used in head-butting contests with rivals for potential mates.

The large, blade-like teeth of *Eocarcharia dinops* were perfect for disabling and killing live prey and ripping through flesh—a clear indication that *Eocarcharia* was a voracious predator.

Fossil bones of another meat-eating dinosaur, *Kryptops palaios*, were found at the same Saharan site and described in 2008. This dinosaur's name means *old wrinkle face*, for the tough, horn-like growths that covered its face. This species roamed the African plains with *Eocarcharia* 110 million years ago.

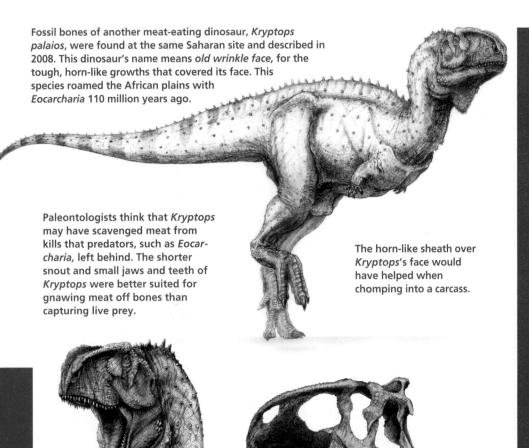

Paleontologists think that *Kryptops* may have scavenged meat from kills that predators, such as *Eocarcharia*, left behind. The shorter snout and small jaws and teeth of *Kryptops* were better suited for gnawing meat off bones than capturing live prey.

The horn-like sheath over *Kryptops*'s face would have helped when chomping into a carcass.

rather than give birth to live young. Producing live young, a typical mammalian characteristic, often works to limit the size and number of offspring, because the females must carry the developing young in their own bodies. In contrast, sauropods most likely produced a large clutch of eggs with many small juveniles hatching simultaneously and growing fast. Another key to the large size and long necks of sauropods was that they did very little chewing of vegetation. Rather, like birds, they used their small heads to tear off and swallow large quantities of plant matter that was digested in a huge stomach and intestines.

Because they did not use large teeth and did not process much food in their mouths, the sauropods were able to develop long necks. These necks enabled them to probe higher parts of trees unavailable to most animals. The problems of having a long, heavy windpipe were overcome by having air sacs in their bones, as do modern birds, which lightened their weight. These air sacs also helped to release excess body heat, which would otherwise have posed a problem for such large animals.

Transitional flounders. In July 2008, paleontologist Matt Friedman of the University of Chicago reported the discovery of a fossil that shows a key step in the development of modern flatfishes. These fish, which include flounders, sole and halibut, have a peculiar body plan—the fish appears to be flattened horizontally. The fish actually lies on its side, with both eyes on the same side of the head. When the flatfish is first hatched, it looks like any other kind of fish. But after a short time, one eye begins to move closer to the eye on the opposite side of the head, and the mouth becomes twisted. One side of the fish then has no eye and is essentially blind. The flatfish spends its adult life lying on the sea bottom on the blind side, with both eyes facing upward.

Paleontologists have long wondered how flatfish originated but had no fossils of transitional forms linking flounders with more symmetrical fish ancestors. Friedman and his team discovered the fossil remains of an ancestral flounder in 40-million-year-old rocks at Monte Bolca, near Verona in northern Italy, that shows this transition. In the well-preserved fossil skull, the left eye remains on the left side but is high on the skull, well above its normal position. These early flatfish were already becoming adapted for lying on one side. Taking clues from modern-day flatfish behavior, Friedman suggested that these ancestral forms raised themselves off the sea floor on their fins and could then search for prey below while keeping a watchful upper eye out for predators from above.

Ancient daisy chains. A report published in October in the journal *Nature* by paleontologists Hou Xian-guang of Yunnan University, China, and three British colleagues shows a stunning example of collective behavior in an ancient species of fossil lobster-like animals. Hou and colleagues discovered the fossils of a previously unknown species of arthropod in the Early Cambrian 525-million-year-old Chengjiang fossil beds in southern China's Yunnan Province. Arthropods are a diverse group of animals that includes spiders, insects, and the *crustaceans,* such as lobsters and crabs. Many modern crustaceans, including some lobsters, show social group behavior at times. For example, deep-sea lobsters sometimes migrate long distances by crawling along the sea floor in long chains. Individuals keep in contact with one another by grasping the tail of the individual in front. However, evidence for any type of group behavior is rarely seen preserved in the fossil record.

The well-preserved fossils at Chengjiang were found in slabs of shale. The fossils show chains of 2 to 20 individuals in which the *telson* (tail spike) and rear appendages of each individual are locked beneath the *carapace* (shell) of the next animal in line. Such a formation suggests that these creatures crawled in long, chain-like groups to remain in contact, perhaps in deep sea environments where there was little light. These fossil specimens provide a unique glimpse of social behavior in some of the earliest animal communities in the oceans. ■ Carlton E. Brett

Panama. On Aug. 14, 2008, some 15,000 Panamanians took to the streets of Panama City, the capital, and other cities to protest the high cost of living and inflation. Demonstrators were also upset by President Martín Torrijos Espino's action in June, granting himself "extraordinary powers" to create four new state security agencies. Human rights advocates and spokespersons for the Roman Catholic Church saw the agencies as part of a move to "remilitarize" the country. In an effort to soothe an increasingly angry public, the Torrijos administration implemented a series of measures, including cash bonuses for public employees, pay hikes for teachers, and tax rebates.

Construction on the canal. The $5.25-billion expansion of the Panama Canal continued in 2008, boosted by the October approval of a $400-million loan from the Inter-American Development Bank (IDB), an international lending agency. The expansion, due to be completed by 2014, will double the capacity of the canal, add thousands of jobs, and bolster government revenue. Since 2004, the IDB has lent Panama more than $500 million for various projects involving water and sanitation, transportation, trade, export promotion, and rural development. ■ Nathan A. Haverstock

See also **Latin America**.

Papua New Guinea. See Pacific Islands.
Paraguay. See Latin America.

in 2008 included those listed below, who were from the United States unless otherwise indicated.

Aglukkaq, Leona (1967?-), was
appointed federal health minister for Canada by Prime Minister Stephen Harper on Oct. 30, 2008, thus becoming the first Inuit person to serve in the Canadian Cabinet. On October 14, Aglukkaq, who held various political offices in Nunavut Territory, won election to Canada's federal Parliament as a Conservative, the party of Prime Minister Harper.

Leona Aglukkaq was born in Inuvik—then part of Canada's Northwest Territories—but was adopted in infancy by a family from the Inuit community of Tulugak. Her family later moved to Gjoa Haven. Leona's adopted family practiced the traditional Inuit way of life, traveling and camping on extended hunts in the summer and settling into their Gjoa Haven home in winter.

In 1999, Canada carved out Nunavut Territory from the eastern flank of the Northwest Territories to provide greater self-government for the Inuit people. Leona Aglukkaq, who had majored in management studies at Arctic College in Iqaluit, Nunavut's largest town, and had held various jobs in local public service, won election to the Nunavut territorial legislature in 2004. There she assumed several leadership positions, including service as house leader and finance minister and, later, as territorial health minister. She resigned in September 2008 to run for election to the federal Parliament in Ottawa.

See also **Canada; Canadian territories.**

Biden, Joe (1942-), became the Democratic
nominee for vice president of the United States following his selection by presidential candidate Barack Obama in August 2008 and was elected to that office in November. Since 1973, Biden had served in the U.S. Senate representing the state of Delaware. In 1988 and 2008, he ran for the Democratic nomination for president.

Joseph Robinette Biden, Jr., was born on Nov. 20, 1942, in Scranton, Pennsylvania, but his family subsequently moved to Wilmington, Delaware. Biden attended the University of Delaware in Newark, graduating in 1965. He obtained a law degree from Syracuse (New York) University Law School in 1968.

After law school, Biden practiced law in Wilmington. In 1970, he was elected to the New Castle (Delaware) County Council. In November 1972, Biden won election to the U.S. Senate, narrowly defeating Delaware's Republican incumbent, J. Caleb Boggs. Biden, then 29, did not attain the minimum required age of 30 for a U.S. senator until several weeks after the election.

On Dec. 18, 1972, Biden's wife and children were in a serious automobile accident in which his wife Neilia and daughter Naomi Christina were killed. Biden's two sons sustained serious injuries in the accident but survived. Biden considered resigning his prospective Senate seat, but Senate Democratic leaders persuaded him to be sworn in on Jan. 5, 1973.

Joe Biden married Jill Tracy Jacobs in 1977; the couple had one daughter and raised Biden's sons from his previous marriage. Biden won reelection to the Senate in 1978, 1984, 1990, 1996, and 2002.

See also **Elections: A Special Report.**

Coen, Joel (1954-), and Coen, Ethan
(1957-), jointly won the Academy Award for best director on Feb. 24, 2008, for their film *No Country for Old Men*. The film, an adaptation of Cormac McCarthy's 2005 novel by the same name, also won the Coen brothers the Oscar for best picture and the Oscar for best adapted screenplay. Javier Bardem, the Spanish actor who played *No Country*'s psychopathic villain, won for best supporting actor.

Joel and Ethan Coen have co-directed, co-written, and co-edited a number of independent films since their first film, the murder thriller *Blood Simple,* in 1984. Many of their films have received critical acclaim and various awards. *Blood Simple* took the United States Film Festival Grand Jury Prize in 1985 and won notice as an unusually strong directorial debut. The brothers' fourth feature film, *Barton Fink* (1991), drew international acclaim, winning the 1991 Cannes Film Festival award for best director and best picture (the Palme d'Or).

Ethan and Joel Coen

Fargo, the Coen brothers' 1996 box-office hit, earned them a best screenplay Academy Award and garnered the best actress award for Frances McDormand, wife of Joel Coen. Other Coen brothers films include *The Hudsucker Proxy* (1994), *The Big Lebowski* (1998), *O Brother, Where Art Thou?* (2000), and *The Man Who Wasn't There* (2001).

Joel and Ethan Coen were born and raised in suburban Minneapolis, Minnesota. Their favorite entertainment was watching old movies on television, and by their teen years the brothers were making their own movies with a home movie camera. Joel studied film at New York University in New York City, and Ethan majored in philosophy at Yale University in New Haven, Connecticut. In the early 1980's, they raised enough money to shoot their script of *Blood Simple,* which was picked up by an independent distributor and launched the Coen brothers' filmmaking career.

See also **Motion pictures.**

Cotillard, Marion (1975-), won the
Academy Award for best actress on Feb. 24, 2008, for her portrayal of iconic, doomed French chanteuse Edith Piaf in *La Vie en Rose.* For her performance in the film, Cotillard also won a Golden Globe award and a César award, the French equivalent of an Oscar. Cotillard was the first woman to receive a best actress Academy Award for a non-English-speaking role since Sophia Loren won in 1961 for *Two Women,* originally released in Italy as *La Ciociara.*

Marion Cotillard was born in Paris on Sept. 30, 1975, to French actor and playwright Jean Paul Cotillard and actress Niseema Theillaud. Marion grew up in Orleans, a small city about 75 miles (121 kilometers) south of Paris, and attended the Orleans Conservatory of Dramatic Arts there. While still a child, she performed in some of her father's theatrical dramas, and in 1994 she made her movie debut in the French film *Histoire d'un garçon qui voulait qu'on l'embrasse* (The Story of a Boy Who Wanted to Be Kissed). In 1998, Cotillard co-starred in the hit French movie *Taxi.* Tim Burton's 2003 film *Big Fish* introduced Cotillard to U.S. filmgoing audiences. She subsequently appeared in *A Good Year* (2006) and other U.S. and French films and television productions.

See also **Motion pictures.**

Cowen, Brian (1960-), became prime minister of the Republic of Ireland in May 2008, following the resignation of his predecessor, Bertie Ahern. In anticipation of the resignation and succession, Cowen was selected leader of Fianna Fáil, Ireland's governing party, in April. Cowen retained Ahern's Cabinet and was widely expected to continue many of the former prime minister's policies. One of those policies, support for a new constitution for

the European Union (EU), of which Ireland is a member, received a blow in June when, in a referendum, Irish voters rejected the proposed EU constitution, 53 percent to 47 percent.

Brian Cowen was born on Jan. 10, 1960, in Tullamore, a small city about 50 miles (80 kilometers) inland from Dublin, the Irish capital. Brian's father, Bernard Cowen, also served as a member of the Irish Parliament.

Brian Cowen was first elected to the lower house of Parliament in 1984. During periods in the 1990's and 2000's when Fianna Fáil was in power, Cowen headed a number of government ministries, including foreign affairs and finance. Prime Minister Ahern appointed him deputy prime minister in 2007. Political observers described Cowen as a highly competent, though sometimes combative, political leader.

See also **Europe; Ireland.**

Day-Lewis, Daniel (1957-), received the
Academy Award for best actor on Feb. 24, 2008, for his portrayal of ruthless, greed-driven Daniel Plainview in the film *There Will Be Blood,* a drama adapted from Upton Sinclair's 1927 novel, *Oil!* Day-Lewis previously won a best actor Academy Award in 1989 for his performance in *My Left Foot.*

Daniel Michael Blake Day-Lewis was born in London on April 29, 1957. His father was Cecil Day-Lewis, a poet laureate of the United Kingdom, and his maternal grandfather was Sir Michael Balcon, head of England's Ealing Studios, which in the 1940's and 1950's released a number of classic English film comedies. Day-Lewis grew up and was educated in the United Kingdom. In 1987, he chose to become a citizen of the Republic of Ireland. Day-Lewis married Rebecca Miller, daughter of the U.S. playwright Arthur Miller, in 1996.

Daniel Day-Lewis studied acting at the Bristol (England) Old Vic School. In the 1970's and early 1980's, he performed onstage in many productions of the Bristol Old Vic and Royal Shakespeare theater companies. Day-Lewis's breakout movie roles were in *My Beautiful Laundrette* and *Room with a View,* both released in 1985. The actor received a New York Film Critics Circle Award for his performances in both films. He delivered notable performances in many other films, including *The Unbearable Lightness of Being* (1988), *The Last of the Mohicans* (1992), *The Age of Innocence* (1993), *In the Name of the Father* (1993), *The Crucible* (1996), and *Gangs of New York* (2003).

See also **Motion pictures.**

Dunwoody, Ann E. (1953-), received an
appointment in June 2008 from President George W. Bush as a four-star general in the United States Army. The U.S. Senate confirmed Dunwoody's appointment in July. Dunwoody is the first woman

Ann E. Dunwoody

Kirchner, Cristina Fernández de

(1953-), president of Argentina, lost a key political battle in 2008 when a nationally organized farmers' strike forced her government to abandon a hike in export taxes on agricultural products imposed in March. Protest against the hikes, which Fernández de Kirchner regarded as a critical part of her government's campaign against rising inflation, prompted the Argentine Congress to strike down the tax program in July. According to Fernández de Kirchner's economists, the taxes on exports were intended to encourage farmers to grow more food crops for domestic consumption and ease food inflation in Argentina.

Cristina Fernández de Kirchner won election to Argentina's presidency in October 2007 and took office in December, succeeding her husband, Néstor Kirchner. Assuming office in 2003 in the wake of a national financial collapse, he obtained special emergency powers and led Argentina out of the crisis and into a period of strong economic growth. Néstor and Fernández de Kirchner ruled essentially by decree until the July 2008 vote in which Congress rejected the export taxes.

Christina Fernández was born in La Plata, Argentina, on Feb. 19, 1953. In the early 1970's, she studied law at a La Plata university, where she met Néstor Kirchner. They married in 1975 and settled in Rio Gallegos, a small city in the far southern province of Santa Cruz, where they forged their political base. In July 2007, President Néstor Kirchner nominated Cristina to represent his Peronist coalition in the upcoming presidential election.

See also **Argentina**.

Lee Myung-bak

(1941-), became president of South Korea on Feb. 25, 2008, having won election to a five-year presidential term in December 2007. Experts in international affairs predicted that Lee's administration would draw closer diplomatically to the United States, in contrast to his predecessors Kim Dae-jung and Roh Moo-hyun, who charted courses more independent of the United States and actively sought accommodation with Communist North Korea. Also in contrast to his predecessors, President Lee championed free market reforms and promised to trim government social programs.

Lee Myung-bak was born on Dec. 19, 1941, in Osaka, Japan, where his parents were working at the time. (Korea was then occupied by Japan.) After the end of World War II (1939–1945), Lee's family returned to Pohang in the southeastern part of the Korean Peninsula (now South Korea), where Myung-bak grew up in poverty. In the early 1960's, Lee worked his way through college by collecting garbage. Following graduation, he went to work for the construction division of the giant Korean company Hyundai, rising to the rank of chief executive officer of Hyundai Construction by the late 1970's. He subsequently held other top executive positions in Hyundai, acquiring the nickname "the Bulldozer" for his ability to achieve difficult objectives. Lee served as mayor of Seoul, South Korea's capital and largest city, between 2002 and 2006.

See also **Korea, South**.

Medvedev, Dmitry

(1965-), became the president of Russia in May 2008 after winning a presidential election in March. Vladimir Putin, Medvedev's predecessor, endorsed Medvedev's presidential candidacy, and Medvedev chose Putin to serve as his prime minister.

The post-Soviet Russian Constitution provides for a strong executive, in which the occupant of the presidential office directs foreign and domestic policy as well as the military and security services. Under the constitution, the prime minister leads the governing coalition in the Duma, the Russian legislature. As Medvedev's administration began governing in 2008, some international experts speculated that Putin, though prime minister, was functioning as the senior partner in the government. During Russia's invasion of neighboring Georgia in August 2008, Putin appeared to play the dominant role in policymaking.

Dmitry Anatolyevich Medvedev was born on Sept. 14, 1965, in Leningrad (now Saint Petersburg), in the then-Soviet Union. He received a law degree from Leningrad State University in 1987 and a Ph.D. degree from the same school in 1990. In the late 1980's, Medvedev joined the Russian Orthodox Church, an action that during Communist rule could have resulted in political and professional repercussions. About the same time, he formed a professional association with Anatoly Sobchak, a Leningrad State University professor with liberal economic and democratic leanings.

By 1990, Russia under the leadership of President Boris Yeltsin was turning away from Communist orthodoxy, and Sobchak was elected to the Leningrad City Council. Upon being elected mayor in 1991, he brought both Medvedev and Vladimir Putin into the city administration, and the two young officials became close political associates.

After President Boris Yeltsin chose Putin as acting president of Russia in 1999, Putin called Medvedev to Moscow to serve in the national government. During the 1990's, Medvedev formed several companies and served as a consultant to another company. In the early 2000's, he directed Gazprom, Russia's largest energy company. In 2005, President Putin appointed Medvedev first deputy prime minister, widely considered a stepping stone to higher office.

See also **Russia**.

Dmitry Medvedev

2010. Officials of the CSO announced Muti's appointment in May 2008. The orchestra's music director serves as its principal conductor and oversees programming and other aspects of the orchestra's activities. Many music critics consider Muti to be one of the world's leading conductors.

Prior to his selection as CSO music director, Riccardo Muti led many orchestras in Europe and North America. He won appointment in 1969 as principal conductor of the Maggio Musicale, an orchestra in Florence, Italy. Muti served as principal conductor of the New Philharmonia (called the Philharmonia beginning in 1977) in London. From 1980 to 1992, he was music director of the Philadelphia Orchestra.

Muti has also conducted at some of the world's leading opera houses, including the Vienna State Opera and Covent Garden in London. Between 1986 and 2005, he served as music director of Milan's world-famous opera house, La Scala. He left La Scala because of disputes with members of the orchestra.

Riccardo Muti was born in Naples, Italy, on July 28, 1941. As a young boy, he studied piano and violin with his father, a physician by profession. He later studied piano as well as composition and conducting at several music conservatories in Italy. Muti first attracted attention in the international music world as a conductor in 1967, when he won first place in the Guido Cantelli Competition for conductors in Milan.

See also **Classical music.**

Meyer, Stephenie (1973-), launched the

fourth and final book in her vampire-romance series of novels, targeted to young adult readers, in August 2008. The book, *Breaking Dawn,* succeeded *Twilight* (2005), *New Moon* (2006), and *Eclipse* (2007). Publication of *Breaking Dawn* became a publishing phenomenon, with major booksellers sponsoring "Harry Potter"-style parties at numerous outlets on Friday night, August 1, before copies of the book went on sale officially at the stroke of midnight on August 2. Because of the popularity of her novels among teens and the intense loyalty of her reading audience, Stephenie Meyer has often been compared with J. K. Rowling, author of the popular "Harry Potter" series of fantasy novels.

The Meyer vampire novels feature Bella, a teenage girl who falls in love with a teenage vampire. The teen vampire, Edward, also in love, struggles against his instinctive desire to bite Bella on the neck and feed on her blood. Author Meyer claims to have written *Twilight,* the first novel in the series, rapidly in the summer of 2003 after having dreamed the story's premise.

Stephenie Meyer was born in Connecticut in 1973, though her family soon moved to Phoenix, Arizona. Stephenie attended college at Brigham Young University in Provo, Utah, earning a bachelor's degree in English. There she met her future husband, Christian, called Pancho. They married, settled in Phoenix, and had three children. Stephenie Meyer received a contract for *Twilight* from Little, Brown and Company, the publisher of the entire series, in November 2003.

Muti, Riccardo (1941-), was in 2008

selected as music director of the Chicago Symphony Orchestra (CSO), to begin in September

Obama, Michelle (1964-), campaigned

with her husband, Barack Obama, as he contested Democratic primaries in dozens of states in the first half of 2008, obtained the Democratic Party's nomination for president in August, led the campaign against Republican nominee John McCain in the fall, and won election to the presidency on November 4. Michelle Obama charmed audiences with her disarming frankness and willingness to chide her husband, tongue-in-cheek, for such mundane failings as not picking up his socks. Like the president-elect, Michelle Obama is a lawyer and community activist. The couple have two daughters.

Michelle LaVaughn Robinson was born in Chicago on Jan. 17, 1964, the daughter of Fraser Robinson, a city worker in the Chicago Department of Water Management, and Marian Fraser, a secretary and homemaker. The Robinsons lived in a bungalow in a predominantly African American middle-class neighborhood on Chicago's

Michelle Obama

August 2007. She was named women's golf Player of the Year in 2006 and 2007. The award is based on points accumulated during an LPGA season.

As the first Mexican player to win a major LPGA championship, Lorena Ochoa has popularized golf, previously a minor sport, in her home country. Since Ochoa's rise to fame, the LPGA has hosted two tournaments annually in Mexico. In 2004, Ochoa established the Ochoa Foundation, which provides funds for underprivileged children in her home city of Guadalajara, Mexico, to attend school.

Lorena Ochoa was born on Nov. 15, 1981, In Guadalajara. She began playing golf at age 5. Ochoa was a star golfer at the University of Arizona at Tucson in 2001 and 2002, winning the National College Athletic Association (NCAA) Player of the Year award both years. Ochoa turned professional in 2002 and was named Rookie of the Year on the LPGA tour in 2003.

See also **Golf**.

South Side. Michelle attended public schools, including one of the city's premier magnet high schools, and she excelled at her studies.

Michelle Robinson attended Princeton University in New Jersey, graduating with a bachelor of arts degree in 1985. (Her brother preceded her at Princeton.) She obtained a law degree from Harvard University in Cambridge, Massachusetts, in 1988 and returned to Chicago to work for a prestigious law firm. During the summer of 1988, Michelle met a summer associate at the law firm—Barack Obama. They married in 1992.

In 1991, Michelle decided to leave the practice of corporate law to work in community affairs and took a job in Chicago's Department of Planning and Development. In 1993, she left city employment to work for Public Allies, a nonprofit community development organization. In 1996, Michelle Obama went to work for the University of Chicago in the city's Hyde Park neighborhood; she eventually became vice president for community and external affairs for the University of Chicago Hospitals. Barack and Michelle Obama settled in the Hyde Park neighborhood, from where Barack Obama launched his political career in 1996.

Ochoa, Lorena (1981-), a
Mexican golfer, won the Kraft Nabisco Championship in April 2008. Kraft Nabisco is one of the four major championships on the Ladies Professional Golf Association (LPGA) tour. The other three are the U.S. Women's Open, the U.S. LPGA Championship, and the Women's British Open. Ochoa won the Women's British Open in

Palin, Sarah (1964-), governor of Alaska,
became the Republican nominee for vice president of the United States following her selection by presidential candidate John McCain in August 2008. McCain and Palin lost to Barack Obama and Joe Biden in November. Palin proved an energetic, though sometimes controversial, campaigner. She attracted much attention with her youth, engaging personality, and informal style. Critics charged that she was inexperienced and unprepared to assume high national office; supporters emphasized her reputation as a political outsider and reformer. On the campaign trail, Palin often assumed the role of hard-hitting critic of Barack Obama, the Democratic nominee for president.

Lorena Ochoa

Sarah Heath was born in Sand Point, Idaho, on Feb. 11, 1964, but moved with her family to Alaska, while still an infant. She graduated from Wasilla High School in 1982 and graduated with a bachelor's degree in journalism from the University of Idaho in Moscow in 1987. In 1984, she competed in the Miss Alaska pageant and was chosen first runner-up as well as Miss Conge-niality. In 1988, she married Todd Palin.

Sarah Palin entered politics in 1992 when she ran for the Wasilla City Coun-cil and won. In 1996, Wasilla voters elected her mayor. Palin sought the Republican nomination for lieutenant governor of Alaska in 2002 but was defeated in the primary election.

Michael Phelps

In 2003, Frank Murkowski, then gov-ernor of Alaska, appointed Palin as chair of the Alaska Oil and Gas Conservation Commission, a state regulatory body that oversees Alaska's extensive energy resources. Palin alienated Murkowski and other powerful state Republicans by pressing for an investigation of a commission member for ethical violations and then by pursu-ing ethics charges against the state's Republican attorney general. Both of these high-profile ethics cases concerned conflicts of interest involv-ing corporations that were exploiting Alaska's energy reserves.

Palin successfully challenged Governor Murkowski in the state's Republican primary in 2006 and went on to win election as governor against Tony Knowles, the Democratic candidate. She was sworn in as Alaska's 11th governor on Dec. 4, 2006.

See also **Elections: A Special Report.**

Paterson, David A. (1954-), was sworn in as governor of New York on March 17, 2008, after Governor Eliot Spitzer resigned in the wake of revelations that he had used the services of a prostitution ring. David Paterson had been elected lieutenant governor of New York on the Democratic ticket with Spitzer in November 2006.

Paterson became the first African American governor and the first visually impaired governor in New York history. On taking office as gover-nor, Paterson pledged to work with the state legislature to tackle such initiatives as revitalizing the economy in depressed upstate areas, building affordable housing, and reducing property taxes. Relations between the New York state Senate and Governor Spitzer had been strained, and the elevation of Paterson, a 20-year veteran of the senate, to the governorship prompted positive responses from many legislators.

David Alexander Paterson was born in Brook-lyn, New York, on May 20, 1954, the son of Basil and Portia Paterson. The infant David was stricken with an infection that destroyed vision in his left eye and left only residual vision in his right eye.

David's father, Basil Paterson, was a labor law attorney who became an important political leader in Democratic state politics. He served in the New York State Senate in the 1960's. In 1978, he served as a deputy mayor of New York City and in 1979 was elected New York secretary of state.

David Paterson enrolled in Columbia Univer-sity in New York City, graduating in 1977 with a bachelor's degree in history. In 1983, he received a law degree from Hofstra Law School in Hemp-stead, New York. Paterson then worked for the district attorney's office in Queens, New York. When a state senate seat unexpectedly opened up in August 1985 upon the death of the incum-bent, David Paterson ran for the seat and won the election. He held the seat until his 2006 elec-tion as lieutenant governor. Paterson became the minority leader in the New York state Senate in 2002. In 1992, David Paterson married Michelle Paige. They have two children.

See also **State government.**

Phelps, Michael (1985-), won eight gold medals at the 2008 Summer Olympic Games in Beijing, a record in a single year's Olympics. Phelps received gold medals in five individual events and three team relay events. In seven of the eight com-petitions, Phelps set world records.

Michael Fred Phelps II was born on June 30, 1985, in Baltimore, and grew up in suburban Balti-more. He started swimming at the age of 7 and began studying with a professional swimming coach at age 11. Phelps competed in the 2000 Summer Olympic Games in Sydney, Australia, at the age of 15. At the 2004 Summer Games in

Athens, Greece, he won six gold medals and two bronze medals.

Michael Phelps also won numerous medals and set records in other competitions. At the World Swimming Championships in Barcelona, Spain, in 2003, he became the first swimmer to set five individual world records in a single meet. In the 2005 world championships in Montreal, Canada, he won five gold medals, three of them in relays. In the 2007 championships in Melbourne, Australia, Phelps won gold medals in all seven events he entered and set five world records.

See also **Olympic Games: A Special Report; Swimming.**

Kevin Rudd

Rudd, Kevin (1957-), prime minister of Australia, withdrew Australia's 550 troops from Iraq in June 2008, fulfilling a campaign promise he had made before the nation's general election in 2007. Rudd's party, the Australian Labor Party (ALP), won a substantial victory in that election. Rudd sharply criticized his long-serving predecessor, Prime Minister John Winston Howard, for having committed Australian troops to the U.S.-led invasion of Iraq in 2003.

Rudd also reversed another of his predecessor's long-standing positions by signing the Kyoto Protocol on global warming. With Rudd's signing of the pact, the United States was left as the only major industrial power not committed to Kyoto.

Kevin Michael Rudd was born in Nambour, Queensland, Australia, on Sept. 21, 1957. In 1981, he obtained a degree in Asian studies from the Australian National University in Canberra, the capital. For the next seven years, Rudd served as an Australian diplomat. He returned to Queensland politics in 1988, working as chief of staff for a politician who was elected premier of the state in 1989.

In 1998, Rudd won election to the Australian House of Representatives, subsequently winning reelection several times. ALP members of the House elected him head of the ALP in 2006.

See also **Australia; Australia, Prime Minister of**.

Ryan, Kay (1945-), was designated poet laureate for the United States by the Library of Congress in July 2008. Appointed annually by the Library of Congress's librarian, the poet laureate receives a monetary award and is encouraged to promote the reading and writing of poetry in the United States.

Often described as a miniaturist—and sometimes compared with Emily Dickinson—Kay Ryan typically creates brief poems with unusually short lines, leavened generously with internal rhyming and flashes of sly wit. Because she has developed a distinct style entirely her own and has lived largely apart from fashionable literary and artistic circles, Ryan has acquired the reputation of being a literary outsider. In 1983, Kay Ryan published her first book of poetry, *Dragon Acts to Dragon Ends,* but her work became known to a larger audience only in the mid-1990's with the 1994 publication of her collection *Flamingo Watching.*

Kay Ryan grew up in small towns in rural California. In the 1960's, she attended the University of California at Los Angeles. For most of her adult life, Ryan has taught remedial English at the College of Marin in Kentfield, California. She and her long-time partner, Carol Adair, married in San Francisco when that city began issuing marriage licenses to same-sex couples in 2004.

See also **Poetry.**

Warren, Rick (1954-), a California-based evangelical minister, hosted on Aug. 16, 2008, a nationally televised interview with presidential candidates Barack Obama and John McCain. Warren, founder and senior pastor of Saddleback Valley Community Church of Orange County, California, one of the nation's largest churches, is widely regarded as one of the most influential evangelical ministers in the United States. The evangelical movement in the United States is comprised of thousands of conservative Protestant congregations.

Rick Duane Warren was born on Jan. 28, 1954, in San Jose, California. He grew up in the small northern California community of Ukiah, where his father, James Russell Warren, served as a Baptist minister. Rick Warren attended California Baptist College in San Bernardino, graduating in 1977. He then trained for the ministry at Southwestern Baptist Theological Seminary in Fort Worth, Texas.

In 1980, Rick Warren and his wife Kay, whom Warren married in 1975, started Saddleback Church in a high school gymnasium in Mission Viejo, California. In 2008, the church regularly accommodated more than 20,000 weekend worshipers, and its main campus occupied more than 100 acres (40.5 hectares) in Lake Forest, California.

In the 1990's, Rick Warren expanded his ministry by writing *The Purpose-Driven Church* (1995), a blueprint for ministerial leadership in evangelical churches, and starting pastors.com, a Web site for ministers. Warren and his associates have conducted training seminars for thousands of evangelical pastors.

In 2002, Warren published *The Purpose-Driven Life,* a guidebook for personal spiritual growth within church communities. By 2008, the book had sold 35 million copies, a record for religious book sales exceeded only by the Bible.

See also **Protestantism.**

Zardari, Asif Ali

Zardari, Asif Ali (1955-), won election as Pakistan's president on Sept. 6, 2008, receiving a majority of electoral votes from Pakistan's presidential electoral college, which consists of national and provincial legislators. Zardari is the widower of Benazir Bhutto, twice prime minister of Pakistan. Bhutto was shot and killed by an assassin on Dec. 27, 2007, while campaigning for restoration of democratic government in Pakistan.

Bhutto and Zardari fled Pakistan in 1999 after Pervez Musharraf led a military *coup* (overthrow) that toppled the democratically elected government of Prime Minister Nawaz Sharif. They returned in 2007, after Musharraf's government granted Benazir Bhutto amnesty for a corruption charge that she had been convicted of in *absentia* (while absent from the country) in 1999. Musharraf won reelection as president in a contested poll in October 2007 but resigned under intense political pressure on Aug. 19, 2008.

Zardari, who had served in Bhutto's Cabinet and in the Pakistani Senate, had spent a total of 11 years in Pakistani prisons on several unrelated corruption charges, though he was never convicted of any crime. In 2007, Zardari delayed legal proceedings against him in the United Kingdom by claiming, with supportive testimony by two physicians, that he suffered from depression and *dementia* (disorder of mental processes leading to impaired reasoning). Because of this court testimony, some international experts questioned Zardari's fitness to lead the government of politically volatile Pakistan.

Asif Ali Zardari was born in Sindh province in southeastern Pakistan on July 26, 1955. He married Benazir Bhutto in 1987. Zardari and Bhutto had three children. Their oldest son, Bilawal (1988-), became head of the Pakistan People's Party (PPP), the political party championed by Bhutto and Zardari, in January 2008.

See also **Pakistan.**

■ Rob Knight

Peru. On Oct.10, 2008, the entire Peruvian Cabinet resigned over a scandal involving the state-owned oil company, Petroperu, and Discover Petroleum of Norway. State officials were accused of taking bribes in return for lucrative government contracts. On October 15, President Alan García Pérez appointed Yehude Simon as the new prime minister and head of the new government. Simon was a popular regional governor who had long championed social movements.

Protests and strikes. Rising food and energy prices, corruption, and scandals made 2008 a year of protests in Peru. In July, thousands of demonstrators blocked highways in poor administrative departments, including Ica, Puno, and Cuzco, and briefly shut down rail service to the Inca ruins at Machu Picchu, the country's top tourist destination. On February 19, a state of emergency was declared in the states of Lima, Ancash, and La Libertad in response to widespread protests. Farmers demanded that the government stop farm seizures by banks, lower the cost of fertilizer, and increase subsidies. They blocked roads and railways, stranding about 140,000 travelers around the country. Five people died in the protests and hundreds were arrested.

Opposition to natural gas project. During 2008, the development of huge natural gas deposits in the Amazonian rain forest was the target of opposition from an international coalition of environmentalists and human rights activists. They were anxious to protect an area rich in biodiversity and the welfare of an estimated 12,000 indigenous people. Despite the protests, a consortium led by Hunt Oil, a Dallas-based company, moved ahead with the $3.9-billion project that was to include the construction of a pipeline over the Andes and a plant to liquefy natural gas near the Peruvian coast.

Slow earthquake aid. On August l5, the first anniversary of a powerful earthquake that caused death and destruction along Peru's southern coast, tens of thousands of people protested the slowness of their government's response. Among them were students angry that they still had to attend classes in tents, owing to the slowness of the reconstruction effort.

Resurgence of Shining Path. In 2008, there was evidence of a resurgence of activities by Maoist Shining Path guerrillas, especially in remote areas of Ayacucho province, such as the Apurímac and Huallaga valleys. According to military officers, the numbers of the armed terrorists had quadrupled in recent years to a figure of nearly 800, thanks to financing from the protection they provided for drug traffickers.

■ Nathan A. Haverstock

See also **Latin America.**

Petroleum and gas.

Petroleum and gas. See Energy supply.

Philadelphia. Michael Nutter, who had been a four-term Democratic city councilman, became Philadelphia's 98th mayor on Jan. 7, 2008. Nutter, who was elected on Nov. 6, 2007, was sworn into office in a ceremony attended by 2,200 people at the Academy of Music, the city's venerable concert hall.

Nutter, 51, announced three goals in his inauguration speech: cutting the city's homicide rate by 30 to 50 percent; doubling the number of residents with college degrees; and cutting Philadelphia's 45-percent school dropout rate. "Today marks a new beginning," Nutter said. "A beginning of hope, a sense of optimism, and renewal for the city."

Nutter's plans faced new economic realities, however. By October 2008, when the national economic picture was bleak, Nutter forecast an $850-million shortfall in revenue for Philadelphia over the next five years. He said he was working on a plan to deal with the shortfall and asked city departments for help in making budget cuts. Nutter worked as an investment manager specializing in public finance before joining the City Council.

New police, school, cultural chiefs. On January 7, the mayor appointed former Washington, D.C., police chief Charles H. Ramsey as Philadelphia's chief of police and charged him with reducing the city's homicide rate. During the eight-plus years Ramsey held the job in the nation's capital, the district's homicide rate fell by almost half.

On March 19, the School Reform Commission hired Arlene Ackerman, who had headed San Francisco and Washington, D.C., public schools, as the Philadelphia School District's chief executive officer. The title effectively made her superintendent. On May 28, the commission adopted a $2.3-billion operating budget for the school district for the 2008-2009 school year. Ackerman began her new post on June 2.

Mayor Nutter kept a campaign promise to revive Philadelphia's cultural affairs office, which former Mayor John Street had closed in 2004 for budgetary reasons. On July 18, 2008, Nutter issued an executive order that created the Office of Arts, Culture and the Creative Economy. To head the cabinet-level office, he named Gary Steuer, a New Yorker who had been executive director of the Arts and Business Council of Americans for the Arts. Philadelphia had been the nation's largest city with no cultural affairs department.

Trial of state senator. Federal prosecutors opened their $3.5-million fraud case on October 22 against state Senator Vincent J. Fumo, a Philadelphia Democrat with a wide network of appointees and a reputation as a powerful dealmaker. Fumo decided not to seek reelection in 2008, ending three decades in office.

A federal grand jury indicted Fumo on 139 counts in February 2007. The government alleged that Fumo, 65, defrauded a nonprofit charity called Citizens' Alliance for Better Neighborhoods. Prosecutors also claimed that Fumo defrauded the city's Independence Seaport Museum, obstructed an investigation by the Federal Bureau of Investigation and Internal Revenue Service, and used state Senate employees for personal errands. The charges carry a possible 10-year jail term.

World Series. The Philadelphia Phillies won baseball's World Series championship after defeating the Tampa Bay Rays 4-3 on Oct. 29, 2008, in a game that had been suspended midway for two days after heavy rain. The Phillies had not won a World Series since 1980, a year that marked the first championship for the ball club. More than 1 million people turned out to celebrate at a parade downtown on Oct. 31, 2008.

New museum building. Please Touch, a museum for children, reopened on October 18 in extensively renovated Memorial Hall in the city's huge Fairmount Park. The hall originally was built for the 1876 Centennial Exposition. The new $88-million, 38,000-square-foot (3,530-square-meter) space is three times as large as the downtown building it had previously occupied.

■ Howard S. Shapiro

See also **City**.

Philippines. The Philippines Supreme Court on Aug. 4, 2008, blocked the signing of an agreement aimed at ending decades of conflict between the government of the predominantly Roman Catholic nation and Muslims on Mindanao Island in the south. This led to intensified fighting between government forces and an estimated 12,000 Islamic insurgents.

The government had reached the Memorandum of Agreement on Ancestral Domain with the Moro Islamic Liberation Front, which fought for more autonomy for Muslims on Mindanao. In 1996, after an estimated 50,000 to 150,000 deaths in guerrilla warfare, another Islamic insurgent group accepted a peace settlement that established a Muslim homeland on the island. Its administration had been riddled with corruption and incompetence, however.

The 2008 agreement with the Front would have expanded the homeland, giving greater autonomy to some 4 million Muslims in more than 700 towns and villages. Officials of Catholic areas of Mindanao, however, feared Muslim encroachment on their territory. Arguing that the agreement would split the nation, they won the court's blocking order. Angered, Front militants launched attacks on government forces and villages on Mindanao. An estimated 150 people died in the fighting, and about 300,000 others fled their homes.

The Supreme Court ruled 8 to 7 on October 14 that the agreement was unconstitutional. The Front turned to seeking support for the agreement at the United Nations and the Organization of the Islamic Conference, a group of Muslim countries.

Insurgent problems continued. Abu Sayyaf, an Islamic extremist organization believed to be linked to the terrorist organization al-Qa`ida, challenged government forces on islands south of Mindanao. In February, the head of President Gloria Macapagal-Arroyo's security staff uncovered an Abu Sayyaf plot to assassinate the president and bomb buildings in Manila, the capital.

Guerrillas with the New People's Army (NPA), a Communist group that had sporadically fought the government for more than 30 years, ambushed army troops on October 24, killing six. The troops were headed to a small village to plan a medical mission. On November 8, two soldiers died when army troops captured an NPA camp.

Economic problems grew during 2008, some a result of domestic trouble and some caused by the worldwide financial downturn. After a record 7.3-percent economic growth in 2007, growth slowed in 2008 while the population continued to grow at an annual rate of more than 2 percent.

Inflation in August reached its highest rate in 17 years at 12.5 percent. With soaring world prices for rice, a basic in Filipino diets, food costs became a major problem for many Filipinos. Domestic rice farmers produced only about 85 to 90 percent of the nation's needs. In 2008, the Philippines became the world's top rice importer.

President Macapagal-Arroyo set a goal of achieving rice self-sufficiency by 2010. In 2008, she announced a nearly $1-billion-per-year program to increase rice production by building and repairing irrigation systems, building farm roads, distributing improved seeds, increasing lending to farmers, and other measures.

President Macapagal-Arroyo had promised to reduce the proportion of people living in poverty by 2010 to only about 17 to 20 percent. The government reported in March 2008, however, that poverty in the Philippines had risen from 30 percent in 2003 to 32.9 percent in 2006.

Demonstrations against Macapagal-Arroyo continued during 2008. She had been repeatedly accused of corruption and of improperly influencing vote counting in the 2004 presidential election. Since becoming president in 2001, she had survived three impeachment attempts and four attempted military *coups* (overthrows). A large demonstration against her in 2008 marked the anniversary of a popular uprising in February 1986 that forced President Ferdinand E. Marcos to flee.

■ Henry S. Bradsher
See also **Asia; Disasters; Food: A Special Report.**

Physics. Sept. 10, 2008, was a momentous day for physicists who study the tiniest bits of matter. On that date, the first beam of *protons* (positively charged subatomic particles) was injected into the Large Hadron Collider (LHC)—marking the start of operation of the world's most powerful *particle accelerator.* Particle accelerators are devices that speed up subatomic particles to high energies and collide them to reveal information about properties of matter. Hadrons are a large group of subatomic particles that includes protons, neutrons, and hundreds of kinds of unstable particles.

The LHC, located at the international CERN laboratory near Geneva, Switzerland, is designed to produce proton beams that have energies as great as 7 trillion electron volts—seven times the previous world's record. The LHC was constructed in a circular tunnel 17 miles (27 kilometers) in circumference, on the French-Swiss border.

At the heart of the LHC are two pipes kept at near-perfect vacuum conditions. Particles circulating in the pipes are held on course by 1,700 powerful electromagnets. Coils of superconducting wire, which carry electricity with no resistance, power these magnets. To keep the coils in a superconducting state, liquid helium cools them to -456 °F (-271 °C). The two pipes carry two beams of particles circulating in opposite directions. At eight points around the ring, the beams cross and head-on collisions of particles can result. New particles are created in these collisions as energy is converted into mass.

The goal behind the LHC's initial tests in September was to inject the proton beams into the LHC and allow the protons to coast in stable orbits. This delicate process required synchronizing the two beams within a fraction of a *nanosecond* (billionth of a second). The next planned step was to accelerate the beams to higher energy levels. Unfortunately, mechanical problems developed a few days after the LHC began operation, resulting in the shut-down of the machine for repair. Physicists expected the LHC to resume operation by early 2009.

The principal scientific goal of the LHC is to test scientific theories that predict the existence of certain particles, such as the *Higgs boson,* which is theorized to provide mass to all other particles. Detection of the Higgs boson may contribute to resolving the central mystery of physics—the relation between gravity and the other forces in nature. Other research conducted with the LHC is expected to shed light on such exotic physics concepts as *dark matter* (an invisible substance thought to make up most of the matter in the universe) and *dark energy* (a form of energy thought to cause the universe to expand more and more rapidly).

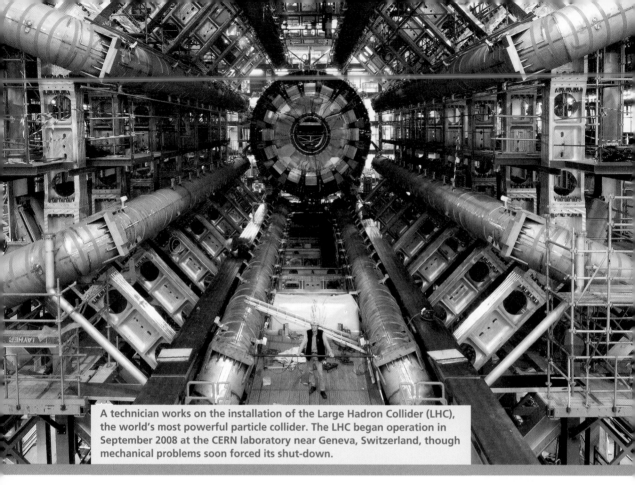

A technician works on the installation of the Large Hadron Collider (LHC), the world's most powerful particle collider. The LHC began operation in September 2008 at the CERN laboratory near Geneva, Switzerland, though mechanical problems soon forced its shut-down.

Super swimsuit. In August 2008, the practical application of physics research played a modest but important role in the 25 world records established in swimming at the 2008 Summer Olympic Games in China. All but one of these records were set by swimmers who wore an "LZR Racer" outfit, designed by scientists at United Kingdom-based Speedo International, the leading manufacturer of competition swimsuits. The design of the LZR Racer was based on the idea of reducing the drag force produced by water flowing over a swimmer's body. To create the design, Speedo scientists used complex computer simulations modeling water flow, called Computational Fluid Dynamics. Although the suit resulted in drag reductions of only a few percent, such reductions can be crucial in swimming, where winning margins are often measured in only hundredths of a second.

Scientists incorporated compression panels into the LZR Racer to flatten out some of the body's bumps, notably on the chest and thighs. Drag from seams was eliminated by welding the suit's panels together with a powerful ultrasound process, rather than by sewing. The resulting high-technology swimsuit cost more than $500—but it could be worn only a few times before losing its shape. ■ Robert H. March

See also **Nobel Prizes.**

Poetry. The Internet continued to expand the audience for poetry in 2008 well beyond its usual outlets in bookshops and classrooms. With a growing array of online poetry archives, Web sites and online journals featuring new poems, and blogs devoted to the dissemination and discussion of poetry, poems have become more widely available than ever before.

The Poetry Archive. One example of the many excellent Web sites relating to poetry belonged to the Poetry Archive. Founded in 2005 by British Poet Laureate Andrew Motion and recording producer Richard Carrington, the organization aimed to preserve and promote authors' recordings of their poems. Their site, which featured such recordings, received over 125,000 unique visitors per month in 2008. These monthly visitors accessed more than a million pages of poetry content.

On the site, Motion stated that the archive "is well on its way to becoming the world's largest and best equipped collection of poets reading from their own work." Established in collaboration with the Chicago-based Poetry Foundation, this audio collection "conserves voices that would otherwise be lost" and serves to remind readers that the aural experience of poetry—the sounds the poem makes when spoken aloud—is an indispensable aspect of the art form. Poetry existed as an oral tradition long before it became a written one.

Funding provided by the Poetry Foundation allowed for the addition of 100 American poets to the archive in 2008. Americans added to the site included Gwendolyn Brooks, William Carlos Williams, and U.S. poet laureate Kay Ryan. In autumn 2008, Ryan had succeeded Charles Simic for that one-year position. Not all recordings on the site were of recent poets. The oldest in the collection were made by poets from the 1800's, including Robert Browning and Walt Whitman.

"Poetry Daily" is another online resource that made contemporary poems available to a large audience in 2008. "Poetry Daily" featured a different poem every day of the week. The poems were selected by editors Don Selby and Diane Boller from recent books and literary journals. Following its spotlighted appearance on a given day, the poem then remained available in the site's archive for a year. The site also included a weekly prose feature on poetry, as well as a news page, which included links to articles and reviews from English-language newspapers and journals around the world.

As Selby and Boller wrote on the site, "Well over 1,000 books of poetry are published in the United States alone each year, but they can be difficult to find, even in areas brimming with bookstores. The numerous journals presenting new poetry and poets can be even more elusive." The purpose of Poetry Daily, they explain, is to make it easier for people to discover new poetry that they want to read.

Beyond its online archive, Poetry Daily has published two print volumes of poems selected from the site: *Poetry Daily: 366 Poems from the World's Most Popular Website* (2003) and *Poetry Daily Essentials 2007,* which included poems by such contemporary poets as Simon Armitage, Martín Espada, Albert Goldbarth, Marilyn Hacker, Edward Hirsch, June Jordan, Kay Ryan, C. K. Williams, Charles Wright, and many others.

The Writer's Almanac. A companion Web site to *The Writer's Almanac,* Garrison Keillor's immensely popular broadcasts on National Public Radio, featured daily podcasts of Keillor reflecting on writers and writing, as well as readings of one or two poems. Keillor's radio program was one of the most influential outlets for bringing poetry to a wider audience in the United States in 2008. In addition to selecting poems for broadcast, Keillor edited two popular print anthologies of poetry: *Good Poems* (2003) and *Good Poems for Hard Times* (2005).

■ David Yezzi

See also **Literature; People in the news** (Kay Ryan).

Poland. A public feud between Prime Minister Donald Tusk and President Lech Kaczynski dominated Polish politics during 2008. Tusk's liberal Civic Platform Party formed a coalition government in October 2007 that replaced the previous right-of-center government led by President Kaczynski's twin brother, Jaroslaw. According to the Polish constitution, the office of president is primarily ceremonial, but Lech Kaczynski stirred controversy in 2008 by publicly opposing policies of the Tusk government and taking an active role in foreign policy.

In October, Prime Minister Tusk led an official delegation to a summit meeting of the European Union (EU) in Brussels, Belgium. The delegation flew in the government jet provided for officials. President Kaczynski then chartered a private jet and showed up at the Brussels summit uninvited, creating confusion among the delegates.

Also on his own volition, President Kaczynski flew to Tbilisi, the capital of Georgia, in August to lend support to Georgia's President Mikheil Saakashvili, whose country was then under invasion by Russian forces. In response to these incidents, Prime Minister Tusk requested that Poland's Constitutional Court issue a definitive ruling on the president's foreign policy role. As of late 2008, the court had not issued its ruling.

Differences over EU policies also divided the president and prime minister. In April, Tusk obtained ratification for the EU Lisbon Treaty by the Polish parliament, but President Kaczynski, a frequent critic of the EU, refrained from signing the treaty through the rest of the year. The Lisbon Treaty, a replacement for a constitutional plan that was rejected in 2005, was designed to streamline decision making within EU institutions.

Economic reforms. In April 2008, the government launched a privatization drive that targeted 750 enterprises in which the government had ownership stakes. Under Communism, all companies were owned by the government, but after the reinstatement of capitalism in the early 1990's, the government began selling off companies. The 2008 privatization plan tagged companies for sale in the insurance, transportation, chemical, pharmaceutical, and timber industries.

Antimissile system. In August, Polish and U.S. officials agreed on a U.S. plan to install parts of a missile defense system on Polish soil. Officials of the administration of U.S. President George W. Bush claimed that the installation was necessary to protect central and eastern Europe from a nuclear attack by a rogue nation, such as Iran. Russian leaders, however, protested that the antimissile system was a provocation to Russia.

■ Sharon L. Wolchik

See also **Europe; Russia.**

Pollution. See Environmental pollution.

Popular music. The music industry closed out the third quarter of 2008 with a 12-percent drop in albums sold compared with the same period in 2007. According to Nielsen SoundScan, which monitors album sales at point of purchase in the United States, about 298 million albums were sold during 2008's third quarter. Industry executives hoped a strong fourth quarter would help the industry rebound during the year. The industry also continued its transformation toward a marketplace centered around digital singles and away from one built around albums (including CD's and digital releases). Retailers noted a trend in the renewed popularity of vinyl records, with sales doubling to 1.3 million LP's sold.

MySpace Music. The major music companies entered into a joint venture with the social-networking Web site MySpace, based in Beverly Hills, California, to make music available for free online listening. The service, called MySpace Music, was a product of a joint venture between MySpace, owned by the News Corporation, based in New York City; Warner Music Group, Sony BMG, and Universal Music Group, all based in New York City; and London's EMI Group. A number of independent music distributors, including the digital label The Orchard, also based in New York City, signed on to the deal as well. The site replaced an area of MySpace that allowed musicians to display and sell their own songs. The expanded site gave music consumers a kind of free online jukebox, offering several million songs for instantaneous streaming. Users could assemble playlists of hundreds of songs and post them on their MySpace profile.

Launched on September 25, MySpace Music planned to make money from selling advertising on the site and from selling downloads of music on the site through a partnership with the Seattle-based Internet dealer Amazon.com. Songs could be downloaded for 79 cents to 99 cents per track. The music companies hoped the service would recoup revenue from slumping CD sales and compete with Apple Inc.'s iTunes Store, based in Cupertino, California, which accounted for more than 70 percent of the digital market.

No royalty rate hike. The Copyright Royalty Board, the three-judge panel that sets rates on music copyright fees, opted in October not to raise rates on digital music downloads for the next five years. The fees, which go to music publishers, will remain at 9 cents per song. Music publishers wanted to raise the rate to 15 cents per song. Amazon, Apple, MySpace Music, and Rhapsody, an online music service run by Seattle-based RealNetworks, are among the major companies that must pay music publishers for each digital track they sell.

Record Store Day. Of the more than 3,000 record stores in the United States that have closed since 2003, nearly half were independent shops.

Hoping to lure back customers, a consortium of trade groups and 300 independent record stores across the United States and the United Kingdom presented the first annual Record Store Day on April 19, 2008. The event was a celebration of the independent record store and the culture of CD and vinyl record collecting. Festivities included in-store guests and performances, one-day-only releases, promotional sales, sampler discs, and giveaways. Numerous artists, including Paul McCartney, Bruce Springsteen, and Peter Gabriel, actively supported the event. Organizers planned a second annual Record Store Day for April 18, 2009.

Top sellers. Alicia Keys's third album, *As I Am,* released in late 2007, was 2008's top seller with nearly 4 million copies sold in the United States. The Eagles' greatest hits collection, *Eagles: Their Greatest Hits 1971–1975,* released in 1976, passed Michael Jackson's *Thriller* in 2008 to become the biggest-selling album in U.S. history. The Eagles's seventh album, *Long Road Out of Eden,* released in 2007, sold over 3 million copies by late 2008. Nearly six years in the making, it was the band's first studio album since 1979. The British band Coldplay sold more digital downloads than any album in digital history with its fourth album *Viva la Vida or Death and All His Friends.* The album sold 354,000 downloads two weeks after its June 11, 2008, release. In July, the Jonas Brothers became the first group to sell more than 100,000 digital downloads for three consecutive singles. The singles included "Burnin' Up" and "Pushin' Me Away" from the album *A Little Bit Longer,* released in August, and "Play My Music," from the *Camp Rock* Disney Channel Original Movie soundtrack album, released in June. The *Camp Rock* album sold over 1 million copies in the United States by September.

Amy Winehouse was in the news in 2008 as much for her legal, health, drug, and other personal problems as for her musical successes. The British singer/songwriter won Grammy Awards for Record of the Year, Song of the Year, and Best Female Pop Vocal Performance for the single "Rehab," and her album *Back to Black* won the Record of the Year award. She also earned a Grammy as Best New Artist. Winehouse's five wins earned her an entry in *Guinness World Records 2009* for most Grammy Awards won by a British Female Act. *Back to Black,* released in 2006, was the best-selling album worldwide during the first half of 2008, selling nearly 4 million copies.

Madonna and Mariah KO the King. In April, Mariah Carey beat out Elvis Presley as the solo artist with the most number-one singles on *Billboard*'s Hot 100 in the rock era. Carey's "Touch My Body," from her 11th album, *E=MC²,* debuted digitally on April 2. The song had a record-setting 286,000 downloads in its first week. It was Carey's 18th number-one single, putting her in second place for

Bo Diddley
The Man Behind the Beat

He walked "47 miles of barbed wire," he used "a cobra-snake for a necktie," he had a "tombstone head and a graveyard mind," and at age 79, the music world minded Bo Diddley dying.

Rock 'n' roll pioneer Bo Diddley died on June 2, 2008. He had a key role in the transition from American rhythm and blues to rock music in the 1950's. Diddley used his handmade rectangular guitar as a percussion instrument, and his characteristic pounding beat is still popular. Widely imitated, he was known as "the originator" because his original, unique sound and performing style influenced such rock legends as Buddy Holly, the Everly Brothers, the Beatles, the Rolling Stones, Eric Clapton, and Jimi Hendrix.

He will, however, be best remembered as the force behind "the Bo Diddley beat." The syncopated, rumba-like African rhythm, whether one called it the "hambone" style or the "shave-and-a-haircut, two-bits" beat, became Diddley's signature sound. It is heard on his first single, "Bo Diddley" (1955), with its self-referential, nursery-rhyme-like lyrics, as well as such other hits as "Pretty Thing" (1956) and "I Need You Baby (Mona)" (1957). The Bo Diddley beat has been the backbone of hundreds of songs recorded by rock artists ranging from Elvis Presley, The Who, Bruce Springsteen, and U2, to new wave and punk bands such as Bow Wow Wow and the Clash. Even newer artists, such as the White Stripes, have used variations of the beat in their music.

Although he was a hero and an inspiration to many musicians, Diddley was frustrated that he never earned royalties from the songs of others who had borrowed his beat. "I opened the door for a lot of people, and they just ran through and left me holding the knob," he told *The New York Times* in 2003.

Bo Diddley was born Otha Ellas Bates in December 1928 in McComb, Mississippi. He was adopted as a child by his mother's cousin and took her last name of McDaniel. He moved with his family to Chicago in the early 1930's. There are varying explanations of how he received the nickname "Bo Diddley." Diddley played violin as a child and taught himself to play the guitar as a teenager. He became a professional musician in 1951 and signed a recording contract with Chess Records in 1955.

Diddley developed many guitar special effects and innovative recording techniques. He often echoed sounds with his booming voice and produced a vibrating effect on his guitar to create an eerie, distorted sound. He was known for his swaggering, wisecracking, and slangy lyrics, as on such hits as "I'm a Man" (1955), "Who Do You Love?" (1956), "Hey Bo Diddley" (1957), "Say Man" (1959), and "You Can't Judge a Book by the Cover" (1962). He was also known for his wild performing style, in which he shook his legs, walked on his toes, jumped, and wrestled his guitar or played it over his head.

Diddley was elected to the Rock and Roll Hall of Fame in 1987. He performed at inaugural balls for Presidents George H. W. Bush and Bill Clinton. Diddley performed until the last year of his life, when he suffered a stroke while on tour. He died at his home in Archer, Florida. Bo Diddley is gone but the beat goes on. ■ Shawn Brennan

the most number-one singles in the rock era. Only the Beatles had more number-one hits, at 20. The same week, Madonna had the number-two song with "4 Minutes," from her album *Hard Candy.* The song was her 37th single in the top 10, beating out Presley as the artist with the most top-10 hits in the history of the chart. The song, featuring Jason Timberlake and Timbaland, sold 217,000 downloads in its first week of wide release. This was the first time since Nielsen SoundScan began tracking digital sales in 2003 that two titles debuted at the same time on the Hot Digital Songs chart with more than 200,000 downloads each. It was also the best single week of digital sales for both artists.

Sticky, sweet, and sour. The 50-year-old Material Girl also broke concert records in 2008 with her "Sticky & Sweet Tour." Madonna's tour began in August and wrapped up in December,

with sold-out concerts throughout Europe and the Americas. The concert featured a controversial video montage that grouped Republican U.S. presidential candidate John McCain with Nazi dictator Adolf Hitler and Democratic presidential candidate Barack Obama with pacifist Indian leader Mohandas K. Gandhi. Madonna and her husband, British film director Guy Ritchie, were divorced in November after eight years of marriage.

Fourth-quarter frenzy. Several releases in the fourth quarter were expected to help bolster recorded music sales in 2008. AC/DC's 15th album, *Black Ice,* the Australian band's first in eight years, debuted at number one on the *Billboard* 200, selling more than 784,000 copies after the first week of its exclusive Wal-Mart release on October 20. The soundtrack album for the Disney movie *High School Musical 3* debuted at

GRAMMY AWARD WINNERS IN 2008

Record of the Year: "Rehab," Amy Winehouse

Album of the Year: *River: The Joni Letters,* Herbie Hancock

Song of the Year: "Rehab," Amy Winehouse

New Artist: Amy Winehouse

Pop Vocal Album: *Back to Black,* Amy Winehouse

Pop Vocal Performance, Female: "Rehab," Amy Winehouse

Pop Vocal Performance, Male: "What Goes Around...Comes Around," Justin Timberlake

Pop Instrumental Album: *The Mix-Up,* Beastie Boys

Pop Instrumental Performance: "One Week Last Summer," Joni Mitchell

Pop Performance by a Duo or Group with Vocals: "Makes Me Wonder," Maroon 5

Traditional Pop Vocal Album: *Call Me Irresponsible,* Michael Bublé

Solo Rock Vocal Performance: "Radio Nowhere," Bruce Springsteen

Rock Performance by a Duo or Group with Vocals: "Icky Thump," The White Stripes

Hard Rock Performance: "The Pretender," Foo Fighters

Metal Performance: "Final Six," Slayer

Rock Song: "Radio Nowhere," Bruce Springsteen

Rock Album: *Echoes, Silence, Patience & Grace,* Foo Fighters

Alternative Music Album: *Icky Thump,* The White Stripes

Rhythm-and-Blues Vocal Performance, Female: "No One," Alicia Keys

Rhythm-and-Blues Vocal Performance, Male: "Future Baby Mama," Prince

Rhythm-and-Blues Performance by a Duo or Group with Vocals: "Disrespectful," Chaka Khan, featuring Mary J. Blige

Rhythm-and-Blues Song: "No One," Dirty Harry, Kerry Brothers, and Alicia Keys

Rhythm-and-Blues Album: *Funk This,* Chaka Khan

Contemporary Rhythm-and-Blues Album: *Because of You,* Ne-Yo

Contemporary Blues Album: *The Road to Escondido,* JJ Cale and Eric Clapton

Traditional Blues Album: *Last of the Great Mississippi Delta Bluesmen: Live in Dallas,* Henry James Townsend, Joe Willie "Pinetop" Perkins, Robert Lockwood, Jr., and David "Honeyboy" Edwards

Rap Solo Performance: "Stronger," Kanye West

Rap Performance by a Duo or Group: "Southside," Common, featuring Kanye West

Rap Album: *Graduation,* Kanye West

Rap Song: "Good Life," Aldrin Davis, Mike Dean, Faheem Najm, and Kanye West

Contemporary Jazz Album: *River: The Joni Letters,* Herbie Hancock

Jazz Vocal Album: *Avant Gershwin,* Patti Austin

Jazz Instrumental, Solo: "Anagram," Michael Brecker

Jazz Instrumental Album, Individual or Group: *Pilgrimage,* Michael Brecker

Large Jazz Ensemble Album: *A Tale of God's Will (A Requiem for Katrina),* Terence Blanchard

Country Album: *These Days,* Vince Gill

Country Song: "Before He Cheats," Josh Kear and Chris Tompkins

Country Vocal Performance, Female: "Before He Cheats," Carrie Underwood

Country Vocal Performance, Male: "Stupid Boy," Keith Urban

Country Performance by a Duo or Group with Vocals: "How Long," Eagles

Country Vocal Collaboration: "Lost Highway," Willie Nelson and Ray Price

Country Instrumental Performance: "Throttleneck," Brad Paisley

Gospel Performance: (tie) "Blessed & Highly Favored," The Clark Sisters; "Never Gonna Break My Faith," Aretha Franklin and Mary J. Blige

Gospel Song: "Blessed & Highly Favored," Karen Clark-Sheard

Traditional Folk Album: *Dirt Farmer,* Levon Helm

Contemporary Folk/Americana Album: *Washington Square Serenade,* Steve Earle

Amy Winehouse performs at the Rock in Rio music festival in Arganda del Rey, near Madrid, in July 2008. Winehouse won five Grammy Awards in 2008—more than any other British female artist in history.

number two the following day, selling more than 500,000 copies in its first week.

Guns N' Roses' sixth album, *Chinese Democracy*, in production for over a decade, was released before Thanksgiving. The release of the album had been postponed so many times that earlier in the year the U.S. manufacturer of Dr. Pepper challenged the band by offering to give away a free can of the soft drink to all Americans if the album was released in 2008. The album was released exclusively at Best Buy stores and online. It was the band's first album of original material since 1991.

Country artist Taylor Swift's second album, *Fearless,* released in November 2008, debuted at number one with sales of over 590,000 in its first week. Kanye West's fourth album, *808s & Heartbreak,* released later in the month, was the rapper's third to debut at number one. It sold 450,000 copies in its first week—less than his last two albums did.

After an erratic 2007 fraught with personal problems, Britney Spears was regarded by many industry observers as 2008's comeback performer with her sixth album, *Circus.* Released on December 2, the singer's 27th birthday, the album debuted at number one and sold more than half a million copies in its first week. The hit single "Womanizer" set the record for the biggest digital sales debut by a female artist with 286,000 downloads sold.

■ Shawn Brennan

Population. The United Nations (UN) Commission on Population and Development focused on urbanization—that is, the migration of people from rural to urban areas—during its April 2008 session at UN Headquarters in New York City. According to a UN report prepared for the session, the world's growing urbanization could have positive impacts on fighting poverty, inequality, and environmental degradation. However, positive impacts would be dependent on governments putting measures into practice ahead of time to capitalize on the benefits of urbanization and prevent negative consequences.

In 2008, for the first time in history, the number of people living in cities worldwide (3.4 billion) was about equal to the number of people living in rural areas, according to the UN report. In North America, Australia, and New Zealand, more than 80 percent of the population lived in urban areas. The urbanization level in Latin America and the Caribbean was 78 percent; in Europe, 72 percent; in Asia, 41 percent; and in Africa, 38 percent.

Urbanization was being driven by the concentration of investment and employment opportunities in urban areas, as well as by the transition to mechanized agriculture and the resulting labor surpluses in rural areas. By one estimate, 80 percent of the world's gross domestic product (GDP) was generated by urban areas in 2008.

and contraception. The World Bank, a UN affiliate, reported on July 10 that despite a huge increase in global availability of contraception, there were 51 million unintended pregnancies in less developed countries each year among women not using contraception, and there were 25 million pregnancies each year due to contraception failure or due to incorrect or inconsistent use of contraception.

Refugees and IDP's. The Office of the UN High Commissioner for Refugees reported in June 2008 a total of 16 million refugees and 51 million internally displaced persons (IDP's) worldwide at the end of 2007. Of the IDP's, 26 million were displaced as a result of armed conflict, and 25 million were displaced by natural disasters.

■ J. Tuyet Nguyen

See also **Census.**

Portugal. The Socialist Party government led by Prime Minister José Sócrates worked to reform the efficiency of public administration in 2008. The government also worked with unions and business associations to make it easier to dismiss inefficient workers and to improve parental leave policies. Anticipating elections in 2009, Manuela Ferreira Leite, who became leader of the opposition center-right Social Democrats in May 2008, criticized the government's large-scale public works projects. However, the criticism failed to gain traction in public opinion polls when the global economic crisis toward the end of the year seemed to recommend these sorts of policies.

Gay marriage. In October, Portugal's parliament rejected a proposal to allow same-sex marriages. The vote against the proposal followed months of heated debate in the predominantly Roman Catholic country. An overwhelming majority of deputies from both the ruling Socialist Party and the opposition Social Democrats defeated two bills backed by the smaller Left Bloc and Verdes (Green) parties that would have reversed an existing ban on same-sex marriages. In response, groups representing gays staged mock marriages outside parliament, maintaining that they suffered discrimination under existing laws.

Electric car network. In July 2008, Portugal, in a partnership with automakers Renault and

2008 put Portuguese banks under pressure. In November, the government announced the nationalization of Banco Portugues de Negocios after it accumulated huge losses and teetered on the verge of collapse. In addition, the government offered 4 billion euros ($5 billion) to Portuguese banks to ensure their solvency.

Economy. European Union economists forecast that Portugal's *gross domestic product* (GDP, the value of all goods and services produced in a country in a year) would grow by only 0.5 percent in 2008, down from 1.9 percent in 2007.

■ Jeffrey Kopstein

See also **Bank: A Special Report; Europe.**

President of the United States. See **United States, President of the.**

Prince Edward Island. See **Canadian provinces.**

Prisons. Statistics released by the United States Department of Justice (DOJ) in December 2008 revealed that the number of adults in U.S. state or federal prisons, in local jails, or on probation or parole reached 7.3 million at the end of 2007. This number was an increase from the 7.2 million recorded a year earlier. Approximately 3.2 percent of the U.S. adult population, or 1 in every 31 adults, was in prison or jail or on probation or parole in December 2007. This percentage has been stable since 1999. At the end of 2007, 70 percent of adults under correctional supervision in the United States were on probation or parole, and 30 percent were in prison or jail.

The DOJ report noted that federal prisons operated at 136 percent of capacity in 2007, while state prisons operated at rates between 96 percent and 113 percent of capacity. The states with the largest increases in prisoner numbers in 2007 were Arizona, Florida, and Kentucky.

Strain on state budgets. A February 2008 report by the Pew Center on the States, a policy research institute based in Washington, D.C., noted that the growing population of incarcerated individuals in the United States was causing a great strain on state budgets. According to the report, the states spent an average of almost 7 percent of their budgets on corrections in 2007—more than any other area of state expenses except

Rowan Williams (center), archbishop of Canterbury and head of the Church of England, enters Canterbury Cathedral in July at the start of the Lambeth Conference, a worldwide meeting of bishops of the Anglican Communion.

for health care, education, and transportation. States spent a total of $49 billion on corrections in 2007, representing a 315-percent increase over the $11 billion spent in 1987.

To cut expenses, the authors of the Pew report recommended that more nonviolent offenders be given alternative punishments to prison, such as community service, substance abuse treatment, and electronic monitoring.

Immigrants and prison. Men who are immigrants—including illegal immigrants—are less likely than native-born men to be incarcerated for crimes in California, according to a study released in February 2008 by the Public Policy Institute of California, a nonpartisan think tank in San Francisco. The authors of the report noted that, among individuals aged 18 to 40, native-born men were in state prisons at rates 2 to 3 times greater than those of foreign-born men. When inmates of county jails and other correctional institutions were included in the calculations, U.S.-born men were 8 to 10 times more likely to be incarcerated than immigrant men. According to the authors, the report's findings suggested that, contrary to popular belief, illegal immigrants do not commit a disproportionate amount of crime in the United States. ■ Alfred J. Smuskiewicz

See also **Crime; Immigration; State government.**
Prizes. See **Nobel Prizes; Pulitzer Prizes.**

Protestantism. Several Protestant denominations struggled in 2008, as they have for years, with disputes over homosexuality and the church. Much controversy centered on the ordination of homosexuals and the blessing of same-sex unions. Some Protestants believe that homosexuals are entitled to the same rights as heterosexuals, including the right to join the clergy and to marry. Other Protestants argue that homosexual behavior is morally wrong. Protestant denominations struggled to reduce tensions and hold church bodies together.

On April 30, a majority of delegates to the United Methodist General Conference voted to maintain the church's position that the practice of homosexuality is "incompatible with Christian teaching." The General Conference is the top policymaking body of the United Methodist Church, the largest Methodist denomination in the United States. However, the General Conference also approved a new resolution in 2008 to oppose discrimination against women and homosexuals. The resolution said the church opposes "all forms of violence or discrimination based on gender, gender identity, sexual practice or sexual orientation."

On June 27, the General Assembly of the Presbyterian Church (U.S.A.), the largest Presbyterian denomination in the United States, voted to overturn a long-standing ban on the ordination of gays and lesbians. The decision of the General Assembly, the church's national governing body, will not take effect unless it is approved within a year by a majority of the church's 173 regional councils, called *presbyteries*, in the United States. At the same meeting, however, the General Assembly refused to revise its definition of marriage to cover same-sex unions, calling marriage a "covenant between a woman and a man." Some Presbyterian leaders predicted years of confusion and conflict over the issue of gay rights.

Changing views about homosexuality and gender roles also continued to generate stress in the Episcopal Church in 2008. The church had consecrated a homosexual bishop in 2003 and elected its first female presiding bishop in 2006. Some Episcopal clergy also blessed same-sex unions. These actions triggered disputes both within the church and in the worldwide Anglican Communion, the international organization to which the Episcopal Church belongs.

The Lambeth Conference of the Anglican Communion met in Canterbury, England, in July and August 2008. The conference is a worldwide meeting of bishops that takes place about every 10 years. More than 200 conservative bishops boycotted the conference because of their opposition to the Episcopal Church's actions.

The conflicts led to splits within the Episcopal Church. Some parishes left the church and placed themselves under the authority of bishops in Africa, where most Anglicans reject gay clergy and same-sex marriage. From December 2007 to November 2008, 4 of the 110 dioceses of the Episcopal Church severed their ties to the church: the dioceses of San Joaquin, California; Pittsburgh, Pennsylvania; Fort Worth, Texas; and Quincy, Illinois. In December 2008, they formed a new division called the Anglican Church in North America.

New Baptist Covenant. More than 10,000 Baptists gathered in Atlanta from January 30 to February 1 for the first meeting of the New Baptist Covenant. The New Baptist Covenant is a loose alliance of more than 30 moderate Baptist organizations from throughout North America. Former U.S. President Jimmy Carter helped organize the alliance. The New Baptist Covenant reaffirmed what its members called "traditional Baptist values," including fighting poverty and respecting religious diversity. The alliance aimed to give moderate Baptists a stronger national voice and serve as a counterweight to the conservative Southern Baptist Convention, which has been closely aligned with the Republican Party.

Tax probes. A number of Protestant organizations in the United States faced challenges to their tax-exempt status in 2008. Churches and religious organizations are generally *exempt* from— that is, excused from paying—income tax. The Senate Finance Committee, which oversees tax laws, began an investigation late in 2007 into six television evangelists. Senator Charles E. Grassley (R., Iowa), the senior Republican on the Finance Committee, accused the evangelists of misusing their tax-exempt status to pay for lavish personal lifestyles. All six were supporters of the "Prosperity Gospel," the belief that financial prosperity is a sign of God's favor. By late in 2008, the committee was still trying to obtain detailed financial information from some of the evangelists.

In May, the Internal Revenue Service (IRS) ended a three-month investigation into the United Church of Christ (UCC). The IRS said that the denomination had not violated restrictions on political activity by tax-exempt organizations. The IRS probe focused on a speech given by Senator Barack Obama (D., Ill.) at a national meeting of the UCC in June 2007, after he became a candidate for president. Federal rules forbid churches from becoming directly or indirectly involved in campaigns of political candidates. Obama, a long-time member of the UCC, was one of about 60 speakers who addressed the meeting in Hartford, Connecticut. ■ Martin E. Marty

Psychology. See Mental health.

Public health. More than 1,300 people throughout the United States became ill in 2008 in a mysterious outbreak of a rare strain of *Salmonella* bacteria. Officials with the United States Food and Drug Administration (FDA) and the Atlanta-based Centers for Disease Control and Prevention (CDC) struggled to pinpoint the source of the outbreak, which began in Texas in April and continued into summer. *Salmonella* infections, typically caused by food contaminated with animal or human fecal matter, result in such symptoms as fever, diarrhea, vomiting, and abdominal pain. Severe illness may develop in some people.

Public health officials first attributed the outbreak to contaminated tomatoes. However, they later announced that contaminated jalapeño and serrano peppers originating at farms in Mexico were the more likely sources of infection. The CDC noted that there were probably multiple food sources of the outbreak.

Food from clones for sale. The FDA in January approved the sale of meat and dairy products from cattle, swine, and goat *clones* and their offspring. Officials with the FDA acknowledged that while many consumers may be reluctant to buy clone foods, their studies showed that food derived from clones was safe and no different from conventionally produced food.

Teen girls and STD's. Approximately one in

four teenaged girls in the United States has at least one kind of sexually transmitted disease (STD), government researchers led by physician Sara Forhan of the CDC reported in March. The researchers analyzed data on 838 girls, between the ages of 14 and 19 years, who had participated in the 2003-2004 National Health and Nutrition Examination Survey, an annual government survey on health issues. The girls had been tested for four STD's: chlamydia, herpes simplex virus, human papillomavirus (HPV), and trichomoniasis. According to the analysis, 18 percent of the girls were infected with HPV, 4 percent with chlamydia, 3 percent with trichomoniasis, and 2 percent with herpes simplex virus. Fifteen percent of the girls had more than one STD.

Drug-resistant TB. Drug-resistant strains of tuberculosis are spreading in many countries at a faster rate than was previously believed, the World Health Organization (WHO) warned in February 2008. The WHO, an agency of the United Nations, noted that there were nearly half a million new cases every year of tuberculosis that is resistant to common drugs. Moreover, extensively drug-resistant tuberculosis, a form of the disease that is virtually untreatable because it resists almost all drugs, had been recorded in 45 countries. ■ Alfred J. Smuskiewicz

See also **AIDS; Drugs; Food; Medicine; Safety.**

Puerto Rico.
On Nov. 4, 2008, Luis Guillermo Fortuño Burset, 48, of the New Progressive Party was elected governor of the Commonwealth of Puerto Rico. He defeated incumbent Governor Aníbal Acevedo Vilá of the Popular Democratic Party. Fortuño had been Puerto Rico's Resident Commissioner to the United States Congress since 2005. Acevedo ran an uphill race to hold on to his post, as he and members of his administration awaited trial on corruption charges in 2009.

On March 24, 2008, a federal grand jury indicted Acevedo and 12 of his associates on 19 counts of tax fraud, illegal fund-raising, and exchanging campaign contributions for government contracts. Acevedo denied any wrongdoing and continued to campaign for reelection despite his indictment on five further criminal counts on August 19.

Drug raids. On August 26, 59 alleged members of a drug ring were arrested following raids on housing projects in several small towns, including the mountain villages of Cayey, Coamo, Jayuya, and Santa Isabel, and the coastal communities of Guayama and Salinas. The raids were carried out by local police in conjunction with the U.S. Federal Bureau of Investigation, Drug Enforcement Administration, and National Guard. Gang members operating in these rural areas were indicted on charges of trafficking in heroin, cocaine, marijuana, and prescription drugs.

Puerto Rican exodus. In the first half of 2008, food prices in Puerto Rico increased by 12 percent, and the cost of housing rose 15 percent. Inflation, unemployment, and crime rates have soared since 2006. These conditions have driven an average of 65,000 Puerto Ricans to immigrate to the United States annually. Nearly 700,000 Puerto Ricans live in Florida; by comparison, 3.9 million people lived in Puerto Rico in 2007.

From 1945 to 1955, more than 500,000 Puerto Ricans immigrated to the United States, most of them farm workers. Many more laborers arrived in the 1970's. However, recent immigrants have included many middle-class professionals. The Puerto Rico Surgeons Association reported an average loss of 800 physicians a year. Many other professionals were hired for the ever-increasing demand in the United States for highly skilled bilingual workers.

San Juan Star folds. On Aug. 29, 2008, *The San Juan Star*, Puerto Rico's only English-language daily, ceased publication, a victim of rising costs and declining revenues. The newspaper was founded in 1959 and won a Pulitzer Prize in 1961 for editorial writing. ■ Nathan A. Haverstock

See also **Latin America.**

Pulitzer Prizes
in journalism, letters, drama, and music were announced on May 29, 2008, by Columbia University in New York City on the recommendation of the Pulitzer Prize Board.

Journalism. *The Washington Post* won the public service prize for exposing mistreatment of wounded veterans at Walter Reed Army Medical Center in Washington, D.C. The prize for breaking news reporting went to the staff of *The Washington Post* for its coverage of the 2007 massacre on the Virginia Polytechnic Institute and State University (Virginia Tech) campus in Blacksburg in which a student gunman killed 32 students and himself. The investigative reporting award was shared by the *Chicago Tribune* staff for its exposure of faulty governmental regulation of toys, car seats, and cribs; and by Walt Bogdanich and Jake Hooker of *The New York Times* for their stories on toxic ingredients in products imported from China.

Amy Harmon of *The New York Times* won the explanatory reporting prize for her examination of the ethical issues that accompany DNA testing. David Umhoefer of the *Milwaukee Journal Sentinel* won the local reporting prize for his stories on the skirting of tax laws to pad pensions of county employees. Jo Becker and Barton Gellman of *The Washington Post* won the national reporting award for their exploration of Vice President Dick Cheney. Steve Fainaru of *The Washington*

Post won the international reporting prize for his series on private security contractors in Iraq.

Gene Weingarten of *The Washington Post* won the feature-writing prize for his chronicling of a world-class violinist who performed in a subway station. Steven Pearlstein of *The Washington Post* won the commentary award. Mark Feeney of *The Boston Globe* won for visual arts criticism. Michael Ramirez of *Investor's Business Daily* in Los Angeles won for editorial cartooning. Adrees Latif of Reuters won for breaking news photography. Preston Gannaway of the *Concord* (New Hampshire) *Monitor* won the feature photography prize.

Letters, drama, and music. Junot Diaz won the fiction prize for *The Brief Wondrous Life of Oscar Wao.* Tracy Letts won the drama prize for *August: Osage County.* Daniel Walker Howe took the history award for *What Hath God Wrought: The Transformation of America, 1815-1848.* John Matteson won the biography prize for *Eden's Outcasts: The Story of Louisa May Alcott and Her Father.* The poetry prize was shared by Robert Hass for *Time and Materials* and Philip Schultz for *Failure.* Saul Friedländer won the nonfiction prize for *The Years of Extermination: Nazi Germany and the Jews, 1939-1945.* David Lang's *The Little Match Girl Passion* won for music.   ■ Shawn Brennan

Qatar. See **Middle East.**

Quebec. See **Canadian provinces.**

Radio. The radio industry in the United States faced mergers, bailouts, sagging stocks, layoffs, and bankruptcy as satellite, terrestrial, and Internet radio stations struggled to stay alive in 2008.

Sirius XM. On July 25, the U.S. Department of Justice and the Federal Communications Commission (FCC) approved a merger of Sirius Satellite Radio of New York City with the country's other satellite service, XM Satellite Radio Holdings Inc. of Washington, D.C., to create a single satellite radio network in the United States. Neither company had ever posted a net profit, and both recorded billions of dollars in losses building their operations. Sirius, which bought out its rival four days after receiving FCC approval, was expected to save about $400 million in 2009. The new company, renamed Sirius XM Radio Inc., had more than 18.5 million subscribers, making it the second largest radio business in the United States. The new Sirius XM offered more than 300 channels of programming, including radio offerings from personalities such as Howard Stern, Oprah Winfrey, and Martha Stewart, to professional sports broadcasts, news, and music. However, subscribers had to pay at least an additional $4 per month if they wished to receive added programming as part of the company's "Best of Both" package, which began in October 2008. Sirius XM was expected to compete with traditional radio as well as digital audio players like iPods. However,

Sirius XM's retail sales leveled off after the merger. Declining auto sales also impacted the company: Sirius XM had deals with all the major car makers for pre-installed satellite radios in their vehicles. By November, Sirius XM's stock had plunged more than 90 percent for the year. Analysts speculated that the company could be headed for bankruptcy.

Industry deals. On July 30, Clear Channel Communications, Inc., of San Antonio, the largest U.S. radio station owner, announced that it had completed a privatization deal with a group of private equity firms led by Bain Capital, LLC, and Thomas H. Lee Partners L.P., both based in Boston. Ending a 21-month effort, the $24-billion transaction ranked as one of the largest media buyouts in U.S. history.

One of Clear Channel's highest profile personalities, conservative talk radio host Rush Limbaugh, celebrated 20 years in radio in July 2008 by signing a contract extension through 2016 worth over $400 million. It was the highest contract ever signed in any broadcast medium. Limbaugh's show was said to attract 20 million regular listeners.

In November 2008, radio company Westwood One, based in New York City, was delisted by the New York Stock Exchange after its stock prices fell below minimum share price. Other companies facing delisting by year's end included Citadel Broadcasting Corporation, based in Las Vegas; Regent Communications, based in Cincinnati; Radio One, based in Lanham, Maryland; and Spanish Broadcasting System, based in Coconut Grove, Florida.

Internet radio. In August, Pandora, one of the most popular U.S. Internet radio services, nearly collapsed because of royalty rate hikes. In 2007, a U.S. congressionally appointed panel decided on a rate hike for the music royalties charged to Internet radio stations. In 2008, Pandora faced royalty fees amounting to 70 percent of its projected revenue of $25 million—about $17 million. In September, Congress passed a bill allowing sites like Pandora to extend negotiations with SoundExchange, the organization that collects royalties, into 2009.

Airwaves ruling. In November 2008, the FCC approved a proposal to make an unlicensed portion of the radio spectrum available for public use. The ruling was expected to benefit businesses and consumers in the wireless space. Opponents of the proposal included television networks and Broadway producers, who argued that signals sent over the frequencies could interfere with broadcasts and wireless microphones during live productions.

National Public Radio (NPR) announced in December that it would lay off 7 percent of its work force and cut two of its daily programs to close a $23-million shortfall. It was NPR's first major reduction in 25 years.   ■ Shawn Brennan

Religion. See **Eastern Orthodox Churches; Islam; Judaism; Protestantism; Roman Catholic Church.**

Republican Party. The Republican Party (or GOP, for Grand Old Party) lost the race for the presidency and lost seats in both houses of Congress in elections on Nov. 4, 2008. The GOP had faced long odds given the realities of a faltering economy and the fact that President George W. Bush's popularity reached historical lows in public opinion polls in the fall of 2008.

Presidential election. Senator John McCain (R., Arizona) lost his bid to extend GOP control of the White House on November 4. Senator Barack Obama (D., Illinois) captured 365 electoral votes, compared with McCain's 173 electoral votes. Obama also won the popular vote with 67.1 million votes, compared with 58.4 million votes for McCain. According to election officials, more than 125 million people voted in the 2008 contest.

GOP response. Republican National Committee (RNC) Chairman Mike Duncan pledged that his party would "take a deep breath and listen to the American people" for advice following the GOP's drubbing in November. He also said that congressional Republicans would act as a check on the Democrats' expanded power in Washington, D.C.

The nominating contests. McCain captured the Republican nomination after outlasting his main opponents, former Governors Mitt Romney of Massachusetts and Mike Huckabee of Arkansas, in a series of primaries from January to March. Other competitors included actor and former Senator Fred Thompson of Tennessee and former New York City Mayor Rudy Giuliani. United States Representative Ron Paul (R., Texas) received the backing of libertarian-minded voters for his opposition to the Iraq War and the federal income tax.

Huckabee won the first contest in Iowa on January 3. McCain won in New Hampshire on January 8. He and Romney then split the month's other contests leading up to Florida's January 29 primary, where the Arizona senator narrowly defeated Romney. Giuliani, who entered 2008 as the favorite, had staked his campaign on winning delegate-rich Florida. He finished third, however, and dropped out of the race the next day.

More than 20 states voted on "Super Tuesday," February 5. McCain took many of the day's biggest prizes, including California, Illinois, and New York. Romney won in seven states, and Huckabee won in five. The day established McCain as the race's clear leader, but the results pointed to a continued weakness of the Arizona senator among socially conservative voters. McCain and Huckabee each won states on February 9. McCain did not lose another race, however, and locked up the nomination after a sweep of states on March 4.

Governorships. Republicans won 4 of 11 races for governor in November. Winning reelection were Republicans Mitch Daniels of Indiana, John Hoeven of North Dakota, Jon Huntsman, Jr., of Utah, and Jim Douglas of Vermont.

Missouri was the site of the lone governorship to change parties. In that race, Democratic state Attorney General Jay Nixon defeated Republican Congressman Kenny Hulshof in a bid to replace departing Governor Matt Blunt, who did not seek reelection. After the election, Republicans held 21 governorships, compared with 29 for Democrats.

Scandals. Senator Ted Stevens (R., Alaska) was convicted on October 27 of seven felony counts of lying to federal prosecutors. Stevens had been accused of concealing hundreds of thousands of dollars in gifts and services from a private oil services company. Stevens indicated he would appeal the guilty verdict, which did not prevent him from standing for reelection the following week. Stevens was defeated by Anchorage Mayor Mark Begich. Stevens's sentencing was set for early 2009.

U.S. Senate elections. Senate Republicans lost seven seats to Democrats in 2008. Along with Alaska's Stevens, defeated GOP incumbents included Elizabeth Dole in North Carolina, Gordon Smith in Oregon, and John Sununu in New Hampshire. Senator Saxby Chambliss (R., Georgia) won a run-off election on December 2 after neither he nor his main challenger, Democrat Jim Martin, received 50 percent of the vote on November 4. The winner of the race between Senator Norm Coleman (R., Minnesota) and comedian Al Franken was unknown at year's end. Democrats also won Republican seats not being contested by incumbents in Colorado, New Mexico, and Virginia.

House of Representatives. Republicans in the House also lost ground to their Democratic counterparts in November. Democrats held a 257-to-178 majority, an increase of more than 20 seats from the last House election in 2006. In a sign of the difficulties the GOP faced in the Northeast, Representative Chris Shays, 21-year House veteran and a Connecticut moderate, lost his seat to Democrat Jim Himes. Shays's loss marked the first time since the GOP's founding in 1854 that the party had no representatives from New England.

Fund-raising. The RNC, the Republican Senatorial Committee, and National Republican Congressional Committee raised a total of $518.8 million in the election cycle from Jan. 1, 2007, to mid-October 2008, according to the Federal Election Commission. The Democratic National Committee, Democratic Senatorial Campaign Committee, and the Democratic Congressional Campaign Committee raised a total of $462.4 million over the same period.   ■ Ken Shenkman

See also **Cabinet, U.S.; Congress of the United States; Elections: A Special Report; People in the news** (Sarah Palin)**; State government; United States, Government of the; United States, President of the.**

Roman Catholic Church.

Pope Benedict XVI made his first trip to the United States in April 2008. It included two huge public Masses, in Washington, D.C., and New York City; a reception on the White House lawn; a visit to ground zero, the site of the World Trade Center terrorist attacks on Sept. 11, 2001; a speech at the United Nations; and a youth rally in New York City.

Benedict squarely faced the accusations of sexual abuse by priests that had rocked the Roman Catholic Church in the United States. Many Catholics were disturbed not only by the charges of abuse but also by the failure of some bishops to discipline accused priests or remove them from their positions. During the pope's flight from Rome, the first question he answered, chosen from a number submitted by reporters, dealt with the sex abuse crisis. The pope told reporters, "We are deeply ashamed," signaling that he would meet the issue head on. Benedict urged the church to be vigilant in looking out for abuse and to better screen applicants for the priesthood. "It's more important to have good priests than to have many priests," he said.

Benedict held a private meeting at the Vatican embassy in Washington, D.C., with several victims of sexual abuse by clergy. It was believed to be the first meeting between a pope and victims of such abuse. Many Catholics hailed the meeting as a healing gesture. During an address to American bishops, Benedict declared that the sexual abuse of children was "evil" and "a sin" and that the crisis was "sometimes very badly handled" by the bishops.

In the same address to American bishops, Benedict expressed sorrow over "the scandal given by Catholics who promote an alleged right to abortion." He called for the Gospel to be preached against what he referred to as "a dictatorship of relativism." Benedict has frequently denounced the moral view called *relativism,* which argues that what is right or wrong depends on the particular culture, historical period, or circumstances. What is right in one case may be wrong in another, this view claims.

Southwestern growth. By the early 2000's, the Southwest had become the center of growth for the U.S. church. A steady influx of mostly Hispanic immigrants since the early 1990's had boosted the Catholic population. Sunday Masses overflowed, and church leaders struggled to build the new parishes and schools they needed. The pope acknowledged the growing importance of the Southwest in November 2007 by naming

Pope Benedict XVI, on his first visit to the United States, greets people attending a huge public Mass that he celebrated at Yankee Stadium in New York City in April 2008.

Archbishop Daniel DiNardo of the Archdiocese of Galveston-Houston as Texas's first cardinal.

Women press for ordination. The debate over the place of women in the Catholic Church continued in 2008. An organization called Roman Catholic Womenpriests continued to ordain women in defiance of church law. The organization began with the so-called Danube Seven, seven women ordained by an independent bishop on a boat in the Danube River in 2002. By late 2007, Womenpriests had ordained an estimated 50 priests, mostly women, worldwide.

Roman Catholic Womenpriests says its ordinations are valid because its first bishops were ordained by Catholic bishops in good standing and in ceremonies that adhered to the laws of the church. Such ceremonies would maintain *apostolic succession,* a connection with Jesus Christ's apostles that validates a bishop's authority. Catholics believe that bishops can trace their succession in an unbroken line to the original apostles, who handed down their authority to the first bishops, who in turn handed down authority to their successors. Church authorities, however, condemned the ordinations by Roman Catholic Womenpriests. The church authorities say that ordinations of women are invalid and that anyone involved is automatically excommunicated. ■ Thomas W. Roberts

Romania. Voters overwhelmingly rejected the government of Prime Minister Calin Popescu-Tariceanu in parliamentary elections on Nov. 30, 2008. The leftist Social Democrats and the rightist Liberal Democrats each received about 34 percent of the votes; Popescu-Tariceanu's center-right Liberal Party placed third with 19 percent. In December, President Traian Basescu asked Theodor Stolojan of the Liberal Democrats to form a new coalition government. Prime Minister Popescu-Tariceanu had headed the government since late 2004.

In October 2008, protesters marched in Bucharest, the capital, after the parliament voted a controversial 50-percent pay increase for teachers on the state's payroll. Many of the demonstrators were state-funded workers in other occupations who did not receive a raise.

After several years of robust growth fueled by large inflows of capital, Romania's economy, like many others in Europe, showed signs of slowing in late 2008. The country's gross domestic product (GDP)—the value of all goods and services produced in a country in a year—grew by about 7 percent both in 2007 and 2008. Analysts projected, however, that GDP would grow by less than 5 percent in 2009. ■ Sharon L. Wolchik

See also **Europe; Economics, World.**

Rowing. See Sports.

Russia experienced political turnover, international conflict, and deep economic turmoil in 2008. Dmitry Medvedev, outgoing Russian president Vladimir Putin's handpicked successor, triumphed in March presidential elections that were boycotted by most international monitoring groups. The Russian government's relations with the West worsened over the course of the year. The low point came when armed conflict broke out in August between Russia and the pro-Western regime of Georgian President Mikheil Saakashvili over the separatist Georgian region of South Ossetia. Russia also experienced a severe economic crisis during the second half of the year, which the Russian government blamed on spillover effects from the financial turmoil in the United States.

Presidential elections. First Deputy Prime Minister Dmitry Medvedev dominated Russia's March 2 presidential elections. Russia's Central Election Commission reported that Medvedev, a relative economic liberal and close ally of outgoing President Vladimir Putin, took 70.2 percent of the vote. Putin had publicly tapped Medvedev for the presidential post in December 2007, virtually ensuring his victory. Medvedev's closest rival in the presidential race, Communist Party leader Gennady Zyuganov, took 17.8 percent of the vote. Ultranationalist Vladimir Zhirinovsky received 9.4 percent, and relative unknown Andrei Bogdanov of the Democratic Party received 1.3 percent.

On February 7, the Organization for Security and Co-operation in Europe (OSCE) canceled its plans to observe the elections. OSCE officials complained that the Russian government demanded that the OSCE overly restrict both the number of election observers and the amount of time they could spend working in Russia before the poll. The Council of Europe's parliamentary assembly, the only Western organization to monitor the election, condemned it as neither free nor fair.

Politics. As expected, the newly elected President Medvedev named outgoing President Putin to serve as his prime minister after the elections. Putin also agreed to become the leader of the ruling pro-Kremlin United Russia party at the party's annual congress in April, though he did not formally become a member of the party.

Prime Minister Putin announced on May 12 that the Industry and Energy Ministry would become two separate ministries: the Ministry of Industry and Trade and the Ministry of Energy. The new Ministry of Industry and Trade, headed by Viktor Khristenko, also absorbed the trade portfolio previously held by the reorganized Economic Development Ministry.

On October 30, President Medvedev accepted the resignation of Murat Zyazikov, who had led the troubled North Caucasus region of Ingushetia since 2002. Medvedev replaced the former KGB

A woman crosses herself before a portrait of Nicholas II, the last czar of Russia. Nicholas and his family were imprisoned by revolutionaries and were killed in 1918. On Oct. 1, 2008, Russia's Supreme Court ruled that Nicholas and his family had been the victims of political repression.

colonel with relative unknown Yunus-Bek Yevkurov. Zyazikov had been widely criticized for corruption and an inability to contain large-scale rebel violence in the volatile region.

On Nov. 5, 2008, during a key address, President Medvedev proposed changes to the constitution that would extend the presidential term from four to six years and the terms of lower-house (State Duma) legislators from four to five years. The Duma and the Federation Council (the upper house of parliament) quickly approved the measures. Although many observers speculated that the amendments were intended to allow Prime Minister Putin to reassume the presidency before Medvedev's term expires in 2012, Putin firmly rejected such speculation.

On Nov. 16, 2008, the long-standing liberal opposition Union of Right Forces party agreed to disband and join the new Kremlin-supported party Right Cause. International affairs experts noted that the dissolution left Yabloko as the only meaningful liberal opposition party in Russia.

Conflict with Georgia. The Russian government established closer political and economic ties with the breakaway Georgian republics of Abkhazia and South Ossetia in April, to the dismay of Georgian President Mikheil Saakashvili and the West. Russia, a long-time ally of Serbia, did so in response to the North Atlantic Treaty Organiza-

tion (NATO) recognizing the independence of Kosovo from Serbia in March. Both Georgian republics have large populations with Russian citizenship, and both had exercised de facto independence with Russian support since the early 1990's. Saakashvili had repeatedly pledged to bring the republics back under Georgian state control.

Tensions increased in April 2008 as the Russian government accused the Georgian government of intending to invade Abkhazia and sent additional troops to the region. In turn, the Georgians accused Russian troops of shooting down a reconnaissance drone over Abkhaz territory.

In August, the primary arena of conflict moved to South Ossetia and turned increasingly serious. On August 7, Georgian troops bombed and briefly occupied the South Ossetian capital of Tskhinvali. While Saakashvili claimed that Russian forces had provoked the attack by shelling Georgian villages in the preceding days, the Russians vehemently denied the charge. The Russian government responded to the Tskhinvali attack with massive force, quickly taking military control of South Ossetia and sending its forces into Georgia proper.

On August 15, President Saakashvili signed a cease-fire agreement brokered by French President Nicolas Sarkozy, chair of the European Union's (EU) rotating presidency. Medvedev signed the following day. The agreement required both sides to withdraw their troops and turn over 4-mile (7-kilometer) buffer zones outside Abkhazia and South Ossetia to EU troops. On August 26, the Russian parliament unanimously voted to recognize South Ossetia and Abkhazia as independent states. On August 29, the Georgian and Russian governments broke diplomatic ties.

A formal memorandum between Sarkozy and Medvedev signed on September 8 further clarified the cease-fire agreement. Russia withdrew its troops from Georgia but maintained a force in the breakaway republics. The EU restarted partnership talks with Russia that it had suspended after the August conflict. On November 24, President Medvedev approved formal friendship, cooperation, and mutual assistance treaties with Abkhazia and South Ossetia.

Economic crisis. A rapid drop in international oil prices, political uncertainty due to the conflict with Georgia, and the global financial crisis combined to plunge the Russian economy into ever-worsening turmoil from July onward. Despite assurances from the government and the Central Bank of Russia that they would maintain a strong ruble, the ruble's value declined steadily against the U.S. dollar, sparking capital flight and a public rush to convert rubles to dollars and euros. Between July and November Russia spent more than $130 billion of its nearly $600 billion in foreign reserves to support the ruble and the Russian financial sector.

Russia's stock exchanges repeatedly halted trading during the fall in the face of collapsing share prices. The Russian government was forced to bail out several medium-sized banks and loaned billions of dollars to the state oil company Rosneft and to wealthy businessmen Mikhail Fridman and Oleg Deripaska to enable them to pay back their foreign debts. On November 20, Prime Minister Putin announced an additional $14.5 billion in stimulus measures, including major reductions in taxes on corporate profits and small businesses. As a result of the evolving crisis, the United Nations-affiliated World Bank predicted a dramatic decline in growth to 3 percent in 2009, down from 6 percent in 2008.

Disaster. The accidental release of poisonous freon gas on board a Russian nuclear submarine killed 20 people and left another 21 ill on November 8. It was the most serious incident for the Russian navy since the sinking of the submarine *Kursk* killed 118 sailors in 2000.

Death. Patriarch Alexei II, the head of Russia's powerful Orthodox Church since 1990, died on Dec. 5, 2008, at the age of 79. ■ Juliet Johnson

See also **Eastern Orthodox Churches; Europe; Georgia; People in the news** (Dmitry Medvedev).
Rwanda. See Africa.

Grandchildren of Russian novelist Alexander Solzhenitsyn pay their respects at his funeral on August 5. Eight years in Soviet labor camps provided Solzhenitsyn with the knowledge and drive to write his famous 1962 novel, *One Day in the Life of Ivan Denisovich.*

June 30, 2008, marked the 100th anniversary of the Tunguska Event, a mysterious explosion in Siberia.

On June 30, 1908, an explosion shook the remote Tunguska River area of Siberia. Witnesses saw a bright white light split the sky, followed by a distant roar. The blast leveled trees over about 775 square miles (2,000 square kilometers) of forest. People 40 miles (64 kilometers) away were thrown to the ground by wind and heat.

In the 100 years since what has become known as the Tunguska Event, investigators have worked to piece together what happened. Science-fiction writers and UFO enthusiasts have imagined that the explosion marked the crash of an alien spacecraft. The evidence, however, points to a chunk of asteroid or comet that exploded under the extreme heat and pressure of entering Earth's atmosphere.

How big was the space rock that caused the Tunguska Event? It's an important question because there are quite a few small objects in space and fewer large ones. If a giant asteroid caused the blast, there is little chance another such object will hit Earth soon. But if the object was small, then Tunguska-like events—with enough power to wipe out a major city—may be worryingly common.

Some simulations have suggested the explosion packed as much power as 700 *megatons* (million tons) of TNT. Impactors large enough to produce this kind of explosive power would be quite rare. But these models were based on atomic bomb explosions. Newer studies suggest that the damage at Tunguska was caused not by the explosion, but by the still-plummeting fireball and the shockwave it produced, which slammed into the ground moments later. Such models point to a much smaller rock, the kind that might strike Earth about once every 300 years.

In 2008, a team of scientists located a possible fragment of the Tunguska meteor buried under a Siberian lake. If an expedition can reach the meteorite, we may learn more about the Tunguska Event and the danger it represents.

Safety. The safety of Americans is at risk because the United States National Guard and military reserves are unprepared to respond effectively to a wide range of disasters, from tornadoes and hurricanes to an attack with chemical or biological weapons. That was the conclusion of a February 2008 report by a congressional commission headed by retired Major General Arnold L. Punaro of the U.S. Marines. The report faulted the Department of Defense (DOD) for not adequately funding domestic preparedness. The DOD, however, disputed the report's conclusions.

Product safety reform. In August, United States President George W. Bush signed the Consumer Product Safety Improvement Act, legislation containing sweeping reform of the U.S. consumer product safety system. Congress took action on the legislation after a record number of safety-related product recalls in 2007.

The legislation required stricter tests for toys and included a ban on lead and harmful substances known as phthalates in toys. It also provided greater public access to complaints about products and more power for state attorneys general to enforce safety laws. In addition, the bill revamped the Consumer Product Safety Commission, the government agency in charge of protecting consumers from unsafe products.

Plastic problems. A chemical widely used to make plastic nursing bottles, water bottles, linings for food cans, and some dental fillings may cause hormone-related health problems, according to a report released in April 2008 by the U.S. Food and Drug Administration (FDA), Centers for Disease Control and Prevention, and National Institutes of Health. The report noted that the chemical—bisphenol A (BPA)—resulted in precancerous growths, reproductive disorders, and behavioral problems in laboratory animals. In September, researchers at the Peninsula Medical School in the United Kingdom and the University of Iowa in Iowa City linked exposure to BPA to increased risks of diabetes mellitus and heart disease.

Despite these reports, the FDA maintained that there was no reason for consumers to stop using plastic products containing BPA. Authorities in Canada, however, banned BPA from nursing bottles in 2008.   ■ Alfred J. Smuskiewicz

See also **Armed forces; Disasters; Food; Public health; Toys and games.**

Sailing. See Boating.

Saint Kitts & Nevis. See Latin America; West Indies.

Saint Lucia. See Latin America; West Indies.

Saint Vincent & the Grenadines. See Latin America; West Indies.

Samoa. See Pacific Islands.

São Tomé and Principe. See Africa.

Saskatchewan. See Canadian provinces.

Saudi Arabia. United States President George W. Bush met with Saudi King Abdullah during a visit to Saudi Arabia in January 2008. President Bush sought to shore up Saudi support for boosting oil output to lower world prices of this commodity, assisting with the rebuilding of Iraq, fighting Islamist terrorism, and offsetting Iran's military power in the Persian Gulf region. To achieve the last objective, President Bush announced a $20-billion arms sale to Saudi Arabia and other Arab gulf countries. The arms sale included Joint Direct Attack Munition technology, which could be used to convert standard munitions into precision-guided "smart" bombs.

President Bush visited Saudi Arabia again in May, repeating his request for an increase in oil production. In addition, the U.S. Senate proposed legislation to freeze parts of the arms deal if Saudi Arabia did not increase oil output. After the visit by President Bush, Saudi officials announced that they had agreed to raise the kingdom's oil output by 300,000 barrels a day.

Russian railway deal. In January, Russian Railways, the government-owned railway company of Russia, won an $800-million contract to build a rail line 323 miles (520 kilometers) long, from King Khalid International Airport in Riyadh, the Saudi capital, to the Al-Zabira junction on Saudi Arabia's North-South Railway project. The rail line was one of four parts of the railway project, which was expected to cover a distance of 1,490 miles (2,400 kilometers) when complete.

Terror indictments. Saudi authorities indicted 991 people in October on charges of participating in terrorist attacks. Prince Nayef, the interior minister of Saudi Arabia, announced that terrorists had been responsible for more than 30 attacks in the kingdom since May 2003, resulting in the deaths of more than 160 people. The prince added that Saudi security forces had foiled approximately 160 other terrorist attacks.

Saudi churches? In March 2008, Archbishop Paul-Mounged el-Hachem, the Vatican ambassador to several gulf nations, announced that the Holy See was negotiating with Saudi authorities for permission to build the first Roman Catholic churches in Saudi Arabia. The negotiations stemmed from a November 2007 meeting between King Abdullah and Pope Benedict XVI.

Film festival. The first international film festival in Saudi Arabia was held in May 2008 in the eastern city of Damman. Although public cinemas were banned in Saudi Arabia during the 1970's and 1980's, most Saudis own television sets, and videos and CD's of movies are available for viewing in the home.   ■ Mary-Jane Deeb

See also **Energy supply; Middle East; Terrorism.**

School. See Education.

Senegal. See Africa.

Serbia. Kosovo's unilateral declaration of independence on Feb. 17, 2008, dominated Serbia's domestic politics and international relations for much of the year. Kosovo, traditionally a province of Serbia, had been administered by the United Nations (UN) since 1999, when NATO forces intervened in response to Serbia's armed invasion of Kosovo and forced eviction of much of the province's ethnic Albanian population. Most of these Kosovars later returned to their homes.

In extended negotiations between Serbia and Kosovo, Serbian leaders insisted that Kosovo, home to a large Albanian majority and a Serb minority, must remain an integral part of Serbia. The talks broke down, and Kosovo's government proclaimed independence. The United States and a number of nations in the European Union (EU) promptly recognized Kosovo's independence.

In Serbia, the reaction was violent. Mobs in Belgrade, the capital, set fire to the U.S. embassy and attacked the embassies of several other countries that had extended recognition to Kosovo. Rioters also ransacked some foreign-owned businesses in Belgrade.

Serbia's governing coalition then split over the Kosovo crisis. Hardliners, including Prime Minister Vojislav Kostunica, wanted to suspend membership negotiations with the EU to protest recognition extended to Kosovo by some EU member states. However, pro-Western pragmatists, such as President Boris Tadic, wanted to press forward with the EU talks. The Kostunica government fell on March 7, when parliament voted down a proposal to halt EU negotiations.

Political transition. President Tadic's pro-Europe Democratic Party outpolled the extreme nationalist Radical party in parliamentary elections on May 11. In July, Tadic's party formed a coalition government with the Socialist Party, the party of former president Slobodan Milosevic. Mirko Cvetkovic, the finance minister in the previous government, became prime minister.

War crimes. EU officials and Serbian leaders on April 29 signed a Stabilization and Association Agreement, the first step toward eventual EU membership. EU officials emphasized, however, that progress on Serbia's candidacy would depend on cooperation with the war crimes tribunal at the Hague, the Netherlands, in bringing to justice several alleged war criminals from the Bosnian War (1992-1995). On July 21, Serbian police arrested Radovan Karadzic, the alleged mastermind of the 1995 Srebrenica massacre in which Bosnian Serb soldiers killed more than 7,000 Bosnian Muslim men and boys. However, a close associate of Karadzic, General Ratko Mladic, remained at liberty as of late 2008.   ■ Sharon L. Wolchik

See also **Europe; Kosovo.**

Sierra Leone. See Africa.

Former Serb leader Radovan Karadzic appears before a judge at the International Criminal Tribunal for the former Yugoslavia at The Hague, the Netherlands, in July 2008. Allegedly the mastermind behind the 1995 mass murder of Muslim men and boys during the Bosnian war, Karadzic was charged with genocide.

Bode Miller of the United States sweeps down a slope on Jan. 13, 2008, in Wengen, Switzerland, during a downhill race on the Alpine skiing World Cup circuit. Miller won his second World Cup overall title on March 13. He captured the super-combined title on February 3.

Singapore. On July 8, 2008, the International Bar Association's Human Rights Institute released a report criticizing Singapore's ruling People's Action Party (PAP) for using defamation lawsuits to silence the opposition and the press. The report expressed concern about the independence and impartiality of Singapore's judges, suggesting that they support the government on political matters.

The Supreme Court of Singapore on Oct. 14, 2008, ordered the Singapore Democratic Party (SDP), along with its head, Chee Soon Juan, and his sister, to pay $416,000 in defamation damages for implying that Prime Minister Lee Hsien Loong and his father, former Prime Minister Lee Kuan Yew, were involved in corruption. Chee, who had been personally bankrupted by an earlier defamation suit by Lee Kuan Yew and another former prime minister, Goh Chok Tong, said that the new ruling might bankrupt the SDP.

Prime Minister Lee warned in an August 17 speech that Singapore's low birth rate meant that the island state's population would drop by half in one generation. The government had long urged couples to have more children, and Lee announced approximately $496 million in new child incentives, including extended maternity leave. ■ Henry S. Bradsher

See also **Asia.**

Skating. See Hockey; Ice skating; Sports.

Skiing. American skiers enjoyed their best season in a generation in 2008 as Bode Miller and Lindsey Vonn each captured World Cup overall titles, the first United States sweep of those crowns since Phil Mahre and Tamara McKinney pulled it off in 1983. U.S. skiers took 3 of the 10 discipline crowns.

Men. Miller, who captured the super-combined title on Feb. 3, 2008, wrapped up his second overall title (the first was in 2005) on March 13, 2008, in Bormio, Italy, when Switzerland's Didier Cuche bowed out of the final slalom of the year. Miller finished with 1,409 points, well ahead of Austria's Benjamin Raich (1,298) and Cuche (1,263).

Miller was denied a chance to win the downhill title when the final race of the season on March 12 was canceled, allowing Cuche to take the discipline by five points. American Ted Ligety captured the giant slalom title on March 14 by winning the final race of the season, at Bormio, to hold off Raich.

Austria's Hannes Reichelt won the final supergiant of the season on March 13 by just .001 second and captured the title by one point over Cuche, who finished 16th in the race. Italy's Manfred Moelgg took the slalom title on the final race of the season on March 15, with a sixth-place finish. France's Jean-Baptiste Grange, who led going into the final race, slipped on his second run and finished last.

Women. Vonn, the season's downhill champion, captured the overall title—her first—on March 14, with her 11th-place finish in the final slalom of the season. She finished with 1,403 points to beat the 2007 overall champ, Austria's Nicole Hosp. Denise Karbon locked up the giant slalom title on March 1, 2008, the first Italian woman to win that discipline in 11 years, when the race in Zwiesel, Germany, was canceled. Germany's Maria Riesch captured two individual disciplines, the super-combined and the super-giant, and Austria's Marlies Schild won the slalom title.

Cross-country skiing. Finland's Virpi Kuitunen won her second straight World Cup overall title with a seventh-place finish in the women's 30-kilometer race at Oslo, Norway, on March 8. Czech Lukas Bauer clinched the men's overall title on March 5, despite missing the race in Drammen, Norway, because his main rival also missed the race.

Ski jumping. Thomas Morgenstern of Austria wrapped up his first title with six competitions remaining on the schedule by finishing fifth on February 17 in Willingen, Germany. He won the first six competitions at the start of the 2007-2008 season, a record.   ■ Michael Kates

See also **Sports.**

Slovakia. In May 2008, the European Commission, the executive arm of the European Union (EU), declared that Slovakia had met the economic criteria required to adopt the euro currency and recommended that Slovakia be admitted to the eurozone, the bloc of EU countries using the euro, on Jan. 1, 2009. Slovakia will be the first formerly Communist Warsaw Pact nation to use the euro. The country's economic growth surpassed 7 percent in 2008.

In April, Prime Minister Robert Fico obtained parliamentary approval for a stringent "right of reply" law that applies to all media. The law required media, including newspapers, to provide a forum for responses from anyone taking issue with a published story. Critics alleged that the intended purpose of the legislation was to give politicians a measure of control over the press.

In May, the Slovak parliament ratified the Lisbon Treaty. The treaty, a replacement for a proposed constitution that EU members rejected in 2005, is to streamline decision making within EU institutions.

Slovakia declined to recognize Kosovo after that Balkan country declared independence in February 2008. Analysts speculated that Slovak leaders did not want to encourage separatist sentiments among Slovakia's Hungarian minority.   ■ Sharon L. Wolchik

Soccer. Big money and global marketing bankrolled playing success on the professional soccer field in 2008. England's Premier League continued to lead world clubs in earnings—with a three-year broadcast-rights deal worth over $4 billion, and the top-earning Manchester United earning $450 million in 2006-2007 (the last year for which figures were available), according to the 2008 Football Money League report by the British financial consulting firm Deloitte LLP. The Premier League had seen more than 20 changes of club ownerships since 2005, with over $2 billion changing hands. The latest injection of foreign capital came with the acquisition of Manchester City by Abu Dhabi United Group. The new owners' spending started with the signing of Real Madrid's Brazilian star Robinho for nearly $60 million.

Coaching changes. In England, Chelsea coach Avram Grant (successor to Jose Mourinho, who moved to Italy's Inter Milan) was sacked in favor of Portugal coach Luiz Felipe Scolari. Kevin Keegan walked out on Newcastle; Gianfranco Zola replaced Alan Curbishley at West Ham; Harry Redknapp left Portsmouth for Tottenham Hotspur. Mark Hughes switched from Blackburn to Manchester City after ex-England coach Sven-Goran Eriksson signed to manage the Mexico national team.

World soccer. Manchester United took the FIFA Club World Cup (played in December 2008 in Japan) beating Liga de Quito (Ecuador) 1-0. (FIFA is the Fédération Internationale de Football Association, the governing body for international soccer.) ES Setif (Algeria) captured the Arab Champions League final in May, beating WAC Casablanca (Morocco) by 1-0.

The CONCACAF (The Confederation of North, Central America and Caribbean Association Football) Champions Cup was won in April by 2007 champions Pachuca of Mexico, who beat Costa Rica's Deportivo Saprissa 3-2 on aggregate over two matches. In South America's Copa Libertadores, Liga de Quito made history in June 2008 by beating Fluminense (Rio de Janeiro) on penalties after the scores finished 5-5 over a two-game final. They were the first team from Ecuador to win the prestigious trophy. In the Copa Nissan Sudamericana, Internacional took Brazil's first title, beating Argentina's Estudiantes 2-0 in December, also over two legs.

The final of Africa's CAF (Confederation of African Football) Champions League matched CotonSport Garoua (Cameroon) with Al-Ahly (Egypt). The Egyptians won the November final 4-2 on aggregate to take their sixth consecutive championship and earn entry as the CAF representative in the 2009 Confederations Cup. In zonal competition for qualification in the 2010 World Cup in South Africa, the United States team made its first visit to Cuba in more than 60 years on September 6, winning 1-0, and then won the home match 6-1 in October in Washington, D.C.

European club soccer. England's Premier League champions Manchester United edged out Chelsea on the final day, May 11. The FA (Football Association) Cup went to Portsmouth, victors over second-tier Championship team Cardiff 1-0 at London's rebuilt Wembley stadium on May 17. Celtic were Scottish league champions, and rivals Rangers won the Scottish Cup, defeating Queen of the South 3-2 on May 24. The big clubs' domination was unlikely to be seriously challenged while they could pay out huge transfer fees and massive wages. Chelsea's John Terry and other Premier League stars, for example, earned around $230,000 a week .

In Serie A (Italy), the traditional dominance of the "big four"—Inter Milan, AC Milan, Roma, and Juventus—was challenged by Fiorentina and other upstarts. Nevertheless, Inter Milan recorded their third Italian championship in a row (and their 16th overall).

In Spain, Real Madrid and Barcelona continued to dominate the Primera Liga, though Sevilla, Valencia, and Villareal threatened this traditional state of affairs. In Germany's Bundesliga, Bayern Munich, with six titles in nine seasons, took their 21st German championship overall and a domestic league and cup double (their third in four seasons) in May, while Lyons won a seventh consecutive championship in France. Encouragingly, it was still possible for lesser clubs to reach the top. Hull City won promotion to England's Premier League for the 2008-2009 season, and 1899 Hoffenheim climbed high in the Bundesliga, having been an amateur side in the 1990's.

European Champions League. Seventy-six clubs from 53 affiliated associations took part in the UEFA (Union of European Football Associations) Europeans Champions' League in 2007-2008. Spain, Italy, and England each supplied four club teams, with other nations fielding from one to three teams, based on domestic league or cup standings. Three of the four semifinalists (Liverpool, Chelsea, and Manchester United) came from the Premier League. Manchester United triumphed in the final in Moscow on May 21, defeating Chelsea 6-5 on penalty shoot-out goals after 120 minutes of high-speed action ended in a 1-1 stalemate. Zenit St Petersburg (Russia) won the UEFA Cup by 2-0 over Rangers (Scotland) at Manchester (England) on May 14.

Euro 2008. The European nations' championship tournament, cohosted by Switzerland and Austria, produced exciting matches, yet few moments of the highest class. The four semifinalists were Germany, Spain, Turkey and Russia. In the final at Vienna, Austria, on June 29, Spain defeated Germany 1-0, thanks to a goal from Fernando Torres. It was Spain's first victory in an international tournament since 1964.

Olympic Games. At the 2008 Summer Olympic Games in Beijing in August, the men's gold medal winners were Argentina, who beat Nigeria by 1-0. The United States won its 1,000th gold medal, thanks to its women's soccer team and scorer Carli Lloyd, who earned the Americans a 1-0 win in the medal final against Brazil. With the next Olympic Games scheduled for London in 2012, there was speculation that host nation the United Kingdom might field a unified national team. Historically, the four divisions of the United Kingdom (England, Wales, Scotland, and Northern Ireland) have entered separate teams in international soccer competitions.

Major League Soccer (MLS). Top-grade pro soccer in the United States continued to flourish. The 2008 MLS playoffs (three teams each from Eastern and Western standings) resulted in the redesigned Philip F. Anschutz Trophy going to Columbus Crew, 3-1- winners against New York Red Bulls on November 23. The Lamar Hunt U.S. Open Cup saw U.S. League outfit Charleston Battery go down 1-2 to DC United of the MLS on September 3. In the 2008 MLS All Stars game, MLS All-Stars maintained their winning streak against international opposition, defeating England's West Ham United 3-2. LA Galaxy continued to pull in the biggest crowds, thanks to stars such as David Beckham (loaned to AC Milan at season's end) and ace striker Landon Donovan.

SuperLiga. This premier tournament climaxed in August. It brought together four U.S. and four Mexican teams, with the winner taking home a $1-million prize, the largest incentive in North American soccer history. The four U.S. teams were 2007 Supporter's Shield winner D.C. United; Western Conference champion Chivas USA; MLS Cup 2007 winners Houston Dynamo; and MLS Cup finalist New England Revolution. From the group phase, the 2008 finalists were both American: New England Revolution defeating Houston Dynamo 6-5 in a penalty shootout (2-2 at full time) at Gillette Stadium in Foxborough, Massachusetts, on August 5.

Women's soccer. In British domestic competition, Arsenal set a record of nine FA Women's Cup victories, beating Leeds United 4-1 in May 2008, in their third win in successive finals. The Olympic success of the American women's squad, who on August 21 secured the third U.S. gold medal in women's soccer history, was a triumph for new Swedish head coach Pia Sundhage. A year of squad disharmony had followed the team's third-place finish in the 2007 World Cup in China. ■ Brian Williams

See also **Sports.**

Social Security. In their 2008 reports, the Social Security and Medicare trustees projected that, without reforms, the Social Security trust fund would be exhausted by 2041, and the Medicare hospital insurance trust fund would be exhausted by 2019—in each case, the same year that the trustees had projected in 2007. The 2008 reports, issued on March 25, also predicted that both funds' payments to beneficiaries would grow rapidly between 2010 and 2030 and that Medicare payments would continue to grow rapidly after 2030. Social Security payments would begin to exceed tax receipts in 2017, the trustees said, and Medicare hospital insurance payments were expected to begin exceeding tax and premium revenues in 2008. The rise in payments was expected because of the retirement of *baby boomers*—the 76 million Americans born from 1946 to 1964—and, in the case of Medicare, because of rising health care costs. The first baby boomers began receiving their first Social Security benefits in 2008.

On Oct. 16, 2008, the Social Security Administration announced that monthly Social Security and Supplemental Security Income benefits would increase by 5.8 percent in 2009. This cost-of-living adjustment was higher than the 2.3-percent increase in 2008. ■ Mike Lewis

See also **Health care issues.**

Solomon Islands. See **Pacific Islands.**

South Africa. On Sept. 21, 2008, President Thabo Mbeki resigned one day after the National Executive Committee (NEC) of the ruling African National Congress (ANC) demanded he leave office. The shock came amid suggestions that he may have interfered in a corruption case against Jacob Zuma, who had ousted Mbeki as ANC leader in December 2007. During his presidency, Mbeki was often criticized for blaming the nation's AIDS epidemic on poverty and for being lenient with the corrupt regime of President Robert Mugabe of neighboring Zimbabwe.

Mbeki—who had been elected South Africa's president after Nelson Mandela retired in 1999—was replaced as interim head of state by Kgalema Motlanthe, the ANC deputy leader. The changes opened the way for Zuma to become the nation's president after general elections scheduled for April 2009. The South African president is not elected by popular vote, as is the case in most republics, but by the members of both houses of Parliament in a joint parliamentary session. Mbeki's sacking also laid the groundwork for the launch of a breakaway group from South Africa's ruling party in December 2008.

Corruption case. Nine days before Mbeki's resignation, Judge Chris Nicholson threw out a bribes and fraud case against Zuma, who had been facing corruption charges for years, on a technicality. The long-running allegations dated back to a multibillion-dollar arms deal South Africa signed in the late 1990's. In June 2005, Zuma's financial adviser, Schabir Shaik, had been sentenced to 15 years in prison for soliciting bribes for Zuma from a French armaments company to help win the huge defense contract in 1999.

In his 2008 ruling, Nicholson referred to a "titanic political struggle" between Zuma and Mbeki and said two successive justice ministers had meddled in Zuma's prosecution, a claim denied by Mbeki. However, the judge did not rule on Zuma's guilt or innocence. Zuma had also been prosecuted for rape charges, but he was acquitted in April 2006.

ANC split. Mbeki's enforced departure from the presidency exposed deep divisions within the ANC, heightening speculation of a major split inside the ruling party. By the end of 2008, the key fault line lay between factions loyal to Thabo Mbeki and the supporters of populist ANC party leader, Jacob Zuma. Dissident members of the ANC, led by former party chairman and defense minister Mosiuoa Lekota, launched their own party called the Congress of the People (COPE), claiming that the ANC leadership had lost touch with democracy and the people. Analysts said that the ANC's huge electoral support had given South Africa characteristics of a one-party state and that a split would provide a viable opposition.

COPE's first electoral test came in early December when its candidates stood as independents in local elections in the Western Cape province. They won 10 out of 27 seats previously held by the ANC. The result suggested that COPE could present a formidable threat to the ANC at a national level.

Riots. On May 21, following nine days of widespread *xenophobic* (fear of foreigners) violence against black foreign migrants, President Mbeki ordered the South African National Defense Force (SANDF) into the country's townships to aid the police. The rampaging mobs had hacked at their victims with knives and other weapons and set some victims on fire in scenes reminiscent of the township violence of the apartheid years, when the nation had an official policy of racial segregation. Apartheid ended with the election of Nelson Mandela as president in 1994.

Since 2000, some 3 million Zimbabwean refugees had fled violence and poverty to settle in South Africa. Millions of other immigrants came from other neighboring countries, as well as from countries as far afield as Nigeria and Somalia. The refugees had often been accused of pushing up unemployment, crime, and worsening housing shortages.

The attacks, which began in mid-May, spread from Johannesburg and other northern areas to Durban and the Cape. The violence left at least 56 dead, and hundreds of others maimed and injured. Some 50,000 foreign Africans were forced from their homes before the return of relative calm by the end of May. Critics claimed that President Mbeki was conspicuous by his absence—during the worst of the violence, he was attending meetings elsewhere in Africa—and called for his resignation. Others said that his refusal to come to grips with the grave economic and political problems in Zimbabwe had been a key factor in the arrival of refugees.

Police scandal. Jackie Selebi, South Africa's national police commissioner, resigned as president of the International Criminal Police Organization (Interpol—a body with 187 member countries) on Jan. 13, 2008. Prosecutors had indicated that he would face corruption charges for allegedly taking payoffs from Glenn Agliotti, a convicted drug smuggler. In return, Selebi allegedly tipped off Agliotti about police anti-drug activities. Selebi was given an extended leave of absence from his duties as police chief while the prosecution prepared its case.

The scandal was an embarrassment for President Mbeki, who had long defended Selebi and had agreed to abolish the Directorate of Special Operations (also known as the Scorpions), the team investigating Selebi, in December 2007. The Scorpions were disbanded in October 2008. In 2008, South Africa had one of the highest crime rates in the world, with some 50 murders and 125 rapes reported every day.

Elephant cull. In a controversial decision, the government decided that South Africa would for the first time since 1994 reintroduce elephant *culling* (selective killing) after May 1, 2008. The reintroduction of the practice was designed to tackle a surge in the elephant population—from 8,000 in 1994 to over 18,000 in 2008. Ecologists claimed that the animals' huge appetites were reducing parts of the Kruger National Park and other game reserves to flatland, threatening areas of high biodiversity. However, some conservationists argued that the environmental impact was less severe than claimed, and animal rights activists threatened to call for a tourist boycott of the country in protest.

Nelson Mandela, South Africa's highly respected president from 1994 to 1999, celebrated his 90th birthday on July 18, 2008. The event was marked by a series of parties, including a huge rock concert on June 27 in Hyde Park, London.

■ Simon Baynham

See also **Africa; Zimbabwe.**

South America. See **Latin America** and the various country articles.

Space exploration. The International Space Station (ISS) grew dramatically in 2008 with the addition of new European and Japanese laboratories. Chinese astronauts conducted their first spacewalk, and India launched an orbiter to the moon. The United States National Aeronautics and Space Administration's (NASA's) Phoenix lander touched down near the North Pole of Mars. Other space probes reported new findings as they explored several planets in the solar system and their satellites.

International Space Station. During the 10 years that the ISS has been under construction, what had been essentially a long, skinny tube consisting of three modules has grown into a sprawling complex a little wider than a football field. And it is still growing. During three busy space shuttle missions in 2008, astronauts added Europe's Columbus laboratory and most of Japan's Kibo (*hope* in Japanese) lab to the station, along with the Canadian-built dexterous manipulator dubbed Dextre.

Columbus went first, carried aboard the space shuttle Atlantis in February. The crews used the shuttle and station robotic arms to plug the pressurized cylinder into the side of the Harmony node, which had been added to the station in 2007. After Columbus was checked for leaks, the crews set up the racks of experiments that scientists will use to learn how life forms that evolved in Earth's gravity adapt to its absence and how familiar materials behave in that environment.

The installation process was repeated twice more—in March and June 2008—when the shuttles Endeavour and Discovery installed Kibo. First Endeavour carried into orbit a small pressurized module that will serve as Kibo's attic (storage space) and temporarily mounted it on Harmony. Endeavour's crew also donned space suits to assemble Dextre and place it on the outside of Columbus for a series of tests. Eventually, the station crew will use the robot with its two 11-foot (3.4-meter) arms to replace worn-out hardware by remote control, eliminating risky spacewalks.

In June, Discovery carried up the main Kibo laboratory. After it, too, had been checked for leaks, the shuttle and station crews pulled experiment racks out of the Kibo attic and set them up inside the lab. At 36 feet (11 meters) in length, Kibo became the largest pressurized laboratory in space. An additional mission in 2009 will add a "porch" (outside platform) to Kibo for experiments in the vacuum of space.

In April 2008, NASA astronaut Peggy Whitson completed her second trip to the ISS. In 2002, Whitson served as a crew member on the station. In 2008, she returned as commander of Expedition 16—the first woman to command the space

Earth appears in an image captured by a camera aboard Chandrayaan-1, India's first spacecraft to travel beyond low-Earth orbit. The Indian Space Research Organization launched Chandrayaan-1 in October from its launch site off the Bay of Bengal. After circling Earth several times, the spacecraft in November went into orbit around the moon, its primary mission.

China, India, and Japan celebrated landmark space missions in 2008.

Craters on the moon appear in stunning detail in an image (left) taken by Chandrayaan-1. The probe allowed India to join China, Japan, Russia, the United States, and the European Space Agency in exploring the moon. The craft was to construct a three-dimensional atlas of the surface as well as maps of chemical and mineralogical deposits.

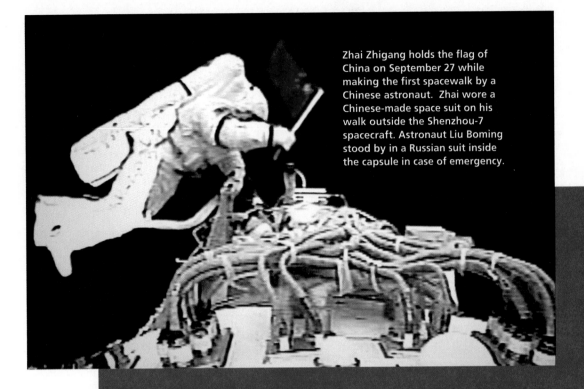

Zhai Zhigang holds the flag of China on September 27 while making the first spacewalk by a Chinese astronaut. Zhai wore a Chinese-made space suit on his walk outside the Shenzhou-7 spacecraft. Astronaut Liu Boming stood by in a Russian suit inside the capsule in case of emergency.

Mission Specialist Akihiko Hoshide of the Japanese Aerospace Exploration Agency—a partner in the International Space Station—works aboard the Kibo laboratory (below). Kibo (*hope* in Japanese) represents Japan's contribution to the international effort. It was carried aloft by the space shuttle Discovery in June.

A white substance, identified by scientists as ice, shines through the red dirt of Mars at the base of a trench dug by the robotic arm of NASA's Phoenix lander in June. The lander, which searched for evidence of life on Mars, confirmed the presence there of water-ice, detected by an orbiting probe in 2002.

station. When she landed, she set the U.S. record for total time in space—377 days. Whitson returned to Earth aboard a Soyuz capsule with Russian cosmonaut Yuri Malenchenko and Yi So-yeon, who became South Korea's first space traveler during her 9 days aboard the ISS. Yi herself had traveled to the ISS aboard a Soyuz with Russian cosmonaut Sergei Volkov, whose father, Alexander Volkov, spent 391 days in space in the 1980's and 1990's.

In addition to Russia's Progress unpiloted cargo capsules, which fly food, fuel, air, and other supplies to the ISS from Russia's Baikonur launch site, Whitson's crew hosted the new European Automated Transfer Vehicle (ATV) as well. The ATV, launched from French Guiana in April 2008, is also a pilotless cargo ship. It is to take over some station resupply duties when the space shuttles stop flying around 2010. The first ATV, named Jules Verne after the pioneering French science-fiction writer, docked at the station in a nearly flawless demonstration of its capabilities. After its supplies were unloaded, it was filled with trash and sent to burn up in the atmosphere over the Pacific Ocean. Future ATV's may be equipped with heat shields that will allow them to be reused.

The final shuttle flight of 2008 was launched to the ISS on November 14. It carried additional equipment that will allow larger crews to live and work aboard the orbiting outpost. A shuttle flight to repair the Hubble Space Telescope was postponed until 2009.

China's first spacewalk. On Sept. 25, 2008, China sent three astronauts into space, where they conducted that nation's first spacewalk. Zhai Zhigang, Liu Boming, and Jing Haipeng—all fighter pilots—lifted off in their Shenzhou 7 spacecraft atop a Long March 2F rocket from China's Jiuquan launch center. During the three-day mission, Zhai tested a new Chinese-made spacesuit in the vacuum of space, with Liu standing by in a Russian suit in case of problems. Chinese astronauts became only the third group—after those from the United States and the Soviet Union—to perform a spacewalk.

India reaches for the moon. India undertook its first mission beyond low Earth orbit on October 22, as its Chandrayaan-1 orbiter took off from a spaceport off the coast of Andhra Pradesh for the moon. The spacecraft is to orbit the moon for two years, mapping its surface and searching for helium-3 (a fuel required for nuclear fusion) and for water. India joined China, Japan, Russia, the United States, and the European Space Agency in lunar exploration.

NASA's Phoenix lander touched down on schedule on May 25 in the northern latitudes of Mars, a region selected because the ice cap there may play a role in shaping the planet's climate. The spacecraft's science team confirmed the long-expected presence of water at the site. But they also found unexpected data in the dust and ice its robotic arm scooped into high-tech laboratory beakers and a heater, including the presence of perchlorate, a chemical that could provide food for primitive life forms. In November, NASA declared an end to the mission, as a dust storm and the Martian winter drained the spacecraft's batteries.

Exploring Mercury and Saturn. In January and October 2008, NASA's Messenger probe made

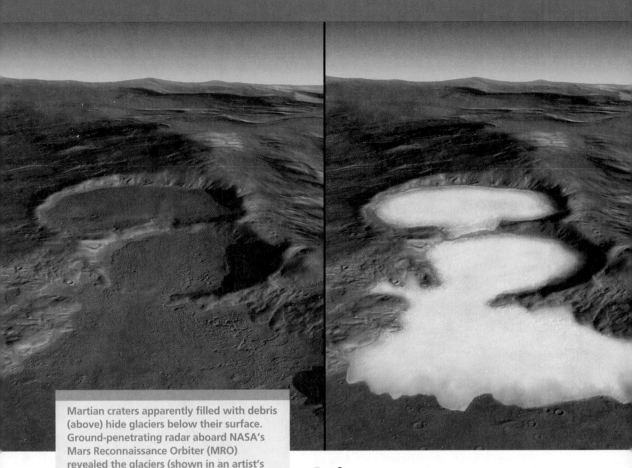

Martian craters apparently filled with debris (above) hide glaciers below their surface. Ground-penetrating radar aboard NASA's Mars Reconnaissance Orbiter (MRO) revealed the glaciers (shown in an artist's conception, above right), in November at middle latitudes, where they had not been suspected before. The glaciers may be vast and up to 0.5 mile (0.8 kilometer) thick.

two close fly-bys of Mercury as it worked its way into orbit around the closest planet to the sun. Launched in 2004, the space probe's January fly-by was the first visit to Mercury since 1975. Although at a distance Mercury looks a lot like the cratered face of Earth's moon, planetary scientists saw long cliffs and troughs in the close-up view that do not occur on the moon. A third fly-by is set for 2009, before Messenger goes into orbit for at least a year of close study in 2011.

In orbit around Saturn since 2004, NASA's Cassini spacecraft continued in 2008 to return spectacular images of the ringed planet and its moons. During several close fly-bys, the nuclear-powered probe traveled through ice geysers erupting from deep cracks near the south pole of the tiny moon Enceladus, where researchers believe liquid water lies not far underground. Radar data from Cassini also suggest that there is an ocean of water and ammonia beneath the surface of Titan, the largest of Saturn's moons.

■ Frank Morring, Jr.

See also **Astronomy**.

Spain. On March 9, 2008, the governing Socialist Workers' Party (PSOE) led by José Luiz Rodríguez Zapatero narrowly defeated the conservative opposition People's Party (PP) in a national election. Zapatero's party performed better than it had in the 2004 election. Nevertheless, the PSOE did not win an outright majority of seats. The party was forced, once again, to form a minority government in which each major piece of legislation requires the agreement of smaller regional and separatist parties. The opposition PP campaigned against Zapatero's record of devolution of power to regional governments and openness to abortion and gay marriage. The strategy largely failed because Spain's economy has performed so well since 2004, when Zapatero was elected following a terrorist attack on trains in Madrid.

Regional discontent. Spain's Catalan and Basque regions continued to press for more regional autonomy. The Basque regional premier, Juan José Ibarretxe, in May 2008 called for a referendum on two issues. The first involved peace talks with the armed separatist group ETA, whose initials stand for Basque Homeland and Freedom in the Basque language. ETA ended a cease-fire agreement in December 2006 and resumed bombing in its 40-year struggle to win independence for the Basque region.

The second issue concerned who has the right

to decide whether the Basque region should be given greater autonomy—the Basque people or all the people of Spain. Zapatero claimed that such a referendum violates the Constitution. In September 2008, Spain's highest court agreed with Zapatero and rejected the plan.

The global stage. In November, Zapatero called for his country's inclusion in the group of 20 countries invited by United States President George W. Bush to Washington, D.C., to discuss the future of global financial markets. He argued that Spain's high GDP and role in international investment merit the country's inclusion in the group of economically powerful nations. Even though Zapatero was not invited, analysts considered his move an important first step in Spain's assuming a larger role in global economic affairs.

Economy. Spain's strong economic growth, based on steadily rising real estate and housing prices, came to a crashing halt in 2008, when housing prices tumbled and global financial markets lurched into crisis. The government instituted programs to buy bank loans, guarantee bank borrowing, and support mortgage payments for homeowners who lost their jobs. Because of the slowdown in the construction industry, the unemployment rate rose quickly. European Union (EU) economists projected that Spain's unemployment rate would top 15 percent by the end of the year, the highest in Europe. EU economists also forecast that Spain's economy would grow by only 1.3 percent in 2008, down from 3.7 percent in 2007.

■ Jeffrey Kopstein

See also **Bank: A Special Report; Europe.**

Sports. In 2008, Carlos Sastre became the third Spaniard in a row to claim bicycling's crown jewel, the Tour de France. But doping scandals once again cast a shadow over the race with four positive drug tests—including one on the race's final day—as well as police raids of hotels where several racing teams were staying and the arrest of a number of cyclists.

In professional team sports, the Boston Celtics captured their first title since 1986 but placed 17th overall in the National Basketball Association (NBA). The Celtics became just the third NBA team since 1950 to win the title a year after missing the play-offs, joining the 1975 Golden State Warriors and the 1977 Portland Trail Blazers.

The Detroit Red Wings in 2008 won their fourth Stanley Cup in 11 years in the National Hockey League (NHL). The New York Giants stunned unbeaten New England to win the 2008 Super Bowl in the National Football League (NFL) and denied the Patriots' bid to become the first team to go 19-0. The Philadelphia Phillies captured Major League Baseball's World Series.

In the Professional Golf Association (PGA),

Tiger Woods captured another major title before season-ending surgery, opening the door for Padraig Harrington of Ireland to win the season's final two majors. In tennis, Spain's Rafael Nadal won two majors and overtook Roger Federer as the world's number-one player, ending the Swiss player's 4 ½-year hold on the top ranking. Federer moved to second for all-time majors won after capturing his 13th, the U.S. Open, in September.

Danica Patrick became the first female driver in a major auto racing circuit to win a race. She came in first in the Indy Racing League's Japan 300 in Motegi, Japan, on April 20.

Tour de France. Sastre, who finished in the top 10 five times in the previous six Tour de Frances, won the 2,212-mile (3,560-kilometer) race on July 28, beating the 2007 runner-up, Cadel

Cyclists wind through the Alps between Embrun and Prato Nevoso, France, during the 2008 Tour de France. Carlos Sastre of Spain won the race on July 28, beating Cadel Evans of Australia by 58 seconds.

Evans of Australia, by 58 seconds. Austria's Bernhard Kohl was third, 1 hour and 13 seconds behind Sastre. The 33-year-old Sastre took the lead during the most difficult Alpine climb—Stage 17 into the Alpe d'Huez—and never gave it back.

Four riders were expelled for failing drug tests, including one on the final day. Two more riders tested positive after the race. Veteran Spanish rider Manuel Beltrán was the first to be expelled. A teammate of champion American cyclist Lance Armstrong, Beltrán had led Armstrong up steep climbs during Armstrong's 2003, 2004, and 2005 Tour de France victories. Beltrán tested positive following the first stage on July 5, 2008. He was taken away by French police as officers raided the team's hotel, and he was expelled on July 6.

Race officials were hoping the 2008 Tour would mark a turning point in the sport's battle against blood doping after a series of high-level scandals the past two years. All cyclists were given pre-Tour blood testing. Some, like Beltrán, were targeted because of abnormal results in their pretest.

At the track cycling world championships in late March in Manchester, England, the United Kingdom claimed nine gold medals and broke three world records.

Awards. University of Florida quarterback Tim Tebow became the first sophomore ever to win the Heisman Trophy. Tebow also won the 78th Amateur Athletic Union (AAU) Sullivan Award, which is presented to the top amateur athlete in the United States. Tebow is the only player in National Collegiate Athletic Association

(NCAA) history to rush and pass for at least 20 touchdowns in a single season.

Biathlon. At the World Championships in Östersund, Sweden, in early February, Ole Einar Bjoerndalen of Norway won the 12.5-kilometer pursuit for his eighth career individual gold medal at the competition. Maxim Tchoudov of Russia won the 10-kilometer sprint. In women's competition, Andrea Henkel of Germany captured the 10-kilometer pursuit and the 7.5-kilometer sprint. Emil Hegle Svendsen of Norway won the men's 20-kilometer individual and 15-kilometer mass, and Yekaterina Yuryeva of Russia won the women's 15-kilometer event.

Bobsled and skeleton. In February in Altenberg, Germany, Sandra Kiriasis of Germany became the first woman to capture the two-woman title at three bobsled World Championships, teaming with Romy Logsch. Kiriasis won her sixth straight season title. German Andre Lange piloted to both the two-man and four-man titles, with Kevin Kuske as his brakeman. Lange had also won the men's two-man and four-man season titles. Germany won the team title. The United Kingdom's Kristan Bromley won the men's skeleton title and Anja Huber of Germany, the women's skeleton title at the World Championships in February. Bromley and Canada's Michelle Kelly won the World Cup skeleton titles for the 2007-2008 season.

Equestrian. Anky van Grunsven of the Netherlands won the 2008 World Cup Final dressage title in Hertogenbosch, the Netherlands, in March. Meredith Michaels-Beerbaum of Germany took the individual show jumping championship, in Göteborg, Sweden, in April.

Luge. Germany won 9 of 10 medals at the world championships on January 25-27 in Oberhof, Germany. André Florschütz and Torsten Wustlich won the men's doubles, with teammates Tobias Wendl and Tobias Arlt in second. In men's single, Felix Loch led a German sweep, and Tatjana Hüfner led a German sweep of the women's single. Germany also won the team event.

Marathon running. Kenyan Robert Cheruiyot became just the fourth man to win four Boston Marathons with his victory on April 21. He finished in 2 hours, 7 minutes, 46 seconds to join Canadian Gerard Cote and Americans Bill Rodgers and Clarence DeMar as men who have won at least four Boston Marathons. In the closest finish in the 112-year history of the women's Boston Marathon, Ethiopia's Dire Tune finished in 2 hours, 25 minutes, 25 seconds to beat Russia's Alevtina Biktimirova by two seconds. Ethiopian Haile Gebrselassie ran the second-fastest marathon ever, 2 hours, 4 minutes, 53 seconds, at the Dubai Marathon on January 18 but fell short of his own world record by 27 seconds.

Nordic combined. German Ronny Ackermann won his third overall title, after previously taking the championship in 2002 and 2003.

Rodeo. Trevor Brazile won his sixth All-Around World Champion Cowboy title in the National Finals Rodeo on Dec. 13, 2008.

Rowing. Canada's Victoria City Rowing Club and Kingston Rowing Club teamed up to capture the marquee event, the Grand Challenge Cup, on July 6 at the Henley Royal Regatta in Henley-on-Thames, United Kingdom, beating a crew from the University of Southern California by two lengths. A team from England's Leander Club beat Studenten Universitiet Okeanos and Delftsche Laga, the Netherlands, by two-thirds of a length to win the Ladies' Challenge Plate. In the Remenham Challenge Cup for international women's eights, a team of England's Leander Club and Wallingford Rowing Club beat a team of England's Furnivall Sculling Club and Leander Club by three lengths.

Sled-dog racing. Lance Mackey of Fairbanks, Alaska, won his second straight Iditarod Trail Sled Dog Race on March 12, finishing the 1,100-mile (1,770-kilometer) course in 9 days, 11 hours, 46 minutes, and 48 seconds. Mackey, who has won the race from Anchorage to Nome, Alaska, four times, shook four-time champion Jeff King at the final checkpoint by pretending to take a nap and then slipping back on to the course while his rival slept.

Soap Box Derby. Girls won five of six individual titles for the first time at the All-American Soap Box Derby on July 26 in Akron, Ohio, sweeping the three major divisions for just the second time. Courtney Rayle, of Mechanicsville, Maryland, won the Masters Division at the age of 16 years, 11 months to become the oldest winner in that division. Other winners were Hayley Beitel (Super Stock), Johanna Barnowski (Stock), Brandon Feagan (Rally Masters), Caitlin Smith (Rally Super Stock), and Megan Newcomer (Rally Stock).

Speed skating. At the World Short Track Championships in Gangneung City, South Korea, American Apolo Anton Ohno claimed the men's overall title, and China's Wang Meng won the women's overall title on March 9. Ohno won by capturing a gold medal in the 500 meters, finishing second in the 1,000 meters, and third in the 3,000 meters. Lee Ho-Suk of South Korea, who won the 1,000 meters, finished second. On the women's side, Wang won gold in the 500 meters, 1,000 meters, and 1,500 meters to easily beat Zhou Yang of China for the overall title. South Korea and China both captured five golds at the event, with South Korea finishing atop the medal table with 13 total medals.

At the World Sprint Speed Skating Championships in Heerenveen, the Netherlands, in January, South Korean Lee Kyou-hyuk won both the 500-meter and 1,000-meter races to take the men's overall title. Jenny Wolf led a 1-2 finish for German women, winning the overall title over Anni Friesinger. Wolf won the 500-meter race, and Ireen Wüst of the Netherlands won the 1,000 meters.

Triathlon. Spain's Javier Gomez took the men's competition at the world championship on June 8 in Vancouver, Canada, winning in 1 hour, 49 minutes, 48 seconds. The United Kingdom's Helen Tucker won the women's competition for her first world title, finishing in 2 hours, 1 minute, and 37 seconds.

Other champions:

Archery. The International Archery Federation's Championships in July in Taipei, Taiwan: men's compound, Rod Menzer, United States; women's compound, Jamie Van Natta, United States; men's recurve, Sebastian Rohrberg, Germany; women's recurve, Jessica Tomasi, Italy; men's barebow, Sergio Cassiani, Italy; women's barebow, Becky Nelson-Harris, United States.

Badminton. World University Championship in May in Braga, Portugal: men's singles, China's Pengyu Du; men's doubles, Indonesia's Bona Septano and Mohammad Ahsan; women's singles, China's Yihan Wang; women's doubles, Thailand's Kunchala Voravichitchaikul and Duanganong Aroonkesorn; mixed-doubles, Thailand's Patiphat Chalardchalaem and Voravichitchaikul.

Curling. World champions: men, Canada; women, Canada; mixed, Switzerland.

Fencing. World championships in April in Beijing, China: men's foil, Italy's Andrea Cassara; men's team foil, Italy; women's epee, Germany's Britta Heidemann; women's team epee, France.

Field hockey. Champions Trophy gold medal: men (in June in the Netherlands), Australia; women (in May in Germany), Argentina.

Lacrosse. Men's NCAA champion, Syracuse University in New York; women's NCAA champion, Northwestern University in Evanston, Illinois.

Motorcyle racing. MotoGP World Champion: Valentino Rossi, Italy.

Table tennis. World Team Champions: men, China; women, China.

Legendary broadcaster dies. Jim McKay, the host of "ABC's Wide World of Sports" for its entire 37 years, died on June 7 at the age of 86. McKay's familiar voice was a part of 12 Olympic Games, including coverage of the hostage situation at the 1972 Munich Games.   ■ Michael Kates

See also **Australian rules football; Baseball; Basketball; Boating; Boxing; Football; Golf; Hockey; Horse racing; Ice skating; Olympic Games: A Special Report; Skiing; Soccer; Swimming; Tennis; Track and field.**

Sri Lanka. In January 2008, the government of Sri Lanka formally ended a 2002 cease-fire agreement with the Liberation Tigers of Tamil Eelam (LTTE). The Tigers had been fighting a war since 1983 for a separate state for the Hindu Tamil minority in the north and east of a mostly Sinhalese Buddhist nation. On June 19, 2008, the World Health Organization, a United Nations affiliate, reported new estimates indicating that 215,000 people had died in the fighting since 1983. The new figure was three times as high as previous estimates.

As fighting escalated in January 2008, the government said the cease-fire had "ceased to have any meaning" and accused the LTTE of using the truce to arm and recruit more fighters. Estimates of Tiger fighters ranged from 5,000 to 10,000, facing an army of 160,000.

Offensive. After ending the cease-fire, the army launched an offensive intended to finally destroy the Tigers. The army chief, General Sarath Fonseka, said in January that he believed the rebels would be defeated in 2008. Government forces, with the cooperation of LTTE defectors, eliminated rebel power in eastern Sri Lanka. A former Tiger commander who had left the LTTE in 2004 won control of the formerly LTTE-controlled Eastern Province in elections held on May 10, 2008.

Fierce fighting throughout the year reduced LTTE control in the country's north. The army closed in on Kilinochchi, the jungle headquarters of Tiger leader Velupillai Prabhakaran. An estimated 200,000 Tamils were forced to flee the area to avoid army gun battles with guerrillas as the bitter war ground on indecisively in late 2008.

Even if the army took control of areas long held by the Tigers, observers warned, sporadic guerrilla warfare could continue. The government showed little sign of preparing political, economic, and cultural changes that might reduce Tamil separatist demands.

Suicide bombers struck repeatedly in Sri Lanka in 2008. A government minister and 13 others were killed while attending a marathon on April 6. Buses in the capital, Colombo, were hit a number of times, with 24 people killed in an April 25 attack. The city's packed railway station was bombed on February 3, killing 11. In the southern town of Buttala, 32 people died on January 16 when rebels bombed a bus and then shot passengers as they attempted to flee.

Economy. Economic growth fell in 2008 while inflation rose above 20 percent. The war and resettlement of refugees cost the government some 30 percent of its budget. Sri Lanka's important garment business faced import restrictions in Europe because of complaints there over Sri Lanka's human rights record.   ■ Henry S. Bradsher

See also **Asia; Terrorism.**

State government. State budgets felt the sting of high unemployment, the financial sector meltdown, and the credit crisis in 2008. Democrats gained a stronger hold on statehouses in the elections. State wins reflected a Democratic resurgence led by Barack Obama's historic win of the United States presidency and the Democratic sweep of the U.S. Congress.

On December 9, Illinois Governor Rod Blagojevich was arrested on federal corruption charges related to the selection of Obama's U.S. Senate successor. Many of the state's political leaders—as well as Obama—called on the governor to resign. The following week, an Illinois House panel began impeachment proceedings against Blagojevich. On December 30, Blagojevich named a former state attorney general, Roland Burris, to fill the Senate seat vacated by President-elect Obama. Senate Democratic leaders responded by issuing a joint statement in which they vowed to block the appointment: "This is not about Mr. Burris; it is about the integrity of a governor accused of attempting to sell this United States Senate seat."

Elections. On November 4, 11 states elected governors. Voters in three states chose new governors. Delaware elected Democrat Jack A. Markell, state treasurer, to replace term-limited Democratic Governor Ruth Ann Minner. Missouri voters chose Democrat Jeremiah W. (Jay) Nixon, attorney general, as their next governor. Republican Missouri Governor Matt Blunt did not seek a second term. In North Carolina, Democratic Lieutenant Governor Beverly Perdue became the state's first female governor, taking over from term-limited Democratic Governor Mike Easley.

In eight other states, current governors won new terms. Incumbent Democratic governors reelected were Brian Schweitzer of Montana, John Lynch of New Hampshire, Christine Gregoire of Washington, and Joe Manchin of West Virginia. Incumbent Republican governors reelected were Mitch Daniels of Indiana, John Hoeven of North Dakota, Jon M. Huntsman, Jr., of Utah, and Jim Douglas of Vermont. Nationwide, the gubernatorial party split stood at 29 Democrats and 21 Republicans after the election.

Voters in 44 states elected 5,824 legislators. The elections resulted in Democrats controlling both legislative chambers in 27 states; the Republican Party (GOP) controlled both chambers in 14 states. After the elections, Democrats dominated both legislative chambers and the governors' offices in 17 states; Republicans controlled 8 states.

Ballot issues. Voters in 36 states also determined the fate of 153 statewide ballot issues on November 4. A host of hot-button issues captured national attention. Arizona, California, and Florida adopted constitutional bans on same-sex marriages. The battle was most intense in California where 11,000 same-sex couples had legally married following the Golden State's June 17 high court decision allowing such unions. California, Colorado, and South Dakota voters refused to further restrict a woman's right to abortion. Washington became the second state to sanction physician-assisted suicide for the terminally ill, joining neighboring Oregon. Michigan voters legalized stem-cell research and approved marijuana for medical purposes. Massachusetts decriminalized possession of an ounce (28 grams) or less of marijuana. Nebraska banned affirmative action. Voters also rejected proposals to rewrite state constitutions in Connecticut, Hawaii, and Illinois.

Gambling measures met varied fates. Arkansas approved a state-run lottery. Maryland legalized slot machines, allowing up to 15,000 at five facilities. Massachusetts banned greyhound racing, effective in 2010. Ohio defeated a casino proposal.

Missouri adopted a measure to require that 15 percent of the state's electricity come from clean alternative sources by 2021. California and Colorado voted against renewable energy proposals seen as costly. California, however, approved borrowing billions of dollars for high-speed rail, hospitals for children, and loans for veterans. Montana expanded children's health care coverage. Maryland approved letting the general assembly enact early voting for elections in the future. Massachusetts voters defeated a proposal to eliminate the state income tax. North Dakota and Oregon rejected tax changes as well.

Governors. In March 2008, New York Governor Eliot Spitzer resigned shortly after it was revealed he had used a prostitution ring under investigation by the federal government. Lieutenant Governor David A. Paterson, a fellow Democrat, succeeded to the office. Paterson was the state's first African American governor and the first legally blind person to hold a governor's office. In August, first-term Alaska Governor Sarah Palin became the first female candidate nominated by the Republican Party to run for U.S. vice president.

Revenue and employment. State officials saw revenues drop drastically. In response, many states laid off employees and cut services. Massachusetts Governor Deval Patrick cut 1,000 jobs and $1 billion in state spending. The governors of California, New Jersey, and New York each called legislative sessions to deal with multibillion-dollar shortfalls. State pension funds across the nation suffered billions of dollars in losses with the financial market slide. High jobless rates strained state unemployment insurance trust funds. California, Michigan, New York, and Ohio were expected to run out of money at the current rate of claims by 2009.

Capital punishment. In April 2008, the U.S. Supreme Court upheld Kentucky's use of lethal injection for capital punishment. The decision

SELECTED STATISTICS ON STATE GOVERNMENTS

State	Resident population*	Governor†	Legislature† House (D)	House (R)	Senate (D)	Senate (R)	State tax revenue‡	Tax revenue per capita‡
Alabama	4,627,851	Bob Riley (R)	62	43	§21	13	$ 8,868,000,000	$1,920
Alaska	683,478	Sarah Palin (R)	18	22	10	10	3,443,000,000	5,040
Arizona	6,338,755	Janet Napolitano (D)	25	35	12	18	12,397,000,000	1,960
Arkansas	2,834,797	Mike Beebe (D)	#71	28	27	8	7,392,000,000	2,610
California	36,553,215	Arnold Schwarzenegger (R)	51	29	26	14	114,737,000,000	3,140
Colorado	4,861,515	Bill Ritter (D)	38	27	21	14	9,206,000,000	1,890
Connecticut	3,502,309	M. Jodi Rell (R)	114	37	24	12	12,848,000,000	3,670
Delaware	864,764	Jack Markell (D)	25	16	16	5	2,906,000,000	3,360
Florida	18,251,243	Charlie Crist (R)	44	76	14	26	35,738,000,000	1,960
Georgia	9,544,750	Sonny Perdue (R)	§74	105	22	34	18,637,000,000	1,950
Hawaii	1,283,388	Linda Lingle (R)	45	6	23	2	5,094,000,000	3,970
Idaho	1,499,402	C. L. "Butch" Otter (R)	18	52	7	28	3,537,000,000	2,360
Illinois	12,852,548	Rod Blagojevich (D)	70	48	37	22	29,517,000,000	2,300
Indiana	6,345,289	Mitch Daniels (R)	§52	47	17	33	14,098,000,000	2,220
Iowa	2,988,046	Chet Culver (D)	56	44	32	18	6,470,000,000	2,170
Kansas	2,775,997	Kathleen Sebelius (D)	48	77	9	31	6,893,000,000	2,480
Kentucky	4,241,474	Steve Beshear (D)	65	35	**15	22	9,895,000,000	2,330
Louisiana	4,293,204	Bobby Jindal (R)	††52	50	‡‡22	15	10,864,000,000	2,530
Maine	1,317,207	John Baldacci (D)	**96	54	20	15	3,582,000,000	2,720
Maryland	5,618,344	Martin O'Malley (D)	**104	36	33	14	15,094,000,000	2,690
Massachusetts	6,449,755	Deval Patrick (D)	**143	16	35	5	20,664,000,000	3,200
Michigan	10,071,822	Jennifer Granholm (D)	67	43	17	21	23,849,000,000	2,370
Minnesota	5,197,621	Tim Pawlenty (R)	87	47	46	21	17,780,000,000	3,420
Mississippi	2,918,785	Haley Barbour (R)	74	48	27	25	6,395,000,000	2,190
Missouri	5,878,415	Jay Nixon (D)	74	89	11	23	10,705,000,000	1,820
Montana	957,861	Brian Schweitzer (D)	50	50	23	27	2,320,000,000	2,420
Nebraska	1,774,571	Dave Heineman (R)	unicameral (49 nonpartisan)				4,071,000,000	2,290
Nevada	2,565,382	Jim Gibbons (R)	28	14	12	9	6,305,000,000	2,460
New Hampshire	1,315,828	John Lynch (D)	225	175	14	10	2,175,000,000	1,650
New Jersey	8,685,920	Jon Corzine (D)	48	32	23	17	29,107,000,000	3,350
New Mexico	1,969,915	Bill Richardson (D)	45	25	27	15	5,205,000,000	2,640
New York	19,297,729	David Paterson (D)	109	41	§32	29	63,162,000,000	3,270
North Carolina	9,061,032	Bev Perdue (D)	68	52	30	20	22,613,000,000	2,500
North Dakota	639,715	John Hoeven (R)	36	58	21	26	1,783,000,000	2,790
Ohio	11,466,917	Ted Strickland (D)	53	46	12	21	24,811,000,000	2,160
Oklahoma	3,617,316	Brad Henry (D)	40	61	22	26	8,906,000,000	2,460
Oregon	3,747,455	Ted Kulongoski (D)	36	24	18	12	7,743,000,000	2,070
Pennsylvania	12,432,792	Ed Rendell (D)	104	99	§20	29	30,838,000,000	2,480
Rhode Island	1,057,832	Don Carcieri (R)	69	6	**33	4	2,766,000,000	2,610
South Carolina	4,407,709	Mark Sanford (R)	53	71	19	27	8,689,000,000	1,970
South Dakota	796,214	Mike Rounds (R)	24	46	**14	20	1,257,000,000	1,580
Tennessee	6,156,719	Phil Bredesen (D)	49	50	14	19	11,345,000,000	1,840
Texas	23,904,380	Rick Perry (R)	§74	75	§12	18	40,315,000,000	1,690
Utah	2,645,330	Jon Huntsman, Jr. (R)	22	53	8	21	5,889,000,000	2,230
Vermont	621,254	James Douglas (R)	§§95	48	23	7	2,559,000,000	4,120
Virginia	7,712,091	Tim Kaine (D)	##44	52	21	19	18,972,000,000	2,460
Washington	6,468,424	Christine Gregoire (D)	64	34	31	18	17,693,000,000	2,740
West Virginia	1,812,035	Joe Manchin III (D)	79	21	28	6	4,654,000,000	2,570
Wisconsin	5,601,640	Jim Doyle (D)	**52	46	18	15	14,483,000,000	2,590
Wyoming	522,830	Dave Freudenthal (D)	§18	41	7	23	2,025,000,000	3,870

*July 1, 2007, estimates. Source: U.S. Census Bureau.
†As of January 2009. Source: National Governors' Association; National Conference of State Legislatures; state government officials.
‡2007 figures. Source: U.S. Census Bureau.
§One vacant/undecided at press time.
#One Green Party

**One independent.
††Three independents.
‡‡Two vacant/undecided at press time.
§§Five Progressive Party, two independents.
##Two independents, two vacant/undecided at press time.

infants at hospitals or other designated facilities without fear of prosecution. The Nebraska law, however, did not specify the age limit for children. During the year, dozens of older children and teenagers from around the country were abandoned by their parents at Nebraska facilities. Legislators determined the law was being abused and limited the age to 30 days. New Jersey became the third state to enact a family-leave law.

Gay marriage. On October 10, the Connecticut Supreme Court overturned a state ban on same-sex marriage. New York Governor Paterson said his state would recognize same-sex unions performed in other states.

Education. Pennsylvania provided its biggest aid increase in 20 years to schools and ordered more equitable financing between districts. The $9.6 billion approved for elementary and secondary education includes a 5.5-percent hike in basic funds. At least 10 states took action to crack down on teachers who sexually abuse students.

Energy and environment. At a climate-change conference at Yale University, 18 states, led by California, pledged to act to reduce greenhouse emissions. Massachusetts passed a number of green measures, mandating a low-carbon fuel standard similar to California's for vehicles. Massachusetts also planned to cut greenhouse-gas emissions and develop wind, wave, and tidal power. Delaware joined a major offshore wind-energy project, making it the first state to meet some of its energy needs from offshore wind turbines. Ohio passed a bill requiring one-fourth of electric power sold by its utilities to come from alternative energy sources by 2025.

Pennsylvania Governor Ed Rendell signed legislation requiring state utilities to cut annual electric-power use by 1 percent by 2011. Florida Governor Crist signed an energy bill codifying many climate-friendly measures. Hawaii's legislature passed a law requiring all households to heat water using solar power. Alaska issued a license, for which federal approval is necessary, to the Trans-Canada company to build a natural gas pipeline from the North Slope to the lower 48 states. ■ Elaine McDonald

See also **Elections: A Special Report.**

ended a seven-month moratorium on all executions nationwide. The Nebraska legislature was left to determine an acceptable method of execution when the state supreme court in February ruled out using the electric chair. In June, the Supreme Court invalidated a Louisiana capital punishment law for the rape of a child.

Health. Florida Governor Charlie Crist pushed through a plan to expand health insurance to uninsured residents ages 19 to 64. New Jersey moved to expand health insurance coverage to more residents. Maine made health care more affordable to healthy younger workers under 30. The state also banned smoking in vehicles with child passengers. Iowa expanded health coverage for children and adopted a statewide ban on smoking in public places, except casinos. Pennsylvania approved a statewide smoking ban. California adopted the first state law to prohibit restaurants from preparing food with trans fats.

Family. Nebraska Governor Dave Heineman called a special session in late 2008 to amend a safe-haven law passed earlier in the year. Such laws are designed to allow parents to leave unwanted

Stocks and bonds. In 2008, the stock market in the United States went through its worst year since 1931, during the Great Depression. Stock market indexes dropped more than 40 percent as some of the nation's largest banks collapsed amid a severe financial crisis, which the U.S. Department of the Treasury and Federal Reserve (the Fed—the nation's central bank) could not tame. The crisis infected the general economy throughout the world as falling stock prices pointed to a global recession.

The stock market decline began in October 2007 and worsened throughout 2008. Prices plunged as the investment bank Bear Stearns & Co. collapsed in March. Stock prices again fell sharply in October after investment bank Lehman Brothers failed, and the federal government was forced to bail out Fannie Mae (Federal National Mortgage Association); Freddie Mac (Federal Home Loan Mortgage Corporation); the insurance giant American International Group, Inc. (AIG); and some of the nation's largest banks.

In just over 13 months, the Dow Jones Industrial Average (an index of the stock prices of 30 major companies) dropped 46.7 percent. On Oct. 9, 2007, the Dow climbed to a record high of 14,164 points. By Nov. 20, 2008, the Dow had slid to 7,997 points, its lowest since 2003. In late November 2008, the market managed to rally more than 10 percent. But investors remained cautious, fearing another downturn as the U.S. *gross domestic product*—the value of all goods and services produced in a country in a year—declined and unemployment rose.

Volatility was extraordinary as the market sometimes swung 700 to 1,000 points in a single day. The New York City-based investment research firm Standard & Poor's reported that the market in 2008 had undergone more moves of 3 percent or greater than at any other time since 1933. By mid-December 2008, fluctuations calmed slightly, even though analysts reported that the nation was in a recession.

The housing-credit crisis. The market downturn grew out of the worst housing recession since the Great Depression. Home prices plunged throughout 2008, and many homeowners with adjustable rate mortgages lost their homes.

Because U.S. lending institutions had packaged many of these *subprime* mortgages (a type of loan granted to people with poor credit histories) into bonds and other securities and sold them worldwide, financial institutions globally suffered billions of dollars in losses. However, financial statements failed to reveal the extent of the losses, and suspicion grew in the financial system. Lenders withheld loans to each other because they feared they would not be repaid. As confidence in banks eroded, a credit crisis developed. It became difficult for consumers and banks and other businesses to access the money they needed, and the economy slowed dramatically.

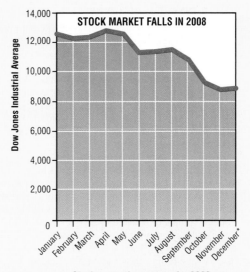

STOCK MARKET FALLS IN 2008

Dow Jones Industrial Average

January February March April May June July August September October November December*

Closing month averages for 2008
* December figure is as of the 16th.

Share prices fell more than 40 percent during 2008, due to a credit crisis involving defaulting subprime mortgages. The Dow reached its lowest at 7,997 points on November 20, then rallied slightly in December.

Rescue efforts. On October 3, the U.S. Congress passed a $700-billion emergency plan—the Troubled Asset Relief Program (TARP)—proposed by the U.S. Treasury and the Fed. The money was intended to shore up the financial system to avert a world-wide panic and depression. However, investors lost confidence in TARP because government leaders seemed to be using the funds through trial and error. In response, the stock market fell futher.

In November, the nation's three automakers—Chrysler Corporation, Ford Motor Company, and General Motors Corporation (GM)—requested a bailout because the financial crisis had severely cut into car sales, leaving automakers on the verge of bankruptcy. On December 19, U.S. President George W. Bush announced that the government would provide $17.4 billion in loans to Chrysler and GM, the two most troubled companies.

Bonds. The financial crisis originated in the bond market. Concern initially centered on mortgage-related bonds but later spread to virtually all bonds except U.S. Treasury bonds. Investors feared that recessionary pressures would cause financial troubles in corporations, cities, and states and lead to huge defaults to bondholders.

Conservative investors poured money into U.S. Treasury bonds despite some of the lowest yields in history. By December, 30-day Treasury bonds were yielding only about 0.10 percent—the lowest in 50 years. Yet, the popularity of the safe bonds forced prices up, and investors in 20-year Treasury bonds were by December earning a 15-percent return for the year.

As states and cities reported shortfalls due to impaired tax receipts, yields on municipal bonds became unusually high compared with Treasury bonds. In November, municipal bond yields averaged 5.4 percent, while long-term Treasury bonds were yielding only 3.7 percent.

As the economy worsened, investors began to expect defaults in corporate bonds, and yields soared to compensate investors for taking risks. By November, 20-year corporate yields rose to 8 percent, and high-yield bonds, which are the riskiest bonds in troubled companies, yielded more than 21.5 percent.

The Madoff scandal. In December 2008, federal prosecutors charged Bernard L. Madoff, a businessman and former chairman of the NASDAQ stock exchange, with one of the largest investment frauds in history. Madoff allegedly ran a giant Ponzi scheme that cost his clients as much as $50 billion. A Ponzi scheme, named for 1920's scam artist Charles Ponzi, involves making investors believe they are receiving profits from successful financial dealings when they are actually being paid with money from other investors. When investment money stops coming in, the scheme collapses.   ■ Gail MarksJarvis

See also **U.S. Government: A Special Report.**

Sudan. Under intense international criticism, Sudan withdrew its nomination to assume the rotating presidency of the African Union (AU) in January 2008. The AU is an organization working to achieve cooperation among African nations. Sudan was condemned because of its human rights record and its handling of the crisis in Darfur, a region in Sudan where government forces and rebel groups had been fighting since 2003. Sudan failed in similar attempts to assume the AU presidency in 2006 and 2007.

Rebel office in Israel. In February 2008, the Sudan Liberation Movement (SLM), one of the major rebel groups in Darfur, announced that it would open an office in Israel. The SLM's leader, Abdul Wahid al-Nur, praised the Israeli government for helping to protect Darfurians from genocide (systematic extermination of a cultural or racial group). Approximately 1,700 refugees from Darfur lived in Israel in 2008.

Intervention in Chad. Three rebel groups in Chad that were armed by the Sudanese government attacked the Chadian capital of N'Djamena in February, reaching the palace of Chad's president, Idriss Déby. The rebels launched their attempt to overthrow Déby from bases in western Sudan. Experts in African affairs explained that Sudan's government sought to overthrow Déby because of his support for rebels in Darfur.

After the Chadian rebels were routed by Chad's army and Sudanese rebel allies, the French minister of defense flew to N'Djamena to reassure President Déby that France would protect Chad against foreign incursions.

Attack on Khartoum. An estimated 3,000 rebel fighters from Darfur staged an attack on Khartoum, the capital of Sudan, on May 10. The rebels advanced to within a few miles of the center of the city before being beaten back by government forces. After the attack, Sudanese authorities reportedly arrested more than 100 individuals believed to be supporters of the rebels, including a number of military officers.

Despite the failure of the attack, the leaders of the Justice and Equality Movement (JEM), a large rebel group, claimed victory. Sudanese officials accused the government of Chad of backing the rebels, noting that JEM fighters helped defend Chadian President Déby in his palace during the February coup (overthrow) attempt.

Some experts in African affairs pointed out that the May attack on Khartoum was likely staged in response to the February attack on N'Djamena. However, other experts believed that the attack on Khartoum was an attempt by the JEM to reach a power-sharing agreement with the Sudanese government by asserting its own strength.

The International Criminal Court (ICC), at The Hague in the Netherlands, indicted President Umar Hassan Ahmad al-Bashir of Sudan on charges of genocide (extermination of an entire people) in July. The action was the ICC's first-ever indictment of a sitting president. Luis Moreno-Ocampo, the ICC prosecutor, charged Bashir with 10 counts of mass crimes, 3 counts of which were for genocide. In the genocide counts, the Sudanese leader was accused of conducting the "ethnic cleansing" of three Darfur tribes by using a rebel insurgency under his control to murder, rape, and deport members of the tribes. Many Sudanese did not recognize the authority of the ICC and protested against the indictment.

UN-AU mission extended. In August, the United Nations (UN) Security Council extended the mandate of the UN-AU Mission in Darfur, a multinational peacekeeping mission in the troubled region. Fourteen member states of the Security Council voted in favor of the extension, while the United States abstained from voting. The U.S. abstention was cast in the context of an attempt by the U.S. government to defer the ICC indictment of President Bashir. United States officials viewed the indictment as an obstacle to ongoing negotiations between the Sudanese government and Sudanese rebels.   ■ Mary-Jane Deeb

See also **Africa; France; United Nations.**

Supreme Court of the United States.

The highest-profile decisions of the Supreme Court's 2007-2008 term dealt with gun rights, the detention of terrorism suspects, and capital punishment.

Gun rights. In a landmark 5-to-4 decision on June 26, 2008, the court struck down the District of Columbia's ban on handgun ownership, ruling that the Second Amendment to the U.S. Constitution protects a person's right to possess firearms for self-defense or other lawful purposes. The Second Amendment reads: "A well-regulated militia, being necessary to the security of a free state, the right of the people to keep and bear arms shall not be infringed." The decision marked the first time in history that the court affirmed an individual constitutional right to own and carry a gun for personal use. The court rejected the notion that the Second Amendment right must be contingent upon service in a militia.

Voting in the majority were the court's conservatives—Chief Justice John Roberts and Justices Samuel Alito, Antonin Scalia, and Clarence Thomas—and the court's centrist swing voter, Justice Anthony Kennedy. The court's liberals—Justices Stephen Breyer, Ruth Bader Ginsburg, David Souter, and John Paul Stevens—dissented.

The D.C. law was the strictest gun control law in the United States. In addition to prohibiting handgun ownership, it required that shotguns and rifles be kept unloaded and disassembled or secured with a trigger lock.

Scalia wrote the majority opinion, and Stevens and Breyer wrote dissenting opinions. All of the opinions included extensive analysis of the text of the Second Amendment, what its purported meaning was at the time of drafting and ratification, and how it had been interpreted throughout its history. All of the opinions also stated that the Second Amendment right is not absolute. In the majority opinion, Scalia listed examples of permissible restrictions under the amendment, including bans on gun possession by felons and the mentally ill, bans on carrying guns in schools and government buildings, and laws imposing conditions on the commercial sale of guns. In the dissenting opinions, Stevens argued that the amendment was intended to protect the right of arms possession for militia service rather than for self-defense, and Breyer argued that the D.C. law was a constitutionally permissible response to the problem of urban crime.

Guantánamo detainees. On June 12, the court ruled 5 to 4 that prisoners at the U.S. naval base at Guantánamo Bay, Cuba, were entitled to the constitutional privilege of habeas corpus—that is, the right to challenge their detention in federal court. The Guantánamo detainees had been captured abroad in the wake of the Sept. 11, 2001, terrorist attacks on the United States and designated as "enemy combatants" by the administration of U.S. President George W. Bush. This designation represented the government's claim that these individuals belonged to the terrorist network al-Qa`ida or the Taliban regime in Afghanistan that supported al-Qa`ida. Both the Bush administration and Congress had sought to deny habeas corpus rights to these detainees. Administration officials argued that because Cuba had legal sovereignty over Guantánamo, the U.S. Constitution did not apply there, but the Supreme Court rejected this argument. The court also ruled that the procedures set up by Congress to review the status of detainees were an inadequate substitute for habeas corpus. Kennedy joined the four liberal justices to form the majority.

Capital punishment. On June 25, 2008, in a 5-to-4 decision, the court struck down a Louisiana law that authorized the death penalty for the crime of child rape. The court ruled that the law violated the U.S. Constitution's Eighth Amendment, which bans cruel and unusual punishments. Capital punishment should not be imposed for crimes that do not result in the victim's death, the court ruled. The four liberal justices, along with Kennedy, made up the majority.

On April 16, in a 7-to-2 decision, the court ruled that Kentucky's method of capital punishment—a lethal injection of three drugs—did not violate the Eighth Amendment. The court rejected the claim that Kentucky was carrying out lethal injections in a manner that posed an unconstitutional risk of serious pain. Most other states in 2008 had an execution method and procedure similar to Kentucky's. Ginsburg and Souter were the dissenting justices.

Voting. In a 6-to-3 decision on April 28, the court upheld an Indiana law requiring voters to present government-issued photo identification at the polls. According to the court, the parties challenging the law had failed to demonstrate that it imposed a substantial burden on voters. In addition, the court ruled, the state's interest in deterring voter fraud arguably outweighs the law's possible burden on voters. Breyer, Ginsburg, and Souter cast the dissenting votes.

First Amendment. The court, in a 7-to-2 decision on May 19, upheld a federal law passed in 2003 prohibiting the pandering and solicitation of child pornography. The court had ruled in 1982 that the freedom-of-speech protection in the U.S. Constitution's First Amendment does not apply to the distribution of child pornography. According to the 2008 decision, the First Amendment also does not apply to offers to provide or requests to obtain child pornography, regardless of whether child pornography is actually distributed. Ginsburg and Souter dissented in the case.

On June 26, the court voted 5 to 4 to strike down the so-called "millionaire's amendment" in campaign finance law. Under this provision, congressional candidates who spent more than $350,000 of personal funds on their campaign would become subject to extra financial disclosure requirements; the opposing candidate would be allowed to raise three times the normal limit per individual contributor; and the opponent's party would be allowed to spend as much as it wanted on the campaign. The court ruled that the provision imposed an unconstitutional burden on a candidate's First Amendment right to spend his or her own money on campaign speech. The conservative justices, plus Kennedy, formed the majority.

Securities fraud lawsuits. On January 15, in a 5-to-3 decision, the court limited the ability of investors who had been defrauded by a company to sue secondary actors—such as banks, accountants, consultants, suppliers, or vendors—that may have helped facilitate the fraud. The court ruled that for lawsuits against a secondary actor to proceed, plaintiffs must show that their investment decisions relied on misstatements or misrepresentations made by the secondary actor. The conservative justices, plus Kennedy, made up the majority. Breyer did not participate because his stock holdings created a conflict of interest.

Job discrimination. On May 27, in two separate decisions, the court allowed workers to pursue claims that their employers had retaliated against them after they filed job discrimination complaints. In one decision, the court ruled 7 to 2 that an 1866 civil rights law protects workers from retaliation if they complain about racial discrimination. Scalia and Thomas dissented. In the other decision, the court ruled 6 to 3 that a 1967 law prohibits retaliation against federal workers who complain about age discrimination. Roberts, Scalia, and Thomas dissented.

Oil spill damages. On June 25, 2008, the court decided 5 to 3 that the $2.5-billion punitive damages award to the victims of the *Exxon Valdez* oil spill was excessive. In 1989, the *Exxon Valdez,* an oil tanker, struck a reef off Alaska's southern coast, spilling millions of gallons of crude oil. The court ruled that the appropriate ratio between punitive damages and compensatory (actual economic) damages should be one to one. Exxon Mobil Corporation had paid $507.5 million in compensatory damages to Alaska Natives, landowners, and commercial fishermen, so the company should have to pay no more than that in punitive damages, the court ruled. Breyer, Ginsburg, and Stevens cast the dissenting votes. Alito did not participate in the case because he owned ExxonMobil stock. ■ Mike Lewis

See also **Courts.**

Surgery. See Medicine.
Suriname. See Latin America.
Swaziland. See Africa.

Sweden. The four-party, center-right coalition government of Prime Minister Fredrik Reinfeldt remained stable in 2008 and was expected to remain in power through the end of its four-year term in 2010. The government modified its program of welfare and tax reforms in light of the global financial crisis. Nevertheless, polls in early 2008 showed that public approval of the coalition had decreased and support for the opposition was rising because of the economic situation.

The government temporarily halted a plan to sell its stakes in six wholly or partially state-owned companies when their share prices dropped dramatically. The sell-off constituted a cornerstone of the government's plan to reduce the national debt and restructure the country's tax system. Sweden's banks remained in fairly good condition throughout 2008. Even so, the country's largest savings bank, Swedbank, suffered some losses because of loans it had made in the Baltic states.

In October, Swedish automobile manufacturing giant Volvo announced a cut of more than 4,000 jobs at plants mainly in Sweden due to a sharp drop in sales. In November, the country's manufacturing industry took a further blow when Norway announced that it would replace its aging combat aircraft with United States-built Joint Strike Fighters rather than Swedish Saab's Gripens.

Foreign policy. In May 2008, Sweden and Russia engaged in a trade dispute over new export tariffs on wood from Russia. The tariffs would dramatically increase the price of wood and threaten Sweden's large paper industry. The Swedish government contended that the Russian move violated the principles of free trade and that, if the measure were not reversed, Sweden would oppose Russia's entry into the World Trade Organization, headquartered in Geneva, Switzerland.

In November 2008, Sweden's parliament ratified the reform treaty of the European Union (EU—Europe's main economic bloc) by a large majority, becoming the 24th member of the 27-member organization to do so. The Lisbon Treaty, as the pact is informally called, is designed to streamline decision making within the EU. In December, Sweden signed a treaty banning cluster bombs, even though it produces them. The treaty must be ratified by 30 nations to go into effect.

Sweden prepared to assume the EU's rotating, six-month presidency in July 2009. Climate change and free trade practices were projected to be among the main concerns of its presidency.

Economy. Sweden was affected in 2008 by the international financial crisis. EU economists forecast that the country's *gross domestic product* (the value of all goods and services produced in a country in a year) would decline to 1.4 percent, from 2.7 percent in 2007. ■ Jeffrey Kopstein

See also **Bank: A Special Report; Europe; Finland.**

Swimming. American Michael Phelps set the stage for the record eight gold medals he earned at the 2008 Summer Olympic Games with a spectacular series of swims at the United States Olympic trials in Omaha, Nebraska, in late June and early July. Phelps won all five of his events, set two world records, and qualified for eight events (including three relays) at the Summer Games in Beijing.

Most of the roughly 50 world records set in 2008 were made by swimmers wearing Speedo's LZR Racer, introduced in February. The Racer's design and fabric significantly reduce drag in the water, producing faster times.

U.S. Olympic trials. Phelps won his first race in Omaha and set his first mark in the 400-meter individual medley (IM) on June 2 with a time of 4:05.25. Phelps set his second mark in the 200-meter IM on July 4, 2008, finishing in 1:54.80. He also won the 100-meter butterfly, 200-meter butterfly, and 200-meter freestyle. Aaron Peirsol's 1:54.32 in the 200-meter backstroke on July 4, 2008, tied Ryan Lochte's 2007 mark.

In women's competition in Omaha, Katie Hoff and Dara Torres stole the show. Hoff, like Phelps, won all five of her races (800-meter freestyle, 400-meter freestyle, 200-meter freestyle, 200-meter IM, and 400-meter IM). Her time of 4:31.12 on June 29, 2008, in the 400-meter IM beat Stephanie Rice's mark, set in March, by .34 second. Torres won both the 50-meter and 100-meter freestyle, setting an American record in the former, and became the first swimmer to qualify for five Olympic Games.

On June 30, Hayley McGregory broke Natalie Coughlin's mark in the 100-meter backstroke set in February with a 59.15, only to see Coughlin reclaim the record one heat later with a swim of 59.03. Margaret Hoelzer swam a 2:06.09 in the 200-meter backstroke on July 5 to break the mark set by Zimbabwe's Kirsty Coventry earlier in 2008.

European championships. Six world records fell at the March event held in Eindhoven, the Netherlands. Alain Bernard of France set records on three consecutive nights, establishing marks in the 50-meter freestyle (21.50) and twice in the 100-meter freestyle (47.60 then 47.50). Dutch swimmer Marleen Veldhuis set a new mark for women in the 50-meter freestyle (24.09). Federica Pellegrini of Italy set a new standard in the 400-meter freestyle (4:01.53). The Dutch women also set a new mark in the 4-by-100-meter freestyle with a time of 3:33.62.

Japan Open. Japan's Kosuke Kitajima trimmed nearly a second off American Brendan Hansen's world record time in the 200-meter breaststroke on June 8 with a swim of 2:07.51 at the Japan Open in Tokyo. ■ Michael Kates

See also **Olympic Games: A Special Report.**

Switzerland. Normally stable Swiss politics remained unsettled for most of 2008. The right-wing Swiss People's Party (SVP)—which had won the most votes in the October 2007 general election—moved into opposition in December 2007, an unprecedented step in a government that traditionally does not have an opposition. Custom in Swiss politics dictates that the four largest parties divide up seats in the country's seven-member cabinet—known as the Federal Council—based on the proportion of the vote received in the general election. The SVP was entitled to two seats in the cabinet. The party chose one of its leading personalities, Christoph Blocher, for one of the positions, but Parliament rejected him in favor of another SVP politician, Eveline Widmer-Schlumpf. After ignoring party instructions to refuse the position, Widmer-Schlumpf was expelled from the party. The SVP then declared itself to be in opposition.

The other SVP politician to take a cabinet post, Samuel Schmid, who became defense minister, was pressured in 2008 to resign. He was accused of covering up previous knowledge of sexual harassment charges brought against one of his appointees, the chief of the Swiss armed forces. SVP leaders had considered Schmid too moderate on many issues, and the party viewed his resignation as an opportunity to return to government. On December 10, the SVP won a sufficient share of parliamentary votes to elect Ueli Maurer to the cabinet. Maurer, a close associate of Blocher's, was considered similarly divisive. Nevertheless, the other major parliamentary groups agreed that the SVP was entitled to representation in the cabinet.

New citizenship rules. The SVP suffered a blow in June 2008 when a referendum it had initiated to toughen citizenship requirements was defeated. Many Swiss suspected that the purpose of the new rules was to make it more difficult for foreign-born residents from certain countries to become citizens while favoring others.

Swiss banks fell under a shadow in July when United States authorities accused UBS, Switzerland's largest financial institution, of helping U.S. citizens hide assets to avoid paying taxes. Swiss authorities responded by partially relaxing their banking secrecy rules and allowing U.S. investigators and regulators access to banking records in cases of suspected fraud. In April, UBS reported that it had lost billions of dollars in mortgage-backed securities in the U.S. housing market.

The Swiss economy was expected to continue to grow in 2008, though at a slower rate because of the global economic downturn. Swiss economists forecast that the economy would grow by 1.9 percent in 2008, compared with 3.3 percent in 2007. ■ Jeffrey Kopstein

See also **Bank: A Special Report; Europe.**

Fighters with the militant pro-Syria group Hezbollah stand at attention in front of a giant poster of fellow fighters near Beirut, the capital of Lebanon, in February during a tribute to Hezbollah commander Imad Mughniyeh, who was killed in a car bombing in Syria. Hezbollah blamed Israel for the killings, though Israeli officials denied involvement.

Syria. In February 2008, the administration of United States President George W. Bush froze the U.S. assets of Rami Makhluf, a cousin of Syria's President Bashar al-Assad, and restricted Makhluf's dealings with U.S. financial institutions. According to the Bush administration, Makhluf, through his business monopolies, worked against the interests of ordinary Syrian businesses and kept his major economic assets under the control of the Assad regime. The U.S. Department of State has accused the Assad regime of using terrorism to destabilize Iraq, Lebanon, and the Palestinian territories.

Arab summit boycotted. The annual Arab League Summit was convened in Damascus, the capital of Syria, in March. The government of Lebanon boycotted the meeting because Syria's allies, led by the militant organization Hezbollah, had prevented the Lebanese parliament from convening to elect a new president of Lebanon. The leaders of Egypt, Saudi Arabia, and Jordan showed their support for Lebanon by not attending the summit and sending only low-level delegations to the gathering.

Hezbollah commander assassinated. Imad Mughniyeh, a leading operative of Hezbollah who planned and executed numerous major terrorist operations against the United States, other Western countries, and Israel, was killed by a car bombing in Damascus in February. Although Hezbollah accused Israel of being responsible for Mughniyeh's murder, many experts in Middle East affairs believed that President Assad eliminated Mughniyeh out of fear that the Hezbollah commander might provide information about Syria's terrorist activities to the international tribunal at The Hague in the Netherlands. The tribunal, which was to begin work in 2009, was established primarily to prosecute those responsible for the assassination in 2005 of former Lebanese Prime Minister Rafik al-Hariri—a murder in which Syria was believed to be involved.

General Muhammad Suleiman was killed by a sniper at a seaside resort in the northern Syrian port city of Tartous in August 2008. General Suleiman reportedly had close associations with Mughniyeh and was also President Assad's "right-hand man" and liaison officer to Hezbollah.

Talks with Israel. The Syrian government began indirect peace talks with Israel in 2008, with Turkish officials acting as mediators. To help move these negotiations forward, President Nicolas Sarkozy of France reversed his country's isolation of Syria and visited Damascus in September to meet with President Assad and the leaders of Turkey and Qatar. Despite these international efforts, peace talks between Syria and Israel failed to advance in 2008. ■ Marius Deeb

See also **Iraq; Israel; Lebanon; Middle East.**

Taiwan. Ma Ying-jeou of the Kuomintang Party (KMT) became president of Taiwan on May 20, 2008. Ma won 58 percent of the vote in the March 22 election, defeating Frank Hsieh of the Democratic Progressive Party (DPP). Ma, a Harvard-educated lawyer, was the mayor of Taiwan's capital, Taipei, from 1998 to 2006. Vincent Siew of the KMT was elected as Ma's vice president.

Ma succeeded the DPP's Chen Shui-bian, who as president had angered China by leaning toward independence for Taiwan. China claims Taiwan, and Taiwan officially considers itself a province of China. The DPP had advocated renouncing this more theoretical than actual tie for the self-governing state, though Chen cautiously avoided going that far. China, which in recent years had built up a strong military force across the 100-mile (160-kilometer) Taiwan Strait, had repeatedly threatened to invade the island if it claimed independence.

Parliament. As president, Chen had been limited by KMT control of parliament. The KMT reinforced this control by winning 81 out of 113 seats in Jan. 12, 2008, elections. Chen called this "the worst defeat since the founding" of the DPP.

China ties. In his inaugural speech, Ma broke with Chen's confrontational approach to China and called for increased cooperation. Ma also called for an end to China's efforts to isolate Taiwan diplomatically. China continued, however, to block the island's participation in many international organizations and tried to lure away some two dozen countries that recognized Taiwan diplomatically as representing all of China.

The first official meeting between Taiwan and China since 1999 was held in the Chinese capital, Beijing, on June 12, 2008. Representatives agreed to establish permanent governmental offices in each other's capitals to facilitate closer relations. Talks led to improved trade and transportation links, but the DPP said Ma was moving too fast on new ties. Taiwan already had large industrial investments in China, where labor costs were cheaper than on the island. On November 4, representatives from China and Taiwan signed additional trade and transportation agreements, including increasing the number and frequency of business and cargo flights.

Scandal. On Aug. 15, 2008, Chen announced his resignation from the DPP and confessed that his wife, Wu Shu-chen, had wired campaign funds to accounts abroad. Chen admitted having $21 million in such accounts. He was jailed on November 12. On December 12, Chen, his wife, and 13 others were indicted on graft charges.

■ Henry S. Bradsher

See also **Asia; China.**
Tajikistan. See Asia.
Tanzania. See Africa.

Taxation. United States lawmakers enacted three major pieces of economic legislation in 2008. All of them contained tax provisions.

Tax provisions in bailout bill. The financial bailout package that President George W. Bush signed on October 3 included dozens of significant tax provisions that the Senate had attached to the bill on October 1. Their net cost was expected to be about $110 billion over 10 years.

Several of the tax provisions extended the life of expiring tax credits or created new credits to promote reduced energy use or investment in alternative energy. For example, credits were extended for people who made energy-efficient improvements to their homes, and credits were created for owners of plug-in electric vehicles. Another provision implemented a fix in the alternative minimum tax (AMT) to prevent millions of people from having to pay the AMT in the 2008 tax year. (The AMT—aimed at wealthy taxpayers when it was created in 1969—was never indexed for inflation, putting many middle-class taxpayers at risk of being ensnared by it each year.)

Other provisions extended the life of a personal deduction for higher education expenses, a research and development credit for businesses, and an option to deduct state and local sales taxes in lieu of state and local income taxes (an attractive option for people who pay no state income tax). Also, the refundable child tax credit was expanded to benefit more poor families; tax relief was provided to victims of recent natural disasters; and banks that had invested in Fannie Mae and Freddie Mac preferred stock were allowed to treat their losses as ordinary rather than capital losses for tax purposes. (Fannie Mae and Freddie Mac are large mortgage finance corporations that plunged in value in 2008 as a result of the U.S. housing crisis and were taken over by the U.S. government on September 7.)

Economic stimulus bill. On February 13, President Bush signed an economic stimulus package providing about $170 billion in tax relief over two years. Under the plan, individuals and families received income tax rebates in 2008, and businesses were able to write off a larger portion of their equipment purchases in 2008.

Tax provisions in housing bill. The housing relief package that President Bush signed on July 30 created a one-time refundable tax credit of up to $7,500 for first-time home buyers purchasing homes from April 9, 2008, to July 1, 2009. The credit had to be paid back over 15 years, essentially making it an interest-free loan. The housing bill also created a property tax deduction for homeowners not itemizing deductions on their tax returns.

■ Mike Lewis

See also **Bank: A Special Report; United States, Government of the: A Special Report.**

Telecommunications. In 2008, Apple Inc. of Cupertino, California, introduced a new version of its popular iPhone, as well as new features for the device. T-Mobile released a similar phone that runs on software developed by Google Inc., based in Mountain View, California. Telecommunications companies were also the subject of a fierce debate involving a United States surveillance law.

The iPhone 3G. In July 2008, Apple released a new version of the iPhone, featuring a faster "3G" (third-generation) Internet connection and a global positioning system (GPS). Like the earlier version of the iPhone released in 2007, the device features a touchscreen and computerlike features. It also functions as a camera and as a digital music and video player.

The new iPhone's price—$199 or $299, depending on the version—was about half the price of the original iPhone. However, iPhone consumers also had to purchase a two-year phone and Internet network plan from AT&T Inc., based in Dallas. The new iPhone's plan was more expensive per month than the old iPhone's plan.

Apple also released a new feature called Apps for all versions of its iPhone, as well as its iPod Touch music and video player. Apps are computer programs—such as games, planners, and Internet-enabled news and shopping features—that work with the device's touchscreen.

Google's phone. In October 2008, T-Mobile, based in Germany, released a new phone that runs on Google's new Android software. The phone, called the G1, has a large touchscreen, a camera, high-speed Internet access, and other computerlike features similar to the iPhone.

Google's Android software, unlike Apple's iPhone software, is open source—that is, its computer code is publicly available. Google hopes that the openness of its software will encourage computer developers to make innovative new programs for the phone. The G1 also differs from the iPhone in its mechanical keyboard beneath the touchscreen. The G1 costs $179, plus a two-year contract with T-Mobile.

FISA and telecom immunity. In July 2008, the U.S. Congress passed a bill revising the Foreign Intelligence Surveillance Act (FISA). The bill granted immunity to telecommunications companies that, according to some members of Congress, illegally cooperated with the administration of U.S. President George W. Bush to monitor the telephone calls of certain American citizens. Congress had fiercely debated whether or not to grant immunity to the companies.

The original FISA was enacted in 1978. It controlled the government's use of surveillance and wiretapping by requiring government agencies to request warrants through a special court. After the September 11, 2001, terrorist attacks in New York City and on the Pentagon in Arlington, Virginia, the Bush administration began collecting surveillance on Americans without consulting the FISA court. Various telecommunications companies cooperated with the Bush administration, opening their networks to the government.

The Bush administration argued that such warrantless wiretaps were necessary to keep America safe. They said the FISA process was too slow for them to effectively monitor and keep up with potential terrorist communications. Critics claimed the warrantless wiretaps were illegal violations of Americans' privacy. Some sought to prosecute the telecommunications companies that worked with the Bush administration, saying they violated their customers' privacy without legal court orders.

Congress tried to pass a bill updating FISA so that it allowed the government to monitor terrorist communications while protecting privacy concerns. Several Democratic members of Congress, including presidential candidate Barack Obama, opposed versions of the bill that granted legal immunity to the telecommunications companies. When President Bush threatened to veto any bill that did not include immunity, the Democrats compromised. ■ Daniel Kenis

See also **Electronics; Internet.**

Television. As Hollywood recovered from a writers' strike in 2008, television networks continued to compete for viewers who, in increasing numbers, chose to watch TV programs on their computers. Coverage of the Summer Olympic Games and a heated presidential race brought in record numbers of television viewers. And TV households prepared for a switchover from analog to digital broadcasting.

Strike settlement. A 100-day contract strike by the Writers Guild of America against the Alliance of Motion Picture and Television Producers was settled on February 12. It was the first Hollywood writers' strike in 20 years. Television and film writers wanted more money when films and TV shows were sold on Internet sites, such as the iTunes Store operated by Apple Inc., of Cupertino, California. Under the new contract, writers received an annual pay increase of from 3 to 3.5 percent. Some 50,000 film and television workers were out of work during the strike, costing the Los Angeles economy an estimated $1.5 billion. During the strike, the average prime-time ratings declined by 6.8 percent compared with the same period in 2007.

Internet TV. In March 2008, the online video service Hulu, based in Los Angeles, was launched. Its Web site, hulu.com, offered free, ad-supported streaming video of a large selection of hit TV shows, movies, and clips. Content providers

Jon Hamm (right) stars as high-pressure New York City advertising executive Don Draper in the AMC series "Mad Men." John Slattery portrays the agency boss, Roger Sterling. The series, set in the early 1960's, was the first from a basic cable network to win an Emmy for best drama series.

included Fox Broadcasting Company, based in Beverly Hills, California; NBC Universal, Inc., based in New York City; Metro-Goldwyn-Mayer Inc., based in Los Angeles; Sony Pictures Television, based in Culver City, California; the Warner Bros. Television Group, based in Burbank, California; Lions Gate Entertainment Corp., based in Santa Monica, California; and the National Basketball Association and the National Hockey League, both based in New York City. The company, a joint venture of NBC Universal, Inc., and News Corporation, both based in New York City, saw the service as a step forward in giving viewers entertainment on their terms.

The 2008 Summer Olympic Games in Beijing in August was the most-viewed event in American television history. More than two out of three people worldwide tuned in for the games. According to the national audience measurement service Nielsen Media Research, 4.7 billion viewers worldwide tuned in to some of the television coverage. NBC received record-breaking ratings for its coverage of the games—the first to be produced and broadcast entirely in high-definition TV.

PRIMETIME EMMY AWARD WINNERS IN 2008

COMEDY
Best Series: "30 Rock"
Lead Actress: Tina Fey, "30 Rock"
Lead Actor: Alec Baldwin, "30 Rock"
Supporting Actress: Jean Smart, "Samantha Who?"
Supporting Actor: Jeremy Piven, "Entourage"

DRAMA
Best Series: "Mad Men"
Lead Actress: Glenn Close, "Damages"
Lead Actor: Bryan Cranston, "Breaking Bad"
Supporting Actress: Dianne Wiest, "In Treatment"
Supporting Actor: Zeljko Ivanek, "Damages"

OTHER AWARDS
Miniseries: "John Adams"

Reality/Competition Series: "The Amazing Race"

Variety, Music, or Comedy Series: "The Daily Show with Jon Stewart"

Made for Television Movie: "Recount"

Lead Actress in a Miniseries or Movie: Laura Linney, "John Adams"

Lead Actor in a Miniseries or Movie: Paul Giamatti, "John Adams"

Supporting Actress in a Miniseries or Movie: Dame Eileen Atkins, "Cranford"

Supporting Actor in a Miniseries or Movie: Tom Wilkinson, "John Adams"

Presidential election coverage brought in a record number of television viewers in 2008. More than 40 million people watched convention speeches on three nights in August and September by Democratic presidential candidate Barack Obama, Republican presidential candidate John McCain, and Republican vice presidential candidate Sarah Palin. The three convention speeches were watched by more people than the "American Idol" finale, the Academy Awards, and the opening ceremony of the 2008 Summer Olympic Games in Bejing. The Republican National Convention in St. Paul, Minnesota, was the most-watched convention on television ever, beating a record set by the Democratic National Convention in Denver a week earlier.

The vice presidential debate between Palin and Democratic vice presidential candidate Senator Joe Biden on October 2 was seen by nearly 70 million viewers, making it the second most-watched TV debate in history. The ratings for the vice presidential debate were much higher than for any of the three presidential debates between Obama and McCain. The second Obama-McCain presidential debate, on October 7, was the highest-rated of the three, with 63 million viewers.

A guest appearance by Palin on "Saturday Night Live"(SNL) also helped bring the NBC late-night comedy show its highest ratings in 14 years. A popular impersonation of Palin on the show by SNL alumna Tina Fey heightened interest in the candidate's appearance on the October 18 show.

On October 29, a highly polished 30-minute Obama campaign commercial aired on seven broadcast and cable networks. The commercial, paid for by the campaign, cost about $4 million and topped network prime-time ratings with more than 34 million viewers. It was the first such political "infomercial" since presidential candidate Ross Perot's series of half-hour campaign ads in 1992.

Obama's historic presidential win on November 4 brought in more than 71 million viewers, making it the highest-rated election night since 1980. ABC was the most-watched among the networks, with 13.1 million viewers. CNN was first among cable networks, with 12.3 million viewers.

60th Annual Prime-time Emmy Awards. "30 Rock," the NBC situation comedy created by Tina Fey based on her experiences at SNL, won an Emmy for best comedy series for the second year in a row. Fey and co-star Alec Baldwin each won for best lead actors in a comedy series. "Mad Men," the drama set in the early 1960's about the cutthroat advertising world of New York City's Madison Avenue, won seven Emmys after its first season. The AMC series became the first show from a basic cable network to be nominated and to win an Emmy for best drama series. The series also won an Emmy for best writing, as well as five technical awards. Another notable Emmy winner was the acclaimed HBO miniseries *John Adams,* which won 13 awards, including best miniseries. Paul Giamatti and Laura Linney won best lead actor awards in a miniseries or movie for their portrayals of the second U.S. president and First Lady Abigail Adams.

Series finales and cancellations. Several notable TV series ended in 2008. MTV's music video show "Total Request Live" (TRL) was canceled after a decade. FX's award-winning police drama "The Shield" ended after seven seasons. On the CW, the comedy series "Girlfriends" was canceled after eight seasons; the reality series "Beauty and the Geek" and the award-winning animated series "The Batman" were canceled after five. CBS's Emmy-winning satirical legal drama "Boston Legal," NBC's crime drama "Las Vegas," and HBO's critically acclaimed police drama "The Wire" all ended after five seasons. TLC's reality series about tattoo artists, "Miami Ink," was canceled after four seasons. CBS's "Jericho" and FX's "Dirt" were canceled after two seasons.

TOP-RATED U.S. TELEVISION PROGRAMS

The following were the most-watched television programs for the 2007-2008 regular primetime season, which ran from Sept. 24, 2007, to May 21, 2008.

1. "American Idol" (Tuesday) (FOX)
2. "American Idol" (Wednesday) (FOX)
3. "Dancing with the Stars" (Monday) (ABC)
4. "Dancing with the Stars" (ABC)
5. "Dancing with the Stars Results" (Tuesday) (ABC)
6. "Dancing with the Stars Results" (ABC)
7. "Desperate Housewives" (ABC)
8. "House" (FOX)
9. "CSI" (CBS)
10. "NBC Sunday Night Football" (NBC)
11. "Grey's Anatomy" (Thursday) (ABC)
12. "Survivor: China" (CBS)
13. "Moment of Truth" (FOX)
14. "NCIS" (CBS)
15. "House" (Monday) (CBS)
16. "CSI: Miami" (CBS)
17. "Two and a Half Men" (CBS)
18. "Extreme Makeover: Home Edition" (ABC)
19. "60 Minutes" (CBS)
20. "Without a Trace" (CBS)

Copyright – Nielsen Media Research, 2008.

The writers' strike sealed the fate of many new shows in 2008. NBC's science-fiction series "The Bionic Woman" and Fox's comedy "Back to You," which began in the fall of 2007, were canceled in 2008 after one season when production was halted due to the strike. The acclaimed HBO series "Tell Me You Love Me" was picked up for a second season in October 2007 but was canceled in July 2008 when series creator Cynthia Mort decided to move on. Other shows canceled in 2008 after one season included ABC's "Oprah's Big Give"; the CW's "Aliens in America"; and CBS's "Kid Nation," which met with controversy after questions arose whether the show violated child safety and labor laws.

New fall shows. The writers' strike was a contributing factor in the smaller crop of new fall shows in 2008. Among the most promising new shows on CBS were "The Mentalist," about a private investigator who uses his keen powers of observation to help police solve cases; "Worst Week," a comedy in which a young couple gets quickly acquainted with their soon-to-be in-laws; and the sci-fi drama "Eleventh Hour," which was compared to "The X Files." Fox's "Fringe," which was also compared to "The X Files," was expected to be a hit. ABC bet on a stellar cast to lure viewers to its new crime drama "Life on Mars," about a policeman who wakes up in 1973 after being knocked unconscious in a traffic accident. Adapted from the successful British series of the same name, the U.S. version starred Michael Imperioli of "The Sopranos" and Harvey Keitel. The CW's "90210," a spin-off of the 1990's drama "Beverly Hills, 90210," was the highest-rated scripted debut show in the channel's history, with almost 5 million viewers.

Industry layoffs. In December 2008, Viacom Inc., of New York City, announced that it would cut nearly 7 percent of its work force, or 850 workers, and freeze salaries for its top managers. NBC Universal announced that it would lay off 500 employees, including several long-time correspondents for NBC News.

Digital television transition. The Digital Television Transition and Public Safety Act of 2005 required all full-power broadcast television stations in the United States to stop broadcasting on analog airwaves and begin broadcasting only in digital signals on Feb. 17, 2009. In early 2008, digital-to-analog converter set-top boxes became available for purchase at electronics retailers. The cost of the box ranged from $40 to $70. Beginning January 1, each U.S. household was eligible to receive two $40 coupons to be used toward the purchase of two converter boxes. The National Telecommunications and Information Administration carried out the government-sponsored coupon program.　　■ Shawn Brennan

See also **Elections: A Special Report; Internet; Motion pictures; People in the news** (Rick Warren).

Tennis. Spain's Rafael Nadal gained the upper hand in his thrilling rivalry with Switzerland's Roger Federer in 2008. Nadal broke the top-ranked player's five-year stranglehold on Wimbledon in a match for the ages a month after winning his fourth straight French Open. Nadal took over the number-one ranking on August 17, ending Federer's record-setting 237-week reign as the game's top player. Federer rebounded to win his fifth straight U.S. Open and moved to second all-time in majors won with 13, one behind the retired Pete Sampras.

In women's tennis, Belgium's Justine Henin became the first top-ranked woman in history to retire while ranked number one. Henin won 41 singles titles, including 10 in 2007, and spent 117 weeks as the No. 1 player during her career. But she was struggling in 2008 when she made her mid-May announcement. On the court, each of the Williams sisters captured a major, with Serena's victory at the U.S. Open giving her the number-one ranking for the first time since August 2003.

Australian Open. Russia's Maria Sharapova, seeded fifth, captured her third major title with a 7-5, 6-3 victory over fourth-seeded Ana Ivanovic in Melbourne on Jan. 26, 2008. Sharapova rolled to the title without dropping a set in all seven matches. Number 3 seed Novak Djokovic became the first Serbian man to win a major title—and ended a run of 11 straight majors captured by either Federer or Nadal—with his 4-6, 6-4, 6-3, 7-6 (2) victory over unseeded Jo-Wilfied Tsonga of France on January 27.

Jonathan Erlich and Andy Ram won in men's doubles; Alona and K. Bondarenko won women's doubles; and Tian Tian Sun and Nenad Zimonjic won the mixed doubles title.

French Open. Nadal blasted an overmatched Federer 6-1, 6-3, 6-0 on June 8 in Paris in the most one-sided men's final in a Grand Slam tournament in 24 years. Nadal improved to 28-0 all-time at the French Open. Federer had not won fewer than five games in a match since 2002. Serbian Ana Ivanovic won her first career Grand Slam event with a 6-4, 6-3 victory over Dinara Safina. The second seed's victory propelled her to the number-one ranking. Pablo Cuevas and Luis Horna captured the men's doubles title; Anabel Medina Garrigues and Virginia Ruano Pascual won in women's doubles; and Bob Bryan and Victoria Azarenka won in mixed doubles.

Wimbledon. Nadal defeated Federer 6-4, 6-4, 6-7 (5), 6-7 (8), 9-7 in a 4-hour, 48-minute marathon on July 6, the longest final in Wimbledon history, which was also interrupted by several rain delays. Federer was attempting to become the first player to win six straight men's titles but saw his run of 40 straight wins at Wimbledon, and 65 straight on grass, snapped.

Rafael Nadal of Spain, in the near court, hits a ball at Swiss star Roger Federer at the Wimbledon Finals on July 6, 2008. Nadal's brilliant victory broke Federer's streak of five consecutive Wimbledon championships.

Venus Williams captured her fifth Wimbledon title with a 7-5, 6-4 victory over younger sister Serena on July 5, the seventh all-Williams Grand Slam singles title match. Hours later, the sisters won the women's doubles title. Daniel Nestor and Nenad Zimonjic won in men's doubles; Bob Bryan and Samantha Stosur won in mixed doubles.

U.S. Open. In a final delayed a day by rain, Federer waxed United Kingdom's Andy Murray 6-2, 7-5, 6-2 on September 8 for his fifth straight title. The last man to accomplish such a feat at the U.S. Open was Bill Tilden in the 1920's. Murray had upset Nadal in the semifinals. In the women's final, delayed a day to September 7, Serena Williams beat Jelena Jankovic 6-4, 7-5, for her third U.S. Open title and ninth major. Mike and Bob Bryan won in men's doubles; Cara Black and Liezel Huber won in women's doubles; Leander Paes and Black won in mixed doubles.

Davis Cup. Spain defeated Argentina 3-1 at Mar del Plata, Argentina, on November 21-23, in spite of the absence of Rafael Nadal, who was out with an injury. The fifth match was canceled by mutual consent. Feliciano Lopez and Fernando Verdasco each won a singles match for Spain and then combined to win the doubles match for their country's three points. ■ Michael Kates

See also **Olympic Games: A Special Report; Sports.**

Terrorism. South Asia became a major terrorist battleground in 2008, with thousands of deaths and injuries in India and Pakistan. Africa experienced a resurgence of terrorist activity, and the Middle East continued to endure high levels of civil violence.

South Asia. In India, terrorist attacks, many of them related to the conflict between Hindu nationalists and the Muslim minority, became common in 2008. The northeastern state of Assam and the northwestern cities of Ahmadabad, Jaipur, Mumbai (formerly known as Bombay), and New Delhi suffered the most violence. On November 26, terrorists began a series of attacks against the commercial center of Mumbai, taking more than 170 lives and wounding at least 300 people in three days. The targets, which included two luxury hotels, a railway station, and a Jewish center, were apparently chosen for their association with India's wealthy business class or with foreigners. Officials from India and the United States claimed Lashkar-e-Taiba (LeT), a militant group based in Pakistan, was responsible for the attacks. However, LeT denied any involvement.

Pakistan's tribal areas continued to serve as a sanctuary for many terrorist groups in 2008. Government forces and terrorist groups, many of them Islamic extremists, engaged in a series of attacks and counterattacks that took many lives. On February 16, just two days before the national election, two suicide attacks in northwest Pakistan killed 39 supporters of the late Prime Minister Benazir Bhutto. On September 20, a car full of explosives was detonated next to the Marriott Hotel in Islamabad, close to Prime Minister Yousaf Raza Gilani's home and the parliament. A natural gas pipe leak caused by the explosion set off a fire that engulfed the entire building and destroyed it completely. More than 60 people died and several hundred were injured.

In Sri Lanka, the continuing conflict between the Sinhalese government and the Tamil minority caused terrorist activities to persist in 2008. In January and the first week of February, a political group called the Liberation Tigers of Tamil Elam was responsible for a number of attacks on commuter buses, killing about 50 people and injuring at least 100.

Africa. In Algeria, terrorist attacks averaged four a month throughout 2008. In August, the bloodiest month, 12 attacks left 80 people dead and more than 140 injured. The Al-Qa`ida Organization in the Islamic Maghreb claimed responsibility for many attacks on police officers, army recruits, government representatives, and foreign nationals.

In Somalia, the Ethiopian-backed government battled fighters of the Islamic Courts movement, who used suicide and vehicle bombs, firearms, grenades, and land mines. A surge in piracy on the seas off Somalia also made the region unstable. About 60 ships were hijacked and 300 crew members were taken captive in 2008.

Middle East. In Shiraz, Iran, a bomb exploded inside the Shohada Hosseiniyeh mosque on April 12, killing 14 worshipers and injuring almost 200 others. Members of an anti-Islamic group called the Kingdom Assembly of Iran claimed responsibility for the attack.

On July 24 in Gaza, a city in the Gaza Strip, a bomb exploded near a police parking lot of the militant Palestinian group Hamas. Nine people died, including several senior Hamas members, and 15 were injured.

On March 18, the Yemen Soldiers Brigades, an al-Qa`ida-affiliated terrorist group, aimed three bombs at the United States Embassy in Yemen's capital city of Sanaa. None of the bombs struck the embassy, however. Two hit a nearby school, killing 2 people and wounding 19 others. On September 17, terrorists again mounted an assault on the embassy but instead struck an area outside the embassy compound, killing 16 people and injuring 16 others. ■ Richard Rubenstein

See also **Algeria; India; Iran; Pakistan; Somalia; Sri Lanka; Yemen.**

An Indian commando battles terrorists holed up in the Taj Mahal Palace & Tower hotel in Mumbai on November 29, the last day of a three-day attack on the city. More than 170 people died before commandos overcame the militants.

Thailand in 2008 was wracked by turmoil as the urban, middle, and upper classes in the capital, Bangkok, opposed elected governments backed by supporters in provincial areas.

Thaksin Shinawatra had become prime minister in 2001 and was then ousted in 2006 by a *coup* (overthrow) on charges of corruption and abuse of power. His followers, who had formed the People Power Party (PPP) after Thaksin's Thai Rak Tai party was officially dissolved, won a parliamentary majority in elections on Dec. 23, 2007, and formed a ruling coalition. The PPP leader, Samak Sundaravej, became prime minister on Jan. 28, 2008.

Protests. In May, demonstrators took to the streets in Bangkok to protest against Samak, charging that his government was a proxy for Thaksin. On September 9, Thailand's Constitutional Court ordered Samak to resign because he was being paid to work as a television chef while serving as prime minister, which violated a ban on government ministers taking money from private companies. He was succeeded by Thaksin's brother-in-law, Somchai Wongsawat.

The People's Alliance for Democracy (PAD), which had led the May demonstrations, continued to protest against the PPP government. Protesters blocked off the prime minister's office, forcing the government to operate from a secondary Bangkok airport. Samak declared a state of emergency on September 2 but revoked the order 12 days later because it was hurting Thailand's important tourist industry. On November 26, protesters blockaded Bangkok's main airport, forcing a suspension of all flights and further disrupting vital commerce and tourism.

Government ousted. On December 2, the Constitutional Court disbanded the PPP for electoral fraud in the 2007 election. The 2008 ruling also banned Somchai from politics for five years. Protesters then ended their weeklong airport siege, which had stranded an estimated 300,000 passengers. On December 15, the opposition Democratic Party (DP) won the backing of enough former PPP supporters to elect DP leader Abhisit Vejjajiva as prime minister.

Thaksin, who left Thailand after his 2006 ousting, returned on Feb. 28, 2008. Although he faced charges of corruption and abuse of power, the Supreme Court granted him bail to attend the Olympic Games in China in August. Instead of returning, he jumped bail and flew to London, leaving more than $2 billion in assets frozen in Thailand. On October 21, the Supreme Court convicted Thaksin of abusing his office in a land purchase by his wife. His wife was acquitted, but Thaksin was sentenced to two years in prison, and efforts began to extradite him from the United Kingdom.   ■ Henry S. Bradsher

See also **Asia; Cambodia.**

Theater. A steep economic downturn in late 2008, accompanied by numerous bank, mortgage, and insurance company failures, had a marked effect on American theaters and caused several Broadway shows and regional theater companies to close their doors. Producers of the musicals *Hairspray* (2002), *Monty Python's Spamalot* (2005), *The New Mel Brooks Musical Young Frankenstein* (2007), *Spring Awakening* (2007), and *13* (2007) all announced in late 2008 that their shows would close in January 2009.

Young Frankenstein's run ended after just over a year. The second of Mel Brooks's movies to be presented as a musical on Broadway, *Young Frankenstein* failed to live up to the strong track record established by Brooks's smash hit, *The Producers* (2001). *Young Frankenstein*'s co-producer Robert F. X. Sillerman said his partners planned to focus their efforts on the play's first national tour in September 2009. It was unclear by the end of 2008 whether *Young Frankenstein* would recoup its backers' investments.

The economic crisis also caused difficulties for resident theater companies, such as the Oregon Shakespeare Festival (OSF) in Ashland, which had successfully weathered past recessions. Founded in 1935, OSF is among the oldest and largest professional nonprofit repertory theaters in the United States. Its eight-and-a-half-month season, from February to October, includes 11 plays performed on 3 different stages. OSF's annual operating budget was more than $26 million. Despite strong ticket sales in 2008, OSF suffered from poor returns on its investments and endowment fund. OSF's deficit for 2008 was $750,000. It projected a $1-million shortfall for the 2009 season. OSF's executive director, Paul Nicholson, said that ticket prices would be raised by 3 to 4 percent in 2009 to help offset the theater's losses.

In early November 2008, the eight-year-old Milwaukee Shakespeare theater company announced that it would cease operations. Despite record subscription sales for the year, the company was unable to withstand the loss of its primary funder, the Argosy Foundation, whose annual grant of almost $1 million constituted nearly 75 percent of the company's annual budget. Milwaukee Shakespeare's co-founder and chief funder Chris Abele, who is president and chief executive officer (CEO) of his family's Argosy Foundation, attributed the discontinuation of the company's annual grant to the downturn in the market, which had left Argosy cash poor.

Two by Mamet. Broadway revivals of two works by American playwright David Mamet opened in fall 2008. *Speed-the-Plow,* a three-character play directed by Neil Pepe, opened on October 23. It starred Jeremy Piven, from the television series "Entourage"; Raúl Esparza, who appeared in

Kelli O'Hara and Paulo Szot (standing) star in the 2008 Broadway revival of the Rodgers and Hammerstein musical *South Pacific*. The hugely successful revival was the musical's first in New York City in nearly 60 years. It originally opened in 1949.

Harold Pinter's *The Homecoming* (1965) in 2007; and Elisabeth Moss from the television series "Mad Men," in her Broadway debut. The play is a satiric take on the American movie business. Piven was replaced in mid-December by Norbert Leo Butz, who won a Tony Award for Best Actor in a Musical in 2005 for *Dirty Rotten Scoundrels*.

Running concurrently on Broadway was the short-lived revival of the play that established Mamet's reputation, *American Buffalo*. Directed by Robert Falls, the show featured as a trio of petty crooks John Leguizamo and, in their Broadway debuts, Cedric the Entertainer and Haley Joel Osment. Produced when Mamet was 27 years old, the play originally opened at Chicago's Goodman Theatre and won a 1976 Obie Award. The play went on to win several Tony awards.

The two 2008 Mamet productions competed at the box office and over theaters to house the shows. Producers of both shows attempted to secure the Ethel Barrymore Theatre. In the end, *Speed-the-Plow* played at the Barrymore, and *American Buffalo* had its brief run at the Belasco Theatre. While *Speed-the-Plow* was still running by the end of 2008, *American Buffalo* closed in

late November after a run of only eight performances and largely negative reviews.

Mamet gained additional attention in 2008 for a March article he wrote for *The Village Voice* titled "Why I Am No Longer a 'Brain-Dead Liberal,'" in which the playwright announced his political about-face. The article coincided with the production of his new political play *November* (2008), which he described as "a laugh a minute ... disputation between reason and faith, or perhaps between the conservative (or tragic) view and the liberal (or perfectionist) view. The conservative president in the piece holds that people are each out to make a living, and the best way for government to facilitate that is to *stay out of the way,* as the inevitable abuses and failures of this system (free-market economics) are less than those of government intervention." The play, starring Nathan Lane, Laurie Metcalf, and Ethan Phillips, received mixed reviews.

Steppenwolf's stellar season. The Chicago-based Steppenwolf Theatre Company received recognition and acclaim in 2008 when its production of *August: Osage County* (2007)—which moved to Broadway in late 2007—received five

Tony awards, including best play, best direction, and best performance by a leading actress. Playwright Tracy Letts also won the 2008 Pulitzer Prize for drama for the play. The darkly comic play, which focuses on a family reunion in Oklahoma, was characterized by some critics as reminiscent of Eugene O'Neill's autobiographical family drama *Long Day's Journey into Night* (1956). Letts and the play's director, Anna D. Shapiro—as well as most of the designers and cast—are members of Steppenwolf, where the original production premiered in June 2007.

TONY AWARD WINNERS IN 2008

Best Play: *August: Osage County*

Best Musical: *In the Heights*

Best Play Revival: *Boeing-Boeing*

Best Musical Revival: *South Pacific*

Leading Actor in a Play: Mark Rylance, *Boeing-Boeing*

Leading Actress in a Play: Deanna Dunagan, *August: Osage County*

Leading Actor in a Musical: Paul Szot, *South Pacific*

Leading Actress in a Musical: Patti LuPone, *Gypsy*

Featured Actor in a Play: Jim Norton, *The Seafarer*

Featured Actress in a Play: Rondi Reed, *August: Osage County*

Featured Actor in a Musical: Boyd Gaines, *Gypsy*

Featured Actress in a Musical: Laura Benanti, *Gypsy*

Direction of a Play: Anna D. Shapiro, *August: Osage County*

Direction of a Musical: Bartlett Sher, *South Pacific*

Book of a Musical: Stew, *Passing Strange*

Original Musical Score: Lin-Manuel Miranda, *In the Heights*

Orchestrations: Alex Lacamoire and Bill Sherman, *In the Heights*

Scenic Design of a Play: Todd Rosenthal, *August: Osage County*

Scenic Design of a Musical: Michael Yeargan, *South Pacific*

Costume Design of a Play: Katrina Lindsay, *Les Liaisons Dangereuses*

Costume Design of a Musical: Catherine Zuber, *South Pacific*

Lighting Design of a Play: Kevin Adams, *The 39 Steps*

Lighting Design of a Musical: Donald Holder, *South Pacific*

Choreography: Andy Blankenbuehler, *In the Heights*

Regional Theater: Chicago Shakespeare Theater

Special Tony Award: Robert Russell Bennett, composer

Steppenwolf was founded in the basement of a church in Highland Park, Illinois, in 1974. The theater took its name from the title of a novel by the German novelist Hermann Hesse. Among Steppenwolf's original members are cofounder Gary Sinise and John Malkovich, both of whom have had distinguished careers on the stage and in films. In 1988, Steppenwolf presented the world premiere of *The Grapes of Wrath*, based on John Steinbeck's Pulitzer Prize-winning 1939 novel and starring Sinise as Tom Joad. The production won the 1990 Tony Award for best play. Steppenwolf also helped to launch the careers of other well-known American actors, including Joan Allen, Gary Cole, Glenne Headly, John Mahoney, Laurie Metcalf, and Martha Plimpton.

Remembering Paul Scofield. British actor Paul Scofield died on March 19, 2008, at the age of 86. He was among the last of the great era of British stage actors that included John Gielgud, Laurence Olivier, and Ralph Richardson. An intensely private man in his personal life, Scofield declined a knighthood and preferred the theater over Hollywood. His greatest stage roles included Sir Thomas More in Robert Bolt's *A Man for All Seasons* (1960); Antonio Salieri in Peter Shaffer's *Amadeus* (1979); Tobias in Edward Albee's *A Delicate Balance* (1966); the "whiskey priest" in Graham Greene's *The Power and the Glory* (1956); and the title characters in *Hamlet* (1956) and *King Lear* (1962), as well as numerous other great Shakespearean roles performed under the direction of Peter Brook. Scofield was for many years Brook's star actor on stage.

Describing Scofield's portrayal of Hamlet, the great British theater critic Kenneth Tynan said: "No living actor is better equipped for Hamlet. On him the right sadness sits and also the right spleen; his gait is a prowl over quicksands, and he can freeze a word with an irony at once mournful and deadly." In an opinion poll in 2004, the members of England's Royal Shakespeare Company voted Scofield's portrayal of King Lear as the greatest performance in a Shakespearean play. Brook also directed Scofield in a 1971 film adaptation of *King Lear*. A 2002 audio version of the play starring Scofield was directed by Kenneth Branagh and co-produced by Scofield and Branagh.

Scofield won an Academy Award for his portrayal of More in the 1966 motion-picture adaptation of *A Man for All Seasons*. Scofield's other memorable film roles included the Ghost in Franco Zeffirelli's *Hamlet* (1990); the poet and Columbia University professor Mark Van Doren in *Quiz Show* (1994); and Judge Thomas Danforth in Arthur Miller's *The Crucible* (1996). ■ David Yezzi

See also **Labor; Pulitzer Prizes.**

Togo. See **Africa.**

Tonga. See **Pacific Islands.**

Toronto in 2008 marked the 10th anniversary of a new kind of city government. In 1998, the province of Ontario had forced seven municipalities—the then-city of Toronto, five of its suburbs, and a metropolitan government—to amalgamate into a single "megacity."

City Hall. On Jan. 28, 2008, Mayor David Miller introduced Toronto's first balanced budget since amalgamation. The City Council approved the $8.2-billion operating budget on March 31. (All monetary figures are in Canadian dollars.) Budgets in earlier years had had large shortfalls, causing city officials to beg the provincial government for last-minute bailouts. Ontario cities are not allowed to borrow to meet operating expenses. The 2008 budget was balanced with a residential property tax increase of 3.75 percent; new taxes on land transfers and vehicle registrations; increases in recreational fees; new garbage fees; savings and efficiencies; and expected assistance from the provincial government.

On July 28, 2008, Shirley Hoy, Toronto's respected city manager, announced that she would resign on October 6. Miller promptly recommended that the City Council pick Deputy City Manager and Chief Financial Officer Joseph Pennachetti to replace Hoy. Some councilors criticized Miller for presenting Pennachetti's candidacy as a done deal, and they called for a wider search to fill the position. Nevertheless, the council on September 24 voted to ratify Miller's choice.

Explosions. Early in the morning of August 10, residents of the city's Downsview neighborhood were rocked by explosions at a propane storage facility. Two people died as a result of the blasts. Hundreds of residences were damaged, and the city had to temporarily evacuate thousands of people living within 1 mile (1.6 kilometers) of the facility because of dangerous fumes. Early investigations revealed no evidence of sabotage, but the presence of the propane facility in a densely populated neighborhood prompted calls for a reexamination of the city's zoning practices.

Arts and culture. Renovation of the Art Gallery of Ontario (AGO) by the renowned Toronto-born American architect Frank Gehry was completed in 2008, with a grand opening on November 14. The newly enlarged and redesigned museum includes dramatic sculptural staircases, Douglas-fir timbers, extensive use of glass, and thousands of new artworks. The AGO renovation was one of several projects undertaken in the early 2000's to transform Toronto into an international center for cultural tourism. Other projects included the construction of the Four Seasons Centre for the Performing Arts, the expansion of the Royal Ontario Museum, and the building of a permanent home for the Toronto International Film Festival.

Torontonians demonstrated the importance of the arts to the city's public life on October 4 and 5 with Toronto's third Nuit Blanche. An estimated 800,000 to 1 million people attended the all-night event, which featured displays by contemporary artists and performing companies in the city's core.

In September, Harbourfront Centre's Premiere Dance Theatre, one of Toronto's small architectural gems, celebrated 25 years of showcasing modern dance with a weeklong retrospective and a name change. The theatre was renamed the Fleck Dance Theatre in recognition of Harbourfront Centre arts patrons Jim and Margaret Fleck.

Economic woes. The spreading world financial crisis in 2008 triggered extreme ups and downs in the Toronto Stock Exchange, as it did in stock markets around the world. Investors faced an uncertain future as the year ended.

However, Mayor Miller did begin to respond to demands that Toronto prepare for the prospect of hard times. On September 29, he announced the formation of two new civic corporations. One, called Build Toronto, was charged with developing underutilized city-owned property. The other, called Invest Toronto, was charged with marketing and promoting the city and seeking out new investment.   ■ David Lewis Stein

See also **Bank: A Special Report; Canada; Canadian provinces.**

Toys and games. Despite an economic downturn in the United States, the nation's toy industry remained strong in 2008. According to the NPD Group, a leading data collection and research company in the toy industry, retail sales of toys were expected to reach about $23 billion, up slightly from $22.1 billion in 2007.

Active play became a growing toy category in 2008. Playthings in this category are designed to encourage active lifestyles. An example is U-Dance, a motion-sensing electronic game from Hasbro, Inc., of Pawtuckett, Rhode Island. Sensors strapped onto a dancer's feet produce images and tunes on a television screen, without wires or a mat. The Me2 from iToys Inc. is a pedometer that children wear. As they move, they earn points that they can use to play online. Animal Scramble from Wild Planet Entertainment, Inc., teaches animal names, sounds, and colors. Children race to tag toy animals placed around a room or outdoors, using a toy giraffe equipped with a radio frequency identification device.

Integrated technology. Many new toys combine a physical toy with opportunities for digital play on the Internet. Techno Source's Clickables Fairy Collection includes a jewelry box, "clickable" bracelets and charms, and an electronic handheld game. The toys are based on Tinkerbell and other Disney fairy characters and

Gary Gygax
The Dungeon Master

Dungeons and Dragons is played with maps, dice, and the imagination.

Gary Gygax, co-creator of *Dungeons and Dragons,* was the father of the role-playing game. Gygax combined the dice and other conventions of board games with elements of storytelling and improvisation. The result enabled players to take on the role of heroes in a world of swordplay, magic, and monsters. "There's a call to adventure," Gygax once noted in explaining the game's appeal. "It's something in the inner psyche of humanity …." He died on March 4, 2008.

Ernest Gary Gygax was born on July 27, 1938, and lived most of his life in Lake Geneva, Wisconsin. As a child, he enjoyed games but showed little interest in formal learning. He dropped out of high school and drifted from job to job. Gygax found work as an insurance underwriter but spent his spare time at a new hobby, wargaming. Nights and weekends, he gathered with friends to re-create historic battles in miniature on their kitchen tables. They used tiny toy soldiers to represent troops, rulers to measure the troops' movements, and dice to resolve skirmishes.

A fascination with games led Gygax to tinker with the rules. He introduced dragons, trolls, and other mythical creatures. He created battles that revolved around individual heroes rather than huge armies. With fellow gamer Dave Arneson, Gygax compiled these innovations into what would become *Dungeons and Dragons*. Their creation was a new kind of game played largely in the imagination. Each player adopted a character—a knight or wizard, for example—whose abilities were recorded numerically on paper. One player, called the dungeon master, served as master storyteller, inventing and describing a fantasy world. The other players decided what actions their characters would perform—exploring dungeons, casting spells, and attacking monsters. Dice were rolled to determine their success.

In 1973, Gygax founded the company Tactical Studies Rules (TSR) to publish *Dungeons and Dragons*. The game's combination of make-believe and math appealed to college students, and many introduced it to younger siblings. Like other youth trends, *Dungeons and Dragons* sparked a moral panic, this time among adults who mistook the game's occult-inspired imagery for earnest devil-worship. Notoriety probably helped to increase its popularity. By the mid-1980's, TSR had grown to a company of 600. But with each new release, *Dungeons and Dragons* grew more complex. Gygax worried that the new rules ruined the fun and scared away would-be players. In 1985, he sold his remaining stake in TSR.

Millions of people have played *Dungeons and Dragons* or its many successors. But such pen-and-paper games have never enjoyed mainstream popularity. Perhaps Gygax's broadest legacy can be seen in computer gaming. Popular online fantasy games like *Everquest* and *World of Warcraft* are little more than computerized *Dungeons and Dragons,* with the dice exchanged for computer code and creative visualization replaced by high-resolution graphics. Gygax lamented the computerization of the role-playing game, feeling it supplanted the hobby's most rewarding aspects—imagination and social interaction. After leaving TSR, he created other role-playing games, but none approached the original in popularity. As the hobby grew, however, Gygax matured into the roles of its patriarch, ambassador, and mascot.   ■ Jeff De La Rosa

on Disney's popular Web site Pixie Hollow, where children can enter a fairy-themed virtual world. By touching together sensors embedded in the Clickables toys, girls can exchange information and become friends in the online world.

For children interested in art and photography, the VTech KidiArt Studio offers a digital camera, software, and creative activities. Children can add special effects to photos and create stop-motion animations.

Elmo Live from Fisher-Price is an animated plush toy based on the "Sesame Street" character. Elmo Live tells stories; sings and dances to music; and plays interactive games when someone touches its foot, stomach, back, or nose.

Science toys. "Green" toys that encourage respect for the environment took many forms in 2008. Aurora World's line of Eco-Plush toy animals have coverings made from soybean fiber and stuffings of kapok, a sustainable rain forest crop. The toys depict many endangered species, such as the polar bear, panda, and lemur.

Planet Earth Monopoly by USAopoly, the Planet Earth DVD board game by Imagination Games, and Planet Earth puzzles by the Canadian Group were based on the award-winning television series, first broadcast in 2006. The games and puzzles teach about natural habitats and animals.

Dinosaur toys remained popular in 2008. Playskool's Kota the Triceratops uses electronics to animate a lifelike toy dinosaur large enough for children to sit on. Kota reacts to touch and sound, makes realistic noises, and even "eats."

Jakks Pacific's Discovery Kids series of toys features a handheld electronic device called the Scanopedia. When the Scanopedia scans toy animals in the Smart Animals series, it triggers sound effects and reveals facts about each animal.

Classic toys appeared in new versions in 2008. Hasbro introduced the Easy-Bake Decorating Sensation Frosting Pen to use with its 45-year-old working toy oven, the Easy-Bake Oven. Crayola celebrated the 50th anniversary of its 64-crayon box. Crayola conducted an online survey in which children worldwide voted for their eight favorite crayon colors and gave them new names.

Toy safety. In August, U.S. President George W. Bush signed sweeping new toy safety legislation. The Consumer Products Safety Improvement Act set strict new safety standards and testing requirements for toys and other children's products sold in the United States.

Bratz ruling. In December, a federal judge ordered MGA Entertainment Inc. to stop making its popular Bratz dolls. A jury found that the creator of the Bratz dolls developed the idea while working at Mattel, maker of the rival Barbie dolls. ■ Adrienne Citrin

See also **Electronics.**

Track and field. Jamaican sprinters Asafa Powell and Usain Bolt staged a thrilling rivalry in 2008, with Bolt establishing himself as the fastest man on the planet. He set world records at the 2008 Summer Olympic Games in Beijing, in both the 100 meters (9.69) and 200 meters (19.30). Powell tied Bolt's previous record for the second fastest 100 meters on September 2, with a time of 9.72 seconds in Lausanne, Switzerland.

In their final meeting of 2008, Bolt overcame a bad start at the Van Damme Memorial in Brussels, Belgium, on September 5 to run the fastest 100 meters into a headwind in history. He finished in 9.77 seconds, 0.06 second ahead of Powell, the only runner to beat him this season.

Pamela Jelimo, an 18-year-old Kenyan, won the Golden League's $1-million jackpot after capturing all six of her 800-meter races in Golden League meets, culminating at the Van Damme Memorial. Croatian high jumper Blanka Vlasic lost in the final meet, allowing Jelimo to keep the entire $1 million. Tyson Gay ran a 9.68 in the 100 meters on June 29 but it was wind-aided and, therefore, not a world record.

Double amputee Oscar Pistorius failed to make the South African 4x400 relay because his 400-meter qualifying time was off the qualifying standards. Pistorius had initially been prohibited from competing in the Olympics when the International Association of Athletics Federations ruled his carbon-fiber blades provided an advantage over able-bodied runners. But the Court of Arbitration overturned that decision.

Racing shame. Track coach Trevor Graham received a lifetime ban from the U.S. Anti-Doping Agency on July 15 for his role in helping his athletes obtain performance enhancing drugs. Among them were Marion Jones, Justin Gatlin, and Tim Montgomery. Justin Gatlin's four-year ban on doping charges was upheld, denying the sprinter a shot at the Olympics.

Marion Jones, who won five medals, including three golds, at the 2000 Summer Olympics in Sydney, served just under six months of a prison sentence in 2008 after pleading guilty to lying to investigators about using performance-enhancing drugs and her role in a check-fraud scheme. Jones, who was released on September 5, had admitted to using performance enhancers after years of negative testing and vehement denials. She was stripped of her medals, as were her teammates on her relay teams.

Montgomery, the world record holder in the 100-meter dash until losing that award for doping, was sentenced to nearly four years in prison for writing bad checks. He also received a five-year sentence on October 11 for selling heroin.

Other men's records. Cuban hurdler Dayron Robles broke the 110-meter record held by China's

Liu Xiang on June 12 in Ostrava, Czech Republic. Robles's time of 12.87 seconds broke the mark by 0.01 second. Russian Vladimir Kanaykin set a new mark in the 20-kilometer race walk with a time of 1 hour 16:53 seconds on June 8 in Saransk, Russia. Ethiopia's Haile Gebrselassie set a record for the marathon with a time of 2 hours 3 minutes 59 seconds on September 28 in Berlin.

Other women's records. Russian pole vaulter Elena Isinbaeva broke her own world record on numerous occasions in 2008, going 16 feet, 6 ½ inches (5.04 meters) just before the Olympic competition, then topping that mark by ¼ inch (.64 centimeter) in Beijing.

Ethiopia's Tirunesh Dibaba set a new record for the 5,000 meters with a time of 14 minutes 11.15 seconds on June 6 in Oslo, Norway. Dire Tune of Ethiopia set a record for the one-hour run with a distance of 18,517 meters (60,751 feet) on June 12 in Ostrava, Czech Republic. Russian Gulnara Galkina set a record in the 3,000-meter steeplechase with a time of 8 minutes 58.81 seconds on July 17 at the Olympics. Barbora Spotáková of the Czech Republic broke the previous javelin record with a throw of 72.28 meters (237 feet) on September 13 at Stuttgart, Germany.   ■ Michael Kates

See also **Disability; Olympic Games: A Special Report.**

Transit. See Transportation.

Transportation. World crude oil prices continued to rise during 2008, soaring to almost $150 a barrel in July. Contributing factors to the price increase included a growing global demand for crude oil, concern over the amount of oil remaining in oil reserves, fears about political instability in oil-producing regions, and speculation by investors about oil prices. As a result of higher oil prices, the cost of gasoline in the United States rose to an average of more than $4 a gallon during the summer.

Public transportation. The dramatic rise in gasoline prices contributed to a significant increase in ridership on public transportation in the United States. Environmental concerns and such new technologies as on-board wireless Internet service and in-rail car media networks also have made public transportation more attractive in recent years.

According to the American Public Transportation Association (APTA), public transportation ridership increased more than 5 percent during the period from April to June 2008, compared with the same period in 2007. APTA predicted that ridership in 2008 likely would set a 50-year record. The U.S. Federal Highway Administration reported that in June, Americans drove more than 12 billion miles (19 billion kilometers) fewer than they had during June 2007.

Air travel also was affected by rising oil prices. Domestic and international airlines raised

WORLD TRACK AND FIELD RECORDS ESTABLISHED IN 2008

Event	Holder	Country	Where set	Date	Record
WOMEN INDOOR					
1,500 meters	Elena Soboleva	Russia	Valencia, Spain	March 9	3:57.71
60-meter hurdles	Susanna Kallur	Sweden	Karlsruhe, Germany	February 10	7.68
Pole vault	Elena Isinbaeva	Russia	Donetsk, Ukraine	February 16	4.95m
MEN OUTDOOR					
100 meters	Usain Bolt	Jamaica	Beijing, China	August 16	*9.69
200 meters	Usain Bolt	Jamaica	Beijing, China	August 20	*19.30
Marathon	Haile Gebrselassie	Ethiopia	Berlin, Germany	September 28	*2:03:59
110-meter hurdles	Dayron Robles	Cuba	Ostrava, Czech Republic	June 12	12.87
20-kilometer race walk	Vladimir Kanaykin	Russia	Saransk, Russia	June 8	1:16:53
50-kilometer race walk	Denis Nizhegorodov	Russia	Cheboksary, Russia	May 11	*3:34:14
4X100-meter relay	Jamaica	Jamaica	Beijing, China	August 22	*37.10
WOMEN OUTDOOR					
5,000 meters	Tirunesh Dibaba	Ethiopia	Oslo, Norway	June 6	*14:11.15
1-hour run	Dire Tune	Ethiopia	Ostrava, Czech Republic	June 12	18,517m
3,000-meter steeplechase	Gulnara Galkina	Russia	Beijing, China	August 17	*8:58.81
Pole vault	Elena Isinbaeva	Russia	Beijing, China	August 18	*5.05m
Javelin throw	Barbora Spotáková	Czech Republic	Stuttgart, Germany	September 13	*72.28m

m = meters
* = not yet ratified.   Source: International Association of Athletics Federations (IAAF).

airfares, attributing their action to the high price of jet fuel. Some airlines also began charging passengers fees for services, such as checking luggage, that previously had been free, to help cover their higher costs. According to the International Air Transport Association (IATA), a global trade organization, the airline industry could face financial losses of more than $5 billion for the year. The IATA also reported slowing growth in the number of airline passengers in August.

In addition to high fuel costs, a global credit crisis affected the aviation industry. By fall 2008, dozens of airlines had gone bankrupt. They included ATA, Aloha, Eos, Frontier, Maxjet, Nationwide, Oasis Hong Kong, Silverjet, Skybus, XL, and Zoom airlines.

The automobile industry experienced adverse effects in 2008 from high gas prices and the global credit crisis. Major automobile manufacturers, including U.S.-based Chrysler, Ford, and General Motors and Japan-based Nissan and Toyota, reported a dramatic dip in U.S. sales of more than 30 percent in September, compared with sales in September 2007. Following the credit crisis, banks restricted lending and consumers had difficulty obtaining loans to purchase cars.

On Dec. 19, 2008, President George W. Bush announced that he had authorized a $17.4-billion short-term loan package to the ailing U.S. auto industry, stating that allowing the industry to fail was not "a responsible course of action." The money was to come from the $700-billion fund pledged to bail out the U.S. financial sector.

Rail legislation passed by the U.S. Congress in 2008 called for railroads nationwide to install a safety system called *positive train control* (PTC) by 2015. This system automatically activates a train's brakes if the engineer fails to heed traffic signals. The legislation also limits the number of hours that train crews may work and authorizes federal subsidies of more than $12 billion over 5 years for Amtrak, also known as the National Railroad Passenger Corporation. The subsidies will help cover such expenses as equipment purchases, rail repair and expansion, and repayment of Amtrak's debt.

Passage of the legislation followed a deadly train collision, on Sept. 12, 2008, involving a Los Angeles Metrolink commuter train and a Union Pacific freight train. The crash, which killed 25 people and injured many others, occurred when the commuter train's engineer missed a stop signal. The legislation's passage also came at a time of record-breaking ridership on Amtrak trains. According to the corporation, its trains carried more than 28 million passengers during the fiscal year ending in September 2008.

Spanair tragedy. A Spanair passenger jet headed to the Canary Islands crashed at the Madrid-Barajas Airport on August 20, killing all but 18 of the 172 people on board. The McDonnell Douglas-82 aircraft crashed near the runway after failing to gain enough altitude to take off successfully. A report issued following the accident said that faulty wing flaps, which provide lift during takeoff, might have caused the crash. Two mechanics who had performed repairs on the plane and the head of Spanair's maintenance staff were under investigation for carelessness.

I-35W bridge in Minneapolis. A new $234-million bridge connecting busy Interstate 35W over the Mississippi River opened ahead of schedule on September 18. The old bridge had collapsed on Aug. 1, 2007, killing 13 people and injuring more than 100 others. Officials said the 40-year-old steel-truss bridge likely had collapsed because of a number of factors, including corrosion, vibrations, weathering, and weight. Hundreds of sensors built into the new bridge record data about how it handles such stress factors and transmit the information to a control center for analysis. The sensors also monitor traffic flow and security and activate an anti-icing system on the bridge in cold weather.   ■ Dawn Krajcik

See also **Automobile; Aviation; Bank: A Special Report; U.S. Government: A Special Report.**

Trinidad and Tobago. See Latin America; West Indies.

Tunisia. See Africa.

Turkey. The Grand National Assembly (parliament) of Turkey passed a constitutional amendment in February 2008 to end the ban on women wearing Islamic headscarves at universities. Turkey's ruling Justice and Development Party (AKP) had argued that banning the headscarves was a denial of individual rights and religious liberty. The amendment was passed despite massive public protests against lifting the ban.

In June, the Constitutional Court (Turkey's highest court) ruled to annul the constitutional amendment because it violated the *secular* (separation of religion and politics) principles of Turkey. The high court also cut off a substantial portion of state aid to the AKP.

Ergenekon arrests. In September, a court in Istanbul ordered the arrests of six people for plotting to overthrow the government of Prime Minister Recep Tayyip Erdogan. These people were the latest of more than 100 individuals who were arrested since mid-2007 on accusations that they were members of an alleged terrorist network called Ergenekon. Critics of the arrests claimed that the government detained the individuals in retaliation for their attempts to have the AKP banned and for organizing anti-AKP demonstrations throughout Turkey.

Confiscated religious properties. The Grand National Assembly approved a law in February

2008 that allowed Jewish and Christian foundations to reclaim places of worship and other properties confiscated by the government in 1974, at the time of the Turkish invasion of Cyprus. This law was a key reform demanded by the European Union (EU) as one of the conditions for Turkey's entry into the EU. The law also allowed Muslim foundations to receive financial aid from foreign countries.

Important state visits. In January 2008, Prime Minister Kostas Karamanlis of Greece became the first Greek head of state to visit Turkey in 49 years. In May, Queen Elizabeth II and Prince Philip of the United Kingdom made their first visit to Turkey since 1971. In September 2008, President Abdullah Gül of Turkey visited Armenia, the first such visit by a Turkish leader in modern history. Experts in international affairs noted that these visits signaled a willingness on the part of the AKP to resolve differences with the West in order for Turkey to accede to the EU.

Kurds in Iraq. Throughout 2008, Turkish forces made numerous cross-border raids into Iraq to attack strongholds of the Kurdistan Workers Party (PKK). The PKK sought an independent state in the region that would include southeastern Turkey. United States and EU officials cautioned Turkey to restrain their attacks in Iraq to avoid destabilizing the region.   ■ Mary-Jane Deeb

See also **Europe; Iraq.**

Turkmenistan began 2008 in a natural gas row with neighboring Iran. Turkmenistan halted natural gas exports to Iran in a pricing dispute in late December 2007. The move set off a chain reaction in which Iran reduced gas supplies to Turkey and Turkey cut gas shipments to Greece during an unusually cold winter. Turkmenistan resumed supplies to Iran on April 25, 2008, after Iran agreed to a significant price hike.

President Gurbanguly Berdimuhammedov continued to lift Turkmenistan out of its earlier self-imposed international isolation during 2008. He reestablished diplomatic relations with Azerbaijan; restored the Gregorian calendar; abolished the February 19 holiday honoring deceased dictator Saparmurad Niyazov's birth; and introduced a new constitution. The constitution, adopted on September 26, called for a 125-member elected parliament and endorsed market economic principles. In an unprecedented move for a Turkmen leader, Berdimuhammedov also invited observers from the Organization for Security and Cooperation in Europe (OSCE) to observe elections to the new parliament on December 14. International observers expressed concern that the only political party represented in the elections was the pro-government Democratic Party.   ■ Juliet Johnson

See also **Asia; Azerbaijan.**

Tuvalu. See Pacific Islands.

Uganda. Some two years of peace negotiations between Uganda and the Lord's Resistance Army (LRA)—a rebel group based mainly in northern Uganda and southern Sudan—were disrupted in 2008 when LRA leader Joseph Kony failed to appear at a signing ceremony. The rebel guerrillas were expected to sign a pact on April 10 to end their two-decade-long insurgency against President Yoweri Museveni's National Resistance Movement (NRM) government, which had originally seized power in 1986.

The LRA subsequently continued its insurgency. In mid-May, the group abducted at least 100 children from neighboring countries to use as fighters, porters, or sex slaves.

War crimes court. During 2008, security analysts reported that Kony had not signed the agreement because he feared that he and four other ranking LRA commanders would be tried and hanged by the International Criminal Court (ICC) in The Hague, the Netherlands. In 2005, the ICC had issued arrest warrants to try Kony and senior LRA leaders for multiple abuses against humanity. In an attempt to convince the ICC that the matter could be settled internally, Uganda's judiciary on May 23, 2008, announced a new special court to deal with serious war crimes arising from the LRA insurgency.

However, by the end of 2008, the ICC indictments still remained a sticking point to the implementation of any peace deal. Independent observers claimed that Kony was stalling to forcibly recruit fresh fighters and acquire new weapons.

Regional relations. Following a violent skirmish between forces from Uganda and Congo (Kinshasa) in the summer of 2007 over ownership of an island in Lake Albert on their mutual frontier, Congo agreed in 2008 to accept an independent ruling that the island belonged to Uganda. The dispute had arisen after the discovery of oil in the area. The agreement occurred against the background of efforts by both nations to improve border security in the largely lawless eastern Congo and appeals by Uganda for its neighbor to fight cross-border crime.

Museveni's fourth term. In July, Museveni confirmed that he intended to run in the 2011 presidential race as the NRM candidate for a fourth consecutive five-year term. At the previous polls held in 2006—the first multiparty elections to have been held in Uganda since 1980—Museveni obtained 59 percent of the presidential vote. Opposition parties responded to the president's announcement by stating that they would field one common candidate in 2011 to defeat Museveni and his ruling NRM.

■ Simon Baynham

See also **Africa.**

A Ukrainian woman protests the visit of a delegation from the North Atlantic Treaty Organization (NATO) in June. Ukrainians were deeply split in 2008 about President Viktor Yushchenko's hope to get Ukraine into the military alliance.

Ukraine continued to suffer from an ongoing political crisis in 2008 as President Viktor Yush-chenko and Prime Minister Yulia Tymoshenko sparred repeatedly, leading their ruling coalition to a dramatic September collapse. Tymoshenko's bloc and Yushchenko's Our Ukraine parties had formed a tenuous coalition after parliamentary elections in 2007. The two leaders' relationship had grown tense soon after the 2004 "Orange Revolution" brought their first pro-Western coali-tion to power and worsened over time. The politi-cal uncertainty sparked by their conflict in 2008 delayed efforts to negotiate a $16.5-billion loan from the United Nations-affiliated International Monetary Fund (IMF) to help resolve Ukraine's economic crisis and dashed Yushchenko's attempts to gain support for the nation's entry into the North Atlantic Treaty Organization (NATO).

Power struggle. Tymoshenko and Yushchen-ko first clashed in 2008 over Ukraine's rising infla-tion and slowing economic growth. Tymoshenko shepherded through parliament a law imposing price controls on staple goods in May, but Yushchenko vetoed the measure on June 20.

The two leaders again butted heads after a military confrontation between Russia and Geor-gia in August. Yushchenko condemned Russia's actions and openly supported pro-Western Geor-gian President Mikheil Saakashvili. In contrast, on September 2, Tymoshenko's bloc voted with Viktor Yanukovich's pro-Russian Party of Regions to defeat a measure blaming Russian leaders for inciting the conflict. On the same day, Tymoshen-ko's bloc and the Party of Regions joined forces to pass a measure weakening the president's powers while boosting the powers of the prime minister. Yushchenko accused Tymoshenko of attempting a political *coup* (overthrow), and the ruling coalition collapsed on September 16.

Election disagreement. On October 9, Yushchenko dissolved parliament and called for early elections to be held on December 7. How-ever, Tymoshenko's bloc repeatedly prevented parliament from voting on a bill to finance the elections, arguing that Ukraine could not afford the cost while in the midst of the global financial crisis. On October 30, Tymoshenko's bloc allowed parliament to vote on the election finance mea-sure, which fell four votes short. This cleared the way for parliament to pass legislation that the IMF had required before it would release emergency funding to battle Ukraine's deep economic crisis. The IMF board formally approved the loan pack-age on November 5. On November 12, Yush-chenko capitulated to Tymoshenko and postponed the planned election until 2009. ■ Juliet Johnson
See also **Europe; Georgia; Russia.**

Unemployment. See **Economics; Labor.**

UNITED KINGDOM

Gordon Brown's Labour Party government had a difficult year in 2008 as the economy of the United Kingdom (U.K.) was affected by the worldwide economic crisis. Labour had been elected in 1997, led by Tony Blair. Brown took over as prime minister in 2007 after serving as Blair's chancellor of the exchequer (finance minister) for the previous decade. Labour's record on the economy had been strong, but the opposition Conservative Party claimed that the U.K.'s vulnerability to the global financial crisis revealed flaws in Brown's record. The Conservatives, led by David Cameron, led in opinion polls throughout 2008.

Cabinet. In January, Work and Pensions Minister Peter Hain resigned after revelations that he had failed to declare a number of donations during his campaign for the deputy leadership of the Labour Party in 2007 (a contest won by Harriet Harman). Hain became the subject of a police inquiry because the donations were allegedly made in an improper manner. He was replaced by James Purnell. Hain had also been minister for Wales and was replaced in that position by Paul Murphy.

Parliament. Controversy arose in 2008 over the inappropriate use of public funds by members of parliament (MP's) and political parties. George Osborne, the Conservative *shadow chancellor* (opposition party member who monitors treasury issues), admitted in January that he had not properly declared campaign contributions amounting to 490,000 pounds ($734,000). He was also embarrassed in October by allegations that he had asked a leading Russian businessman, Oleg Deripaska, to make a donation to the Conservative Party through a British company Deripaska owned. Such a donation would be illegal because only British citizens may contribute to British political parties.

Conservative MP Derek Conway was suspended in January for an inappropriate use of public funds when he employed his sons as research assistants. Conway decided not to stand in the next general election. In June, the parliamentary commissioner for standards began an investigation into whether Conservative Party Chair Caroline Spelman had paid her children's nanny with public funds. The police also investigated allegations that the Labour Party had accepted donations from property developer David Abrahams in an improper manner.

In November, the shadow immigration minister, Damian Green, was briefly arrested for having received confidential information from a source in the Home Office. His home and office in the House of Commons were searched. During a debate in Parliament, opposition politicians questioned the legality of the arrest. Speaker of the House of Commons Michael Martin admitted that the police had no search warrant, leading to calls for Martin's resignation for having allowed the search to take place.

Constitution. In March, Justice Secretary Jack Straw proposed a bill that included such constitutional changes as giving Parliament the right to approve or reject the use of armed forces abroad, improving the independence of the civil service, and restoring the right to demonstrate outside Parliament. In addition, Straw suggested changing the voting system from "first past the post" (in which the candidate with the most votes wins) to a system that apportions votes among multiple candidates if one candidate fails to win more than 50 percent of the votes. He also included the possibility of making voting compulsory and moving the voting day from Thursday to the weekend. By the end of 2008, Parliament had not passed the bill.

The 10 pence tax band. A simplification of the taxation system introduced by Gordon Brown in 2007, when he was still chancellor of the exchequer, stirred controversy in 2008, when the change was to be implemented. Brown had eliminated the 10 pence tax band—the lowest level of income tax, in which people pay 10 pence to the pound. The MP's passed the legislation in 2007 but, in 2008, critics complained that the move would hurt the poorest taxpayers. In May, the new chancellor, Alastair Darling, introduced a rebate package for those who had paid more taxes because the 10 pence band was eliminated.

Financial crisis. Following the credit crisis in the United States, the British economy began to move into recession during 2008. Housing prices fell, as did the value of sterling (upon which the British pound is based). Unemployment and inflation rose. Investors lost confidence in business, and the number of homes repossessed because their owners could not pay their mortgages increased.

In February, the government nationalized savings bank Northern Rock after failing to find a new owner for the bank in the private sector. Northern Rock specialized in mortgage lending. The bank failed in 2007, leading to panic among its customers, who rushed to withdraw their deposits. To maintain the bank, the Bank of England loaned Northern Rock 26 billion pounds ($39 billion) and the treasury guaranteed a further 30 billion pounds ($45 billion).

Nevertheless, for much of the year, Brown insisted that the British economy was basically sound. However, Darling admitted in August that the nation was facing its worst economic crisis in 60 years. The U.K.'s recent prosperity had been based on an overvalued housing market and on financial services, which were vulnerable to the global crisis.

To sustain the housing market, Brown made 1.6 billion pounds ($2.4 billion) available to first-time buyers. In September, he brokered a deal in which Lloyds Bank took over the ailing HBOS (the U.K.'s largest mortgage lender). Brown also nationalized the mortgage bank Bradford and Bingley and sold its branches to the Spanish bank Santander. One month later, Brown propped up banking in the U.K. by providing the largest banks with government funding in exchange for ownership shares and by offering loans to ease borrowing. This dramatic step—which cost 400 billion pounds ($591 billion)—was viewed as a form of nationalization and was taken to prevent a run on the banks. In November, the Bank of England cut interest rates by 1.5 percent to 3 percent—an unprecedented

drop and the lowest rate in half a century—to stimulate the economy. Government plans to combat the recession appeared in the November Pre-Budget Report. Darling announced a temporary 2.5 percent cut in the *value added* (sales) tax to encourage consumer spending. He also increased government borrowing and national insurance as well as the income tax rate for top earners.

Brown reshuffled his Cabinet in October, in an effort to bring more experienced members into the Cabinet. He recalled Peter Mandelson (often viewed as Brown's political enemy) to become business secretary. The appointment was seen as evidence that Brown's government was setting aside differences to focus on the economy. Former Foreign Secretary Margaret Beckett was also brought back as housing minister. In late 2008, Brown established a National Economic Council to shape economic policy and handle the recession.

Terrorism. In February, five men were convicted for their involvement in the "second wave"

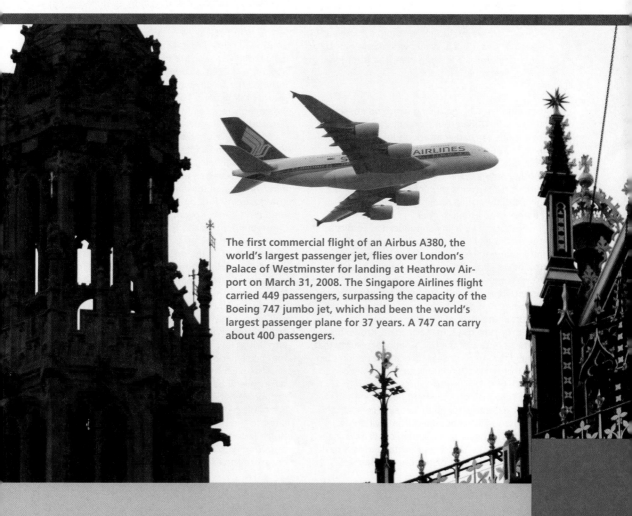

The first commercial flight of an Airbus A380, the world's largest passenger jet, flies over London's Palace of Westminster for landing at Heathrow Airport on March 31, 2008. The Singapore Airlines flight carried 449 passengers, surpassing the capacity of the Boeing 747 jumbo jet, which had been the world's largest passenger plane for 37 years. A 747 can carry about 400 passengers.

The traditional horsehair wigs and black robes worn by British civil court judges for centuries were replaced in October 2008. Modern robes developed by fashion designer Betty Jackson—without wigs—were introduced. However, judges in criminal courts, as well as *barristers* (lawyers who argue cases in court) will continue to wear the traditional wigs and robes.

of London bombings, during which bombs set on the London Underground on July 21, 2005, failed to explode. An earlier attack on July 7, 2005, had killed 52 people and injured 700 others. Also in February, Mohammed Hamid was found guilty of inciting others to murder and of creating training centers for terrorists throughout the U.K. One of his associates, Atilla Ahmet, pleaded guilty to charges of soliciting murder.

In September, a jury announced its verdict at the trial of eight British Muslims accused of attempting to blow up airplanes by carrying liquid explosives aboard flights from London to several North American cities in 2006. One of the men was acquitted, and three were convicted of conspiracy to commit murder. The jury was unable to reach a verdict in the cases of the four others.

Forty-two days. In March 2008, Brown presented a review of the U.K.'s national security that argued that terrorism constituted the nation's biggest threat. He claimed that the police needed to be able to detain terrorist suspects for up to 42 days. Tony Blair's government had attempted to permit detention for up to 90 days. However, the measure ran into opposition from civil rights groups. The government settled on 28 days as the maximum under which a suspected terrorist could be detained without being formally charged.

Brown insisted that 42-day detention was necessary. Many Labour MP's rebelled over the issue and, in June 2008, a counterterrorism bill that included the 42-day measure barely passed in the House of Commons. The 42-day measure was overwhelmingly rejected in the House of Lords in October, and the bill was passed without it.

Muslims. Issues related to the integration of Muslims into the wider British community were raised in 2008. Michael Nazir-Ali, the Anglican Bishop of Rochester, provoked criticism in January when he alleged that some places in the U.K. were "no-go areas" for non-Muslims. The leader of the Anglican Church, Rowan Williams (Archbishop of Canterbury), provoked controversy when he suggested in February that the introduction of some forms of Shari`ah (Islamic law) into British law was unavoidable. His comments were intended to recognize that certain aspects of Shari`ah, such as those concerning marriage and inheritance, were already used by Muslims in the U.K., just as Orthodox Jews in the U.K. used rabbinical courts. Critics argued that Shari`ah should not be incorporated into British law. Williams apologized and claimed that his remarks had been misunderstood.

Also in February, the press revealed that the security services had secretly recorded Muslim Labour MP Sadiq Khan as he visited a jailed member of his constituency who was due to be extradited to the United States on terrorism charges. Home Secretary Jacqui Smith claimed that the recording was lawful. However, she ordered a review of the existing codes of practice.

Scotland. The Scottish National Party (SNP), which became the largest party in the devolved Scottish Parliament in 2007, presented its first budget in February 2008. The party, led by Alex Salmond, had formed a minority administration. The budget was passed because Labour and the Liberal Democrats abstained from the vote.

The SNP seeks to make Scotland independent of the U.K. and promised a *referendum* (vote) on the issue in 2010. In May 2008, Wendy Alexander, the leader of the Labour opposition, called for a referendum immediately—a move that was opposed by Brown and the Labour leadership. Alexander argued that Scottish support for independence was low and that such a fact would be exposed in a referendum. Salmond's strategy was to use a sustained period of SNP government as a vehicle to convince Scots of the merits of independence. In October, however, the failure of Scotland's two largest banks during the global financial crisis—and their rescue by the British government—pointed out the problem with such a plan.

Alexander resigned as leader of Scottish Labour in June, after complaints that she had received illegal campaign donations. She was replaced by Iain Gray in September.

Iraq and Afghanistan. In March a parliamentary committee reported that the cost of the U.K.'s contribution to the allied military presence in Iraq and Afghanistan in 2007-2008 was 3.3 billion pounds ($4.9 billion). The need to improve equipment had boosted costs from 2006-2007 despite a reduction in the number of British troops in Iraq. In April 2008, the Law Lords (Britain's highest court of appeal) rejected a request from the mothers of two soldiers who had been killed in Iraq for a public inquiry into the legality of the Iraq War (2003-).

In February 2008, a media source leaked the news that Prince Harry—son of Prince Charles, the Prince of Wales, and Princess Diana—had been serving with the army in Afghanistan since December 2007. The report led to concerns about the safety of Prince Harry and that of troops serving with him. The British Defense Ministry called the prince back from Afghanistan.

Elections. In May 2008, the Labour Party was defeated in local elections throughout England and Wales, experiencing its worst electoral performance since 1968. Forty-four percent of the electorate voted for Conservative Party candidates. Labour Party candidates came in third with 24 percent, just behind the Liberal Democrats, who secured 25 percent of the vote. Labour lost 334 council seats, and the Conservatives gained control of an additional 12 councils.

In London, Labour Mayor Ken Livingstone was defeated in May 2008 by the Conservative candidate,

THE CABINET OF THE UNITED KINGDOM*

Gordon Brown—prime minister; first lord of the treasury; minister for the civil service

Alistair Darling—chancellor of the exchequer

David Miliband—secretary of state for foreign and Commonwealth affairs

Hilary Benn—secretary of state for environment, food, and rural affairs

Geoff Hoon—secretary of state for transport

Alan Johnson—secretary of state for health

Shaun Woodward—secretary of state for Northern Ireland

John Hutton—secretary of state for defence

Jim Murphy—secretary of state for Scotland

Lord Mandelson—secretary of state for business, enterprise, and regulatory reform

Andy Burnham—secretary of state for culture, media, and sport

Jacqui Smith—secretary of state for the home department

Yvette Cooper—chief secretary to the treasury

Harriet Harman—leader of the House of Commons; lord privy seal; minister for women and equalities

Ed Balls—secretary of state for children, schools, and families

Baroness Royall of Blaisdon—leader of the House of Lords; lord president of the council

Jack Straw—secretary of state for justice; lord chancellor

Douglas Alexander—secretary of state for international development

James Purnell—secretary of state for work and pensions

Paul Murphy—secretary of state for Wales

John Denham—secretary of state for innovation, universities and skills

James Purnell—secretary of state for work and pensions

Edward Miliband—secretary of state for energy and climate change

Hazel Blears—secretary of state for communities and local government

*As of Dec. 1, 2008.

HOUSE OF COMMONS

Queen Elizabeth II opened the 2008-2009 session of Parliament on December 3, 2008. As of that date, the House of Commons was made up of the following:

350	Labour Party
193	Conservative Party
63	Liberal Democrats
9	Democratic Unionist Party
7	Scottish National Party
5	Sinn Féin
3	Plaid Cymru
3	Social Democratic and Labour Party
5	Independent
1	Independent Conservative
1	Independent Labour
1	Respect
1	Ulster Unionist Party

In addition, the unaffiliated speaker and 3 deputies attend sessions but do not vote.

MP and journalist Boris Johnson. Livingstone, who had served as mayor for two terms, had been criticized for some of his appointments, including his race relations adviser, Lee Jasper. Jasper was accused of improperly channeling public money to projects run by his friends. Jasper resigned in March when London's *Evening Standard* published e-mails of a suggestive nature that he had sent to a business contact. Johnson won 53 percent of the vote to Livingstone's 47 percent.

Labour also performed badly in several by-elections, for which Prime Minister Brown's unpopularity was widely blamed. In November, however, the Labour candidate retained the Scottish seat of Glenrothes with a large majority. The victory was seen as evidence that voters were giving the prime minister credit for his handling of the financial crisis.

Princess Diana. The inquest into the deaths of Princess Diana and Dodi Fayed in 1997 in a car crash in Paris ended in April 2008. The jury decided that the couple were killed by their chauffeur, Henri Paul, who was drunk while driving at a high rate of speed, and by the journalists who pursued them while trying to photograph the couple. Paul also died in the crash.

■ Rohan McWilliam

See also **Bank: A Special Report; Europe; Ireland; Northern Ireland.**

United Kingdom, Prime Minister of.

Gordon Brown had a difficult year in 2008, leading some members of his own party to consider replacing him. However, he ended the year with praise both at home and abroad for his response to the global financial crisis and the downturn in the British economy. Brown became prime minister in 2007, having served as chancellor of the exchequer (finance minister) under Tony Blair after the Labour Party won the 1997 general election. Brown was credited with Labour's strong economic record. However, confusion over whether to call a general election in late 2007 lost him support, and his government appeared to lack direction as the economy moved toward recession.

In 2008, opinion poll ratings for Brown and the government were low, with Brown trailing David Cameron, the leader of the opposition party, the Conservatives. Brown's final budget as chancellor in 2007 was considered a betrayal of the poor, the very people Labour was meant to represent. In late 2008, Brown made a strong speech to the Labour Party conference. He offered financial assistance to British banks to facilitate lending and called for greater international coordination of fiscal and monetary policy. Some opinion polls showed a modest improvement in support for Brown's government.

■ Rohan McWilliam

See also **Bank: A Special Report; United Kingdom.**

United Nations.

The United Nations (UN) General Assembly opened its 63rd annual session on Sept. 16, 2008. Newly elected president Miguel d'Escoto Brockmann, a Roman Catholic priest and former foreign minister of Nicaragua's leftist Sandinista government, began his term in office. D'Escoto called for the democratization of the UN and an end to domination by superpowers.

Dozens of heads of state and government attended the General Debate in the assembly, focusing on the world's economic crisis and on how rising food and energy costs are making it difficult for the world's poorest people to secure subsistence. Secretary-General Ban Ki-moon warned UN members that they were facing a development emergency, saying "The cost of inaction—even in what may constitute tough economic times—will be devastating. ..."

On September 25, governments, foundations, and businesses pledged $16 billion to fight poverty, hunger, disease, and other socio-economic ills. The World Bank, a UN agency, reported on October 8 that high food and fuel prices will result in an increase of 44 million malnourished people in 2008, for a total of 967 million malnourished people around the world.

Disaster. Cyclone Nargis struck Myanmar (also known as Burma) on May 2, causing the deaths of more than 138,000 people. Millions of others became destitute. UN officials appealed to Myanmar's military government to allow the delivery of humanitarian supplies by international relief workers. On May 22, Secretary-General Ban and Emergency Relief Coordinator John Holmes flew to Myanmar to assess the damage. They initially sought $187 million from the international community to help the victims of the cyclone and later requested an additional $300 million. However, by November, only half the funds had been provided. International donors cited lack of accountability and an obstruction of relief efforts by the military regime as reasons for the shortfall in donations.

Africa. The conflict in Sudan's western region of Darfur between the Arab-led government in Khartoum and African rebel groups continued in 2008 despite diplomatic efforts. Secretary-General Ban reported on April 4 that four years after the UN took on the responsibility to end the conflict, the situation had worsened. The international community had spent nearly $1 billion each year since 2005 on humanitarian and recovery assistance in Darfur. During 2008, attacks on the joint UN-African Union peace operation killed 12 peacekeepers. (The African Union is an organization of more than 50 African nations.)

On July 14, prosecutor Luis Moreno-Ocampo requested that the International Criminal Court (ICC) in The Hague, the Netherlands, issue a warrant for the arrest of Sudanese President Umar al-Bashir. Al-Bashir was charged with crimes against humanity, war crimes, and genocide. An estimated 300,000 people have been killed in Darfur since 2003. Al-Bashir rejected the charges, and the African Union warned that arresting him would harm the peace process. ICC attorneys began reviewing the case in October 2008.

On November 20, the Security Council voted unanimously to increase by about 3,000 troops the UN's peacekeeping force in eastern Congo (Kinshasa). The force, which had been composed of about 17,000 troops, was attempting to stop the fighting among ethnic militias, Congolese troops, and Tutsi rebels from Rwanda that had broken out during the early 2000's. However, despite the presence of the world's largest UN peacekeeping force, a humanitarian disaster developed in late 2008 as some 250,000 people were caught in the cross fire.

AIDS. The Joint United Nations Program on HIV/AIDS (UNAIDS) issued a progress report to the 17th International Conference on HIV/AIDS, held in Mexico City in August. According to UNAIDS, global efforts to combat the epidemic worldwide had resulted in a decline of new HIV infections and AIDS-related deaths. In 2007, about 33 million people worldwide were living with HIV, and 2 million others died of the disease. About 2.7 million people became infected with HIV in 2007, down from 3 million in 2001. The report noted that some 105 countries have set targets toward achieving universal access to HIV prevention, treatment, and support by 2010.

Human rights. The UN General Assembly approved in July 2008 the nomination of South African Navanethem Pillay as the new UN High Commissioner for Human Rights. The purpose of the office is to promote and protect human rights around the world. Pillay, who has served as a judge on the International Criminal Court, began her four-year term on September 1.

Pope Benedict XVI visited UN headquarters in New York City on April 18. He urged the organization to remain, in the words of Pope John Paul II, a "moral center" where all nations can feel at home and develop a shared awareness of being a family of nations.

Security Council. In 2008, five new members were elected to the Security Council for a two-year term beginning Jan. 1, 2009—Austria, Japan, Mexico, Turkey, and Uganda. They joined the five permanent members—China, France, Russia, the United Kingdom, and the United States—and five members completing a two-year term, Burkina Faso, Costa Rica, Croatia, Libya, and Vietnam.

■ J. Tuyet Nguyen

See also **Agriculture: A Special Report; Congo (Kinshasa); Myanmar; Roman Catholic Church; Sudan.**

United States, Government of the.

The U.S. government had its hands full with a major mortgage, financial, and credit crisis during much of 2008. The crisis had begun in 2006 and 2007, when U.S. housing values started to fall and mortgage delinquencies and home foreclosures started to skyrocket. The housing slump created major troubles for financial markets, because many banks and other financial firms had invested heavily in complex securities backed by mortgages. Financial firms were forced to write-down the value of those securities, to the tune of billions of dollars, and investors fled from firms perceived to be overly exposed to those securities, causing the firms' stock prices to plummet. The depleted capital levels at many financial firms led to a severe tightening of credit, making it more difficult for both financial and nonfinancial firms, as well as consumers, to borrow money. Several financial firms collapsed, and others were taken over. The credit crunch began to noticeably disrupt overall economic activity in 2008, both in the United States and abroad.

The financial crisis prompted numerous emergency responses from the U.S. government. By the end of 2008, the amount committed by the government to financial markets—in the form of loans, direct investments, and emergency aid, as well as guarantees on bank deposits, bank-issued debt, and money market funds—exceeded $7 trillion.

In late 2007 and throughout 2008, the U.S. Federal Reserve System (the Fed), the country's central bank, cut interest rates several times and made numerous expansions in its lending programs for financial and credit markets. In February 2008, Congress enacted income tax rebates and business tax incentives to try to stimulate spending and investment. In March, the Fed financed a take-over of the Wall Street investment bank Bear Stearns & Co. by the banking firm JPMorgan Chase. In July, IndyMac Bank, a major mortgage lender, was seized and placed under the control of the Federal Deposit Insurance Corporation (FDIC). Also in July, Congress passed legislation to try to prop up two huge mortgage finance companies, Fannie Mae and Freddie Mac, and to authorize the government to insure $300 billion worth of mortgages in an effort to help homeowners at risk of foreclosure. In September, after the troubles of Fannie Mae and Freddie Mac became more critical, the companies were placed under the full control of the newly created Federal Housing Finance Agency.

Later in September, U.S. officials refused to finance a buyout of the Wall Street investment bank Lehman Brothers, forcing the firm to declare bankruptcy. The Lehman collapse helped spark a major upheaval in financial markets worldwide. Shortly afterward, the Fed agreed to lend the giant financial insurance firm American International Group (AIG) $85 billion in exchange for an

80-percent stake in the firm. Also, the Treasury Department announced that it would guarantee money market funds. In late September, another major mortgage lender, Washington Mutual, was seized and placed under FDIC control. The FDIC then sold the bank's operations and assets to JPMorgan Chase.

In early October, at the urging of executive branch officials, Congress enacted legislation creating a $700-billion financial bailout fund called the Troubled Asset Relief Program (TARP), to be administered by the Treasury Department. The legislation also extended several expiring tax breaks and provided for more federal insurance for bank deposits. The original intended use for TARP funds was to purchase troubled mortgage-backed assets from financial firms. However, Treasury Secretary Henry Paulson later abandoned that idea. In October, Treasury officials announced that $250 billion in TARP funds would be used to buy stock in several major banks, thus partially nationalizing the banks. In November, $40 billion in TARP funds was designated to buy stock in AIG as part of a restructured $150-billion Fed rescue plan for that company. Later that month, $20 billion in

TARP funds was designated to buy stock in the giant banking firm Citigroup (on top of $25 billion already designated for Citigroup in October) as part of a rescue plan that also included a partial government guarantee of more than $300 billion in troubled assets held by Citigroup. In late November, Fed and Treasury officials announced a plan to encourage lending in the consumer finance and housing markets. The plan called for the Fed to lend up to $200 billion to investors willing to purchase assets backed by consumer loans, such as auto, credit card, and student loans. The Treasury Department designated $20 billion in TARP funds for this effort. The plan also provided for the Fed to buy $600 billion in mortgage-related assets from Fannie Mae and Freddie Mac.

Auto industry. In late 2008, the giant automakers General Motors (GM), Chrysler, and Ford appealed to the U.S. government for emergency aid to the industry. The automakers had had one of their worst sales years in decades, and the credit crunch exacerbated their financial woes and put them at risk of collapse. In December, after Congress opted not to provide loans, President George W. Bush announced that $17.4 billion in TARP funds would be lent to GM and Chrysler, on the condition that the companies prove their financial viability by March 31, 2009. (Ford indi-

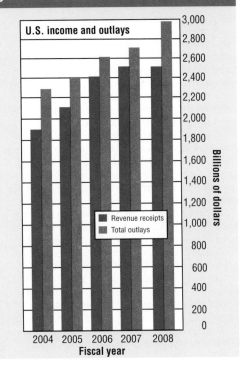

FEDERAL SPENDING   United States budget for fiscal 2008*

Billions of dollars

National defense	624.1
International affairs	28.8
General science, space, technology	24.0
Energy	0.5
Natural resources and environment	30.2
Agriculture	22.1
Commerce and housing credit	27.8
Transportation	77.7
Community and regional development	22.5
Education, training, employment, and social services	89.1
Health	280.6
Social security	617.0
Medicare	390.8
Income security	432.7
Veterans' benefits and services	84.7
Administration of justice	47.4
General government	16.0
Interest	248.9
Undistributed offsetting receipts	-86.2
Total budget outlays	**2,978.7**

*Oct. 1, 2007, to Sept. 30, 2008.
Source: U.S. Department of the Treasury.

SELECTED AGENCIES AND BUREAUS OF THE U.S. GOVERNMENT*

Executive Office of the President
President, George W. Bush
 Vice President, Richard B. Cheney
 White House Chief of Staff, Joshua B. Bolten
 Presidential Press Secretary, Dana M. Perino
 Assistant to the President for Domestic Policy,
  Karl Zinsmeister
 Assistant to the President for National Security Affairs,
  Stephen J. Hadley
 Office of Science and Technology Policy—
  John H. Marburger III, Director
 Council of Economic Advisers—Edward P. Lazear, Chairman
 Office of Management and Budget—
  James A. Nussle, Director
 Office of National Drug Control Policy—
  John P. Walters, Director
 U.S. Trade Representative, Susan C. Schwab

Department of Agriculture
Secretary of Agriculture, Ed Schafer

Department of Commerce
Secretary of Commerce, Carlos M. Gutierrez
 Bureau of Economic Analysis—J. Steven Landefeld, Director
 Bureau of the Census—Stephen H. Murdock, Director

Department of Defense
Secretary of Defense, Robert M. Gates
 Secretary of the Air Force, Michael B. Donley
 Secretary of the Army, Preston M. Geren III
 Secretary of the Navy, Donald C. Winter
 Joint Chiefs of Staff—
  Admiral Michael G. Mullen, Chairman
  General James E. Cartwright, Vice Chairman
  General Norton A. Schwartz, Chief of Staff, Air Force
  General George W. Casey, Jr., Chief of Staff, Army
  Admiral Gary Roughead, Chief of Naval Operations
  General James T. Conway, Commandant, Marine Corps

Department of Education
Secretary of Education, Margaret Spellings

Department of Energy
Secretary of Energy, Samuel Wright Bodman

Department of Health and Human Services
Secretary of Health and Human Services,
 Michael O. Leavitt
 Centers for Disease Control and Prevention—
  Julie Louise Gerberding, Director
 Food and Drug Administration—Andrew C. von Eschenbach,
  Commissioner
 National Institutes of Health—Raynard S. Kington, Acting
  Director
 Acting Surgeon General of the United States,
  Rear Admiral Steven K. Galson

Department of Homeland Security
Secretary of Homeland Security, Michael Chertoff
 U.S. Citizenship and Immigration Services—vacant
 U.S. Coast Guard—Admiral Thad W. Allen, Commandant
 U.S. Secret Service—Mark J. Sullivan, Director
 Federal Emergency Management Agency—R. David Paulison,
  Administrator

Department of Housing and Urban Development
Secretary of Housing and Urban Development,
 Steve Preston

Department of the Interior
Secretary of the Interior, Dirk Kempthorne

Department of Justice
Attorney General, Michael B. Mukasey
 Federal Bureau of Prisons—Harley G. Lappin, Director
 Drug Enforcement Administration—
  Michele Leonhart, Acting Administrator
 Federal Bureau of Investigation—
  Robert S. Mueller III, Director
 Solicitor General, Gregory G. Garre

Department of Labor
Secretary of Labor, Elaine L. Chao

Department of State
Secretary of State, Condoleezza Rice
 U.S. Ambassador to the United Nations,
  Zalmay Khalilzad

Department of Transportation
Secretary of Transportation, Mary E. Peters
 Federal Aviation Administration—
  Robert A. Sturgell, Acting Administrator

Department of the Treasury
Secretary of the Treasury, Henry M. Paulson, Jr.
 Internal Revenue Service—Douglas Shulman, Commissioner
 Treasurer of the United States, Anna Escobedo Cabral
 Office of Thrift Supervision—John M. Reich, Director

Department of Veterans Affairs
Secretary of Veterans Affairs, Lieutenant General James B. Peake

Supreme Court of the United States
Chief Justice of the United States, John G. Roberts, Jr.
 Associate Justices—

John Paul Stevens	Clarence Thomas
Antonin Scalia	Ruth Bader Ginsburg
Anthony M. Kennedy	Stephen G. Breyer
David Hackett Souter	Samuel Anthony Alito, Jr.

Congressional officials
 President of the Senate pro tempore, Robert C. Byrd
 Senate Majority Leader, Harry Reid
 Senate Minority Leader, Mitch McConnell
 Speaker of the House, Nancy Pelosi
 House Majority Leader, Steny H. Hoyer
 House Minority Leader, John Boehner
 Congressional Budget Office—Robert A. Sunshine, Acting Director
 Government Accountability Office—Gene Dodaro, Acting
  Comptroller General of the United States
 Library of Congress—James H. Billington, Librarian of Congress

Independent agencies
Central Intelligence Agency—General Michael V. Hayden, Director
Commission of Fine Arts—Earl A. Powell III, Chairman
Commission on Civil Rights—Gerald A. Reynolds, Chairman
Consumer Product Safety Commission—
 Nancy A. Nord, Acting Chairwoman
Corporation for National and Community Service—
 David Eisner, CEO
Environmental Protection Agency—Stephen L. Johnson, Administrator
Equal Employment Opportunity Commission—
 Naomi Churchill Earp, Chairwoman
Federal Communications Commission—Kevin J. Martin, Chairman
Federal Deposit Insurance Corporation—
 Sheila C. Bair, Chairwoman
Federal Election Commission—Donald F. McGahn II, Chairman
Federal Reserve System Board of Governors—
 Ben S. Bernanke, Chairman
Federal Trade Commission—William E. Kovacic, Chairman
General Services Administration—Jim Williams, Acting Administrator
National Aeronautics and Space Administration—Michael D. Griffin,
 Administrator
National Endowment for the Arts—Dana Gioia, Chairman
National Endowment for the Humanities—Bruce M. Cole, Chairman
National Labor Relations Board—Peter C. Schaumber, Chairman
National Railroad Passenger Corporation (Amtrak)—
 Joseph H. Boardman, President and CEO
National Science Foundation—Arden L. Bement, Jr., Director
National Transportation Safety Board—
 Mark V. Rosenker, Acting Chairman
Nuclear Regulatory Commission—Dale E. Klein, Chairman
Office of the Director of National Intelligence—
 Mike McConnell, Director
Peace Corps—Ronald A. Tschetter, Director
Securities and Exchange Commission—
 Christopher Cox, Chairman
Selective Service System—William A. Chatfield, Director
Small Business Administration—Sandy K. Baruah, Acting Administrator
Smithsonian Institution—G. Wayne Clough, Secretary
Social Security Administration—Michael J. Astrue, Commissioner
U.S. Postal Service—John E. Potter, Postmaster General

*As of Dec. 31, 2008.

United States Attorney for Northern Illinois Patrick Fitzgerald announces the filing of federal corruption charges against Illinois Governor Rod Blagojevich on Dec. 9, 2008. Fitzgerald accused the governor of conspiring to enrich himself through a number of "pay to play" schemes, including attempts to sell the U.S. Senate seat vacated by President-elect Barack Obama.

cated that it did not need a loan but would be badly damaged by the collapse of GM or Chrysler.)

Hiring and firing at Justice. Three reports about politicized hiring and firing at the U.S. Department of Justice (DOJ) were issued in 2008 by two DOJ divisions, the Office of the Inspector General and the Office of Professional Responsibility. One report, issued on September 29, was about the controversial removal of nine U.S. attorneys in 2006. According to the report, the process used to remove the attorneys was unsystematic and arbitrary; the attorneys were not told why they were being removed or given a chance to address performance concerns; and DOJ officials in 2007 gave inconsistent, misleading, and inaccurate statements about the reasons for the removals. The primary blame for these failures, according to the report, lay with the two senior DOJ leaders at the time, Attorney General Alberto Gonzales and Deputy Attorney General Paul McNulty, who failed to adequately oversee the removal process. In 2007, Gonzales and other DOJ officials testified that the firings had been routine and based on performance. However, the report concluded that only two attorneys had been removed for performance reasons and that there was significant evidence of political motives in the removals of at least three attorneys. The most troubling removal, according to the report, was that of New Mexico

U.S. Attorney David Iglesias. The evidence showed that he was removed because several New Mexico Republican politicians—including U.S. Senator Pete Domenici—had complained to DOJ and Bush administration officials about Iglesias's handling of voter fraud and public corruption cases in the state. On the day the report was issued, Attorney General Michael Mukasey appointed Connecticut Acting U.S. Attorney Nora Dannehy to continue investigating the attorney firings and to determine whether any criminal offense had been committed.

The other two reports, issued on June 24 and July 28, 2008, found that DOJ officials under both Gonzales and his predecessor, John Ashcroft, had illegally favored conservative candidates and rejected candidates perceived as left wing when hiring summer interns, entry-level attorneys, and career attorneys in nonpolicymaking roles, including immigration judges. The July 28 report focused especially on the hiring practices of Monica Goodling, the DOJ's White House liaison and senior counsel to the attorney general from 2006 to 2007; and Kyle Sampson, chief of staff to the attorney general from 2005 to 2007. ■ Mike Lewis

See also **Afghanistan; Armed forces; Bank: A Special Report; Congress of the United States; Election: A Special Report; Social Security; Supreme Court; Taxation; U.S., Government of the: A Special Report; United States, President of the; Welfare.**

Economic Crisis:

The

*For background information
on the banking crisis, see
Bank: A Special Report.

Government
Jumps In

By John D. Boyd

The worldwide crisis in credit markets, with powerful banks and
financial institutions afraid to lend to one another, deepened
to historic levels in September and October 2008.* A number
of top U.S. financial firms either collapsed, had to be propped up by
government loans, or were forced into mergers. The U.S. Congress
provided a $700-billion rescue fund and gave broad powers to
Treasury Secretary Henry M. Paulson, Jr., to keep banks and other
financial institutions from collapsing. Even these controversial
measures were not, however, enough to contain the crisis. In early
October, stock markets around the world began to crash. A number of
nations, in a coordinated move, responded by sharply cutting interest
rates, pouring public money into frozen credit markets, giving blanket
guarantees to bank deposits, and partly nationalizing banks to shore
up this critical industry.

It was, simply, the greatest threat to the world's financial system
since the stock market crash and panic that preceded the Great
Depression of the 1930's. Indeed, economists and government

**Billions of U.S.
taxpayer
dollars were
spent in 2008
in a federal
attempt to
thaw frozen
credit markets.**

The road to bailout

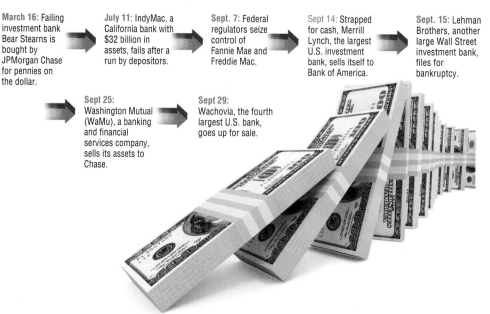

March 16: Failing investment bank Bear Stearns is bought by JPMorgan Chase for pennies on the dollar.

July 11: IndyMac, a California bank with $32 billion in assets, fails after a run by depositors.

Sept. 7: Federal regulators seize control of Fannie Mae and Freddie Mac.

Sept 14: Strapped for cash, Merrill Lynch, the largest U.S. investment bank, sells itself to Bank of America.

Sept. 15: Lehman Brothers, another large Wall Street investment bank, files for bankruptcy.

Sept 25: Washington Mutual (WaMu), a banking and financial services company, sells its assets to Chase.

Sept 29: Wachovia, the fourth largest U.S. bank, goes up for sale.

officials in 2008 warned that unless the escalating crisis was contained, and contained quickly, it could destroy markets and produce enough economic retrenchment to trigger another depression.

Earlier efforts

The crisis that first seized credit markets in late 2007 spurred the U.S. government to take extraordinary measures beginning in early 2008. Treasury Secretary Paulson had been chairman and chief executive officer at Goldman Sachs, the premier Wall Street investment bank, and had stocked his Treasury advisory team with Goldman alumni steeped in the workings of markets. Ben Bernanke, chairman of the Federal Reserve (the Fed—the U.S. central bank) had been an academic economist before coming into government; he had special expertise in the events that produced the Great Depression and how the Fed and other institutions had or had not responded. Under their leadership, the Fed made a series of interest rate cuts and loans that were designed to provide liquidity and keep capital moving as the value of mortgage-linked securities eroded in the face of widespread foreclosures and falling housing prices.

The Fed repeatedly cut the federal funds rate, the interest rate on overnight loans between banks, in late 2007. On Jan. 22, 2008, it slashed the rate by three-quarters of a point to 3.5 percent, an unusually deep cut; the rate was lowered again, by half a percentage point, to 3 percent, just days later, on January 30; and cut again on March 18 and April 30; on October 8, it was dropped to 1.5 percent from 2 percent and then cut a half-point to 1 percent on October 29. On December 16, the Fed cut the rate to 0.25 percent, or virtual zero, a historic low.

Long before Congress passed the $700-billion bailout bill on October 3, the Fed, with Treasury's blessing, tried to ease jammed credit

The author:
John D. Boyd is an associate editor specializing in freight transportation, economics, and international trade at *Traffic World* magazine, a unit of United Business Media.

flows by injecting billions of dollars into banks or short-term money markets through new loan programs. (Money markets are global trading systems for business and bank loans of about 12 months or less through the use of Treasury bills and commercial paper—promissory notes issued by corporations, usually through a bank.) In February and March, the Fed had offered $400 billion in loans to both commercial and investment banks and even accepted longer term mortgage-backed securities as collateral, which expanded the type of debt the Fed was willing to hold.

On July 13, Paulson announced a plan to prevent the collapse of mortgage giants Fannie Mae and Freddie Mac. Stocks of both companies had dropped by nearly half during the week of July 6. (Fannie Mae [the Federal National Mortgage Association] and Freddie Mac [Federal Home Loan Mortgage Corporation] are federally chartered but operate as for-profit companies. Both create secondary trading markets in differing types of home loans as a way to provide more money for would-be home buyers.) The plan allowed the firms, for the first time, to borrow from the Fed and increased the amount they could borrow from the Treasury Department.

Paulson and Bernanke also pushed major financial firms to strengthen their balance sheets or seek mergers. In March 2008, the Fed and Treasury brokered the merger of a top U.S. investment bank, The Bear Stearns Companies, after market fears about its large mortgage-related portfolio abruptly caused overnight money markets to quit funding Bear Stearns's short-term debt needs. Bear Stearns was the smallest of the five largest U.S. investment banks, a group that was topped by Goldman Sachs and included Merrill Lynch, Morgan Stanley, and Lehman Brothers. Investment banks underwrite stocks and business debts and trade and hold large investment portfolios of their own and for customers. Before the credit crisis, they also traded heavily in and held a wide range of securities tied to mortgages, instruments that created vast amounts of extra capital while spreading the risks around the globe. By the mid-2000's, they had surpassed regular banks as the major source of capital that fuels business activity.

Because Bear Stearns was a critical link in various money markets, a party to trillions of dollars of obligations through its various dealings, Paulson and Bernanke decided they could not allow it to fail, which they later explained could cause interwoven global markets to stop functioning.

The New York City-based commercial bank JPMorgan Chase agreed on March 16 to acquire Bear Stearns at a fire-sale price of $236 million, down from a

market value of $20 billion a year earlier. A key to the deal was a $29-billion loan from the Fed to cover some of the riskier holdings. Bear Stearns shareholder protests soon led Morgan to increase the price it paid to about $1.2 billion.

Bernanke was criticized for this "bailout" when many homeowners faced foreclosure, even though Bear Stearns investors lost heavily and most of its 14,000 employees lost their jobs. Some lawmakers questioned the Fed's unusual exercise of power. Bernanke told Congress on April 2 that the Fed acted "to prevent a disorderly failure of Bear Stearns and the unpredictable but likely severe consequences of such a failure for market functioning and the broader economy."

For a number of months, the action appeared to work. As late as August, some observers said that the Bear Stearns deal had been the turning point when the government had gotten on top of the crisis. The deal gave other firms with troubled portfolios time to make orderly changes but sent the message that they could lose their companies. Trouble signs continued, however. Credit markets remained weak and halting, and stocks were volatile. Then on July 11, IndyMac, a California-based savings and loan with $32 billion in assets, failed after a bank run.

The crisis reemerges

On September 7, U.S. regulators seized control of Fannie Mae and Freddie Mac. Earlier Treasury support had been insufficient to save them, and regulators placed them under new management. The government also pledged to invest up to $200 billion to cover default losses.

Within days, Lehman Brothers, the fourth-largest Wall Street investment bank, was close to collapse, but this time Paulson drew the line, reportedly telling the heads of the remaining large investment banks and top commercial banks that there would be no more federal funds committed to propping up firms.

During a weekend of crisis meetings in New York City between Paulson and top Wall Street executives, Merrill Lynch, a venerable stock brokerage that had expanded into investment banking, agreed to be bought by Charlotte, North Carolina-based Bank of America. Lehman, however, got no takers after the bankers looked closely at its holdings. On September 15, it filed for bankruptcy.

Things rapidly unraveled after that. The Lehman announcement sent stocks tumbling on markets around the world. Lehman was much larger than Bear Stearns and handled more funds from other parties or trading of its own. Lehman customers, which included large money market funds, suddenly found their assets frozen in the bankruptcy and, therefore, had trouble making payouts to their own customers. Credit markets locked up tightly.

The largest corporate and industrial insurer in the United States, American International Group (AIG), which held a huge portfolio of ailing mortgage-related securities, found it could no longer tap short-term debt markets for operating funds. Reversing their stance against no more federally funded bailouts, Paulson and Bernanke on September 16 promised AIG an $85-billion loan that later grew to more than $150 billion. In return, the Treasury Department took an 80-percent stake in AIG.

Soon after, the two remaining independent Wall Street investment banks, Goldman Sachs and Morgan Stanley, desperate for federal money, were forced to restructure as commercial bank holding companies, subject to Fed regulation but able to tap Fed loan resources. An era on Wall Street was over: All five of the top investment banks were gone, either through collapse, merger, or restructuring.

The Fed's $85-billion bailout of AIG failed to quell investor fears. The Dow Jones Industrial Average dropped nearly 450 points in trading on the New York Stock Exchange on September 17; it had fallen 800 points, or 7.1 percent, in three days. Stocks also declined in London, Paris, Frankfurt, Hong Kong, and Tokyo.

The great bailout

On September 18, Paulson and Bernanke went to Congress to warn that the crisis had escalated to the point that they needed new power and funds to stabilize markets. They proposed buying up troubled home loans as a way of halting the downward spiral of their value. They called it the "troubled asset relief program," but many in Congress and the media called it history's biggest bailout. Although the plan would cost taxpayers "hundreds of billions of dollars," noted Secretary Paulson, "it will cost Americans far less than the alternative. . . . Their retirement savings, their home values, their ability to borrow for college depend on it."

On September 19, Treasury announced that it would, for the next year, guarantee money market funds against losses up to $50 billion. The Fed announced that its emergency lending program would be expanded to provide loans to commercial banks for acquisition of asset-backed securities from money market funds. At that point, money market funds held some $3.4 trillion in investments. However, the total value had declined by nearly $170 billion in just one week, and Putnam Investments, faced with an avalanche of investor redemption requests, announced that it was forced to liquidate its $12.3-billion Putnam Prime Money Market Fund. Treasury officials voiced their concern that this falling value of money market funds was causing further liquidity strains in world markets. "This action should enhance market confidence and alleviate investors' concerns about the ability for money market mutual funds to absorb a loss," declared Treasury officials.

The Paulson proposal set off intense debate among lawmakers angered by the lack of regulatory oversight that had allowed the panic to unfold. They pointed out that the administration of President George W. Bush was rushing to bail out Wall Street when millions of families were suffering and losing their

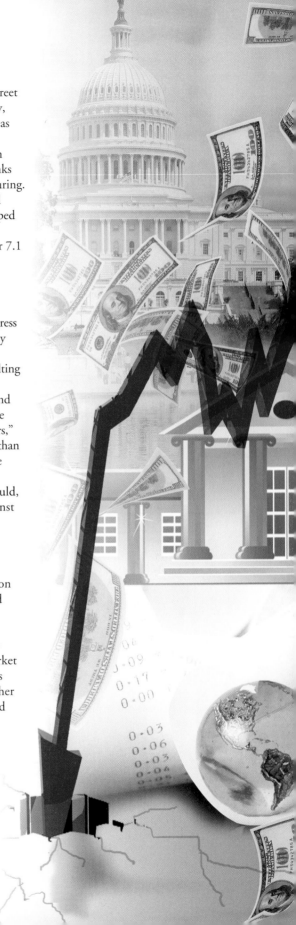

homes without any kind of help from the government. Members of Congress were also worried by the large costs involved, the extreme powers Paulson sought, and how it would all affect voters just before the congressional and presidential elections in November.

The financial crisis and the election

As talks continued between congressional leaders and the administration on how to reshape the bailout to suit both branches of government, voters began to look closely at the two main presidential candidates: Senator Barack Obama (D., Illinois) and Senator John McCain (R., Arizona). According to political experts, the economic crisis triggered a shift in public opinion toward the candidates. Obama was young, 47, a former professor, and a legal scholar. McCain, a war hero, was at 71 the oldest man ever to run for president. McCain responded to the crisis by announcing that he would suspend his campaign and return to Washington, D.C., to help push the rescue plan through Congress. At McCain's urging, President Bush convened a meeting of government leaders, including McCain and Obama, on September 25. McCain announced that because of the crisis the first presidential debate scheduled for September 26 should be postponed. Obama insisted that they debate as planned, and the two resumed their campaigns. Obama subsequently took a clear lead in the polls, and many observers linked that lead to his calm, steady appearance during the crisis.

The destruction continues

On the day of the first presidential debate, Seattle-based Washington Mutual Inc.—a savings and loan with $307 billion in assets—was seized by federal regulators in what was described as the biggest bank failure in U.S. history. JPMorgan Chase bought many of its assets, including 2,300 branch offices, for $1.9 billion.

At the same time, officials at Charlotte-based Wachovia Corporation—the nation's fourth-largest bank holding company, with assets of $783 billion in 2007—watched helplessly as shareholders fearful of the Wachovia mortgage portfolio dumped their holdings. As the stock slid, depositors began to withdraw deposits. On September 29, Wachovia agreed to sell itself to Citigroup of New York City for $2.19 billion. In 2007, Wachovia had assets of $783 billion. Wells Fargo later topped Citigroup's offer. Congress imposed numerous conditions on the market rescue plan before it first came to a vote on September 29 in the House of Representatives. In a 228-205 vote, the House rejected the plan. Opponents claimed that the legislation was too hastily written, not fully considered, and rewarded failed Wall Street speculators with taxpayer money. The Dow reacted with a record 778-point drop, then the biggest single-day point drop in New York Stock Exchange history. The Senate then retooled the bill to include oversight provisions and popular tax breaks and passed the measure. The House followed suit, and President Bush signed it into law on October 3.

Economic contagion

By the time Congress passed the $700-billion rescue legislation, the credit lockdown had swept ferociously into Europe and Asia. It pushed the nation of Iceland into bankruptcy, threatened top banks in the United Kingdom, and forced Russia to suspend its crashing stock market.

To combat panic and restore trust, the Fed and some other central banks had already expanded the range of banking assets they would accept as collateral, including mortgage-backed securities. On October 7, the Fed announced it also would buy unsecured, short-term corporate debt to unfreeze money markets. (Companies issue short-term debt to help meet daily business needs, much like the overnight federal loans that banks use.) The move put the Fed in the position of buying as much as $1 trillion in corporate promissory notes backed by no collateral.

On October 8, the Fed, European Central Bank, Bank of England, Bank of Canada and several governments simultaneously cut rates by ½ percent to show global coordination. It failed, however, to calm the markets and end the volatility.

Paulson then switched gears, telling top bankers on October 13 that the Treasury would use up to $250 billion from rescue plan funds to take ownership stakes in all major U.S. banks, much like a British plan that was helping restore market confidence. The idea was to capitalize the banking system while giving the Treasury more control over how they operate. The banks had no choice but to accept what was, in fact, partial nationalization.

On November 12, Paulson explained that the rescue program would not be used to purchase troubled assets as originally planned, but rather, funds would be used to support financial markets. According to Paulson, 40 percent of consumer credit in the United States is derived through selling market securities backed by pools of such debt as auto and student loans and credit card balances. "This market, which is vital for lending and growth, has for all practical purposes ground to a halt," he noted, adding that bailout money could also be used to keep mortgage borrowers from going into default and losing their houses. The stock market reacted by falling 411.30 points to close at 8282.66.

Every week brought new major efforts to blunt the crisis. On November 23, the government unveiled a "backstop" aid plan for Citigroup, the largest U.S. bank by assets, after its stock plunged 60 percent the prior week. Federal agencies agreed to stand behind most of the bank's troubled $306 billion portfolio and invest $20 billion directly on top of $25 billion already put into Citigroup earlier. In exchange, the Fed received $7 billion of preferred stock shares and imposed new restrictions. On November 24, the Fed announced that it would spend $800 billion to buy up consumer loans and $200 billion to help unstick intermediate markets for such household debt as auto and student loans; $500 billion more was aimed at mortgage-related securities.

More was on the way. President-elect Obama urged Congress to prepare a stimulus bill that included massive public works projects to be ready when he would take office on Jan. 20, 2009. According to lawmakers, the package could total another $700 billion.

United States, President of the.

Barack Obama, a Democratic U.S. senator from Illinois, was elected the 44th president of the United States on Nov. 4, 2008. Obama made history as the first African American to be elected president. He defeated his Republican opponent, U.S. Senator John McCain of Arizona, by a vote of 365 to 173 in the Electoral College and by 53 percent to 46 percent in the popular vote. Obama and his vice presidential running mate, U.S. Senator Joe Biden of Delaware, were to be inaugurated on Jan. 20, 2009.

Obama's election was remarkable not only because of his racial background—his father was a black man from Kenya, his mother a white woman from Kansas—but also because just four years earlier, he had been a little-known Illinois state senator. He had achieved national prominence in July 2004, during his campaign for the U.S. Senate, when he delivered the keynote address at the Democratic National Convention in Boston. Almost immediately after that speech, many people began touting him as presidential material. He announced his candidacy for president in February 2007, just two years after becoming a U.S. senator.

In the 2008 Democratic primaries, Obama ran neck-and-neck with Senator Hillary Rodham Clinton of New York. He narrowly clinched the nomination in June and was officially nominated in August. It was the first time a major party had chosen an African American as its candidate.

Vetoes. President George W. Bush vetoed four bills in 2008, but Congress overrode three of the vetoes. On March 8, he vetoed a bill that would have prohibited the Central Intelligence Agency (CIA) from using certain harsh interrogation techniques on terrorism suspects, including a form of simulated drowning known as waterboarding. He claimed that the bill would have diminished the effectiveness of CIA interrogations. On May 21 and June 18, he vetoed two versions of a five-year agricultural policy measure commonly known as the farm bill. (The second version was passed to correct a clerical error in the first.) He called the spending in the farm bill excessive and particularly objected to increases in farm subsidies. Congress overrode both farm bill vetoes. On July 15, the president vetoed a bill designed to prevent cuts in Medicare reimbursements to physicians. He said he supported the bill's objective but opposed the way Congress funded it, which was to reduce subsidies to private insurance firms that offer coverage under the private Medicare Advantage program. Congress overrode this veto. ■ Mike Lewis

See also **Cabinet, U.S.; Democratic Party; Elections: A Special Report; Republican Party; United States, Government of the; United States, Government of the: A Special Report.**

Uruguay. See Latin America.

Uzbekistan.

Islam Karimov was sworn in for a third consecutive seven-year term as president of Uzbekistan on Jan. 16, 2008. Western election observers had uniformly condemned the Dec. 23, 2007, elections as undemocratic. Opposition leaders had argued that Karimov was constitutionally prohibited from serving a third term.

Karimov pardoned several jailed human rights activists early in 2008 in an attempt to soften Western criticism and sanctions. The sanctions were imposed after his government's violent crackdown on protesters in the eastern city of Andijon in May 2005. On March 13, 2008, the International Committee of the Red Cross announced that it had been allowed to resume visiting prisoners in Uzbek jails. That same day, the United States ambassador to Uzbekistan praised the country's "small but significant" steps in improving its human rights record. In September, the Uzbek Senate announced that it had pardoned some 44,000 prisoners in 2008. On October 13, the European Union (EU) agreed to lift most of its sanctions on Uzbekistan, including visa bans on top Uzbek government officials, enacted after the Andijon crackdown. However, an EU-imposed arms embargo remained in place. ■ Juliet Johnson

See also **Asia.**

Vanuatu. See Pacific Islands.

Venezuela.

On Nov. 23, 2008, the people of the capital city of Caracas effectively turned their backs on President Hugo Chávez by electing Antonio José Ledezma Díaz, the candidate of a coalition of opposition parties, as their mayor. The outcome of the balloting in the commercial hub of the country was heavily influenced by rampant crime and festering piles of uncollected trash in the city's burgeoning slums—once rock-solid bastions of support for Chávez—as well as unfilled potholes amid a general breakdown of metropolitan area services.

Oil prices fall. The political setback occurred as the Chávez regime was attempting to cope with the impact of plummeting prices for the oil on which Venezuela depends for half its earnings. A 63-percent drop in the cost of a barrel of oil from July to November—plus a 20-percent reduction in its domestic production—threatened the continuance of food subsidies and a host of other popular social programs credited with having reduced poverty in Venezuela.

Oil to China. In seeking to modernize his nation's petroleum industry, Chávez turned to China and Russia for help. On a September visit to Beijing, he reached an agreement with China's President Hu Jintao on building three new refineries in China to process Venezuelan crude oil and four new tankers to transport it there. With these investments, Venezuela's oil exports to China were expected to increase from the 2008 level of 250,000 barrels a day to 1 million by 2012.

Space satellite. As a gesture of friendship, China launched Venezuela's first space satellite into orbit on Oct. 29, 2008. The satellite, built at a cost of $406 million over three years, provided improved Internet, radio, telephone, and television communication in Latin America. Uruguay had a 10-percent financial stake in the project.

Russian relations. On two trips to Russia in 2008, Chávez cultivated closer relations on a wide range of matters with new Russian President Dmitry A. Medvedev. The two leaders agreed to jointly finance a $6.5-billion oil refinery and to form a bilateral energy consortium both to produce and market oil. They expressed the hope that this arrangement might eventually include two of Venezuela's energy-rich Andean neighbors, Bolivia and Ecuador.

In July, three Russian oil and natural gas giants, TNK-BP, Lukoil, and Gazprom, committed themselves to joint oil exploration of the vast reserves of the Orinoco basin in concert with Petróleos de Venezuela, the state-owned oil company. As a spin-off of this effort, the Escorpión Vigilante, an offshore platform for the drilling of natural gas and oil, commenced operations in the Gulf of Venezuela on November 7.

To the consternation of the United States government, Chávez continued to stockpile Russian-made arms in 2008. These included antiaircraft missile systems, attack helicopters, and diesel-fueled submarines. As part of this buildup—the cost of which had reached $5.5 billion since 2005—Venezuela took delivery in August of 24 high-performance Sukhoi fighter aircraft. "They're for defensive purposes," declared Chávez, who had often expressed his fear of a possible American invasion. "We're not going to attack anybody."

Joint naval maneuvers. In late November, President Medvedev and Chávez posed for photographers on the deck of a Russian destroyer at the inauguration of joint Russian-Venezuelan naval exercises in Caribbean waters. Chávez used the occasion of the maneuvers, which included the Russian nuclear-powered cruiser *Peter the Great* and three Venezuelan frigates, to praise Russia for raising its profile in the Americas.

Diplomats go home. In September, President Chávez expelled Patrick Duddy, the U.S. ambassador to Venezuela, claiming the envoy was involved in a plot to overthrow the governments of Venezuela and Bolivia. United States officials denied the charges, but Venezuelan Ambassador Bernardo Álvarez was recalled from the United States the same month. ■ Nathan A. Haverstock

See also **Bolivia; Latin America.**

Vietnam struggled with major economic troubles in 2008. Rising inflation early in the year caused unrest among low-paid workers. A shortage of skilled workers, partly caused by a poor educational system, limited the nation's ability to move from producing simple goods to exporting more profitable, sophisticated products.

Despite official efforts to deal with the economic trouble, overall inflation continued to rise. In July, inflation hit 27 percent, the highest rate in Asia. Food prices were nearly 73 percent higher in 2008 than in 2007. Some people, unable to live on low factory wages, moved in 2008 from cities to rural areas from which they had migrated in search of work. Since 1993, Vietnam's poverty rate had fallen from 58 percent of the population to just 15 percent, but in 2008 some people began slipping back into poverty.

A journalist who claimed to have exposed government corruption in a 2005 gambling scandal was sentenced to two years in prison on Oct. 15, 2008. The court ruled that he had "abused freedom and democracy" by fabricating stories about high-ranking government officials. One of his police sources was jailed for one year for "revealing state secrets." Another police official was let off with a warning. ■ Henry S. Bradsher

See also **Asia; Agriculture: A Special Report.**

Vital statistics. See Census; Population.

Washington, D.C. The Supreme Court of the United States ruled in 2008 that a District of Columbia (D.C.) ban on handgun ownership violated the constitutional rights of citizens. The court, in a 5-to-4 decision on June 26, said that the strict law, which banned handgun ownership unless a resident owned a gun before the law went into effect in 1976, violated the Second Amendment to the U.S. Constitution. The amendment guarantees, in part, that "the right of the people to keep and bear arms shall not be infringed." The decision was the high court's first affirmation of an individual right to bear arms. Justice Antonin Scalia wrote the majority opinion.

In 2007, the U.S. Court of Appeals for the D.C. Circuit had ruled in a 2-to-1 decision that the handgun ownership ban was unconstitutional, also citing the Second Amendment. The Supreme Court's decision upheld that ruling.

Washington Mayor Adrian M. Fenty said he was disappointed with the June 2008 ruling and predicted it would lead to more handgun violence. The city's police department began registering handguns after the Supreme Court's decision.

On September 17, the U.S. House of Representatives voted 266-152 to overturn gun laws in the District. The city began loosening its gun ownership requirements, even though the U.S. Senate failed to consider the House bill before adjournment. Washington has its own governmental process, but Congress ultimately oversees its laws.

Embezzlement plea. Harriette M. Walters, a manager at the D.C. Office of Tax and Revenue, pleaded guilty on September 16 to charges of tax evasion, money laundering, and wire fraud in what federal authorities called the biggest corruption scandal in the history of D.C. government. Prosecutors claimed that a scam run by Walters took in more than $48 million over about 20 years.

Prosecutors said she ran an operation that created and cashed in phony tax refunds, stole other refund checks, and took money from citizens who owed tax penalties. Walters, 51, entered into a plea agreement with prosecutors to serve between 15 and 18 years in prison. She was the 10th person in the fraud operation to plead guilty.

New ballpark. More than 41,000 Washington Nationals fans and others helped open the District's $611-million Nationals Park on March 30, when President George W. Bush threw out the ceremonial first pitch. The new stadium is south of Capitol Hill, near the Anacostia River. At the opening-night game, the Nationals defeated the Atlanta Braves, 3 to 2.

Papal visit. Pope Benedict XVI celebrated Mass for about 46,000 people in the new Nationals Park on April 17. The pope acknowledged "the pain which the Church in America has experienced as a result of the sexual abuse of minors," a reference to pedophile priests who had abused children. The pope's trip to Washington also included a 90-minute visit with President Bush in the White House and a prayer service at the Basilica of the National Shrine of the Immaculate Conception.

Pentagon Memorial. On September 11, a $22-million memorial to victims of a terrorist attack seven years earlier was dedicated at a 2-acre (0.8 hectare) site on the west side of the Pentagon. On Sept. 11, 2001, terrorists hijacked American Airlines Flight 77 and crashed the airplane into the Pentagon, the headquarters of the Department of Defense in Arlington, Virginia, part of metropolitan Washington. The Pentagon Memorial commemorates the 184 people who were killed in the attack. Each victim is represented by a bench that lies along the airplane's deadly path.

Martin Luther King Memorial. On Sept. 18, 2008, the U.S. Commission of Fine Arts, which oversees projects on the National Mall, approved the start of construction for a 28-foot (8.5-meter) statue that will be a memorial to civil rights leader Martin Luther King, Jr.

Visitor Center. The $621-million Capitol Visitor Center opened on December 2, about $360 million over budget . The three-level center, just east of the U.S. Capitol, contains exhibits, theaters, gift shops, and restrooms. ■ Howard S. Shapiro

Water. See Environmental pollution.

Weather. A series of Pacific storms slammed ashore in the western United States, starting off 2008 with high winds, heavy rain, and snow. California was hard hit on January 4 and January 5 when a storm dumped more than 10 inches (25 centimeters) of rain in some places. The downpours spurred an earthen canal east of Reno, Nevada, to break, causing the flooding of 800 houses. More than 800,000 residents lost electric power as winds clocked as high as 163 miles (262 kilometers) per hour over the Sierra Nevada downed power lines. Snowfall in parts of the Sierra exceeded 100 inches (254 centimeters). Another powerful storm blasted California at the end of January, bringing more than 15 inches (38 centimeters) of rain to some southern areas. Heavy snow from the storm also smothered parts of the Rockies. Thunderstorms erupted from the Midwest to the Southeast from January 7 to January 10, spawning more than 100 tornadoes. Wisconsin had its first January tornadoes since 1967.

Overseas, harsh winter weather plagued China, where conditions were described as the worst in 50 years. Freezing temperatures, heavy snow, and ice affected more than 78 million people and led to at least 100 deaths from January 1 to January 10. Nearly 400,000 houses were damaged. Many people were unable to return home for Chinese New Year celebrations because rail and highway systems were paralyzed. Snow cover across the northern hemisphere reached its greatest January extent on record.

Winter across the contiguous United States was colder and wetter than average in 2008. The Northeast had its wettest February since record keeping began in 1895, and New York state had its wettest winter ever. It was the snowiest winter on record in Madison, Wisconsin, and Caribou, Maine, with 101.4 inches (257.6 centimeters) and 197.8 inches (502 inches), respectively. A storm smothered Columbus, Ohio, with 15.5 inches (39.4 centimeters) on March 7 and March 8, the city's biggest snowstorm on record.

Severe weather also plagued areas east of the Rockies in late winter and spring. From February 4 to February 6, thunderstorms spawned over 130 tornadoes from the Ohio Valley to the Southeast, forcing early closing of some presidential primary polling places. The twisters killed 57 people, the deadliest tornado outbreak in the nation since 1985. On March 14 and March 15, 2008, thunderstorms in the Southeast spawned 51 tornadoes. A tornado formed in downtown Atlanta, killing 1 person and causing $150 million in damage. The severe weather season reached a peak in May as 460 tornadoes were counted across the nation, more than double the May average. From May 1 to May 2, 11 tornadoes killed 7 people and destroyed 400 homes, primarily in Arkansas. An

EF-5 tornado, the strongest on the Enhanced Fujita Tornado scale, ripped through Parkersburg, Iowa, on May 25. The twister killed seven people and destroyed or damaged more than 500 homes and businesses. Nationally, 1,296 tornadoes were tallied in the first six months of 2008, more than the average number for an entire year.

On May 2, 2008, powerful Cyclone Nargis struck Myanmar (also known as Burma). The storm was accompanied by a 12-foot (3.7-meter) storm surge at the coast. Torrential rain over the Irrawaddy Delta led to disastrous flooding, including in Myanmar's largest city, Yangon. Nearly 85,000 people were killed and 53,000 remained missing.

Searing heat came early to parts of the West. Seattle had its earliest 90 °F (32 °C) reading on record on May 17. Farther south, Death Valley reached 120 °F (49 °C) on May 19, its hottest day so early in the year.

Recurrent heavy rain in June led to record flooding in parts of the Midwest. Rainfall was 200 percent over normal in much of Missouri, Iowa, southern Wisconsin, central Illinois, southern Indiana and central Ohio. On June 13, much of Cedar Rapids, Iowa, was submerged when the Cedar River crested at 19.1 feet (5.8 meters) above flood stage. The American Farm Bureau estimated weather-related crop damage to be over $8 billion across the Midwest. The wet June helped make the first half of 2008 the wettest in Iowa, Missouri, and Ohio since record keeping began in 1895.

As heat intensified over the Southwest in mid-June 2008, lightning strikes sparked over 800 wildfires in northern California. The fires, which by early November had burned more than 1.24 million acres (500,000 hectares) and destroyed about 1,700 homes, came after the driest spring on record in many areas of California.

Hurricane season. Two hurricanes started off the season in July. Bertha developed on July 3 in the central Atlantic and soon weakened to a tropical storm as it stalled south of Bermuda. The storm dissipated on July 20, becoming the longest-lived July Atlantic tropical cyclone on record. Hurricane Dolly, which formed in the Caribbean Sea, made landfall in the Yucatán Peninsula before making a second landfall on South Padre Island, Texas, on July 23. The storm led to a record daily rainfall of 6.68 inches (17 centimeters) in Brownsville, contributing to Brownsville's wettest July on record.

A cluster of severe thunderstorms raced across northern Illinois on August 4. Three tornadoes were confirmed and a wind gust of 94 miles (151 kilometers) per hour was recorded near downtown Chicago. More than 500,000 residents lost power. Travelers at O'Hare International Airport were evacuated to lower levels, and a baseball crowd of over 40,000 at Wrigley Field sought shelter as tornado sirens sounded.

Tropical Storm Fay crossed the eastern coast of the island of Hispaniola on August 15. The storm caused extensive flooding in Haiti and Cuba before making its first Florida landfall in the lower Keys on August 18. Over the next six days, Fay meandered north, producing locally torrential rain along its path. More than 20 inches (50.8 centimeters) of rain were measured near Melbourne and 11.44 inches (29.1 centimeters) at Tallahassee. Fay became the first tropical cyclone to make four landfalls in Florida—or any other state. Rainfall from the remnants of the storm helped alleviate drought in the interior Southeast.

Hurricane Gustav left a trail of destruction from the Greater Antilles to the central Gulf Coast in late August and early September. The storm brought deadly flooding to Haiti, Jamaica, and Cuba as it swept across the island nations from August 26 to August 28. Gustav carried winds of 150 miles (240 kilometers) per hour in the northwest Caribbean but weakened before making landfall near Grande Isle, Louisiana, with highest winds of 115 miles (185 kilometers) per hour on September 1. The hurricane caused more than 100 deaths—most of them in Haiti—and forced the largest prestorm evacuation in U.S. history as more than 2 million residents of eastern Texas and Louisiana fled.

Hurricane Hanna formed on August 28 and lashed the southern Bahamas in early September before weakening to a tropical storm as it drifted south. After causing floods and mudslides in September in Haiti, where it was blamed for at least 529 deaths, Hanna accelerated north. On September 6 and 7, the storm brought 2 to 8 inches (5 to 20 centimeters) of rain from the eastern Carolinas to southern New England.

On September 13, Hurricane Ike came ashore on Galveston Island, Texas, becoming the sixth consecutive Atlantic tropical cyclone to make landfall in the United States. Ike had earlier struck Haiti and Cuba with winds up to 125 miles (200 kilometers) per hour. The storm battered northeast Texas, flooding Galveston Island and Bolivar Peninsula with a 10-to-15-foot (3-to-5-meter) storm surge. The remnants of the storm moved northeast and merged with a cold front resulting in widespread power outages in the Ohio Valley and the biggest single-day rainfall in Chicago, 6.64 inches (16.8 centimeters) on September 13. At least 5 million people lost power from Texas to the Midwest.

On December 12, a very severe ice storm left more than 1 million homes and businesses without electric power in New England. The governors of both Massachusetts and New Hampshire declared states of emergency and sent out the national guard. ■ Fred Gadomski and Todd Mine

Weightlifting. See Sports.

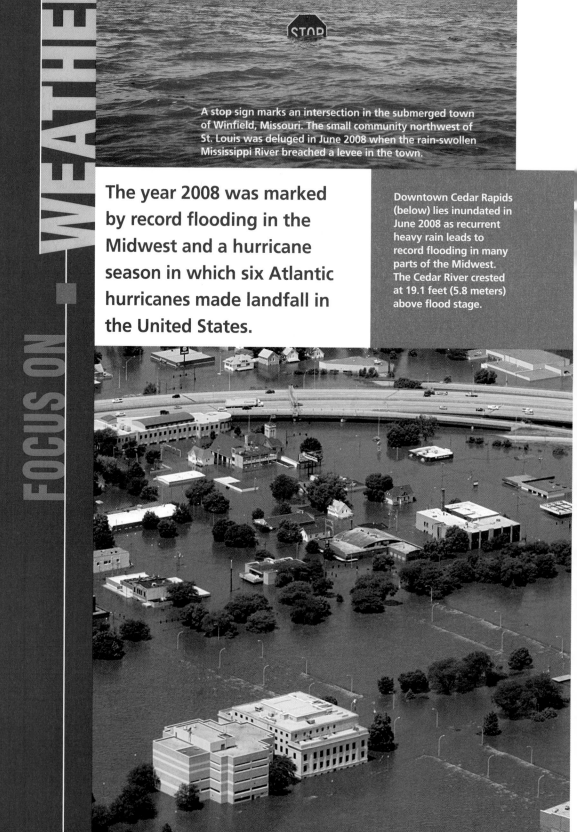

A stop sign marks an intersection in the submerged town of Winfield, Missouri. The small community northwest of St. Louis was deluged in June 2008 when the rain-swollen Mississippi River breached a levee in the town.

The year 2008 was marked by record flooding in the Midwest and a hurricane season in which six Atlantic hurricanes made landfall in the United States.

Downtown Cedar Rapids (below) lies inundated in June 2008 as recurrent heavy rain leads to record flooding in many parts of the Midwest. The Cedar River crested at 19.1 feet (5.8 meters) above flood stage.

A lone house stands amid the rubble in Gilchrist, Texas, in September, after Hurricane Ike tore through the area. Ike struck Cuba and Haiti with wind speeds up to 125 miles (200 kilometers) per hour before flooding Galveston Island and Bolivar Peninsula with a storm surge as high as 15 feet (5 meters).

Welfare. According to the United States Administration for Children and Families (ACF), the country's welfare rolls declined from March 2007 to March 2008 by about 2 percent. The number of families receiving cash aid under the Temporary Assistance for Needy Families (TANF) program dropped from 1,687,043 to 1,626,659 during this period, and the number of individuals dropped from 3,933,158 to 3,784,726. TANF cash aid is provided, for up to five years, to needy families with dependent children, with the requirement that the parents must be working, training for work, or seeking work.

By 2008, the number of families and individuals receiving welfare payments had fallen significantly since welfare reforms were enacted in 1996, according to ACF data. From August 1996 to March 2008, the number of families fell from 4,408,508 to 1,626,659—a 63-percent decline. The number of individuals fell from 12,242,125 to 3,784,726—a 69-percent decline.

In 2008, the U.S. Food and Nutrition Service reported that 25 million people participated in the Food Stamp Program in 2006—67 percent of the 37 million who were eligible. The program provides benefits to low-income people to help them buy food. Also in 2008, Congress reauthorized the program and renamed it the Supplemental Nutrition Assistance Program. ■ Mike Lewis

West Indies. The tourism industry, a mainstay of many Caribbean economies, suffered in 2008 from the devastation caused by a series of fierce tropical storms that struck the region. Many international travelers put their plans on hold, pending relief and cleanup operations. The number of summer cruise passengers dropped by more than 13 percent from 2007. Tour bookings of all sorts were down across the board. In addition, record prices for jet fuel led U.S. airlines to cut back on flights to several island airports.

Elections in the Dominican Republic. On Aug. 16, 2008, Leonel Fernández Reyna of the governing Dominican Liberation Party was sworn in for his third consecutive term as president of the Dominican Republic. Fernández was born in the capital, Santo Domingo but grew up in the large Dominican community in New York City.

Shortly before his reelection in May 2008, Fernández inaugurated the $710-million Santo Domingo Metro, the second subway system in the Caribbean. His administration also increased subsidies on such foods as milk, chicken, and eggs and distributed the goods throughout the country.

Elections in Grenada. Tillman Thomas, 63, of the National Democratic Congress (NDC) was sworn in as prime minister of Grenada on July 9, 2008. In an election held the previous day, the NDC won 11 of 15 seats in Parliament, ousting

the New National Party, which had governed the island since 1995. Thomas, a veteran lawmaker and former minister, promised better management of Grenada's fragile economy.

Jamaican Olympic gold. Athletes from Jamaica won six gold medals, more than any other Latin American country, at the 2008 Summer Olympics in Beijing. Three of the medals went to track star Usain Bolt, who set world records for his performances in the 100- and 200-meter races and as a member of a four-man relay team. Jamaica's Shelly-Ann Fraser won the women's 100-meter race, and Veronica Campbell-Brown won the 200.

Dominican Pulitzer. Dominican-born author Junot Díaz, 39, won the 2008 Pulitzer Prize in fiction for his first novel, *The Brief Wondrous Life of Oscar Wao*. Diaz lives in New York City.

The passing of an icon. On November 4, legendary Jamaican musician Byron Lee died at age 73. Lee and his band, the Dragonaires, released their first album in 1962 and their last in 2000. Lee helped bring reggae, calypso, and soca music to an international audience.

■ Nathan A. Haverstock

See also **Latin America; Literature; Olympic Games: A Special Report.**

Yemen. See Middle East.

Yukon. See Canadian territories.

Zambia. See Africa.

Zimbabwe. The political, economic, and security crisis in Zimbabwe deepened in 2008, as 84-year-old President Robert Mugabe and his ruling Zimbabwe African National Union–Patriotic Front (ZANU-PF) maneuvered to repress the opposition Movement for Democratic Change (MDC), led by Morgan Tsvangirai. According to political experts, the March presidential and parliamentary polls were marred by allegations of government intimidation and vote-rigging.

Elections. On March 29, Tsvangirai officially won 47.9 percent of the vote in the presidential election, compared with Mugabe's 43.2 percent. The MDC, which insisted that Tsvangirai had won just over half of the vote, also ended the ZANU-PF's stranglehold on Parliament by winning 109 seats in the 210-member House of Assembly; ZANU-PF won 97. Tsvangirai fell short of the absolute majority needed to avoid a second round of elections. A minority MDC faction had backed a third candidate, former ZANU-PF finance minister Simba Makoni, who took some 8 percent of the votes. The two MDC factions reunited for parliamentary purposes on April 28.

However, five days before the June 27 presidential runoff election, Tsvangirai announced that he was pulling out because of the violence unleashed by ZANU-PF operatives against the MDC: at least 86 MDC supporters had been killed;

more than 2,000 jailed; and over 10,000 beaten during the previous three months. Tsvangirai's decision handed victory and a sixth term in office to Mugabe, extending his 28 years in power since independence from the United Kingdom in 1980. The MDC declared the result invalid.

International mediation. Following the March 29, 2008, elections, South African President Thabo Mbeki and other leaders of the Southern African Development Community (SADC) attempted to mediate a peaceful resolution to Zimbabwe's crisis. A power-sharing agreement was eventually announced in Harare, Zimbabwe's capital, on September 15. The agreement retained Mugabe as president and placed Tsvangirai in the new post of prime minister. The MDC was allocated 16 of the Cabinet's 31 posts. However, the pact remained in virtual deadlock for the rest of 2008 as Mugabe stonewalled over the distribution of the security and home affairs ministries. In December, his refusal to compromise led to calls from some African leaders for him to be deposed by force as scores of soldiers, frustrated with being unpaid, clashed with police.

Economic developments. On October 9, the World Food Program, a United Nations (UN) affiliate, warned that 28 percent of Zimbabwe's children under the age of 5 were malnourished and nearly half of the population would starve without food aid over the coming six months. During 2008, Mugabe's regime was frequently accused by humanitarian agencies of diverting aid money intended for the nation's most vulnerable people to ZANU-PF and of using food aid as a political weapon. Zimbabwe was self-sufficient in food until 2000, when the government began confiscating mainly white-owned land to redistribute to black farmers, destroying commercial agriculture, the mainstay of the economy.

Mugabe also imposed a ban on aid agencies early in 2008 after accusing them of campaigning for the MDC—allegations they denied. With talks between ZANU-PF and the MDC paralyzed, billions of dollars of international aid were blocked.

Zimbabwe's inflation continued to skyrocket in 2008. According to the Cato Institute, a Washington, D.C., think tank, in November it was running at 89.7 sextillion (1 followed by 21 zeros) percent a month.

Cholera epidemic. In August, an outbreak of cholera began raging across Zimbabwe. Aid officials estimated in December that at least 978 people had died from the disease and that there may be up to 60,000 cholera cases by early 2009. The epidemic caused thousands of people to flee to neighboring countries for medical treatment.

■ Simon Baynham

See also **Africa; Food: A Special Report.**

Zoology. See Biology; Conservation; Ocean.

Zoos. An important exhibit featuring Madagascar opened in 2008, as researchers identified new species from the island. Zoos also welcomed many new arrivals, from panda bears to manta rays.

Island sanctuary. In June, a major new exhibit on Madagascar opened at the Bronx Zoo in New York City. Madagascar is a large island that separated from the southeast coast of Africa more than 150 million years ago. Many of the animals on Madagascar, including an entire group of primates called lemurs, live nowhere else in the world. Tragically, these unique natural wonders are in danger of disappearing. Zoos and conservation groups have warned for years that life on Madagascar is threatened by the actions of human beings, especially deforestation.

In 2008, the Bronx Zoo converted its 105-year-old Lion House into a breathtaking new exhibit on Madagascar. Inside the building, ring-tailed lemurs dart through a forest of spiny trees. A crocodile lurks in a limestone cave, while 100,000 Madagascar hissing cockroaches crawl around a giant replica of a baobab tree. All told, more than 150 animals representing 30 species are housed in the 20,000-square-foot (1,858-square-meter) building.

More Madagascar. Another zoo announced the discovery of two new lemur species in February. Researchers with the Henry Doorly Zoo in Omaha, Nebraska, discovered the species during an expedition to Madagascar. In January, the same zoo reported the birth of two baby fossas. The fossa is another native of Madagascar that resembles a cat but is more closely related to the mongoose. Fossas are the main hunters of lemurs. Both animals will be part of a major new exhibit on Madagascar under construction at the zoo.

New exhibit, new cubs. A pair of rare Sumatran tigers produced a litter of three cubs at the Honolulu Zoo in Hawaii in September. The cubs were the first tigers born at the zoo since 1981. Before the zoo's new enclosure opened in 2007, the parents lived at the Fort Wayne Children's Zoo in Indiana, where they also had three cubs.

Steinhart reopens. The Steinhart Aquarium in San Francisco reopened in September 2008, in its new home at the California Academy of Sciences. The aquarium occupies the lower level of the $500-million facility; but some exhibits, such as a Philippine coral reef, extend upwards onto the building's main floor. The pool of the museum's domed tropical rain forest exhibit, on the main floor, is visible to visitors walking through the aquarium below. Major exhibits simulate the California coast and a swamp in the southeastern United States, featuring a white alligator. The 212,000-gallon (802,507-liter) coral reef exhibit houses a vast number of small reef fish, which are often overlooked in reef exhibits that focus on large fish.

Russian bears. The Minnesota Zoo in Minneapolis celebrated its 30th anniversary in June with a new "Russia's Grizzly Coast" exhibit. The exhibit features Russia's exotic Far East wilderness, including the large brown bears that give the exhibit its name. Visitors tour simulated coniferous forests, volcanic mountains, and wave-lashed coastlines. In addition to the grizzlies, the exhibit houses Amur leopards, wild boars, and sea otters.

New elephant quarters. The Houston Zoo unveiled its new McNair Asian Elephant Habitat in June. Two elephants, Mac and Methai, cut the ribbon in the opening ceremony. The new facility has a 7,000-square-foot (650-square-meter) barn with large sliding windows that allow visitors a peek behind the scenes. In August, 25-year-old Tess and her calf, Tucker, came to the habitat from the California elephant training and breeding facility, Have Trunk Will Travel.

Giraffes, dragons, and more. The Cincinnati Zoo opened its new Giraffe Ridge in June. Covering 27,000 square feet (2,508 square meters), this exhibit features three male and two female giraffes. An elevated platform brings visitors eye to eye with the giraffes. Visitors on the platform can feed the giraffes, giving the animals a chance to show off their 18-inch (46-centimeter) tongues.

The Smithsonian National Zoological Park in Washington, D.C., opened an enclosure for the world's largest lizards, the giant Komodo dragons. The Georgia Aquarium in Atlanta launched an American alligator exhibit. The Toledo Zoo in Ohio opened an exhibit housing tuataras, lizard-like creatures from New Zealand that have changed little in the last 200 million years.

The Point Defiance Zoo and Aquarium in Tacoma, Washington, completed a $35-million makeover by expanding its children's area. As part of the makeover, the zoo previously opened an Asian Forest Sanctuary for Sumatran tigers, white-cheeked gibbons, and other Asian species.

New arrivals. Zoo Atlanta welcomed a rare giant panda cub in August. Its parents had already produced one cub there. Atlanta is one of four zoos in the United States with giant pandas. The San Francisco Zoo welcomed three Sumatran tiger cubs in March. The cubs were the first born there since 1956. The zoo lost a Siberian tiger in December 2007. Police shot the tiger after it escaped its enclosure, killing a teenager. The Georgia Aquarium welcomed a huge manta ray in August 2008. Nine feet (2.7 meters) across, the 456-pound (207-kilogram) manta ray was flown from Durban, South Africa, to Atlanta. The manta ray was rescued from shark nets last year. The aquarium is the only one in the United States to exhibit a manta ray. ■ Edward Ricciuti

See also **Conservation.**

A white rhinoceros successfully gave birth to a male calf at the Budapest Zoo in Hungary on Oct. 22, 2008. In a first for the species, the mother was artificially inseminated using sperm that had been frozen.

2009
SUPPLEMENT

New encyclopedia
articles are devoted to
the following topics:

© Johanna Huber, SIME/4Corners Images

Austria is known for its picturesque mountain scenery. The Alps and their foothills dominate Austria's landscape. Heiligenblut village, *shown here,* lies in a Central Alpine valley in the Carinthia region of southern Austria. Thick forests also cover much of the land.

Austria

Austria is a small country in central Europe famous for its beautiful mountain scenery. The towering Alps and their foothills stretch across the western, southern, and central parts of the country. In many areas, broad, green valleys separate the mountains. Austria has many lovely, mirrorlike lakes. Thick forests cover much of the land.

Austria has no coastline. It shares boundaries with the countries of Switzerland and Liechtenstein to the west, Germany and the Czech Republic to the north, Slovakia and Hungary to the east, and Slovenia and Italy to the south.

Vienna is the capital and largest city of Austria. It lies on the Danube River in the northeastern part of the country. Most of Austria's people live in cities and towns.

Austrians take great pride in the fact that their country has long been a leading cultural center of Europe. The cultural institutions and scenic beauty of Austria attract millions of tourists each year.

Austria was once the core of one of the great powers of Europe. Austria began as a military border territory of the Holy Roman Empire in the late 900's and became a *duchy* (territory ruled by a duke) of the empire in 1156. In the late 1200's, the Habsburg (also spelled *Hapsburg*) family gained control of Austria and became identified with Austria. The House of Habsburg, also known as the House of Austria, developed into the most powerful dynasty in the empire. From 1438 to 1806, except from 1740

Steven Beller, the contributor of this article, is the author of A Concise History of Austria *and other books on Austrian history and culture.*

to 1745, the Habsburgs ruled the empire. The Holy Roman Empire ended in 1806, and the Austrian Empire, founded in 1804, replaced it. The Austrian Empire became the Dual Monarchy of Austria-Hungary in 1867. This kingdom split into several states at the end of World War I in 1918, with the territories of present-day Austria forming the Austrian republic. The republic endured two decades of economic difficulty and political unrest.

From 1938 to 1945, Austria was part of the German *Third Reich* (Third Empire), the Nazi term for the empire in which they hoped to unite all Germanic peoples. After Germany's defeat in World War II (1939-1945), the Allies occupied Austria until 1955. Since then, Austria has been a neutral country. It has benefited from both economic

Facts in brief

Capital: Vienna.
Official language: German.
Official name: Republik Österreich (Republic of Austria).
Area: 32,383 mi^2 (83,871 km^2). *Greatest distances*—east-west, 355 mi (571 km); north-south, 180 mi (290 km).
Elevation: *Highest*—Grossglockner, 12,461 ft (3,798 m) above sea level. *Lowest*—Neusiedler Lake, 377 ft (115 m) above sea level.
Population: *Estimated 2008 population*—8,221,000; density, 254 per mi^2 (98 per km^2); distribution, 66 percent urban, 34 percent rural. *2001 census*—8,032,926.
Chief products: *Agriculture*—barley, cattle, corn, grapes, hay, hogs, milk, oats, potatoes, rye, sugar beets, wheat. *Manufacturing*—chemical products, electrical equipment, furniture, glass, iron and steel, lumber, machines and tools, motor vehicles, paper and pulp, processed foods and beverages, textiles and clothing. *Mining*—coal, gypsum, iron ore, magnesite, natural gas, petroleum, salt, stone, tungsten.
National anthem: "Land der Berge, Land am Strome" ("Land of Mountains, Land at the River").
Money: *Basic unit*—euro. One hundred cents equal one euro. The schilling was taken out of circulation in 2002.

Article outline

I. **Government**
  A. The president
  B. The chancellor and Council of Ministers
  C. The Federal Assembly
  D. Provincial and local government
  E. Political parties
  F. Courts
  G. Armed forces
II. **People**
  A. Ancestry
  B. Language
  C. Way of life
  D. Social welfare
  E. Recreation
  F. Education
  G. Religion
  H. The arts
III. **Land and climate**
  A. Land regions
  B. Climate
IV. **Economy**
  A. Natural resources
  B. Service industries
  C. Manufacturing
  D. Agriculture
  E. Tourism
  F. International trade
  G. Transportation
  H. Communication
V. **History**

© fl online/Alamy Images

The Federal Assembly building in Vienna is the meeting place of both houses of the Austrian legislature. The building, designed in the Greek Classical style, dates from the late 1800's.

and political stability and has become a prosperous nation. In 1995, Austria joined the European Union (EU), an organization of European nations that works for economic and political cooperation among its members.

Government

Austria is a federal republic made up of nine provinces: Burgenland, Carinthia, Lower Austria, Salzburg, Styria, Tyrol (or Tirol), Upper Austria, the city of Vienna, and Vorarlberg. Austria's Constitution was adopted in 1920. All Austrian citizens who are 16 years and older may vote.

The president is Austria's head of state. The people elect the president to a six-year term. The president may serve any number of terms but no more than two in a row. The president's duties include appointing ambassadors, signing treaties, and swearing in certain officeholders. The president also acts as commander in chief of the armed forces. The president does not have the power to declare war or to *veto* (reject) bills passed by Austria's parliament, the Federal Assembly.

The chancellor and Council of Ministers run the Austrian government. The *chancellor* (prime minister) serves as head of government. Generally, the president appoints as chancellor the leader of the political party with the most seats in the Nationalrat. The Nationalrat is the more important of the two houses of the Federal Assembly. On the chancellor's advice, the president also appoints members of the Council of Ministers to head the government departments. The chancellor and Council of Ministers set government policies and are responsible to the Nationalrat. The Nationalrat may force the chancellor and Council of Ministers to resign by rejecting their policies in a *vote of no confidence.*

The Federal Assembly consists of two houses, the Nationalrat (National Council) and the Bundesrat (Federal Council). Members of the Nationalrat are elected by the people to four-year terms. But new elections may take place sooner if the Nationalrat dissolves itself, or if the president dissolves it on the chancellor's advice. The Bundesrat's members are elected by the country's nine *Landtags* (provincial legislatures). Members of the Bun-

Austria's civil flag has three stripes of red, white, and red. The state flag includes the coat of arms in the center.

The coat of arms was adopted in its present form in 1945. Use of an eagle to symbolize Austria dates from the 1200's.

WORLD BOOK map

Austria is a landlocked country in central Europe. Eight other European countries surround Austria.

Austria political map

═══ International boundary	┼┼┼ Railroad and tunnel
─── Province boundary	⊛ National capital
┼┼┼ Expressway and tunnel	★ Provincial capital
┼┼┼ Other road and tunnel	• Other city or town

WORLD BOOK map

Austria map index

Provinces

Burgenland	277,569	C	7
Carinthia	559,404	D	4
Lower Austria	1,545,804	B	6
Salzburg	515,327	D	4
Styria	1,183,303	D	4
Tyrol	673,504	D	2
Upper Austria	1,376,797	B	5
Vienna	1,550,123	B	7
Vorarlberg	351,095	D	1

Cities and towns

Amstetten	22,595	B	5
Ansfelden	14,789	B	5
Arnoldstein	6,832	E	4
Bad Aussee	5,086	C	4
Bad Goisern*	7,602	C	4
Bad Hofgastein	6,727	D	4
Bad Ischl	14,081	C	4
Bad Vöslau*	10,998	C	7
Baden	24,502	B	7
Berndorf*	8,642	C	6
Bischofshofen	10,087	C	4
Bludenz	13,701	D	1
Braunau	16,337	B	4
Bregenz	26,752	C	1
Bruck an der Leitha*	7,311	B	7
Bruck [an der Mur]	13,439	C	6
Deutschlandsberg	7,983	D	6
Dornbirn	42,301	C	1
Ebensee	8,452	C	4
Ebreichdorf*	8,788	C	7
Eisenerz	6,435	C	5
Eisenstadt	11,334	C	7
Enns	10,611	B	5
Feldkirch	28,607	D	1
Feldkirchen	14,030	D	5
Ferlach	7,602	E	5
Fohnsdorf	8,523	D	5
Freistadt	7,353	B	5
Friesach	5,462	D	5
Frohnleiten*	6,592	D	6
Fürstenfeld	5,982	D	6
Gänserndorf*	7,928	B	7
Gerasdorf*	8,231	B	7
Gleisdorf	5,224	D	6
Gmünd	5,861	B	5
Gmunden	13,184	C	4
Götzis*	10,097	D	1
Graz	226,244	D	6
Guntramsdorf*	8,421	B	7
Hall in Tyrol	11,492	D	2
Hallein	18,399	C	4
Hard*	11,471	C	1
Hartberg	6,547	D	6
Hermagor	7,232	E	4
Herzogenburg*	7,738	B	6
Hohenems*	13,891	D	1
Hollabrunn	10,685	B	6
Horn	6,411	B	6
Imst	8,689	D	2
Innsbruck	113,392	D	2
Judenburg	10,130	D	5
Kapfenberg	22,234	C	6
Kitzbühel	8,574	C	3
Klagenfurt	90,141	E	5
Klosterneuburg	24,797	B	7
Knittelfeld	12,740	D	5
Köflach	10,671	D	6
Korneuburg	11,032	B	7
Krems	23,713	B	6
Kufstein	15,358	C	3
Laa	6,137	A	7
Laakirchen*	9,130	C	4
Landeck	7,336	D	2
Langenlois*	6,875	B	6
Langenzersdorf*	7,261	B	7
Lauterach*	8,678	C	1
Leibnitz	6,892	D	6
Leoben	25,804	C	6
Leonding	22,203	B	5
Lienz	12,079	D	3
Liezen	6,908	C	5
Linz	183,504	B	5
Lustenau	19,709	C	1
Marchtrenk*	11,274	B	5
Mattersburg	6,256	C	7
Mistelbach	10,644	B	7
Mittersill	5,584	D	3
Mödling	20,405	B	7
Mürzzuschlag	9,569	C	6
Neunkirchen	11,028	C	6
Oberwart	6,696	D	7
Perchtoldsdorf	13,998	B	7
Pinkafeld	5,181	C	7
Purkersdorf*	7,762	B	7
Radenthein*	6,620	D	4
Rankweil*	11,171	D	1
Reutte	5,719	C	2
Ried	11,404	B	4
Rottenmann	5,489	C	5
Rum*	8,352	D	2
Saalfelden	15,093	C	4
Salzburg	142,662	C	4
St. Andrä	10,719	D	5
St. Johann im Pongau	10,260	D	4
St. Johann in Tyrol	7,961	C	3
St. Pölten	49,121	B	6
St. Valentin*	8,983	B	5
St. Veit	12,839	D	5
Schrems	5,830	A	5
Schwaz	12,212	D	3
Schwechat	15,286	B	7
Seekirchen*	9,344	C	4
Sierning	8,516	B	5
Spittal	16,045	D	4
Steyr	39,340	B	5
Stockerau	14,452	B	7
Tamsweg	5,936	D	4
Telfs	12,833	D	2
Ternitz	15,232	C	6
Traiskirchen	15,669	B	7
Traun	23,470	B	5
Trofaiach*	8,385	C	5
Tulln	13,591	B	6
Vienna (Wien)	1,550,123	B	7
Villach	57,497	E	4
Völklabruck	11,697	C	4
Voitsberg	10,074	D	6
Völkermarkt	11,373	D	5
Vorchdorf*	7,265	C	4
Waidhofen [an der Thaya]	5,750	A	6
Waidhofen [an der Ybbs]	11,662	C	5
Wattens	7,291	D	2
Weiz	8,926	D	6
Wels	56,478	B	5
Wiener Neudorf*	8,428	B	7
Wiener Neustadt	37,627	C	7
Wilhelmsburg*	6,660	B	6
Wolfsberg	25,301	D	5
Wörgl	10,885	C	3
Ybbs	5,684	B	5
Zell am See	9,638	D	4
Zeltweg*	7,834	D	5
Zwettl [Niederösterreich]	11,630	B	6

*Does not appear on the map; key shows general location.
2001 census.

desrat serve as long as the Landtag that chose them stays in power. The number of members a province has in the Bundesrat varies according to population.

Provincial and local government. The people in each province elect Landtag members to terms of up to five or six years, depending on the province. Each Landtag chooses the governor of the province. The provinces are subdivided into more than 2,000 *municipalities* (units of local government). Voters in each municipality elect a governing council, which selects one of its number to serve as mayor. Vienna is both a province and a municipality. Its municipal council serves as the provincial legislature, and its mayor serves as governor.

Political parties. Two political parties control the great majority of seats in the Nationalrat. They are the center-left Social Democratic Party of Austria and the conservative Austrian People's Party. Other parties include the environmentalist Greens and two parties on the far right—the Alliance for the Future of Austria and the Freedom Party of Austria.

Courts. The Supreme Court is Austria's highest court of appeal in civil and criminal cases. The Constitutional Court determines whether laws are constitutional, and the Administrative Court is the highest court for cases that challenge the activities of government agencies. Four regional courts hear appeals of decisions made by lower courts. Various special courts handle juvenile matters and labor disputes.

Armed forces. Austrian men must serve at least six months in the army, usually with additional periods of follow-up training later. Most men serve between the ages of 18 and about 22. Women serve in the armed forces on a voluntary basis.

People

Most of Austria's people live in the lowland areas of the country—in the east and just south of the Danube River. About a fifth of the people live in Vienna, the country's capital and largest city.

Ancestry. Many different groups of people have settled in Austria. Each group mixed with other people and so helped shape the ancestry of present-day Austrians. In ancient times, the people of Austria included Celts and Romans. Later, various Germanic and Slavic groups settled in Austria. After the 1300's, Austria attracted people from many parts of central Europe and parts of the Habsburg empire, such as Italy and Spain. Many immigrants came to Austria during the Cold War, the rivalry between Communist and non-Communist nations that lasted from the late 1940's to the early 1990's. Large numbers of people fleeing from Communism in Czechoslovakia and Hungary settled in Austria. In the 1990's, the tensions surrounding the breakup of Yugoslavia led some people from that region to immigrate to Austria.

Language. Almost all Austrians speak German, the country's official language. In different parts of the country, the people speak *dialects* (local forms) of German.

A number of Austrians speak another language as their first language. In the province of Burgenland, for example, there are communities of people who speak Croatian. Carinthia has a number of people who speak Slovenian. Small groups of people in Vienna speak either Czech or Slovak. Other languages spoken as a first language include Magyar (also called Hungarian), Serbian, and Turkish.

Way of life. Most city dwellers in Austria live in apartment buildings. Others live in single-family homes. Many farm and village families live in single-family homes. Housing styles vary from region to region. In Burgenland, many homes are simple in design and covered with a kind of plaster called *stucco.* The provinces of Tyrol and Vorarlberg have many wooden houses called *chalets* similar to those of Switzerland. Most chalets have a steep, pointed roof with wide, overhanging eaves.

Austrians wear clothing much like that worn in other European countries and in North America. On special occasions, many Austrians wear traditional national or regional costumes. Men may wear a green-trimmed, gray wool suit consisting of a coat and *knickers*—short, loose-fitting trousers gathered just below the knee. Women may wear a peasant costume called a *dirndl,* which has a full skirt, an apron, and a close-fitting top that is worn over a blouse and laced up the front.

Many Austrian dishes have been influenced by Czech, German, or Hungarian cooking. Popular meats in Austria include beef, chicken, pork, sausage, and veal. An Austrian dish called *Wiener schnitzel* (breaded veal cutlet) has become a favorite in many countries. Popular side dishes in Austria include dumplings, noodles, and potatoes. Austrians drink beer or wine with many meals. The delicious cakes and pastries created by Austrian bakers have become world famous.

Festivals and holidays play an important part in Austri-

Salzburg, one of Austria's major cities, attracts visitors from all over the world. The people shown here are gathered at one of the city's many outdoor cafes. Hohensalzburg Fortress, the city's chief landmark, stands in the background.

an life. Some festivals date from pre-Christian times. One such festival held in parts of the Tyrol has become part of the late winter merrymaking that precedes the solemn religious season of Lent. Some people pretend to chase away the "evil spirits" of winter. Wearing special costumes and masks, they march through the streets and wave large sticks in the air.

Social welfare. The Austrian government provides comprehensive welfare services. Under the national social insurance program, workers may receive disability, maternity, old-age, sickness, survivors', or unemployment benefits. Austria also has a national health insurance program for all citizens. The costs of both programs are shared by insured people; employers; and the federal, provincial, and local governments.

Since 1919, Austrian law has limited the workday to eight hours and has guaranteed employed people annual holidays. Today, most employed people who have been on the job for one year or longer receive at least a 25-day vacation with pay each year. In 1975, the workweek became limited to 40 hours.

Recreation. Austrians love the outdoors, and their country's many forests, lakes, and mountains offer opportunities for a variety of outdoor sports. In winter, the people especially enjoy ice skating, skiing, and tobogganing. Other popular winter sports include bobsledding, ice hockey, and ski jumping. Favorite summer sports include boating, fishing, hiking, mountain climbing, swimming, and water skiing. The people also enjoy bicycling, camping, picnicking, and playing soccer.

Austrians love the arts as well as sports. Ballets, concerts, motion pictures, operas and operettas, and plays are all popular.

Education. Almost all adult Austrians can read and write. Austrian children between the ages of 6 and 15 are required to attend school. Most students attend free public schools. The rest attend private schools, which may charge a tuition fee.

Austria has several universities, technical colleges, and fine arts colleges. The University of Vienna is the country's largest university.

Religion. About 75 percent of the people in Austria are Roman Catholics, and about 5 percent are Protestants. Austria has small Jewish and Muslim populations, who mostly live in Vienna. The Austrian government gives financial support to many religious institutions, including the private schools of the Roman Catholic Church and several other recognized religions.

The arts. Austria has been a leading cultural center in Europe. The country has made outstanding contributions in architecture, literature, painting, and theater. However, Austria's most important cultural achievements have been in music.

Music. Austria has produced many great composers. During the late 1700's and early 1800's, Joseph Haydn helped make the symphony one of the most important forms of musical composition. Haydn and Wolfgang Amadeus Mozart became the leading composers of the Classical period of music. Mozart wrote masterpieces in a wide range of musical forms. Many people consider his *Don Giovanni* (1787) the world's greatest opera.

The German composer Ludwig van Beethoven spent most of his life in Austria. Most of his nine symphonies and his opera, *Fidelio* (three versions: 1805, 1806, 1814), were composed and first performed in or near Vienna. In the early 1800's, Franz Schubert of Vienna created chamber music, symphonies, and over 600 *lieder* (German-language art songs). Hugo Wolf continued the lieder tradition in the late 1800's. Gustav Mahler and Anton Bruckner wrote many symphonies, which are considered some of the finest Austrian contributions to music during the Romantic era. Johannes Brahms, a German composer who combined the Romantic and Classical traditions, also lived in Vienna. Johann Strauss and his son, Johann Strauss, Jr., composed their famous waltzes and operettas in Vienna.

Arnold Schoenberg became one of the most revolutionary composers of the 1900's. He developed a new system of composition called the *twelve-tone technique.* Schoenberg influenced many composers, including his fellow Austrians Alban Berg and Anton Webern.

Austria continues to make important musical contribu-

© INTERFOTO/Alamy Images

Scenic resort towns lie along many lakes in the Salzkammergut area of central Austria. In St. Gilgen, *shown here,* a waterfront scene shows boats and visitors on Lake Wolfgang. Mountains of the Alps rise in the background.

The Vienna Boys' Choir performs a holiday concert at the Vienna Konzerthaus. With performances around the world, the choir has achieved international fame.

tions today. The Vienna Boys' Choir, Vienna Philharmonic, Vienna State Opera, and Vienna Symphony have achieved international fame. The Salzburg Festival is one of the great annual musical events. Students from all over the world study at Austria's fine music schools.

Architecture. Austria has some of Europe's best examples of Baroque architecture. Beginning in the 1600's, buildings in the Baroque style featured elaborate decorations and an abundance of paintings and sculptures. The architects intended these buildings to express the power

The interior of Innsbruck Cathedral, a Roman Catholic church, has tall columns and a richly decorated ceiling in the Baroque style. Catholics are a majority of Austria's population.

and glory of the Roman Catholic Church, the Austrian aristocracy, and the Habsburg dynasty. The finest examples of Austrian Baroque architecture include the *Karlskirche* (Church of St. Charles, named for St. Charles Borromeo) in Vienna and the Church of the Holy Trinity in Salzburg. Johann Bernhard Fischer von Erlach designed both churches. Other examples include the Belvedere Palace in Vienna, designed by Johann Lucas von Hildebrandt, and the Benedictine monastery in Melk, designed by Jakob Prandtauer.

Austria also has many churches, palaces, and other buildings designed in the Rococo style of the 1700's. Rococo architecture is even more decorated than Baroque, but lighter.

During the late 1800's and early 1900's, Otto Wagner developed a simplified, *functionalist* style of architecture, based on the belief that a building's function should determine its style. Adolf Loos further developed this architectural functionalism. Wagner and Loos are regarded as two of the founding figures of the Modern Movement in architecture.

Literature. People in Austria love the theater, and many of the country's most important writers have been playwrights. Franz Grillparzer wrote plays in the early to middle 1800's that drew on classical German drama as well as Austrian folk plays. Ferdinand Raimund wrote plays in the folk tradition with elements of fairy tales, while Johann Nestroy wrote political satires often disguised as fantasies.

During the late 1800's and early 1900's, such writers as Arthur Schnitzler and Hugo von Hofmannsthal created a Viennese literary tradition famous for its artistic style and psychological depth. Such authors as Robert Musil, Franz Werfel, and Stefan Zweig further developed this tradition of psychological fiction. These authors of such fiction were inspired partly by the theories of Sigmund Freud, the Austrian physician who developed psychoanalysis as a method of treating mental illness. Karl Kraus became one of the greatest satirists of the early 1900's. In 2004, Elfriede Jelinek became the first Austrian writer to receive the Nobel Prize in literature.

Painting. Gustav Klimt, who worked in the late 1800's and early 1900's, was one of Austria's first modern painters of international importance. He is known for his flat, two-dimensional, decorative portraits. Two of Klimt's followers—Egon Schiele and Oskar Kokoschka—became the leading artists of Austrian Expressionism, a movement that emphasized strong emotional content.

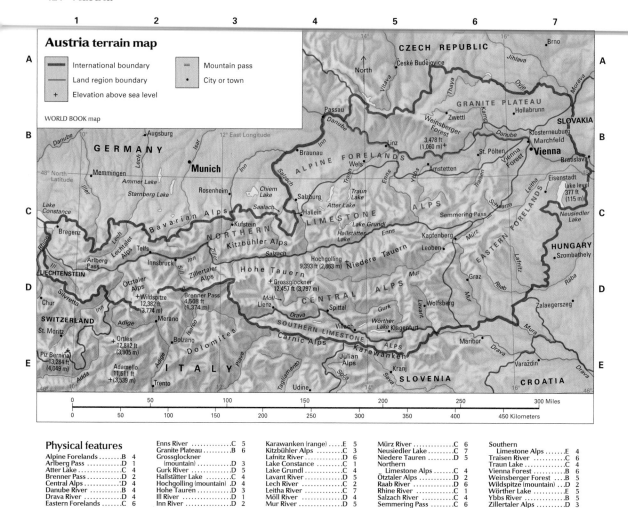

Austria terrain map

━━	International boundary	▪	Mountain pass
──	Land region boundary	•	City or town
+	Elevation above sea level		

WORLD BOOK map

Physical features

Alpine Forelands	B 4	Enns River	C 5	Karawanken (range)	E 5	Mürz River	C 6	Southern	
Arlberg Pass	D 1	Granite Plateau	B 6	Kitzbühler Alps	C 3	Neusiedler Lake	C 7	Limestone Alps	E 4
Atter Lake	C 4	Grossglockner		Lafnitz River	D 6	Niedere Tauern	D 5	Traisen River	C 6
Brenner Pass	D 2	(mountain)	D 3	Lake Constance	C 1	Northern		Traun Lake	C 4
Central Alps	D 4	Gurk River	D 5	Lake Grundl	C 4	Limestone Alps	C 4	Vienna Forest	B 6
Danube River	B 4	Hallstätter Lake	C 4	Lavant River	D 5	Ötztaler Alps	D 2	Weinsberger Forest	B 5
Drava River	D 4	Hochgolling (mountain)	D 4	Lech River	C 2	Raab River	D 6	Wildspitze (mountain)	D 2
Eastern Forelands	C 6	Hohe Tauern	D 3	Leitha River	C 7	Rhine River	C 1	Wörther Lake	E 5
		Ill River	D 1	Möll River	D 4	Salzach River	C 4	Ybbs River	B 5
		Inn River	D 2	Mur River	D 5	Semmering Pass	C 6	Zillertaler Alps	D 3

Land and climate

Mountains cover about three-fourths of Austria. The Alps stretch across the western, southern, and central parts of the country. A separate mountainous area, the Granite Plateau, lies in the north. The country's highest point, the mountain Grossglockner, rises 12,461 feet (3,798 meters) above sea level in central Austria.

The Danube, the country's longest river, flows 217 miles (350 kilometers) from west to east through northern Austria. Almost all Austrian rivers flow into the Danube. Austria's largest lake is Neusiedler Lake. Part of this lake lies in Hungary. The Austrian part covers 52 square miles (135 square kilometers).

Land regions. Austria has six main land regions. They are (1) the Granite Plateau; (2) the Eastern Forelands; (3) the Alpine Forelands; (4) the Northern Limestone Alps; (5) the Central Alps; and (6) the Southern Limestone Alps.

The Granite Plateau forms Austria's northernmost region. It consists of hills and mountains that are made up mostly of granite and partly covered by thick forests.

The Eastern Forelands lie southeast of the Granite Plateau. The northern part is a lowland called the Vienna Basin. Its fertile soil helps make it Austria's chief agricul-

tural area. The southern part consists of rolling hills and broad valleys, with the land becoming flatter in the east.

The Alpine Forelands lie south of the Granite Plateau and west of the Eastern Forelands. The region is made up of hills and low mountains.

The Northern Limestone Alps rise south and southwest of the Alpine Forelands. The mountains in this region consist of limestone. The region is marked by high plateaus; steep, forested slopes; and jagged peaks. Several large lakes formed by ancient glaciers dot this mountainous region.

The Central Alps are separated from the Northern Limestone Alps to the north by a series of valleys. Unlike the Northern Limestone Alps, the Central Alps do not consist of limestone but of such rocks as granite and gneiss. The Central Alps have Austria's highest mountains. Glaciers cover many parts of the mountains.

The Southern Limestone Alps lie south of the Central Alps. A series of valleys separates the two regions. The physical features of the Southern Limestone Alps resemble those of the Northern Limestone Alps.

Climate. Austria has four sharply defined seasons. The country's climate is influenced by both west and east

The Danube, the longest river in Austria, flows from west to east through the northern part of the country. It runs through the city of Krems, *shown here,* in the northeast.

winds. Warm, moist winds blowing eastward from the Atlantic Ocean affect the climate of western and central Austria. These winds bring rain, snow, and other forms of precipitation and help produce moderate temperatures throughout the year. Dry winds blowing westward from the Asian plains are hot in summer and cold in winter. Partly as a result of these winds, eastern Austria has less precipitation and more extreme temperatures than western and central Austria.

Within the western, central, and eastern areas, Austria's climate varies from place to place, partly because of differences in altitude. Local winds also influence the climate. For example, warm, dry winds called *foehns* cause sudden rises in temperature in some mountain valleys in winter. Because they may rapidly melt mountain snow, foehns sometimes cause destructive avalanches.

January temperatures in Austria average about 27 °F (–3 °C). July temperatures average about 67 °F (19 °C). The country receives an average of about 25 inches (64 centimeters) of precipitation yearly.

Economy

Austria's economy is based mostly on private ownership of businesses. The country's economy was severely damaged by the breakup of the Habsburg dynasty in 1918. Wartime destruction and defeat in World War II (1939-1945) brought further economic distress to Austria. However, postwar financial aid from the United States helped boost Austria's economy.

In the late 1940's, the Austrian government *nationalized* (transferred from private to state ownership) most of the companies in several chief industries, including coal and metal mining; electric power production; iron and steel production; and oil drilling and refining. In the 1980's and 1990's, the government *privatized* many of these industries, returning them to private ownership.

After the early 1950's, Austria rapidly became an industrialized nation. Today, service industries have overtaken manufacturing as the country's leading industry. Austria

has become a prosperous country with little poverty or unemployment.

Natural resources. During the Middle Ages, from about the 400's to the 1400's, Austria was famous for its minerals, especially iron from the Erzberg (Iron Ore Mountain) in the Styria province and silver from the Tyrol province. Today, mineral deposits either have become depleted or are too low in quality to meet the country's needs. The Erzberg still has much iron ore, but Austria must import higher-grade ores. Austria has its own petroleum and natural gas reserves in the Lower Austria province, but these reserves are insufficient for the country's demands. As a result, Austria depends upon large imports of petroleum and gas.

Austria is one of the world's leading producers of magnesite, which is used to make such products as heat-resistant bricks and artificial stone. Other mineral deposits include gypsum, salt, stone, and tungsten.

Austria's rich forests, which cover about 45 percent of the country, provide plentiful lumber, paper, and other products. Spruce and fir are the most commercially important trees. Strict conservation laws and extensive replanting programs ensure the preservation of forests.

Austria's swift-flowing rivers are another important natural resource. They provide energy for many hydroelectric power stations, which produce most of the nation's electric power.

Service industries, taken together, account for the largest part of Austria's economy, as measured by the *gross domestic product* (GDP)—the total value of goods and services produced within a country in a year. Community, government, and personal services—including education and health care—employ about a fourth of the country's workers. The privatization of businesses has reduced the government's influence in the economy, but the state still controls several of Austria's major companies. Many foreign investors own shares in Austria's banks, and many Austrians have invested in banks in central and eastern Europe. Such international investment helps to make business services, finance, insurance, and

Austria's gross domestic product

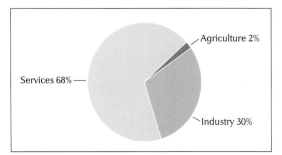

Austria's gross domestic product was $258,776,000,000 in 2003. The gross domestic product is the total value of goods and services produced within a country in a year. *Services* include community, government, and personal services; finance, insurance, real estate, and business services; trade, restaurants, and hotels; and transportation and communication. *Industry* includes construction, manufacturing, mining, and utilities. *Agriculture* includes agriculture, forestry, and fishing.

Production and workers by economic activities

Economic activities	Percent of GDP produced	Employed workers	
		Number of people	Percent of total
Finance, insurance, real estate, & business services	22	439,900	12
Community, government, & personal services	20	983,200	26
Manufacturing	20	734,300	19
Trade, restaurants, & hotels	18	812,300	21
Construction	8	338,600	9
Transportation & communication	8	238,200	6
Agriculture, forestry, & fishing	2	210,900	6
Utilities	2	34,800	1
Mining	*	6,100	*
Total	100	3,798,300	100

*Less than one-half of 1 percent.
Figures are for 2003.
Source: International Labour Organization; International Monetary Fund; Statistics Austria.

real estate an important service industry group. Hotels, restaurants, retail, and trade in Austria benefit from tourism.

Manufacturing. The production of metal, especially iron and steel, and the manufacture of metal products—including automobiles, locomotives, machines, and tools—once dominated Austrian manufacturing. Today, however, manufacturing has become more varied. Austria's factories now also produce chemical products, cement, electronic equipment, furniture, glass and porcelain products, paper, processed foods and beverages, and textiles.

Factories are scattered throughout Austria, but the heaviest concentration is in the Vienna area. There is a strong emphasis in Austrian manufacturing on high quality rather than mass production. Many factories are small or medium-sized. Austria is known for its craftworkers, who produce excellent glassware, jewelry, needlework, porcelain objects, woodcarvings, and other handicrafts. One of the country's best-known products is Swarovski crystal.

Agriculture. Austria is so mountainous that only about 20 percent of the land can be used for growing crops. But the country's farmers use modern machinery and scientific farming methods. As a result, they can supply more than 80 percent of the food needed by the people. All Austrian farms are privately owned. Since the late 1940's, there has been a trend toward larger farms. But most farms in Austria are still small.

Dairy farming and livestock production are the main sources of farm income. Austria's farmers produce all the eggs, meat, and milk needed by the people. Farm animals graze in the high areas of the country, where it is too rugged and cold to grow crops.

The best croplands are in the Vienna Basin. But farm plots can be found in every province. The farmers produce all the potatoes and sugar beets and most of the oats, rye, and wheat needed in Austria. Other farm crops grown in the country include apples, barley, corn, grapes, hay, hops, pears, and vegetables. Winemaking is an important industry in Austria.

Tourism. Austria is one of Europe's most popular vacation spots. Millions of tourists visit the country every year. Innsbruck, Kitzbühel, and other sports centers in the Alps attract many winter vacationers, especially skiers. In summer, the lakes of Carinthia and of the Salzkammergut area in central Austria are popular recreation spots. Vienna's art galleries, concert halls, and museums also attract many tourists, as do the summer music festivals held throughout the country.

International trade. Austria depends heavily on trade, especially trade of manufactured goods with other European nations. Austria imports some types of machinery and vehicles and exports other types. Other imports include chemicals, foods, and petroleum. Other exports include forest products, especially paper and pulp; iron and steel; and magnesite. The value of Austria's imports is greater than that of its exports. Income from tourism largely makes up the difference.

Austria's chief trading partner is Germany. Both countries are members of the European Union (EU). Most of Austria's trade is with EU members or with members of the European Free Trade Association (EFTA), an economic organization of European nations. EU and EFTA members have removed almost all tariffs and other restrictions on imports of manufactured goods from one another.

Transportation. Austria has an excellent road network. Almost all Austrian families own an automobile. Railroads link almost all cities and towns. The federal government owns about 90 percent of the nation's railroad tracks. Both buses and trains provide fast and frequent passenger service. Many mountain areas have cable railways.

A government-controlled company owns much of the stock in the national airline, Austrian Airlines. The airline operates international and domestic flights. Vienna has Austria's chief airport. The Danube River is a major shipping route for trade between Austria and nearby countries. Passenger vessels also travel on the Danube.

Communication. Austria has a number of daily newspapers. The federal and provincial governments own the nation's radio and television network. There is also an extensive choice of private channels for viewers with cable television. People who own a radio or television set pay a

© HP Huber, SIME/4Corners Images

Skiers glide downhill at a mountain resort in the Tyrol region of western Austria. Ski resorts in Austria's Alps attract numerous tourists and vacationers each year. The country is widely known for its outdoor sports.

© IML Image Group/Alamy Images

Austrian bakeries are known for their delicious cakes and pastries. The chefs shown here are working in the kitchen of a bakery in Vienna. Other foods popular in Austria include dumplings, noodles, and *Wiener schnitzel* (breaded veal cutlet).

license fee. The federal government operates the postal and telephone services. Most families in Austria have a computer, radio, television set, and telephone. Many people also own a cellular telephone.

History

Early years. People have lived in what is now Austria for thousands of years, but historians know little about the earliest inhabitants. They do know that after about 800

The Habsburg lands

In 1282, almost all of what is now Austria, outlined in red, formed part of the Holy Roman Empire. The Habsburg family controlled the areas shown in yellow. In 1526, the Habsburg lands included Bohemia, part of Hungary, and other areas.

——— Boundary of present-day Austria

0   300 Miles
0   300 Kilometers

WORLD BOOK maps

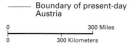

B.C., the people mined and traded iron ore and salt. These people were part of a cultural group known as the Celts, which eventually spread through much of central and eastern Europe. Archaeologists have found the earliest evidence of Celtic culture at the village of Hallstatt, near Salzburg.

By 15 B.C., the Romans had made Austria south of the Danube River part of their empire. In the late A.D. 100's, mainly Germanic tribes from the north began to invade Roman Austria, weakening Roman control. The Roman Empire split into two parts in the late 300's, and the western part collapsed in 476. Various groups—including Avars, Slavs, and a Germanic people who became the Bavarians—invaded and settled in Austria.

In the late 700's, Austria came under the rule of Charlemagne, king of a Germanic people called the Franks. After Charlemagne's death in 814, the Frankish empire gradually broke up. In the 900's, Magyars, the national ethnic group of Hungary, overran Austria. But the king of Germany, Otto I, defeated them in 955. Austria then came under his rule. In 962, the pope crowned Otto emperor of what later became known as the Holy Roman Empire. The Holy Roman Empire lasted until 1806. Austria became the empire's most important state.

In 976, Holy Roman Emperor Otto II had given control of northeastern Austria to Leopold I of the Babenberg family. In 1156, Holy Roman Emperor Frederick I increased the importance of this area by declaring it a duchy. In 1192, the Duchy of Styria, south of the Duchy of Austria, also came under Babenberg rule. In 1238, the Duchy of Austria was divided into two administrative parts, Upper and Lower Austria.

The Habsburgs. The last Babenberg duke died without an heir in 1246. King Ottokar (also spelled Otakar) II of Bohemia then gained control of the Babenberg duchies of Austria and Styria, plus some lands to the south. In 1273, the princes of Germany elected Rudolf I, a member of the Habsburg family of Switzerland, as Holy Roman emperor. Rudolf defeated Ottokar in battle in 1278 and began to acquire for his family the lands that the king had taken.

In the early 1300's, the Habsburgs lost control of the Holy Roman crown. The empire was a patchwork of territories ruled by various families, including the Habsburgs. In 1359, the great-grandson of Rudolf I, Rudolf IV, made a claim, based on forged documents, to the title of archduke of Austria. Other European rulers did not recognize this claim until 1453. In the next few centuries, the Habs-

Important dates in Austria

15 B.C. Romans controlled Austria south of the Danube River.
A.D. 100's Germanic tribes from the north began to invade Roman Austria, and Roman control started to weaken.
476 The Roman Empire collapsed in Western Europe.
976 The Holy Roman emperor put Leopold I of the Babenberg family in control of northeastern Austria.
1278 Holy Roman Emperor Rudolf I began to acquire the duchies of Austria and Styria for the Habsburgs.
1438-1806 Austria's House of Habsburg was the most important dynastic power in the Holy Roman Empire.
1804-1806 The Austrian Empire was established, and the Holy Roman Empire dissolved.
1867 Austria-Hungary was established.
1914 Austria-Hungary's declaration of war on Serbia began World War I.
1918 Austria-Hungary was defeated in World War I. The Habsburgs were overthrown, and Austria became a republic.
1938 Adolf Hitler made Austria part of Germany.
1939-1945 The Allies defeated Germany in World War II.
1945-1955 The Allies occupied Austria.
1955 The Austrian State Treaty guaranteed Austrian independence.
1995 Austria joined the European Union, an economic and political organization of European nations.

burgs acquired many new territories, including most of the regions that make up present-day Austria.

In 1438, a Habsburg had again been elected Holy Roman emperor. From then on, the Habsburgs held the title almost continuously. The House of Habsburg, also called the House of Austria, became the chief dynastic power of the Holy Roman Empire. One of the greatest Habsburgs was Maximilian I. In 1496, he arranged for his son, Philip, to marry the daughter of the king and queen of Spain. Philip's son became King Charles I of Spain in 1516 and Holy Roman Emperor Charles V in 1519. In 1556, Charles gave up the two thrones. Spain went to his son, and Austria and the title Holy Roman emperor went to his brother, Ferdinand I. The Habsburgs thus became divided into Spanish and Austrian branches.

Ferdinand I had become king of Bohemia and claimed

Emperor Francis I and Empress Maria Theresa at Schönbrunn Castle, surrounded by their 12 children (1756), oil on canvas painting by Martin van Meytens; Chateaux de Versailles et de Trianon, Versailles, France (Daniel Arnaudet, Art Resource)

Maria Theresa became ruler of Austria, Bohemia, and Hungary in 1740. This painting shows Maria Theresa, *seated at right,* with her husband, Francis I, *seated at left,* and 12 of their children.

Hungary in 1526. Some Hungarian nobles supported him, and others tried to make a Hungarian nobleman their king. Meanwhile, the Ottoman Empire conquered most of Hungary. Ottoman forces besieged Vienna in 1529 and again in 1683. Both sieges failed. The Habsburgs gained control of almost all of Hungary soon after the 1683 siege.

In 1618, Protestants in Bohemia revolted against their Habsburg ruler, Ferdinand II. Ferdinand was a strong supporter of the Counter Reformation, a movement that led to renewal within the Catholic Church. The Protestants in Bohemia were defeated in 1620. But their revolt led to the start of the Thirty Years' War (1618-1648), a series of political and religious wars that involved most European nations. The Peace of Westphalia, which ended the war, weakened Habsburg authority in the Holy Roman Empire but strengthened the family's control over their lands in Austria. The peace treaty declared that the ruler of each state within the empire could determine the religion of that territory. The Habsburgs forced Catholicism on Austria's large Protestant population.

Wars in the 1700's and 1800's. The last Habsburg king of Spain died in 1700. Both Austria and France claimed the throne. The War of the Spanish Succession (1701-1714) followed. Austria won Belgium and Spain's Italian lands. A French prince became king of Spain.

Charles VI, the Habsburg heir, became Holy Roman Emperor in 1711. In 1713, Charles publicly announced a decree based on a secret family succession agreement that was made in 1703. Charles added a provision to the ordinance stating that the Habsburg lands should remain united. He also included that, in the event of not having a direct male heir, his daughters' succession claims should take priority over those of the daughters of his older brother and predecessor, Joseph I. Joseph's daughters normally would have come before Charles's daughters in the line of succession. This decree served to strengthen the succession claim of Charles's prospective children over those of Joseph. Known as the *Pragmatic Sanction,* this law became especially significant when it became clear that Charles indeed would have no direct male heir. Charles sought and obtained the acceptance of this document, first from the nobles of all of the Habsburg-ruled lands by 1724, and then from the rulers of the principal European states. By doing so, Charles secured the succession of his oldest daughter, Maria Theresa, as the Habsburg heir.

After Charles VI died in 1740, several states challenged Maria Theresa's right to rule. In the War of the Austrian Succession (1740-1748), Maria Theresa established her rights as ruler of Austria, Bohemia, and Hungary. But she lost one of her lands, Silesia, to Prussia. In the Seven Years' War (1756-1763), she tried to regain Silesia but failed.

Austria suffered many defeats in the Napoleonic Wars of the late 1700's and early 1800's. In these wars, Napoleon I of France fought successfully for many years against an alliance of major European powers, including Austria. Napoleon conquered large parts of the Holy Roman Empire, and in 1806 Emperor Francis II dissolved the empire. Francis had declared himself emperor of Austria in 1804 to ensure that he would still have imperial standing. After 1806, he reigned as Emperor Francis I of Austria. Napoleon was finally defeated in 1815.

Austria-Hungary in 1914

The Austrian Emperor Franz Joseph set up the Dual Monarchy of Austria-Hungary in 1867. It consisted of the Austrian Empire and the Kingdom of Hungary. Austria-Hungary reached its greatest size in 1914, the year World War I began. The country broke up in 1918, at the end of the war.

Austrian Empire

Kingdom of Hungary

Boundary of present-day Austria

0   200 Miles
0   200 Kilometers

WORLD BOOK map

Metternich and revolution. The major political figure in Austria from 1809 to 1848 was Prince Klemens von Metternich, who served as minister of foreign affairs. Metternich played a leading role at the Congress of Vienna. The congress was a series of meetings of European political leaders that arranged the peace settlement following the Napoleonic Wars. The congress returned to Austria most of the land it had lost. Austria exchanged Belgium for Venetia, an area in northeast Italy. The congress also set up the German Confederation, a loose union of independent states. Austria and Prussia began a struggle to lead the confederation.

During the 1800's, early liberalistic and nationalistic ideas swept across Europe. These ideas, particularly the belief that people had a right to govern themselves, triggered revolutions in many areas of Europe. Because Metternich feared revolution, he tried to put down all nationalist movements in the Austrian Empire. But in 1848, revolution began in France and spread to Austria, Bohemia, the German states, and Hungary. In Vienna, revolutionaries demanded that Metternich resign and that a constitutional government be set up. Metternich fled to England. Revolts also broke out in the Austrian-controlled states in Italy. But by late 1849, the Austrian army had put down all revolts.

At this time, Italy and Germany were not unified countries but were each divided into numerous small states. During the 1860's and 1870's, unification movements in Italy and Germany weakened the Austrian Empire. In Italy, the kingdom of Sardinia, which included the island of Sardinia and the Piedmont region of Italy, led the unification movement. Austria declared war on Sardinia in 1859, but Italian and French forces defeated the Austrians. As a result, Austria lost the Lombardy region of northern Italy and could not prevent Italian unification. In 1866, Prussia used a minor dispute to spark the Seven Weeks' War, in which Italy and Prussia quickly defeated Austria. Austria had to give Venetia to the new Kingdom of Italy, and the German Confederation was dissolved. Prussia formed a new German empire without Austria.

Austria-Hungary. In 1867, Emperor Franz Joseph agreed to Hungarian demands for greater *autonomy* (self-rule) and status. In the resulting Dual Monarchy of

Austria-Hungary, both the Austrian Empire and the Kingdom of Hungary were ruled by the Habsburg monarch. The two countries were united in their conduct of foreign, military, and joint financial affairs. But each country had its own government to handle all other matters.

In the late 1800's and early 1900's, Slavs and other minority groups in Austria-Hungary also demanded the right to govern themselves. Serbia led a movement to unite the region's Slavs. In 1908, Austria-Hungary added the territory of Bosnia-Herzegovina in southeast Europe to its empire. Serbia wanted control of this area because many Serbs lived there. In 1914, Gavrilo Princip, a Serb from Bosnia-Herzegovina, assassinated Archduke Franz Ferdinand, heir to the Austro-Hungarian throne. Austria-Hungary then declared war on Serbia, starting World

Wide World
The German dictator Adolf Hitler, *front left,* visited Vienna in April 1938. His troops had seized Austria the month before. Hitler had then announced the union of Austria and Germany, which lasted until Germany's defeat in World War II in 1945.

War I (1914-1918). In this war, the Central Powers—Austria-Hungary, Germany, and other nations—fought the Allies—France, Russia, the United Kingdom, and later the United States. The Allies won the war.

After World War I. A defeated Austria-Hungary signed an armistice on Nov. 3, 1918. On November 12, the last Habsburg emperor was overthrown, and Austria became a republic. Many Austrians wanted to make Austria part of Germany. However, the Treaty of St.-Germain, signed by Austria and the Allies in 1919, forbade such a union. In addition, the treaty established Austria's present boundaries. In 1920, Austria adopted a democratic constitution.

Austria had many political problems after the war. The two major parties—the conservative Christian Social Party and the socialist Social Democratic Workers' Party—often clashed with each other. The Austrian Nazi Party also became an increasing menace. In March 1933, Chancellor Engelbert Dollfuss of the Christian Social Party adjourned the Federal Assembly. In February 1934, he outlawed the Social Democratic Party. Dollfuss then ruled Austria as a dictator. But Austrian Nazis assassinated him in July 1934 because of his strong opposition to Adolf Hitler, the Nazi dictator of Germany. Dollfuss was succeeded by Kurt von Schuschnigg, who struggled to maintain Austrian independence against Nazi pressure.

In March 1938, German troops marched into Austria and seized the country unopposed. Hitler then announced the *Anschluss* (union) of Austria and Germany. Austria became part of Nazi Germany, whose quest for power led to World War II (1939-1945). Hitler's forces conquered most of continental Europe and, in the "Final Solution" of the Holocaust, killed about 6 million Jews. Austrians took full part in both the military campaigns and the Holocaust. The Allies, including France, the Soviet Union, the United Kingdom, and the United States, defeated Germany in 1945.

After World War II, Austria was divided into American, British, French, and Soviet zones of occupation. But the four powers allowed Austria to set up a single *provisional* (temporary) government based on the 1920 Constitution. Following elections in November 1945, a national government was formed. It included leaders of both the People's Party (formerly the Christian Social Party) and the Socialist Party (formerly the Social Democratic Party). This *coalition* government—that is, a government including two or more parties—helped stabilize Austria. In 1955, the Allies ended their occupation of the country. The Austrian State Treaty of 1955, between the Allies and Austria, guaranteed Austrian independence. To obtain its independence, Austria agreed to be permanently *neutral*—that is, completely uninvolved in international military affairs. Later in 1955, Austria joined the United Nations (UN).

As a neutral nation, Austria became an important channel for the exchange of ideas between the non-Communist countries of Western Europe and the Communist countries of Eastern Europe. Vienna was the site of some of the Strategic Arms Limitation Talks (SALT) that led to a 1972 treaty between the Soviet Union and the United States limiting nuclear arms. Vienna also became the home of a number of UN agencies.

Austria had coalition governments until 1966, when the People's Party, led by Chancellor Josef Klaus, won a majority of seats in the Nationalrat. In the 1970 elections, the Socialist Party became the strongest party, though it lacked a majority. The party formed Austria's first Socialist government, with Bruno Kreisky as chancellor. The Socialists gained a majority in the Nationalrat in the 1971 elections and kept it until 1983.

In the 1983 elections, the Socialists won the most seats in the Nationalrat but fell short of a majority. They formed a coalition with the Freedom Party to keep control of the government. Kreisky resigned as chancellor following the elections. Fred Sinowatz of the Socialist Party succeeded him.

Kurt Waldheim, a former secretary-general of the UN, was elected president of Austria in 1986. During the election campaign, records surfaced indicating that Waldheim might have been involved in Nazi war crimes during World War II. He denied taking part in war crimes, and an investigation found no evidence that he had done so. However, he had lied about his wartime record, which led to both domestic and international outrage. After Waldheim's election, Sinowatz resigned as chancellor and was succeeded by another Socialist, Franz Vranitzky.

Elections in 1986 brought an increase in support for the right-wing Freedom Party, led by Jörg Haider. Vranitzky refused to enter a coalition with Haider and instead formed a new coalition government with the People's Party in 1987. Vranitzky began a policy of facing up to Austria's past. He became the first Austrian chancellor publicly to accept Austria's responsibility for war crimes committed when Austria was part of Nazi Germany, from 1938 to 1945. The coalition of the Socialist and People's parties retained its majority in elections in 1990, 1994, and 1995. In 1991, the Socialist Party changed its name to the Social Democratic Party. Chancellor Vranitzky retired in 1997. Viktor Klima, also of the Social Democratic Party, then became chancellor.

Recent developments. Elections in 1999 gave Haider's Freedom Party the second largest number of seats in the Nationalrat. In early 2000, the People's Party formed a coalition with Haider's group. Governments around the world reacted with concern because they disapproved of Haider's right-wing views. In response, Haider resigned his leadership of the Freedom Party, but the coalition remained in place after his resignation and after the Freedom Party lost some of its seats in the 2002 elections.

In 2005, Haider and the leaders of the Freedom Party left the party to form a new one, the Alliance for Austria's Future. In 2006, Nationalrat elections led to a coalition between the Social Democratic Party, led by Alfred Gusenbauer, and the People's Party. Gusenbauer then became chancellor. Steven Beller

Additional resources

Mazdra, Marian. *Austria.* Gareth Stevens, 2005. Younger readers.
Sanna, Jeanine. *Austria.* Mason Crest, 2006. Younger readers.
Steininger, Rolf, and others, eds. *Austria in the Twentieth Century.* Transaction Pubs., 2002.
Tan, Ronald. *Welcome to Austria.* Gareth Stevens, 2006. Younger readers.

Language is a system of communication. It connects *signals*—such as sounds, hand signs, or letters—to meanings. It allows people to speak to each other and to write their thoughts and ideas. The use of language is one of the most important of human abilities. Other species have ways of communicating with one another, but experts disagree about whether such communication should be considered "language."

The process people use to connect a language signal to its meaning is extremely complicated. Signals must be learned in specific orders to form words. In addition, languages feature certain rules of word and sentence structure that must be mastered. Yet, despite the complex skills needed to acquire language, most young children throughout the world gain the ability to speak or sign a language without much conscious effort. Further, children develop their command of language at a time when other complex mental skills are beyond their capabilities. As a result, scientists and *linguists* (scholars who study language) think people have an *innate* (inborn) ability to learn and use language.

The sounds of language

The complexity of language is linked to the intricacy of the human *vocal tract* and the ability people have to hear subtle differences in sounds. What linguists call the vocal tract is a branching tube running up from the *larynx* (voice box) into the head. One branch of the tract goes through the mouth, the other through the nose. Most speech sounds are made when air is expelled from the lungs and passes the *vocal folds* (vocal cords) in the larynx. Some sounds require vibrating the vocal folds. Other sounds are made by bringing mouth sur-

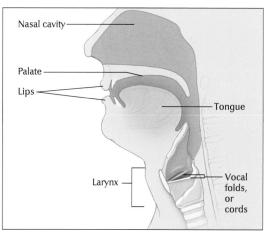

WORLD BOOK illustration by Christine Gralapp

The human vocal tract, shown here in blue, is where speech is produced. The tract includes the *larynx* (voice box) and other structures in the head and neck. The intricacy of the vocal tract is one factor that allows for the complexity of human language.

faces close to each other to create audible turbulence, such as by touching the tongue to the roof of the mouth behind the teeth (as in *s*).

Using the vocal tract, people produce distinguishable sounds. The key to speech is twofold—that is, not only can speakers make different sounds, but listeners can tell the sounds apart.

Linguists call sounds that distinguish one word from another *phonemes*. In English, for example, the sounds

Related signs in American Sign Language

Some signs in American Sign Language share certain features, such as *handshape, location,* or *movement.* Artists working in American Sign Language use the relationship between signs as authors in other languages might use the relationship between words that rhyme. For example, poets working in American Sign Language might "rhyme" the signs *candy* and *apple,* which differ in handshape but are the same in location and movement.

Candy | Apple | Jealous

Signs differing only in handshape

Summer | Ugly | Dry

Signs differing only in hand location

Tape | Chair | Train

WORLD BOOK illustrations by Adam Weiskind

Signs differing only in hand movement

of the letters *d* and *g* are phonemes. Most dialects of English have about 40 phonemes, which is about average for a language. Some languages, however, have more than 100 phonemes, and others have only about a dozen.

Because the audible difference in sounds—for example, between *d* and *g*—can be subtle, linguists questioned how people came to learn to distinguish these differences. Scientific studies showed that even newborn babies could make such distinctions, indicating that this ability is something with which people are born.

The parts of language

Words and morphemes. Phonemes are in themselves meaningless, but combining them into larger units can make a word. And, unlike its component phonemes, a word has meaning. Some words, such as *house,* are simple in the sense that none of its parts are meaningful. Other words, such as *greenhouse* and *unthinkable,* are complex. Greenhouse is a *compound word,* made by joining two independent words together to make a new word. In such words as *unthinkable,* however, the prefix *un-* is not an independent word. Linguists call such units *bound morphemes*—that is, sounds that must be bound to a word. *House,* on the other hand, is called a *free morpheme* because it can stand alone as a word.

There are many ways to form, combine, and change words, depending on the language. English, for example, uses a *productive bound morpheme* of *-s* to mark plurals:

book (singular), book*s* (plural)
cat (singular), cat*s* (plural)

Consequently, when a new noun enters the English language, it will usually take an *-s* ending to make it a plural. In a study done by linguist Jean Berko Gleason in 1958, children were presented with made-up words they could not have seen before, such as *wug.* (The children were told that a wug was a small birdlike creature.) In that study, most of the children agreed that the plural of *wug* must be *wugs,* even though none of them could have learned this ahead of time. This indicates that children at this stage have learned a rule about how to create the plural form of singular nouns—a rule that applies to many words in the language, even words that children have never before encountered.

Syntax is the arrangement and ordering of words to convey meaning. It is especially important in English. For example, word order in an English sentence can convey who is acting and who is being acted upon. The sentences below clearly differ in meaning:

A *dog* bit a *man.*
A *man* bit a *dog.*

Grammar. Linguists call the collection of mechanisms, rules, and operations that speakers of a language know concerning syntax, word formation, and structure the *grammar* of a language.

People are often unaware of many details of the grammar that they know, much as people are largely unconscious of the mechanical details of walking. For example, few English speakers consciously know the grammatical rule that states that, with few exceptions, productive plurals are not permitted on the first word in

Major language families and languages

The colors on the map represent the chief language families. The names identify the main languages in the families. The chart on the opposite page shows the approximate percentage of the world's people that speaks the languages in the chief families.

a compound word. For example, a piece of furniture that contains many *books* can be a *bookcase,* but not a *bookscase.* Linguists find, however, that though few English speakers can state the rule, even preschool-age children who speak English are usually able to form the correct plural of compounds. Even young language users unconsciously know a great deal about the grammar of their language.

Signed languages

People who cannot hear sometimes have difficulty managing spoken languages. For this reason, some deaf people use *signed,* or *sign, language.*

Language scholars began to carefully analyze signed languages in the mid-1900's. They soon discovered that these languages have a rich and elaborate organization. Signed languages are just as expressive as spoken language, and thoughts can be expressed just as quickly by signing as speaking. There are many distinct signed languages used by deaf people all over the world.

Signed languages use the hands as the signaling device and the eyes as the receiver, as spoken languages use the vocal tract and the ears. Linguists do not know for certain the extent to which these different modes of communicating affect the structure of the languages. But they do know that signed languages share many proper-

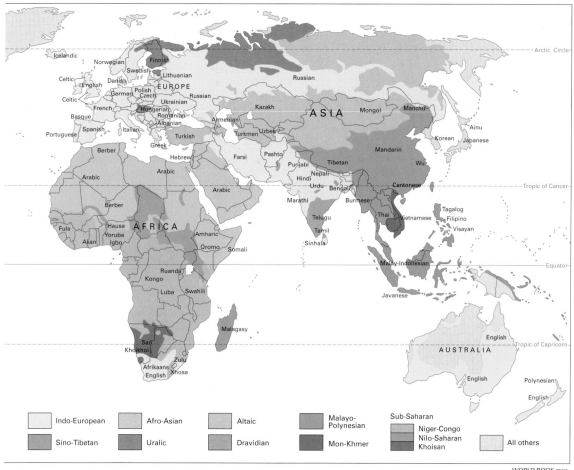

Icelandic
Norwegian
Swedish
Finnish
Lithuanian
Russian
Celtic
English
Danish
German
Polish
Czech
Ukrainian
Russian
EUROPE
Celtic
French
Hungarian
Romanian
Albanian
Kazakh
ASIA
Mongol
Manchu
Basque
Spanish
Italian
Turkish
Turkmen
Uzbek
Armenian
Ainu
Portuguese
Greek
Korean
Japanese
Berber
Hebrew
Farsi
Pashto
Mandarin
Arabic
Punjabi
Tibetan
Wu
Arabic
Nepali
Hindi
Berber
Arabic
Urdu
Bengali
Cantonese
Marathi
Burmese
Hausa
AFRICA
Amharic
Telugu
Thai
Vietnamese
Tagalog
Filipino
Fula
Yoruba
Oromo
Tamil
Visayan
Akan
Igbo
Somali
Sinhala
Ruanda
Malay-Indonesian
Kongo
Luba
Swahili
Javanese
Malagasy
English
AUSTRALIA
San
Khoikhoi
Zulu
English
Afrikaans
Xhosa
English
Polynesian
English

Arctic Circle
Tropic of Cancer
Equator
Tropic of Capricorn

Indo-European	Afro-Asian	Altaic
Sino-Tibetan	Uralic	Dravidian

Malayo-Polynesian	
Mon-Khmer	

Sub-Saharan
Niger-Congo
Nilo-Saharan
Khoisan
All others

WORLD BOOK map

ties with spoken ones.

For example, signs in American Sign Language (ASL) have predictable properties of form, just as words do in English. It is possible to classify signs in terms of their *handshape, location,* and *movement.* If signs share certain features, but differ in another, they can be said to "rhyme." Signers feel such signs to be related to each other, even though the signs differ dramatically in meaning. ASL has a rich tradition of poetry and storytelling, and sometimes an artist will use the formal relation between signs—that is, their similarity of form, as opposed to meaning—for an effect, just as hearing poets do. For example, as a hearing poet might rhyme *slow* and *glow,* a signing poet might "rhyme" the signs for *apple* and *jealous.* Just as *slow* and *glow* differ only in the initial phoneme, so *apple* and *jealous* differ only in handshape, but are the same in movement and location.

Signed languages are ordinary human languages that differ only in the way in which they are transmitted and received. Thus, deaf children learn sign language, with all its complexity, just as easily as hearing children learn their *ambient* (surrounding) spoken language. Furthermore, native signers appear to use the same brain locations to store particular aspects of their language as speakers do. The vast majority of signers and speakers both store a language they learn as a first language in

the left *hemisphere* (half) of the brain. But, whether it is a sign language or a spoken language, languages learned later in life as a second language are stored in another location.

In addition, signed languages break down under brain damage much the way spoken languages do. For example, a *lesion* (injury) to the left frontal lobe of the brain in speakers often leads to difficulty in planning the complex movements of the mouth necessary for speech. Such a lesion in a signer can also lead to difficulty in planning the elaborate movements of the hands required for signing.

Other species and language

Scientists know that many species have elaborate, shared communication systems. Some fish, for example, have complicated courtship dances that communicate something to other fish of their species. Some scientists consider these systems of animal communication as a kind of language.

Some scientists have wondered if animals could learn human language, and they have performed experiments attempting to teach language to other species with high intelligences. These scientists believed that if language primarily depended on general intelligence, chimpanzees and other relatively smart apes ought to be able

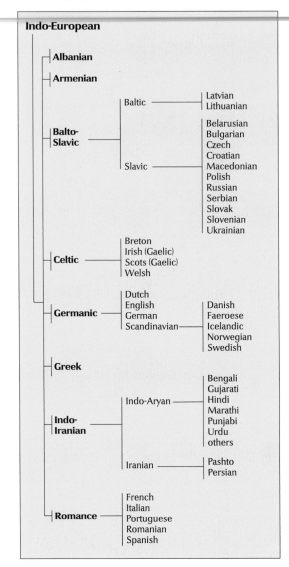

Indo-European

Albanian

Armenian

Balto-Slavic
Baltic — Latvian / Lithuanian
Slavic — Belarusian / Bulgarian / Czech / Croatian / Macedonian / Polish / Russian / Serbian / Slovak / Slovenian / Ukrainian

Celtic — Breton / Irish (Gaelic) / Scots (Gaelic) / Welsh

Germanic — Dutch / English / German / Scandinavian — Danish / Faeroese / Icelandic / Norwegian / Swedish

Greek

Indo-Iranian
Indo-Aryan — Bengali / Gujarati / Hindi / Marathi / Punjabi / Urdu / others
Iranian — Pashto / Persian

Romance — French / Italian / Portuguese / Romanian / Spanish

Indo-European is the most widespread language family today. About half the people in the world speak a language in this family. Scholars divide the Indo-European languages into several groups, such as Balto-Slavic, Germanic, and Romance.

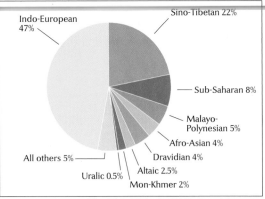

Indo-European 47%
Sino-Tibetan 22%
Sub-Saharan 8%
Malayo-Polynesian 5%
Afro-Asian 4%
Dravidian 4%
Altaic 2.5%
Mon-Khmer 2%
Uralic 0.5%
All others 5%

Sidney S. Culbert, University of Washington, and other sources.

to learn much of a human language. But if language is in some way unique to human beings—requiring special brain "circuits"—animals without these special pathways in the brain should have difficulty acquiring language.

Since about the mid-1900's, chimpanzees have been taught words in a large number of experiments. This research has made clear that the chimpanzee can learn some aspects of human languages. Learning to sign such words as *water,* for example, is not too difficult for them. Other research focusing on the perception and understanding of language has shown that some chimpanzees can interpret fairly complicated requests. Some researchers claim that certain chimpanzees can perform at the level of a 2- or 3-year-old child.

As a result of these experiments, scientists have learned that features of a language that a human being must learn, such as individual words, can be taught to a chimpanzee. However, the features of a language that people are less consciously aware of when learning or speaking a language, such as syntax, are extremely difficult, if not impossible, to teach to chimpanzees. Human children master language when around other speakers without making any special attempt to do so. But chimpanzees who have been extensively trained in a human language still do not seem to have certain types of facility with language that would be found in a young child.

Language change

Some parts of language seem to be fixed, based on the way the brain works. Other parts of language are fairly changeable. Because of the varied relationships in which children need to communicate, the grammar they acquire is likely to be at least a little different from that of their parents. Such a difference is particularly likely if the children encounter languages or dialects that their parents did not experience. These small changes in grammar, word usage, and other aspects of a language can, over many generations, lead to larger changes. For example, English used in the late 1500's and early 1600's by the English playwright William Shakespeare sounds strange to modern-day speakers of English. The earlier English used in the 1300's by the author Geoffrey Chaucer in *The Canterbury Tales*—that is, Middle English—is yet more difficult to understand without interpretation. And the Old English used in England from around 500 to 1100, in which the epic poem *Beowulf* is written, cannot be understood by modern speakers without special training.

Time is not the only factor in language change. When speakers of a language become divided into groups that lose contact with one another, the language of each group continues to change in its own way. After several centuries, the individual groups speak so differently that they may not be able understand one another. Nevertheless, linguists can often determine the original language from which these new languages evolved.

Language families

During the 1800's, observers of languages began noticing how languages change. These scholars determined a way to reconstruct older, sometimes long-dead languages, on the basis of changes that were known to have occurred to existing languages that could be directly observed. One of the basic principles of such reconstruction is that languages that have come from a common source will look more alike if they have only recently diverged. Through observation and analysis, linguists traced back languages that they believed had descended from a common *proto-language*. They used that knowledge to construct a system of grouping languages into broad *language families*. However, not all linguists are in agreement concerning certain language families or the classification of certain languages.

Indo-European is the most prominent language family. It includes many of the languages of Europe, as well as languages of India, such as Hindi. Speakers of Indo-European languages now reside in other parts of the world as well. Languages from this family have become the most important tongues in Australia and New Zealand, and in the countries of North, Central, and South America.

The Indo-European family has several living branches. They are (1) Albanian, (2) Armenian, (3) Balto-Slavic, (4) Celtic, (5) Germanic, (6) Greek, (7) Indo-Iranian, and (8) Romance. Not all Indo-European scholars group the branches in this way. For a breakdown of these branches, see the *Indo-European language* table in this article.

Many simple, basic words are similar in Indo-European languages. For example, the English word *mother* is *mata* in Sanskrit, a language used in ancient India; *meter* in Greek; *mater* in Latin; *madre* in Spanish; and *Mutter* in German.

Speakers of the parent Indo-European language probably lived in the area north of the Black Sea. From there, they likely migrated in several directions, changing the language along the way. The earliest Indo-European language of which we have a record is Hittite, which was used by an ancient people who lived in what is now Turkey. Greek and Sanskrit were other early Indo-European languages.

Other language families. Scholars have constructed other language families in addition to Indo-European.

The Sino-Tibetan family includes Chinese, with its many dialects, Thai, Burmese, and Tibetan. These languages are the leading languages of East Asia.

The Afro-Asian family includes Arabic and Hebrew, the Berber tongues of North Africa, and the Amharic of Ethiopia. Most of the people who speak these languages live in North Africa, the Near East, and northeast Africa.

The Uralic family includes Finnish, Estonian, and Hungarian (or Magyar). Languages in this family can be found in northern Europe and northwestern Asia.

The Altaic family includes Turkish and Mongolian, which are largely limited to Turkey and Mongolia. Some linguists also include Japanese and Korean in the Altaic family, but their inclusion is controversial.

The Dravidian family is made up of Tamil, Telugu, and other languages. Most speakers of these languages are in southern India and parts of Sri Lanka.

The Malayo-Polynesian family includes the languages of Indonesia, the Philippines, Hawaii, New Zealand, Madagascar, and most other islands of the Pacific and Indian oceans.

The Mon-Khmer family has most of its speakers in Southeast Asia and parts of India. This family is sometimes called *Austro-Asiatic*.

The Nilo-Saharan family is made up of languages spoken in countries around the upper branches of the Nile River in Africa. This family includes Luo, which is spoken in Kenya.

The Niger-Congo family includes the Bantu languages, such as Swahili, as an important subgroup.

The Khoisan family features languages famous for the "clicking sounds" they have. These languages are spoken around the Kalahari Desert.

Language loss. There are about 7,000 languages spoken in the world. Of those languages, however, linguists believe that as many as half will die out within the next 100 years. Consequently, large parts of entire language families would be lost. The areas that seem to be most threatened with the possible extinction of languages include Australia, central South America, eastern Russia, the Pacific Coast, eastern Siberia, and the southwestern United States. These areas all have *indigenous* (native) people who are losing their language and moving to a more dominant language, such as English or Portuguese. Linguists try to record languages and describe the grammars of them before the last speaker dies.

The science of language

At some time between 400 and 200 B.C., the Indian grammarian Panini produced the first language study to meet strict linguistic criteria. He compiled a written grammar of Sanskrit that linguists still admire as a model of precise and sophisticated description. Then little was done in the study of languages for centuries. During the Middle Ages, from about the A.D. 400's through the 1400's, many people mistakenly believed that all languages came from Biblical Hebrew.

In the late 1700's, such scholars as Friedrich Schlegel, Jakob Grimm, and Franz Bopp, all of Germany, studied languages by the *comparative method*. They compared the world's languages and noted relationships among them. This work eventually led to a classification of languages into families.

During the early 1900's, Ferdinand de Saussure, a Swiss scholar, introduced several important concepts to linguistics, such as the distinction between what people know about their language and how people use that knowledge when speaking. Saussure also focused on the systematic nature of languages. He is widely considered to be the father of modern linguistics. Linguists still follow Saussure's example in seeking to develop careful descriptions of existing languages. In the United States, one special focus of this work is in American Indian languages, many of which have become or may soon become extinct.

The last half of the 1900's saw the emergence of the American linguist Noam Chomsky's theory of *generative grammar*, a way of studying people's knowledge (sometimes their unconscious knowledge) of their language. Chomsky emphasized precise mathematical characterizations of languages and their grammars. Chomsky's work has drawn attention to those aspects of language that appear to be innate in human beings. As a result, many experts today consider linguistics to be a means of studying some of the fundamental aspects of human nature. Michael Flynn

© Kim Karpeles, Digital Railroad

The cities and towns of Mexico are known for their colorful *plazas,* or public squares, which have long served as centers of public life. The busy plaza shown here is in the city of Guanajuato, the capital of Guanajuato state in central Mexico.

Mexico

Mexico is the northernmost country of Latin America. It lies just south of the United States. The Rio Grande, one of the longest rivers in North America, forms about two-thirds of the boundary between Mexico and the United States. Among all the countries of the Western Hemisphere, only the United States and Brazil have more people than Mexico. Mexico City is the capital and largest city of Mexico. It also is one of the world's largest metropolitan areas in population.

Towering mountains and high, rolling plateaus cover more than two-thirds of Mexico. Mexico also has tropical forests, deserts, and fertile valleys. Few other countries have such a wide variety of landscapes and climates within such short distances of one another.

To understand Mexico, one must consider its history. Centuries ago, the *indigenous* (native) population of Mexico, also called Amerindians or Indians, developed several advanced civilizations. These civilizations built large cities, developed a calendar, invented a counting system, used a form of writing, and established vast empires. The last indigenous empire in Mexico—the Aztec Empire—fell to Spanish invaders in 1521. For the next 300 years, Mexico was a Spanish colony. The Spaniards took Mexico's agricultural and mineral riches. They also introduced many changes in farming, government, industry, population,

---

Jürgen Buchenau, the contributor of this article, is Professor of History at the University of North Carolina at Charlotte.

and religion. The descendants of the Spaniards became Mexico's ruling class. Most of the indigenous people remained poor and uneducated.

During the Spanish colonial period, a third group of people developed in Mexico. These people had both indigenous and European ancestors—and, in some cases, African ancestors as well. These Mexicans of mixed ancestry became known as *mestizos.*

Mexico gained independence from Spain in 1821. Over the next 50 years, the country experienced civil war, economic decline, and foreign intervention that resulted in the loss of half its territory. An uprising called the Mexican Revolution began in 1910, when the people of Mexico overthrew a long-standing dictatorship. The revolutionaries promised to work for greater social justice, democratic reform, and economic development. As a result of the revolution, the government took over huge, privately owned landholdings and divided them among millions of landless farmers. The government also established a national school system and built many hospitals and housing projects. To deal with the pressure of rapid population growth on the economy, the government especially encouraged the development of manufacturing and petroleum production.

The great majority of Mexicans are mestizos. Indigenous people make up the second largest population group. Both groups generally take great pride in their Indian heritage. A number of government programs emphasize the indigenous role in Mexican culture. In 1949, the government made the last Aztec emperor, Cuauhtémoc *(kwow TEHM ohk),* the symbol of Mexican nationality. Cuauhtémoc faced the Spanish invaders so bravely that he

© World Pictures/Alamy Images

Cactuses grow in the Sierra Madre del Sur, a rugged mountain range that extends along Mexico's southern Pacific coast. This photograph shows part of the Sierra Madre in the state of Oaxaca.

became a Mexican hero.

Manufacturing, agriculture, mining, and tourism are all important to Mexico's economy. Leading manufactured products include automobiles, chemicals, processed foods, and steel. Cropland covers about one-seventh of Mexico's area. The rest of the land is too dry, too mountainous, or otherwise unsuitable for crops. However, Mexico is one of the world's leading producers of cacao beans (from which chocolate is made), coffee, corn, oranges, and sugar cane.

Mexico is rich in minerals. It is one of the leading producers of silver in the world and also has large deposits of copper, gold, lead, salt, and sulfur. Mexico became the world's leading oil exporter in 1921. In the 1970's, after decades of low production, Mexico reemerged as a major exporter of petroleum products.

Since the late 1900's, Mexican leaders have tried to develop the economy by fostering ties with other countries, particularly the United States. However, Mexico continues to face difficult economic and social problems, and a majority of its people still live in poverty.

Government

Mexico is a federal republic with an executive branch, a legislative branch, and a judicial branch. The executive branch, headed by a president, is the decision-making center of the government. It establishes government policies, proposes laws, and controls the distribution of federal tax revenues.

Mexico has 31 states and 1 federal district. Each state has an elected governor and legislature. The Federal District is governed by the elected mayor of Mexico City. All

Outline

I. Government
  A. National government   D. Courts
  B. State and local   E. Armed forces
     government
  C. Politics

II. People
  A. Population   C. Language
  B. Ancestry

III. Way of life
  A. City life   E. Holidays
  B. Rural life   F. Recreation
  C. Food and drink   G. Religion
  D. Clothing   H. Education

IV. Arts
  A. Architecture   D. Music
  B. Painting   E. Motion pictures
  C. Literature

V. The land
  A. The Pacific Northwest
  B. The Plateau of Mexico
  C. The Gulf Coastal Plain
  D. The Southern Uplands
  E. The Chiapas Highlands
  F. The Yucatán Peninsula
  G. Plant and animal life

VI. Climate
VII. Economy
  A. Service industries   F. Energy sources
  B. Manufacturing   G. Trade
  C. Agriculture   H. Tourism
  D. Mining   I. Transportation
  E. Fishing   J. Communication

VIII. History

Mexico in brief

General information

Capital: Mexico City.
Official language: Spanish. But about 7 percent of Mexicans use Nahuatl, Maya, Zapotec, or some other American Indian language.
Official name: Estados Unidos Mexicanos (United Mexican States).
National anthem: "Himno Nacional de México" ("National Anthem of Mexico").
Largest cities:
Mexico City (8,591,309)
Guadalajara (1,647,720)
Ecatepec (1,620,303)
Puebla (1,346,176)
Netzahualcóyotl (1,224,924)

Flag Research Center

Mexico's flag, adopted in 1821, features a version of the country's coat of arms. The green stands for independence, white for religion, and red for union.

Coat of arms. A legend says the Aztec people built their capital Tenochtitlan (now Mexico City) where they saw an eagle perched on a cactus and devouring a snake.

Land and climate

Land: Mexico lies in North America. It is bordered by the United States on the north and by Guatemala and Belize on the southeast. The Gulf of Mexico and the Caribbean Sea lie to the east; the Pacific Ocean to the west and south. A chain of high volcanic mountains extends east-west across southern Mexico, just south of Mexico City. Lower mountain chains extend northwestward from each end of the volcanic chain, forming a great U-shape of mountains. Much of north-central Mexico is a high plateau rimmed by these mountain ranges. The Pacific Coast in the far south is rugged and has densely forested areas. The long peninsula of Baja California in the northwest is mostly desert with some mountains. The Yucatán Peninsula in the southeast is flat and forested. Mexico's chief rivers are the Rio Grande (at the U.S. border) and the Balsas.

WORLD BOOK map

Area: 756,066 mi² (1,958,201 km²). *Greatest distances*—north-south, 1,250 mi (2,012 km); east-west, 1,900 mi (3,060 km). *Coastline*—6,320 mi (10,170 km).
Elevation: *Highest*—Pico de Orizaba (also called Citlaltépetl), 18,410 ft (5,610 m). *Lowest*—near Mexicali, 33 ft (10 m) below sea level.
Climate: Northwest and north-central Mexico are mostly desert, with hot summers and cool to mild winters. The northeast coast has moderate rainfall with mild winters and warm summers. Central Mexico is dry, with temperatures varying according to altitude. High locations, such as Mexico City, have mild temperatures the year around. Low-altitude locations are warmer. Southern Mexico, including Yucatán, is warm and moist the year around.

Government

Form of government: Federal republic.
Chief executive: President (elected to 6-year term).
Legislature: Congress of two houses—128-member Senate and 500-member Chamber of Deputies.
Judiciary: Highest court is the Supreme Court of Justice.
Political subdivisions: 31 states, 1 federal district.

People

Population: *Estimated 2008 population*—110,915,000. *2000 census*—97,483,412.
Population density: 147 per mi² (57 per km²).
Distribution: 76 percent urban, 24 percent rural.
Major ethnic/national groups: Almost entirely Mexican. Most Mexicans are of mixed American Indian and Spanish ancestry; some are entirely Indian or entirely of European descent; a few have partly African or East Asian ancestry.
Major religions: More than 75 percent Roman Catholic; some Protestants, Jews, and American Indian religions.

Population trend

Millions

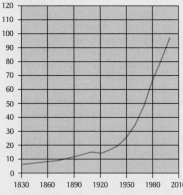

Year	Population
1831	6,382,000
1873	9,210,000
1895	12,632,000
1910	15,160,000
1921	14,335,000
1930	16,553,000
1940	19,654,000
1950	25,791,000
1960	34,923,000
1970	48,225,000
1980	66,847,000
1990	81,249,645
2000	97,483,412

Economy

Chief products: *Agriculture*—avocados, bananas, barley, beans, coffee, corn, cotton, lemons, mangoes, oranges, potatoes, sorghum, sugar cane, tomatoes, wheat. *Manufacturing*—chemicals, iron and steel, motor vehicles, processed foods. *Mining*—copper, gold, lead, natural gas, petroleum, salt, silver, sulfur, zinc.
Money: *Basic unit*—Mexican peso. One hundred centavos equal one peso.
Foreign trade: *Major exports*—electrical machinery, motor vehicles, telecommunications equipment. *Major imports*—electrical and electronic equipment, industrial machinery, motor vehicles. *Major trading partners*—China, Germany, Japan, United States.

Mexicans who are at least 18 years old can vote.

National government. Mexico's president has a significant role in the national government. All prominent political figures in the executive branch depend directly on the president for their jobs. The president appoints a cabinet that directs government operations. Important cabinet members include the secretary of government and the secretary of finance and public credit. The president also originates much legislation. Some presidents have introduced constitutional amendments to support their own policies.

The president is elected by the people to a six-year term and may serve only one term in office. If the president does not finish the term, the legislature chooses a temporary president to serve until a special or regular presidential election is held.

Mexico's legislature is called the Congress. It consists of a Senate and a Chamber of Deputies. The Senate has 128 members who are elected to six-year terms. The Chamber of Deputies has 500 members elected to three-year terms. Three hundred of the deputies are elected from the country's electoral districts. The remaining 200 seats are filled by deputies who do not represent a particular district. Members of Congress may serve multiple, but not consecutive, terms.

State and local government. The people elect state governors to six-year terms and state legislators to three-year terms. The president may remove governors from office with the Senate's approval. Each state is divided into *municipios* (townships). Each municipio has a president and a council elected to three-year terms. Less than 10 percent of all tax revenues go directly to state and local agencies. State agencies depend on the national government, and local authorities on state agencies, for funds to carry out public works projects.

Politics. Mexico has a number of political parties. The most important include the Partido Revolucionario Institucional (Institutional Revolutionary Party), also known as the PRI; the Partido Acción Nacional (National Action Party), or PAN; and the Partido de la Revolución Democrática (Party of the Democratic Revolution), or PRD.

The PRI, established in 1929 as the Partido Nacional Revolucionario (National Revolutionary Party), dominated Mexican politics and government until the end of the 1900's. In 2000, a non-PRI candidate was elected president for the first time in 71 years.

Courts. Mexico's highest court at the federal level is the Supreme Court of Justice. The president appoints 21 members and several alternates to the court. The federal judicial system also includes hundreds of circuit and district courts. The highest court in each state is a Superior Court of Justice.

Mexico's courts play a limited role. The courts rarely declare a law unconstitutional and generally support the president's policies. Mexicans may use the courts to protect their individual rights through an *amparo* (protection) procedure. In amparo cases, the courts may decide that a law has resulted in unfair treatment and that an exception should be made. However, the law in question is not changed. Most Mexicans cannot afford to use the legal process.

Armed forces. About 240,000 men and women serve in Mexico's army, navy, and air force. The army is the largest branch of the armed forces. It has about 185,000

members. Mexican men are required to serve part-time for a year in the army after reaching the age of 18.

People

Population. Mexico's population has increased rapidly as a result of a traditionally high birth rate and a sharply reduced death rate. The reduced death rate is due in part to improved living conditions and expanded health services since the early 1950's. Since 1970, the most rapid population growth has occurred in the states of Campeche, México, Morelos, and Quintana Roo.

More than half of the people of Mexico are under 20 years of age. The relatively young population and its high growth rate have placed tremendous pressure on such services as education, health care, and social security. The strain on basic services is especially serious in urban centers. Many cities lack adequate housing, drinking water, and public transportation.

The high rate of population growth has also contributed to a shortage of jobs in Mexico. Since the 1980's, far more people have entered the labor force than have retired, and the economy has generally failed to create enough jobs. This situation has led to a high rate of unemployment. It has also stimulated increasing migration of Mexicans to the United States.

Ancestry. The majority of Mexicans are mestizos. Their white ancestors were mostly Spaniards who came during and after the Spanish conquest of 1519 to 1521. Their indigenous ancestors lived in Mexico when the Spaniards arrived. Some mestizos are also descended from Africans brought to colonial Mexico to serve as slaves. Being a mestizo is generally a matter of pride.

Indigenous people make up Mexico's second largest population group. Being indigenous in Mexico does not depend chiefly on ancestry. It is mostly a matter of lifestyle, language, and viewpoint. For example, Mexicans are considered indigenous if they speak an Amerindian language or wear clothing typical of an indigenous people. Such peoples include the Nahua of central Mexico; the Mixtec, mainly from Oaxaca state; and the Maya of southeast Mexico. In the heavily indigenous south, Amerindian traditions influence mestizo ways of life.

Most of Mexico's political, business, intellectual, and military leaders are mestizos, though whites remain influential. In addition to whites, the people of Mexico include some Asians of unmixed ancestry.

Language. Almost all Mexicans speak Spanish, the official language of Mexico and most other Latin American countries. Many words used in the United States came from Mexico, including *canyon, corral, desperado, lariat, lasso, macho, patio, politico, rodeo,* and *stampede.*

Most indigenous Mexicans speak Spanish along with their own ancient language, but millions of them primarily use their indigenous language in daily life. Altogether, they speak more than 60 Amerindian languages and dialects. Major Amerindian languages include Maya, Mixtec, Nahuatl, Otomí, Tarascan, and Zapotec.

Way of life

The way of life in Mexico includes many traditions from the nation's long indigenous past and the Spanish colonial period. But Mexico changed rapidly in the 1900's. In many ways, life in its larger cities has become similar to that in the neighboring United States. Mexican villagers follow

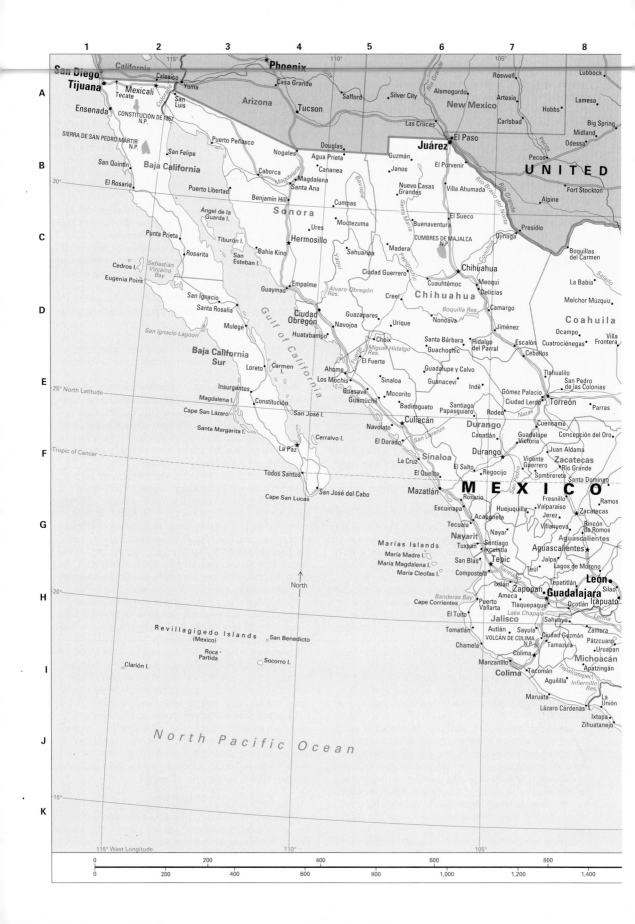

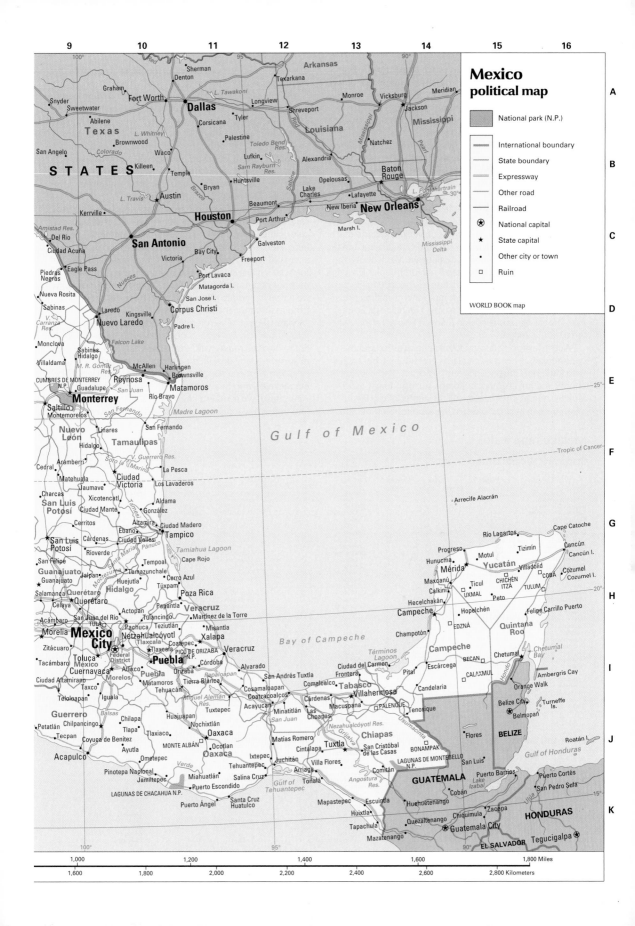

Mexico
political map

	National park (N.P.)
	International boundary
	State boundary
	Expressway
	Other road
	Railroad
⊛	National capital
★	State capital
•	Other city or town
□	Ruin

WORLD BOOK map

Arkansas

Sherman
Denton
Graham
Texarkana
Longview
Monroe
Vicksburg
Meridian
Fort Worth
Dallas
Snyder
Sweetwater
Corsicana
Tyler
Shreveport
Jackson
Abilene
Louisiana
Mississippi
San Angelo
Texas
L. Whitney
Brownwood
Waco
Palestine
Toledo Bend Res.
Alexandria
Natchez
Baton Rouge
S T A T E S
Killeen
Temple
Sam Rayburn Res.
Colorado
Huntsville
Lufkin
Opelousas
Amistad Res.
Austin
Bryan
Beaumont
Lafayette
New Iberia
New Orleans
Kerrville
L. Travis
Brazos
Houston
Port Arthur
Galveston
L. Pontchartrain
Del Rio
San Antonio
Bay City
Freeport
Marsh I.
Mississippi Delta
Ciudad Acuña
Victoria
Piedras Negras
Eagle Pass
Nueces
Port Lavaca
Matagorda I.
Nueva Rosita
San Jose I.
Sabinas
Laredo
Kingsville
Corpus Christi
V. Carranza Res.
Nuevo Laredo
Padre I.
Monclova
Falcon Lake
Sabinas Hidalgo
Villaldama
M. R. Gómez Res.
McAllen
Harlingen
Brownsville
CUMBRES DE MONTERREY N.P.
Reynosa
Matamoros
Guadalupe
San Juan
Monterrey
Río Bravo
Saltillo
San Fernando
Madre Lagoon
Montemorelos
Nuevo León
Linares
San Fernando
Hidalgo
Tamaulipas
Gulf of Mexico
Arámberri
Soto la Marina
V. Guerrero Res.
Cedral
La Pesca
Matehuala
Jaumave
Los Lavaderos
Charcas
Ciudad Victoria
Xicotencatl
Aldama
San Luis Potosí
Ciudad Mante
González
Cerritos
Altamira
Ciudad Madero
Arrecife Alacrán
San Luis Potosí
Cárdenas
Ciudad Valles
Tampico
Ebano
Río Lagartos
Cape Catoche
San Felipe
Rioverde
Tamiahua Lagoon
Tizimín
Cancún
Guanajuato
Jalpan
Tempoal
Cape Rojo
Progreso
Motul
Cancún I.
Guanajuato
Tamazunchale
Hunucmá
Villadolid
Salamanca
Querétaro
Huejutla
Cerro Azul
Mérida
Yucatán
Cozumel
Celaya
Hidalgo
Túxpam
Maxdanú
CHICHÉN ITZÁ
Cozumel I.
Acámbaro
Querétaro
Poza Rica
Ticul
COBÁ
Morelia
San Juan del Río
Papantla
Calkini
UXMAL
Peto
TULUM
TULA
Actopan
Martínez de la Torre
Hecelchakán
Zitácuaro
Pachuca
Tulancingo
Campeche
Hopelchén
Felipe Carrillo Puerto
Toluca
Teziutlán
Misantla
Champotón
Quintana Roo
Tacámbaro
Mexico City
Netzahualcóyotl
Xalapa
EDZNÁ
Federal District
Tlaxcala
Coatepec
Bay of Campeche
Chetumal Bay
Ciudad Altamirano
Puebla
PICO DE ORIZABA
Veracruz
Términos Lagoon
Campeche
BECÁN
Chetumal
Cuernavaca
Orizaba
Córdoba
Ciudad del Carmen
Escárcega
CALAKMUL
Morelos
Atlixco
Alvarado
Frontera
Pital
Ambergris Cay
Taxco
Puebla
Tierra Blanca
San Andrés Tuxtla
Candelaria
Orange Walk
Teloloapan
Matamoros
Papaloapan
Cosamaloapan
Comalcalco
Tabasco
Belize City
Turneffe Is.
Iguala
Tehuacán
Coatzacoalcos
Cárdenas
Villahermosa
PALENQUE
Belmopán
Guerrero
Miguel Alemán Res.
Tuxtepec
Acayucan
Macuspana
Tenosique
Balsas
Chilapa
Huajuapan
Minatitlán
Las Choapas
Petatlán
Chilpancingo
Nochixtlán
San Juan
Usumacinta
Tlapa
Nezahualcóyotl Res.
Flores
BELIZE
Roatán I.
Tecpan
Coyuca de Benítez
Tlaxiaco
Oaxaca
Matías Romero
Chiapas
Acapulco
Ayutla
MONTE ALBÁN
Ocotlán
Cintalapa
San Cristóbal de las Casas
Gulf of Honduras
Oaxaca
Ixtepec
Tuxtla
BONAMPAK
Ometepec
Verde
Tehuantepec
Juchitán
Villa Flores
LAGUNAS DE MONTEBELLO N.P.
San Luis
Pinotepa Nacional
Salina Cruz
Arriaga
Comitán
Puerto Cortés
Jamiltepec
Miahuatlán
Tonalá
Angostura Res.
GUATEMALA
Lake Izabal
San Pedro Sula
LAGUNAS DE CHACAHUA N.P.
Puerto Escondido
Gulf of Tehuantepec
Cobán
Puerto Barrios
Puerto Ángel
Santa Cruz Huatulco
Mapastepec
Escuintla
Huehuetenango
Ulúa
Huixtla
Chiquimula
Zacapa
HONDURAS
Tapachula
Quezaltenango
Guatemala City
EL SALVADOR
Tegucigalpa
Mazatenango

1,000   1,200   1,400   1,600   1,800 Miles

1,600   1,800   2,000   2,200   2,400   2,600   2,800 Kilometers

the older way of life more than urban Mexicans do. Even in the villages, however, government programs are doing much to modernize people's lives. Schools, health clinics, roads, electric power and running water, and government-sponsored television are bringing people in small towns into mainstream Mexican life.

Mexican households have five or six people on average. It is common for several generations to live together. Many urban women have jobs. Women in farming areas often help cultivate the fields. Mexican girls have less personal freedom than girls do in Canada and the United States. Farm boys work in the fields, and many youths in the cities have part-time or full-time jobs.

City life. The most urban areas of Mexico include the metropolitan areas of Mexico City and Guadalajara and the states of Nuevo León and Baja California. Mexico City, the country's capital, has more than 8 million people. The city's metropolitan area has a population of about 20 million. Nine other Mexican cities have more than 1 million people. These cities are, in order of size, Guadalajara, Ecatepec, Puebla, Netzahualcóyotl, Juárez, Tijuana, León, Monterrey, and Zapopan.

Many Mexican cities and towns began as indigenous communities. After the Spaniards arrived, they built cities with traditional European layouts. Each city had a major church and government buildings surrounding a *plaza* (public square). The plaza is still the center of city life in Mexico, even in large cities. In the evenings and on Sun-

day afternoons, people gather in the plaza to socialize or listen to music.

The city centers are filled with high-rise buildings, and modern houses and apartment buildings occupy the suburbs. Older parts of towns and cities have rows of homes built in the Spanish colonial style. Most of these houses are made of stone or *adobe* (sun-dried clay) brick. Small balconies extend from some windows. A Spanish-style house also has a *patio* (courtyard), which is the center of family life. This gardenlike area may have a fountain, flowers, vines, and pots of blooming plants.

Mexican cities have grown as people have moved from rural areas to find jobs and a better life. As a result, many cities suffer from serious social and environmental problems. Houses in many of the poor sections are made of scraps of wood, metal, and other found materials. Most of them lack electric power and running water. The large number of automobiles results in frequent traffic jams. Air pollution in Mexico City causes many people to suffer from respiratory and eye diseases.

Many people who migrate to cities have no regular jobs. Others do not earn enough to support themselves. Entire families must work, sometimes at two or three jobs, to survive. Many unskilled poor people find jobs as construction workers, street cleaners, or street vendors. Others make a living by washing clothes or cleaning homes. After they have lived in a city for a while, many of the poor find higher-paying jobs in factories.

Mexico map index

States and Federal District

Name	Population	Area In mi²	In km²	Map key
Aguascalientes	943,506	2,112	5,471	G 8
Baja California	2,487,700	26,997	69,921	B 2
Baja California Sur	423,516	28,369	73,475	E 3
Campeche	689,656	19,619	50,812	I 14
Chiapas	3,920,515	28,653	74,211	J 13
Chihuahua	3,047,867	94,571	244,938	D 6
Coahuila	2,295,808	57,908	149,982	D 8
Colima	540,679	2,004	5,191	I 7
Durango	1,445,922	47,560	123,181	F 7
Federal District	8,591,309	571	1,479	I 10
Guanajuato	4,656,761	11,773	30,491	H 9
Guerrero	3,075,083	24,819	64,281	J 9
Hidalgo	2,231,392	8,036	20,813	H 10
Jalisco	6,321,278	31,211	80,836	H 7
México	13,083,359	8,245	21,355	I 9
Michoacán	3,979,177	23,138	59,928	I 8
Morelos	1,552,878	1,911	4,950	I 10
Nayarit	919,739	10,417	26,979	G 7
Nuevo León	3,826,240	25,067	64,924	F 9
Oaxaca	3,432,180	36,275	93,952	J 11
Puebla	5,070,346	13,090	33,902	I 10
Querétaro	1,402,010	4,420	11,449	H 9
Quintana Roo	873,804	19,387	50,212	H 15
San Luis Potosí	2,296,363	24,351	63,068	G 9
Sinaloa	2,534,835	22,521	58,328	F 6
Sonora	2,213,370	70,291	182,052	C 4
Tabasco	1,889,367	9,756	25,267	I 13
Tamaulipas	2,747,114	30,650	79,384	F 10
Tlaxcala	961,912	1,551	4,016	I 10
Veracruz	6,901,111	27,683	71,699	H 11
Yucatán	1,665,707	14,827	38,402	H 15
Zacatecas	1,351,207	28,283	73,252	F 8

Cities and towns

Acámbaro .....110,487 ..H 9
Acapulco ....721,011 ..J 9
Acayucan ....78,156 ..J 12
Aguas-
   calientes ....643,360 ..G 8
Ahome ....358,663 ..E 5
Apatzingán ...117,849 ..I 8
Alizapán de
   Zaragoza* ..467,262 ..I 10
Atlixco ....117,019 ..I 10
Caborca ....69,359 ..B 3
Campeche ..216,735 ..H 14
Canatlán ....31,113 ..F 7

Cancún ....419,276 ..G 16
Cárdenas .....216,903 ..I 13
Celaya ....382,140 ..H 9
Centro* ....519,873 ..I 13
Cerro Azul ...24,706 ..H 10
Chetumal‡ .....94,158 ..I 15
Chihuahua ...670,208 ..C 6
Chilapa ....102,716 ..J 10
Chilpancingo ..192,509 ..J 9
Ciudad del
   Carmen ....221,908 ..I 13
Ciudad
   Guzmán ......86,587 ..I 7

Ciudad
   Hidalgo* ....106,198 ..H 9
Ciudad Lerdo ..112,272 ..E 7
Ciudad
   Madero .....182,012 ..G 10
Ciudad
   Mante ....112,453 ..G 10
Ciudad
   Obregón‡ ...311,443 ..D 4
Ciudad
   Valles ......146,411 ..G 10
Ciudad
   Victoria ....282,686 ..F 10
Coatepec ....73,459 ..I 11
Coatzacoal-
   cos ....267,037 ..I 12
Colima ....129,454 ..I 7
Comalcalco ...164,640 ..I 13
Comitán ......104,986 ..J 13
Compostela ....65,804 ..H 7
Córdoba ......176,952 ..I 11
Cortazar* ......81,157 ..H 9
Cosamalo-
   apan ....54,059 ..I 11
Cozumel ....60,025 ..H 16
Cuauhtémoc ..124,279 ..D 6
Cuautla* ......153,132 ..I 10
Cuernavaca ...337,966 ..I 10
Culiacán .....744,859 ..F 5
Delicias ......116,132 ..D 7
Dolores
   Hidalgo* ...128,675 ..H 9
Durango ......490,524 ..F 7
Ecatepec* ...1,620,303 ..I 10
El Fuerte ......89,556 ..E 5
Ensenada ....369,573 ..A 1
Etchojoa* .....56,164 ..D 4
Fresnillo .....182,744 ..G 8
Garza
   García* ....126,147 ..E 9
Gómez
   Palacio ....272,806 ..E 7
Guadalajara ..1,647,720
   †3,669,021 ..H 8
Guadalupe ...668,780 ..E 9
Guanajuato ...141,215 ..H 9
Guasave ......277,201 ..E 5
Guaymas .....130,108 ..D 4
Hermosillo ...608,697 ..C 4
Hidalgo del
   Parral .....100,881 ..D 6
Iguala ....123,883 ..I 9
Irapuato .....440,039 ..H 8
Jerez ....54,746 ..G 8
Jiutepec* ....170,428 ..I 10
Juárez .....1,217,818 ..B 6
Lagos de
   Moreno ....127,949 ..H 8

La Paz ....196,708 ..F 4
La Piedad
   Cavadas* ....84,785 ..H 8
Lázaro
   Cárdenas ...170,878 ..I 8
León ....1,133,576 ..H 8
Linares ....69,023 ..F 9
Los Mochis‡ ..162,659 ..E 5
Manzanillo ...124,014 ..I 7
Martínez de
   la Torre ...118,815 ..H 11
Matamoros ...416,428 ..E 10
Matamoros* ...91,858 ..E 8
Matamoros .....70,532 ..I 10
Matehuala .....78,053 ..F 9
Mazatlán .....380,265 ..F 6
Mérida ....703,324 ..H 15
Mexicali .....764,902 ..A 2
Mexico City ..8,591,309
   †17,786,983 ..I 10
Minatitlán ...152,983 ..J 12
Monclova .....193,657 ..E 9
Monterrey ..1,108,499
   †3,273,332 ..E 9
Morelia ......619,958 ..I 9
Naucalpan* ...857,511 ..I 10
Navojoa ......140,495 ..D 5
Netzahual-
   cóyotl ...1,224,924 ..I 10
Nogales ......159,103 ..B 4
Nuevo
   Laredo .....310,277 ..D 9
Oaxaca ....256,848 ..J 11
Ocosingo* ....171,495 ..J 13
Ocotlán ....84,181 ..H 8
Orizaba ......118,488 ..I 11
Pachuca ......244,688 ..H 10
Papantla .....170,123 ..H 11
Pátzcuaro .....78,127 ..I 8
Penjamo* .....143,927 ..H 9
Piedras
   Negras ....127,898 ..C 9
Poza Rica ....152,678 ..H 11
Puebla .....1,346,176 ..I 10
Puerto
   Vallarta ...183,741 ..H 7
Querétaro ....639,839 ..H 9
Reynosa ......419,776 ..E 10
Río Bravo ....103,901 ..E 10
Salamanca ...226,864 ..H 9
Salina Cruz ...76,392 ..K 12
Saltillo ......577,352 ..E 9
Salvatierra* ...94,322 ..H 9
San Andrés
   Tuxtla .....142,251 ..I 12
San Cristóbal
   de las
   Casas .....132,317 ..J 13

San Francisco
   del Rincón* .100,149 ..H 8
San Juan
   del Río .....179,300 ..H 9
San Luis ....145,276 ..A 2
San Luis
   Potosí .....669,353 ..G 9
San Martín Tex-
   melucan* ...121,093 ..I 9
San Miguel de
   Allende* ...134,645 ..H 9
San Nicolás de
   los Garzas* ..495,540 ..E 9
San Pedro de
   las Colonias ..88,451 ..E 8
Santa
   Catarina* ..226,573 ..E 9
Santiago
   Ixcuintla ....95,311 ..G 7
Silao ....134,037 ..H 8
Tamazunchale ..88,991 ..H 10
Tampico ......294,789 ..G 10
Tapachula ....271,141 ..K 13
Taxco ....99,907 ..I 9
Tecomán ....99,296 ..I 7
Tehuacán .....225,943 ..I 11
Tehuantepec ...53,168 ..J 12
Temapache* ..102,824 ..H 10
Tepatitlán ...118,948 ..H 8
Tepic ....305,025 ..H 7
Teziutlán .....81,001 ..H 11
Tierra
   Blanca ......89,143 ..I 11
Tijuana ....1,212,232 ..A 1
Tlalnepantla ..720,755 ..I 10
Tlaquepaque ..475,472 ..H 7
Tlaxcala ....73,184 ..I 10
Toluca ....665,617 ..I 9
Torreón ......529,093 ..E 8
Tula de
   Allende* ....86,782 ..H 10
Tulancingo ...121,946 ..H 10
Tuxpan ....31,185 ..G 7
Túxpam ......126,475 ..H 11
Tuxtla ....433,544 ..J 13
Uruapan .....265,211 ..I 8
Valle de
   Santiago* ..130,557 ..H 9
Venustiano
   Carranza* ..462,089 ..I 10
Veracruz .....457,119 ..I 11
Xalapa ....390,058 ..I 11
Yuriria* ....73,602 ..H 9
Zacapu* ....69,739 ..I 8
Zacatecas ....123,700 ..G 8
Zamora ....161,191 ..H 8
Zapopan ....1,002,239 ..H 7
Zitácuaro ....137,970 ..I 9

*Does not appear on map; key shows general location.
†Population of metropolitan area, including suburbs.
Sources: 2000 census, except ‡, which are 1990 census figures.

Population density

The population of Mexico is concentrated in the south-central region of the country, particularly around Mexico City. The cities shown on the map are among the largest in Mexico.

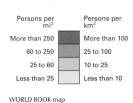

Major urban centers

● More than 10 million inhabitants

● 1 million to 10 million inhabitants

• Less than 1 million inhabitants

Persons per mi²	Persons per km²
More than 250	More than 100
60 to 250	25 to 100
25 to 60	10 to 25
Less than 25	Less than 10

WORLD BOOK map

Rural life. About 1 out of every 4 Mexicans lives on a farm or in a small village. Most farmers live near their fields. The villages are poor, with little access to such basic social services as health care and education. Most young people leave their villages to find work in Mexican cities and towns or in the United States.

Village homes stand along simple dirt or cobblestone roads. In most villages, a Roman Catholic church rises on one side of the plaza, which forms the center of the community. Shops and government buildings line the plaza's other sides.

Almost every village, and every city and town, has a marketplace. Going to market is one of the chief activities of people in farming areas. They generally spend one day each week there, doing business and chatting with friends. The people bring clothes, food, and other goods that they wish to sell or trade. They display them in rented stalls or spread them on the ground. Farmers often trade their goods instead of selling them, and much bargaining takes place.

The shape and style of village houses vary according to the climate. People on the dry central plateau build homes of adobe, brick, cement block, or stone, with flat roofs made of red tile, sheet metal, or straw. Some of these houses have only one room, a dirt floor, and few or no windows. The kitchen may be a structure called a *lean-to,* built of poles and cornstalks placed against an outside wall. If a house does not have a lean-to kitchen, the family may build a cooking fire on the floor.

In areas of heavy rainfall, many houses have walls built of poles coated with lime and clay. This mixture lasts longer than adobe does in the rain. The houses have sloping roofs that allow rain to run off easily. Some indigenous people in southern Mexico build round houses. In Yu-

© Didier Dorval, Masterfile

Homes in central Mexico typically are made of adobe, brick, cement block, or stone, with flat roofs. This photograph shows a residential area in Zacatecas, the capital of Zacatecas state.

© Chip & Rosa Maria Peterson

© Russell Gordon, Digital Railroad

Extremes of poverty and wealth can be seen in these views of Mexico City. Poor people live in shacks on the outskirts of the city, *left.* Wealthy residents can afford to live in luxury apartment buildings, such as those in the city's Interlomas area, *above.*

catán, most village houses are rectangular with rounded ends. The roofs are made of palm leaves.

Most indigenous people live in villages in central and southern Mexico and the Yucatán Peninsula and are poor. Dishonest outsiders, both Mexican and foreign, have treated them unfairly, sometimes taking their land, exploiting them for cheap labor, or charging them higher prices for goods and services. As a result, conflicts have occurred between indigenous communities and their wealthier neighbors.

Food and drink. Thousands of years ago, the indigenous inhabitants of what is now Mexico discovered how to grow corn. It became their most important food. Today, corn is still the chief food of most Mexicans, especially in rural areas. Mexican cooks generally soften the corn before cooking by soaking it in a mild chemical solution called *limewater.* Then they boil the corn and grind it into meal.

The main corn-meal food is the *tortilla,* which is a thin, flat bread shaped by hand or machine and cooked on an ungreased griddle. Tortillas also can be made with wheat flour. The tortilla is the bread of most Mexicans. They eat tortillas plain or as part of *tacos* (folded tortillas filled with chopped meat or cheese, then sometimes fried), *enchiladas* (rolled-up tortillas filled with chopped meat or cheese and covered with hot sauce), or *tostadas* (fried tortillas served flat with meat, cheese, beans, lettuce, and onions). In northern Mexico, wheat tortillas are more common. A burrito is a large wheat-flour tortilla filled with such ingredients as cheese, beans, vegetables, rice, and hot sauce.

Many Mexicans eat *frijoles* (beans) that are boiled and mashed, then fried and refried in lard. Poorer Mexicans may eat frijoles every day, often using a folded tortilla to scoop them up. Rice is also boiled and then fried. Other popular foods include *atole* (a thick, soupy corn-meal dish) and *tamales* (corn meal steamed in corn husks or banana leaves and usually mixed with pork or chicken). Most Mexicans like their food highly seasoned with chili pepper or other hot peppers. Turkey is a popular holiday dish. It is often served with *mole* sauce made of chocolate, chili,

sesame seeds, and spices.

Poorer families eat little meat because they cannot afford it. They may vary their basic diet of corn and beans with fruit, honey, onions, tomatoes, squash, or sweet potatoes. Favorite fruits include avocados, bananas, mangoes, oranges, and papayas. The fruit and leaves of the prickly pear cactus are eaten boiled, fried, or stewed. Wealthier Mexicans have a more balanced diet.

Popular beverages in Mexico include water flavored with fruit juice and cinnamon-flavored hot chocolate beaten into foam. Mexicans also drink coffee, milk, and mineral water, and they are especially fond of soft drinks. Alcoholic beverages include beer and wine as well as two popular distilled liquors called *mescal* and *tequila,* both made from the juice of the maguey plant.

Clothing. Urban Mexicans wear clothing like that worn in the United States and Canada. Villagers wear simple

© Frederica Georgia, Photo Researchers

Bullfighting is a popular spectator sport in Mexico. Almost all large cities and many small towns have bull rings.

clothes that vary according to region and climate. The designs of these clothes date back centuries. In central and southern Mexico, men generally wear plain cotton shirts and trousers and leather sandals called *huaraches*. Wide-brimmed felt or straw hats called *sombreros* protect them from the hot sun. During cold or rainy weather, they may wear *ponchos* (blankets with a slit in the center for the head). At night, they may wrap themselves in colorful *serapes*, which are blankets carried over one shoulder during the day. Village women wear blouses and long, full skirts. They usually go barefoot or wear sandals. The women cover their heads with fringed shawls called *rebozos*. A mother may tie her baby to her back with a rebozo.

Some clothing worn by villagers is homemade. Hand weaving is an ancient indigenous art, and many Amerindian communities are famous for their beautiful home-woven fabrics. Styles of weaving vary throughout Mexico, and the colors and design of a poncho or serape can show where it came from. For example, blankets with a striped rainbow pattern come from the Saltillo area in northern Mexico.

Some indigenous people wear distinctive clothing. In Oaxaca state, Amerindians wear large capes made of straw. On holidays, indigenous women on the Isthmus of Tehuantepec wear a wide, white, lacy headdress called a *huipil grande*. In Yucatán, Maya women wear long, loose, white dresses that are embroidered around the neck and the bottom hem.

Mexicans sometimes wear national costumes on special occasions. The men's national costumes include the dark blue *charro* suit, made of doeskin or velvet. It has a *bolero* (short jacket) and tight riding pants with gold or silver buttons down the sides. A flowing red bow tie, spurred boots, and a fancy white sombrero complete the costume. The best-known women's costume is probably the *china poblana*. It is usually worn for the *jarabe tapatío*, also

known as the Mexican hat dance. According to legend, the china poblana was named for a Chinese princess of the 1600's who was kidnapped by pirates and sold to a merchant of Puebla. It consists of a full red-and-green skirt with beads and other ornaments, a colorfully embroidered short-sleeved blouse, and a brightly colored sash.

Holidays. Mexicans celebrate their Independence Day, September 16, and other holidays with colorful *fiestas* (festivals). Every city, town, and village holds a yearly fiesta to honor its patron saint. Most fiestas begin before dawn with ringing bells and a shower of fireworks. During the fiestas, the people pray and burn candles to their saints in churches decorated with flowers and paper garlands. They dance, gamble, hold parades, and buy refreshments in the marketplace and public square. Folk dances are an important feature of fiestas. In the Mexican hat dance, dancers perform a lively sequence with hopping steps and heel-and-toe tapping.

In smaller towns and villages, cockfights and amateur bullfights also take place during fiestas. In larger towns and cities, most fiestas include less religious worship than do the village fiestas. The people watch plays and professional bullfights, ride merry-go-rounds and Ferris wheels, and buy goods at merchants' booths.

Guadalupe Day, celebrated on December 12, is Mexico's most important religious holiday. It honors Our Lady of Guadalupe (often called the Virgin of Guadalupe), Mexico's patron saint. Catholics believe that on Dec. 12, 1531, the Virgin appeared to an indigenous peasant on Tepeyac Hill, in what is now Mexico City.

On the nine nights before Christmas, friends and neighbors gather to act out Mary and Joseph's journey to Bethlehem. This activity is called the *posada*. Each night after the posada, the children play the *piñata* game. Piñatas are containers made of earthenware or papier-mâché. Many are shaped like animals and filled with candy and toys. A piñata is hung above the children's heads. The youngsters are blindfolded and take turns striking the piñata with a stick. After the container breaks, the children scramble to collect the scattered presents. On Twelfth Night, 12 days

© Richard Steedman, The Stock Market

Traditional garments worn by Mexico's Huichol Indians, *shown here,* are embroidered with colorful, detailed patterns.

© Gräfenhain Günter, SIME/4Corners Images

Folk dances, such as the *jarabe tapatío,* also called the Mexican hat dance, *shown here,* are a feature of many Mexican fiestas.

Worshipers wave palm branches in a church procession through the streets of Puebla on Palm Sunday. Religion plays an important role in the lives of most Mexicans. The majority of Mexico's people belong to the Roman Catholic Church.

Melinda Berge, Bruce Coleman Inc.

after Christmas, parents fill their children's shoes with presents.

Other important holidays include New Year's Day (January 1); Constitution Day (February 5); Holy Week (the week before Easter); Cinco de Mayo (May 5); Día de los muertos (November 2); and Revolution Day, the anniversary of the Mexican Revolution of 1910 (November 20).

Recreation. Soccer is the most popular sport in Mexico, followed by baseball. People often play soccer or baseball on vacant lots, and many play on teams in amateur leagues. Mexico also has professional soccer and baseball leagues. Basketball and jai alai, a game that resembles handball, are popular as well.

Many Mexicans enjoy watching bullfights. Most large cities have bull rings. Mexico City has the largest bull ring in the world. It seats about 55,000 people.

On Sundays—the only day most Mexicans do not work—many families go to the park to relax and picnic. Mexicans also enjoy watching movies and television, dancing at nightclubs, and entertaining friends and relatives at home. Many wealthier Mexicans visit the country's historic sites and resorts along the coast.

© Henry Romero, Reuters/Landov

Día de los muertos, which means *day of the dead,* is a holiday honoring those who have died. This Mexican family is decorating the graves of deceased relatives with flowers.

Religion. More than three-fourths of Mexico's people belong to the Roman Catholic Church. Mexico also has some Protestants, Jews, and other religious groups.

Catholic missionaries first arrived from Spain in the early 1500's. They converted millions of indigenous people to Catholicism. But respect for the rain, sun, and other forces of nature remained an important part of indigenous religion. Mexican religious practices still combine ancient beliefs and traditions with Catholicism.

During the Spanish colonial period, the Catholic Church was closely linked with the Mexican government as the official state church. The church became wealthy and powerful and prohibited other religions. Beginning in the mid-1800's, the government greatly reduced the church's political and economic power by prohibiting churches from owning property and participating in politics. However, these laws were not always enforced. In 1991, Mexico's legislature passed constitutional amendments to end some of these restrictions.

Since the mid-1900's, the number of Protestant churches in Mexico has increased greatly. The growth of Protestantism has resulted in large part from missionary activities by Protestants from the United States.

Education. Throughout the Spanish colonial period, the Catholic Church controlled education in what is now Mexico. During the 1800's, the newly independent government and the church struggled for power, and the government won control of the schools. Mexico's Constitution, adopted in 1917, prohibited religious groups and ministers from establishing or teaching in schools. However, the laws often were not enforced. Constitutional changes passed in 1991 legalized church-owned schools and religious instruction in them.

During the early 1900's, less than 25 percent of Mexicans over 6 years old could read or write. Since the Revolution of 1910, and especially since the early 1940's, the government has done much to promote free public education. It has built thousands of new schools and established teachers' colleges. The government spends large sums on education each year. Today, most Mexican adults can read and write.

Mexican law requires all children from the age of 6 through 14 to go to school. After kindergarten, a child has six years of elementary school, followed by three years of basic secondary school. Graduates of basic secondary school may go on to a three-year upper secondary school. Many upper secondary schools are privately run. Colleges operate some of these schools to prepare students for college work. Other upper secondary schools offer business and technical courses.

About 85 percent of school-age children in Mexico attend school. About 90 percent complete elementary school, and about 60 percent finish some secondary school. Few attend upper secondary school or college.

Courses of higher education at Mexico's universities, specialized colleges, and technical institutes last from three to seven years. The oldest and largest Mexican university is the National Autonomous University of Mexico in Mexico City.

Arts

The arts have been an important part of Mexican life since the days of early indigenous civilizations. The Maya and Toltec peoples constructed beautiful temples and painted *murals* (wallpaintings) in them. The Aztec composed music and poetry. The Spaniards brought a love of literature and beautiful buildings. Indigenous craftworkers built thousands of churches based on Spanish designs. In the 1900's, Mexico produced many important architects, painters, composers, and writers.

Architecture of ancient Mexican civilizations was related chiefly to religion. The Teotihuacano and Aztec, among others, built stone temples on flat-topped pyramids and decorated them with murals and sculptured symbols. These symbols represented the feathered serpent Quetzalcoatl and other gods. Many ancient structures still stand near Mexico City and in Chiapas, Oaxaca, and Yucatán states.

After the Spanish conquest, the earliest mission churches had a simple design. Later churches, especially those built in the 1700's, had a more ornamental style. The huge

Metropolitan Cathedral in Mexico City, begun in 1573 but not completed for hundreds of years, shows the influence of many different architectural styles. In the 1900's, many Mexican architects combined ancient designs with modern construction methods. Their work includes the buildings of the National Autonomous University of Mexico, by Félix Candela and Carlos Lazo, and the striking National Museum of Anthropology, in Mexico City, by Pedro Ramírez Vázquez. Some other examples are the Jardines de Pedregal apartment buildings, by Luis Barragán, and the 44-story Latin American Tower in Mexico City.

Painting. Ancient Mexican civilizations left many impressive murals, like those at Bonampak in Chiapas state. During the Spanish colonial period, many artists painted murals in churches or portraits of government officials. Mexican painting gained worldwide renown after the Mexican Revolution of 1910. Beginning in the 1920's, José Orozco, Diego Rivera, and David Siqueiros painted the story of the revolution on the walls of public buildings. Rivera's wife, Frida Kahlo, is one of the best-known painters in Mexican history. Other important Mexican painters during the middle and later 1900's included Rufino Tamayo and José Luis Cuevas. Beginning in the 1950's, many Mexican painters turned away from revolutionary themes and followed international trends.

Literature. Outstanding colonial writers included the dramatist Juan Ruiz de Alarcón and the poet Sor Juana Inés de la Cruz. In 1816, José Joaquín Fernández de Lizardi wrote *The Itching Parrot,* probably the first Latin American novel. After 1910, revolutionary themes became important in novels by such writers as Mariano Azuela and Martín Luis Guzmán. These themes also appear in the works of such later writers as Carlos Fuentes, Juan Rulfo, and Agustín Yáñez. Leading Mexican poets of the 1900's included Amado Nervo, Octavio Paz, Carlos Pellicer, Alfonso

Fresco (1964); Museum of National History, Mexico City; © Estate of David Alfaro Siqueiros/SOMAAP, Mexico/VAGA, New York City (Giraudon/Art Resource)

The story of the Mexican Revolution is told in murals by David Siqueiros and other well-known Mexican artists. This part of a Siqueiros mural shows the revolt led by Emiliano Zapata to gain land for Mexican peasants.

SANTO
EL ENMASCARADO DE PLATA
en

SANTO
VS. LOS
VILLANOS
DEL RING

con
WOLF RUVINSKIS - EDUARDO BONADA
JEAN SAFONT - DICK MEDRANO
RAY MENDOZA - BENI GALAN
HAM LEE - EL NAZI - RAMIRO ORCI
SILVIA FOURNIER Y GRACIELA LARA
DIRECCIÓN ALFREDO B. CREVENNA

© Everett Collection/Rex USA

Popular Mexican films of the mid-1900's included motion pictures starring the celebrated professional wrestler El Santo. This photograph shows a poster for one of El Santo's films.

Reyes, and Marco Antonio Montes de Oca. The 1900's also saw the emergence of important women writers, such as Rosario Castellanos and Ángeles Mastretta.

Music. Early indigenous people used drums, flutes, gourd rattles, sea shells, and their voices to make music. This ancient music is still played in some parts of Mexico. Much church music was written during the colonial period. Folk songs called *corridos* have long been popular in Mexico. They may tell of the Mexican Revolution, a bandit or a sheriff, or the struggle between church and state. In the 1900's, Mexican composers, including Carlos Chávez and Silvestre Revueltas, used themes from corridos or ancient indigenous music.

Today, strolling musicians called *mariachis* perform along streets and in restaurants. Mariachi groups include singers and guitar, trumpet, and violin players. The music of *marimbas* (instruments similar to xylophones) is also popular.

Motion pictures. Mexico has one of Latin America's largest motion-picture industries. Some of the first movies produced in Mexico chronicled the violence of the 1910 revolution. The 1930's and 1940's are considered the golden age of Mexican cinema. The most famous Mexican actor of this period was Mario Moreno. Moreno's comic character Cantinflas represented the average poor, urban Mexican. The Spanish-born director Luis Buñuel made many of his most important films in Mexico in the 1950's and 1960's, including *Los Olvidados (The Young and the Damned,* 1950).

In the 1960's and 1970's, Mexican filmmakers began making action and horror movies. One extremely popular action hero was El Santo, a professional free-style wrestler who starred in more than 50 films.

The 1990's and early 2000's brought the development of the Nuevo Cine Mexicano (New Mexican Cinema). Unlike older films, which were produced mainly for a Mexican audience, movies from the Nuevo Cine Mexicano have achieved global fame. Famous filmmakers from this period included Carlos Carrera, Alfonso Cuarón, Alejandro González Iñárritu, and Guillermo del Toro.

The land

Mexico has six main land regions: (1) the Pacific Northwest, (2) the Plateau of Mexico, (3) the Gulf Coastal Plain, (4) the Southern Uplands, (5) the Chiapas Highlands, and (6) the Yucatán Peninsula. Within these six land regions are many smaller ones that differ greatly in altitude, climate, and land formation. Many kinds of plants and animals also live in Mexico.

The Pacific Northwest region is generally dry. The Baja California Peninsula (Peninsula of Lower California), the region's westernmost section, consists largely of rolling or mountainous desert. During some years, the desert receives no rain at all. It has a few oases where farmers grow dates and grapes. The northwestern corner and southern end of the peninsula get enough rain for a little farming. The lowest point in Mexico is in the far northern area, near Mexicali. This area, 33 feet (10 meters) below sea level, is the southern end of the huge Imperial Valley of California.

The mainland coastal strip of the Pacific Northwest region has fertile river valleys that contain some of Mexico's richest farmland. Farmers irrigate these valleys with water from the Colorado, Fuerte, Yaqui, and other rivers. Steep, narrow mountain ranges extend in a north-south direction in the state of Sonora, east of the coastal plain. The ranges lie parallel to each other and separate the upper river valleys. In these basins are cattle ranches, irrigated farmland, and copper and silver mines.

The Plateau of Mexico is the largest of the six land regions. It has Mexico's largest cities and most of the country's people. The plateau consists of five sections.

The Cordillera Neo-Volcánica (Neo-Volcanic Range), a series of volcanoes, extends across Mexico at the southern edge of the plateau. The range is also called the *Eje Neo-Volcánico Transversal* (Transverse Neo-Volcanic Axis) or the Transverse Volcanic Range. A number of the volcanoes are active. The volcanic soils are fertile and receive enough rain for agriculture. Farmers have grown corn, beans, as well as other crops on the slopes since the days of ancient indigenous civilizations. Pico de Orizaba (Citlaltépetl), at 18,410 feet (5,610 meters), is the highest mountain in Mexico. Ixtacihuatl and Popocatépetl, two volcanoes that stand more than 17,000 feet high (5,180 meters), rise southeast of Mexico City. Far to the west, near the city of Guadalajara, is Lake Chapala. It covers approximately 420 square miles (1,100 square kilometers). However, this figure varies with changes in rainfall and human consumption.

The Mesa Central (Central Plateau), which lies north of the Neo-Volcanic Chain, is the heart of Mexico. It averages about 7,000 feet (2,100 meters) above sea level. The rainfall in this section is enough to raise corn, beans, wheat, and barley. The Aztec capital of Tenochtitlan stood at the mesa's southern edge, in the beautiful Valley of Mexico. Mexico City was built on the same site and became the capital during the colonial period. Several small lakes, including the famous Lake Xochimilco, are in the Mexico City area.

The western part of the Mesa Central is called the Bajío, meaning *flat*. This region covers one of the most productive agricultural areas in the country. The Bajío also includes the manufacturing centers of Guadalajara, León, Querétaro, and San Luis Potosí.

The Mesa del Norte (Northern Plateau) makes up more than half the Plateau of Mexico. It extends from the Mesa

Central north to the United States. The Mesa del Norte is highest in the south and west, with altitudes of 6,000 to 9,000 feet (1,800 to 2,700 meters). In the north and east, it is less than 4,000 feet (1,200 meters) high. Low mountains rise from 2,000 to 3,000 feet (610 to 910 meters) above the mesa. The mesa receives little rainfall except in the higher mountains, where frost is a constant threat to crops. Only in irrigated places, such as the Saltillo and Torreón areas, is farming successful.

The mesa's low mountains have rich deposits of metal ores. The Spaniards began developing these mines in the 1500's. They also established huge ranches in the dry hills and plains nearby to supply the miners with beef, horses,

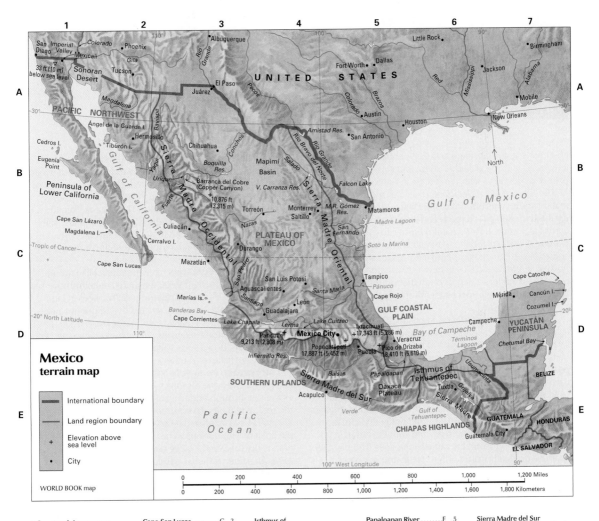

Mexico
terrain map

— International boundary

— Land region boundary

+ Elevation above sea level

• City

WORLD BOOK map

	Miles					
0	200	400	600	800	1,000	1,200 Miles
0	200	400	600	800	1,000	1,200	1,400	1,600	1,800 Kilometers

Physical features

Amistad Reservoir	......B	4	
Angel de la Guarda			
Island	.................B	1	
Balsas River	..............E	4	
Banderas Bay	.............D	3	
Barranca del Cobre			
(Copper Canyon)	......B	3	
Bavispe River	............A	2	
Bay of Campeche	.....D	6	
Boquilla Reservoir	.....B	3	
Cancún Island	...........D	7	
Cape Catoche	C	7	
Cape Corrientes	........D	3	
Cape Rojo	...............D	5	
Cape San Lázaro	C	1	

Cape San Lucas	C	2	
Cedros Island	...........B	1	
Cerralvo Island	C	2	
Chetumal Bay	...........D	7	
Chiapas Highlands	.....E	6	
Colorado River	.........A	1	
Conchos River	..........B	3	
Cozumel Island	.........D	7	
Eugenia Point	...........B	1	
Falcon Lake	..............B	4	
Fuerte River	..............B	2	
Grijalva River	............E	6	
Gulf Coastal Plain	.....D	5	
Gulf of California	.......B	2	
Gulf of Mexico	C	6	
Gulf of Tehuantepec	....E	5	
Infiernillo Reservoir	.....D	4	

Isthmus of			
Tehuantepec	.........E	6	
Ixtacihuatl (volcano)	.....D	5	
Lake Chapala	...........D	3	
Lake Cuitzeo	.............D	4	
Lerma River	..............D	4	
M. R. Gómez			
Reservoir	..............B	4	
Madre Lagoon	C	5	
Magdalena River	.......A	2	
Magdalena Island	C	2	
Mapimí Basin	............B	4	
Marías Islands	C	3	
Nazas River	C	3	
Oaxaca Plateau	........E	5	
Pacific Northwest	......A	1	
Pánuco River	............D	5	

Papaloapan River	.......E	5	
Paricutín (volcano)	......D	4	
Peninsula of Lower			
California	.............B	1	
Pico de Orizaba	........D	5	
Plateau of Mexico	C	4	
Popocatépetl			
(volcano)	.............D	4	
Río Bravo del Norte			
(river)	.................B	4	
Rio Grande (river)	.......B	4	
Salado River	..............B	4	
San Fernando River	C	5	
San Pedro River	C	3	
Santiago River	..........D	3	
Sierra Madre			
(mountains)	...........E	6	

Sierra Madre del Sur			
(mountains)	...........E	4	
Sierra Madre			
Occidental			
(mountains)	C	2	
Sierra Madre Oriental			
(mountains)	C	4	
Sonoran Desert	.........A	1	
Soto la Marina River	...C	5	
Southern Uplands	......E	4	
Términos Lagoon	.......D	6	
Tiburón Island	..........B	2	
Urique River	..............B	2	
Usumacinta River	......E	6	
V. Carranza Reservoir	...B	4	
Yaqui River	...............B	2	
Yucatán Peninsula	......D	7	

The rugged mountains of Mexico's Sierra Madre Occidental are divided by deep, steep-walled canyons carved by swiftly flowing streams. The mountain range borders the western edge of Mexico's wide Central Plateau.

© E. R. Degginger, Bruce Coleman Inc.

and mules. In the Durango and Chihuahua areas, *vaqueros* (cowboys) became skilled at riding and roping cattle. American cowboys later copied these skills.

The Sierra Madre Occidental is a long mountain range that forms the western rim of the Plateau of Mexico. Until the 1900's, when paved roads and a railroad were built across the range, it was a natural barrier to transport between the plateau and the west coast. The range includes some of Mexico's most rugged land. Short, steep streams flowing to the Pacific Ocean have cut canyons more than 1 mile (1.6 kilometers) deep through the mountains. The largest canyon is the spectacular Barranca del Cobre, cut by the Urique River.

The Sierra Madre Oriental, the plateau's eastern rim, is actually a series of mountain ranges. In many places between the ranges, highways and railroads climb up to the plateau from the east coast. Monterrey, near large deposits of coal and iron ore, is the major center of the Mexican steel industry.

The Gulf Coastal Plain. North of Tampico, this region is largely covered by tangled forests of low, thorny bushes and trees. This part of the plain is generally dry, and farming is possible only along rivers and with the aid of irrigation. South of Tampico, the rainfall increases. The plant life changes gradually from north to south and becomes a tropical rain forest in Tabasco state. The southern part of the plain has some rich farmland.

Many of Mexico's longest rivers flow into the Gulf of Mexico from the coastal plain. They include the Rio Grande, which forms about 1,300 miles (2,090 kilometers) of Mexico's border with the United States. Large petroleum deposits lie beneath the plain and offshore. Huge sulfur deposits occur near the Gulf in the Isthmus of Tehuantepec. The isthmus, which is about 135 miles (220 kilometers) wide, is the narrowest part of Mexico.

The Southern Uplands consist largely of steep ridges and deep gorges cut by mountain streams. The region includes a large, hot, dry valley just south of the Neo-Vol-

canic Chain. The Balsas River drains the valley. The Sierra Madre del Sur, a rugged mountain range, rises southwest of the valley along the Pacific Ocean. The famous beach resort of Acapulco is on this coast. A little farming takes place on the steep mountainsides. The Oaxaca Plateau makes up the eastern part of the Southern Uplands. The ancient Zapotec capital of Monte Albán stood on the plateau. In addition, much of the gold of the Aztec Empire probably came from the plateau.

The Chiapas Highlands have great blocklike mountains that rise more than 9,000 feet (2,700 meters) above sea level. There are also many relatively flat surfaces at high altitudes. These tablelands are farmed by indigenous peasants who speak Maya dialects and other ancient languages. Some modern farming has developed in the region's deep, broad river valleys. With irrigation, farmers grow coffee, fruits, and other crops.

The Yucatán Peninsula is a low limestone plateau with no rivers. Limestone dissolves in water, and rainfall reaches the sea through underground channels dissolved out of the rock. Great pits have formed where the roofs of these channels have fallen in. The pits were the sacred wells of the ancient Maya people. The northwestern part of the region is dry bushland. Agave plants that grow there provide *henequen* fiber, which is used to make twine. Rainfall increases to the south, where tropical rain forests cover the land.

Plant and animal life. Forests cover about a fifth of Mexico. Forests of the northwestern and central mountains provide ebony, mahogany, rosewood, walnut, and other valuable hardwoods used to make furniture. Large pine forests in these mountains also supply timber for Mexico's pulp and paper industry. Mexico has thousands of kinds of flowers, including azaleas, chrysanthemums, geraniums, orchids, and poinsettias. Hundreds of varieties of cactus grow in Mexico's northern deserts.

Deer and mountain lions live in Mexico's mountains. The country's northern deserts have coyotes, lizards,

Tropical rain forests grow in the southern areas of the Gulf Coastal Plain and on the Yucatán Peninsula. The crowns of the tall trees, *shown here,* form a thick canopy that blocks most light from the forest floor.

© Tom McHugh, Photo Researchers

prairie dogs, and rattlesnakes. Mexico also has some alligators, jaguars, opossums, and raccoons. Chihuahuas, the world's smallest dogs, originally came from Mexico.

Mexico has hundreds of kinds of birds, including the beautifully colored quetzals of the southern forests. Other birds include flamingos, herons, hummingbirds, parrots, and pelicans. Fish and shellfish are plentiful in Mexico's coastal waters, lakes, and rivers. Freshwater fish include bass, catfish, and trout. Many kinds of tropical fish inhabit coral reefs along the Caribbean coast of the Yucatán Peninsula. Marlin, swordfish, and tarpon are among the game fish caught in coastal areas.

Climate

Mexico's climate varies sharply from region to region. These differences are greatest in tropical Mexico, south of the Tropic of Cancer. There, large variations in altitude result in three main temperature zones. The *tierra caliente* (hot land) includes regions up to 3,000 feet (910 meters) above sea level. It has long, hot summers and mild winters with no frost. The *tierra templada* (temperate land), from 3,000 to 6,000 feet (910 to 1,800 meters), has temperatures that generally stay between 50 and 80 °F (10 and 27 °C). Most crops can grow in the temperate zone. The *tierra fria* (cold land) lies above 6,000 feet (1,800 meters). Frost is rare up to 8,000 feet (2,400 meters), but it may occur at almost any time. The highest peaks in the tierra fria are always covered with snow.

In tropical regions of Mexico, most rain falls in summer, usually as short, heavy, afternoon showers. Toward the south, the rainy season starts earlier and lasts longer.

Most of the northern half of Mexico consists of deserts and semideserts. The lack of rainfall has limited agricultural development in the north. Only the mountainous sections receive enough rainfall to grow good crops without irrigation. Most of northern Mexico's rainfall occurs during the summer, but northwestern Baja California receives most of its rainfall in the winter. Above 2,000 feet (610 me-

ters), summer days are hot and nights are cool. During the winter, days are warm and nights are cold. The coastal lowlands are hot, except on the cool Pacific coast of Baja California.

Economy

Until the mid-1900's, the Mexican economy was based mainly on agriculture and mining. In the 1940's, the government began to promote the development of industry. Mexico now produces many of the manufactured goods that its people use. In the early 2000's, however, Mexico lost many manufacturing jobs to China and other East Asian countries.

In the 1970's, Mexico became a major exporter of oil to the United States. Income from oil production, which the government controls, spurred the development of manufacturing and service industries. During the middle and late 1970's, the price of oil was high. Mexico used its expected income from oil production as collateral to borrow money for many construction projects. In 1981, however, the price of oil began to fall. Mexico soon found it difficult to repay its loans, and the government had to cut spending severely. The economy declined, and many Mexicans lost their jobs. In the late 1980's and early 1990's, the economy improved because the government sold off state-owned companies, attracted foreign investment, and controlled inflation.

Since the mid-1990's, the Mexican economy generally has struggled against global competition. However, *remittances* (money sent) from relatives in the United States have grown significantly and now serve as a major source of national income. Millions of Mexicans living in the United States send home billions of dollars to their families each year.

Service industries are those economic activities that produce services, not goods. Service industries account for about two-thirds of the total value of goods and services produced in Mexico. Service industries also provide

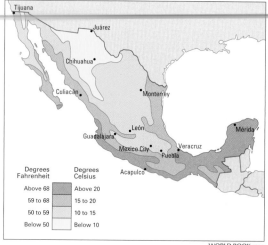

In winter, Mexico has warm weather in the south and cooler weather in the north and at high elevations. Average January temperatures in Mexico City range from 42 to 66 °F (6 to 19 °C).

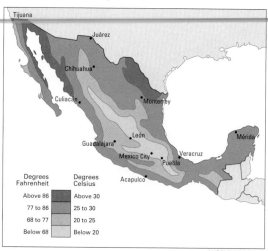

In summer, Mexico's climate is warm in the central regions of the country and hot along the coasts. July temperatures in Mexico City range from 53 to 73 °F (12 to 23 °C).

Average monthly weather

	Mexico City						Monterrey				
	Temperatures				Days of rain or snow		Temperatures				Days of rain or snow
	°F		°C				°F		°C		
	High	Low	High	Low			High	Low	High	Low	
Jan.	66	42	19	6	4	Jan.	68	48	20	9	6
Feb.	69	43	21	6	5	Feb.	72	52	22	11	5
Mar.	75	47	24	8	9	Mar.	76	57	24	14	7
Apr.	77	51	25	11	14	Apr.	84	62	29	17	7
May	78	54	26	12	17	May	87	68	31	20	9
June	76	55	24	13	21	June	91	71	33	22	8
July	73	53	23	12	27	July	90	71	32	22	8
Aug.	73	54	23	12	27	Aug.	92	72	33	22	7
Sept.	74	53	23	12	23	Sept.	86	70	30	21	10
Oct.	70	50	21	10	13	Oct.	80	64	27	18	9
Nov.	68	46	20	8	6	Nov.	71	55	22	13	8
Dec.	66	43	19	6	4	Dec.	65	50	18	10	6

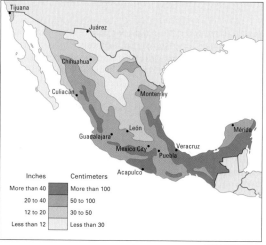

Most of Mexico's precipitation falls during a rainy season that lasts from June to September. Northern Mexico is generally dry. Heavy rains fall in the south and on the Yucatán Peninsula.

more than half of Mexico's jobs. Schools, hospitals, stores, hotels, restaurants, and police and fire protection belong to this sector. Banking, trade, transportation, and communication are also service industries.

Manufacturing. Mexico City is Mexico's leading industrial center. Businesses in the city and its suburbs make about half the country's manufactured goods. Guadalajara, Juárez, Monterrey, and Tijuana are also important manufacturing centers. Government programs encourage the spread of industry to other areas.

Since the 1980's, the government has promoted industrial growth aimed at supplying foreign markets. Factories called *maquiladoras* near Mexico's northern border manufacture and assemble a variety of products for export to U.S. companies. These products include electronic equipment, automobile parts, and clothing.

Mexico's leading products include chemicals, iron and steel, motor vehicles, processed foods, processed petroleum, and tobacco. Other important products include beer, cement, clothing, household appliances, and wood pulp and paper.

Mexico has long been famous for the skill of its craftworkers, who follow beautiful indigenous or Spanish-colonial designs. Their products, which vary by area, include silver jewelry from Taxco, glassware and pottery from Guadalajara and Puebla, and handwoven baskets and blankets from Oaxaca and Toluca. Many of these goods are sold to tourists.

Agriculture. The various farming regions of Mexico differ greatly in altitude, rainfall, and temperature. As a result, many kinds of crops can grow. However, mountains and insufficient rainfall make most of the country naturally unsuited for agriculture. Crops are grown on only about 15 percent of Mexico's total land area.

The best farmland is in the southern part of Mexico's plateau region. Rich soils, enough rainfall, and a mild climate there permit intensive cultivation. The northern part of the plateau has little rainfall and serves mainly as grazing land for cattle.

Fertile soils exist in the rainy, hot regions of southern and eastern Mexico and in the eastern coastal plains. However, turning these areas into productive farmland requires much work, including clearing and draining the land and controlling floods, insects, and plant diseases. The west coast of Mexico also has fertile soils, but much of the land is mountainous and dry. Irrigation has developed some rich cropland in dry regions.

Among the wide variety of crops grown in Mexico, corn takes up more farmland than any other crop. It is the basic food of the Mexican people. Other major crops include avocados, bananas, coffee, lemons, mangoes, onions, oranges, potatoes, sorghum, sugar cane, tomatoes, and wheat. Mexican farmers also raise barley, beans, chili peppers, coconuts, grapes, pineapples, and safflower seeds. Mexico exports many tropical fruits and winter vegetables to the United States. Farmers cultivate cacao and vanilla in tropical wet areas of the country.

Farmers and ranchers raise livestock throughout Mexico. Beef cattle graze in the dry northern pasturelands, and dairy cattle are found chiefly in central Mexico. Farmers throughout the country also raise chickens, goats, hogs, horses, sheep, and turkeys.

Until the 1900's, most Mexicans made a living by farming land near their villages or working on large estates called *haciendas* for wealthy landowners. The Mexican Constitution of 1917 provided for land reform. By 1964, the government had broken up most of the haciendas and distributed the land to the peasants.

The Constitution also recognized the old system of *ejidos (eh HEE dohs),* farmlands held in common by communities. Today, most farmers work alone on individual sections of the ejidos. However, some farmers work the land as a group and share the crops. Ejidos make up about half of Mexico's total cropland. The remainder is divided between small family farms and large haciendas that the

Mexican government has not broken up. Since the 1990's, the ejido system has fallen into crisis. The owners of many ejidos have sold or abandoned their land to look for work in Mexican cities or in the United States.

Agriculture provides 16 percent of all jobs in Mexico, but it accounts for less than 5 percent of the total value of Mexican goods and services. The government has tried to increase agricultural production by promoting modern farming methods. However, educational programs, financial aid, and public works projects intended to achieve this goal have not benefited most small family farmers and those living on ejidos. As a result, Mexico has some highly modern and productive commercial farms owned by a few prosperous people, but the vast majority of rural Mexicans are poor.

Mining. A wide variety of minerals are mined in Mexico. The country ranks as one of the world's leading silver producers, mining about one-seventh of the world's annual production. Most silver mines are in the central regions of the country.

Mexico is also a leading producer of petroleum. It pumps more than 1 billion barrels of petroleum each year. Oil wells operate chiefly in the states of Campeche, Tabasco, and Veracruz, along the coast and in the Gulf of Mexico. Petróleos Mexicanos (PEMEX), a government agency, runs the petroleum industry. In addition, Mexico produces much natural gas.

Mexico also mines large quantities of copper, gold, gypsum, lead, salt, sulfur, and zinc. Other valuable minerals include antimony, bismuth, fluorite, and manganese. Large iron ore deposits support the nation's steel industry.

Fishing. Although Mexico has an extensive coastline, fishing accounts for less than 1 percent of the national income. Significant ports include the cities of Ensenada and La Paz on the Baja California Peninsula, Guaymas in the state of Sonora, and Mazatlán in the state of Sinaloa. Fishing crews catch anchovies, oysters, sardines, shrimp, and tuna.

Economy of Mexico

This map shows the major uses of land in Mexico, as well as where the leading farm, fishing, mineral, and forest products come from. It also locates the country's chief manufacturing centers.

Chiefly cultivated land

Grazing land

Chiefly forest land

Generally unproductive land

Fishing

• Mineral deposit

• Manufacturing center

WORLD BOOK map

Mexico's gross domestic product

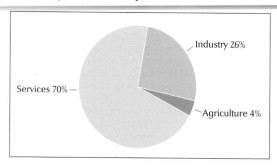

- Industry 26%
- Services 70%
- Agriculture 4%

Mexico's gross domestic product (GDP) was $676,496,000,000 in 2004. The GDP is the total value of goods and services produced within a country in a year. *Services* include community, government, and personal services; finance, insurance, real estate, and business services; trade, restaurants, and hotels; and transportation and communication. *Industry* includes construction, manufacturing, mining, and utilities. *Agriculture* includes agriculture, forestry, and fishing.

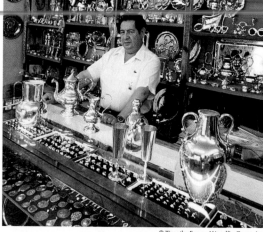

© Timothy Eagan, Woodfin Camp, Inc.

Beautiful silver objects, including vases, tableware, and jewelry, line the shelves of this shop in San Miguel de Allende. Mexico is one of the world's leading producers of silver.

Production and workers by economic activities

Economic activities	Percent of GDP produced	Employed workers Number of people	Employed workers Percent of total
Community, government, & personal services	26	8,607,700	20
Trade, restaurants, & hotels	20	12,438,200	30
Manufacturing	18	7,350,700	17
Finance, insurance, real estate, & business services	13	1,769,400	4
Transportation & communication	10	1,888,700	4
Construction	6	2,741,800	7
Agriculture, forestry, & fishing	4	6,937,900	16
Utilities	1	239,700	1
Mining	1	169,500	*
Total†	100	42,143,600	100

*Less than one-half of 1 percent.
†Figures do not add up to 100 percent due to rounding.
Figures are for 2004.
Sources: International Labour Organization; International Monetary Fund; Mexico's National Institute of Statistics, Geography and Informatics.

Energy sources. Wood is the main source of energy for poor people. Petroleum deposits provide cheap fuel oil and natural gas for industrial use. Coal, natural gas, and petroleum generate the vast majority of Mexico's electric power. Most of the rest is produced by hydroelectric or nuclear power. Manuel M. Torres Dam, Mexico's largest hydroelectric plant and one of the world's highest dams, is on the Grijalva River in the state of Chiapas. Laguna Verde, Mexico's only nuclear power plant, is in the state of Veracruz. The government handles almost all power production and distribution.

Trade. Mexico's leading exports include petroleum and petroleum products. Other mineral exports include copper, gold, iron, silver, and zinc. The main industrial exports include electrical machinery, motor vehicles, and telecommunications equipment. Mexico also exports coffee and fruits and vegetables. The leading imports include electric and electronic equipment, industrial machinery, and motor vehicles.

About three-fourths of Mexico's trade is with the United States, but trade with European countries, China, and

© Frances Stephane, SIME/4Corners Images

Cancún, on the Caribbean coast of the Yucatán Peninsula, is a popular resort city. The area's warm, sunny climate and white sandy beaches attract large numbers of visitors every year. Tourism is one of Mexico's main sources of income from abroad.

Oil refineries in Mexico process large amounts of petroleum, one of the country's leading products. Petróleos Mexicanos (PEMEX), a government agency, runs the petroleum industry.

© Albano Guatti, The Stock Market

Japan is increasing. Trade with other Latin American countries is relatively unimportant. However, Mexico is trying to increase such trade through the Latin American Integration Association, an economic union of Mexico and several other Latin American nations. Mexico also belongs to a regional trading bloc that includes Canada and the United States. This bloc was created by the North American Free Trade Agreement (NAFTA), which has eliminated nearly all *tariffs* (taxes on imports) and other trade barriers.

Tourism. Along with exports of manufactured goods and petroleum, tourism serves as one of Mexico's largest sources of income from abroad. Each year, millions of tourists, mostly from the United States, visit Mexico. The tourist industry is also a major source of employment for the Mexican population. Tourists visit Mexico City, the old Spanish colonial cities of central Mexico, and the ruins of Maya cities on the Yucatán Peninsula. Beautiful beach resorts attract many vacationers from the United States and Canada, especially in winter. Popular resort areas include Acapulco, Cabo San Lucas, Ensenada, Huatulco, Manzanillo, Mazatlán, Puerto Escondido, Puerto Vallarta, and Zihuatanejo on the Pacific coast, and Cancún and Cozumel Island on the Caribbean coast.

Transportation in Mexico ranges from modern methods to ancient ones. Mexico has a good highway system. Airlines, bus service, and railroads connect all the major cities and towns. But some farmers still carry goods to market on their heads and backs, or by burros and oxcarts.

Mexico City is an important center of international air travel. There are also large international airports in Cancún, Guadalajara, and Monterrey. The government owns the country's extensive railway network.

More than 100 ocean ports provide access to Mexico. These include Tampico and Veracruz on the Gulf of Mexico, and Guaymas, Manzanillo, and Mazatlán on the Pacific Ocean. Mexico also has a small merchant fleet.

Communication. The first book known to be published in the Western Hemisphere was a *catechism* (book used to teach religion) printed in Mexico City in 1539. Today, books and magazines published in Mexico City are read widely throughout Mexico and all of Latin America. Mexico has more than 300 daily newspapers representing many different political opinions. The largest newspapers

include *El Financiero, El Heraldo de México, El Nacional, El Universal, Esto, Excélsior, La Jornada, La Prensa, Ovaciones,* and *Reforma,* all published in Mexico City.

Telephone lines connect all parts of the country. Many people use cellular phones. Internet usage is increasing as more Mexicans gain access to computers.

History

Ancient times. The first people who lived in what is now Mexico arrived there before 8000 B.C. They were peoples of unknown tribes who migrated from the north. These first Mexicans were hunters who lived in small, temporary communities. They followed the herds of buffalo, mammoths, mastodons, and other large animals that roamed the land. About 7500 B.C., the climate became drier. The herds could not find enough grass to eat and died off. The people then lived on small wild animals or the berries and seeds of wild plants.

About 7000 B.C., the inhabitants of what is now the Puebla region discovered how to grow plants for food and became farmers. They grew corn, which became their most important food, and avocados, beans, peppers, squashes, and tomatoes. They were among the first people to cultivate these vegetables. They also raised dogs and turkeys for food. As the wandering bands of hunters became groups of farmers, they established permanent settlements.

The growth of villages. By 2000 B.C., large farm villages stood along Lake Texcoco in the fertile south-central Valley of Mexico, and in the southern highlands and forests. The farmers used irrigation to improve their crops. The villages grew, and new classes of people developed, including potters, priests, and weavers. The people traded polished stones, pottery, and sea shells with distant communities.

By 1000 B.C., the villagers were building flat-topped pyramids with temples on them. Some villages, including Cuicuilco near what is now Mexico City, became religious centers. Members of other communities came to worship in the temples. Because these people were farmers, they worshiped gods that represented such natural forces as the rain and the sun. The villages grew into towns, from the Valley of Mexico to the Gulf of Mexico and to the Pacific Ocean, and south to what is now Guatemala.

The Olmec people of the southern Gulf Coast made the first great advance toward civilization in the Mexico region. Between about 1200 and 400 B.C., the Olmec developed a counting system and calendar. They also carved beautiful stone statues.

The Classic Period. Great civilizations thrived between A.D. 250 and 900, the Classic Period of Mexico. Huge pyramids dedicated to the sun and the moon were built at Teotihuacán, near what is now Mexico City. In the religious centers of southern Mexico and northern Central America, the Maya built beautiful homes, pyramids, and temples of limestone. They recorded important dates on tall, carved blocks of stone and wrote in a kind of picture writing. In what is now the state of Oaxaca, the Zapotec people leveled a mountaintop and built their capital, called Monte Albán.

The reasons for the fall of these Classic civilizations are not clear. The climate probably became even drier about A.D. 900, and the people could not produce enough crops to feed the large population. Perhaps city dwellers attacked their neighbors to get more land, or farmers revolted against the priests who had ruled them. In the north, Chichimec tribes destroyed a large number of cities.

The Toltec and the Aztec. Many wars followed the Classic Period. During the 900's, the Toltec people established an empire with a major city at Tula, north of present-day Mexico City. Toltec influence spread throughout central and southern Mexico. Invading Chichimec tribes destroyed the Toltec Empire about 1200.

The Aztec (also called the Mexica) built the last and greatest indigenous empire during the mid-1400's. The Aztec Empire extended between the Pacific and Gulf coasts, and from the Isthmus of Tehuantepec north to the Pánuco River. The Aztec capital, Tenochtitlan, stood on an island in Lake Texcoco at the site of Mexico City. According to Aztec tradition, Tenochtitlan was founded in 1325. Modern scholars believe it was founded somewhat later. When the Spaniards arrived in 1519, the city and its suburbs had a population of about 200,000.

The Aztec were fierce warriors who believed it was their duty to sacrifice the men they captured in battle to their gods. Every year, they sacrificed thousands of prisoners of war. The Aztec also composed beautiful music and poetry and were skilled in medicine. They grew rich with gold, silver, and other treasures collected annually from the cities and tribes they conquered.

The Spanish conquest. The Spaniards began to occupy the Caribbean region during the 1490's and first set foot in Mexico in 1517. That year, Diego Velázquez, the governor of Cuba, sent ships under Francisco Fernández de Córdoba to explore and search for treasure. Córdoba found the Yucatán Peninsula and brought back reports of large cities. Velázquez then sent Juan de Grijalva to the area in 1518. Grijalva explored the Gulf coast from Yucatán to what is now Veracruz.

A third expedition of about 600 men sailed from Cuba under Hernán Cortés in February 1519. Cortés's 11 ships followed Grijalva's route along the coast. Cortés defeated large indigenous armies with his horses and cannons. He founded Veracruz, the first Spanish settlement in what is now Mexico.

Reports of the explorers reached the Aztec emperor Montezuma II (also spelled *Moctezuma*) in Tenochtitlan. The tales of Spanish guns and horses—which the indigenous people had never seen before—and of soldiers in armor made him fear the Spaniards. Montezuma sent messengers with rich gifts for Cortés, but he also ordered the Spanish explorer to leave. Instead, Cortés marched toward Tenochtitlan. He was joined by thousands of the Aztec's indigenous enemies, who hoped he would destroy Montezuma's empire. Montezuma allowed the invaders to enter Tenochtitlan in November 1519. The Spaniards were far too few to control Tenochtitlan by themselves. However, Cortés soon seized Montezuma and held him hostage to secure his own men's safety.

In June 1520, the Aztec revolted. After a week of bitter fighting, the Spaniards tried to sneak out of the city. The Aztec discovered them and killed hundreds of Spaniards during *la noche triste* (the sad night). The rest, including Cortés, were saved by their indigenous allies. Six months later, Cortés returned to the Tenochtitlan area at the head

Important dates in Mexico

c. 2000 B.C. Village life developed in the Valley of Mexico.

c. A.D. 250-900 Great Indian civilizations thrived during the Classic Period.

c. 900-1200 The Toltec Empire controlled the Valley of Mexico.

c. 1325-1350 The Aztec founded Tenochtitlan (now Mexico City).

1519-1521 Hernán Cortés conquered the Aztec Empire for Spain.

1810 Miguel Hidalgo y Costilla began the Mexican struggle for independence.

1821 Mexico won independence.

1836 Texas won independence from Mexico.

1846-1848 The United States defeated Mexico in the Mexican War and won much Mexican territory.

1855 A liberal government under Benito Juárez began a period of reform.

1863 French troops occupied Mexico City.

1864 Maximilian of Austria became emperor of Mexico.

1867 Liberal forces led by Benito Juárez regained power.

1876-1880 and **1884-1911** Porfirio Díaz ruled Mexico as dictator.

1910-1911 Francisco I. Madero overthrew Díaz.

1917 A revolutionary constitution was adopted.

1929 The National Revolutionary Party (now called Institutional Revolutionary Party) was formed.

1934 The government began a major program of land distribution to farmers.

1938 Mexico took over foreign oil company properties.

1953 Women received the right to vote in all elections.

1968 Government troops put down student demonstrations in Mexico City.

1970's Major new petroleum deposits were discovered on the Gulf of Mexico coast.

1985 Two earthquakes struck south-central Mexico, killing about 10,000 people.

1994 NAFTA (North American Free Trade Agreement) took effect, providing for the gradual elimination of trade barriers among Mexico, the United States, and Canada.

1997 The Institutional Revolutionary Party lost its majority in the Chamber of Deputies for the first time.

2000 Vicente Fox Quesada of the National Action Party was elected president. He became the first non-PRI candidate elected to that office in 71 years.

Ruins of an ancient Maya temple stand at Palenque in the state of Chiapas. The temple was built about A.D. 650, during a period when great *indigenous* (native) civilizations thrived in Mexico.

© Ales Liska, Shutterstock

of an invading force that included tens of thousands of indigenous troops. By May 1521, this coalition had surrounded the Aztec capital and cut off the city's food and water. Battles, sickness, and starvation weakened the Aztec army. In August, Cuauhtémoc, the last emperor, surrendered the city. Cortés sent soldiers to take over the rest of the Aztec Empire. Some indigenous people resisted, but most accepted Spanish rule without a fight.

Spanish rule. After the fighting ended, the Spaniards faced the problem of how to govern the large number of people in the colony. To keep the Amerindians from revolting, King Charles I of Spain allowed them to speak their own languages and be governed by their own officials. However, they had to pay a special tax called a *tribute* and work for the Spaniards when help was needed. They were also required to convert to Catholicism.

Tenochtitlan and other indigenous cities became Spanish cities ruled by white people. The Spaniards destroyed Tenochtitlan and built their own new city on top of the ruins. The Europeans unknowingly introduced a number of diseases to the indigenous population. Along with harsh labor conditions and the forced resettlement of many indigenous communities, these diseases caused a great decline in the native population. When the Spaniards arrived, there may have been from 15 million to 25 million indigenous people living in Mexico. Between 1519 and 1600, the indigenous population dropped to approximately 1 million.

The arrival of Europeans and, later, Africans in Mexico led to the emergence of a new, racially mixed society. The whites included *peninsulares* (people born in Spain) and *creoles* (Europeans born in America). The creoles and mestizos considered themselves superior to the indigenous people. From 1520 to 1810, the Spaniards imported about 200,000 African slaves to Mexico. Most were brought to Mexico, then part of the colony called New Spain, before 1700.

During the 1540's, the Spaniards discovered silver mines in the north-central part of their colony. The silver brought much wealth to the creoles and peninsulares, and the mines attracted more Spanish immigrants. The creoles used the power of the royal government to make the indigenous people work for them. They established hacien-

das, where they produced food and clothing for the new mining communities. Some indigenous peasants lived on the haciendas. Others lived there when they had work and lived in their own villages the rest of the time.

The indigenous people were poor, but there was little they could do to change their situation. However, they were allowed to live separately according to their customs. As a result, the houses they lived in, the food they ate, and the way they worked changed little over the nearly 300 years of Spanish rule. Spanish laws gave the indigenous people the right to keep the lands they had owned before the conquest, but greedy landowners found ways to take over these lands. The Amerindians blended the Roman Catholic faith with their own culture and respected their Spanish priests. However, the colonial period included several riots and rebellions that demonstrated indigenous discontent with Spanish rule.

At first, the creoles were content to be ruled by Spain because the king was far away and he usually permitted them to govern themselves. Authorities in Spain made the

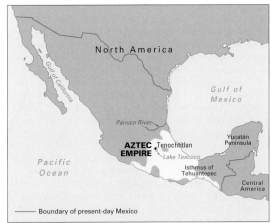

WORLD BOOK map

The Aztec Empire reached the height of its power during the early 1500's, covering much of what is now south-central Mexico. In 1521, Spaniards led by the explorer Hernán Cortés conquered the Aztec and destroyed their civilization.

Drawing with colored ink on parchment by an unknown artist; Biblioteca Apostolica Vaticana (Vatican Library)

Hernán Cortés conquered Mexico for Spain in the early 1500's. The picture writing in this manuscript portrays Cortés meeting the Aztec ruler Montezuma II in 1519. An Aztec artist created the manuscript at Montezuma's request.

laws, but few Spanish officials worked in New Spain. The officials could not enforce the laws if the creoles objected. In the late 1700's, King Charles III tried to reorganize the colonial government, giving more power to Spanish-born individuals and less to the creoles. He also raised taxes. Few creoles sought independence, but many wanted more control of their affairs.

Revolt against the Spaniards. In 1807, French forces occupied Spain and imprisoned King Ferdinand VII. Confusion spread in Spain's colonies. Some creoles plotted to seize Mexico's colonial government. One such person was Miguel Hidalgo y Costilla, a priest from what is now Guanajuato state. In the early hours of Sept. 16, 1810, he called indigenous people and mestizos to his church in the town of Dolores. He made a speech known as the *Grito de Dolores* (Cry of Dolores), in which he called for a rebellion against Spanish rule. Today, late on September 15, Mexico's president rings a bell and repeats the Grito de Dolores. Mexicans celebrate September 16 as Independence Day.

Hidalgo's untrained followers armed themselves and attacked Spanish officials and those who supported the Spaniards. At first, Hidalgo gained support for his cause. However, most of his followers were Amerindians and mestizos rather than creoles. Some indigenous communities refused to support the rebels because of their violent ways. Eventually, Hidalgo was forced to retreat. Spanish troops captured and executed him in 1811.

José María Morelos y Pavón, another priest, continued Hidalgo's struggle. In 1813, Morelos held a Congress that

issued the first formal call for independence. The Congress wrote a constitution for a Mexican republic that included many social reforms to benefit mestizo and indigenous people. Unlike Hidalgo, Morelos used ambush tactics against small, isolated Spanish military units. His campaign was more successful than Hidalgo's, but in 1815 he also was captured and executed. By 1816, Spanish troops had captured or killed many of the rebels, but small guerrilla groups continued to operate in the countryside.

King Ferdinand VII had returned to the Spanish throne in 1814. In an effort to help Spain recover from the Napoleonic Wars, he taxed the creoles. He also organized a large army to put down any revolutionary movement. Ferdinand's actions convinced many creoles that they could no longer trust Spain.

Independence. In 1820, a revolt by political liberals swept Spain. Ferdinand's power weakened, and many creoles saw their chance for independence. A group of powerful creoles supported Agustín de Iturbide, who had served in the Spanish army in the war against José María Morelos y Pavón. Iturbide had been given command of a Spanish army to crush the last rebel leader, Vicente Guerrero. But instead of fighting Guerrero, Iturbide met with him peacefully. In February 1821, the two leaders agreed to make Mexico independent. They joined their armies and won the support of liberal and conservative creoles. Only a small portion of the Spanish forces in Mexico remained loyal to Spain. By the end of 1821, the last Spanish officials withdrew from Mexico, and Mexico became independent.

Following independence, the creoles could not agree on a form of government. Conservatives called for a monarchy, but liberals wanted a republic. The conservatives could not persuade a member of the Spanish royal family to be king. Iturbide, who had the backing of the army, became Emperor Agustín I in 1822. Iturbide was a poor ruler, and most groups turned against him. In 1823, a military revolt drove him from power.

Mexico's Congress then followed the wishes of the liberals and began to write a constitution for a federal repub-

Fresco (1949) by José Clemente Orozco in the State Capitol, Guadalajara (© Robert Frerck)

Miguel Hidalgo y Costilla set off Mexico's struggle for independence in 1810. Mexico won freedom from Spain in 1821.

lic. But the creoles still disagreed on how the constitution should be written. Conservatives desired a strong central government and wanted Roman Catholicism to be the national religion, as it had been under Spanish rule. Liberals wanted the central government to have less power and the states more, and they called for freedom of religion. The groups finally reached a compromise, though many conservative creoles did not support it.

In 1824, Mexico became a republic with a president and a two-house Congress heading the national government, and governors and legislatures heading the states. Guadalupe Victoria, a follower of Hidalgo and Morelos, became the first president.

Difficulties of the early republic. The mid-1800's were a difficult period in Mexico. Many creoles did not support the Constitution, and Mexicans had little experience in self-government. Military men often revolted. One such man, General Antonio López de Santa Anna, served as president 11 times between 1833 and 1855. Santa Anna was elected president in 1833, but he soon tired of his duties and left the government in the hands of his vice president, Valentín Gómez Farías. Gómez Farías passed many reforms that lessened the influence of the church and the military. Although Santa Anna had long favored liberal policies, he joined with conservatives in a successful revolt against the government in 1834. He soon took over the country as a dictator.

Texas was then part of Mexico, but many people from the United States lived there. When Santa Anna changed the Constitution in 1836 to concentrate greater power in the central government, Mexicans and Americans in Texas revolted. Santa Anna defeated a Texas force in the Battle of the Alamo at San Antonio in 1836. But later that year, Texas forces defeated Santa Anna's army at San Jacinto and captured him. Santa Anna signed a treaty recognizing the independence of Texas. In addition to what is now the state of Texas, the new republic of Texas included parts of present-day Colorado, Kansas, New Mexico, Oklahoma, and Wyoming.

The Mexican government did not recognize Santa Anna's treaty. Texas joined the United States in 1845, but Mexico still claimed it. Border disputes developed between Mexico and the United States. In April 1846, Mexican troops attacked U.S. soldiers who had entered the disputed area. In May, the United States declared war on Mexico.

United States soldiers occupied what was then Mexican territory in Arizona, California, and New Mexico. In February 1847, U.S. General Zachary Taylor fought Santa Anna, who was president again, at the Battle of Buena Vista near Saltillo, Mexico. Both sides claimed victory. Taylor became a national hero in the United States and was elected president the next year. Other U.S. forces landed at Veracruz under General Winfield Scott. In September 1847, Scott captured Mexico City after the bitter Battle of Chapultepec. Six military students are said to have thrown themselves from Chapultepec Castle to their deaths during this battle, rather than surrender. Today, the Monument to the Boy Heroes, honoring the students, stands in Chapultepec Park in Mexico City.

The Treaty of Guadalupe Hidalgo, signed in February 1848, ended the Mexican War. Under the treaty, Mexico gave the United States the land that is now California, Nevada, and Utah; most of Arizona; and parts of Colorado,

WORLD BOOK map

The Republic of Mexico was established in 1824. It covered much of what is now the western and southwestern United States. In the mid-1800's, Mexico lost vast territories to the United States and sold additional lands to its northern neighbor.

New Mexico, and Wyoming. Mexico also recognized Texas, south to the Rio Grande, as part of the United States. Mexico received $15 million from the United States. In the Gadsden Purchase of 1853, the United States paid Mexico $10 million for land in what is now southern Arizona and New Mexico.

Reform. The Mexican War exhausted Mexico's economy, and great political confusion developed. Santa Anna seized power again in 1853 and ruled as a dictator. The liberals, who had been gaining strength since the war, drove Santa Anna from power in 1855.

Benito Juárez, a Zapotec from Oaxaca, and others gave the liberal movement effective leadership. They promoted the private ownership of land and wanted to eliminate the privileges of the Roman Catholic Church. After they took over the government in 1855, the liberals passed laws to break up the large estates of the church and the lands held in common by indigenous villages. In 1857, a new constitution brought back the federal system of government.

These reforms led to a conservative revolt in 1858. Juárez fled Mexico City. The liberals declared him president, and he set up a government in Veracruz. During the civil war that followed, known as the War of the Reform, a conservative government operated in Mexico City. The Catholic bishops supported the conservatives because of the liberals' opposition to the church. In 1859, Juárez issued his Reform Laws in an attempt to end the church's political power in Mexico. The laws ordered the separation of church and state, and the take-over of all church property. The liberal armies defeated the conservatives late in 1860, and Juárez returned to Mexico City in 1861.

The French invasion. The Mexican government had little money after the War of the Reform. Juárez stopped payments on the country's debts to the United Kingdom, France, and Spain. Troops of those three nations occupied Veracruz in 1862. The British and Spaniards soon left Mexico after they saw that the French were more interested in political power than in collecting debts. The French emperor, Napoleon III, took this opportunity to invade and conquer Mexico. Napoleon knew that the United States would oppose the invasion, but he was confident the U.S. government could not intervene because it was fighting the American Civil War (1861-1865). French troops occupied Mexico City in 1863, and Juárez escaped from the capital.

In 1864, Mexican conservatives, aided by Napoleon III, named Maximilian emperor of Mexico. Maximilian was a brother of the emperor of Austria. Juárez and the liberals fought guerrilla-style battles against Maximilian and the French invaders. In 1866, the United States pressured France to remove its troops. In addition, Napoleon III feared that war would break out in Europe. In 1866 and 1867, he withdrew his forces from Mexico. Juárez's forces then captured and shot Maximilian, and the conservative movement broke up. Juárez then returned to Mexico City. He served as president from 1867 until his death in 1872.

The dictatorship of Porfirio Díaz. Frequent revolts took place after Juárez's death. In 1876, Porfirio Díaz, a mestizo general, overthrew Juárez's successor. Díaz developed good relations with the conservatives and with some liberal state leaders who cooperated with him. He used the army to control his opponents. Díaz served as president from 1876 to 1880, and again from 1884 to 1911. The strength of his allies and the people's fear of the army helped Díaz rule as a dictator. Many people who sided with him became wealthy.

Mexico's economy improved under Díaz. He attracted foreign investment to connect Mexico with the rest of the world, particularly the United States. Investors' money helped build railroads, develop mines and oil wells, and expand manufacturing. However, the government kept industrial wages low and crushed attempts to form labor unions. Indigenous communities lost their land to big landowners. The great majority of Mexicans remained poor and uneducated. Economic improvements primarily benefited big landowners, business owners, and foreign investors.

The Revolution of 1910. Opposition to Díaz's rule began to grow after 1900. Francisco Indalecio Madero, a liberal landowner, decided to run for president against Díaz in 1910. During the campaign, Madero became widely popular. Díaz had him imprisoned until after the election, which Díaz won. Madero then fled to the United States.

In November 1910, Madero issued a call for revolution. He had opposed violence, but he saw no other way to overthrow Díaz. Revolutionary bands developed throughout Mexico. They defeated federal troops, destroyed railroads, and attacked towns and estates. In May 1911, members of Díaz's government agreed to force him from office, in the hope of preventing further bloodshed. Díaz resigned and left Mexico, and Madero was elected president later that year.

Madero meant well, but he could not handle the many groups that opposed him. Some groups wanted a dictatorship. Others demanded greater reforms than Madero enacted. General Victoriano Huerta seized control of the government in 1913, and Madero was killed.

Some Mexicans supported Huerta's dictatorship, hoping for peace. But Madero's followers united behind Venustiano Carranza, the governor of Coahuila, and bitter fighting continued. Powerful military leaders from northern Mexico, including the famous Pancho Villa and Álvaro Obregón, led the war against Huerta. United States President Woodrow Wilson sided with Carranza's revolutionaries. In 1914, U.S. forces seized Veracruz. Wilson hoped to prevent the shipment of arms from the seaport to Huerta's army. Later in 1914, Carranza's forces occupied Mexico City, and Huerta left the country.

The Constitution of 1917. The victorious revolutionary leaders soon began to struggle with one another for power. Carranza's and Obregón's armies fought those of Villa and the indigenous leader Emiliano Zapata. Villa and Zapata demanded more extreme reforms than Carranza planned. In 1915, the United States supported Carranza and halted the export of guns to his enemies. In revenge, Villa crossed the U.S.-Mexico border in 1916 and raided Columbus, New Mexico. His men killed 18 Americans. About five times as many Mexicans also died in the raid. President Wilson sent General John J. Pershing into Mexico, but Pershing's troops failed to capture Villa.

In 1916, Carranza's power was recognized throughout most of Mexico. He called a convention to write a new constitution. The Constitution, adopted in 1917, combined Carranza's liberal policies with more radical social reforms. It gave the government control over education and over farm and oil properties. It also eliminated some privileges enjoyed by the Roman Catholic Church, limited Mexico's president to one term in office, and recognized labor unions. But Carranza did little to carry out the new constitutional program. In 1920, he was killed during a revolt led by Obregón, who then became president.

Reforms of the early 1900's. Obregón distributed some land among the peasants, built many schools throughout the countryside, and supported a strong labor union movement. Plutarco Elías Calles, who had fought Huerta and Villa alongside Obregón, became president in 1924. Calles carried on the revolutionary program. He encouraged land reform, reorganized the country's financial system, and enforced constitutional controls over the Roman Catholic Church. In protest, the Catholic bishops closed their churches from 1926 to 1929. This action led to a peasant rebellion.

The assassination of Obregón in 1928 caused a political crisis. Obregón had just been elected president but had not yet taken office. When Calles's term ended, Emilio Portes Gil became interim president. But Calles remained the real power behind the presidency. In 1929, Portes Gil reached an agreement with Catholic officials that allowed the Catholic Church to operate churches and schools without interference. In return, church leaders promised to stay out of political affairs.

Calles and his allies formed the National Revolutionary Party (PNR) in 1929. Before the formation of the PNR, Mexican political parties had been temporary groups organized by presidential candidates. The PNR stood for the goals of the Mexican Revolution and included all important political groups. It was reorganized as the Party of the Mexican Revolution in 1938 and as the Institutional Revolutionary Party in 1946.

By 1930, the push for reform had slowed down. The Great Depression, a worldwide economic slump, hit Mexico hard and prevented high government spending on social reforms. Calles and many other old leaders also opposed extreme changes. Younger politicians called for speeding up the revolutionary program. As a result, in 1933, the PNR adopted a six-year plan of social and economic reform. The party chose General Lázaro Cárdenas

Rebel forces commanded by Emiliano Zapata marched toward Mexico City after the overthrow of Mexican dictator Victoriano Huerta in 1914. Zapata and Pancho Villa struggled for power against revolutionary leader Venustiano Carranza. But by 1916, Carranza controlled most of Mexico.

UPI/Bettmann

as its presidential candidate and charged him with carrying out the reform plan.

After Cárdenas became president in 1934, he ended Calles's power. He divided among the peasants about 49 million acres (19 million hectares) of land. This was more than twice as much land as all previous presidents combined had given the peasants. Cárdenas also promoted government controls over foreign-owned companies and strongly supported labor unions. In 1938, during an oil workers' strike, the government took over the properties of American and British oil companies in Mexico. The companies and the British government protested angrily. The U.S. government recognized Mexico's right to the properties as long as the companies received fair payment. In the 1940's, Mexico agreed to pay the companies for their lost property.

During and after World War II. Mexico's economy grew rapidly in the 1940's. Manuel Ávila Camacho, who was president from 1940 to 1946, did much to encourage industrial progress. World War II (1939-1945) also contributed to industrial growth. Mexico entered the war on the side of the Allies in 1942. It sent an air force unit to the Philippines to fight the Japanese. About 250,000 Mexican immigrants also fought in the U.S. Army. However, Mexico's contribution to the war effort was mostly economic. The country supplied raw materials and many laborers to the United States. It also made military equipment in factories that the United States had helped set up. The value of Mexican exports had nearly doubled when the war ended in 1945.

The economy continued to improve after the war. Industry and other economic activities expanded through the 1960's. Aided by generous government assistance, new factories made such products as automobiles, cement, chemicals, clothing, electrical appliances, processed foods, and steel. The government expanded highway, irrigation, and railroad systems. Many new buildings went up, especially in the capital. Agricultural exports to the United States increased, and a growing number of foreign tourists visited Mexico.

The late 1900's. During the late 1960's, many Mexicans, especially students, accused the government of human rights violations and other abuses of power. On Oct. 2, 1968, soldiers fired on a crowd of student demonstrators in Mexico City's Tlatelolco district. Hundreds of people were killed. During the 1970's and early 1980's, many people involved in antigovernment movements disappeared

and were presumably killed. Many Mexicans and members of human rights groups blamed military and security forces for the disappearances.

Worldwide problems of recession and inflation led to a decrease in economic production and sharp price increases in Mexico during the 1970's. In 1976, Mexico *devalued* (lowered the value of) its currency, the peso, twice. The devaluations were efforts to stabilize the economy by reducing the cost of Mexican exports and thus making them more competitive abroad.

Luis Echeverría Álvarez, who was president of Mexico from 1970 to 1976, increased government control over foreign-owned businesses. He also took steps that strained Mexico's friendship with the United States. For example, he improved Mexico's relations with socialist governments in Cuba and Chile in spite of U.S. opposition to those governments. Illegal immigration of Mexicans into the United States, plus drug smuggling from Mexico to the United States, caused more problems between the two countries.

José López Portillo became president in 1976. He reduced government controls over both foreign and domestic businesses to encourage private investment in Mexico. Vast petroleum deposits were discovered in and near the Gulf of Mexico in the 1970's. Mexico became a major oil exporter. Its relations with the United States also improved. In the late 1970's, the government greatly increased spending on public works and industry to create more jobs.

Despite Mexico's new-found oil wealth, many people remained poor. Many farmers still lacked modern agricultural equipment and irrigation systems, and wages for farm laborers remained low. Each year, more rural Mexicans moved to cities to look for jobs. This migration and a high rate of population growth contributed to overcrowding and unemployment in urban areas. Millions of Mexicans moved to other countries, especially the United States, to try to make a better living.

The Mexican government expected the income from petroleum to help balance its spending. But by 1981, decreased demand and lower prices for petroleum contributed to an economic crisis in Mexico. The government could not pay its foreign debt, and the value of the peso plummeted during the 1980's. Unemployment and prices rose sharply.

In 1982, Miguel de la Madrid Hurtado became president. He cut down on government spending, especially

The Zapatista Army of National Liberation, a rebel group made up mostly of Maya, led a revolt against the passage of the North American Free Trade Agreement (NAFTA) in 1994. Since that time, the group has continued its efforts to improve the lives of indigenous Mexicans.

AP/Wide World

aid for the poor. But Mexico's economic problems continued. The problems worsened in the early 1980's, when thousands of refugees from civil wars in El Salvador, Guatemala, and Nicaragua entered Mexico and settled in camps near its southern border.

On Sept. 19 and 20, 1985, earthquakes struck south-central Mexico, including Mexico City. They caused about 10,000 deaths and $5 billion in property damage. The government's slow, ineffective response to the tragedy made many Mexicans critical of the Institutional Revolutionary Party (PRI), which had been in power since 1929.

Opposition to the PRI grew during the mid-1980's. In 1988, the party's candidate, Carlos Salinas de Gortari, was elected Mexico's president in the closest election in many decades. Many people believed that Salinas won the election by fraud, and he entered office amid much criticism. That same year, an opposition coalition—the National Democratic Front—and an opposition party—the National Action Party—won almost half of the seats in the Chamber of Deputies. As a result, the president could no longer rely on the vote of two-thirds of the Chamber that was required to amend the Constitution.

Salinas promised to remove government restrictions on the economy and to reform Mexican politics. He attempted to stimulate economic growth and overcome Mexico's huge foreign debt by further reducing government ownership of businesses and by encouraging large-scale foreign investment in Mexico. Under these reforms, Mexico's economy improved, and the PRI won a majority of seats in the Chamber of Deputies in 1991 elections.

In 1993, Mexico, Canada, and the United States ratified the North American Free Trade Agreement (NAFTA). The treaty, which went into effect on Jan. 1, 1994, provided for the gradual elimination of trade barriers among Mexico, the United States, and Canada.

A few hours after NAFTA went into effect, Maya rebels took control of several towns in Chiapas state. The rebel group called itself the Zapatista Army of National Liberation, in memory of the revolutionary leader Emiliano Zapata. The rebels' spokesperson, a non-Indian who hid his identity with a mask, claimed that NAFTA would harm his supporters economically. However, the major cause of the revolt was the poor living conditions in the region. About 100 people were killed in fighting between the Zapatistas and government troops. The government regained possession of the towns within two weeks and declared a cease-fire on January 12. The Zapatistas continued to campaign against the poverty and discrimination faced by indigenous Mexicans.

In August 1994, Ernesto Zedillo Ponce de León of the PRI was elected president. The PRI's previous candidate for president, Luis Donaldo Colosio, had been murdered after he called for fundamental changes in the party. Shortly after taking office in December, Zedillo faced an economic crisis. Mexico's economy had developed weaknesses, caused in part by large foreign debts and years of the government spending more than it received. The economic weaknesses prompted Zedillo to devalue the peso, but the sudden devaluation triggered a crisis. An emergency economic plan and an international aid package helped ease the crisis in 1995, but the economy still struggled.

The Mexican government passed a series of election reforms in 1996. To help prevent voting fraud, the reforms created an independent federal elections board. They also provided for the direct election of the mayor of Mexico City. Previously, the mayor had been appointed by the president.

In elections held in 1997, the PRI lost its majority in the Chamber of Deputies. In 2000, Vicente Fox Quesada of the National Action Party was elected president of Mexico. He became the first non-PRI candidate to be elected to that office in 71 years.

Recent developments. Felipe Calderón of the National Action Party narrowly won Mexico's presidential election in 2006. The runner-up claimed fraud, but a partial recount of the votes confirmed Calderón's victory. In 2008, Mexico's government passed legislation to reform the criminal justice system. The new legislation provided for public court hearings and for the presumption of innocence, until proven guilty, of people charged with crimes. Under the old system, judges decided cases privately based on written evidence. The reforms were scheduled to be fully in effect by 2016.   Jürgen Buchenau

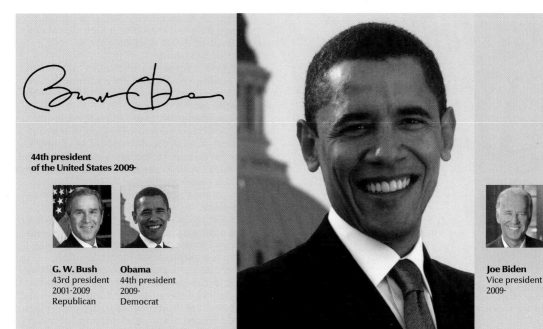

44th president
of the United States 2009-

G. W. Bush
43rd president
2001-2009
Republican

Obama
44th president
2009-
Democrat

Joe Biden
Vice president
2009-

Obama, *oh BAH muh,* **Barack,** *buh RAHK* (1961-   ), became in 2008 the first African American to be elected president of the United States. Obama, a Democrat, had represented Illinois in the United States Senate since 2005. Before being elected to the U.S. Senate, Obama served for eight years in the Illinois Senate. In the 2008 presidential election, Obama defeated Senator John Mc-Cain, a Republican from Arizona. In a heated fight for the Democratic nomination, Obama had defeated Hillary Rodham Clinton, a U.S. senator from New York and former first lady.

Obama had served only two years in the U.S. Senate before announcing his run for the presidency. During the 2008 presidential campaign, Obama's opponents charged that he was too inexperienced to be president. Obama, however, pledged "a new kind of politics" and sought to represent a strong change in direction from the administration of President George W. Bush. Bush, a Republican, faced low approval ratings, due in part to a struggling economy and the unpopular Iraq War, which had begun in 2003.

Obama, the child of a black Kenyan father and a white American mother, stressed that his mixed-race status gave him the perspective to understand Americans' differing views on issues related to race and ethnicity. He spent his boyhood in Hawaii and Indonesia, and he said his experiences as an "outsider" helped him see the United States as others see it. He believed that such a viewpoint could help him repair the nation's international reputation, which many people believed was damaged by the Iraq War.

Obama became only the third sitting U.S. senator to be elected president. Warren Harding, in 1920, and John F. Kennedy, in 1960, were the others.

Early life

Family background. Barack Hussein Obama, Jr., was born on Aug. 4, 1961, in Honolulu. His first name comes from the Swahili word *baraka,* which means *blessing.*

Obama's father, Barack Hussein Obama, Sr. (1936-1982), was born in the village of Nyang'oma Kogelo, near Kisumu, in western Kenya. His family were members of the Luo, one of the country's largest ethnic groups.

Obama's mother, Stanley Ann Dunham (1942-1995), was born in Kansas. She was named after her father, Stanley Dunham (1918-1992), a furniture salesman. Her mother, Madelyn (1922-2008), became a bank executive after the family moved to Hawaii during the late 1950's.

In 1959, Obama's father traveled to Hawaii after earning a scholarship to the University of Hawaii. There he met Stanley Ann, called Ann, and the two married the next year. Initially, both sets of parents disapproved of the union. It was uncommon at the time for people of different races to marry.

Important dates in Obama's life

1961	(Aug. 4) Born in Honolulu.
1967	Moved to Indonesia.
1971	Returned to Hawaii.
1983	Graduated from Columbia University.
1991	Graduated from Harvard Law School.
1992	(Oct. 3) Married Michelle Robinson.
1996	Elected to the Illinois Senate.
2004	Elected to the U.S. Senate.
2008	Elected president of the United States.

UPI/Landov

Obama's grandparents Stanley and Madelyn Dunham visited Barack while he was a student at Columbia University. Obama lived with the Dunhams for much of his childhood.

When young Barack, called Barry, was 2 years old, his father left the family to study at Harvard University. Barry's parents divorced in 1964, and the elder Obama later returned to Kenya, where he worked in several government positions. The father saw his son only once more before dying in a 1982 automobile accident in Nairobi, Kenya.

Boyhood. Barry spent his earliest years in Honolulu with his mother in his grandparents' home. Friends described Barry as a happy child who loved spending time at the beach with his grandparents, whom he called "Toot" and "Gramps."

In 1967, when Barry was 6 years old, his mother remarried. Lolo Soetoro, an Indonesian student studying at the University of Hawaii, became Barry's stepfather. The family soon moved to Jakarta, Indonesia. Barry attended two schools there. Ann worked as an English teacher and as an anthropologist.

Obama had eight siblings, including Maya, a teacher who was born in Indonesia to Barack's mother and stepfather. In Kenya, Barack's father had seven other chil-

dren. They were Abongo, called Roy, an accountant; Auma, a social worker; Mark; David, who died in a motorcycle accident; Abo, a store manager; Bernard, a businessman; and George.

In 1971, Obama received a scholarship to attend the Punahou School, a well-known private school in Honolulu. He moved back to Hawaii to stay with his grandparents while attending school.

Obama excelled at his studies and made a diverse group of friends in the ethnic melting pot of Hawaii. But he sometimes struggled to define his racial identity as a black child being raised by his white mother and grandparents. "I was trying to raise myself to be a black man in America," he wrote, "and beyond the given of my appearance, no one around me seemed to know exactly what that meant."

Obama was a reserve player on the Punahou School basketball team that won the state title in 1979. For his success at making long-range jump shots, his teammates gave him the nickname "Barry O'Bomber."

College. After graduation from high school, Obama enrolled at Occidental College in Los Angeles. He was popular among his classmates and became known as a serious student and an accomplished basketball player. While at Occidental, Obama participated in demonstrations to encourage the college to withdraw its investments from South Africa because of that country's policy of *apartheid* (rigid racial segregation). Obama credited the experience with getting him involved in public policy issues.

During his time at Occidental, Obama began to call himself Barack, his given name. Friends said Obama made the change to be taken more seriously and perhaps also to feel a stronger connection to his African

UPI/Landov

Obama as a toddler is held by his mother, Ann Dunham, in the early 1960's. Dunham met Obama's father, Barack Obama, Sr., a Kenyan, when both were students at the University of Hawaii.

Obama taught constitutional law at the University of Chicago Law School from 1992 to 2004. During his time as a university lecturer, Obama also worked as a lawyer and as a state senator.

heritage. In 1981, Obama transferred to Columbia University in New York City. Obama received a bachelor's degree in political science from the university in 1983.

Community organizer. In 1985, Obama moved to the South Side of Chicago to work for a community development organization in low-income African American neighborhoods. In this role, Obama worked to bring reform to schools and public housing, and to help residents organize for job-training and health-related issues.

About this time, Obama met his half-sister Auma. He later traveled to Kenya to visit his father's country and to meet his extended family.

Law school. Obama entered Harvard Law School in 1988 and graduated *magna cum laude* (with great honor) in 1991. In law school, he became the first African American to serve as president of the *Harvard Law Review. Law Review* members are selected on the basis of their grades and writing ability, and membership is a prized

honor. The members prepare articles for publication and elect a president to oversee their work. As president of the *Law Review,* Obama gained praise from fellow law students, both liberal and conservative, for his willingness to provide a forum for differing viewpoints.

Obama's family. In 1988, while working as a summer associate at a Chicago law firm, Obama met Michelle Robinson (1964-   ). Michelle was a lawyer who later became a hospital executive. The couple married on Oct. 3, 1992. They have two children: Malia (1998-   ) and Natasha, commonly called Sasha (2001-   ). Obama's mother died of ovarian cancer in 1995.

Early career

After graduating from Harvard, Obama practiced law in Chicago, specializing in civil rights issues. He also began teaching constitutional law at the University of Chicago.

While still in law school, Obama had begun writing what became the autobiography *Dreams from My Father: A Story of Race and Inheritance* (1995). In the book, Obama writes about his family. He describes the father from Kenya with whom he shared a name but barely knew; his strong-willed, idealistic mother; and his maternal grandparents who helped raise him. The book details his experiences as a community organizer in Chicago and how that work helped him find a place in the African American community. The book had only modest sales after its initial publication. But after Obama gave a celebrated speech at the 2004 Democratic National Convention, the book became a best seller.

Entry into politics

State senator. In 1995, Obama began campaigning for a seat in the Illinois Senate. He won the November 1996 race and took office in 1997. In the state Senate, he focused on such issues as health care, poverty, crime, ethics, and education. For much of his early legislative career, Obama's Democrats were the minority party in the state Senate. Many of his early proposals failed, but he became known as a politician who would listen respectfully to opponents and their views.

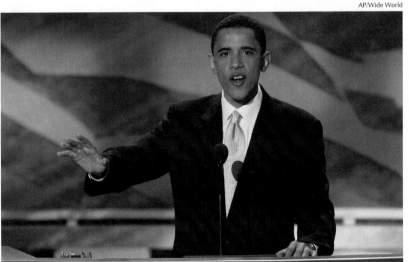

The 2004 Democratic National Convention in Boston helped make Obama a rising star in his party. Senator John Kerry of Massachusetts, the party's presidential nominee, asked Obama to deliver the convention's keynote address. Obama was a candidate for the U.S. Senate at the time. The speech discussed "the politics of hope."

Obama's family includes, *from left,* his wife, Michelle, and daughters Sasha and Malia. In this picture, the family departs an airplane in Indianapolis. Obama campaigned in the city prior to Indiana's Democratic primary in May 2008.

© Jason Reed, Reuters/Landov

Obama did have some successes in the Illinois Senate, notably in ethics reform and criminal justice issues. In 1998, he sponsored legislation that banned nearly all gifts from lobbyists. The law also required lawmakers to report all contributions and expenditures into an electronic database. In 2003, Obama cooperated with law enforcement officials and conservative legislators to reform police procedures. They enacted new rules requiring the police to videotape interrogations and confessions in death penalty cases. The new rules came after reports showed that many inmates on death row had been innocent of their crimes.

United States senator. In 2003, Obama decided to run for a U.S. Senate seat that was held by a retiring Republican. He easily won the Democratic nomination in 2004. In the November election, Obama faced Alan Keyes, a conservative commentator who before the campaign had been living in Maryland. Obama won the election with 70 percent of the vote. He took office in January 2005, becoming the only African American in the Senate.

Convention speech. The summer before the 2004 election, Senator John Kerry, the Democratic presidential nominee, asked Obama to give the keynote address at the Democratic National Convention in Boston. The speech solidified Obama's status as a rising star within the party. He discussed what he called the "politics of hope," saying, "It's the hope of slaves sitting around a fire singing freedom songs; the hope of immigrants setting out for distant shores; . . . the hope of a skinny kid with a funny name who believes that America has a place for him, too."

Legislative accomplishments. In the Senate, Obama voted with his party on a majority of bills. But he also made a point of cooperating with Republicans on several issues. In 2006 and 2007, Obama worked with Senator Richard Lugar, a Republican from Indiana, on the Lugar-Obama threat reduction initiative. The act, signed into law by President Bush in January 2007, expanded the role of the United States in helping other nations destroy stockpiles of conventional weapons, including shoulder-fired missiles.

A second autobiography. Obama's second autobiographical book, *The Audacity of Hope: Thoughts on Reclaiming the American Dream* (2006), presented his views on the differences and similarities between Republicans and Democrats and on such topics as values, religion, race, and foreign policy. He wrote that politics can reflect the common values and hopes that bind Americans together despite their different views.

The book took its name in part from a sermon titled "The Audacity to Hope" by Jeremiah A. Wright, Jr., the pastor of Trinity United Church of Christ in Chicago. Obama had attended the church since the 1980's.

Presidential nomination. In February 2007, Obama held a rally in Springfield, Illinois, to announce that he would seek the 2008 Democratic nomination for president. His rivals for the nomination included Governor Bill Richardson of New Mexico, former U.S. Senator John Edwards of North Carolina, U.S. Representative Dennis Kucinich of Ohio, and U.S. Senator Hillary Rodham Clinton of New York.

Late in 2007, Obama trailed Clinton by more than 20 percentage points in national polls. On Jan. 3, 2008, he scored a surprise victory in the Iowa caucuses, but Clinton won the New Hampshire primary about a week later.

A historic choice. By February, most of the Democratic hopefuls had dropped out of the race, and the nomination came down to a contest between Obama and Clinton. The match-up ensured that for the first time, a major party would nominate either an African American or a woman candidate for president.

Clinton and Obama took similar positions on many issues, including immigration reform and tax policy. Both candidates offered similar plans regarding the withdrawal of U.S. troops from Iraq. Obama stressed that he had strongly opposed the war even before it began. In 2002, when the administration of President Bush was proposing to invade Iraq, Obama gave a speech declaring: "I know that even a successful war against Iraq will require a U.S. occupation of undetermined length, at undetermined cost, with undetermined consequences . . . I am not opposed to all wars. I'm opposed to dumb wars."

The race for the 2008 Democratic nomination was one of the closest in history. In this image, Obama's main rival, Senator Hillary Rodham Clinton, joined him onstage before a debate.

Clinton, who had voted in Congress for the measure to authorize the war, claimed she had the greater experience to handle international crises.

Controversies. Media coverage of the nominating campaign often centered on verbal blunders and other controversial remarks by the candidates or their associates.

Sermons by Obama's pastor, Jeremiah A. Wright, Jr., drew heavy media attention. Wright had accused the U.S. government of creating HIV, the virus that causes AIDS, to harm African Americans. Wright also said that U.S. foreign policy was partly responsible for the September 11 terrorist attacks. Obama distanced himself from his pastor's remarks, concerned that such accusations would undermine his message of racial unity. Obama left the church in May 2008.

Clinton, in turn, faced criticism for her claim of having

been shot at by snipers upon landing in Bosnia in 1996. News coverage of the landing proved her story false.

Some of Obama's opponents tried to take advantage of public fears regarding terrorism and Muslim extremist groups hostile to the United States. They spread rumors that Obama was a Muslim and often mentioned his Muslim-sounding middle name Hussein. Opponents also questioned Obama's patriotism, noting that he had been critical of some U.S. foreign policy and did not wear a U.S. flag pin on his lapel. Later in the campaign, Obama began wearing such a pin, which earlier he had called a substitute for true patriotism.

Race in the United States. On March 18, in a Philadelphia speech, Obama responded to the issue of race in the campaign, in part inspired by the heated reaction to his pastor's remarks. Obama spoke of his unusual racial identity and discussed such issues as white resentment of affirmative action programs and the continued legacy of discrimination against blacks. He asked Americans for their help to put aside such resentments and to focus instead on shared goals, such as better health care and economic and educational opportunities.

Securing the nomination. The contest between Obama and Clinton intensified on February 5—a day known as "Super Tuesday" because almost half the states held nominating contests. Obama and Clinton ended the day nearly tied in the race for delegates to the national convention. In other February contests, however, Obama gained victories in a number of states. Some of the victories came in caucus states where Clinton had chosen not to seriously compete.

In May, Obama received praise for rejecting a "gas-tax holiday" proposed by both Clinton and McCain. Obama said the proposal—which called for the suspension of the federal tax on gasoline during the summer months—would jeopardize the transportation projects the tax funded and do little to reduce the costs of fuel. A survey of economists supported Obama's stance, and public opinion polls at the time indicated that most voters agreed with him.

In early June, after the last primaries had concluded in

Three televised debates between Obama and his Republican opponent, Senator John McCain of Arizona, *left,* were key events leading up to the 2008 election. This picture shows the first debate, at the University of Mississippi in Oxford.

Running mates Obama and Joe Biden, U.S. senator from Delaware, accepted the Democratic nomination for president and vice president at the party's 2008 national convention in Denver.

© Keith Bedford, Bloomberg News/Landov

South Dakota and Montana, Obama gained enough delegates to secure the Democratic nomination. He reached the necessary total with the help of so-called *superdelegates*—Democratic party leaders and officials who can vote for a candidate regardless of the results of their state's primary election or caucus. A few days after the primaries ended, Clinton publicly conceded the nomination and promised to support Obama in the general election against McCain.

Political observers described the tight Clinton-Obama race as the longest and most expensive nominating contest in the history of the United States. Each candidate raised hundreds of millions of dollars, setting fundraising records.

The 2008 election

In August, at the Democratic National Convention in Denver, Obama formally became the party's presidential nominee. At Obama's request, the delegates nominated Senator Joe Biden of Delaware as their candidate for vice president. Obama and Biden faced the Republican nominees McCain and Alaska Governor Sarah Palin.

Obama's book *Change We Can Believe In: Barack Obama's Plan to Renew America's Promise* (2008) was published soon after the conventions. It details Obama's ideas on how to fix the nation's problems and contains the text of his major speeches.

During the general election campaign, both Obama

Obama's election

Place of nominating convention	Denver
Ballot on which nominated	1st
Republican opponent	John McCain
Electoral vote (incomplete)*	364 (Obama) to 162 (McCain)
Popular vote	64,152,671 (Obama) 56,561,037 (McCain)‡
Age at inauguration	47

* Final election results for Missouri and Nebraska were unavailable at press time.
‡ Estimated.

and McCain worked to rally their political bases while reaching out to independent voters. Obama and other Democrats attempted to link McCain with President Bush, whose approval ratings were at record lows. They highlighted McCain's similarities to Bush on such issues as taxes and the Iraq War, and they urged voters to reject a "third Bush term." Meanwhile, Obama's opponents argued that his pledges of "a new kind of politics" were unrealistic and that his policies, especially with regard to taxation and government spending, were too liberal.

Major issues during the campaign included energy policy, international affairs, and the economy. Both candidates pledged to reduce the nation's dependence on foreign oil, but they differed on the steps needed to achieve such a goal. The candidates strongly contrasted in their views on the Iraq War and negotiating with hostile nations. Obama favored a timetable for withdrawing troops from Iraq and said the United States should not be afraid to negotiate with its enemies. McCain opposed a timetable and said that negotiations could hurt U.S. interests by legitimizing enemy regimes. During the summer and fall, many U.S. financial firms suffered huge losses, largely related to risky mortgages called *subprime mortgages.* The economy slumped badly. In October, Congress passed legislation that provided up to $700 billion for the government to purchase bad debts from troubled lenders. Most political experts said the troubled economy helped Obama and the Democrats win the election.

One of the greatest contrasts between Obama and McCain was the 25-year age gap separating them. In polls, many voters expressed concerns about McCain's age. At 72 years old, he would have been the oldest president inaugurated for a first term. Obama, born during the "baby boom" generation from 1946 to 1964, presented himself as a more youthful candidate and an agent of change in national government. His campaign used the effective slogan "Change We Can Believe In."

In the November election, Obama defeated McCain. Obama became the nation's 44th president.

Yanek Mieczkowski

© Brent Jones   © age fotostock/SuperStock

Radio broadcasting originates in a studio and can be heard almost anywhere. A disc jockey at a radio station, *left,* announces and plays recorded music. Many people use portable radios, *right,* to listen to broadcasts.

Radio

Radio is one of our most important means of communication. It enables people to send words, music, images, codes, and other signals over long distances. People on ships and in aircraft and spacecraft keep in contact with other people far away on land, air, or sea by using radio. People also use radio to communicate far into space.

The most widespread and familiar use of radio is for the form of one-way communication known as broadcasting. Radio broadcasts feature music; news; discussions; interviews; sports coverage; drama; educational, cultural, and religious programs; and commercial advertising. Many people wake up to clock radios and listen to radio while in their automobiles. Many also enjoy listening to radio programs during their leisure hours. Some people listen to their favorite radio shows on their computers.

Radio broadcasting once had much the same entertainment role as television has today. From the 1920's to the early 1950's, millions of families gathered around their radios every night. They listened to dramas, light comedies, variety shows, live music, and other kinds of programs. This period, which is sometimes called the Golden Age of Broadcasting, ended with the rise of television during the 1950's.

Radio has many uses in addition to broadcasting. People in many occupations use radio for two-way, wireless communication. Scientists send radio waves into the sky to learn about the weather. Telephone companies send messages across the ocean by radio. Many people operate amateur radio stations.

The contributors of this article are Donna L. Halper, Assistant Professor of Communication, Lesley University, Cambridge, Massachusetts; and David W. Matolak, Associate Professor of Electrical Engineering and Computer Science, Ohio University.

Radio works by changing sounds or other signals into radio waves, a form of energy called *electromagnetic radiation.* Radio waves travel through the air and through space. They also go through some solid objects, such as the walls of buildings. A radio receiver changes them back into the original sounds.

Many people contributed to the development of radio, and no one individual can be called radio's inventor. The Italian inventor Guglielmo Marconi sent the first radio communication signals in 1895. Today, radio waves that are broadcast from thousands of stations, along with waves from other sources, fill the air around us continuously.

Uses

Broadcasting ranks as the most familiar use of radio by far. Every day, millions of people throughout the world listen to news, sports, music, and other radio programs that are broadcast for their entertainment and information.

People also use radio in dozens of other ways. Many uses involve *two-way communication,* in which radio equipment is used both to send and to receive messages. In broadcasting and in most two-way communication, radio transmits sounds, such as voice and music. But in other uses, radio sends communication signals other than sounds. Such signals include the radio beams used in navigation and the remote control signals used in operating certain kinds of equipment.

Broadcasting. Most radio broadcasts originate at radio stations. There is at least one radio station in almost every country in the world, and altogether there are thousands of stations.

Some radios are powered by current from electrical outlets. These radios are usually kept in the home, where electrical outlets are readily available. But many radios are powered by batteries. People listen to these

Radio terms

AM stands for *amplitude modulation,* a broadcasting method in which the strength of the carrier waves is varied to match changes in the audio-frequency waves.

Amplitude is the strength of a wave.

Audio-frequency waves are electric or sound waves that fall within the range of human hearing, typically 20 to 20,000 hertz.

Automatic Frequency Control (AFC) is an electric circuit in an FM receiver that automatically remains locked on to the frequency of the selected transmission.

Bandwidth is the frequency range occupied by a transmitter signal.

Broadcast band is a group of radio frequencies. One band is for AM broadcasting, and one is for FM broadcasting.

Call letters are the initials that identify a radio station, such as station KRKO in Everett, Washington.

Carrier waves are radio waves that "carry" the sounds of a program by being combined with audio-frequency waves.

Channel is the radio frequency assigned to a station.

Detector is an electronic circuit that recovers the portion of a radio signal that represents the program.

Digital Audio Broadcasting (DAB) is a system for transmitting sound and other information as a numeric code.

FM stands for *frequency modulation,* a broadcasting method in which the frequency of the carrier waves is varied to match changes in the audio-frequency waves.

Frequency is the number of complete cycles per second of an electric wave.

Ground waves consist of the radio waves that spread along the ground away from a broadcasting antenna.

Ham is a name for the operator of an amateur radio station.

Hertz is a unit used to measure frequency. One hertz equals one cycle per second.

Kilohertz means 1,000 hertz.

Line-of-sight refers to the direct line in which radio waves travel. Waves in the FM band travel this way, without "bending" over mountains or the curve of Earth.

Live broadcast consists of sounds made at the moment of the broadcast, without having been prerecorded.

Long-wave band is the frequency band ranging from 148 to 283.5 kilohertz. It is used for radio broadcasts in Europe and in parts of Asia and northern Africa.

Medium-wave band is the frequency band ranging from 535 to 1,705 kilohertz used for AM radio broadcasts throughout the world.

Megahertz means 1 million hertz.

Multiplexing means sending two or more signals on a shared channel, as in stereophonic transmissions.

Network is an organization that provides radio programming for a group of stations that belong to it. It also refers to a collection of radio transmitters and receivers that communicate with one another.

Oscillator is an electrical device that produces an electric or electromagnetic signal at a desired frequency. It may use mechanical vibrations or electronic means to produce the signal.

Podcast is a digital audio or video recording that is available on the Internet. Many podcasts are recordings of programs that were initially broadcast on radio or TV.

Prerecorded means recorded on phonograph records, tapes, or audio compact discs for broadcast at a later time.

Radio data system (RDS) is an FM-based method for transmitting data along with an audio program.

Radio waves are electromagnetic waves in the radio frequency band.

Satellite radio is a system that uses satellites to broadcast many channels of coded digital audio signals to special radio receivers. Companies typically offer satellite radio service by subscription.

Selectivity is a radio's ability to pick a desired radio signal from among the many received by the antenna.

Short-wave band is the frequency band ranging from 3 to 30 megahertz. It is used worldwide for radio broadcasts and other services.

Sky waves consist of the radio waves that come from a transmitting antenna and go into the sky.

Stereophonic sound comes from at least two radio speakers to match as closely as possible the sounds people would hear with their two ears.

Stream means to send audio or video data over the Internet.

Superheterodyne is a tuning method in which the desired incoming radio station signal is converted to an intermediate frequency before a detector recovers the signal.

Webcast is a broadcast made on the World Wide Web.

---

radios almost everywhere—in homes and yards, at beaches and picnics, and even while strolling down the street. In addition, nearly all automobiles have a radio.

In some parts of the world, radios provide the people with one of the few links they have to the world outside their village or town. In some places, there is no electric power and batteries are too scarce or expensive for people to buy them. People in such communities sometimes use a special wind-up radio that requires no other source of power. Many people do not own radios, and they listen to radio programs in public gathering places instead.

Two-way communication. Two-way radio provides communication in an almost endless variety of jobs— whenever there is a need for wireless contact between one point and another. Some of the most important of these uses are in (1) public safety, (2) industry, (3) defense, and (4) private communication.

In public safety. Police officers and firefighters use two-way radios in their patrol cars and fire engines. They also carry small, portable two-way radios called *walkie-talkies.* They use these radios to get directions from their headquarters and to communicate with one another. Airplanes and ships use two-way radios for safe operation and for rescue missions. Special ambulance

teams use radio to help save lives after rushing to the scene of an accident. These specialists radio the details of a victim's condition to a doctor in a hospital. The doctor then directs the emergency treatment of the victim by radio.

In industry. Two-way radio has become a standard tool of the transportation industry. Taxi drivers receive radioed instructions on where to pick up customers. Airplane pilots receive landing and take-off instructions by radio. Ships, trains, and many trucks and buses are equipped with two-way radios.

Radio also helps save time, money, and work in many other industries. Construction workers use it to communicate from street level to the top of a skyscraper. With the aid of two-way radio, farmers, ranchers, and lumber workers receive information when they need it and get equipment delivered where they want it.

In defense, radio plays a key role by linking a country's defense units. Military personnel use radio equipment in planes and tanks and on ships. Large communications centers and handy walkie-talkies help provide instant contact between military units.

In private communications. Many licensed radio operators called *hams* send and receive long-distance messages by radio as a hobby. Children play with walkie-talkies that broadcast over short distances. Many people use two-way radios in such places as cars and pleasure boats. One popular type of radio used by private citizens for short-distance, two-way communication is called *citizens band radio*. Radio signals also enable people to communicate using portable cellular telephones and through wireless local area networks.

Other uses. Radio waves can carry many more kinds of information than just sounds. Radio signals make possible the operation of navigational aids, remote control devices, and data transmission equipment. In addition, radio has several highly specialized uses.

Navigation. Radio beams made up of special navigation signals help airplane pilots stay on the proper flying course. Many ships have devices for mapping their position with the aid of signals radioed from shore. Airplanes and ships also rely on radar—a special form of radio—for their safe operation.

Remote control by radio can be used to guide the flight of a model airplane or a real plane that has no pilot. Radio-controlled devices also direct railroad cars in switching yards. In addition, radio-controlled devices do such jobs as opening garage doors or changing television channels.

Data transmission. Radio equipment can send large quantities of information at great speeds. Data transmission usually occurs between one electronic device and another. For example, radio equipment on the ground may transmit data to a computer in a spacecraft orbiting Earth.

Special uses. Criminals and law enforcement officials sometimes use hidden radio devices called *bugs* to listen in on conversations in attempt to gather information. High-energy radio waves cook food in microwave ovens.

Radio programming

Radio programming varies from country to country. In most countries, a majority of programs broadcast are designed for entertainment. The rest provide some type of information. Advertisements are broadcast during and between the programs of commercial stations. Noncommercial stations, also called *educational* or *public*

stations, have few or no commercials. Radio stations compete with one another for listeners. Most stations choose programs to appeal to a specific audience, called a *target demographic.* For example, stations in the United States that play rock music try to attract teenage and young adult listeners.

Entertainment. Recorded music is the chief kind of radio entertainment. Most stations specialize in one kind of music, such as rock, classical, country, or jazz. Some stations broadcast several kinds of music.

Most radio stations that broadcast music have *disc jockeys* who introduce and comment on the music. They play an important role. Commercial stations try to hire disc jockeys whose announcing styles and personalities appeal to the station's largest audience.

Additionally, entertainment programs include comedy shows, serials, and plays that are performed live or recorded in a studio by actors. Some plays are written especially for radio.

Information. Programs that provide information include newscasts, talk shows, and live broadcasts of sports events. Newscasts are broadcast at regular times—every half-hour or hour on some stations. In addition, radio stations present on-the-spot news coverage of such events as political conventions, disasters, and speeches by national leaders. Radio stations also broadcast such specialized news as weather forecasts, traffic reports, and stock market information. Other information features include public service announcements about community events and government services. A few stations broadcast only news.

Talk shows present discussions on a variety of topics and interviews with people from many professions. Each show has a host who leads the discussion or does the interviewing. The subject of a program may be a current political topic, such as an election or a government policy, or it may deal with a social issue, such as crime, pollution, poverty, racism, or sexism. Many talk shows allow listeners to take part in the program. Listeners are invited to telephone the station to ask questions or give their opinions about the topic.

Sports events, like news, have always been an important part of radio programming. Sports announcers try

© Richard Hutchings, Photo Researchers

An airplane pilot radios the control tower for instructions. During flight, radio beams help pilots stay on course.

© Paul David Drabble, Alamy Images

A soldier uses a handheld two-way radio called a *walkie-talkie* to communicate with a military unit.

© Alex Segre, Alamy Images

A police officer uses a walkie-talkie to communicate with other officers. Emergency personnel also use walkie-talkies.

to capture a game's action and excitement for the listeners. Games in many professional sports, such as baseball, basketball, cricket, football, hockey, and soccer, are broadcast locally on radio. Radio stations also broadcast many college and some high school sports contests. Stations that broadcast only sports and discussions of sports are also popular.

How radio programs are broadcast

Radio stations are places where radio broadcasts begin. The *studio* is the part of the radio station from which programs are broadcast. It is soundproofed so that no outside sounds can interfere with the broadcasts. Many studios have two separate areas—the *main studio* and the *control room*. The main studio is the place where the performers do their jobs. The control room contains the equipment needed to prepare and broadcast programs. This equipment includes the *control board,* a panel with the switches, knobs, buttons, and other devices used to regulate the sounds of the broadcasts. A large window in the wall between the main studio and the control room enables people in each area to see one another.

Putting a show on the air involves such jobs as researching current events, script writing, announcing, and controlling the broadcasting equipment. Some shows have a producer who contacts guests and helps prepare interviews. At a small station, the same person may write scripts, announce, play recordings, and even operate the controls. A large station has a staff that plans programs, including the writing of news and other scripts. An announcer may use a script or may simply *adlib* (speak without a script).

During the Golden Age of Broadcasting, the production of some radio programs was a complex process involving many people. Writers wrote scripts for comedies, dramas, and variety shows. A director guided actors and actresses, who stood around a microphone reading their lines. An announcer introduced the show, closed it, and read the commercials. Sound-effects specialists created such sounds as thunder, footsteps, creaking doors, and galloping horses. An orchestra played appropriate music. Most radio stations were in hotels, and many radio shows were broadcast *live* (while they were being performed). These shows were often performed on the stage of a hotel ballroom or a theater-like studio in front of an audience.

Today, the production of most radio programs is less complicated. Only a small number of radio shows are broadcast in front of a live studio audience. Most shows today take place in the radio studio, where only the on-air staff is heard. New technology has even enabled some radio hosts to broadcast directly from their homes. Most programs consist of conversation and recorded music. In addition, many radio stations use computers to do much of the work formerly done by people, such as operating technical equipment, recording program information, and even running the control board. Automation saves money by reducing the number of employees needed to run the station.

From sound waves to electric waves. A radio program consists of speech, music, and other sounds. These sounds may either be live or *prerecorded*. Prerecorded sounds are not broadcast when first produced.

Most are stored on tapes or audio compact discs (CD's) and broadcast later. Almost all the music and commercials heard on radio are prerecorded.

To understand how radio broadcasting works, it is necessary to know what sound is. All sounds consist of vibrations. The number of vibrations each second is the *frequency* of the sound. For example, the sound of a person's voice consists of vibrations of the air that are caused by the person's vibrating vocal cords. The faster the vocal cords vibrate, the higher the frequency. The slower the vocal cords vibrate, the lower the frequency. Sound travels through the air in the form of waves called *sound waves.*

During a live radio broadcast, a microphone picks up speech and other sounds that make up the program. When sound waves enter the microphone, they cause an electric current that runs through the microphone to vary. The variations in the current form electric *audio-frequency waves* that match the program's sound waves. Prerecorded sounds are also changed into audio-frequency electric waves before being broadcast.

From electric waves to radio waves. The electric waves representing the live and prerecorded sounds of the program travel over wires to the control board. A technician uses switches on the control board to select, adjust, and mix the material to create the *program signal* that will be broadcast. The program signal travels from the control board to the transmitter, either by wire or by a special beam of radio waves.

Low-power transmitters may be in the studio. High-power transmitters are generally far away from the studio, at the site of the *transmitting antenna,* the device that sends radio waves through the air. Special types of radio waves called *microwaves* are sometimes used to send the program signal from the studio to a distant transmitter in a narrowly focused "beam."

In the transmitter, the program signal is combined with electric waves called *radio-frequency waves.* Radio-frequency waves have a much higher frequency than do the audio-frequency waves that make up the program signal. Radio-frequency waves are also known as *carrier waves* because they "carry" the program signal from the transmitter to radios. Carrier waves are used because they travel through the atmosphere better than the original audio-frequency waves can. The frequency of the carrier waves produced in the transmitter is the station's *broadcast frequency*—that is, the frequency to which a radio must be tuned to hear that station.

Transmitting radio waves. After the program signal is combined with the carrier waves, the transmitter *amplifies* (strengthens) the combined radio signal and sends it to the antenna. The antenna then broadcasts the radio signal through the air.

Radio waves travel at the speed of light. This speed is 186,282 miles (299,792 kilometers) per second. By contrast, sound waves move through the air at the speed of only about ⅕ mile (0.3 kilometer) per second.

Most radio broadcasts are transmitted in one of two ways, depending on how the carrier waves and program signal are combined. These two kinds of radio transmission are *amplitude modulation* (AM) and *frequency modulation* (FM). In AM band transmission, the *amplitude* (strength) of the carrier waves is varied to match changes in the program signal coming from the radio studio. In FM band transmission, the amplitude of the carrier waves remains constant. But the frequency of the carrier waves is varied to match changes in the program signal. The radio wave signal properties described here depend on the carrier frequencies used by the AM and FM broadcasting systems.

Transmitting AM band signals. An AM antenna sends out two kinds of radio waves—*ground waves* and *sky waves.* Ground waves spread out horizontally from the transmitting antenna. They travel through the air along Earth's surface and follow the curve of Earth for a short distance. Sky waves spread up into the sky. When they reach a layer of the atmosphere called the *ionosphere* or the *Kennelly-Heaviside layer,* they are reflected down to Earth. AM broadcasts are thus reflected beyond Earth's curve. The ionosphere rises at night and so reflects AM waves farther than it does during the day. As a result, radios can receive broadcasts from distant stations more clearly at night.

Transmitting FM band signals. An FM radio antenna sends out waves that travel in the same directions as AM waves, but FM waves that travel skyward are not reflected. Instead, they pass through the atmosphere and go into space. The FM waves that spread horizontally travel in what is called *line-of-sight.* This means that FM waves cannot be received farther than the horizon as seen from the antenna.

Transmitting short-wave signals. Many broadcasting stations operate in the short-wave bands. Short-wave broadcasts travel over long distances. In some sparsely populated areas, only short-wave broadcasts can be received. Generally, programs transmitted by short-wave stations are addressed to audiences far away.

Most short-wave broadcasting stations transmit on several frequencies to ensure worldwide reception at different times of the day and year. Programs consist mainly of international and national news, commentaries, interviews, music and other cultural programs, sports events, radio plays, and language courses. The governments of some countries block short-wave broadcasts during periods of political unrest.

The ionosphere reflects short waves best when the solar activity is greatest. Thus, short-wave transmissions travel farther during the day than at night. They also travel farther in the winter, when the sun is farther away. However, eruptions on the sun's surface called *solar flares* may disturb the ionosphere enough to interfere with communication or even cause blackouts of short-wave reception.

Digital audio broadcasting (DAB). Beginning in the early 1990's, several countries began experimenting with digital audio broadcasting (DAB). For DAB broadcasts, sound is *sampled* by taking thousands of segments of sound per second and translating each into *digital* (numeric) code. The digital data are compressed by eliminating parts of the signal that do not change from sample to sample, and the signal is transmitted.

DAB can deliver sound of the same quality provided by a compact disc. DAB can also deliver data services. Some AM and FM radio transmitters must be modified to broadcast DAB. Special receivers are required to receive DAB.

One form of digital audio broadcasting is *satellite radio.* Satellite radio systems use satellites to broadcast more than 120 channels of coded digital audio signals directly to special radio receivers or to ground-based *repeaters* that rebroadcast the signals. Computer chips (circuits) in the receivers decode the signals to produce high-quality audio signals. The satellites may be in either a *geostationary orbit,* remaining in a constant position relative to Earth, or a circular or *elliptical* (oval-shaped) orbit around Earth. Companies typically offer satellite radio service by subscription. Some offer adapters that allow conventional radios to receive satellite radio signals.

Webcasting and podcasting. In the mid-1990's, some radio stations began transmitting, or *webcasting,* over the Internet. Radio stations carry computer signals to and from the Internet via wireless *local area networks* (LAN's). LAN's are small networks that connect computers in one office, school, or building. Stations may *stream* their programming—that is, simultaneously broadcast into the air and onto the Internet. Stations may also *podcast,* or release a digital audio recording on the Internet.

Broadcasting power and frequency. Another factor that influences the distance a radio program can be

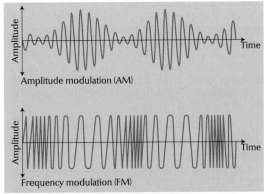

WORLD BOOK diagrams by Mark Swindle

Broadcast waves are a combination of two kinds of electric vibrations. Audio-frequency waves represent voice and other sounds. Radio-frequency waves "carry" audio waves after being combined with them in one of the ways shown at the right.

AM and FM. In AM, the *amplitude* (strength) of the radio-frequency waves is varied to match the audio waves. In FM, the *frequency* (number of vibrations per second) of the radio-frequency waves is varied to match the audio waves.

Radio waves. An AM antenna radiates *ground waves,* which may extend a short distance beyond the horizon, and *sky waves,* which bounce off the ionosphere and may also bounce off Earth. An FM antenna radiates *line-of-sight waves,* which cannot be detected beyond the horizon.

broadcast is the power of the transmitter. The strongest AM stations have a power of 50,000 watts. They can be heard far away, especially at night when reflected waves travel farther. For example, 50,000-watt stations in Chicago can be heard at night by listeners in Florida, about 1,000 miles (1,600 kilometers) away. The weakest AM stations operate at 250 watts and usually serve only one or two towns.

The power of FM stations ranges from 100 watts, which can broadcast about 15 miles (25 kilometers), to 100,000 watts, which can broadcast about 65 miles (105 kilometers). Some noncommercial FM educational stations operate at as little as 10 watts and reach an area of only a few miles or kilometers.

Each station broadcasts on a different *channel,* also called an *assigned frequency.* The use of different carrier frequencies keeps stations from interfering with one another's broadcasts. Frequency is measured in units called *hertz* (cycles per second). One kilohertz equals 1,000 hertz, and 1 megahertz equals 1,000,000 hertz. AM stations transmit within the medium-wave band, which ranges from 535 to 1,705 kilohertz. FM stations transmit within a very high frequency (VHF) band that ranges from 88 to 108 megahertz. The short-wave band ranges from 3 to 30 megahertz. The L-band, within which most DAB signals are broadcast, ranges from 1,452 to 1,492 megahertz.

How radio programs are received

Radios detect radio-frequency signals, separate the program signals from the carrier waves, and then change the program signals into sound waves. Different types of radios can receive different broadcast bands. Many radios can receive both AM and FM, the most popular broadcast bands. *Multiband radios* can pick up AM, FM, and other bands, such as police, marine, aviation, and short-wave bands.

One of the simplest radio receivers is the *crystal radio.*

This type of receiver uses an electronic device called a *crystal rectifier* to detect changes in the strength of an AM signal. These changes in signal strength represent the program's original sound waves. A crystal radio works on just the power of the radio waves it receives and needs no electric power source. However, a listener must use earphones because a crystal radio can produce sound only at a low volume. Furthermore, this type of radio does not receive FM broadcasts well. Because of such limitations, most radios made today are electrically powered.

The electric power for a radio can come from batteries or from an electrical outlet in a house or other building. A typical radio that runs on household power has a component called a *power transformer* that lowers the household voltage to the level the radio requires.

The main parts of an electrically powered radio include (1) the antenna, (2) the tuner, (3) the intermediate-frequency amplifier and detector, (4) the audio-frequency processor and amplifier, and (5) the speaker. A radio that can receive more than one type of signal also has a switch for selecting the band.

The antenna is a length of wire or a metal rod that converts radio waves in the atmosphere to electrical signals at the antenna *terminal* (end point). The antenna may be entirely inside the radio, or part of the antenna may be outside the radio but connected to it, as is the case in automobile radios. An antenna receives radio waves from many stations at the same time.

The tuner is the part of the radio that can be adjusted to particular frequencies. A display on the radio shows the frequencies, or channels, of the stations that may be tuned in. For example, station WQAM in Miami broadcasts on a frequency of 560 kilohertz. To tune in WQAM, a listener selects number 560 (abbreviated as 56 or 5.6 on some radio displays).

Today, most radio receivers use the *superheterodyne* tuning method because of the advantages it offers. The

Main parts of an AM/FM transistor radio

Emerson Radio Corp. (WORLD BOOK photo)

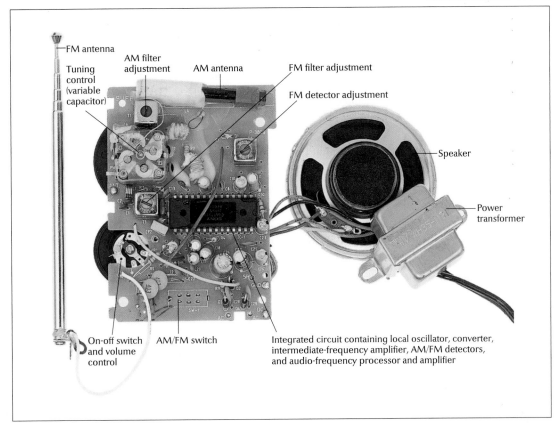

FM antenna

Tuning control (variable capacitor)

AM filter adjustment

AM antenna

FM filter adjustment

FM detector adjustment

Speaker

Power transformer

On-off switch and volume control

AM/FM switch

Integrated circuit containing local oscillator, converter, intermediate-frequency amplifier, AM/FM detectors, and audio-frequency processor and amplifier

tuner of a superheterodyne radio consists of three main parts: (1) an amplifier, (2) a local oscillator, and (3) a mixer/converter. The amplifier strengthens the antenna signal. The local oscillator generates a signal of a specific frequency, which the mixer/converter combines with the amplified antenna signal. The combined signal, called the *intermediate frequency,* contains a particular radio program. When a listener adjusts the tuning control, the local oscillator frequency changes and a different radio program is selected to be on the intermediate frequency. The intermediate frequency is 10.7 MHz for FM and 455 KHz for AM. Use of the same intermediate frequency to process many radio frequencies simplifies the radio's design. It also allows for improved *selectivity*—that is, the radio's ability to pick a desired radio signal from among the many received by the antenna.

The intermediate-frequency amplifier and detector receive the intermediate-frequency signal produced by the tuner. The amplifier strengthens the signal, which then enters the detector. The detector removes the intermediate-frequency components from the signal and leaves only the *audio-frequency signal*—the part that represents the program.

The audio-frequency processor and amplifier strengthen the audio-frequency portion of the signal. Volume, bass, and treble controls can be used to adjust

the loudness and tone of the sound before it goes to the speaker.

The speaker is the final link between the broadcasting studio and the listener. It changes the electrical signal back into sound waves that represent the original program sounds. The basic parts of a speaker are a magnet and a coil of wire called the *voice coil.* The voice coil is attached to a cone, which is usually made of paper. The electric current from the amplifier passes through the coil and exerts varying push and pull against the magnet's field. The cone vibrates in time with the electric current flowing through the coil. The cone's vibrations create sound waves that match those that first went into the microphone or were recorded earlier, and the original program sounds come out of the speaker.

Stereophonic receivers can detect *stereophonic,* or *stereo, multiplex* signals. These signals are formed by sending two separate audio-frequency signals on a single carrier frequency at the same time. The two audio-frequency signals are called the *right channel* and the *left channel.* Stereo multiplex signals better re-create for the listener the sensation of hearing live sounds than do *monophonic* signals, which transmit only one channel.

Both stereo and monophonic receivers have a superheterodyne circuit. However, stereo receivers have an additional circuit called a *demultiplexer.* This circuit changes the multiplex signal back into its original left and right channels. The two parts of the signal then enter separate audio-frequency processors and amplifiers. Stereo receivers have at least two speakers, one for each channel.

DAB receivers are required to pick up DAB signals. Such receivers recombine a DAB signal's components and restore the original sound even if reception has been affected by interference.

Radio data system (RDS) receivers pick up special signals that provide data in addition to audio broadcasts. Radio stations throughout the world have adopted an FM-based multiplex system for such signals. The additional data provide listeners with new features, including the ability to find stations based on type of program, such as classical music, rock and roll, or news. A special demultiplexer circuit is needed in the radio to receive and use the information. RDS radios are popular in cars in many countries.

The radio industry

Radio has several important industrial roles. Broadcasting stations provide jobs for thousands of workers around the world. Radio commercials help other businesses sell every kind of product and service—from dog food to automobiles to insurance. The recorded music played by disc jockeys is often an important factor affecting the sale of music. Stores throughout the world sell millions of radio receivers each year.

Stations and networks. There are two main types of radio stations—commercial stations and public stations.

Cameramann International, Ltd.

The manufacture of radios provides job opportunities for a variety of skilled workers, from technicians to electronics engineers. The technician shown here is assembling radio parts.

Commercial stations, which are owned by private companies, make profits from advertisements. Public stations are funded at least partly by the government. However, in some countries, public stations also take advertisements. Some countries also have nonprofit radio stations, many of which are operated by educational institutions. A radio station may employ only a few workers or as many as several hundred.

The organization of radio broadcasting varies from country to country. In the United States, for example, almost all commercial radio stations are privately owned businesses. Most European countries have both commercial stations and nonprofit stations. Most countries have at least one commercial radio station.

Commercial radio stations broadcast programs to attract listeners. They sell broadcasting time to advertisers who want to reach these listeners. Sponsors pay the stations for time during and between the programs to advertise their products. Stations that attract the largest audiences receive the highest fees. Many commercial stations have an *affiliation* (working agreement) with a national *network*. A network is an organization that provides some of the programming for its affiliated radio stations. It may also sell some of the stations' advertising time. Networks send radio signals to their affiliates using communications satellites.

Careers. The radio industry offers a variety of career opportunities. Stations and networks need program planners and announcers, news reporters and newscasters, technicians, and maintenance workers. Other personnel write scripts, sell advertising time, and work in such general business activities as accounting and public relations. An employee of a small radio station may be called on to do any of these jobs at one time or another. Therefore, a job with a small station provides excellent experience for a person starting a radio career. Most people who hold a key job at a large station first gained experience by working at small stations.

Employees of large stations or networks generally specialize in one of four kinds of work. These kinds of work are (1) programming, (2) engineering, (3) sales, and (4) general administration.

The programming department is headed by a program director. This department includes journalists who gather the news and write news reports and other material to be broadcast. Other members of the programming department include announcers, copywriters, and production personnel. The engineering department includes the technicians who operate and maintain the broadcasting equipment. Members of the sales department are responsible for selling broadcasting time to sponsors. The general manager of the station or network heads the department of general administration and has overall responsibility for the organization's operation. The general administration department includes accountants, secretaries, and other office workers.

Careers outside of broadcasting are available to people trained in the operation and repair of radio equipment. Many people skilled in radio repair go into business for themselves.

Government regulation of radio

The government of every country regulates the use of radio in some way. Without regulation, radio stations and other radio users would broadcast signals that would interfere with one another and make it impossible for communications to be understood. Another reason for regulation is to ensure that stations adhere to the terms of their broadcast licenses. Many governments regulate radio in a way that enables them to use the medium to promote their own ideas and policies. They also effectively prevent the broadcast of ideas that government leaders oppose.

Many nations have private and government-owned stations. In most other countries, the government owns all the stations. In the United States, the federal government does not control any radio stations that broadcast to the general public.

In general, a country allows radio broadcasters the same degree of freedom it allows its citizens. Most democratic countries allow wide freedom in broadcasting. Many totalitarian governments severely regulate and censor broadcasting for political purposes.

In the United States, the Federal Communications Commission (FCC) regulates all nonmilitary communication by radio. The FCC assigns frequencies and call letters for various types of radio operations, including broadcasting, amateur radio operation, and marine and aviation radio. In addition, the FCC issues licenses to stations and certain other users of transmitting equipment. The FCC does not censor radio programs or tell stations what programs they should broadcast. But it can impose a fine on or revoke the license of a station that violates broadcasting rules.

In Canada, the Canadian Broadcasting Corporation (CBC) provides the programs for the government stations. The Canadian Radio-television and Telecommunications Commission supervises government and private stations. In the United Kingdom, the British Broadcasting Corporation (BBC) regulates the government-owned stations. The Office of Communications (commonly called Ofcom), a government agency, regulates privately owned stations.

History

The development of radio in the late 1800's revolutionized communication. At that time, people had two other means of quick, long-distance communication—telegraph and telephone. But the signals sent by both these devices had to travel through wires. As a result, telegraph and telephone communication was possible only between places that had been connected by wires. Radio signals, on the other hand, passed through the air. Thus, radio enabled people to communicate quickly between any two points on land, at sea, and—later—in the sky, and even in space.

Radio broadcasting, which began on a large scale during the 1920's, caused major changes in the everyday lives of people. It brought a tremendous variety of entertainment into the home for the first time. It also enabled people to learn about news developments as they happened or shortly afterward.

Early development. Radio, like many other inventions, developed from the theories and experiments of many people. Joseph Henry, a professor at the College of New Jersey (now Princeton University), and a British physicist, Michael Faraday, discovered one of the first important ideas in the early 1830's. Both men had experi-

mented with electromagnets. Separately, they each developed the theory that a current in one wire can produce a current in another wire, without the wires being connected. This idea is called the *induction theory.*

In 1864, the British physicist James Clerk Maxwell helped explain the induction theory by suggesting the existence of electromagnetic waves that travel at the speed of light. During the late 1880's, the German physicist Heinrich Hertz did experiments that proved Maxwell's theory.

Nikola Tesla, an American inventor from Austria-Hungary, has been credited with the invention of the radio, based on his early patents for radio communications equipment. In 1891, he invented the Tesla coil, a type of high-frequency transformer. This device is a vital component of radio transmitters.

In 1895, Guglielmo Marconi, an Italian inventor, combined earlier ideas and his own ideas and sent the first radio communication signals through the air. He used electromagnetic waves to send telegraph code signals a distance of more than 1 mile (1.6 kilometers). In 1901, Marconi's radio equipment sent code signals across the Atlantic Ocean from England to Newfoundland (now Newfoundland and Labrador), Canada.

During the early 1900's, electrical engineers developed devices called *vacuum tubes* that could be used to detect and to amplify radio signals. Lee De Forest, an American inventor, created a vacuum tube called a *triode* in 1906. This tube became the key element in radio reception.

There are many claims for the first broadcast of human speech over the air. Most historians give credit to Reginald A. Fessenden, a Canadian-born physicist. In 1906, Fessenden spoke by radio from Brant Rock, Massachusetts, to ships offshore in the Atlantic Ocean. The American inventor Edwin H. Armstrong did much to improve radio receivers. In 1918, he developed the superheterodyne circuit. In 1933, he discovered how to make FM broadcasts.

Culver

Guglielmo Marconi invented a way of sending telegraph signals by radio in 1895. His invention helped lead to the development of broadcasting. This photograph shows him with some of his wireless equipment.

The first practical use of the "wireless," as radio was then called, was for ship-to-ship and ship-to-shore communication. Radio helped save the lives of thousands of victims of sea disasters. The first sea rescue involving the use of radio took place in 1909, after the S.S. *Republic* collided with another ship in the Atlantic Ocean. The *Republic* radioed a call for help that brought rescuers who saved almost all the passengers.

Dozens of new uses were soon found for radio. By the 1930's, airplane pilots, police officers, and military personnel were using radio for wireless communication.

The start of broadcasting. Experimental radio broadcasts began about 1910. In that year, Lee De Forest produced a radio program from the Metropolitan Opera House in New York City. The program starred the famous opera singer Enrico Caruso.

Many people consider radio station WWJ (then known as 8MK), in Detroit, the first commercial radio station. It began regular broadcasts on Aug. 20, 1920. Others claim the distinction for station KDKA in Pittsburgh. KDKA grew out of an experimental station that began in 1916 in Wilkinsburg, a suburb of Pittsburgh. KDKA's broadcast of the 1920 U.S. presidential election results on Nov. 2, 1920, is generally considered the beginning of professional broadcasting, even though 8MK also broadcast the election. The first license to broadcast regularly went to station WBZ in Springfield, Massachusetts. The U.S. government issued the license on Sept. 15, 1921.

Network broadcasting began as early as October 1921. At that time, WJZ in New York City and WGY in Schenectady, New York, broadcast the World Series. The two stations formed a simple network connected by telephone lines. Network broadcasting—or, as it was called, *chain broadcasting*—soon included stations across the United States. The Radio Corporation of America (RCA) formed the National Broadcasting Company (NBC), which was the first permanent national network, in 1926.

In the 1920's, radio stations began operating in many other countries as well. The British Broadcasting Corporation (BBC) began broadcasting in 1922. Stations began operations in Australia in 1923 and in Japan in 1925.

The Golden Age of Broadcasting began in the United States about 1925 and lasted until the early 1950's. During this period, radio was a major source of family entertainment. Every night, many families gathered in their living rooms to listen to comedies, adventure dramas, music, and other kinds of radio entertainment. Children hurried home from school to hear afternoon adventure shows. In the daytime, millions of people listened to dramas that were called *soap operas* because soap manufacturers sponsored many of them.

Radio brought to the home the music of famous band leaders, including Tommy Dorsey, Duke Ellington, Benny Goodman, Harry James, Guy Lombardo, and Glenn Miller. Exciting radio dramas of the Golden Age included "Buck Rogers in the 25th Century," "Gangbusters," "The Green Hornet," "Inner Sanctum," "Jack Armstrong, the All-American Boy," "The Lone Ranger," "The Shadow," and "Superman." Some radio soap operas were "The Guiding Light," "John's Other Wife," "Just Plain Bill," "Ma Perkins," "One Man's Family," "Our Gal Sunday," and "Stella Dallas."

Radio's famous comedians included Fred Allen, Jack Benny, Eddie Cantor, and Bob Hope. The ventriloquist Edgar Bergen and his dummy, Charlie McCarthy, hosted a weekly comedy program with famous stars as guests. Situation comedies included "Fibber McGee and Molly," "The Great Gildersleeve," "Duffy's Tavern," "Henry Aldrich," and "Our Miss Brooks." The husband-and-wife comedy team of George Burns and Gracie Allen gained fame in radio.

The popularity of "Amos 'n' Andy," a situation comedy, and the impact of a dramatic program called *The War of the Worlds* help illustrate the enormous influence radio entertainment had on people. "Amos 'n' Andy" was broadcast each weekday throughout the 1930's. While the program was being broadcast—from 7:00 to 7:15 p.m. Eastern Standard Time—many movie theaters stopped their films and turned on radios so the audiences could listen to the program. Some stores and restaurants played radios over public address systems so that customers would not miss it. Although "Amos 'n'

A "crystal" radio of the early 1920's worked without batteries or other source of power, but a listener needed earphones to hear it.

Bettmann

A radio of the mid-1920's was powered by electric energy and had a trumpetlike loudspeaker.

Culver

By the early 1940's, radios had become "streamlined." Members of a family often got together to listen to programs.

Bettmann

Andy" was immensely popular, it also became controversial. The actors and actresses on the radio show were whites who portrayed blacks. Many people have criticized the program for portraying African Americans as a stereotyped group to be laughed at. Some people tried to have the show taken off the air.

The War of the Worlds, broadcast on Oct. 30, 1938, was one program in a series of dramas put on by Orson Welles's Mercury Theatre on the Air. The program was adapted from the science-fiction novel of the same name by the British author H. G. Wells. It took the form of on-the-spot news reports describing an invasion of New Jersey by aliens from Mars. The announcer told the radio audience that the show was fictional. Even so, large numbers of listeners believed the invasion was actually taking place, and widespread panic resulted. Thousands of people called the police and other authorities for instructions on what to do. Many people fled their homes, some taking furniture with them. Still others were treated in hospitals for shock.

Some radio news reporters of the Golden Age became almost as well known as the top entertainers. They included Kathryn Cravens; Elmer Davis; Gabriel Heatter; H. V. Kaltenborn; Fulton Lewis, Jr.; Edward R. Murrow; Lowell Thomas; Dorothy Thompson; and Walter Winchell.

Newscasts became especially important during World War II (1939-1945). Millions of people turned to radio every day for latest news on the war. The governments of countries that fought in the war made widespread use of broadcasts to their own and other countries for propaganda purposes. The Voice of America, an agency of the United States government, began broadcasting overseas in 1942 to inform the world of America's role in the war.

Franklin Delano Roosevelt, president of the United States from 1933 to 1945, used radio effectively. He held informal talks called "fireside chats." The talks did much

Brown Bros.

President Franklin Delano Roosevelt broadcast "fireside chats" to the nation during the 1930's and 1940's. These talks helped him gain popular support for his government policies.

to help Roosevelt gain support for his policies. Earlier presidents, beginning with Woodrow Wilson in 1919, had spoken on radio. However, Roosevelt was the first to fully understand the great force of the medium and the opportunity it provided for taking government policies directly to the people. Other political leaders, including Winston Churchill of the United Kingdom and Charles de Gaulle of France, made use of radio to address their nations.

Also popular and often influential were religious broadcasters. Listeners tuned in to hear sermons and commentary by such religious radio pioneers as the

NBC

A sound-effects expert used odd-looking equipment to create realistic sounds for Golden Age dramas. This picture shows water being sprayed into a bucket to make the sound of rain.

Culver

George Burns and Gracie Allen were famous radio performers during the Golden Age. The husband-and-wife team starred in a popular weekly situation comedy from 1932 to 1950.

Protestant minister S. Parkes Cadman, the evangelist Aimee Semple McPherson, the rabbi Stephen S. Wise, and the controversial Roman Catholic priest Charles Coughlin.

The Golden Age was also the era of the "radio homemakers," such as Ida Bailey Allen and Mary Margaret McBride. These women hosted daily programs directed at stay-at-home wives and mothers. The programs featured guest experts who gave advice on child-rearing, cooking, health, and other issues. These heavily sponsored shows appealed to women as an important consumer market for broadcasters and advertisers.

Radio since the 1950's. The rise of television in the 1950's ended the Golden Age of radio broadcasting. People turned to TV for comedies, dramas, and variety shows, and these kinds of shows all but disappeared from radio. Many people believed television would cause radio broadcasting to become an unimportant communication medium with a small audience. Instead, radio's audience has continued to grow, in spite of its competition from television.

After the Golden Age of Broadcasting, music became the major form of radio entertainment. Rock music, which was a new form of music in the 1950's, became an important kind of music on radio. Broadcasts of rock music gained many listeners—especially teenagers—for radio. Talk shows and stations that broadcast only news also helped radio gain listeners. Thorough coverage of a topic or news event continues to be an important feature of such programs.

Portable radios also helped increase radio's popularity. Such devices, including tiny *personal radios* with headphones, have made radio a source of individual, rather than family, enjoyment. In addition, automobile radios are now commonplace.

Still another aid to radio's growth has been the development of stereophonic broadcasting. Stereo broadcasts began on a large scale in the 1960's. In 1961, the FCC allowed only FM stations to broadcast in stereo in the United States to help them compete with AM stations. FM's better sound quality enabled it to surpass AM in popularity by the late 1970's. The FCC authorized AM stereophonic broadcasting in 1982.

In the late 1980's and early 1990's, researchers developed *digital audio broadcasting* (DAB), a system that converts sounds to *digital* (numeric) code before transmission. DAB was introduced at a world conference in Spain in 1992. In 1998, the first commercial DAB operation began in the United Kingdom. Because DAB can carry multiple signals, radio programs similar to those broadcast today may be supplemented by images, text, graphics, and other data. For example, information about local traffic problems could be transmitted over a DAB data channel. Drivers might receive this information as text, synthesized speech, or maps. An LCD (liquid crystal display) on the receiver might display the name and composer of any music played, the radio station's telephone number, or an electronic program guide.

The 1990's also saw an increase in the popularity of the "talk radio" format in the United States. Notable radio personalities who have found large, loyal listenerships with this format include the conservative political commentator Rush Limbaugh and the controversial entertainer Howard Stern. Beginning in 2006, Stern helped popularize subscription-based satellite radio when he made a highly publicized move from "terrestrial" (land-based) radio to Sirius Satellite Radio Inc. of New York City.

Satellite radio has now become an important new form of radio. Most satellite radio receivers are portable units mainly for use in automobiles, but equipment is also available for use with a home stereo, a portable radio, or a personal computer. Many models of cars now come equipped with satellite radio receivers. In 2008, the U.S. Department of Justice and the FCC approved a merger of Sirius with the country's other satellite service, XM Satellite Radio Holdings Inc. of Washington, D.C., to create a single satellite radio network in the United States.

In 2006, a coalition of major radio station operators in the United States launched an effort to promote HD Radio—a technology that transmits programs digitally over existing AM and FM frequency bands. In its campaign, the alliance stressed the high-quality sound of HD Radio, as well as the fact that, unlike satellite radio, listeners could tune in to HD Radio for free. Thousands of AM and FM stations now broadcast with HD Radio technology. HD Radio has also become an option in many models of cars. However, a major challenge for HD Radio has been the higher cost of a digital radio compared with a regular AM-FM radio.

Donna L. Halper and David W. Matolak

Important dates in radio

1864	James Clerk Maxwell predicted the existence of electromagnetic waves that travel at the speed of light.
1880's	Heinrich Hertz proved Maxwell's theory.
1895	Guglielmo Marconi became the first person to send radio communication signals through the air.
1906	Reginald A. Fessenden broadcast voice and music by radio.
1909	Passengers of the S.S. *Republic* were saved in the first sea rescue using radio.
1918	Edwin H. Armstrong developed the superheterodyne circuit.
1919	Woodrow Wilson became the first U.S. president to make a radio broadcast. He spoke from a ship to World War I troops aboard other vessels.
1920	Two U.S. stations, WWJ of Detroit and KDKA of Pittsburgh, made the first regular commercial broadcasts.
1922	The British Broadcasting Company, later the British Broadcasting Corporation, made its first broadcast.
c. 1925-1950	Radio was a major source of family home entertainment, during the Golden Age of Broadcasting.
1934	The Telecommunications Act created the Federal Communications Commission (FCC) in the United States.
1947	Scientists at Bell Telephone Laboratories (now part of Lucent Technologies) developed the transistor.
1960	John F. Kennedy and Richard M. Nixon held the first radio and television debates between two U.S. presidential candidates.
1961	Soviet space officials held the first radio talks with a space traveler, cosmonaut Yuri Gagarin.
1960's	Stereophonic radio broadcasting began.
1969	Radio signals carried to Earth the first words spoken by astronauts on the moon.
1982	AM radio stations in the United States began broadcasting in stereo.
1998	The world's first commercial digital audio broadcasting (DAB) service began in the United Kingdom.
1999	Subscription satellite radio broadcasting began.
2004	Internet radio podcasting began.
2006	HD Radio began.

Index

How to use the index

Each index entry gives the page number or page numbers—for example, **Aubry, Martine,** 228. This means that information on this person may be found on the page indicated.

A page number in italic type means that there is an article on this topic on the page or pages indicated. For example, there is an Update article on **Australia** on pages 68-72. The page numbers in roman type indicate additional references to this topic.

An entry followed by "reprint" refers to a new or revised encyclopedia article in the supplement section, as in **Austria.** This means that there is an article on pages 418 through 430.

When there are many references to a topic, they are grouped alphabetically by clue words under the main topic. For example, the clue words under **Automobile** group the references to that topic under several subtopics.

The "see" and "see also" cross-references—for example, **Aviation**—refer the reader to other entries in the index.

The indications (il.) or (ils.) mean that the reference on this page is to an illustration or illustrations only, as in **Baghdad.**

Acknowledgments

The publishers acknowledge the following sources for illustrations. Credits read from top to bottom, left to right, on their respective pages. An asterisk (*) denotes illustrations and photographs created exclusively for this edition. All maps, charts, and diagrams were prepared by the staff unless otherwise noted.

8 © Pedro Ugarte, AFP/Getty Images
9 AP/Wide World
10 © Adam Pretty, Getty Images
12-15 AP/Wide World
16 © Jin Lee, Bloomberg News/Landov
19-23 AP/Wide World
24 © Danny Moloshok, Reuters
27 © Gleb Garanich, Reuters
28 © Jim Young, Reuters
31 AP/Wide World
32 © John Gress, Reuters/Landov
35 © John Moore, Getty Images
39 © Philimon Bulawayo, Reuters
45-49 © Shutterstock
52 AP/Wide World
54 Studio Gang Architects
57 © Ali Al-Saadi, AFP/Getty Images
59 The Gross Clinic (1875), oil on canvas painting by Thomas Cowperthwait Eakins; Jefferson College, Philadelphia (Bridgeman Art Library)
61 © Reuters
66-67 NASA/JPL-Caltech
69 © William West, AFP/Getty Images
75 AP/Wide World
76 AP/Wide World; Toyota Motor North America
77 General Motors; American Honda Motor Co.
78 AP/Wide World
82-88 © Shutterstock
89 © Bill Kostroun, Reuters/Landov
94 © Gabriel Bouys, AFP/Getty Images
98 © Aizar Raldes, AFP/Getty Images
102 © Richard Cummins, SuperStock
104 © Library and Archives Canada
105 © Chris Wattie, Reuters
111 © Todd Korol, Reuters/Landov
118 AP/Wide World
122 © Susan Zheng, UNEP/Peter Arnold, Inc.
123 © Liu Xiaoyang, China Images/Alamy Images
125 © Fritz Hoffmann, National Geographic/Getty Images
127 © Alistair Berg, Alamy Images
128 AP/Wide World
129 © Hulton Archive/Getty Images
130 © Lou Linwei, Alamy Images
131 © Jason Lee, Reuters/Landov
133 AP/Wide World
138 © Enrico Nawrath, Bayreuther Festspiele GmbH
139 U.S. Department of Defense
147 AP/Wide World
148-149 © Digital Vision/SuperStock
151 © Shutterstock

153 © David Muenker, Alamy Images; © Ed Darack, Science Faction/Getty Images
155 © Shutterstock
156 Natural Resources Conservation Service; © Phillip Augustavo, Alamy Images
157 © Walter Bibikow, Jon Arnold Images/Alamy Images
159 © David McNew, Getty Images
160 © Bill Bachmann, Alamy Images
162 AP/Wide World
168 Charles Hope, Alberta Ballet Company Artists
169 AP/Wide World
170 © Pictorial Parade/Getty Images
171 © Hulton Archive/Getty Images
172 Children's Hospital Boston; © Touchstone/Everett/Rex Features
173 © Michael Ochs Archives/Getty Images; © MGM/ZUMA Press
174 © Focus/Everett/Rex Features
175 © Michael Ochs Archives/Getty Images
176 © CBS/Landov; AP/Wide World
177 © Niklaus Stauss, Keystone/Landov; © Brendan Smialowski, Meet the Press/Getty Images
178 © Keystone/Landov
179 © Steve Kagan, Time & Life Pictures/Getty Images
180 © Bert Reisfeld, dpa/Landov
182 AP/Wide World
183 © Pictorial Press/Alamy Images
187 © Getty Images
196-200 AP/Wide World
201 © Keith Bedford, Bloomberg News/Landov
202 AP/Wide World
203 YouTube; © Justin Sullivan, Getty Images
208 © Corbis
210-214 © Shutterstock
215 © Nir Elias, Reuters/Landov
217 © AFP/Getty Images
222-231 AP/Wide World
232 © Carlos Gutierez, UPI/Landov; © Crisian Brown, Intendencia Region de los Lagos/Reuters
236 AP/Wide World
240 © Jason Reed, Reuters
244 AP/Wide World
246 © India Today Group/Getty Images
251-272 AP/Wide World
278 Tom Evans*
281-283 AP/Wide World
288 © Paramount Vantage/ZUMA Press; © Miramax Films/ZUMA Press
289 © Canal Plus/ZUMA Press
292 © Brian Sokol, Getty Images
293 © Keyur Khamar, Bloomberg News/Landov

295 © Peter Jackson, Reuters/Landov
296 © Karin Zeitvogel, AFP/Getty Images
297 © Ben Stansall, AFP/Getty Images
298 © Chip East, Reuters
299 © Time & Life Pictures/Getty Images; © Chris McGrath, Getty Images
304 © Luo Xiaoguang, Xinhua/Landov
306 © Hou Deqiang, Xinhua/Landov
308 AP/Wide World
310 © Adam Pretty, Getty Images
312 © Kyodo/Landov
316-318 AP/Wide World
320 © Todd Marshall, Project Exploration; © Mike Hettwer, Project Exploration
321 © Todd Marshall, Project Exploration
323 © Francis Specker, Landov
325 AP/Wide World; © Lee Celano, Landov
327-329 AP/Wide World
330 © Commonwealth of Australia
334 © CERN PhotoLab
337 AP/Wide World
339 © Juan Medina, Reuters/Landov
341-348 AP/Wide World
349 © Sergei Karpukhin, Reuters
350 © Topham/The Image Works
352 © Jerry Lampen, Reuters/Landov
353 © Shaun Botterill, Getty Images
358 Indian Space Research Organisation
359 AP/Wide World; NASA/JSC
360 NASA/JPL-Caltech/University of Arizona/Texas A&M University
361 NASA/University of Texas at Austin
363 © Bogdan Cristel, Reuters
368-374 AP/Wide World
377 AMC TV
380 © Kevin Lamarque, Reuters
381 © Pedro Ugarte, AFP/Getty Images
383 © Christopher Anderson, Magnum Photos
386 AP/Wide World; © Ray Stubblebine, Wizards of the Coast/Reuters
391-393 AP/Wide World
394 © Graeme Robertson, Getty Images
400 © David Banks, UPI/Landov
401 AP/Wide World
402-407 © Shutterstock
412 © Win McNamee, Getty Images; © Liz Martin, ZUMA Press
413 © David J. Phillip, Reuters
416 AP/Wide World